CHILD OF MY

Also by Sue Ryder

AND THE MORROW IS THEIRS
(The Burleigh Press, Bristol 1975)

Sue Ryder

CHILD OF MY LOVE

THE HARVILL PRESS
LONDON

First published in Great Britain by Collins Harvill in 1986

This revised edition published in 1997 by
The Harvill Press
84 Thornhill Road
London N1 1RD

1 3 5 7 9 8 6 4 2

A CIP catalogue record for this book
is available from the British Library

ISBN 1 86046 432 7 (hbk)
ISBN 1 86046 378 9 (pbk)

Designed and typeset in Sabon at
Libanus Press, Marlborough, Wiltshire

Printed and bound in Great Britain by Butler & Tanner Ltd
at Selwood Printing, Burgess Hill

This book is dedicated
to all those millions
who gave their lives during
two World Wars
in defence of human values
and to the countless others who are suffering
and dying today as a result of persecution,
hunger and disease.

Child of my love, fear not the unknown morrow,
Dread not the new demand life makes of thee.
Thy ignorance doth hold no cause for sorrow
For what thou knowest not is known to Me.

FRANK J. EXLEY

Our Lady of Częstochowa

The exquisite and world-famous painting of the Black Madonna, reproduced on the front cover, hangs above the altar in the Chapel of Our Lady in the monastery of Jasna Góra (the bright mountain) which is set on the topmost height of the Kraków–Częstochowa Jura in Poland. The painting is on wood and it is thought to have been part of the booty seized from Ruthenia by the Duke of Opole in 1384. It is clear that even at that time the painting was considered a priceless relic and was regarded with the greatest reverence.

After its transfer to Jasna Góra, the devotion to Our Lady of Częstochowa grew up around it and made the monastery a flourishing centre of pilgrimage. Today the Black Madonna has more visitors than Lourdes. Thousands of pilgrims travel hundreds of miles on foot, especially on the Feast of the Assumption of Our Lady on 15 August. According to legend, the painting was originally made by St Luke the Evangelist from the table top on which the Holy Family used to work and eat at Nazareth.

In 1430 the monastery was sacrilegiously attacked. The painting was deliberately slashed by swords and sabres and terribly damaged. After the attack it was taken to Kraków where it was painstakingly restored with a care and devotion previously unknown in mediaeval Poland. The two slashes which can still be seen across the Madonna's cheek were left untouched to remind people of the infamous attack.

Over the centuries, kings, peasants and soldiers came to pay homage to their Queen at Częstochowa. Before the celebrations of Poland's Christian millennium in 1966, a copy of the picture, blessed by Pope Pius XII, was sent from parish to parish, strengthening the faith of the people, and this custom still continues.

Contents

List of Illustrations

Author's Note

There are many people whose advice and assistance have proved invaluable to me in the preparation of this book. I offer them all my heartfelt gratitude.

In particular, I would like especially to thank Michael Humfrey and Pam Richards for their help with the editing of the First and Second Edition of the book. I owe a limitless debt to my Personal Secretary, the late June Backler, for her endless support during the long period of gestation of the first edition. My heartfelt appreciation goes to Christine Curd who took over for the second edition and who has shown immense patience and perseverance.

I also wish to thank Professor Gilbert, Gervase Cowell and Pat O'Conner who all contributed and assisted me. I have not found it easy to write this book, and I could never have finished the task without the constant prayers and encouragement of my late beloved husband, Leonard Cheshire, who also contributed some of the photographs.

THE SUE RYDER FOUNDATION is a Living Memorial to all those millions who gave their lives during two World Wars in defence of human values, and to the countless others who are suffering and dying today as a result of persecution.

Whatever you do and wherever you pray, think about their supreme sacrifice.

This is an International Foundation which is devoted to the relief of suffering on the widest scale. It seeks to render personal service to those in need and to give affection to those who are unloved, regardless of age, race or creed, as part of the Family of man.

The work is a summons to seek out and face the reality of human suffering and to do something about it. It is a call to deny ourselves, and to give ourselves to those who have need of us, wherever they may be.

It is a challenge to us all:

> "For the cause that lacks assistance,
>   For the wrong that needs resistance,
>   For the future in the distance,
>   And the good that I can do."

George Linnaeus Banks.

Preface
to the original edition

For the pattern is the action and the suffering.
T.S. ELIOT

This book contains the fragments of many people's lives, which have been part of my own experience and which have gone into the building of the Foundation.

Despite the fact that histories of the last two World Wars have been written from the national perspective of nearly every country engaged in them, inevitably there are countless unwritten stories of individual courage, sacrifice and suffering that are being lost to us. The generations of men and women who went to war are slowly but surely dying out, whilst others take for granted the peace they paid so high a price for.

Who can recount their deeds and say to others *remember . . .* they offered their all that evil and wickedness be overcome?

I pray that the Foundation, the Living Memorial, will always remain a tribute to those to whom it is dedicated. I also hope that I may leave behind a group of believers to go forth to set up new foundations in other lands to provide the cornerstone of spiritual inspiration for the future.

People who guide the destinies of the world *must* learn from the tragic failure of the politicians of the years between the Wars to avert confrontation between nations. The terrible lessons must not be forgotten.

What is the message that I want to leave with you? Musicians, painters and well-known writers live on in the lives of millions of future generations who enjoy the gifts they have created. The valuable legacy they leave to the world is not of riches but in how they used their great artistic gifts. Yet all of us have been endowed with some gift which we can use to benefit humanity. I have always been surprised by the number of well-meaning people with a genuine desire to help who have looked at the enormity facing humanity and said, "The problem is too big – there is nothing I, as an individual, can do to help." The truth is that there are few problems confronting humanity that are incapable of solution if only a sufficient number of human beings apply their hearts and energies.

I believe that nothing in my life could ever have occurred except through God's will and also by the example of countless people. It is through *them* that I have learnt; I have laughed and joked with them and been rewarded with so much love. Throughout the writing of this book I have been conscious not only of the persons and places named in it but also of many more whom I have not been able to mention. I think of the thousands who on my path through life have inspired me by their courage in extreme adversity, by their power to draw out the best in men and women of good will.

When you have read all, or any, of these Chapters please do not simply put the book down – I ask you to remember that every journey begins with a single step.

SUE RYDER

PART ONE

Listening and Learning

Home is where You Start From

I WAS BORN ON 3 July 1923, in Leeds, Yorkshire. My mother had had four previous children delivered at home, but as she had lost a baby and I was the youngest by six years, she was advised to use the facilities of a hospital. She loved children and liked large families, though she told me she dreaded the pain of giving birth. My father's first wife had died, leaving him with five children. Charles Foster Ryder married my mother, Mabel Elizabeth Sims, in Oxford on 11 July 1911.

We lived in Scarcroft near Leeds and, until the early thirties, for four months of the year at Thurlow in Suffolk. Though Scarcroft was a Village on the main Leeds-Wetherby road, our pleasant home was almost within walking distance of terrible slums. As a child I visited the people living there, and the children would come over to us for outings and to play in our fields and garden. I remember preparing food and bags of sweets for them, and enjoyed joining in the excitement of their outings away from the back-to-back houses and narrow cobbled streets – the only places they had to play. The bad housing conditions appalled me. It was usual to find only one bedroom in a house, which meant that the children had to sleep with their parents and sometimes a sick person too. Several children would share the same bed. The dreariness of their surroundings, with no lavatory, often no water tap, little to eat and frequently no change of clothes or shoes horrified me. Often children would put a piece of cardboard in their shoes to cover up a hole in the sole; others ran about barefoot. I found it profoundly shocking that there were people who ate off newspapers instead of tablecloths, and slept without sheets because they had none, but I greatly admired their sense of pride and the cheerful way they scrubbed their small houses on their knees, including the front doorsteps, in a perpetual struggle against the industrial grime and smog of their environment. The air was constantly polluted by the smog and poisonous emissions from factory chimneys (the Clean Air Act was not passed until 1956). I felt dismayed to see people existing in such conditions and I can say with certainty that this indelible impression has been a contributory factor to the direction my life has taken. I was moved, at this very early age, to think of how human beings could live in better conditions and with dignity.

In the early 1930s, and on until the 1940s, more than two million people in Britain were living in totally unfit dwellings.

Among this population, only one in seventeen babies survived after birth.

Leeds in the thirties had 35,100 of the oldest type of back-to-back house, all built prior to 1872. They were approximately 228 square feet each and were built seventy to eighty per acre. The houses comprised of a ground floor consisting of one room with a single window and door onto the street, and a room, perhaps divided into two, above. The downstairs room served as a combined kitchen, scullery, parlour, wash-house and larder. The sanitary conveniences were in confined courts and yards or sandwiched between the houses where there was room, and they were few, dark and ill ventilated. Identical houses were built onto three sides of each house, the door of the house at the back opening onto the next street.

The second group numbered 29,082 and were built between 1872 and 1890. These were two- and three-roomed houses in blocks of eight. The sanitary conveniences were built in open spaces at the end of the blocks. It was rare for houses in the first and second groups to have baths.

The third group consisted of 14,224 houses and were built after 1890 and into the 1930s. This type was approved under the Housing and Town Planning Act of 1909. They were three- to five-roomed houses with a scullery and garden or forecourt in the front. They had water closets in the forecourt.

The appalling housing conditions were exacerbated by the atrocious occupancy factor. In 1921, 1,139 houses were shared by two families and another 196 by three or more families, whilst in 1931 this had increased to 1,427 for the former and 423 for the latter.

From this it can be seen that the problem of overcrowding required a massive programme of building new houses. Some people remote from the slums thought that this programme was unnecessary but most of us felt it would be a better idea to gut the interior of these houses and refurbish them, thus keeping the essential community together, when and wherever possible. My Mama, who was a strong voluntary worker, the District Nurses, from whom I learnt so much, and many other practical people, were partially successful in carrying out this idea, but were always fund-raising. Mercifully high-rise flats had not then appeared in Britain.

Leeds was only one of many cities with appalling slums, and whenever I had the opportunity I visited these too.

A major hazard from the overcrowded conditions and one that was rife in Leeds, was pulmonary tuberculosis. A distinction was made between "spit positive" and "spit negative" cases since it was from the former that the disease was spread rapidly. The report dated September 1929 of the Medical Officer of Health stated that ". . . only 40 per cent of the spit positive cases have a room to themselves, the remaining 60 per cent sharing a bedroom with an average of two other persons, whilst only 52 per cent of the spit positive cases have a separate bed. Actually at the time of collecting the information 87 spit positive cases were sharing beds with 96 other people".

Mama and her friends worked very hard, and voluntarily, on improvements, serving on hospital and school boards, and trying to better these appalling conditions. Political controversy sometimes hindered and dimmed the progress, even counterbalanced the efforts being made to help people, and I remember my parents lamenting to their friends and placing before them petitions, ideas and plans – what they and others considered was overall co-ordinated effort. One of my earliest recollections is of going the rounds to friends and others asking them to subscribe towards a certain improvement, such as providing an extra "shared" lavatory or the installation of a water tap or even a communal bath. Their reactions were quite revealing. Some exclaimed, "Those people won't know what to do with a bath – they'll use it to put coal in", to which my mother would reply: "Ah, then it is our fault for not providing the recipients with a coal hole!" On the whole, however, the donors were shocked and compassionate. The names of those who had been approached were listed and anyone whose attitude had been a bit negative received a second call, when possible, and was told that "Mrs Snooks" was delighted and enjoyed using the water tap, or other commodity which had been supplied. Outings or holidays were also arranged – it was essential for those existing in such awful conditions to be given the opportunity to enjoy being in the fresh air in the country and at the seaside. All these different actions and activities naturally meant continuous fund-raising.

Those were the days when the state left a great deal of responsibility to members of the community, and family units were still strong; people knew each other and helped each other in times of distress. Wilfred Owen, the famous poet (1893–1918), was among those who did care, and before 1914 he wrote:

> I am holding aloof from the short-breads; and I mean to give some to a gentle little girl of five, fast sinking under consumption – contracted after Chickenpox. Isn't it pitiable? She is going to a hospital (weeks hence *of course*), and may be beyond the reach of doctors by that time. She can't take unappetising food, poor Violet; but how is aught to be provided her; when the Father is perennially out of work, and the Mother I fancy half-starving for the sake of four children. This, I suppose, is only a typical *case*; one of many Cases! O hard word! How it savours of rigid, frigid professionalism! How it suggests smooth and polished, formal, labelled, mechanical callousness!

His words summarise poverty as he saw it then, and as it is still known today in so many places.

The Yorkshire spirit of hospitality and frankness was very evident in the villages and on the farms we visited; we were invited into the cottages and offered delicious teacakes and fresh bread, which in those days were baked at home. This was a great contrast to the slums of the towns, but whether in the country, towns, or cities, keeping warm in winter proved to be a problem. There was no electricity, so candles or small kerosene lamps were used, but often we had to raise the funds to purchase them for people.

At our homes in Scarcroft and later Thurlow we had a huge tiled stove which warmed the main hall and a few of the rooms, otherwise it was the coal and wood fire that provided heat. Central heating was unheard of. I quote the following from a local parish magazine:

But most homes then were dependent on the fire for cooking, boiling the kettle, heating the bath water and having one warm spot in winter. The fire was ever present, even on hot summer days, except for those who had paraffin heaters.

In the autumn the fire meant making sure there were faggots for kindling and a good supply of coal and logs. The chopping of kindling and the filling of coal scuttles were unpopular jobs for someone (usually a wrong-doer!). In winter, the fire was the gathering place of the family. As soon as one came in and answered the question "Did you shut the gate?" and the instruction "Take off those muddy boots", one moved to the fire to warm one's hands and then looked for a seat where knees and feet could be warmed. Woe betide the child who dared to sit in dad's chair, even if he was not likely to come in for some time.

In many homes, there was a grandparent who occupied the most draught-free seat and an occasional chore was making paper spills for grandad to use when lighting his pipe. One of the most popular jobs was making toast or toasting a piece of cheese, because it was a good excuse to monopolise the warmest place. If there were small children, this meant moving the fireguard, but there was always a fender, which usually had some brass pieces that had to be polished, but which was just right for putting one's feet on.

In front of the fire, there could be also trivet, where mum warmed the flat iron, while she used part of the kitchen table for ironing. The oven beside the fire was not only used for cooking, but also to heat bricks for bed warming. Just before bedtime, dad might be persuaded to tell a story, as everyone gathered round the fire, and the only noises were the singing of the kettle or mum spitting on the iron to check its warmth and cleanliness.

On Saturday nights, there was the ritual of bathing. In came the galvanized bath, large saucepans of water were heated and starting with the oldest, the children were bathed and dried in front of the fire – same water, with a little hot water added each time! When all were done, there was the mad scamper upstairs to icy bedrooms and the scramble into bed, hopefully warmed by a brick.

In winter, the gathering of the family round the fire after tea meant the uniting or welding together of the family, in the same way that regular meals together served the same purpose. Many of the stories told were like the more famous fables – there was a lesson for the children.

Older readers will remember changing for bed in front of the fire before moving to the icy bedroom.

I have vivid memories of the Leeds General Infirmary where I had been operated on for tuberculosis of a gland in my neck. There were prayers in the wards every morning. I loved the surgeons and the nurses. The discipline was strict and the standard of care for the individual was high and very personal. The staff always appeared to have time for us, were ready to answer my many questions, and gave us all the feeling that they really cared for us. Later, at home, I transformed the drawing room into an operating theatre. I persuaded friends staying in the house to join in; we gowned, scrubbed down and masked, and one of us was carried onto the operating table. The local doctor said to Mama: "Your daughter will certainly became a physician or surgeon, or perhaps a builder."

We were extremely fortunate in having a lovely garden with lawns, a rose garden, a Dutch garden, a rose pergola and a long walk between wide herbaceous borders to the kitchen garden beyond. The orangery led off the drawing room, and through the wrought-iron grilles we could glimpse the rainwater which was channelled off the roof to be stored in an underground tank, for the head gardener, Preston, allowed nothing but rainwater to moisten the precious plants which grew in the orangery – the two Kentias in copper-bound oak tubs, the great trails of crimson pink bougainvillea, the hanging baskets of lobelia of the most intense blue, long trailing fuchsias, and masses of different ferns and moonflowers. I remember the beauty of a white-flowered variety of ivy-leaf geranium called *l'Elegante*, the hydrangea, stephanotis, and the arum lilies of Easter. The conservatory had a warm, earthy smell that was clean and pleasant. For birthdays, Preston prepared lovely sprays of flowers. Alas, I have never had the time to learn about gardens and their landscaping.

Being so much the youngest child, with my brothers and sisters away at boarding school, I naturally spent a great deal of my time during the term with my parents. My father, who was already middle-aged when I was born, was quiet and reserved, spending more time in working on the family farms and reading and writing, than in talking. When he spoke, however, he proved to have an unusually wide vocabulary and the ability to express his thoughts with great clarity. Papa had won at least one prize for history at school, but his father had made him read mathematics at Trinity College, Cambridge, instead of history, which was his natural bent. At Cambridge he rowed and was awarded a cup for sculling at Trinity. His day started with a cold bath and physical exercises. Conservative in dress, he always wore a high, stiff white collar. He was a great believer in outdoor life, liked walking and was a skilful and intrepid horseman. He liked simple food such as baked apples, tomatoes and baked potatoes, indeed he was obliged to as he was born with a small stomach which could cause indigestion. This I have also inherited from him and always tried to keep to a strict diet except naturally during the War and for very many years afterwards, where food was so scarce, especially in Central and other parts of Europe and the Third World, but one became accustomed to that way of life.

As children we were allowed downstairs for Sunday lunch and a cold supper – to which we helped ourselves, as the staff had the evening off. After the age of eight we joined our parents for all meals and in the presence of people from very varying walks of life we learned much. It was customary *always* to rise when an adult entered the room, to open the door for an adult, and to shake hands on meeting. Once two members of the Royal Academy, F. W. Elwell and A. J. Munnings, reproduced the mediaeval timbered-frame barn on canvas: it was a beautiful oil painting. I used to enjoy watching and listening to these two famous artists. Papa enjoyed inviting people for meals and discussions, both formally and informally. Cocktail parties were not in vogue or considered right in our family.

I loved Papa deeply and when we went riding together to visit the farms we would discuss different subjects. At mealtimes, unless there were guests, he would often read, while Mama did crosswords. If we children made too much noise he would say: "Stop this damned nonsense or I will send you out of the dining room." Papa was strict, too, about the common cold. "Go outside and walk," was his answer for a cold cure. We also had an extremely strict nanny who never stopped telling us that "manners maketh man".

It was my mother, however, who had the greatest influence on my childhood, and, indeed, on my entire life, playing an important part in my later work and giving me her unfailing interest, encouragement and active help. She had been brought up in somewhat straitened circumstances by her widowed mother, who nevertheless managed, with the help of friends, to give her a wide education, later taking her abroad to Florence and Paris to study the history of art and languages. My mother was a woman of many talents and interests, which she loved sharing while still learning from others. She was a good writer, conversationalist and mimic, with a deep understanding of architecture, music and painting. The most striking of her gifts was perhaps her very warm and real interest in people, their wants and needs, and even in old age she remained a vital outgoing person. She had a great sense of fun, and a friend once remarked about her that she should either have been a bishop's wife – or an actress. Mama was ingenious at inventing games, and amongst her inventions was one in which everybody was invited to a party wearing something they had bought for 3d or 6d at Woolworths. This included imitation jewellery. It was a great leveller and caused much amusement. A book of party games called *I've Got Your Number* was much enjoyed. Mama was in every way an unworldly person. I remember her, for example, remarking one evening in her room when she had just come in from a long and heavy day of visits, meetings and an official luncheon: "Well, I wish to goodness people would save time and money on food and use them in feeding others in need."

Mama's father, Herbert Sims, had been an Anglican priest who had won a cricket Blue when at Jesus College, Cambridge, and also on occasion played for Yorkshire. He died young at St Cuthbert's Church, Hunslet, a poor parish in Leeds. My grandmother, Elizabeth Sims (Simmie), was strict, alert, tidy and very slim, and I remember her having a very small waist of only eighteen inches. She had few clothes, but wore these with dignity and always changed for dinner. She kept meticulous lists of presents for those in need, and information about them. She was an authority on Bradshaw's famous timetable covering all railway services in Britain. She used to tell me stories of how the poor lived and put up with awful conditions. We talked, too, of the contrasts in town and country houses; of how when maids were employed they felt, in some households at least, a sense of belonging and of security, particularly if their employers were aware of their social responsibilities.

Because both my father's estates and houses were large, some people assumed that we were well off. This was completely wrong as in the twenties and thirties, owing to the Great Depression and other reasons, farming was anything but profitable.

Very recently a former tenant farmer told me: "In the Depression, there were not many gentlemen farmers who merited the respect and gratitude that Mr Ryder did. We have a photograph of him on the mantelpiece of the living room in our farmhouse".

Religion influenced both my parents' lives – and my own – from the beginning. We attended church at Shadwell and Bardsey; for the beautiful part-Saxon, part-Norman church of Bardsey I bought, with the money I had saved from selling my hens' eggs, a crucifix which still hangs there today, and on the oak door a notice reads:

> Only a step from the street
> And the troubled ways of men
> Yet here may God with mortals meet
> And Christ be born again.

We were brought up strictly, too, as regards observing Lent and giving up sweets or whatever we most liked. On Good Friday there was the Three Hours' Service, a hot cross bun and a warm drink, and fasting afterwards. On some Sunday evenings we would gather around the piano to sing hymns while Mama played.

The house at Scarcroft was a busy one and there was always something happening: callers arriving, people coming in for help or advice, visitors to be looked after, and businessmen dropping in to the estate office. Tramps and the homeless were not simply turned away at the door with money: they were asked in to have a hot meal, a bath, a change of clothing, and, when they wanted a bed for the night, each was looked upon as an individual, a person with dignity. We children were always interested to know why they had resorted to the life they led.

It was the era when very few people possessed cars, and walking and bicycling (the latter sometimes on tandems) were popular, especially on Sundays and Bank Holidays. Crowds of people streamed past our home and the sound of their voices carried into the house which was separated from the road by only a stable yard and, further down, a long wood. In the neighbourhood, and no doubt in other parts of the country too, camping was very popular, for comparatively few people could afford holidays. They therefore either camped free or paid 3d to a local farmer for the use of part of a field. We too loved sleeping out, but Mama always tried to cover us with a mackintosh sheet, as the dew was heavy. I remember her coming down in the middle of the night to see if we were all right. One morning, on waking, we saw that three horses had got loose and were coming towards us at full gallop but luckily they veered off at the last moment.

Amongst the many people we visited was Mrs Liversedge in Scarcroft who stored in her capacious memory a large number of cake recipes. Nanny, who helped look after us at home, would expect me to write these down – a good exercise in writing, but quite difficult to accomplish in Mrs Liversedge's case. She lived in an era when false teeth were not made of plastic but of a much heavier material, vulcanite, and, as her mouth had shrunk with age, the dentures were loose and clicked alarmingly all the time she was speaking to me!

Another person who comes to mind is Gertrude Kiddy who lived in a very small cottage on the outskirts of Withersfield. She suffered from an acute kidney disease and was bed-bound in a small upstairs room. Her mother looked after her devotedly and Gertrude lay there uncomplainingly and appeared to look forward to our visits when we took her fresh fruit and other essentials and sat with her.

Although the sick and handicapped who lived in the rural areas may seem to have had a better existence than their counterparts in the towns and cities, for they were not engulfed in the perpetual smog and could enjoy the beauty of a flower or a tree, the majority existed in tiny bedrooms up steep and twisting staircases and were therefore confined within four walls. The rooms had very low ceilings and, with luck, a low window through which they could look out from their iron bedstead with its hard mattress. Wheelchairs were almost unheard of. District nurses were so thoroughly trained that they could deal with almost every situation and demand made upon them. Their experience in obstetrics was wonderful. Very few babies were born in hospital. Families were large in the villages, with as many as nine or eleven children; the Athertons in Thurlow had fifteen children (two were born in our house because of the overcrowding). Clothing and shoes were passed on to them and food provided too, when necessary. Sheets, crockery and other basic commodities were collected for distribution in both the urban and rural areas.

Mrs Cuthbert, who was over a hundred years old, was full of the most entertaining stories of her life in service, especially at Little Thurlow Park, the large and beautiful house built by Sir Stephen Soame (Lord Mayor of London in 1598) where a staircase was "so broad that a coach with four horses abreast could have driven up it". Sadly, this house was burnt down on 23 January 1809 and replaced by a Regency one. Sir Stephen established the free school for the children of Thurlow and the surrounding villages.

Miss Wallace, who was often given a lift by Mama in the car as she found walking difficult owing to her age (she was over ninety), always wore a black hat and "bobbed" as the old car drew up.

Listening to these and countless other individuals gave me a profound insight into their lives and reminded me of what a great deal they had witnessed and endured.

It was also a period of mounting distress. The men who had survived the First World War had been promised a better country in which to live, but instead they were faced with unemployment, a dole that barely held body and soul together, and a period of economic collapse which culminated in the Great Depression. When farming was at its hardest and taxation at its height, my father gave financial aid which he could ill afford to people who were suffering hardship or out of work. (Often this money was borrowed on an overdraft.)

Every year we undertook the journey from Yorkshire to the other family estate at Thurlow in Suffolk, where we spent four months. A special railway coach was reserved for us and our luggage, which was marked with red tape. These memorable journeys ended, however, in the thirties when the Depression also hit my father. I remember him coming into the library one Sunday morning and expressing deep concern at the huge number of unemployed and the financial crisis; he then explained to us the necessity of giving up the house at Scarcroft. From then on we lived permanently at Great Thurlow.

The beautiful Village of Thurlow was spread between the churches of Great and Little Thurlow, with its trees, hedges and cottages in gardens full of flowers – almost as it remains today. There is still the old Jacobean brick house where the fire glowed as we opened the door, the Cock Inn, and the house with the pump outside. There were the forge, the baker's, the cobbler's and the gamekeeper's cottages, the Rose and Crown Inn where the Women's Institute gave concerts. The two shops at each end of the Village were small general stores and sold everything that an average person required. Each order of bacon, cheese, sugar, dried fruit and so forth was weighed on the old iron and brass scales and then done up in greaseproof or tissue paper, or in blue bags folded most carefully at the ends and tied up with string, if necessary. Personal service was of paramount importance. All this took time, but people waited, talked and were patient. What a contrast to the bursting plastic bags and huge supermarkets of today!

A feature of the Village was the almshouses built in 1618 with their tiled roofs, mellow red bricks and well-kept gardens, and I visited them regularly with my mother. To those unable to cook or cope for themselves we took meals, which I often brought to them in the basket on my bicycle. I liked doing this, as I enjoyed talking to people. They were very friendly and open, and I started in this way to have an insight into their disabilities, problems and joys. Each person, adult or child, was an individual to whom one listened and from whom one learnt. There was a great variety in people's stories and circumstances. There was Mrs Wright, who lived on her own to a great age (over ninety): she was bedridden and liked companionship and recalling the past. Dr Wilkin, who was everybody's family doctor, Mrs Tweed, as well as other district nurses and friends who would talk with Mama about their rounds of the sick. The people, the children and the visits remain in my mind very vividly, for I accompanied Mama whenever possible.

Often when we were out riding or walking the hedge-keeper stopped to greet us. He spoke in a high-pitched East Suffolk dialect, and always had something cheerful and enthralling to say about the wildlife of the area. In those days there were far more hedges throughout the country (except in areas where stone was available for walls) than there are now, and it was his pride to keep them neatly cut and the ditches cleared, and also to see to it that the edges of the roads were well maintained. He invariably wore part of his First World War uniform, complete with putties.

Harvesting was a communal activity, when the binder, which was drawn by horses (later by tractor), had cut the corn and placed string round the sheaves, these were shocked (or stooked) in groups of six, eight or ten. Women and children came to pick up ears of corn that had been missed by the rake, walking up and down the field with their backs bent collecting as much as possible for their own use. This was called gleaning or leazing. Hens would sometimes be let loose on the stubble.

Shocking was really very hard work as the straw could be prickly on one's bare arms and legs, and we would work from daybreak until the light faded, usually with only two short breaks for refreshments; but for all that we enjoyed the experience and loved the smell of the corn under the blue August sky and the sight of the clover, poppies and cornflowers; the hedges with hips and haws and feathery "old man's beard"; blackberries ripening and the smell of the horses with their jingling harness. The shocks were left in the field until they were forked up into a horse-drawn cart, to be driven away for stacking and threshing. Much depended on the weather, as it always has done in farming, and the time factor was always in the farmer's mind. Once the corn had been stacked and thatched the farm workers had to turn round and start ploughing and drilling for the next harvest.

After threshing, the grain was sacked and weighed. In Suffolk, a sack was known as a coomb, which weighed anything from twelve to nineteen stone, depending on what was in it – wheat, oats, barley or beans. The men carried the sacks on their backs, put them on the cart by means of a hand-operated lifting machine and drove them to the barn where they stacked them two high. The carrying of sacks of such weight was an art in itself, and men these days are no longer able, nor indeed allowed, to do it.

Charles Dickens reminds me of all this in *Pickwick Papers*:

> There is no month in the whole year, in which nature wears a more
> beautiful appearance than in the month of August. Spring has many
> beauties, and May is a fresh and blooming month, but the charms of this

time of year are enhanced by their contrast with the winter season. August
has no such advantage. It comes when we remember nothing but clear
skies, green fields and sweet-smelling flowers – when the recollection of
snow, and ice, and bleak winds, has faded from our minds as completely
as they have disappeared from the earth – and yet what a pleasant time it
is! Orchards and cornfields ring with the hum of labour; trees bend beneath
the thick clusters of rich fruit which bow their branches to the ground;
and the corn, piled in graceful sheaves, or waving in every light breath that
sweeps above it, as if it wooed the sickle, tinges the landscape with a golden
hue. A mellow softness appears to hang over the whole earth; the influence
of the season seems to extend itself to the very wagon, whose slow motion
across the well-reaped field is perceptible only to the eye, but strikes with
no harsh sound upon the ear.

The country sounds never seemed spoilt by unnatural noises, such as
transistor radios, and both long before and during the War it was common
to hear people whistling and humming popular melodies of the day – a
habit which has now been largely dropped.

Like other villages, Thurlow too had its characters, the most notable of
whom was a woman with the habit of communicating through telegrams
delivered by the patient postman. Mrs Barnes exercised her imagination and
her thoughtfulness for the good of the Village. One telegram told Mama
that a large coach has been hired to take as many people as possible to the
Derby. I do not recall the details of how it was decided who should go, but
I believe notices were put up in the Village shops, pubs and post office.
Anyway, this news travelled fast, and on the appointed morning people filed
into the coach. Mrs Barnes handed Mama a big bunch of red, white and
blue flowers, instructing her to present them to Queen Mary, and also some
money for any members of the party who wanted to have their fortunes told
by the gypsies.

Their arrival at Epsom was delayed because quite a number of the
passengers, who had rarely in the past been given the opportunity of
travelling, soon felt sick. The coach had stopped while newspapers, paper
bags, eau de cologne and smelling salts were hastily sought and bought. It
was nightfall when the weary party returned to Thurlow, but Mrs Barnes –
the worse for the long wait – expected a graphic description of the outing
and then demanded that they sing the National Anthem!

Mrs Barnes' house belonged to my father. It was decided that a window
had to be blocked up. This entailed some loss of light in one of the rooms,
which was not to Mrs Barnes' liking. She struck back with characteristic and sardonic humour by having a large poster painted in front of
her house with the biblical words "The Lord is my Light" for all and sundry
to read.

On other occasions Mrs Barnes despatched boxes full of kippers or
peaches to my mother via Alec Sadler, the postman, for distribution. They
were then followed by a stream of telegrams – "Advise immediately if
kippers have arrived."

Each telegram contained its own element of surprise and variation: "No letter you promised to me Little Black Flag gone up today for New Whash House Big Flag from London." Or "I must show you everything I have written in the village to you I have done my best for everyone before I leave for year."

Mrs Barnes was extremely kind-hearted and generous, but she was an alcoholic and in consequence unpredictable. She would give wedding presents like a piano or a pony, and then ask Mama to go and get them back, so when Alec, the postman, married, he decided to ask for wallpaper as a wedding gift so that she would be unable to ask for its return.

When Mrs Barnes discovered that the Villages of Great and Little Thurlow had no funeral bier, she quickly made good this deficiency and the usual telegrams started to flow again: "Hand hearse giving who got to keep it clean I have cleaned it myself I paid 5/- for last cleaning before my big meeting I shall have something to say." And "Order hearse and get both Vicar and Rector to hold services and organise procession through village."

Mama obediently enquired of both the Rev. Basil le Fleming, vicar of Great Thurlow, and the Rev. Charles Rogers, rector of Little Thurlow, if they were prepared to take either a separate or joint dedication service; they declined both offers. She then had to explain this to Mrs Barnes, who promptly instructed Mama what to substitute for the clergy! A hasty meeting was arranged and people were encouraged to walk behind the hearse, which was draped with a Union Jack. The procession started at the main Village clock outside the Reading Room in Great Thurlow and ended in Little Thurlow Church, joined by Mrs Barnes en route, armed with her awe-inspiring tall stick. The hearse was duly wheeled in and Miss Grace Page played suitable music on the organ, which was pumped by Tony Smith. Mrs Barnes turned to Mama and shouted: "Sing a hymn." Although Mama had prepared what she hoped would be a very brief and suitable dedication service, this was dismissed by Mrs Barnes, and after the completion of each hymn she shouted: "Sing another!" Mama, Miss Page and the choir started to run out of what they considered suitable hymns for such an occasion and it was only after the eighth hymn (which I remember was "Through the night of doubt and sorrow . . .") and Mama's concluding prayer that Mrs Barnes was content to allow the exhausted singers to go home.

Mrs Barnes was in the frequent habit, too, of ringing up her firm of solicitors in Haverhill, and the partners always dreaded the variety of her requests and demands. Mr William Morris, who later became an honorary solicitor of the Foundation, was once urged to go to Thurlow to see Mrs Barnes. On his arrival she greeted him at the front door brandishing a shotgun. She wanted Mr Morris to go round to see Mill Cottage, but they had no key so Mrs Barnes smashed a windowpane and said, "Get inside."

The only hall in the Village large enough for plays and meetings was Mungo Lodge, which was owned by Mrs Barnes. One occasion which I recall most vividly concerned a pre-election meeting there. It was the turn of the Conservative candidate to address the assembly and the candidate happened to be a short man with a bowler hat and walking stick; he was singularly bereft of all humour. The same applied to his companion. Suddenly Mrs Barnes appeared (as was her habit) with a very heavy box of apples which she then proceeded to throw thick and fast at the party on the platform. There was pandemonium in the hall and several people did their utmost to restrain Mrs Barnes. Mama shouted, "Mrs Barnes, Mrs Barnes, you will break your beautiful lamps" and – perhaps as a result of this quick thinking on Mama's part – she was persuaded to leave.

Amongst my father's Cambridge friends was a very revered and kindly figure who was a great gardener. He was known to everybody as Captain Frink and his great granddaughter, the late Dame Elisabeth Frink, became a well-known sculptress. He had an open invitation to come and share our cold supper on Sunday evenings. Topics of conversation during the meal ranged widely. He had a feeling of good neighbourliness towards everyone, and if he thought there was a suspicious lack of activity in a village house or cottage he would use his ladder to see if life continued on the upstairs floor! On several occasions his inquisitive face at the window had surprised and startled women engaged in their belated morning toilet. This particular habit of his had been formed when one of our friends had died suddenly; his motives were entirely those of a good neighbour!

In spite of individual idiosyncrasies, however, there was a very deep sense of community at Thurlow, which makes me feel that I belong there even now; many years after the death of my father and the sale of the family home.

On one side of Great Thurlow Church with its square, solid tower, a pair of white gates and an avenue of chestnut trees led to the Hall. In springtime the grass beneath the trees was golden yellow with aconites and, later, daffodils. The Hall was a large Georgian house, its simple lines softened by the creeper which covered it. A high brick wall hid from view the kitchen garden and the greenhouses, and behind were the rose garden, the lawns descending to the stream, and the old trees – copper beech and oak and yew. I had my own very small patch in the kitchen garden where I spent much time, for I liked to see things grow and bear fruit, and I loved the smell of sun, damp earth, moss and tomatoes. I enjoyed the fun of pinching grapes and leaving only the stalks, much to the gardener's annoyance; punting under the curved bridge; listening to the call of pheasant and partridge; and catching the scent of lilac and acacia.

Up to the age of nine I had lessons at home with my mother, although a French teacher came some years during the summer holidays. I was obliged to converse in French, at mealtimes or one day of the week both at home and at my first school. My mother taught me all the elementary subjects, and I would sit with her on the sofa listening to her talk about different countries and peoples, their cultures, folklore and history. I became interested in music. Each spring there was a local musical festival at Clare in which many villages participated. The standard was quite high and the adjudicators came from well-known schools of music. My mother was a co-founder with Mrs Mary Proby and a hardworking president. The choir master at Thurlow, Percy Kibble, lived at Haverhill. He was a perfectionist and rehearsed relentlessly one evening each week in our drawing-room. Songs (four-part and unison) and madrigals were sung and I can remember the ringing tones of the large-bosomed soprano as she sang "Kind Sir, you cannot have the Heart" from *The Gondoliers*. She performed with joy and enthusiasm and her voice echoed throughout the house. Mr Kibble was my first piano teacher, and although I never became proficient, he must have given me a liking for it, for I see in my mother's diary: "I went to the churchyard and returned to the church to find Sue perched on the organ stool, pulling out stops and playing five-finger exercises with great assurance and effect, Gavin Dudley blowing for her." Alas, I can no longer play, but the love of music has remained and increased, and it means much to me.

Christmas was for us all the highlight of the year. For weeks beforehand a whole team of volunteers prepared and made very many presents, especially for those we knew would not be receiving any. Whatever the weather, my mother drove herself to Yorkshire (considered a considerable distance in those days) to present her gifts, occasionally taking me or one of my brothers with her. Mama kept in close contact with the district nurses and indeed all those with whom she had been associated and worked with, especially in the slums. Her warm-hearted nature made her see how important the personal side of giving was, and each present was made or chosen with special attention to what the recipient would like.

Carol singers and bell-ringers called and were entertained, but above all it was the mystery and beauty of the Christmas story that dominated everything, and all through Advent we prepared for joy of the birth of Christ. Usually the whole family came for Christmas, and I had the companionship of my two half-nieces, Anne and Peggy, who were near my age and who later became an architect and a nurse respectively.

But I was closest to my three brothers: John, who later became an historian; Michael, a physician; and Stephen, who read history but eventually took up farming. Stephen was a good mimic, while Mama was in the habit of constantly playing practical jokes, and I suppose I have inherited her sense of humour. One evening I offered to help out at dinner and dressed up as a parlour maid in a black dress with a white apron. Apparently the only person who recognised me was a retired Admiral, who said to Mama, "How unusual to see someone enjoying a meringue behind the screen near the sideboard". I remember Papa became slightly indignant when I took the port round twice.

On Saturday afternoons we were usually allowed to accompany Papa to the Museum and bookshops in Cambridge, where he would show me the way in which the books were arranged and explain their contents. We spent hours there and John, my eldest brother, would lose count of time as he became so absorbed in reading. Occasionally I would be sent back to fetch him, and one evening he was locked in, not having noticed that the shop was closing. We were expected to be avid readers and were able to look reasonably interested when books written by authors such as Somerset Maugham, H.G. Wells, Aldous Huxley, Dickens, Hardy and C.S. Lewis were mentioned.

From the age of eight I helped to look after the dairy; my half-sister gave me two cows and I began my own small herd of Jerseys. I took this work seriously, studying farm books and magazines so as to be sure that I was doing everything correctly and thoroughly. After milking we separated the milk, and then I would clean the dairy and scrub the flagstones. People from the Village came with their enamel mugs and jars to the door of the top dairy to buy the milk which I would ladle out to them, marking it off on the register. One large family always asked for skimmed milk, which was cheaper, but I did not think that was right, and let them have the ordinary full-cream milk. Butter-making was done in the other dairy near the laundry, at first in the old wooden tubs, which were quite heavy for me to turn, and later in the three-minute churn. I would roll the butter, salt it and make it up into pound and half-pound packs. Then I would clean up the churns and equipment, which involved me in a lot of hand scrubbing.

It was hard work, but I enjoyed it, and at twelve, because my father encouraged me and possibly because he thought I was proficient enough, I entered for a butter-making competition at a local show. Together with Argent, the head dairyman, who instructed me so thoroughly, and his colleague, I also helped deliver the calves and shared in the milking. It was hard work with a herd of twenty-four that had to be milked twice a day.

On rare and special occasions I made Devonshire cream. This was done by pouring milk into shallow round copper pans which stood in the coolest place in the larder to allow the milk to set. We did not own a refrigerator but relied upon large blocks of ice which were kept in a special ice box. The larder faced north and the window was covered in wire mesh. The ice was delivered by horse and cart and the iceman sawed off, outside your house, the quantity you required. When the milk had set, the copper pans were carefully carried onto the kitchen range and heated very gently without allowing the milk to boil. The pans were then returned to the cool of the slate shelves of the larder and left for another twelve hours. The cream was then taken off with a fish slice and the skimmed milk used for cooking.

In the carpenter's shop I learnt from George Womack the use of tools and different kinds of wood, and how to make a table, a trolley and a book-case. One Friday, each month, an architect friend of Papa's came over to stay for the weekend. He was most diligent and I enjoyed spending time with him, going round the properties on the estate and learning a great deal about maintenance of buildings, repairs and restoration work, and the different materials needed to renovate the buildings on the home farm and the various cottages and farmhouses. My father encouraged me to go round and listen to and ask questions of the men who were responsible for the regular maintenance, so I was aware of their trades and the time the work took but, above all, of the quality of the service they gave. I was allowed to choose the colour schemes for the exterior decoration of the farmhouses and cottages. When tractors became redundant or farm machinery out of date, my father also permitted me to bargain with scrap merchants to secure a good price for them.

In the house, Nellie Martin, the scullery maid, taught me how to scrub over very wide areas (on my knees, of course) – mops were never allowed; and from Miss Annie Bainbridge, the head housemaid (affectionately called "Bay"), I learnt how to do housework and all that this entailed without the many mechanical gadgets we have these days. We would "bottom" a room, to use a Yorkshire term, either by removing everything or placing objects of furniture in the middle and covering them with dust sheets. We would then get down to our system of cleaning. Incidentally every tiny piece of soap was saved, dampened, and rolled into tablets or balls ready for re-use.

The staff had a close and well-organised routine. Each knew what was expected of them. Regardless of the number staying in the house, my parents and their guests had their curtains opened and drawn each morning and evening by the head housemaid. In the morning, one of the under-housemaids would also enter each room to clear the grate, lay the fire and light it. Others would make their rounds with special trays of early morning tea served in the old and charming china. Then there was the ritual of bringing in the hot water in brass jugs for the washstand basins. This had to be repeated late every evening after the family and guests finished dinner. The housemaids moved so quietly and looked so pretty in the morning in their pink cotton dresses, white aprons and mop caps and black stockings and shoes. In the late afternoon they would change into black dresses and frilly aprons and caps.

It was unusual for a member of the staff to complain as everyone had proper food and accommodation, at least with our family and with those families whom we knew, but their pay was extremely low.

Staff were often sons and daughters of previous staff, and the senior people sometimes gave decades of loyal service. We became true friends and learnt from childhood always to be polite and greet them regardless of the time of the day. Also we were expected by our parents to learn about their tasks. In their retirement the family looked after them in return for their dedication.

The staff had its own hierarchy. The housekeeper would eat in her own room, next door to the stillroom, where jams were made and fruit bottled. Cooper, our last butler, who died when I was young, would sit at the head of the table and take his meals with the maids. Grace was always said before meals and prayers were said each morning with all the staff present.

Our nanny was extremely strict and when the family were still young there were two nursery maids, but naturally we had to make our own beds and help clean. From my earliest recollection I could never tolerate dirt, dust or untidiness. My reaction today is still to get out my scrubbing brush, floor cloth, hard soap and kneeler. Furthermore, in rare spare moments, I enjoyed sorting and was taught how to wash the clothes properly, to use a wash board, copper dolly, also to mangle and iron with an iron heated on a stove. Everything was then neatly piled and put into drawers ready for distribution.

Scrubbing remains my favourite physical work.

Bay had served in several well-known households. First she was with Sir Hugh and Lady Bell, parents of Gertrude Bell,* at Routon Grange near Northallerton for four years (this house was later demolished). Then she worked for Lady Lawston at Grimston Hall near Tadcaster during 1918–19. Following this she was employed by Mr and Mrs Gascoigne of Lothorton, Garforth, Leeds (now a National Trust House), and then by a Mr and Mrs Charles Webb. She left the latter house to come and work for Mama.

These people all had London houses for the season. Bay once told me, "I clearly remember meeting you and your mother outside the railway station at Harrogate and as we sat together I immediately felt an affinity and was delighted to come and serve your mother for the rest of my working life after the pomp and finery of some beautiful houses." Bay stayed for forty-three years and became Mama's devoted companion. They loved walking, working and doing things together.

I also enjoyed learning from the cooks in the large kitchen with the high ceiling, and saw how to cater for numbers. One of the cooks was Mrs Blada who had fled from Czechoslovakia. Both she and Ruth, the kitchen maid, who was Austrian by origin, had a flair for cooking and baking. They were both Jewish and had succeeded in escaping to England thanks to my parents and their friends who also tried very hard to collect funds and make arrangements to place Jewish children and occasionally other Jewish adults with families in this country, thus saving them from being exterminated by the Nazis. Once, to the consternation of others, Mrs Blada enjoyed plucking a goose to stuff her pillow. She also liked to remind us that her first post in England was as cook to Mr and Mrs Winston Churchill.

There were more conventional pastimes too, blackberrying in our favourite wood, riding over the countryside I loved so much, all the activities of the house – the music and charades, the play-readings and games, the practical jokes and the dances I was allowed to attend, for I

---

* "Gertrude Bell was perhaps the most distinguished woman of our day, in the field of oriental exploration, archaeology and literature and in the service of the Empire in Irak."
The Times obituary, 13 June 1926

was very fond of dancing. On occasions we would enjoy tobogganing down the wide main staircase on a large tin tray. My mother loved reading aloud and making up stories. She also wrote a pageant about the history of Thurlow in which the entire Village joined, helping and taking part. Bay and friends spent hours in the workroom making costumes. The proceeds were divided between the Chinese Red Cross and the building fund for the Village hall. To boost funds, Sir Malcom Campbell brought his famous racing car *Bluebird* to Thurlow for the occasion.

We all had a full and busy life, with no time to get bored, and the participation in community activities brought us together in a way that is almost impossible to describe. There was once a Mr Bulkley who could not pay his rent – apparently nobody knew where he came from and he took over (presumably under false pretences) one of the farms. Our agent told Papa he was armed and felt he could not go back to ask for the rent again. Shortly afterwards Mr Bulkley was living with us. Weeks later Mama and Papa said to each other: "Well, what are we going to do with him?" Neither felt it kind to ask him to leave, as he was alone and odd. He talked to many of us and asked me, amongst many other things, to mend the puncture on his bicycle with a needle and black cotton. Weeks later he rode off, supposedly to open a sweet shop in Cambridge, but he came back frequently and without warning, and knowing that he would always find a bed and food with us.

For Papa, who after all was a very busy man, the constant activity in the house must have sometimes been trying. I remember him wistfully walking about the house finding rooms, including the library, drawing-room and dining-room, full of people. He had a routine for each day, which began with his early morning exercises and continued until late in the evening, and apart from all his other activities he was also a great champion of countries which were trying to gain their independence. Papa and his colleagues would also discuss the growing threat of Nazism and how some people seemed more interested in writing letters to *The Times* about when they first heard the cuckoo!

Mama went to Holy Communion almost every day of her life as she was high Anglo-Catholic. On Sundays the family invariably attended church, either going to the service at Great Thurlow adjoining the grounds or, more often, climbing stiles and walking across the fields to St Peter's, Little Thurlow (rebuilt in the thirteenth century), sometimes as the five-minute bell was ringing and the rector, with flapping cassock, could be seen hurrying across his garden to the Church. In summer the side door of the Church near the altar was left open and we could see the sun glinting on the grass among the headstones; in winter hot air would blow through the gratings in the floor and the candles were lit in the brass candelabra.

Bell-ringing in Britain began in the early fifteenth century and, except for a few nations of the Commonwealth, it remains peculiar to this country. Elsewhere, bells are either chimed or played from a keyboard. Church towers can hold up to twelve bells. The bells are rung in a full circle to set musical patterns and, in theory, no two bells should sound at the same time. The tone depends upon the metal content which is an alloy of copper and tin. In each English village the sound of the church bells varies according to the size and number of bells, and there are said to be 10,000 different peals of bells in England.

In addition to ringing for Sunday services, weddings and other special occasions, each team of bell-ringers usually practises one evening a week. In the past, when a person died in the village, a bell would toll.

Alas, this beautiful tradition of bell-ringing is dying out due to lack of interest among younger people, who appear to prefer a very different kind of secular music!

The Litany of the Saints was said regularly. One of my favourite canticles was the *Benedicite*:

> O all ye Works of the Lord, bless ye the Lord:
> Praise him, and magnify him for ever.
> O ye Angels of the Lord, bless ye the Lord:
> O ye Heavens, bless ye the Lord:
> O ye Waters that be above the Firmament, bless ye
> the Lord:
> O all ye Powers of the Lord, bless ye the Lord:
> O ye Sun and Moon, bless ye the Lord:
> O ye Stars of Heaven, bless ye the Lord:
> O ye Showers and Dew, bless ye the Lord:
> O ye Winds of God, bless ye the Lord:

There was a smell of beeswax, an organ which had to be pumped by hand and, on either side of the altar, there were brass tablets inscribed with the Ten Commandments – ". . . Thou shalt not kill, Thou shalt not covet . . ."

The box pew of the family is still there behind the choir stalls on the left of the altar, high, dark and polished, and today there is a plaque on the wall which reads:

> In loving memory of Charles Foster Ryder, a constant worshipper in this House of God, Lord of the Manor of Little Thurlow.
> *"What doth the Lord require of thee but to do justly and to love mercy and to walk humbly with thy God."*

Underneath, there is an inscription to my mother:

> *"He that dwelleth in love dwelleth in God, and the souls of the righteous are in the hands of God."*

On the other wall a wooden plaque made from his aircraft propeller commemorates William Harold Ryder, my youngest half-brother, who was killed near Arras while flying during the First World War. Papa wore a black tie for the rest of his life. This poem by Wilfred Owen reminds me so much of him:

Anthem for Doomed Youth

What passing bells for these who die as cattle?
  – only the monstrous anger of the guns
    only the stuttering rifles' rapid rattle
Can patter out their hasty orisons.
No mockeries for them; no prayers nor bells,
nor any voice of mourning save the choirs,
The shrill demented choirs of wailing shells;
    and bugles calling for them from sad shires.

What candles may be held to speed them all?
    Not in the hands of boys, but in their eyes
    shall shine the holy glimmers of goodbyes.
The pallor of girls' brows shall be their pall;
Their flowers the tenderness of patient minds,
And each slow dusk a drawing-down of blinds.

2

The Years of Transition

Beginners who may hope to improve.

ALTHOUGH OUR OWN HOME life was happy, the tragedies, sorrows and unsolved problems remaining as the aftermath of the First World War weighed on many people's minds, for there was hardly a family that had not been affected: millions had lost their lives and thousands were left mutilated. Written and verbal descriptions of the battles and the terrible drawings and photographs of disfigured men and buildings haunted me as a child.

Many people living and working around us had been involved in the fighting and nursing, and as a few were willing to talk, I learnt much by listening to them. Several had been affected by the gas attacks on the Western Front from April 1915 onwards. A figure I remember used to bicycle regularly along the local roads, swearing at anybody who passed – he was shell-shocked and disturbed, and had no other occupation than bicycling on through the four seasons of the year.

In general, there was at that time far, far more respect for, and attention to, those who had died than there is today. On Armistice Day the whole nation united to remember them by observing a two-minutes' silence, when *every* person and vehicle stood still, regardless of where they were or what they were doing, often while the names of those from the village who had died in action were read out in church or at the local War memorial, and we sang: "I vow to thee, my country" and "O Valiant Hearts". I remember too, the last few words of John Henry Newman's famous hymn "Lead Kindly Light":

> . . . and with the morn those angel faces smile
> which I have loved long since, and lost a while.

In church, after the beautiful prayers and before the Last Post was played, the following lines, written by Laurence Binyon, were said:

> They shall grow not old, as we that are left grow old:
> Age shall not weary them, nor the years condemn.
> At the going down of the sun and in the morning we
> will remember them.

The sacrifices others had made in defence of liberty and the price they had paid seem even higher considering how this was subsequently taken for granted by many people.

Vera Brittain's autobiography, *Testament of Youth*, published in 1933, gave a vivid and poignant description, especially of the years when she nursed with the Voluntary Aid Detachment during 1915–18. Here I quote part of a letter written during the Cambrai offensive:

> The hospital is very heavy now – as heavy as when I came; the fighting is continuing very long this year, and the convoys keep coming down, two or three a night . . . Sometimes in the middle of the night we have to turn people out of bed and make them sleep on the floor to make room for more seriously ill ones that have come down from the line. We have heaps of gassed cases at present who came in a day or two ago; there are 10 in this ward alone. I wish those people who write so glibly about this being a Holy War, and the orators who talk so much about going on no matter how long the War lasts and what it may mean, could see a case – to say nothing of 10 cases – of mustard gas in its early stages – could see the poor things burnt and blistered all over with great mustard-coloured suppurating blisters, with blind eyes – sometimes temporally [*sic*], sometimes permanently – all sticky and stuck together, and always fighting for breath, with voices a mere whisper, saying that their throats are closing and they know they will choke. The only thing one can say is that such severe cases don't last long; either they die soon or else improve – usually the former; they certainly never reach England in the state we have them here, and yet people persist in saying that God made the War, when there are such inventions of the Devil about . . .
>
> Morning work – i.e. beds, T.P.R.s (temperature, pulses, respirations), washing, medicines, etc., which in Malta I started at 6.0, start here at 3.30! The other morning there were no less than 17 people to wash! . . . Cold is terrific; the windows of the ward are all covered with icicles and the taps outside frozen. I am going about the ward in a jersey and long coat.
>
> The extreme cold had begun very early that winter. By the middle of December our kettles and hot-water bottles and sponges were all frozen hard when we came off duty if we had not carefully emptied and squeezed them the night before – which in our hasty, last-minute toilettes we seldom did, for getting up to go on duty in the icy darkness was a shuddering misery almost as exacting as an illness. Our vests, if we hung them over a chair, went stiff, and we could keep them soft only by sleeping in them. All the taps froze; water for the patients had to by cut down to a minimum, and any spilt in the hut passage between our rooms turned in a few seconds to ice.

Later, Vera Brittain writes:

> I realised it was not the courage and generosity of the dead which had brought this chaos of disaster, but the failure of courage and generosity on the part of the survivors.

Quite apart from the actual fighting at the fronts, fifty-one Zeppelin attacks made on Britain had killed 557 and injured 1,358 people, as well as 857 people killed and 2,058 injured by German aircraft. Mama used to tell that in the night a member of the household would come to her door and say,

"The Germans are over the stable yard." It was, however, the terrible number of thirty-seven million casualties (or more) lost in monstrous circumstances which kept recurring in my mind while we drifted on to the next abyss. We were waiting for another statesman to confirm again what Sir Edward Gray had said on 3 August 1914: "The lamps are going out all over Europe; we shall not see them lit again in our lifetime."

Reading the prose and poetry produced during and after that great and awful conflict – Siegfried Sassoon, Charles Sorley, Rupert Brooke, Julian Grenfell, Wilfred Owen, Geoffrey Dearmer and others – I felt we were being unfaithful to the writers and those for whom they had written.

I quote from the last of the War Poets, Geoffrey Dearmer:

Revelation

Can death give you such dignity, and pride
So beautiful it put our grief to shame?
For now we stumble as we speak your name,
Yet you were just a boy before you died.
We question blankly, pondering heavy-eyed,
Can this be he we used to praise or blame
In careless moments, ere the trial came
When all the bravest hearts in anguish cried?
Then, humbled, we beheld our poor disguise,
False moods and manners clothed in empty speech
Which drowned the silence – till there came a day
That smote our vision to awakened eyes:
For God bent down to bring you to our reach,
But ere we touched you, you had gone away.

Fallen

The days shall darken and sink down to Night,
And Night shall break in the bleak dawn of Day:
The years shall dim his face, our fleeting sight
Shall see his splendid image fade away
Beyond the knowledge of our drifting thought
Which moves in circles to the source again,
Beyond dark seas with shivering stars inwrought,
Beyond war-burdened men in stricken pain.

I searched in rage and passionate despair
Down winding paths of thought, and comradeless
In the full surge and tumult where he died
I turned; and saw my Brother standing there.
His face was like a dawning happiness –
I saw wounds in his hands, his feet, his side.

Gallipoli, October, 1915

The fallen rested in massive cemeteries with mile upon mile of graves. There were 15,277 in different countries, mostly in the Commonwealth War Graves Commission's War cemeteries and plots, but there were also War graves in many civil cemeteries and churchyards throughout the world.

King George V wrote in 1922 in Flanders:

> We can truly say that the whole circuit of the earth is girdled with the graves of our dead . . . and, in the course of my pilgrimage, I have many times asked myself whether there can be more potent advocates of peace upon earth through the years to come than this massed multitude of silent witnesses to the desolation of war.

The following poem was written by Lieutenant-Colonel John McCrael of the Royal Canadian Army Medical Corps who paid the supreme sacrifice in the First World War:

In Flanders Fields

In Flanders fields the poppies blow
Between the Crosses row on row
that mark our place, and in the sky
the Larks, still bravely singing, fly
scarce heard amid the guns below

We are the dead short days ago
We lived felt dawn sunset glow
Loved, and were loved, and now we lie
In Flanders' Fields

Take up our quarrel with the foe
To you from failing hands we throw
The Torch, be yours to hold it high
If you break faith with us who die
We shall not sleep, though poppies grow
In Flanders Field

May 1915

At the top of each headstone was engraved the national emblem or the service or regiment badge, followed by the rank, name, unit, date of death, age and the appropriate religious emblem, and at the foot, in many cases, an inscription chosen by the relatives.

The men and women who were cremated, or had no known grave, or who perished at sea (the Royal Navy lost 38,505 officers and men, and the Merchant Navy 14,661), were commemorated on memorials ranging from small tablets bearing a few names to great monuments bearing many thousands. One such memorial, bearing 54,360 names and designed by Sir Edwin Lutyens, is at the Menin Gate to the Missing of the Ypres Salient, and another is the Thiepval Memorial to the Missing of the Somme (72,073 names). There are another 35,000 names of the missing commemorated on the panels of the Tyne Cot cemetery at Passchaendale.

I was taken, during the early 1930s, to visit the vast War cemeteries which stretch across great areas of France and Belgium. Never will I forget the emotions I felt as we stopped at each place – that terrible, grievous sense of the waste of so many young lives. I thought of all that promise which would remain now forever unfulfilled, and of the irreparable loss borne by their families and their country. The futility of it all was overwhelming.

The late Lord Butler's cousin, Charles Hamilton Sorley, was killed in 1915 at the age of twenty. He and Wilfred Owen shared the same unsentimental streak with its stark lack of self-pity. Owen's bitterness became overpowering, and on New Year's Eve 1917 he wrote to his mother:

> I thought of the very strange look on all faces in that camp; an incomprehensible look, which a man will never see in England . . . It is not despair, or terror, it was more terrible than terror, for it was a blindfold look, and without expression, like a dead rabbit's. And to describe it, I think I must go back and be with them.

He was killed on 4 November 1918, a week before the Armistice.

The following poem by Wilfred Owen expresses the tragic experiences and waste of life:

> Bent double, like old beggars under sacks,
> Knock-kneed, coughing like hags, we cursed
>   through sludge,
> Till on the haunting flares we turned our backs,
> And towards our distant rest began to trudge.
> Men marched asleep. Many had lost their boots
> But limped on, blood-shod. All went lame; all blind;
> Drunk with fatigue; deaf even to the hoots
> Of gas shells dropping softly behind.
>
> Gas! Gas! Quick, boys! – an ecstasy of fumbling.
> Fitting the clumsy helmets just in time:
> But someone still was yelling out and stumbling.
> And floundering like man in fire or lime.
> Dim through the misty panes and thick green light,
> As under a green sea, I saw him drowning.
> In all my dreams, before my helpless sight he plunges
>   at me, guttering, choking, drowning.
>
> If in some smothering dreams you too could pace
> Behind the wagon that we flung him in,
> And watch the white eyes writhing in his face,
> His hanging face, like a devil's sick of sin;
> If you could hear, at every jolt, the blood
> Come gargling from the froth-corrupted lungs,

> Obscene as cancer, bitter as the cud
> Of vile, incurable sores on innocent tongues,
> My friend, you would not tell with such high zest
> To children ardent for some desperate glory
> The old lie: Dulce et decorum est pro patria
>   mori.

Sir Arthur Bryant, the famous historian, wrote:

I once asked Bernard Paget, the Second World War Commander-in-Chief who trained the British armies for D-Day before Montgomery took over, which in his opinion, was the finest army this country had ever produced and he replied "the army that went over the top on 1 July, 1916". By this he did not mean that the latter compared in training or experience with any of the armies in other battles and in the Second World War, but that it was one whose personnel, in human quality and fighting spirit and potential, outshone them all. "All my young England fell today in fight". one of the soldier poets of the time wrote. In that horrific battle and those that preceded and followed it, Britain lost the leaders who would have given her direction for so many decades.

Edward Wyndham Tennant, a schoolboy at Winchester in 1914, had succeeded in joining the Grenadier Guards at the age of 17. A few weeks after his eighteenth birthday, after a year's training in England, he sailed to France with his battalion, writing before the battle of Loos, "I wouldn't be anywhere else but here for the world . . . I have the feeling of Immortality very strongly. I think of Death with a light heart and as a friend whom there is no need to fear." By the time of the Somme he was a finished veteran, with more experience of the hardships and horror, as well as nobilities and sacrifices, of war, than most professional British soldiers.

His death, like that of many others who fell that year, is the measure of all we have lost. Two nights before he died he wrote to his mother: "The spirit of the Brigade of Guards will carry all resistance before it . . . I have never been prouder of anything, except your love for me, than I am of being a Grenadier . . . I feel rather like saying, '*If it be possible let this cup pass from me.*' but the triumphant finish '*nevertheless not what I will but what Thou willest*', steels my heart and sends me into this battle with a heart of triple bronze . . . Your love for me and my love for you has made my whole life one of the happiest there has ever been." His memorial, under the spire of Salisbury Cathedral, records how he "gave his earthly life to such matter as he set great store by: the honour of his country and his home". "How we all loved him," one of his soldiers wrote, "The whole regiment loved him . . . He was the life and soul of everything; fun or danger it was all the same to him." "When things were at their worst," wrote another, "he would go up and down the trenches cheering the men . . . when danger was greatest his smile was loveliest."

It seemed we had devalued the quality of their lives. Somebody who seems to me to have personified the same qualities in a different and later time was Antony Knebworth. His biography, by his father, the Earl of Lytton, is a book that still moves me. This boy was a person I admired, not only for his writing, but also for his outlook on life as expressed in one of his letters:

> It seems to me immensely unimportant whether we live or die, are gay or sad, but very essential never to give up trying one's utmost. Let us be thankful for what was good, hope for the future, love, laugh and praise, and one day perhaps we shall know.

The year 1933 brought the rise of Nazism and in 1935 racial laws were passed in Germany; once again dark shadows lengthened over Europe. We had Jewish friends staying near Thurlow who had managed to get out of Germany, and they told us – and others too – that pogroms had begun and would get worse, and that many thousands of people, including Socialists and Christians, were being arrested and sent to the concentration camps of Dachau, Esterwegen and Oranienburg-Sachsenhausen which had been founded in 1934–5; the rule of terror had begun. Having become so aware of all the implications of the First World War through all that I had heard and read, I began to feel that every day we lived brought us closer to the Second.

* * *

In the meantime I had been sent to my first school as a weekly boarder. I was extremely homesick, not because of the place itself or the lessons, but because I missed my parents and the activities at home so greatly. It was the only thing about which I can clearly remember not agreeing with Mama. At one point I ran away, but after a mile or so decided that it would not have the desired effect, nor would I necessarily be accepted back by Papa, who was a strict disciplinarian and considered that a woman should learn a trade or profession and be independent regardless of her status in life. I wept and wept every night and felt the more desperate when nobody appeared to understand, for they probably thought the mood would pass.

It was at this time that I gradually became aware of the profound, inexplicable delight of classical music and discovered the mystical peace it could bring. I yearned to be able to play, but despite long hours of practice I could never master the piano. Unfortunately, I still know very little about classical music, but there are certain works to which I can listen for hours on end; and if I ever find myself in the presence of musicians I am enthralled by their knowledge and art.

Amongst my other loves was dancing, but though I tried hard I never mastered that either. My tuition commenced when I was about five years old, and when I was nine Miss Stainer (who ran her own school) became my teacher for Greek, ballroom, ballet and tap dancing. I remember her auburn hair, her high-heeled court shoes and elegant dresses. She was always accompanied by two or three teachers and a pianist from her school. The former wore leotards similar to those worn by all the pupils.

Greek dancing was performed outdoors in fine weather, while we practised exercises for hours at the barre before commencing centre practice. This is necessary for the limbering of all the muscles and to learn technique. We had to take everything, including our exercises, very seriously. We would watch the older girls wearing points, but before reaching that stage we had to loosen up our blocked ballet slippers in an attempt to make them more supple and "easy" for our feet to dance in. I particularly remember the great moment first wearing points, but only after three years of training. (It is quite unusual even to be allowed to wear blocks before the age of eleven.) We would put our feet in resin and rub the blocks in it to supple them up. A few girls used to wrap lamb's wool round their toes. This was a painful part of the experience, unknown to those who have never known the joy of being taught ballet. I had good reason to be grateful for this training, particularly because it gave great strength to my legs and feet.

Miss Stainer explained to her pupils that learning dance meant long training and very hard work, especially after exercises at the barre. "The earlier you start the happier you will be. Always keep the joy of dance and mime. Use your head and arms and remember particularly your facial expression." She also taught us a little of the history of dance, and these lessons seemed all too short. "I want you to love classical ballet. Dance is an emotional art but one of the most neglected."

Miss Stainer was a sister of Leslie Howard, one of our most gifted and admired stage and screen actors, who died in 1943 when his unarmed aircraft disappeared on a flight from Lisbon to London. Like millions of others, I remember him best as Ashley Wilkes (husband of Melanie) in that classic film Gone with the Wind, and also as Professor Higgins in Pygmalion.

I behaved very mischievously one day on hearing that parents of would-be pupils were to be shown around the school. Another girl and I stuffed several pillowcases and laid these out on one of the four beds in our room. We covered the "body" with a sheet on which we placed flowers and a prayer book; the curtains were then drawn. There was a loud collective gasp as the mistress opened the door and the visitors saw the touching scene before them. I was hiding behind the door in the loo opposite. Naturally, and properly, we were later sent for and received a severe warning. We were both made to pay a penny to threepence from our pocket money for each article used to stuff the "body", and this meant borrowing. It took us two terms – or more – to pay our fines!

When I left, the headmistress, who bore me no grudge, wrote: "Sue has worked well throughout the term and really knew her work for the examinations. She is cheerful and gay by nature and most helpful and reliable in both form and in the house."

These were generous words. After looking round various schools, Mama went to see Miss Sheldon, Miss Hindle and Miss Bird, co-founders of a comparatively new school at Benenden in Kent, and at the age of twelve I went there as a new girl. Wearing of uniform was essential and strenuously enforced, together with a sense of tidiness and a strict, but humane, general discipline.

The founders and the school had a profound and lasting influence on me. Vera Joscelyne, a member of staff, remembers the school's first term at Bickley and the indomitable Miss Sheldon:

> Conditions were a bit cramped and the girls perched for coaching in whatever room became vacant at the time. We used to sit around sipping our drinks at night while the Leading Ladies (the Founders) regaled us with their daily adventures in house-hunting.
>
> The school at Benenden grew rapidly from twenty-four the first autumn term to one hundred and twenty-six a year later. But it *tried* not to lose that "family" quality. I think this has been due almost entirely to the unifying influence of Miss Sheldon. She cared for people as individuals. She never left anybody out. Quarrels broke up in laughter in her presence. Changes came, retirements and long break of war, but she had set her mark upon the school.
>
> In staff plays I think of Miss Sheldon as a Saxon villein dressed in a sacking tunic, as a haughty Duchess or as a Parisian lady in a red wig. There was the time when she brought the house down by demanding of the prompter in a loud and clear voice, "What did you say?"
>
> She was the eternal optimist. One form in which this evinced itself was her uncomfortable habit of accepting more girls for entry into the school than there was room for. A climax was reached one term when we were reduced to asking our bachelor vicar to remove himself to a cottage and allow us the use of the vicarage. This he obligingly did.
>
> Her faith was as necessary as the air she breathed, the secret perhaps of her serenity and patience with the foibles of others. She was full of hope and of the belief that, if faced sanely, difficulties could be resolved and truth and good intentions would prevail.
>
> She believed, sometimes against the judgement of her staff, that a most tiresome member of the school would ultimately become the golden girl if she would believe in herself – and she was seldom wrong. "Don't you think it is just a phase?" she said at staff meetings of a girl who was being universally condemned.

When the school had started in 1923 the founders could only contribute £300 amongst them towards the initial expense until six months later when a company was formed to ensure the continuity of the school. I think that some of us were conscious in those early days of improvisation, that it was a courageous venture, and we felt it was up to us to help make it a success. This, and the fact that there was "freedom within the law", made us feel responsible and trusted.

We had many contacts with the world outside through visitors, concerts, lectures, and with children from the London Settlements who came to stay, as well as other children. One of the founders, Miss Bird, wrote to me:

You ask about the beginning of the school. We wanted it to be a friendly, normal, happy place where learning to live life as a whole went side by side with a sound academic training. We hoped that you would all find a philosophy which would help you in meeting difficulty, trouble and opportunity, and that in planning your lives you would always be aware of the needs of others and serve them with compassion and understanding. The atmosphere of friendliness, gaiety and the forward-looking spirit of the early days is still part of the school's character and tradition. It seems summed up in the school lesson: "Think on these things"

(Philippians 4, 4–9):

> Rejoice in the Lord always: and again I say rejoice.
> Let your moderation be known unto all men.
> The Lord is at hand.
> Be careful for nothing; but in everything by
> prayer and supplication, with thanksgiving let
> your requests be made known unto God.
> And the peace of God, which passeth all understanding,
> shall keep your hearts and minds through Christ Jesus.
> Finally, brethren, whatsoever things are true,
> whatsoever things are honest,
> whatsoever things are just,
> whatsoever things are pure,
> whatsoever things are lovely,
> whatsoever things are of good report;
> If there be any virtue and if there be any praise,
> think on these things.
> Those things which ye have both learned, and
> received, and heard, and seen in me, do;
> and the God of peace shall be with you.

My memory of you as a schoolgirl is very clear, as if caught by a snapshot. You were standing quite alone in the courtyard, a small, still figure, fair-haired. I watched you for a few minutes and wondered what you were thinking about. In a school community it is rather rare for people to wish to be alone, and I always hoped that I should know something of their future; these people who were friendly and enjoyed life but yet felt the need sometimes for the pleasure of solitude. I still wonder what you were thinking about – perhaps you were planning one of your practical jokes!

Miss Bird ("Birdie"), taught English, Scripture, Public Speaking and Committee Work. She was also responsible for our physical welfare. It was her inspiration (described by Miss Sheldon as "the great think up") to create School Hobbies. What made the enterprise different was that it was entirely the girls' own work. Staff could be asked for guidance but nothing was "taught". Hobby representatives were chosen from each House and they, with a member of staff to act as co-ordinator, were responsible for finding out what each girl was doing. Time to spend on hobbies was allowed throughout the year and, usually at the end of the summer term, everything was given a written assessment and a grade, mostly by external judges. On the judging days the girls themselves organised the performances of music, drama, dancing, fencing, swimming, and so on, from which the best were chosen for Hobbies Day itself. On this day, parents and friends were invited and there was a big display of work.

Hobbies Day still took place until recently and until her death in December 1984 Birdie continued to be a source of much encouragement. The variety of the exhibits has been astonishing. They have included: bell-ringing, and many of those who rang still do so in parish churches and cathedrals; brass-rubbing, with impressive displays in the entrance hall; an automatic egg-fryer (the whole egg went in one end while eager eaters queued at the other for a sizzling helping); the learning of braille, so that blind people could be helped; water divining; an electric-bell system, which was afterwards adapted for regular school use; film productions; novels; and every kind of handwork, from the designing and making of dresses to intricate patchwork quilts. One girl designed an architect's model of a house. Most of the hobbies were individual ones but there was plenty of scope for group work too. Thus, gentle pressure was put on each member of the school to occupy part of her leisure time, which enabled every girl to show her particular flair. The valuable by-product was the preparation of something ready to be shown to others by a certain date – a good training for the years ahead. Some Seniors of seventy years of age are enjoying something that caught their interest sixty years ago! I remember Birdie telling me how important it is to give everyone a chance to *succeed* in something. It is odd that success is so good for the people who are not so clever, and failure, from which you have to recover, is important for clever people. In the same way a life which is all sunshine is less full a life than one which has shadows in it.

Peggy Man (*née* Durnford), an early member of the school, wrote:

> One of Birdie's greatest interests was in Public Speaking and Committee Work – she was lecturer at the Royal College of Nursing for fourteen years, where she helped over a thousand students, and at Denman College and St. Thomas's Hospital. Her lectures were brilliant and are gratefully remembered by many a student to whom she gave confidence to speak in public and to take the chair in committee in later years.

Public Speaking for beginners and a knowledge of committee procedures were two very useful subjects taught at a time when girls might be involved in either of these as soon as they left school. We were taught how to plan talks and the importance of thinking what responses we wanted to get from an audience; increased knowledge, generosity to a charity, amusement, information, etc. We learnt that most good speakers were nervous and how to cope with that situation by becoming audience-conscious, not self-conscious. A nervous speaker who gives way to nervousness makes a nervous audience and the day is lost. Make your audience your friend.

Learn your first and last paragraphs by heart. A confident ending can very much increase the effect of your talk. A knowledge of committee procedure was equally important. People who have it and use it tactfully are invaluable in any association. It is not, as many suppose, a dull subject.

Part of the weekly school routine which I remember especially is the school service on Sunday evening, to which I always looked forward. Nearly every week a different speaker was invited, but the most memorable services were those taken by Miss Bird. Her sermons, especially her "Angel Sermons", have been printed and reprinted and read by countless people who never had the privilege of hearing her give them. Birdie believed in Angels and that one had a special interest in the school, where she saw him. Birdie wrote:

> Dear Seniors,
>
> I have written down these few fables because you, in your friendly way, have asked for them. I have done this with much misgiving. You have grown up since you first heard them at School Service, and you will find them young and wonder why you liked them once, but perhaps they will recapture something of what you felt and thought and prayed about and laughed at when you were here.
>
> Here I reproduce only a few lines from A Conversation:
>
> "What would you give them for a leaving present?" I asked the Angel.
> "I would give them Courage and Sincerity," he said.
> "I hope they will always remember," I said.
> "I think they will," said the Angel with a twinkle in his eyes.
> "Aren't they somebody's initials here?"
> "So they are!" I said.

Prayers have always meant a great deal to me, and the following school prayer is especially memorable:

> Grant, O God, that as the years pass by there may go forth from this place a great company who, strengthened by Thy Grace, and inspired by Thy Spirit, shall serve Thee Faithfully, for the welfare of their fellow-men, and for the honour of Thy great Name: through Jesus Christ our Lord. Amen.

I remember the choir singing Walford Davies's "God be in my Head", St Patrick's Breastplate" and "Ave Verum Corpus" by Mozart and walking afterwards down the drive called Lime Avenue in our navy blue cloaks, the lights twinkling in the leaded windows of the main house behind us. I remember, too, the games field exposed to the winds over the Weald, the cold and the chilblains, and particularly Dinky Dick Read's laughter and her fast running.

We would wind up illicit gramophones, stuffed with silencing serge bloomers, to listen to Jack Buchanan and Fred Astaire while the older girls held highbrow discussions on T.S. Eliot and W.H. Auden. Sometimes in the eighth week of term, always a difficult time, when we were unusually tiresome in school, a whole day's outing would be announced, during which we walked miles with "nosebags", frying pans and sausages – regardless of the weather – and returned in a more tractable frame of mind. I believe the staff also welcomed these outings.

There was a large and good teaching staff, but many of their names and endeavours are forgotten. On festive days there would be talk about past teachers – "Do you remember old so-and-so?" Stories of a remembered eccentric would elicit mirth, but under the mirth was affection as we liked the eccentrics. Nearly all the women at Benenden school had dedicated their lives to teaching. They were of the First World War generation and several had lost brothers and fiances in the War.

History, Geography, English and Economics were my favourite subjects, while Mathematics and Science remained forever beyond my grasp. I followed a special course for three years in order to receive the Westminster Diploma for Domestic Science. This covered a wide variety of work, including budgeting, laundry, diets and how to cook for every type of meal, including luncheons and dinners, for four to four-hundred people. Presentation was essential. It was a hard course, but gave me a good grounding and, to my astonishment, I received a ninety-eight per cent mark on the final oral and practical examinations. Our carpentry teacher we found strict at the time – though later I had every reason to be profoundly grateful for what I had learnt under her guidance. She demanded the very highest standards. "Ma White", as we nicknamed her, seemed exceedingly eccentric and formidable, both to fellow members of the staff and to her pupils.

I had always thought that I would like to follow a career in nursing or study medicine, although I was most doubtful of being able to cope. One of my brothers was a doctor and, as a small girl, I had enjoyed looking at and reading his books. Each House had its own Matron. The one in Guildford had trained at St Thomas's Hospital in London and was nick-named "the Woman". This Matron knew I had developed a special interest in nursing and kindly asked me to regard her as a sort of Sister Tutor. She taught me a great deal and, as it turned out, the knowledge I acquired from her was to prove invaluable in the years to come. However, as was the case with millions of others, Hitler had other plans for my future.

Our Classics mistress, Miss Lucy Spencer, was strict too and so was Miss Willis ("Willy"), who taught us English, and, amongst other things, to precis essays and how to write letters without using the same adjective twice. Willy also made us study and analyse a wide variety of poems to see how well they scanned and what emphases the poet gave to individual words in each line. We learnt quite a lot of poetry by heart, and although we may have resisted at the time, I was very grateful later to be able to reflect on the poems.

Letters were very important to me, and each day some member of the family or a friend would write. I can still see the letters laid out and waiting for me on the quarry-tiled windowsill of the house. I wrote to Mama at length, keeping notes of what to tell her each day and usually starting the letter with a quotation.

Benenden, June 1938

Darlingest Mum,

When I was out walking through the woods and past the rhododendron bushes, ablaze with different, gorgeous colours, many thoughts went through my mind. I wonder how much longer we will enjoy peace and poetry? – probably only a short time now – shorter than many realise or want to hear.

I hope that whatever happens we may retain the ability to pray and listen to God's will. In your little Book, *The Bond of Sympathy*, which I dip into almost every night, these lines from Brook Herford come into my mind:

Go Forth

Go forth into the busy world and love it, interest yourself with its life; mingle kindly with its joys and sorrows; try what you can do for men, rather than what you can make them do for you, and you will know what it is to have men yours, better than if you were their king or master.

Fear Not

Fear is a most expensive guest to entertain, the same as worry is; so expensive are they, that no one can afford to entertain them. (R.W. Trine)

Take Joy Home

Take joy home and make a place in thy great heart for her, and give her time to grow, and cherish her; then she will come and oft will sing to thee, when thou art working in the furrows. (I. Ingleow)

I am tempted to write more, but there is a lot of prep. and anyway I don't want to take up more of your own time.

With lots of love as always
Sue

P.S. Everyone here whom you know often asks after you. I enjoy meeting other people's parents.

In another letter I wrote and told her what I had been doing:

I made a *complete* fool of myself in French this morning. Ten out of Ten for English made up for it a wee bit and, of *all* things, I somehow managed to shoot 3 goals in lacrosse this afternoon. We had talks from a variety of speakers.

Yesterday a woman who is a missionary in East Africa came and talked for one hour about the school there, which is supported by this school and how, when she first went, she had to take over from another who was ill. Forty mission schools are dotted over a vast area and one girls' school where she had to teach. She also told us all about the nursing in the villages around and how she helped with the locals to build a church.

We enjoyed the treat of hearing musicians, amongst them Kuttner, Solomon, Cortot and Myra Hess and the Casals Trio, who came and played to us in the school hall.

Every Saturday morning one of the schools's founders held a session in current affairs. We sat on the main staircase and on the floor in the entrance hall. A synopsis was given of what had appeared in the press, including the *Spectator* and the *New Statesman*, and on the BBC about the principal events of the week. Time was allowed for questions, which covered a very wide range. Discussions at Benenden, as at home and elsewhere, were concerned with the calamitous and deepening crisis. I loved economics, and at the age of about fifteen, I ended an essay of taxation: "The state may use taxation for revenue purposes, moral purposes, social and medical purposes, political and, most important today, war purposes . . . in actual fact, large portions of our taxes go towards paying for past and future wars." This essay was written in 1938 and it was returned with the words "and future" crossed through in red.

I remember, too, the Spanish Civil War and the way in which it polarised the left and right wing; the plight of the homeless and the children in Spain; and on 11 December 1936, with all the then unusual attendance of the press and radio, the abdication of King Edward VIII. I admired the calm way in which King George VI and Queen Elizabeth, under such sudden and unexpected pressure, shouldered their huge burden of becoming King and Queen. They gave the public renewed confidence in the monarchy, which was badly needed. I also remember when Kemal Ataturk, the Turkish ruler, ordered Moslem women to stop using their veils – an astonishing innovation.

Many of us became increasingly concerned about current problems and injustices, both at home and abroad. I wrote to my mother:

> Amongst others who had escaped there is a Jewish girl here from Northern Italy. She's in my dormie, and tells me in graphic detail about the arrests, suspicions and the Fascists. Her family only just got out in time, thousands were left. Many won't realise or believe the fate which awaits them. Equally, the majority of people don't understand the full horror of what is happening and being planned. Afterwards, they'll say it's exaggerated or could have been averted. If one didn't believe in God and justice in the next world, one might despair.

Another younger girl was Ann Hull Grundy who became a famous art historian and collector.

Jewish organisations in this country had requested that all Jewish refugees from Germany should be admitted without distinction, and that Jewish refugees already admitted as visitors, or those who might be admitted as visitors in the future, should be allowed to stay indefinitely. The British Government considered the Jewish proposals, but rejected the possibility of relaxing the regulations so as to allow entry to German Jews lacking financial means or in search of employment. Thus, the principle of "no admission without financial guarantee" was confirmed.

The result of this policy was disastrous for hundreds of thousands of ordinary Jews who desperately sought to leave Germany and Austria to start a new life in Britain and escape their grim fate of extermination by the Nazis.

At school, although only a pupil in a lower class, I was given special permission by Miss Sheldon to attend certain history lessons in the sixth form, and I therefore became more aware of the history of the Jews and other varied events leading up to the War.

In AD 70 a four-year revolt in the Roman province of Judea came to a bloody end with the destruction of the Jewish capital of Jerusalem and the massacre of its citizens by the Roman general, Titus, son of the Emperor Vespasian. The Jews were expelled from their homeland and subsequently settled mainly in the Mediterranean possessions of the Roman Empire.

By the end of the nineteenth century greater political freedom in Europe enabled Jews to form the Zionist movement whose Congress in Base, in 1897, called for a Jewish state to be established in Palestine. In 1903 the British Government offered land in Uganda for the purpose – a proposal rejected by the Jews who wished for a return to their ancient homeland. The area offered was 6,000 square miles, about seventy-five per cent of the area of the present state of Israel.

The most dramatic change favouring Jewish aspirations rose from the publication of the "Balfour Declaration". This document was simply a reply by the British Foreign Secretary, Lord Balfour, to a prominent Zionist, Lord Rothschild, that our Government would support the establishment of a home for world Jewry in Palestine. After the Great War, the new League of Nations, with British support, gave a similar pledge. The United States, although not a member, also endorsed the League of Nations resolution of 1920.

Establishing a Jewish homeland in Palestine faced two major difficulties. Firstly Palestine was already occupied by Arabs, and secondly the British had also given the Arabs promises, through their agent, Colonel T.E. Lawrence, of an independent Arab state in Palestine. "Lawrence of Arabia" attended the Versailles Peace Conference in 1919 and, broken emotionally, retired from public life. He never forgave what he considered an act of betrayal to the Arab leaders whom he had persuaded to fight the Turks when Britain and her Allies had needed their aid.

The result was that neither Arab nor Jew was to rule in the former Turkish province of Palestine. Instead a British Mandate was established which lasted until 1948 when that was replaced by the state of Israel.

We also had many history lessons on the situation in Germany and there was much comment on these matters at the time both inside Germany and abroad. The German postWar conditions bore similarity to Britain's, with large increases in unemployment in the immediate aftermath of the First World War, but there was a profound difference. The Germans could blame foreigners, especially the French, for their economic woes. Principally, however, many of them, especially the Nazis, held the Treaty of Versailles and the politicians and parties who endorsed it as the chief culprits. The Great War had ended in a truce called Armistice, not a surrender (in the view of Nationalists), and yet they had been treated as a conquered people. They resented paying reparations to the French and most bitterly, of being occupied by their troops in 1923 to secure payment. In the rampant inflation which followed the War, the middle class in particular had suffered severely. Not surprisingly, many sons of businessmen and pensioners joined the Nazi party in the early 1920s. Germany differed from Britain in the second half of the 1920s, as the latter was buoyed up by vast loans received from America under the Dawes Plan. With the advent of the Great Depression in the 1930s, unemployment returned to top the six million mark and the attraction of the Nazi and Communist parties dramatically improved. In 1933 Hitler was chosen as Chancellor by the aged President Hindenburg, one year later becoming dictator with the title of "Führer of the German People".

The chief aims of Hitler in power, from 1933 onwards, were to remove the limitation on sovereignty imposed by the "unjust" Treaty of Versailles and re-establish German power and influence in Europe; to solve the "Jewish problem"; and seize "living space" in the lands to the east inhabited by the "lesser" races.

The generally held belief was that once Hitler was in power he would be constrained, both by circumstances and by those cabinet members who were not Nazis. They did not believe his actions would be as extreme as his sayings in his book *Mein Kampf*. As one German proverb puts it: "Food never tastes as hot as it appears from the cooking." It is generally true that most extremist politicians, once they have come to power, ostensibly behave more moderately, but by the end of February 1933 Hitler had shown his true colours. Bruening, Chancellor from 1930–32, went into exile in the summer of 1933, his life in danger. The persecution began immediately after the Reichstag fire on 27 February 1933. President Hindenburg should have intervened, but he was senile and under very considerable pressure.

At the end of World War I, Western Europe and the world at large faced social and economic problems of a scale and complexity never before experienced.

With Germany suffering all the consequences of military defeat, followed by economic collapse, she was further weighed down by the harsh fiscal and other demands laid upon her by the Treaty of Versailles. But this, in turn, had expressed the widespread determination of the Western Allies that Germany should be made to pay for her unprovoked assault on her neighbours. The fact that reparations would, first, prove an economic embarrassment to the receiving nations, and secondly, prove such an economic drain on Germany's resources as to cripple her financially and industrially, was only later realised. Farce was added to farce, when America granted huge loans to Germany, out of which the latter blandly paid her dues under the Treaty to those entitled to them.

Parallel to the German debacle, there existed an almost comparable state of affairs amongst the victorious Allies. Militarily they were supreme, but with their entire economies disrupted in the service of war, and much of their treasure spent or destroyed, they faced a bleak situation of industrial and commercial disruption, unemployment, and war-weariness, which disinclined people to further effort.

Alas, during the years immediately after 1914, few voices were raised against the follies committed by the Versailles Treaty, nor had they any workable solutions to their countries' industrial and economic problems.

Russia alone sought to solve her problems by a social revolution into Communism, commencing in 1917. This was viewed with fear and dismay by the Western Capitalist powers, *and especially by the Poles*, who alone halted the Bolshevik armies near Warsaw and drove them back to the new Soviet Union.

Looking back on the postWar era, 1919–39, it seems clear that there were three important developments in European and world politics that were behind the outbreak of war in the autumn of 1939. These were:

1. For most of this period the Western Allied nations (and the USA) were struggling with severe economic recession, including collapse of the stock markets, and (in Britain) a national strike in 1926 which brought nearly all industrial and commercial activity to a halt. Confusion reigned.

2. Revulsion against the whole idea of war was widespread in the West. The mass of the people desired only a peaceful existence, with prosperity if possible, and were strongly averse to any gloomy crystal-gazing concerning Germany as a possible renewed military threat, with its awful probable implications.

3. Meanwhile, Fascism under Mussolini in Italy, and later Nazism under Adolf Hitler, emboldened both these nations to flout international law and treaty obligations alike, using a step-by-step technique of territorial acquisition and subjugation of weaker neighbours, culminating in the completely unjustified invasion of Poland in 1939.

France, Britain and their former Allies generally remained quiescent during much of this time; indeed, they indulged in extensive disarmament thereby emboldening the two aggressor nations as their outrageous actions met with nothing more than verbal protests.

Alongside all this, another nation, armed and ready for war – Japan – was secretly planning her assault on the Far-Eastern colonial territories of the European nations and the USA. Cause, indeed, for the threatened peoples to be glancing nervously over their shoulders.

In all this swirl of events – many with the most trenchant implications for the continuance of peace and stability in the world – who spoke for Britain and Empire?

Without a doubt, one above all – Mr Winston Churchill. Surely Vansittart and Lord Gray should also be mentioned. Speaking in the House of Commons on 13 July 1934, Mr Churchill summarised what by then was seen to be a disastrous policy for the Western nations – disarmament, and the implications of a belated swing toward rearmament.

I am very glad that the Disarmament Conference is passing out of life into history. It is the greatest mistake to mix up disarmament with peace. When you have peace you will have disarmament. But there has been during these recent years a steady deterioration in the relations between different countries, a steady growth of ill-will, and a steady, indeed a rapid increase in armaments that has gone on through all these years in spite of the endless flow of oratory, of perorations, of well-meaning sentiments, of banquets, which have marked this epoch.

Europe will be secure when nations no longer feel themselves in great danger, as many of them do now. Then the pressure and the burden of armaments will fall away automatically, as they ought to have done in a long peace; and it might be quite easy to seal a movement of that character by some general agreement. I hope, indeed, that we have now also reached the end of the period of the Government pressing France – thus peaceful France with no militarism – to weaken her armed forces. I rejoice that the French have not taken the advice which has been offered to them so freely from various quarters, and which the Leader of the Opposition (Mr Lansbury) no doubt would strongly endorse.

This is not the only Germany which we shall live to see, but we have to consider that at present two or three men, in what may be a desperate position, have the whole of the mighty country in their grip, have that wonderful scientific, intelligent, docile, valiant people in their grip, a population of seventy millions; that there is no dynastic interest such as the monarchy brings as a restraint upon policy, because it looks long ahead and has much to lose; and that there is no public opinion except what is manufactured by these new and terrible engines – broadcasting and a controlled Press. Politics in Germany are not as they are over here. There you do not leave office to go into Opposition. You do not leave the Front Bench to sit below the Gangway. You may well leave your high office at a quarter of an hour's notice to drive to the police station, and you may be conducted thereafter very rapidly to an even graver ordeal.

It seems to me that men in that position might very easily be tempted to do what even a military dictatorship would not do, because a military dictatorship, with all its many faults, at any rate is one that is based on a very accurate study of the real facts; and there is more danger in this kind of dictatorship that there would be in a military dictatorship, because you have men who, to relieve themselves from the great peril which confronts them at home, might easily plunge into a foreign adventure of the most dangerous and catastrophic character to the whole world.

Thus did this great British statesman clearly and accurately analyse the psyche and the intentions of a resurgent militarised Germany, but also the psychological and practical revolution which must come, if the Western powers were to have any prospect at all of checking Germany's aggressive stance, or her eventual chances of waging a successful war against her former victors, and many others besides.

How this transition from democracy to dictorship was accomplished so rapidly and effectively between 1933 and 1939 still remains a mystery to many. I believe a major part of the answer must lie in one of Hitler's own special creations, the Schutz Staffen, (i.e. Elite Security Guard) known more commonly and with dread as the "SS".

From its foundation in 1923 as a security guard, strong, for the party leader, the SS still retained a special relationship to Hitler, even when their numbers grew to thousands. Members were selected on the basis of their health, so-called racial group features such as complexion and facial structures, and their oath to do whatever Hitler required of them. Special "Stud Farms" were supervised to ensure their partners were also true Ayrians. Inge, a German friend of mine in her late twenties, had married a Hungarian who survived from one of four Nazi death camps. Inge was very ill and eventually died of TB, but before and during her illness, she gave me graphic descriptions of SS Stud Farms and unprintable details of plans which were drawn up and carried out to ensure that each individual girl was forced (after a complete examination) to conceive a child for the German race by an SS stallion. Inge never knew if she would ever be released from the Stud Farm. She also told me too that – in keeping with the Nazi philosophy – the first victims of gassings, as early as the mid-1930s onwards, were thousands of Germans, their own countrymen and women resident in mental hospitals. Thus the euthanasia decree came into being.

Their leader, and one of Hitler's most loyal supporters for the twenty-two years of the corps' existence, was Heinrich Himmler and his assistant Reinhard Heydrich, until his assassination by members of the Czech Resistance on 27 May 1942, as described in Chapter 4.

On the night of 30 June 1934 Hitler staked his whole future on the loyalty of the SS when he called them through their leader, Heinrich Himmler, to execute over 1,000 other party members, mainly in the working-class Nazi Brownshirts of "SA", German initials for the "storm-troopers". The SA was founded in 1921 by the Nazis to protect their rallies from physical attacks by street gangs belonging to extremist parties on the left wing of German politics. By 1934 they had grown in number to two million, led by an ex-officer, Captain Erst Roehm. Many of the growing army of unemployed enlisted in the SA for something to do and for the small sums of money they received from party funds. Roehm was loyal to Hitler, as were his followers, but Roehm's aim of replacing the Regular Germany Army by the SA and his Socialistic ideas on nationalisation of big business upset both the Army and the financiers who funded Hitler's political campaigns. In April 1934 representatives of the Armed Forces informed Hitler that he should liquidate the leadership of the SA or they would undertake the task themselves. Hitler agreed and with the help of the SS eliminated the SA leaders on the night of 30 June 1934. After the

"Night of the Long Knives", as this event came to be known, the SA was downgraded to a minor role. With the swift development of full employment plus conscription, the membership of the SA declined to about one third of its pre-purge numbers.

I now quote a passage from Churchill:

> This Massacre, however explicable by the hideous forces at work, showed that the new Master of Germany would stop at nothing, and that conditions in Germany bore no resemblance to those of a civilised State. A Dictatorship based upon terror and reeking with blood had confronted the world. Anti-Semitism was ferocious and brazen, and the concentration-camp system was already in full operation for all obnoxious or politically dissident classes. I was deeply affected by the episode, and the whole process of German rearmament, of which there was now overwhelming evidence, seemed to me invested with a ruthless, lurid tinge. It glittered and it glared.

Those killings on the 30 June 1934 marked the beginning of an horrendous trail that was to lead to the death camps in Germany, Poland and indeed to all parts of Europe. Elsewhere, the SS were given sinister powers, the right to act outside the law including torture, imprisonment or execution of those they considered enemies of the state.

The responsibilities of the corps came to include the Gestapo (Secret Police), intelligence at home and abroad "SD" and the Waffen SS. The Gestapo joined the SS in April 1934, a year after its foundation by Goering in his office in charge of the Prussian Ministry of the Interior. The SS ensured the execution of the Race Laws and were responsible for the pre-War scheme to "export" 450,000 Jews from Europe as well as the "Madagascar" proposal.* This project was to found a new Israel in Madagascar, and was taken seriously by Hitler who told Mussolini of the plan in July 1940. But the idea was later abandoned on practical grounds as the War spread to North Africa. There was also a proposal to resettle Jews in Poland but the German Governor, Hans Frank, vetoed it. The last two schemes were projected by Adolf Eichmann. The "Final Solution" to exterminate millions of Jews, Poles, gypsies, and other nations, was advanced, most probably, by Hitler – not Eichmann – at the SS Conference held in Wansee, Berlin, in July 1942. Eichmann, did however administer the dreadful "Holocaust". He was tried and executed by the state of Israel in July 1962.

At the beginning of the War, I myself saw a map of Europe, listed by the Nazis, coloured in such a way as to make perfectly clear which countries, including Britain, they intended to occupy. First-hand accounts and many vivid descriptions of the persecutions were written by British journalists, but the Government in Britain on the whole ignored them. We were shocked and dismayed by the attitude of Chamberlain, and indeed by many members of the British Government – a few Members of Parliament had

---

* *Hitler and Stalin*, Alan Bullock (a double biography), Harper Collins, 1990.

even attended the Nuremberg rallies. The complacency and the reasons they gave shocked me, for we had heard, and indeed been taught, that the Versailles Treaty would restrain Germany, whereas it did just the opposite. The whole policy of appeasement was appalling and should teach the world a lesson, whenever a bully and dictator arises in the future.

A major weakness was the failure of the French and British to co-operate, especially in military matters, in the face of Hitler's breaches of the Treaty of Versailles. France refused to disarm unless Britain would enter into a firm military alliance with her, which Britain found unacceptable. In these circumstances Hitler was able to withdraw Germany from the International Conference on Disarmament in 1934, and by his own rearming, successfully breach the Versailles Treaty. In 1937 Hitler did agree to a limitation in his naval strength in the Anglo-German Treaty of that year – no doubt a move to secure British neutrality in a future war.

On 13 March 1938, as a result of the *Anschluss*, Austria was incorporated into the Greater German Reich under the name of Ostmark. This triumph of Hitler's caused great excitement amongst the Sudetens and Volksdeutsch, and whenever Nazi rallies were held we heard the slogan "Ein Volk, Ein Reich, Ein Führer" (one people, one realm, one leader).

Also Hitler sought power through the youth of Germany; from the book *The SS: Hitler's instrument of Terror* by Gordon Williams, I quote:

> The Nazis indoctrinated German youths from a very early age. For young boys between the ages of 10 and 14 the Party established the Jungvolk, and for girls the same age the Jungmadel. A boy entering the Jungvolk had to undergo an initiation test, which involved reciting the Horst Wessel song, running 50 metres in 12 seconds and learning weapons drill. The next step was the Hitler Youth, which was compulsory for boys aged between 15 and 18.
>
> The Hitler Youth units that defended Berlin in 1945, fought with a bravery bordering on the insane. They were the flower of the Nazi party, believing themselves superior. This is not really surprising, given the indoctrination they had received. An example of this was provided by Himmler in 1936, when he addressed a meeting of the Hitler Youth: "The German people, especially German youth, have learned once again to value people racially – they have turned away once again from Christian theory, from the Christian teaching which ruled Germany for more than a thousand years and caused the racial decay of the German Folk, and almost caused its racial death."

In September of that year, after an agitated solo mission to Berchtesgaden and Bad Godesberg, Chamberlain agreed with his French counterpart, Edward Daladier, to meet Hitler and Mussolini in Munich. There on 29/30 September, with no representatives of Czechoslovakia present, Chamberlain and Daladier gave in to Hitler's threats. They handed over 10,000 square miles of Czech Sudetenland to Nazi Germany, 5,000 square miles of southern Slovakia to Hungary, and a smaller area in Silesia to Poland. Later, apologists argued that Chamberlain and Daladier had thereby gained time to improve their military defences: but so had Hitler. What really swung the decision was insularity and a fear of war. "How horrible, fantastic, incredible it is," said Chamberlain in a broadcast before going to Munich, "that we should be digging the trenches and putting on gas masks here because of a quarrel in a faraway county between people of whom we know nothing!" The British called up the Home Fleet and started to dig air-raid shelters in the public parks.

Chamberlain received representatives of the British press in Munich before his return to London on 30 September, when he made the following statement:

> I have always been of the opinion if we could get a peaceful solution to the Czechoslovak question it would open the way generally to appeasement in Europe. This morning I had a talk with the Führer, and we both signed the following declaration:
>
> We, the German Führer and Chancellor and the British Prime Minister, have had a further meeting today and are agreed in recognising that the question of Anglo-German relations is of the first importance for the two countries and for Europe.
>
> We regard the agreement signed last night and the Anglo-German Naval Agreement as symbolic of the desire of our two peoples never to go to war with one another again.
>
> We are resolved that the method of consultation shall be the method adopted to deal with any other questions that may concern our two countries, and we are determined to continue our efforts to remove possible sources of difference and thus to contribute to assure the peace of Europe.

This optimistic statement was accepted and welcomed by the majority of the British people. When Chamberlain returned from Munich proclaiming "Peace for our time . . . Peace with honour", not everyone shared the euphoria. In particular, Winston Churchill (1874–1965) had realised the danger posed by the rise to power of Hitler and the Nazis from 1933 onwards.

He continued to warn Parliament of the need to rearm in the face of these dangers, aided by such friends as Robert Vansittart (1881–1957), Civil Service Head, and the scientist, Lord Lindemann (1886–1957). Churchill's impact was however limited. He had been Chancellor of the Exchequer (1924–29) but lost much of his influence after he resigned from the Shadow Cabinet over Indian affairs in 1930.

Even though an old-age pensioner when War eventually came, Chamberlain recalled him to serve in his Cabinet and less than a year later he became Prime Minister of the Wartime Coalition.

On Chamberlain's return from Munich, the Czechoslovakian President, Jan Masaryk, was present to hear the House of Commons go wild with joy. Perhaps it was fortunate that his father Tomas Masaryk had died a year earlier on 14 September (Jan's fifty-first birthday). Long before, in failing health, Tomas had passed the Presidency to Edward Benes, a man sharply but not unfairly described by David Lloyd George as "impulsive, clever but much less sagacious and more short-sighted than Tomas Masaryk". The old President had the measure of Benes. On his deathbed he had told his son, "Very bad times are coming to the nation . . . and for Europe. Benes will have to bear the brunt of it. You must help him. You know much of the world better than he does. Stand by Benes always. Promise me that you will never leave him alone." Jan Masaryk had given his word.

Now, with the frenzied shameful cheers of the House of Commons still ringing in his head, he went to see Chamberlain and the Foreign Secretary, Lord Halifax. His words then might have been his father's: "If you have sacrificed my nation to preserve the peace of the world, I will be the first to applaud you. But if not, gentleman, God help your souls."

It was no wonder that both the Czechs and Slovaks felt the British and the French had betrayed them. Unlike the Poles they had not experienced the historic Russian occupations of their country and consequently looked East for some help. The following quotation by Richard Mayne in the May 1983 edition of *Encounter* illustrates the Nazi political pressures:

> Jan Masaryk was his country's envoy to London and part of his job was precisely to bring notice of his country's plight to Westminster, Whitehall and Number 10 Downing Street. He spent most of his time there explaining to the official gentleman inside that Czechoslovakia was a country and not a contagious disease. It was a necessary task. Britain seemed dangerously inattentative to the trouble that was brewing for his country and Europe.
>
> From 1935 onwards Hitler's aim was to exploit and foster discontent. Secretly, Germany paid 15,000 marks a month to a man chosen by themselves, Konrad Henlein, a member of the Sudetenland party to do this. When Henlein visited Jan Masaryk at the Czechoslovakian Legation in London he came with an "SS" man and said, "My friend accompanies me wherever I go". Masaryk opened the door of his drawing room, whistled for his Aberdeen terrier and said, "My friend here accompanies me wherever I go." For Hitler, Henlein was a puppet and the troubles in the Sudetenland were merely a pretext for annexation. During the summer of 1938 Hitler's demands brought the quarrel to a crisis and threat of war."

So, sadly, President Benes, then Czech President, yielded under "unheard-of pressures" and finally acquiesced. Nevertheless, the Czechs mobilised and reluctantly acquired an Agreement which in effect surrendered all border fortifications to the enemy. The Army in Czechoslovakia consisted of twelve Infantry Divisions (two Brigades each), two Brigades of Mountain Infantry, twelve Light Field Artillery Brigades, and four Cavalry Brigades. In addition, they had a system of Reservists. If they had been allowed to choose their own course and had been supported fully by their Allies, there might have been a different outcome.

Later, Hitler told his generals, "It was clear to me from that moment that I could not be satisfied with the Sudeten territory. That was only a partial solution." Hitler marched into Prague on 15 March 1939 and the Nazi swastika flag flew from Hradcany Castle where Hitler spent the night in the apartment which had once been Tomas Masaryk's. He turned the Czech half of the country into a Nazi "protectorate"; the Slovak half became his first "satellite state".

Hitler had once again succeeded. "We double-crossed the Czechs for our own security" was the City of London gibe.

"That war", a Czechoslovak poet wrote, "was like broken glass in our arteries and our blood". The country was drained by the Nazis. Property worth some 14,000 million dollars was lost in six years. Between March 1939 and May 1945, 350,000 Czechs and Slovaks were deported to concentration camps. Only 100,000 came back. Some 30,000 partisans of the Czechoslovak Resistance Network, *Obradna Naroda* (Defence of a Nation) were killed by the Gestapo.

Meanwhile, that same month, Britain had sent a delegation to Poland, headed by General Sir Edmund Ironside, to enter into a treaty with the Poles (France had done so in 1921) guaranteeing that in the event of a German invasion Britain would stand by them. "The British had signed a blank cheque – blank in a double sense, for we have promised military aid which we were not in a position to supply." Thus, as a deterrent the treaty was totally ineffective, as the Germans well knew.

Such incompetence and naïvety were incredible. We were on a head-on collision course because of our purblind failure to stop Hitler and his followers in their tracks in the early thirties and to awaken as many people as possible to his obsession for world power; at the same time refusing to arm ourselves. In fairness, it should be remembered that some historians still argue that Chamberlain's policy of appeasement was to give Britain time to rearm.

From the time of remilitarisation of the Rhineland and the instruction given by Hitler to his generals in 1936, Churchill, Vansittart and others called for a stern stand and strengthening of Britain's armed forces. We now know that Hitler told his generals that same year that if any attempt was made to block his path the Wehrmacht was to withdraw.

Our old portable blue radio at home was much used and a visitor from Germany insisted upon listening to Hitler's screeching voice at the Nuremberg rallies. She also read out part of *Mein Kampf* and we were revolted by this too and told her so. It gave a dreadful insight into what the Nazis planned for the whole world.

The summer of 1939 was a particularly lovely one and the still, sunny days continued on during the last week of August, the week before war was declared on Germany. Everywhere there was a feeling of tension, and the cloudless golden days seemed to pass unbearably slowly while we waited for news. There were prayers every evening in the Village Church at Great Thurlow; specially fervent parayers for the miracle to avert the War that appeared to be inevitable. In Cardinal Newman's favourite prayer I found a measure of tranquillity, or at any rate a hope of tranquillity, that helped to ease the strain of those days:

O Lord, support us all the day long of this troublous life, until the shades lengthen and the evening comes, and the busy world is hushed, the fever of life is over, and our work is done. . . .

Then Lord, in Thy Mercy, grant us a safe lodging, a holy rest and peace at last: through Jesus Christ our Lord. Amen.

On 3 September 1939 war was declared. The old life had ended for good. Yet another generation had to stand up to aggression from the same nation again; millions more faced slaughter and wounds. Moreover, the map of Europe was to be redrawn, and it was the end of liberty for those on whose behalf Britain and the Empire went to war, and for their descendants. Those of us who cared felt sickened and sad at heart.

Fabian von Schlabrendoroff, in his book *The Secret War against Hitler,* says:

In our efforts to broaden the base of the opposition, we did not limit ourselves to seeking the co-operation of Protestant leaders, but also sought to make contact with prominent Catholics. One of these with whom we met was Heinrich Bruening, Chancellor of Germany from 1930–32. At that time Bruening was living in St Hedwig's Hospital in Berlin, where he was not so much exposed to surveillance by the Nazis. In contrast to the then rather vacillating position adopted by the Centre party, whose candidate he had been, Bruening left no doubt as to where he stood. Rejecting all customary avowals of loyalty to Hitler's regime, Bruening declared: "A man has to choose whether he wants to stand under the swastika or under the cross of Christ. He can decide for only one of them."

We underestimated both the efforts made and the sufferings endured by a number of ordinary German people. They came from a wide range of professions, and included members of the Scout and Girl Guide Movements who were arrested and became some of the first prisoners in the Nazi camps. There were others too, involved in various groups between 1933–44, who showed great courage in their determination to overthrow the Nazis.

There was no doubt in the minds of many people, too, that there was a huge cover-up in the highest ranks of the Foreign Office and the BBC as regards to anti-Semitism. They suppressed news about Germany's attempts to exterminate European Jews, Slavs and gypsies. This evidence is contained in documents from the BBC archives and Government papers at the Public Records Office.

I always felt that if this distressing and sad cover-up had been avoided, and the general public and the Armed Services had been made more aware of the terrible evil of Nazism which they faced, they would have realised the absolute necessity and importance of winning the War.

PART TWO

War

3

Go out into the Darkness

THE CONGREGATION AT GREAT Thurlow was in church as usual at
eleven o'clock on Sunday, 3 September 1939, and there on a portable
radio we heard Neville Chamberlain's announcement from 10 Downing
Street that Britain was at war with Germany. The War had started two days
earlier with Hitler's invasion of Poland, a crime the direct and particular
effects of which were destined to have a special and lasting influence on my
whole life.

We felt a sense of very deep shame and distress when the Prime Minister
in his broadcast mentioned the failure of the ultimatum his Government
had sent to Berlin after the expected invasion and bombing and killing in
Poland had begun – an ultimatum vainly demanding a German withdrawal.
In March 1939, and indeed at Munich the previous year, the Czechs had
been sold down the river, and now, owing to unbelievable political blindness it was too late to be of any assistance to the Poles whose territorial
integrity against Germany we had guaranteed and with whom we had
signed a mutual defence treaty. When I see the pre-War British Embassy in
Warsaw and remember the crowds who assembled there calling for the
Ambassador and cheering him because they vainly believed that we would
send arms, I marvel at the Poles' lack of bitterness today.

Immediately after the broadcast, sirens sounded but people reacted
calmly. It was in fact a false alarm. There followed a series of false alarms
which typified the start of the eight-month period of the phoney War.

The nearest bomb to us was subsequently dropped near the sheep pen on
the Home Farm. My brother Stephen's friend, John McAnally, aged twenty-
one (who was killed on 7 July 1941 as a pilot in 214 Squadron), watched
with us from the door of the cellar, and we talked about the courage of the
Poles and their resistance and how remarkable the cavalry were to fight on
horseback against the German tanks. We expressed indignation at our
inability to help them and the knowledge that we and the French had let
down their country and our common cause.

Newspaper vendors at street corners in towns used to call out the head-
lines of the day, and during this time, billposters urged us to contribute to
the War effort. One such poster, I remember, read "Keep Calm and Dig".

Evacuees from London were given rooms in our home, and for a
few months I worked in a local hospital where the simple training and

subsequent examinations I passed proved extremely useful in the wards, and even more so later on in life. Quite a number of evacuees from the East End were admitted, many of them children who were frightened they might never see their homes or parents again. The majority had never had the opportunity of seeing the country before. They came from slum areas and were used to sharing a bed. Some we had to persuade to bath and change their clothes and many were infected so that on admission their heads were tooth-combed with carbolic. We had to cope with all the difficulties arising from different social attitudes and from personal handicaps – lice, incontinence and smells – as well as the discipline that had to be exerted in teamwork, diagnosis and treatment of illness.

I enjoyed keeping temperature charts and attending to all the little needs of the individuals under the eagle eye of the staff nurse. Rightly, the discipline and routine were strict, and if we failed and got slightly behind, the ward sisters were quick to reprimand us. Everything we did was scrutinised. If a nurse went off duty without putting away a medicine glass, she would be sent for to put it back in the medicine cupboard. I recall having to return to tidy up a patient's bed and then align it with others in the ward. There was constant tiredness to contend with; our feet were swollen from walking through long covered ways between the different departments of the hospital, including the theatre, and it was a constant temptation to snatch forbidden moments of rest sitting on the bread-bins in the small ward kitchen. However hard-pressed and busy, we were never allowed to run except to deal with haemorrhage or fire.

Our uniforms had to be immaculate; starched aprons had to match the hem of the dress – to the calf of the leg. We wore black stockings and polished black shoes, and there were different coloured dresses, belts and caps, to signify the status of all members of staff and any organisations who worked in the hospital. If we were sent for we removed the cotton or organdie cuffs, rolled down our sleeves and put on starched wrist cuffs before reporting to Matron's office.

We did not have curtain cubicles, and whenever a patient wanted a bedpan, wash or blanket bath, we had to carry a heavy wooden screen the length of the long ward. I remember there was a young girl of nine with a heart condition who had convulsions and as we had no oxygen tent she was resuscitated with an oxygen cylinder. She was kept under very strict observation before she eventually died. Surgical cases were kept in bed for at least twelve days. So, too, were many other patients. If a patient deteriorated he was moved up the ward towards the door.

There were great restrictions on lighting because of the blackout regulations and we used a torch on night rounds. Every night four reports had to be written up by the night sister and it was usual to receive three visits by the general night sister.

It was exacting to prepare the trolleys, especially for the surgical ward. Drugs and sterilisers were prepared daily and each needle and syringe sterilised before use. Bandages had to be washed, boiled and re-rolled, and the gauze cut and folded. There were no disposable sputum mugs. Mouth trays were placed on each individual bedside cabinet and there was a special day for washing out all the lockers. I remember, too, the continuous scrubbing of bed mackintoshes. As we did not have proper trolleys, the wet and soiled linen had to be specially folded. Each ward had its own itemised list and when an inventory was taken we occasionally had to borrow from another ward. In those days there was fasting from 10 p.m. prior to an operation. The day started before 6 a.m. in order to get all the bed patients washed, their beds made (three minutes were allowed to make a bed, and this one always did with another nurse), drugs distributed and dressings changed. At four-hourly intervals backs were rubbed down with methylated spirits and boracic powder to avoid bedsores. The Consultant would conduct his weekly ward rounds escorted by his retinue consisting of Ward Sister, Register Physician and Ward House Doctor, and silence had to be maintained.

In June 1940, a few of the wounded were evacuated from France. They were the first grim battle casualties that we had seen, but some of them were full of fun, teased us even to the extent of getting me into trouble with the Sister because I had given a blanket bath to the wrong patient.

After Dunkirk, defensive preparations were made in earnest in the Village of Thurlow, and a very serious-minded man gave lectures, which the majority of Villagers attended, on what action we were to take in the event of an invasion. Pamphlets were distributed titled IF THE INVADER COMES, telling us to be prepared, not to panic, and not to believe or spread false rumours. We fully expected to be invaded. The duties of the Local Defence Volunteers (later the Home Guard) and Air Raid Precautions wardens increased. People became very suspicious if asked for directions as all signposts were taken down, and street names obliterated.

Only after the War did I hear from Major-General Gubbins himself of his involvement in the training and preparation of special units in Britain to organise the Resistance here in the event of a Nazi occupation. I recall him saying that some three thousand men and women were trained to be guerrillas. There were hiding places for over 1,000 secret radios throughout Britain, and for stocks of grenades, explosives, rifles, Tilley lamps, food and water. Each guerrilla was provided with a commando knife and a truncheon! They prepared themselves for the worst.

The troops who had been brought back exhausted from the miracle of Dunkirk continued their training and marching, but it was evident that few carried weapons. Some people were assigned to making Molotov cocktails, while others were told that in the event of an invasion their duties would include looking after the wounded and cooking food in the woods. We were told that the church bells were to be rung everywhere once the parachutists had landed. It was a miracle that the Nazis never invaded and occupied Britain.

At night the glow of the fires from the oil tanks at Tilbury which had been bombed was visible sixty miles away. Several Dorniers were shot down in the vicinity, and one crew surrendered to a farmer who had only a pitch-fork; another German crew were so arrogant that they were taken to an RAF station and shown some of the ground crews playing cricket to convince them that the British were far from panicking.

Churchill's speeches and the general spirit of the country gave a sense of purpose and unity to everyone. His memorable speeches on 4 and 18 June 1940 made us feel determined that, regardless of all odds, we would resist to the last:

4 June 1940

Even though large tracts of Europe and many old and famous States have fallen or may fall into the grip of the Gestapo and all the odious apparatus of Nazi rule, we shall not flag or fail. We shall go on to the end. We shall fight in France, we shall fight on the seas and oceans, we shall fight with growing confidence and growing strength in the air. We shall defend our island, whatever the cost may be. We shall fight on the beaches, we shall fight on the landing-grounds, we shall fight in the fields and in the streets, we shall fight in the hills. We shall never surrender.

And even if, which I do not for a moment believe, this island or large part of it were subjugated and starving, then our Empire beyond the seas, armed and guarded by the British Fleet, would carry on the struggle until, in God's good time, the New World, with all its power and might, steps forth to the rescue and liberation of the Old.

18 June 1940

The "Battle of France" is over. The "Battle of Britain" is about to begin. Upon this battle depends the survival of the Christian civilisation. Upon it depends our British life and the long-continued history of our institutions and our Empire. The whole fury and might of the enemy must very soon be turned on us. Hitler knows that he will have to break us on this island or lose the war.

If we can stand up to him all Europe may be free, and the life of the world may move forward into broad and sunlit uplands. If we fail, then the whole world, including the United States and all that we have known and cared for, will sink into the abyss of a new dark age, made sinister and perhaps more prolonged by the light of a perverted science.

Let us, therefore, do our duty and so bear ourselves that if the British Commonwealth and Empire lasts a thousand years men will still say, "This was their finest hour."

The response by RAF Fighter Command was one of the decisive battles of world history. Perhaps it was fortunate, perhaps not, that so very few of us knew at the time how savagely the margin between possible salvation and defeat was shrinking. But we did "hang breathless" on its fate, and if we thought at all we could but realise and marvel that those pilots were enduring and triumphing over the appalling strain of constant duelling against odds. During the Battle of Britain a number of the dog-fights took place above us, and every day in the early mornings we saw waves of German planes in formation flying inland, a sight and sound *never* to be forgotten. It's true that the heat and passion and fog of battle inflated the claims made immediately on either side, but honest exaggeration certainly gave a needful and worthwhile boost to morale, and victory mattered far more than statistics. Two of the crucial days were 15 August, when we now know the Luftwaffe's losses were seventy-five aircraft and the RAF's were thirty-four, and 15 September, the last, when they lost sixty aircraft and we lost twenty-six. This was also the day when Churchill, on a visit to 11 Group Fighter Command, asked where the reserves were and was told there were none.

> The gratitude of every home in our Island, in our Empire, and indeed throughout the world, except in the abodes of the guilty, goes out to the British and Allied airmen, who, undaunted by odds, unwearied in their constant challenge and mortal danger, are turning the tide of world war by their prowess and their devotion. Never in the field of human conflict was so much owed by so many to so few.
> Churchill Speech about the Battle of Britain.

During the Battle of Britain 537 Allied airmen of Fighter Command were killed as well as others from Bomber and Coastal Commands. That, altogether, cost some 1,500 lives. Between 8 August and 31 August 1940, 2,375 German aircraft are known to have been destroyed in daylight. But by then Hitler had made his fatal mistake. On 7 September the Luftwaffe's main onslaught was switched from airfields, aircraft factories and ports to industrial towns and London, and the invasion of England was called off.

So London and other big British cities had to "take it", and did. Between 7 September 1940 and 16 May 1941 the German Air Force made 141 major raids on twenty-one cities. Principal German night attacks in 1942 were made on twenty-one cities and towns. Day attacks started in 1943 and these numbered seventeen, with fifteen night attacks.

Some statistics (1 May 1940–1 June 1944):

Total number civilians killed and injured in the London Civil Defence Region			80,397
Total for all other Civil Defence Regions			66,380
Bristol:	Killed		1,299
	Injured		3,300
Plymouth:	Killed		1,172
	Injured		4,448
Liverpool and District:	Killed		3,966
	Injured		3,812

There were eighty-five major raids made on London, and eight on Liverpool/Birkenhead, also eight on Birmingham and eight on Plymouth/Devonport. In the raids on Liverpool/Birkenhead, 120,000 houses were damaged.

Many of those enduring the nightly blitz were remarkable people. Few had adequate shelter: the cupboard under the stairs became something far more vital to survival than anyone had ever dreamed it could be. Anderson Shelters were popular and useful. Thousands made a weird communal life for themselves for months on end on the platforms of the London Underground, able to sleep despite the noise because of sheer exhaustion. Some sang and hot drinks were distributed to them whenever possible. They emerged at dawn or after the "All Clear" to discover whether their homes still stood. Unfortunately, some Underground stations received direct hits resulting in heavy casualties. All incidents took place at stations with less than 35-foot cover or as a result of direct hits on booking halls and subways just below the street level. The worst disaster was at Balham during the evening of 14 October, 1940, when a bomb penetrated the northbound station tunnel at its northern end, rupturing water mains and sewers. The explosion was immediately followed by an alarming inrush of water and gravel which half-filled both station tunnels, by then plunged in darkness. Escaping coal gas heightened the horror of the situation and those still alive on the platforms were sealed off by watertight doors at the base of the escalator shaft. One by one, they were evacuated through emergency escape hatches from this grim station-tomb. The bodies of sixty-four shelterers and four railway men were found in the debris and it was three months before the line could be reopened. Nearly seven million gallons of water had to be pumped from the vast hole.

On the day before the Balham disaster, nineteen shelterers were killed and fifty-two injured at Bounds Green when a bomb reached the platforms of the Piccadilly line. All but three of those killed were Belgian refugees who were all sheltering together at one end of the station platform. It is not recorded whether the bomb fell down the ventilation shaft or not, but this seems quite likely.

Amongst other incidents was the dreadful accident which occurred at Bethnal Green just before 8.30 p.m. on 3 March 1943. A salvo of anti-aircraft rockets was fired off about mile from the station entrance in the belief that an air attack was imminent. As people groped their way down the stairs, fierce pushing from those behind knocked them forward and others tumbled on top of them. Those at the top, fearing that the platform doors had been closed against them, pushed all the harder in their blind desire to reach safety. When the police gained control of the situation they found a tangled human mass at the bottom of the stairs. Twenty-seven men, eighty-four women and sixty-two children were found crushed to death amid sixty-two injured.

People adapted themselves with astonishing facility to utterly unfamiliar duties in instant, dire and often macabre peril. I do truly think it was Britain's "finest hour". No one would like to have such an experience again, but it did give us a discipline and unity that we have not recovered since the War.

Richard Hillary, a young Battle of Britain pilot and a most promising writer, author of *The Last Enemy*, was killed in January 1943, aged twenty-three years. Three years earlier, during the Battle of Britain, he was one of the first fighter pilots to be shot down. He survived a ghastly crash-landing in the sea but suffered terrible burns and temporary blindness. After months of hospital care and grafting and patience and fortitude, he returned to duty as a member of ground staff. He was determined to fly again, and after beseeching and badgering his superiors, he was allowed to train as a night fighter pilot, and so he died.

In his book he mentions a journey through London when he was caught in an air raid and the following is part of his description:

Together with the man in the A.F.S. (Auxiliary Fire Service), the taxi-driver and I found our way into the street. He turned to us almost apologetically. "If you have nothing very urgent on hand," he said, "I wonder if you'd help here for a bit. You see it was the house next to you that was hit and there's someone buried in there."

I turned and looked on a heap of bricks and mortar, wooden beams and doors, and one framed picture unbroken.

We dug, or rather we pushed, pulled, heaved and strained, I somewhat ineffectually because of my hands; I don't know for how long, but I suppose for a short enough while. And yet it seemed endless. From time to time I was aware of figures round me: an A.R.P warden, his face expressionless under a steel helmet; once a soldier swearing savagely in a quiet monotone; and the taxi-driver, his face pouring sweat.

And so we came to the woman. It was her feet that we saw first, and whereas before we had worked doggedly, now we worked with a sort of frenzy, like prospectors at the first glint of gold. She was not quite buried, and through the gap between two beams we could see that she was still alive. We got the child out first. It was passed back carefully and with an odd sort of reverence by the warden, but it was dead. She must have been holding it to her in the bed when the bomb came.

Finally we made a gap wide enough for the bed to be drawn out. The woman who lay there looked middle-aged. She lay on her back and her eyes were closed. Her face, through the dirt and streaked blood, was the face of a thousand working women; her body under the cotton nightdress was heavy. The nightdress was drawn up to her knees and one leg was twisted under her.

Around me I heard voices. "Where's the ambulance?" "For Christ's sake don't move her!" "Let her have some air!"

I was at the head of the bed, and looking down into that tired, blood-streaked, work-worn face I had a sense of complete unreality. I took the brandy flask from my hip pocket and held it to her lips. Most of it ran down her chin but a little flowed between those clenched teeth. She opened her eyes and reached out her arms instinctively for the child. Then she started to weep. Quite soundlessly, and with no sobbing, the tears were running down her cheeks when she lifted her eyes to mine.

"Thank you, sir," she said, and took my hand in hers. And then, looking at me again, she said after a pause, "I see they got you too."

Mobilisation meanwhile was acquiring a new meaning. The National Service Act had been rushed through Parliament at the outset of the War. It was to be supplemented later by a law making everybody, men and women alike, aged eighteen to sixty, liable for some type of War work.

I decided to join the FANY as a volunteer.

*　　*　　*

The FANY was the first women's voluntary Corps to be registered in this country.

The First Aid Nursing Yeomanry was the full title of the Corps which was dreamed up and founded in 1907 by a Captain Baker. It was originally a mounted Corps. In both the Sudan and in the South African War, experience had shown that, owing to the length of time wounded had to be left unattended on the battlefields, many lives were lost which might have been saved if first aid could have been given earlier. Members of the Corps were therefore trained to act as mounted auxiliaries to the Royal Army Medical Corps to enable them to reach the wounded quickly. The FANYs were all trained in first aid and horsemanship and some were fully qualified nurses.

In September 1914, the first unit of the FANY went to Belgium and served with Belgian Army. Their service and valour, particularly at Calais, became famous. They became part of the Belgian Army, were recognised as soldiers and had the same rank. Their four years of continuous service with the Belgian Army had its reward when they were the first women to enter Bruges, Ostend, Ghent and Brussels after the German evacuation.

The name Ashley-Smith was mentioned in Corps History whilst I was on my training course. She was a woman full of energy, who disliked bureaucracy and ignored the scorn of Generals in the British Army. She would not wait for the War Office to give permission, and with a party of twelve, including six FANYs, she set off for Folkestone on 26 October 1914, from where they crossed to Calais, complete with ambulances which she had begged and scrounged.

In Hugh Popham's book on the FANY, he writes on the work they undertook at Calais and beyond:-

> Calais was a seething mass of trains, horses, gun-limbers, carts, refugees, and soldiers either on their way to the front or, wounded, on their way back from it. Less than fifty miles to the west the first battle of Ypres was about to reach crisis point. Casualties had been heavy: 8,000 were evacuated through Calais alone during the first five days that the FANYs were there. "Calais swept by storms of wind and rain, cold and wet

and cheerless," as Grace Ashley-Smith wrote later; "the Calais along whose quays one never-to-be-forgotten night, rows of wounded lay, in the darkness and the cold and the rain."

So rife was typhoid among the patients that three wards on the ground floor of a make-shift hospital were turned over exclusively to them, the only such wards in Calais at the time. These gaunt delirious creatures who raved and cried – and occasionally tried to strangle their benefactors – were enough to try the nerves of seasoned nurses, but the girls coped; indeed "coping" almost became a Corps motto in time. "Untrained, yes, but teachable," the redoubtable Sister Wicks wrote of them. "When I think of the spongings these children have to do, with the basin on the floor as there are no chairs – back-aching work; then the two-hourly feeds which can only be given sip by sip, the injections and routine work, I wonder how they do it." They probably wondered themselves.

Even without the shellfire, trips to the front were fairly arduous. The vehicles had only rudimentary windscreens or none, brutal springing, uncertain engines, no self-starters, and tyres depressingly prone to punctures. In these bone-shakers, on tiny oil sidelights (the Carbide headlights, and sometimes even the sidelights, were forbidden), they drove on narrow roads with deep mud on either side constantly having to dodge other traffic, staff cars, gun-limbers, horses and tramping men. Luckily when they did slide off the hard surface, there was usually a cheerful mob of soldiers to heave them out of the morass. The landscape, all gutted houses and stricken trees, was rendered even more desolate by the inundations engineered by the Belgians back in September to halt the German advance.

At this time the FANYs were the only women driving in France: the effect of this on the soldiers is adequately summed up by one wounded man who, on recovering consciousness after a gas attack, opened his eyes and exclaimed in awed tones: "My Gawd, it's a woman!". . .

On they trailed, out of France and into Flanders, into Ypres and out again to Hellfire Corner, where on 24 May, 1915, they came under attack by gas.* "Out of a green haze that hung over everything one unending stream of Tommies, English and Scotch, came down the road, tottering, stumbling, gasping." Fortunately the two girls had (Belgian) respirators, while many of the men had none, and they spent the next six hours doing what they could to relieve the collapsed and retching men.

"Of my impressions of the devastated area," one girl recorded later, "it is impossible to write, the horror of it haunts me still, but one feeling stands out above all others, and it is an intense admiration for the men who could endure so much and yet keep such wonderful spirits through it all."

The FANY serving with the French Army also had the privilege of being the first women into St Mitiel, Metz, Strasbourg and later parts of Germany. They joined the French Army with the rank of *poilu* in 1917, and their efforts since then have been even more extraordinary than in their first freshness. With their ambulance convoys they were sent to places where no

---

* This is often referred to as "the first gas attack", but that took place a month earlier, on 22 April, 1915, by the Germans: gas was, in fact, used sporadically throughout Second Ypres – a forlorn battle that cost the British 60,000 casualties and achieved nothing.

women had hitherto been allowed, and they had at times worked under fire. Very often during those years the FANY quarters were empty houses with only a minimum of comfort – straw for beds and food that was frequently bad. During 1918 there were few nights without raids. The FANYs showed unfailing pluck and sterling, dogged persistence, working often night and day without food or sleep. Their motto is "In Difficulties Unconquered".

A Colonel of the British field ambulance recently told a story to representatives of the FANY of hundreds of British and French wounded lying on stretchers, of FANY ambulances arriving loaded and in the midst of it all an air raid! German planes circling over the clearing station dropped bombs on the wounded. Those who could walk or crawl managed to reach dugouts, and the FANYs tended them during the bombing and all through the night till dawn, and from then till night again. "It made me proud to be English," were the Colonel's closing words.

I again quote from Hugh Popham:

> In the First World War, far from being paid, members themselves paid a subscription of £1 a year to belong to it, found their own uniforms – as was sometimes all too apparent: and for all running expenses were dependent on private generosity. To tap which, FANYs on leave were expected to give lectures and talks in their home towns. They gained 135 decorations, including 1 Legion d'Honneur, 1 Croix de Guerre with Palm, 32 Croix de Guerre (Belgian), 1 Ordre de Leopold Ist Class and several Croix Civiques.

Since 1916 they have also worked with the British Army but they are not part of the Army like the French and Belgian Sections, being but a civilian body. They are not so well known in this country as they might be, owing to the major part of their activities being in France and Flanders.

After the Armistice the FANY offered its services to the Government at home for work in any emergency. In 1926 the Corps was called upon to drive buses and lorries during the General Strike, and only in 1927 the FANY was at last officially recognised by the War Office.

In 1938, 415 members attended the main summer camp at Mytchett. FANY sections were also being founded in other countries. All recruits in Britain (who were volunteers and not conscripted) passed through the Corps training school which was originally at a large country house owned by the Boileaus at Ketteringham in Norfolk, and later near Banbury. It was staffed by members of the Corps. The youngest FANY was sixteen-and-a-half, the average age being about twenty.

If selected for work with Special Operations Executive (SOE), FANYs went to further training schools where they received instructions in the use of small arms and signals. They became cipher operators – enciphering and deciphering secret messages – while others learnt to receive and transmit morse code by wireless; some became packers of parachutes, arms, explosives and every type of equipment. FANYs escorted agents (affectionately called "Bods") throughout their training, often jumping with them on their parachute courses. The FANYs in SOE helped run the training schools, signals and ops stations. The strictest possible security had to be maintained and no contact with the local population was ever allowed. From the ops station the FANYS drove the Bods to the airfields after the signal had come through from the occupied countries that the reception committees were ready and the weather conditions were favourable.

Some FANYs too were dropped behind enemy lines by parachute or landed by Lysander aircraft. They took part in armed resistance and sabotage and, in the course of their everyday duties, travelled many miles carrying information, arms and often wireless parts, bluffing their way through enemy posts. The necessity for being constantly on the alert in enemy-occupied territory was an appalling strain. During the War a number of FANYS were captured, tortured and executed; a few died in concentration camps, others were killed in action, some survived.

"The FANY Corps has the oldest traditions and proudest records of all women's corps in this, and therefore the greatest spirit," quoted Field-Marshal Earl Wavell in 1945 and the following is an extract from a letter written after the War by the head of SOE, Major-General Sir Colin Gubbins:

> I am left tongue-tied when I try to tell you what the FANYs have meant to the organisation and to me. I say "to me" because I took the original decision and had the idea to use them to the utmost, and I am personally sufficiently human to be glad to find my judgement proved right. But to the organisation they were everything, as you well know, and without them we just couldn't have done it. In every theatre they have became a household word for efficiency, guts, cheerfulness, persistence, tenacity and comrade-ship in difficulty, and I am proud to have been the means of their proving their great qualities, and they have been magnificent and invaluable.
>
> I know that what they have themselves learnt will be of inestimable and permanent value to their country.

The FANY celebrated its Diamond Jubilee in October 1967 and at a special service of Thanksgiving and Commemoration in the Guards Chapel, the Very Reverend Nevile Davidson, MA, DD, CH.St.J, Chaplain to the Queen in Scotland and a former Moderator of the Church of Scotland, recalled the early history of the Corps as a band of mounted nurses, and described it as "pioneering, adventurous, compassionate; indifferent to danger and hard-ship, ready for self-forgetting service".

Dr Davidson said: "The history of the FANY across these sixty years has been a record of imaginative voluntary service. Both those adjectives are significant. Yours is the oldest women's voluntary Corps in our country. You and the older comrades who went before you have given to the utter-most of your strength, your skill, your powers of mind and body, without thought of reward or remuneration. That voluntary service has been inspired by love of our country and by the ideals and traditions of freedom and justice handed down to us. You have given of your best without counting the cost.

"Courage and Compassion; they are two qualities which are immensely needed in the world of our own time," Dr Davidson continued. "Physical courage yes, but even more, moral courage: courage to choose and follow the best values, however unpopular. We live today in a world both of exciting opportunities and demanding challenges. A world in which it is easy especially for younger people to lose their way, because so many of the familiar guidelines and signposts have been knocked down. A world in which it is all too easy to accept plausible but misleading slogans, and to allow older standards and ideals to be scoffed at. At such a period in history it takes moral courage to accept and to live by a worthy scale of values. And one of the great needs of this time is for a strong steady moral leadership; not pompous or pretentious or puritanical, but inspired by personal faith and displayed with fortitude.

"No less is the lovely virtue of Compassion needed today. Because even in our pretty affluent country, there are people in need of help: the old, the frail, the foolish, the lonely, the housebound. And often sudden emergencies or disasters in which the assistance of a skilled and trained unit like yours can be of vital value.

"And today you bring all that record of Courage and Compassion to God in thanksgiving: and you bring yourselves to God in renewed dedication, praying that by His help you may always in days to come be able to keep alive in your own service that same spirit of courage and compassion.

"May I refer to your badge: the Circle for Unity and the Cross for Sacrifice. In unity is strength; and I know that the wonderful comradeship of your Corps has always been one of the secrets of its unfailing fortitude.

"And the Cross; which points us to the supreme thing in life; the power that comes to us through Christ, the Divine Warrior who in His own person faced hardship, loneliness, pain, anguish of body and darkness of spirit and came through victorious. There is a wonderful sentence in one of St Paul's letters. 'I can do all things through Christ who strengthens me.' And I am sure that many of you here this afternoon have found in your own experiences something of what he meant. As you faced some task which seemed beyond your abilities, as you accepted some new responsibility which frightened you, as you carried out some duty which almost exhausted you – something strange and marvellous happened. Suddenly you realised that you were not alone, left to your own poor resources, but that at your side stood the Divine Friend and Helper, the strengthening Christ.

"May I leave with you, as I finish, that great assurance of St Paul's: 'You will be able to do all things, you will be equal to every task and ordeal, through Christ who strengthens you.'"

The FANY traditions of voluntary service remain alive today. They are on call for national emergencies to man the documentation Casualty Bureau for the City of London Police. They are also trained for work in Ministry of Defence Communication Centres and their Language Group can provide interpreters in ten languages. The FANY Headquarters is at the Duke of

York's Barracks in Chelsea. Training is as important as ever and they may volunteer for parachuting, gliding, coding, W/T (Wireless Telegraphy) operating, shooting and unarmed combat. Since they were formed their uniforms have been:

1907 – dark blue riding skirt, scarlet service cap and scarlet tunic;
1910 – changed to service khaki divided skirt, khaki tunic and khaki topee;
1914 – service khaki jacket and skirt, service khaki jacket and shirt, service khaki topee, shirt and tie;
1939 – khaki jacket and skirt, battledress and tin hat. Both a khaki peaked service cap and khaki bonnet with the Corps badge were worn. Respirator (in case of gas attacks) had to be carried all the time.

Badge

The Corps badge is formed by a Maltese Cross within a circle. The Cross is a symbol of sacrifice and the circle is a symbol of unity. The meaning of the badge is therefore self-sacrifice to achieve unity and service.

On my training course, each morning began with drill, at that time taken by a sergeant from the Devonshire Regiment, whose accent made his commands quite difficult to follow. Ethel Boileau, the well-known author, who was the Commanding Officer at Ketteringham, inspected us, paying particular attention to our appearance: hair had to be well above the collar, and our shoes polished vigorously every day – the insteps were expected to be as clean and shiny as the uppers. The Sam Browne belts, too, had to be polished to resemble a mirror. The course included route marches, training in Army procedure, military groups, fire drill, security, respiration and stretcher drill, night vision, mechanics, advanced first-aid nursing, convoy driving, night map reading, and driving different types of vehicles ranging from cars to seven-ton lorries. Every FANY driver was expected to maintain her vehicle in first-class condition. We later received 11/2d per week. We were addressed by our surnames only.

In addition to the practical work we had to pass written and oral examinations in all these subjects. We attended lectures in Corps history, and were reminded that during the freezing winters of the First World War the FANYs slept in tents and the girls had to wind up the vehicles every twenty minutes throughout each night to prevent the engines freezing. Some of us were overawed by what the FANYs had endured and the high standards expected of us; we were more than a little apprehensive as to whether we would come up to the mark.

Those in charge wore the round cherry-coloured insignia of a Commander on their epaulettes, which also usually signified that they had served in and survived the First World War. The younger members amongst us nicknamed them "raspberry tarts". They were, however, greatly revered and with comparatively few written rules there was an *esprit de corps* and discipline so strong that as far as I can remember nobody questioned or disregarded what was expected of us.

We remember Ethel Boileau addressing us and saying "And then there is Bingham's Unit, from which no FANY ever returns."

The course lasted for about three weeks, and then lists were put up with our names indicating to which sections we had been posted. I was to report to Bingham's Unit, SOE Headquarters in Baker Street, London, a rabbit-warren of offices and a prosaic threshold to a new world. For several hours I was grilled by security before signing the Official Secrets Act. We were, without realising it, signing our names to a new way of life. The Head of SOE believed in our capacity to do difficult and secret work and that security would be impeccable. He gave encouragement to all, but especially to those of us still in our teens. The familiar, ordinary world was left behind, and I never returned to it.

I am always reminded of King George VI's Christmas broadcast in 1939 and the quotation he used from Minnie Louise Haskins:

> I said to the man who stood at the gate of the year, "Give me a light that I may tread safely into the unknown," and he replied, "Go out into the darkness and put your hand into the hand of God. That shall be to thee better than a light and safer than a known way."

4

These Hearts Were Woven

These hearts were woven of human joys and cares,
Washed marvellously with sorrow, swift to mirth.
The years had given them kindness. Dawn was theirs,
And sunset, and the colours of the earth.

RUPERT BROOKE

SUBVERSIVE ACTIVITY IN VARIOUS forms and in different countries
was directed against Germany even before the outbreak of the Second
World War at the instigation of the British Secret Services. Special
Operations Executive was formally set up as a separate organisation in July
1940, when Winston Churchill drafted a memorandum to his Cabinet
establishing the organisation "to co-ordinate all action by way of subversion and sabotage against the enemy overseas". The Prime Minster was to
remember later that his purpose had been "to set Europe ablaze".

On the very day that Churchill's memorandum was presented to the
Cabinet, Hitler, in an address to the Reichstag, offered to end hostilities
with Britain "as a victor speaking in the name of reason". The establishment of SOE was in a sense, Churchill's defiant answer.

The Minister of Economic Warfare was given ministerial responsibility
for SOE and at the time of its formation Dr Hugh Dalton was the Minster
concerned. He immediately set about implementing its charter.

During the early part of the War many men and women had escaped
to Britain from different occupied countries. While the majority joined
the services, some volunteered or were picked for SOE. Many of these
volunteers had already fought with great bravery in their own countries –
they had also witnessed defeat, withdrawal, bitterness, collapse. They were
Dutch, Norwegian, French, Belgian, Danish, Polish and Czech. The
Norwegians were left bewildered by the Allied withdrawal from their
country and many made their escape to the United Kingdom by an
incredible variety of routes, a few even via the Trans-Siberian railway
and Canada. All were worried about the fate of their families and friends
at home.

In 1941 Dr Dalton was succeeded by the Earl of Selborne who had for
many years been a close personal friend and a Parliamentary colleague of
Winston Churchill. He proved to be an outstandingly successful Minster
from the point of view of SOE.

SOE had only three operational chiefs during its life, all of whom were
known as "CD". The first was Air-Commodore Frank Nelson, who was

succeeded by Sir Charles Hambro. He was in turn succeeded by Brigadier (later Major-General Sir) Colin Gubbins.

Colin Gubbins later described SOE's tasks thus:

> The problem and the plan was to encourage and enable the peoples of the occupied countries to harass the German war effort at every possible point by sabotage, subversion, go-slow practices, etc., and at the same time to build up secret forces therein, organised, armed and trained to take their part only when final assault began ... In its simplest terms, this plan involved the ultimate delivery to occupied territory of large numbers of personnel and quantities of arms and explosives. The first problem was to make contact with those countries, to get information on the possibilities, to find out the prospects of getting local help, and an even more immediate task was to find someone suitable and willing to undertake the first hazardous trip, then to train him and fit him for the job and ensure communications with him when he had landed. But all contacts with occupied territories closed when the last British Forces returned to Great Britain in 1940, so the first man to go back to any country had to be parachuted "blind" as we say, i.e. there was no one waiting to receive him on the dropping ground, no household ready to give him shelter, conceal his kit, and arrange his onward passage ...

During the course of the next five years the men and women of SOE painstakingly fostered the spirit of resistance amongst the populations of occupied territories, first in Europe and subsequently in the Far East in many of the territories occupied by the Japanese. On the foundations thus created they systematically built organised Resistance groups varying in character and size according to the operational needs of the areas in which they were situated. Such groups varied from the close-knit cells created in large cities to the widespread Maquis in areas such as the Massif Centrale of France. The Resistance groups had the dual role of committing controlled acts of sabotage according to the operational requirements of the time and place concerned, and the preparing for armed uprising to assist Liberation by Allied Forces at a later date. In occupied Europe the German and Italian transportation networks were systematically sabotaged. Rolling-stock, railway lines and waterways were destroyed, interrupting vital enemy lines of supply.

The achievements of SOE were many and varied. Tens of thousands of German troops were diverted from fighting fronts to contain Resistance activity behind their own lines and it is now known that the work of SOE had a profoundly depressing psychological effect on the morale of the Germans and of those who collaborated with them in the occupied territories. Among the most striking and important achievements were the destruction of the heavy water plant erected by the Germans in Norway, the destruction (twice) of a strategic bridge across a deep ravine in Greece; and the recovery and dispatch to London of an almost intact experimental V2 rocket which had landed in Poland.

At the time of the invasion of occupied Europe by the Allied Armies (Italy in September 1943 and France in June 1944), SOE stepped up its campaign of harassment behind enemy lines and called into action Resistance groups which it had painstakingly armed and trained in preparation for the various landings. For example, as a result of SOE activity, one Panzer division north of the Pyrenees which was ordered to reinforce the German resistance to the Normandy landings arrived at its sector of the front too late to be effective.

I quote from the Book *The Waffen SS* by George H. Stein:

> The early months of 1944 found the elite 2nd SS Panzerdivision "Das Reich" in southern France recuperating after a hard winter of fighting on the Russian front. While there, the division assisted the local security forces in a drive against partisan bands operating in the mountains of Auvergne. In the small village of Tulle alone, ninety-nine people – men and women – were hanged, and the SS operation soon became known as the "Blood and Ashes Action". Immediately after the Allied invasion of France, the SS Division "Das Reich" was ordered north to help defend Normandy. As elements of the division passed near the village of Oradour-sur-Glane, to the east of Limoges, a French resistance sniper shot and killed an SS officer. In reprisal, the First Battalion of the division's SS Panzergrenadier Regiment 4 "Der Führer" burned the village and massacred its entire population; 642 inhabitants, including 207 children, were shot or burned to death. The SS regiment's action report for the day refers to a "cleansing action" in which the village was burned after "munitions were discovered in almost every house". The mass murder of unarmed men, women, and children was treated as if it had been a military operation, and the SS report listed the casualties as "548 enemy dead" at a cost of "2 men wounded". Apparently two SS men got too close to a fire or were accidentally shot by their comrades. An almost identical case involving an SS division occurred in Greece during the same year. When a convoy belonging to the 4th SS Polizei Panzergrenadierdivision, refitting in northern Greece after a disastrous year on the Russian front, was ambushed by Greek guerrillas near Klissura, members of the SS unit conducted savage reprisals against the local inhabitants.
>
> With the Allied invasion of France in June 1944, Western soldiers clashed with the Waffen SS for the first time since 1940. For the Americans and Canadians it was an entirely new experience, while the British found the SS troops skillful and tough as they remembered them. Moreover, Allied soldiers soon discovered that the Waffen SS thoroughly lived up to the reputation for brutality it had gained along the eastern front.

The Western Allies were also murdered in full uniform in some terrible massacres.

The final, and one of the most vital parts of the Bods' training, involved a mock "interrogation". It was essential that they should learn to cope with the element of surprise. Instructors broke into their rooms in the early hours of the morning when they were in a deep sleep and immediately tested their ability to withhold information from "Gestapo interrogators". For some of the Bods, these scenes were to be repeated in real life in the months ahead.

The courage of the men and women of SOE became a legend in their own time. Casualties amongst them were heavy and many of those captured by the Gestapo were executed with extreme savagery in prisons, concentration camps and elsewhere. Even under the physical and metal stress of torture nearly all of them maintained silence about their activities and contacts and those who went to their deaths did so with extraordinary bravery. The full extent of their contribution towards final victory is still very little known and appreciated, but their memory deserves to be honoured for all time.

In SOE there were different "stations", referred to by numbers and serving different purposes. Amongst others there were training stations where agents were prepared for their future activities, and operations and holding stations where they waited before being dropped. The stations were usually requisitioned or rented country houses, the majority of them in isolated rural areas.

I was posted, very briefly, to the Czech Section, but otherwise served with the Poles. No reasons were ever given regarding postings and no questions ever entertained. As part of my training, I was taught the rudiments of the Czech and Polish languages, but never succeeded in speaking them naturally, though I can follow conversation.

When alone and not embarrassed, I gain confidence, and I liked to be encouraged to talk. We were expected to take the lessons seriously, and I especially remember Professor Rose's book on how to learn Polish. It is an exceedingly difficult language, particularly the pronunciation. My late brother, John, who was a linguist, criticised me for speaking the language badly, and this gave me a complex about it.

It would be very difficult indeed to describe in detail the size and complexity of the Polish Section of SOE, and to explain the activities of the underground in Poland. Their work covered acts of sabotage against enemy installations, collecting vital information for the Allies, organising and training new groups and distributing BBC news. (It was forbidden by the Germans for a Pole to possess a wireless set – all were confiscated and anybody found with one was promptly imprisoned or executed.)

Large numbers of men, women and children belonged to the Resistance and all lived in constant danger of being arrested at any hour of the day or night.

After an extremely tough and arduous training in Britain, the Bods would go to one of the holding ops stations, where they waited in secrecy until the right moon period and when a signal had been received from Poland that the weather conditions were favourable for a parachute drop. The Bods would get ready, often at very short notice, and the FANYs would drive them as quickly as possible to the airfield. In the early days Whitley bombers were used for the drops, but fortunately they were replaced by the

Halifax. The later versions of the latter aircraft were faster than the earlier ones: their cruising speed averaged 220 miles per hour, which meant a flight time of about eight hours, depending on head or tail winds and the location of the dropping zone.

Apart from driving the Bods, our tasks included escorting them to Ringway (the Parachute Training School near Manchester) and to special courses, as well as maintaining their vehicles and working as cipherers. We looked after them, acting as their confidantes, and tried also to bring some kind of stability to a life which, for many, held only a precarious future. Whatever we did to help them, they gave far more back to us. It was a time my companions and I were never to forget.

One of the Bods at Ringway, with help from a few of us, composed the followed poem:

> We, who drop out of the clouds,
> a sheer plunge before floating,
> flung to the whim of the currents
> below the fuselage,
> gather our limbs for the land,
> conscientiously noting
> points of assembly and cover
> to harbour us all.
>
> Out of the hatch we are hurled
> and the body that bore us
> fades to a shadow, its murmur
> a breath of the breeze.
> Weather and earth and the passing
> of arms are below us:
> battle may blaze before half of
> us rise from our knees.

After being lectured severally and at length on security at Baker Street, I was told to take a train to Hertford. I was driven to the railway station in the back of a small van with the canvas flaps down. On arrival at Hertford I was met by a FANY who had just seen off some students. On the way from the railway station to the training school I remember her saying, "Those students have gone to get some decent grub, but we must meet them again tonight and see that they are safely in." This FANY was one of several to have been sent to Special Training School (STS) 17, and she went on, "Anybody who comes here is not expected to ask questions. You will find out what you need to know, but always keep your own mouth shut." She was an auburn-haired New Zealander with a natural complexion and a slightly rugged outdoor look.

When we arrived at the Training School she took me to a small cottage beyond the clock and coach house and said, "You had better come over later to the main building. It is easy to find your way." She then gave me very brief directions and added, "Your duties will be explained to you later. The cover story here at all times is that it is a training school for Allied Commandos." I was rightly made aware that discipline, security and hard work were considered essential, and anybody treating any of these matters lightly would not last long here.

Station 17 started training in August 1941. The house, called Brickendonbury, was built by a London merchant in 1704, and had had extensions added later. There was also a cottage and coach house in the grounds. The property had belonged to Lord Cowdray, and then it became a preparatory school before Baker Street chose it to house Station 17.

There had been some discussion as to whether the Training School should remain "open" with security personnel in the town keeping their eyes and ears open for potential dangers to security, or whether it should be "closed" with dog patrols and so on. The "open" system was retained, but outside visits and contacts were forbidden. Security was broken only once, as far as I can remember, and that was when a party of boys from Haileybury School were found swarming around the aeroplane and tank park.

Though our days were full and passed quickly, a few of the students and FANYs at the School sometimes had an overwhelming urge to get out for a while. This was not permitted, but all the same we would, very occasionally, go out from Station 17 for a swift ride in the surrounding country on the light collapsible bicycles which used to be packed into containers and dropped into enemy-occupied countries. Such escapades earned us a severe ticking-off if we were caught. Sometimes there were bets about climbing the high water-tower near a pub called The Green Man.

STS 17 specialised in industrial sabotage, and some 1,200 men had passed through its various courses by the time War ended in 1945. The Commanding Officer was Lieutenant-Colonel George Rheam. Some other members of the staff I remember were Major Bill Sykes (who had served in Shanghai); he was an expert in pistol shooting and silent killing, but he looked like a retired bishop! Then there was George Howard, a small arms expert; Sergeant England, who gave instruction on demolition; Hatcher, ex-bomb disposal unit who also taught demolition; PT instructors Lieutenant Francis and Sergeants Redhouse and Carter; and Jarrett, who had been head waiter at the Royal Victoria Hotel, Hastings. He was a bit of a leg-puller. One of his pet expressions was "I don't know what will happen to us all." He returned to his old job after the War.

In 1941 little was known about efficient ways of destroying machinery and plant with explosives. The standard Army method of placing "large" quantities of gun cotton in a building and "blowing it up" was obviously unsuitable for clandestine work, because of the difficulty of concealing the bulk of the explosive required during the approach to and at the target. SOE needed to use small quantities that could be reasonably concealed and carried on the person.

Part of the Station was turned into a demolition research area and scrap yards and factories over a wide area were searched for suitable machinery and plant to experiment on (and later for the trainees to practise on).

Small quantities of plastic explosive can cause a great deal of destruction. Some fundamental rules were quickly established and training began in recognising the vital machine or sections of plant and the correct positioning of the explosive charges – and this was often for people quite unfamiliar with machinery.

In addition to industry, airfields (and their planes) and military equipment generally were priority targets in the early years of the War; railways were important throughout and became vital targets towards the end. For training in this work, the school had three planes; a two-engined Manchester, a Tempest or Typhoon with Sabre engine, and a German JU88. In addition it had a Churchill tank, and all stood in a compound on the East drive with a GWR locomotive in a nearby siding.

A general course of three weeks' duration was devised to ensure as far as possible that every student not only had sufficient knowledge to operate efficiently and with confidence but also to act in turn as an instructor when he went into the field. There were also specialist courses and courses associated with a particular target.

The three-week course (referred to as "famous" in the official history of SOE in France by M.R.D. Foot) comprised lectures, visits to industrial plants for practice in the recognition of "vital targets"; practical work in the school grounds, on the local Metropolitan Water Board pumping station, the engine sheds at Hitchin, the local railway, and the airfields at Radlett and Stansted – the latter being a night-fighter base.

Prior to the Dieppe raid in 1942, Colonel Rheam received a telephone call asking him to train thirty instructors in SOE methods of demolition. In the event, thirty-three Canadian Commandos came to STS 17, and only a few knew French. On arrival, one of the Commandos was heard to say, "We don't want any further training," but they were told to obey orders. Some thought it was a peculiar place, not recognisable as the usual Army Training School. Their task was to destroy the dock machinery and other targets at Dieppe. The School considered it a great honour to be asked to give further training to these men. Stormy weather delayed the operation for a month; it finally took place on 19 August 1942 at a cost of 3,642 Allied servicemen killed, wounded or taken prisoner. We heard that Mountbatten and Combined Operations had insisted on this raid.

In March 1941 a group of SOE Norwegian Commandos under the command of Captain Martin Linge, later killed in action, raided the Lofoten Islands off the Norwegian coast, and reported that they had destroyed the fish-oil plant there by "blowing it up". A few days later the SOE clandestine radio operator reported that though the buildings had been largely destroyed, the plant was working again. This incident led to STS 17 training parties of Army personnel for special operation, such as the airborne glider attack on Rjukan and also Canadian 1st Division's raid on

Dieppe – a disaster already mentioned. The School also showed groups of Americans their methods so that they could set up their own organisation. Much other work was done.

One of the most notable operations trained at the School was the attack on the heavy water plant of the Norsk Hydro Elektrisk at Rjukan in Norway, which was carried out by Norwegian personnel.

In the autumn of 1942 it was thought that the Germans might be ahead of the Allies in the attempt to manufacture the atomic bomb, and they were using heavy water as the moderator in their reactor, obtaining their supplies from Rjukan, which had the largest heavy water plant in Europe. STS 17 was informed that it was to be responsible for the specialised technical and demolition training that would be needed to destroy the plant.

A party of some thirty-four men from the British Airborne Division was selected for Operation *Freshman* and, after training, left for Norway on the 19 November 1942 in two Horsa gliders towed by Halifax aircraft. Adverse weather conditions caused both gliders to crash-land miles from the intended landing area. The survivors were rounded up by the German Field Police and shot, though all were members of the British Army and in uniform. (After the War the officer responsible for the crime was executed.) This tragic failure alerted the Nazis to the importance the Allies attached to the destruction of the Rjukan factory, and they rapidly tightened its security arrangements.

The second attack was also entrusted to SOE and a party of six Norwegians under the command of Lieutenant Ronneberg was sent to the School. They were accompanied by Professor Leif Tronstad of Trondheim, the distinguished physicist who had been associated with the factory before the War. He had escaped to Britain and was a member of the combined SOE/Norwegian staff. Without him no real plans could have been made. This sabotage team was from the Linge Company and was code-named *Gunnerside*.

On the 18 October 1942, prior to the *Freshman* Operation and the *Gunnerside* men leaving Britain, a small group of Norwegians had been dropped by parachute in Fjarefit in the Songedal area. They were the advance party under the code-name *Grouse*. They had exceptional knowledge of the target area, its approaches and exits, and besides technical skills and expert training they were exceptionally tough and endured incredible hardships before they met up with colleagues in *Gunnerside*, when their party was re-named *Swallow*.

Intelligence was good, and Professor Tronstad had given such clear information about the heavy water plant that it had been possible to make a mock-up of it. Outbuildings at the School had been altered so that they resembled the target.

The plan was to destroy the high-concentration cells (each over a metre high) and the interconnecting pipework by small charges of plastic explosive linked together and provided with a 25-second fuse. Using dummy charges similar to the operational ones, the party had constantly practised entering the building, placing and fixing the charges and making good their escape, until the time for the whole Operation was reduced to a few minutes.

There remained the problem of gaining access to the heavy water plant in the complex of factory buildings.

Aerial photographs showed the general arrangement of the buildings, the perimeter fence, and the very difficult terrain in which the factory was situated – but they also showed the overhead power lines entering the building at about level, close to the heavy water plant. This was vital information because such cable entries are frequently left unsealed and so could provide a way into a building. And so it proved in this case.

Intelligence from SOE agents in Norway showed that the gates in the perimeter fence and the doors into the factory building were kept locked when in use. The party was therefore provided with a pair of heavy bolt croppers capable of cutting through any padlock and chain likely to be found, which were, in the event, used to get into the factory compound.

Before leaving on their mission, Professor Tronstad (who was killed later in the War) said to the group: "You have been told what happened to the airborne troops and you must reckon that in no circumstances will the Germans take any prisoners. For the sake of those who have gone before and have died, I beg you to do your utmost to make the operation succeed. You know how important it is, and what you do now will be part of Norway's history a hundred years hence."

Bad weather delayed the Operation, and it was February 1943 before the party could be parachuted into Norway. There they were joined by the back-up group of four SOE-trained men (*Grouse*) previously sent to the country, and the long arduous trek over the snow-clad mountains to Rjukan commenced. The members of *Grouse* had lived rough in bitter conditions for months on end.

On 27 February four members of the sabotage got into the factory building through the cable entry, found the high-concentration cells, laid the charges, ignited the fuses and made good their escape, all as planned in the training stages.

The Operation was completely successful, in spite of the heavy guard the Germans had placed on the factory following the airborne attempt. It had been carried out with great skill and determination and without the loss or capture of a single Bod. In all eleven Bods participated. The Nazis were deprived of all Norwegian means of production of heavy water and they started to rebuild the factory, but on 16 November 1943, the power station and adjoining plant were destroyed by American bombers, putting a final end to production.

Although production of heavy water at Rjukan had been brought to an end, it was known from the Norwegians that there were still substantial stocks of the precious substance at Rjukan and that the Germans intended to move these stocks to Peenemunde. This decision and the Germans' detailed plans for the journey quickly became known to Norwegian Resistance and London was informed.

The Chiefs of Staff instructed SOE to destroy the stocks of heavy water at all costs, and that in no circumstances must any of it reach Germany. Orders were transmitted to Norway accordingly.

The Germans had decided to transport the heavy water in special re-inforced containers from Rjukan to Mel on Lake Tinnsjo which was a regular port of call for the steamers which ply the fjords carrying passengers and freight. The closely guarded railway trucks carrying the consignment were to arrive at the little port on a Sunday afternoon just in time to catch the hydro ferry for a larger port, where, heavily guarded all the time, it was to be trans-shipped to Germany.

The SOE men and Resistance workers made their dangerous plans with great care. The hydro railway ferry was due to sail from Mel at 10 a.m. on Sunday 20 February 1944 and the previous evening three of the men succeeded in boarding the ship. One man engaged the ferry watchman in conversation while the other two laid nineteen pounds of high explosive in the form of a sausage in the cramped bilges of the ship in a foot of water. This was detonated by two alarm-clock mechanisms with only a third-of-an-inch clearance in the loose contacts – a third of an inch between them and disaster. On the Sunday morning the ferry sailed and blew up and sank on schedule in deep water and the remainder of the heavy water went down with her. Fourteen Norwegians and four Germans lost their lives, although the Norwegian Resistance reckoned that the Germans lost at least twenty men.

Thus ended the story of Norwegian heavy water for Germany and, with it, all possibility of the Germans overtaking the Allies in the race to produce the atomic bomb.

* * *

At the ops station, when a signal came through we took it in turns to go to the group leaders to tell them: "Ops are on."

One of these friends was a Polish officer we called "Zub". He had fought in the September 1939 campaign, escaped from German captivity, and during the first eighteen months of occupation worked with the cell of the Resistance which was set up to rescue Jews. In the same cell was another worker, Karol Wojtyla, later to become Pope John Paul II. In April 1941, Zub was ordered to proceed as a courier to Budapest and deposit there a microfilm containing important intelligence material. Whilst there, he made contact with a British liaison officer and then made his way to Britain by way of Yugoslavia, Italy and France. After extended debrief-ing in London he was assigned to SOE and completed his parachute training at Ringway, being awarded the Polish parachute badge bearing the consecutive number 12.

Zub received further training at STS 38 in Briggens near Roydon in Hertfordshire, where three FANY's also worked. In his own words:

> This Station was established in January 1941. About 140 students (Bods) were trained there in basic secret warfare – explosives, weapons, judo, secret inks and codes, microscope photography, radio communications. Throughout the War Briggens also acted as a base for the "Forgers", who were three graphic artists previously employed by the Bank of Poland. In Briggens they – and occasionally British experts and printers – worked in great secrecy, forging all types of German identity papers and currencies used on the Continent.
>
> These diverse and – to say the least – unorthodox activities were conducted under the watchful eye of our hosts Lord and Lady Alderham, who were aware of the secret nature of the work and whose patience and hospitality was appreciated by the Bods and the Forgers. It was exceptional that the owners were permitted to remain and were told what was going on. They lost one of their sons, Vicary Gibbs, a Captain in the Grenadier Guards, who was killed advancing on one of the Rhine bridges in 1945. I never discovered what Lord Aldenham, at that time Chairman of Westminster Bank thought of his ancestral home being used as a centre for the design and printing of counterfeit currencies!

Zub worked closely with Captain Kalenkiewicz, "Kotwicz", who was mainly responsible for operational planning and the logistics of support for the Polish Resistance by secret flights over Poland by the Polish crews of Special Duties RAF Squadon 138, and, later, Polish Squadron 301. Zub had brought Father Staniszewski to distribute Holy Communion. Kalenkiewicz refused to carry his poison tablet and wore instead a medallion with the consecrated host in a metal container. The last person who saw them in England was Kay, a FANY. She gave them red and white roses on board their aircraft.

Kalenkiewicz and four other officers were dropped in German-occupied Poland in late December 1941, thus inaugurating the flights which carried 320 SOE-trained agents and tons of supplies over the following two-and-a-half years. After his work with Captain Kalenkiewicz, Zub was attached to the Polish General Staff liaising with SOE Headquarters in Baker Street. Preparation and briefing were completed by the quiet, very well-mannered briefing officers from London, and the Bods were driven down to the airfield along the familiar roads of Hertfordshire, Cambridgeshire or Suffolk. The aircraft originally took off from a runway converted from one of the race courses at Newmarket, but later on they flew from Stradishall and Tempsford airfields. Each nationality had its own changing hut near the airfield and, for security reasons, was kept apart from the others. The FANYs also prepared sandwiches and flasks for the flight – sometimes an agent's last meal was from one of these "hayboxes".

At the ops station and during the journey checks were made to ensure that none of the agents carried any clues that would give them away – such as labels on clothing – and also to ensure that each had his or her compass, forged identification card and money, poison tablet (sometimes hidden in the top inside part of the jacket) and revolver. All messages, passwords and other information had to be memorised and carried by word of mouth only.

Though the pre-mission hours were naturally very tense, there was also a wonderful sense of humour and cheerfulness among the Bods. I can't remember any false bravado; on the contrary, it was real wit that came through. No written word can recapture the warmth of the atmosphere throughout the station. Whenever the atmosphere was especially tense or a feeling of dread pervaded, someone in the small group would rally the spirits of the others. They had, too, an extraordinary humility and a religious faith which was exemplified in the way they prepared themselves for their missions, such as making their confessions to a priest who would come to the ops station especially for this purpose. One of the FANYs would usually stay on at the airfield in one of the huts to await the return of the aircraft and to hear the debriefing. (She would have taken her sleeping bag as there were no beds in the huts.) It was at the debriefing that we would know if anyone had been lost. Occasionally we returned to the ops station to await the signal that the aircraft were on their way back and within three minutes we would be in our vehicle on our way back to the airfield.

After the build-up to a mission it was particularly demoralising for the agents when the aircraft had to return with them still on board because either the reception committee could not be located or visibility in the region of the landing area was too bad. Some Bods had flown on futile missions as many as eight times.

Both the piano and the gramophone were popular at the holdings ops station, for music relaxed the tension. Several of the Bods enjoyed playing the piano and the works of Chopin and Bartók were particularly loved. We learnt the Bods' folk dances and songs, especially the Czech and Polish ones, and played the haunting melodies of the 1930s and those composed in the Bods' own countries during the War.

If I hear any of these tunes now memories come flooding back. I suppose it was all the more poignant as we knew what lay ahead for the Bods and that these occasions might well be their last opportunity on earth to enjoy themselves. I remember, too, that one group said that the tune "Jealousy" would be the code used when we knew we could be reunited in Warsaw. It was not the words, but the music they liked. "All our tomorrows will be happy days"; "Wish me luck as you wave me goodbye"; "Broken chords" and "The gold and silver waltz" by Franz Lehar were others I recall. One of the most popular songs they sang was "Time's for us quickly passing":

> Time's for us quickly passing,
> Of life we're fast bereft,
> A year, a day, a moment,
> Maybe is all that's left.

Of our young days we're thinking,
How youth does quickly fly,
And for its loss we're heaving
A sad and gentle sigh.
Let then all young be happy,
Let's spare them grief and tears,
Let them to brighter future
Look forward, ban all fears.
We have now reached the crossroads,
Today the year does end,
God will protect the brave ones,
His help to all He'll send.

The Bods would often whistle and sing songs to themselves as they went about their duties on the station, and we had to ask them to concentrate on forgetting these tunes in case they hummed them without thinking once they had been dropped and gave themselves away to the enemy.

Christmas at the ops station was unforgettable. The Bods took over the station, including the kitchen, and managed (despite rationing) to prepare part of their tradition; Christmas Eve supper, including *barszcz* (beetroot soup) and fish. Meat is not eaten by Polish Catholics on Christmas Eve, for to them it is a day of abstinence. The Poles observed *wigilia* (vigil). Hay was laid on the table to represent the manager and, after the first star appeared, we handed each other a wafer (*oplatek*) blessed by a priest. This was held in one hand and taken round to everybody present when a special greeting was said; and, according to tradition, we asked each other's forgiveness and God's blessing. An empty chair is always left for the stranger to arrive and as a symbol of Christ's presence. For many of those present, this was their last Christmas on earth.

We learnt and sang their carols and taught them ours. At midnight, Mass was celebrated. We could not exchange presents for obvious reasons, but I remember one Bod who handed me his parachute badge. He wrote, "Until we meet at the Central Station in Warsaw". We were naturally unable to invite them to our own homes because of security, and this made us feel all the more united. I have spent Christmas away from home twenty-one times in all.

The agents delighted in talking about their own countries: it seemed to help them, perhaps because it eased their homesickness and enabled them to express the pride they felt. The Dutch talked of Amsterdam, the canals and the flowers, and of the pre-War breakfast tables laden with different varieties of cheese and sausages. The Norwegians would describe the long northern nights, the way they had been brought up to use skis, and the distances they covered on them while working for the Resistance in the pine forests and the fjords. Peter, a young Norwegian, felt that after the War it would be impossible for him to remain in his own country, for he couldn't imagine settling down to an ordinary life after being an agent. He talked of emigrating, but did not know where he wanted to go. The other Bods were shocked by his attitude. Some said they would study medicine or social work, and they spoke about trying to rebuild their countries because, for some, both their cities and their lives were in ruins. Less than a year was to pass before Peter was captured and shot.

To live and share, however briefly, in the lives of great, yet unknown, people made a profound impression on me and I felt it was a privilege never to be forgotten. I could never have imagined that one would be so honoured. We talked about what they would miss in life and what could be contemplated or imagined in the world beyond. Some would say:

> Let us look at the snow
> Let us look at the sun
> Let us look at the moon
> For us these are very special
> Hope never dies.
> Life may change.
> One day all will be made known.

The Bods were fighting for Britain and for freedom for their own countries, and they knew what lay ahead for them if they were caught. A few of the Bods who had escaped following capture and imprisonment at the hands of the Gestapo returned to Britain to risk their lives again with SOE. Their anger at the occupation of their countries and the atrocities committed there made them prepared to face any risk in an attempt to do battle with the devil. But, on the other hand, there were also those who questioned their ability to cope with the frustrations and the perpetual strain and the surprising degree of boredom involved in living and working in the Resistance. All the men and women who trained as agents had to be in top mental and physical condition and had to possess initiative; they were self-reliant and discreet and capable of standing up to rough and arduous training and work. From many volunteers only a small number were accepted.

The men and women who were trained as radio operators included the bravest, for if they were caught with a set they knew they faced death. To escape detection they frequently had to change the place from which they transmitted messages; and, to avoid capture, they often had to disguise themselves – sometimes at barely a moment's notice. German radio-telegraphists were on duty at their listening posts twenty-four hours a day. The Gestapo always had a flying squad ready to go into action immediately to hunt and seize these Bods. The radio network in Poland started from scratch and contact was always extremely difficult – sometimes only small homemade sets of 15W were available.

The Polish cryptologists were equally brave in all they did, and they were remarkably clever. Their work enabled the Allies to intercept information of incalculable value. The Polish scientists and cryptologists had, in fact, begun to decode German military messages as far back as 1933. The work had started in 1930 when three mathematicians (graduates of the Polish University of Poznań) were part of the Polish Cipher Bureau in Warsaw. Their names were: Marian Rejewski (repatriated, returned in 1947, died February 1980 in Warsaw); Jerzy Rozycki (drowned in 1942); Henryk Zygalski (died in Britain in 1978).

When the Germans occupied Vichy France, Rejewski and Zygalski escaped and joined a Polish signals unit near Stanmore, London. This was headed by Colonel Lisicki who had been in charge of research on military electronics at the Technical Institute in Warsaw prior to the outbreak of war. Rejewski and Zygalski also helped to break other ciphers and assisted in discovering the operating procedures of the German cipher machine known as Enigma. They were never allowed to go to Bletchley.

I worked at the Polish Signal Station at Stanmore and later Professor David Dilks wrote:

> The Poles had always retained control of their own wireless and ciphers for communication between Britain and Poland. Occasional suggestions that the British should have copies of the ciphers, so that assurances could be given to the Russians that the Polish government were not fostering anti-Russian or pro-German activities in Poland were strongly resisted by SOE. Sir Alexander Cadogan, to his credit, believed that it would be out of the question to ask the Poles for all their ciphers, which would be an insulting demand to address to a loyal ally.

A German named Scherbius produced the original version of Enigma and tried unsuccessfully in the 'twenties to promote it as a commercial product. The German High Command decided in the 'thirties that the Scherbius machine was well suited to the communications system needed for the co-ordination of the forces, so they designed their own portable battery-operated machine and put it into large-scale production.

The first Enigma machine produced a highly sophisticated military cipher for the German armed forces. However, the Poles worked out the principle on which the machine operated and they constructed their own duplicate. Later, about thirty more were made in Poland as the Poles reckoned that at least this number would be needed in a future war to decipher enemy messages. Before the War broke out, two of these machines were given to the Allies – one to the French and the other to the British – during the conference held at Pyry near Warsaw on the 24 July 1939 when Commander Denniston, "Professor Sandwich", Gustave Bertrand and Captain Braquenie were present.

The Poles destroyed twenty-seven of their Enigma machines in September 1939. One was smuggled to France in the autumn of that year when the German Army invaded their country. To quote the mathematician and the author, Gordon Welchman:

> The Poles had given us the full advantage of their brilliant work on Enigma. When I come to describe what happened at Bletchley Park, it will be apparent that these individuals were of immense importance in getting us

started on the road that led to Hut 6 Ultra. It should have been made
known long ago that Hut 6 Ultra would never have gotten off the ground
if we had not learned from the Poles, in the nick of time, the details both
of the German military version of the commercial Enigma machine and of
the operating procedures that were in use.

The French and British scientists and cryptologists added their own
tremendous contribution and, to a large extent, enabled Churchill and the
Allied Commanders to know in advance about the long-term strategic plans
of the Germans. Later on the Germans began to suspect that their cipher
might have been broken by the Allies and they even thought of inventing
new machines, but they were frightened of telling Hitler. They were always
changing procedures, keys, and so on, but this did not seriously affect the
Allied intelligence-gathering.

In July 1945 General Dwight D. Eisenhower wrote to General Menzies
(Chief of the British Secret Service) about the intelligence produced by
Enigma: "It has saved thousands of British and American lives and, in no
small way, contributed to the speed with which the enemy was routed and
eventually forced to surrender."

* * *

Little is known of the struggles within the Czech Section where I served
briefly and I would like to recall for posterity the dilemma the Czechs
faced regarding the Butcher of Prague, SS Obergruppenführer Reinhard
Heydrich, who served Hitler and the whole Nazi system as Chief of the
Security Service. He was only thirty-eight and already had a notorious
record.

When he was appointed the new "Protector of Czechoslovakia" he
announced martial law in both Bohemia and Moravia and ordered the
execution of the Czech Generals, Bily and Vojta, amongst many other
people. Pankrac Prison in Prague was filled with political prisoners and
German execution squads were frequently at work in Kobylisy and Ruzyns.

Heydrich was determined to destroy the Slavs and he succeeded in elim-
inating many Resistance groups. This, in turn, engendered a feeling of
humiliation amongst members of the Czech Government in London and
their servicemen.

The question of Heydrich's assassination was considered by President
Benes and the Head of his Intelligence Service, General Frantisek Moravec,
and the Czech authorities approached the then Chief of SOE, Sir Charles
Hambro, for permission to carry out the assassination – though they
probably were not obliged to obtain this.

When the matter was first raised with Sir Charles he consulted the top
echelon of SOE who gave very, very careful consideration to the matter
before replying to the Czechs. Numerous enquiries were carried out, and
eventually a decision was reached that Operation *Anthropoid* go ahead as
requested by the Czech authorities and that SOE should organise the

training; they would in any event have had to convey the selected men to Czechoslovakia to do the job.

Out of dozens of servicemen who had escaped to Britain and who became parachutists, two men were eventually selected: Jan Kubis, aged twenty-eight (a Czech from Moravia), and Josef Gabcik, aged twenty-nine (a Slovak from Poluvsic in the District of Zilina). Both were single. Neither came from Prague or knew the City, therefore had no friends or relatives there. In the words of General Moravec, "The training was very tough and lasted six weeks. The men were kept in isolation from the outside world." Stretched to the utmost, harried, prodded and tested, the trainees were probed for any physical or psychological weaknesses which might cost them their lives. They were trained to use small arms of every kind, to manufacture homemade bombs, do jujitsu, survive in open country on synthetic foods, learn topography and map reading and understand concealment devices. A very exacting physical fitness course completed the curriculum.

The men had to learn the topography of Prague from a large-scale plan. After they had landed every detail of the route which Heydrich followed from his headquarters at Hradcany Castle, and the place where he lived in Brezany, a small Village two miles from Prague, had to be memorised. The attack was to be made on this road as the car slowed down near a corner.

Both Kubis and Gabcik had been strongly advised not to make contact with members of the Resistance; to buy bicycles and to make every attempt after the assassination to get out of Prague "into the relative safety of Slovakia" before it was all too late. Alas, in practice, this did not prove possible, and in hiding they came into contact with two other groups who had been trained in Britain.

The parachutists were dressed and equipped in Czech-made products. This Section, like others in SOE, ensured that every item was of the target country's origin – including matches and cigarettes. The departure of Kubis and Gabcik was postponed because of bad weather, but on 29 December 1941, they took off in a Halifax bomber flown by an experienced British pilot, Ft. Lt. R.C. Hockey (later G/Capt Hockey, DSO, DFC), and were dropped by parachute at 02.24 hours at Nehvizdy, twenty kilometres from Prague.

On 27 May 1942 the news was announced on the Prague radio that the Reichsprotector Heydrich had been severely wounded in a criminal attempt to assassinate him at 10.30 that morning in the south-east suburb of Prague. A bomb had been thrown into his car and had exploded. Two men were seen leaving the scene of the crime on bicycles. The search for them was in progress.

Heydrich was wounded, not dead. Leading Nazi specialists were called to his bedside at the Berov Hospital in Prague. The Nazi police moved swiftly, isolating Prague from the rest of the country. A curfew went into force at 9 p.m. All theatres, cinemas and restaurants were ordered to close. All public transport was stopped and trains could not leave Prague railway station. Roads leading out of the City were blocked, while SS and SA units roamed the empty streets in a house-to-house search which went on all night. A reward of one million Reichmarks (about £100,000) was offered to anyone who could help the police apprehend the men who had attacked Heydrich. Any person who helped to shelter the men or refused to reveal their whereabouts would be shot and all his family with him. The death penalty was also announced for the illegal possession of arms or having guests in the house without police registration, and even for "approval" of the attack. Frank, the sadistic State Secretary, and Kurt Daluege, an SS General, were in charge of the investigation.

Arrests and executions began immediately. People were executed without trial, often without even being interrogated. Special units of the Gestapo and SS came to Prague to help with the hunt and to act as execution squads. Still the parachutists were not found.

The following top priority cable was sent by Himmler to SS Gruppenführer Frank:

Top Priority Cable
Special Train "Heinreich" no. 5745-27 May 1942

To SS Gruppenführer Frank
Prague
For Immediate Delivery
SECRET

1. I agree to the proclamation.
2. The 10,000 hostages to be arrested must above all contain the intellectuals of the Czech opposition.
3. One hundred leaders of this Czech intellectual opposition are to be shot the same night.

I shall telephone you again tonight.

Signed: H. Himmler

Heydrich died on 4 June 1942. There were two funerals, one in Prague and one in Berlin, the latter attended by Hitler and all the top Nazis. The Protectorate Government led by Hacha was there, properly humble. At this occasion Hitler told the cringing Czech ministers that if they wanted to avoid their nation being wiped off the map they must see to it that Heydrich's assassins were caught immediately.

A few days later the Nazis demonstrated what Hitler meant by "wiping off". The barbaric idea was to terrify the Czech people by completely destroying a village, chosen at random. The choice fell on Lidice, a ninety-five house hamlet near the mining town of Kladno, about fifteen miles north-east of Prague.

During the night of 9/10 June 1942, units of the Gestapo and the Wehrmacht encircled Lidice. All the inhabitants were roused from their beds, the men (199) herded onto the Village green, the weeping women and children carted away in trucks. Then the men were shot. The houses were set on fire, the burnt-out walls blown up, the dynamited sites bulldozed and ploughed under. Nothing was to be left to indicate where the Village had stood; even its name had to disappear. But the name of Lidice did not disappear. The inhuman conduct of the Germans fired public opinion all over the world. Several places in the world changed their names to Lidice, to remind mankind for ever of the bestial behaviour of the self-styled master race.

The 195 women of the Village were taken to the Concentration Camp at Ravensbrück. The children, who numbered almost 100, were examined "racially" in another concentration camp. Only nine were pronounced "suitable for Germanisation". These were given German names and false documents and sent into the Reich to be brought up in German families. After the War they were returned to Czechoslovakia. The remaining ninety-five children, adjudged racially impure, were housed in the Concentration Camp of Chelmno, with the ominous notification "special care not indicated". Of these only nine returned, eighty-six ending in the Chelmno gas chambers.

The operation was executed with such German thoroughness that even persons who happened to be absent from the Village on the night of its destruction were gradually located and executed.

The search for the parachutists went on. On 16 June Frank issued a warning that Prague's population would be decimated if the assassins were not found inside a fortnight. The next day it was announced that the assassins had been located. They were "Czech agents parachuted from England", said the radio, and they were hiding in the crypt of the Orthodox Church of St Cyril and St Methodeus, in Ressl Street, in the old part of Prague. The announcement said that the parachutists were encircled and that their capture was only a matter of hours. Obviously the men were resisting.

The parachutists had indeed taken refuge in the Church and were encircled by Gestapo and SS units. After two hours fighting the SS troops finally forced their way up to the choir loft. They found two of the agents, Adolf Opalka and Jaroslav Svarc, had committed suicide by taking poison. The third man, Jan Kubis, was mortally wounded and died shortly afterwards, without regaining consciousness. As the fighting continued the survivors retreated to the crypt in the 200-year-old Church, which became like a fortress. The Germans brought in reinforcements – nineteen officers and 740 other ranks from the Waffen SS, as well as an unspecified number of Gestapo men. They tried tear gas, and the besieged parachutists threw the tear-gas bombs back. Finally, after machine-gun fire and hand grenades failed – the only window was a small opening at street level – the Germans inserted a fireman's hose and pumped in water to flood the cellar, but still the bloody battle continued hour after hour until the parachutists' ammunition ran out. When their bodies were removed and laid out on the street outside, it was seen that each had shot himself with his last bullet.

The following day Prague radio announced that it was all over. The men were dead or dying. But according to the broadcast there were not two, but seven of them. When their names were announced, Gabcik and Kubis headed the list; the rest were other parachutists sent from England. The interior of the Church was totally destroyed, but it has now been restored, and in the crypt there is a small but moving tribute and exhibition to the Bods who died. Whenever I visit this Church one of the priests always says a special Mass.

The executions, however, did not stop and included Bishop Gorazde, three priests and many members of the congregation, including the Chairman of the Council. One day after the parachutists' death, General Elias, the arrested former premier, was also executed. Five days later the Gestapo and the SS razed another Czech village to the ground, this time a tiny hamlet called Lezaky, where our short-wave radio transmitter "Libuse" had been operated by a group of parachutists for some months. On 30 June the Germans executed 115 persons, most of them outstanding workers of the national Resistance movement who had been arrested by the Gestapo during Heydrich's administration, and several captured parachutists. Among them was Colonel Josef Masin, whose irons the executioners refused to remove and who, according to a witness, stood proudly at attention in spite of his bound arms, and shouted "Long live the Czechoslovak Republic!"

Further reprisals were carried out against the relatives and those who had helped the assassins and on 24 October, 252 men and women were executed at Mauthausen Death Camp in Austria.

Only two or three had planned and knew about the Operation, but Jan Kubis and Josef Gabcik had been dropped about twenty miles from their designated point and had to turn to the local undergroud for support, although the intention had been that they should not be involved. One proved a traitor like Judas. About 5,000 Czechs paid with their lives for the death of the maniac, Heydrich, and 3,000 Jews were taken from the Theresienstadt ghetto and exterminated.

The consequences were ghastly. In the words of a Bod who survived: "Perhaps the Czech Section never regained its confidence and hopes – never rebuilt its lost numbers." But if Heydrich had remained alive he would have continued his butcherings.

A plaque on the wall of the Orthodox Church in Ressl Street, where flowers are laid and candles lit, also commemorates the Operation.

Shortly after the attack on Heydrich, a young Czech said to me as we stood with our backs to the gate of the ops station: "This is the beginning of the end for my country, and unless the Allies reach Czechoslovakia first we shall never know democracy and freedom again." We were both aged nineteen. There were few words of comfort I could offer him. I was reminded of the shame I had felt in 1938 when huge crowds in Britain had celebrated Chamberlain's return to London while Prague was in sorrow – and prepared to fight. Since 1989 they have regained their freedom and democracy but had to wait a very, very long time for it.

* * *

Many Polish and other aircrews were attached to the Special Duties Squadrons of the RAF. The crews referred to the slow heavy Whitley aircraft as coffins, but gradually they were replaced by Halifax bombers which flew at 150 miles per hour, and which were adapted to carry an extra fuel tank, thus increasing their range to 2,100 miles.

The courage and endurance of the aircrews and of the Bods they carried were superb; they faced special dangers from fighters and from very heavy flak because they were operating alone or in small groups. They also had to endure appalling weather conditions, bitter cold and the noise of the aircraft, often the absence of heating and seats, and uncertainty as to whether the reception committee would be waiting for them at the dropping zone. The curfew forbade people in occupied Europe to leave their homes between dusk and dawn, so the risks the reception committees took were very great. Containers with Sten guns, Bren guns, Piats (anti-tank guns), revolvers, ammunition, gammon grenades, hand grenades, plastic explosive, instantaneous detonator fuses, safety fuses and detonators were loaded into the bomb bay of the aircraft, while lighter packages of tins of meat, biscuits, margarine, American rations and medical equipment were kept in the hull and thrown out by the dispatcher when the dropping zone was in sight. It was not unheard of for these aircrews to fly five nights in succession if that would help the Resistance and ensure the success of an operation. But, tragically, in such circumstances, exhaustion and heavy casualties were inevitable.

We got to know some of these crews well. I remember John, aged nineteen, the navigator of a Whitley bomber, saying that his home had been bombed and his mother killed in the London Blitz of 1940. His younger brother was serving in the Merchant Navy and his father in the fire brigade, and he showed great concern for them. Some weeks later he told me: "Now I can understand far more about the Bods and the work we are involved in, for since I last saw Dad his team was sent to another town and he was killed in a raid, and Peter's boat has been torpedoed and blown up in the Atlantic by a U-boat." I was struck, however, by the lack of rancour in his tone. Not long afterwards, as I was standing with some Bods by an aircraft that was about to take off, John left the cockpit and, leaning over the fuselage, said, "We must keep smiling, as you all do." He, his crew, and the Bods were lost on their long flight back from Poland, shot down over Denmark. They were returning to Tempsford because they could not find the reception committee.

It would be impossible to give details of the hundreds of missions to occupied Europe which were flown by these crews, or of the courage shown on each. 138 Squadron alone flew 2,562 such missions, dropped 995 parachutists, 29,000 containers and 10,000 packages – and lost seventy aircraft and their crews. Very few received any official recognition or decoration, for they belonged to a world where anonymous heroism both during and after the War was the norm. They seemed to be linked with those who had suffered in the First World War, and with those who have been afflicted ever since – the persecuted, the sick, the hungry, the millions everywhere, up to the present day, whose names and whose heroism are known only to God.

Deep friendships were made, transient but precious, for we were all "ships passing"; and there was the unspoken knowledge between us that we would most probably not see each other again, which made important the short time spent in each other's company. In some ways it was an unreal world; in others it enforced an inescapable reality. Small groups came and small groups left. Each was different, some gayer than others, but the poignancy of their presence was strongly felt by the few of us who served at the station. A strong bond of affection was forged between us in the short time they were with us. A dull void remained after their departure. The situation was always hard to accept.

Farewells have followed me all through my life. I have always felt a sense of sadness and poignancy on leaving both people and places, even though I may have known the individual concerned for only a short time or been to a place on no more than a brief visit. It was especially hard for people who lived so close to each other to leave each other's company, and we admired greatly the way the Bods did this.

Occasionally the ops station was deserted when we returned to it from the airfield because everyone was on a mission, and then it was filled with memories. Sometimes in the night or early hours of the morning a telephone call would come through that we were to return immediately to the airfield, and we found that an aircraft had already landed with its Bods and packages, having had a fruitless flight. At other times we would wait near a runway for the aircraft to return, and then the dispatchers in each aircraft would give us news of what had happened, sometimes bringing back messages or notes scribbled on a cigarette packet. One read: "What was your life? A ray of light that rushed astonished through the darkness of the earth." – Nomads (*The Vigil*).

The writer of the note would be far away in his occupied country facing a situation which called for every ounce of courage and resourcefulness. As we read the message, we could not help wondering what dangers the writer was facing at that moment. Perhaps he had already been killed or betrayed; he might be in a railway carriage travelling to the next destination on his mission; or perhaps he was in a remote mountain village, making contacts, deciding whom he could trust, gambling his life and the mission entrusted to him on the honesty he recognised in another man's eyes. Or perhaps luck had deserted him and he had already been captured and stood with his hands above his head and a Gestapo gun in his back.

SOE necessarily had to operate behind a heavy veil of secrecy: the only address that we used and could give to friends and relations was "Room 98, Horseguards, London SW1" and mail was collected from there and brought to the stations by dispatch riders. There was much coming and going of people from Headquarters in Baker Street but their names were not allowed to be mentioned.

No contact with local people in the area of a station was ever permitted and cover stories were given, though at times these must have struck the locals as somewhat less than convincing. A group of curious people gathered one day on the road outside Audley End House (STS43) near Saffron Walden, Essex (then used as one of the training stations by the Poles), and gazed across the wide lawns as a number of Bods taking part in a training exercise and disguised as Germans held off an attack. And at one railway station I was embarrassed to hear someone mention to me, "Strange noises come from your place and low parachute drops are made up your way."

Security at more secluded stations presented less of a problem, but even here the risk of discovery could not be eliminated. The cover story regarding Station 18 near Watton-at-Stone, Hertfordshire, was that Allied officers were convalescing en route to Scotland. The house and cottage were isolated, but Security had apparently overlooked a woman who came in to work in the laundry. One day she called out saying that she had never seen a shirt button melt in the wash. Two of the FANYs who overheard her quickly got her out of the laundry on some pretext and then, with a couple of hand brooms, rinsed the washing thoroughly. It was the poison tablet sewn to the shirt! As a result of the incident, Security ensured that she never returned.

There was also the day at Ops Station 20 when everyone was engaged in small-arms firing practice and an astonished woman advanced through the woods saying: "I have always understood this place to be a transit centre for the wounded."

Station 20 was small and enclosed, holding Polish agents and occasionally a Czech too. This station lay, together with Station 20B, deep in the woods off Nightingale's Lane near Chalfont St Giles in Buckinghamshire. No outside contact was allowed.

A Polish woman dentist who had been thoroughly scrutinised was allowed to visit the Station to treat the Bods, and I well remember the drill which she operated by a foot pedal. She never froze our gums or gave an injection before extracting a tooth!

All the Bods had escaped from their homeland in extraordinary ways. They were young. Many had been deported to Siberia, and their descriptions of the prisoners' existence were horrifying – a few, they told us, had even resorted to cannibalism to survive. The prisoners had been released as a result of the Sikorski – Stalin Pact of 30 July 1941 and had come by diverse routes to Britain.

Between September 1939 and July 1940 an estimated two to two-and-a-half million Poles from all walks of life were deported to Siberia by the Soviet authorities. These included landowners, university students, civil servants, regular soldiers and other professional people. The Pact of July

1941 allowed some of these unfortunate people to join an Army formed by General Anders to fight with the Allies against the Nazis. After the evacuation of the Polish Army under General Anders to Persia, the Soviets sponsored a Polish Army under General Berling which it is estimated some 43,500 men and women, of those who had failed to reach General Anders' Army whilst it was still in the Soviet Union, joined. Thousands of soldiers from both Armies were involved in some of the bloodiest battles of the War.

In the course of the evacuation from the Soviet Union to Persia unknown thousands of Poles, including children of all ages, died of typhus, hunger, dysentery and other diseases. The mortality rate of those released from the forced labour camps was such that only approximately 70,000 soldiers and 38,000 civilians completed the journey to Persia to join General Anders. Some reached freedom on Easter Day 1942.

Those who were given the opportunity to fight were more fortunate than thousands of other Poles.* In April 1943 the bodies of 4,000 Polish officers were unearthed in mass graves at Katyń, near Smolensk, in Western Russia, by German occupying forces. The Germans immediately blamed the Soviets for the massacre and the discovery was skilfully exploited by Nazi German propaganda as evidence that Britain was in Wartime alliance with murdering barbarians. The Soviet authorities, on the other hand, stuck resolutely to their official version of the Katyń story – that the Poles had been killed by Hitler's men.

For many years the world remained unsure of who was really to blame. After the Germans discovered the graves, the Commander of the Polish AK (Home Army) in that region, General Rowecki, sent an observer to the site and, on receipt of his Report, informed General Sikorski in London. The General notified Churchill, but he was reluctant to encourage the Poles to make any large-scale protest because of Britain's alliance with the Soviets.

In the autumn of 1992 the last piece was revealed of a puzzle that had bedevilled historians and Governments since the discovery of the bodies in April 1943, when a key document was published in Russia which proved that the murders had been directly ordered by Stalin on the recommendation of Beria, his Chief of the Secret Police. This document, which is signed by Stalin, suggests that those condemned to die in March 1940 were not only Polish prisoners of War and internees from three camps known as Kozielsk (Katyń), Starobielsk and Ostaszkow, (14,736 men in all), but also Poles who were in prison in the newly acquired Western districts of the Soviet Union because of their links with the former Polish "Establishment". In Beria's description they ranged from "spies and diversionists" to landowners, factory owners and civil servants – a further 10,685 men.

Beria originally proposed himself as a member of the "troika", or three-man court, that was to "try" the victims. His name, however, is crossed out in Stalin's handwriting and the name of Beria's deputy, Bogdan Kobulov, is

* Adapted from an article by Nicholas Bethell published in *The Times* on Friday 23 October, 1992.

inserted in its place. It was Kobulov who, after Stalin had given his assent, organised the massacres.

The mass murders brought a legacy of embarrassment to successive Soviet leaders, each of whom had been individually informed of the truth about Katyń through documents kept in a special safe. In a paper signed by KGB Chief, Shelpin, in March 1959, he states that, of a total of 21,857 massacred, 4,421 were from Katyń, 3,820 from Starobielsk, 6,311 from Ostaszkow and 7,305 from various prisons in the Western Soviet Union.

Those murdered at Katyń included Polish civilians and members of the intelligentsia; the Poles murdered at Starobielsk, near the large City of Charkov, comprised officers and reservists; and those killed at Ostaszkow comprised Poles who had held positions of authority before the War and included ordinary policemen. All the bodies were buried in mass graves.

Out of 14,500 members of the Polish intelligentsia only 400 survived the massacres, probably because they had been moved earlier from other camps to a camp called Pavlischev Bor.

*　*　*

For ten days I shared a small room at Station 20 with a Polish courier, whose English name was Elizabeth Watson, while she waited for favourable weather before being parachuted back into Poland. In that room she shared many of her thoughts with me. Years later, when our paths were to cross again, she gave me the following account of her activities which graphically illustrates the hazards and unknown heroism of the couriers:

> As a courier between 1941–42 I often had to travel to Berlin, but I could not risk going by the most direct way from Warsaw via Poznań as the Gestapo kept all main trains, especially the international ones, under close observation. I was obliged therefore to use an alternative route via Torun or via Silesia in the south of Poland. The routes also depended on whether I had contact points in the Resistance where I could leave or collect messages.
>
> Once in May 1942 while travelling from Berlin to a contact point in Silesia where I had hoped to spend the night, I was carrying rather a large and heavy suitcase – this had a false compartment which was full of dollars. In this suitcase I also carried some clothing and whatever else I could pack in to disguise the weight of the money. My route lay through a place called Sosnowiec. There I should have found my sister and a colleague who I knew could give me a bed for the night. Because I had the documents of a Reich-German, who therefore was not Polish, I could travel after the hours of curfew. It was the 25 May 1942 when I arrived at my sister's door and knocked, but nobody answered. I then went to a neighbour's house and knocked; she opened the door and went absolutely white with shock on seeing me. She wanted to close the door on me, but I put my foot in and I asked her why she was behaving in this way and what had happened to my sister Klara. She said "The Gestapo are here and they have arrested both your sister and colleague, Nina."

At that time they arrested several cells of people in the Resistance in Silesia and I think there had been a general round-up, but I had not heard of it. I had come from Berlin and found myself in a situation where the Gestapo were on the lookout for any suspicious people, but fortunately the arrests had taken place four days earlier. Nevertheless, they were still watching the house, but by pure chance they had just left to have a meal before I arrived. It was really a miracle as my sister was already being interrogated by the Gestapo. I took my suitcase very quickly and went as calmly as I could to another colleague, Stacha. (Later she was arrested and beheaded in Katowice at the end of July 1942.) I was lucky to find that Stacha was still free; she belonged to a different cell and I was able to stay there until 3 a.m., and she told me what was happening but, of course, I still had the suitcase with me. I also realised that it was my duty to inform as many people as I could about what was happening, so next day I took the suitcase to the station and deposited it in the left luggage department and received a receipt for it.

From the station I went into one of the streets; it was not the main street, but nevertheless quite a busy one, and I managed to meet one or two of our people and I said to them very quickly "Get away from here", but, unfortunately, I made the mistake of remaining there too long. An agent had noticed me and I knew that I was being observed and followed. I boarded a tram still in Sosnowiec, but two Gestapo men in plain clothes got on as well. The tram went to Katowice. I got off there and tried various means to loose them but could not, so I had to proceed to Kraków.

On the way, there was a frontier post at Trzebinia. I was absolutely soaked with perspiration from fear and I thought that when we were checked they would see my papers. The Gestapo presumably told the frontier control people that they were watching me. Of course, they carried with them blacklists in which perhaps one of my many names appeared. I was amazed not to have been arrested.

When I arrived at Kraków I was absolutely exhausted. I was trying all the time to disguise myself completely in whatever way I could to keep ahead of them, but there was absolutely no other way but to go to a colleague and say to her, "Look, help me, try and see if they are still there", My colleague, Celina Zawodzinska (later arrested and transported to Ravensbrück), looked out and saw one of the Gestapo waiting for me so I had to leave her. I asked her to follow this Gestapo member at a safe distance herself to see what happened to me and then disappear before curfew. Furthermore, the Gestapo kept changing.

I arrived late in the evening at Kraków station, by which time it was dark. I waited a long time. At 11 p.m. there was an express train to Warsaw and I entered a compartment reserved for Germans only. Of course, I had a thousand thoughts in my head but, before boarding, I managed to observe on the platform a colleague from Warsaw. She kept walking up and down. I found a tiny piece of paper and wrote on it. "One has broken down under torture and is therefore likely to give away the names of other people. I am under observation and being followed by Gestapo." I was able to get near to her and simply handed her this crumpled piece of paper. She was an extremely experienced member of the Resistance and she turned away as though she did not know me at all; at the same time, of course. I gave her to understand that if I was taken she, in turn, should warn the others. At that moment I felt that at last I could breathe. I later discovered that the reason why the person had given some people away was that the Gestapo had put her on an electric bed and after this and other methods of torture she broke down.

I was still frightened and wanted to jump from the express train. I kept wondering whether to try and get out before daylight, but I realised the dangers, not only from the drop but also of falling onto the track which might have killed me, and I did not want to die. On the other hand, I knew that I had to get out of that train because if I remained on it and arrived in Warsaw I would be arrested. Also, I did not carry a poison tablet. As the train approached the town of Zyrardow (48 kilometres from Warsaw) there was a curve on the line and the train started to slow down a bit. It was about 4 a.m. I knew the moment had arrived when I simply had to get out. I left the compartment as though to go to the toilet and walked along the corridor. I realised, of course, that I was still under observation, but I had left my small insignificant packet in the compartment before going to the toilet. The third carriage was the last; and the last carriage always had a rear window. I went to the last door and saw a Polish railway official; he held the door and I sprang out.

When one is in such a dangerous situation one has odd thoughts, and as I jumped I remembered that I had heard that in America and other countries tramps and people who were homeless often jumped up in the air before going down. However, I fell on knees and arms, which started to bleed, and I rolled over into a ditch. I thought that the Gestapo would stop the train and I hoped that they would not have bloodhounds.

With blistered hands and painful legs I started to make haste towards the woods. I remember two men looking at me curiously, as if I had been mad! I ran further and saw a woman with a shawl over her head who looked like a factory worker. I took off my jacket and a gold ring and gave them to her and she in exchange hurriedly gave me her things and some bread she was carrying which I needed badly as I was so hungry. I threw away my shoes and washed the blood off my legs, feet and arms and tried to disguise myself as a simple girl from the country. The sun had risen, but I continued to walk for miles keeping well away from the railway line and I felt tired. Finally, I came to a railway station and I asked a Pole, "Please give me some money, I must get to Warsaw." The Pole immediately gave me the money I needed and I caught the next train to Warsaw. (During the occupation we were all brother and sisters regardless of being strangers.)

I believed that the Gestapo had lost sight of me so I quickly went to a contact point where my friend, Wanda, gave me a coat and I felt calm and relieved to be with her.

My poor sister Klara – by profession a lawyer – was by now in prison at Sosnowiec together with many of her fellow "workers". She survived difficult interrogations as she knew the German language fluently and was able to give shrewd replies to their continual questions. Despite all this, she maintained she could not give them any information. Klara spent six months in that prison. My other sister, Dela, sent her food parcels but a large proportion of these where stolen and eaten by the SS warders.

Meanwhile, I was still thinking about the suitcase which I had left behind. I had managed to leave the receipt for this with a pharmacist in Katowice. I reported this to the cell in which I worked in the Resistance and a courier named Tadeusz, together with another member of the Resistance, were sent with haste from Warsaw to fetch it. From Kraków, Tadeusz was obliged to cross the frontier to Katowice in Silesia. As he had left in a hurry he did not have the right documents, and on reaching the frontier he secretly paid a guide to help him cross the border illegally.

When Tadeusz reached the pharmacy it was unfortunately closed. He lost valuable time in searching for the pharmacist. This put him in greater danger and when he realised that his contact was nervous he did not feel it was fair to stay the night there and he therefore resorted to hiding in a haystack in a nearby village. By burying himself in the hay he felt all the more dishevelled.

Eventually he succeeded in obtaining the receipt and went to the left luggage office at the railway station at Katowice. As he approached he noticed a German standing nearby who seemed to be taking a great interest in him. At the moment of handing over the receipt to the German clerk, he had the presence of mind to engage them in conversation (only the German language was allowed to be spoken and he knew it fluently). He also knew that some Germans could be bribed and he therefore offered both men a cigar. This enabled him to get out of the station with the suitcase and walk as naturally as possible.

Thanks to his cool courage, the contents of the suitcase, which were invaluable for the work, were saved. All this meant however that I could no longer travel to Berlin as I was now on the wanted list by the Gestapo under my real name of Elizabeth Zawacka, born 19 March 1909 in Torun. So, I had to change my whole appearance: I dyed my hair red and took to wearing a very large hat. I received a new name, forged identity card and waited for a new mission.

I was extremely lucky to be given a seemingly improbable order to prepare myself for a long journey. I was told to cross almost the whole of Europe – several thousand kilometres – and reach the General Staff of the Polish forces in London. I had to take messages and act as Emissary of the Home Army Headquarters to discuss (1) the different routes take by couriers, and (2) as a pre-War instructor of the Women's Military Training Service, I was to report the different problems connected with the organisation of the Polish Military Women's Service in our Secret Army.

A few of my colleagues said this mission would be a reward for the difficulties I had experienced beforehand.

The preparation took a long time. It was difficult to procure foolproof forged documents so that the route could be relatively safe. I had to memorise all the details of the complicated network of our liaison stations spread all over Europe. I also had to learn quite a lot of different things, including some knowledge of the English language. I studied the existing routes and read for weeks different decoded secret documents hitherto hidden in archives.

On the 17 of December 1942 I set out by train from Warsaw to Paris via Berlin and Strasbourg. My new name was Elizabeth Kubitza and I was officially employed as clerk to a petroleum firm which had branches in both Warsaw and Paris. (I was bilingual in German and Polish.)

I reached Paris safely after feeling frightened whilst crossing two frontiers, the first near Kutno between G.G. (General Government) and the Reich, the second one near Strasbourg, Germany/France. The journey from Warsaw to Paris had lasted about forty-eight hours.

In Paris there was a liaison group/cell from Zagroda (a division of the Home Army in Poland) under the code-name *Janka* which operated with Ceux de la Libération Vengeance, part of the French Gaullist organisation and under the command of Colonel Mederic.

Janka was trying to prepare a route for me to the unoccupied part of France and then on to Spain. The way was via Vichy and Perpignan in the East Pyrenees, to Figueras in Spain, and then to the British Consulate in Barcelona. My pseudonym in France was now Mme. Elise Rivière from Alsace. As my mission was so vital and I carried such important messages, I had received an order to be certain of the security of the route, but this route was a new one and had not been tested before by any other courier.

Amongst the people in the French Resistance who were helping us was an engine driver. He drove a special train which sometimes carried Laval (a collaborator with Vichy and the Germans). The train travelled regularly from the Gare d'Orléans Station in Paris to Vichy. I crossed the dangerous border between occupied and unoccupied France. This engine driver took me and another courier called Pankrac. We had to climb the narrow opening into the tender attached to the locomotive which carried water. This was located behind the engine. We had to lie on hard wooden boards over the splashing water in the tender. We lay on these boards from the evening until early the next morning waiting to start. It was mid-December 1942. At 3 a.m. the engine driver, who was clearly upset, came and called to us in the tender, "You must get out because another courier, Wilski, who left on the route you intend to follow is already in the hands of the Gestapo near Narbonne." He (the engine driver) had received a very urgent message from the Pyrenees to give us this warning.

It was still very dark and I remember that I had turned my coat inside out in order to prevent it looking too dirty. We got out and the French driver led us very cautiously through the station to his own flat. There were many Germans on patrol in different parts of the station.

Pankrac went to a different flat. He knew Paris better than I did and had more contact points. He had also been a student there before the War. (He was later sent to Spain. There he was arrested and taken to the Concentration Camp Miranda, from which he was later released. Then he joined General Sikorski at Gibraltar and boarded the same ill-fated aircraft there. In Pankrac's last notes which were found later, he had written, "I reached the summit of my life when I reported to General Sikorski".)

I remained with the engine driver's family for about ten days.

The organiser of routes for Zagroda in France, called Bradl (Kazimierz Leski), suggested to me that I should try another route. We went to Bordeaux and from there to Bayonne. We had two possibilities there. The first was to travel via St Jean de Luz to find a boat which could take me to the Spanish side, to Irun in the Basque country and from there, with luck, to Pamplona. Unfortunately, we could not find a guide so we went to Pau where it was proposed that I should travel in a truck amongst cattle, but this did not seem a sensible or realistic proposition, so I returned to Paris.

The other idea was to receive guidance and help from Andrzej Lipkowski. He had a cousin who was a manager of a bank in Paris and his family had lived in France for many years. He also knew Colonel Mederic. He told me that there might even be a remote opportunity of being picked up by a Lysander aircraft (a light, single engine reconnaissance aircraft with a very short take-off and landing capability) which I thought sounded unbelievable. I had not heard about these pickups before and it seemed a fantastic idea.

I waited in Paris some days over Christmas in order to satisfy myself that I had tried everything. Then I resumed my *other* identity, of Elizabeth Kubitza, and crossed the whole of Germany back to Warsaw. During the two days I was returning from Paris to Warsaw I had no more food coupons and only managed to find a celery salad in Berlin. As always, I was frightened but at any rate I reached my beloved capital and explained the situation to my commanding officer, "Marcysia".

As I was considered to be an experienced courier who had travelled to many different parts of Europe, I was given my head to decide upon which route I should follow from Warsaw the second time. Meantime, I had other work to do for about four weeks while a new and equally essential assignment had been prepared for me to take on. This comprised a few hundred pages of ciphered microfilmed typescript and drawings hidden in a key and cigarette lighter.

So, on the 17 February 1943, I started out again and travelled as Elizabeth Kubitza.

There, in Paris, for the *second* time I reported again to the German Ortskommandantur in order to exchange my food coupons from Warsaw and obtain my original French ones which I had left with them – both lots were forged. I also had to obtain an hotel billet. The Germans would not issue the coupons immediately as they had on the *first* journey, and they told me to stay overnight at the Hotel Cadet near the Metro and to return the following day to collect them. I did not know why they had said this. I was carrying the secret post and felt terrified during the hours of darkness that the Gestapo might arrest me, so I walked up and down the hotel room wondering what on earth to do. I had a sleepness night.

The next morning I returned to the German office where, to my amazement, I heard them saying to one another, "Look at these food coupons . . . they are the right ones and the others (meaning the legal ones) should look like these!" Such was my relief that I went to a coffee shop and treated myself to some coffee, some ham and a glass of wine.

While in Paris I followed a short course in Spanish at the Paris Berlitz School. I then reverted to my French identity of Elise Rivière.

Again, on my second attempt to reach London, the same engine driver hid me in the tender of Laval's train, but this time with no less than eight young Frenchmen who were attempting to escape to join the Free French forces. I was not accompanied by another Polish courier. We all had to lie on the boards over the water. I was carrying my messages again in a lighter and a key.

I cannot remember the time of night we crossed the border between the two zones, but I arrived in Vichy early in the morning. I was able to look at the park. Then we boarded different trains for Toulouse. I had the opportunity of seeing the most beautiful small mediaeval town of Carcassonne. We slept on the station at Toulouse and felt very stiff and tired, but I was in the company of young and optimistic Frenchmen. Then we continued our journey to a village close to Tarascon, near the Spanish frontier. On the way we had numerous checks and had to go through control points manned by French gendarmes under the direction of the German authority. The young Frenchmen were naturally very anxious, but fortunately we reached our destination.

Along the frontier in the different mountain villages quite a number of Spaniards were living amongst the French people. They had escaped from Franco's regime and a few of them were either smugglers or guides. The young Frenchmen in whose company I was, found a young man called Paco Bonne, a young Catalonian, who was to be our first guide, and I gave him some money. I was the only person in the group who had enough money, because in Warsaw I had been given two gold sovereigns and a number of dollars. I asked him whether he could somehow manage to find a compass for me, or even a map of the Pyrenees, but neither could be found.

I wore a blue coat and bound my feet with woollen strips, like gaiters, to protect them as well as possible from the elements. Paco asked us to meet him at a small country inn in a village not far from Tarascon at 8 p.m. that evening. There we waited in a narrow, dimly lit corridor from which a door led into the main room of the restaurant. Suddenly, to our horror, instead of Paco two Germans entered. They were from the Special Mountain Police and wore the Edelweiss insignis on their caps. While one went to telephone, the second started to question each of us about the identity cards we carried. It would have been very difficult indeed to explain what an Alsatian woman, who spoke only moderate French, was doing there. I succeeded in moving to the end of the row and hid behind a cupboard where I managed to remove my coat. The following moments were terrible and my legs felt like jelly.

The Frenchmen were naïve as conspirators and had great difficulty in answering the Germans' questions. As they reached the third or fourth person I slipped through a second smaller door into the restaurant and snatched an apron from an astonished waitress. I noticed that there was a radio playing and quickly turned up the volume. I had also noticed that there was a simple wooden staircase and as I mounted this I felt a hand on my arm and realised it was Paco. He had been waiting upstairs and, seeing the Germans, he realised that was happening. Naturally, he was also frightened. He grabbed me by the arm and took me through a little door which led directly out onto the mountainside. I hid as best I could behind a bush and waited. Later I heard the roar of an engine. My unhappy companions were being taken away by the Germans but, by a miracle, it seemed I had been saved. It was exceedingly cold, especially as I was high up the mountains and it was towards the end of February. Unexpectedly, I felt someone put a warm jacket round me. It was Gilbert, who became a new friend of mine. I was taken to a room where there were some Spaniards and remained there for two or three days.

I kept on asking, "Please give me a map, for I want to go on alone," but understandably they had no map. I still had a little money on me so I could try to cross the mountains again. Meanwhile, Paco Bonne organised a fairly large group of smugglers which included his uncle. This was the *second* attempt and in this group two Jews were included who had succeeded in escaping from Vienna to the Pyrenees. One was tall, the other short, and both were poor and thin. There was a full moon and it was bitterly cold. The place from which we were leaving had ruins of historical Roman baths, and we set off with Paco Bonne and his uncle. We started to climb and came upon a stream which was absolutely frozen. As one or two in the company started to cross it the ice cracked. There was a noise and suddenly we heard a shot ring out – fired by the Germans – and we hid behind some marble columns.

Crouching down we wondered what would happen next. The others had disappeared. Later, one of the Spaniards, a guide, took me by the arm and led me to a mountain hut. Perhaps this man knew that I had a little money, but I was fast running out of this and only three one-dollar notes remained stitched inside my clothing.

When I met Paco Bonne again I had been obliged to admit that I had little or no money, but to strengthen my case I felt it was necessary to tell him that I worked for the Intelligence Service. "If you get me over this fron-tier," I said, "I cannot pay you, but I will recommend you to the Consul as a good guide." He was not very happy with this, but at last I convinced him that this was my *third* attempt. Again, I had to wait two to three days because Paco Bonne had to choose the right night. It was essential to know the movements of the frontier guards and at what time the Germans changed their shifts etc. so we regrouped with the two Jews still included in the party.

In addition to Bonne, there was the young Frenchman called Gilbert, whom I mentioned earlier. He came from the Pas de Calais, northern France. I got to know him quite quickly. He was a woodcutter and in this way he was able to make money and pay a guide, for his aim was to reach North Africa and join the Free French forces.

About twenty of us started to climb the mountains. The going was extremely rough, and after some hours a very severe blizzard descended on us. The guide lost his way. We continued to battle on in this freezing cold with the added hazard of the blizzard. Nevertheless, we somehow managed to keep going at a reasonable pace but the weakest, including the two unfortunate Jews, fell back. One of them simply said he could not go on. I had finished my small ration of chocolate and only had a little sugar left, so I gave him this and we were obliged to leave them.

After walking for hours we found a rough stone mountain hut. The route had proved extremely difficult because it was full of stones which we continually stumbled over in the blizzard. I remember the snow came up to my waist and Bonne had to try and clear a way. Those who remained felt

exhausted. The mountain hut was used during the summer for sheep, and
we had to clear out the snow which had blown inside. We then lay down
and slept for three to four hours. The worst aspect (apart from the weather)
was the fact that the guide had completely lost his way. He had no means
of knowing where we were. My lips were swollen, chapped and bleeding,
and the only fluid I had taken was from licking snow. I had no food left.
We continued walking for about twenty hours when suddenly we came
upon a heap of snow where I saw a frozen arm sticking out: it was one of
the Jews we had left behind. He had fallen into the snow and frozen to
death. Later I realised that the others had deserted us and I was alone with
Paco Bonne and Gilbert. Paco Bonne led, I was in the middle and Gilbert
helped to push me. Bonne confidently said to us, "We shall arrive quite
soon at the frontier." As we went on we came to the cliffs and we paused
to gather our breath and strength. I listened in the stillness and I heard
German voices. Looking down on the snow I saw an empty packet of
German cigarettes. We were terrified. As we came to realise our position
we started to run down the mountain as fast as we could and reached a
dried-up river bed full of stones. Some of these stones were so sharp that
it was a miracle we did not break our bones.

At last the weather improved, and after about an hour Paco Bonne
realised where we were. In fact, we were far too near a hut used by the
German frontier patrols. Paco knew that at certain times the frontier shifts
changed, but we continued to be exceedingly concerned and wondered
whether the guards were alone or accompanied by dogs. We hid in a deep
ditch. The snow covered us and the Germans passed by, fortunately
without dogs. We resumed walking and after some hours we came to
another mountain hut where an acquaintance of Paco Bonne's was waiting.
He led us up into the loft and I slept for 24 hours. When they woke me
they brought some food. I had recovered my strength and returned to the
same village. Then we had to start thinking how we were to make a fourth
attempt. Paco Bonne either could not or would not undertake the journey,
and so his uncle agreed to do so. He did not appear to be particularly
friendly. Two other Frenchmen had joined Gilbert and me, so there were
five of us this time.

We had to continue to plod through the night in order not to be seen by
the German frontier guards. This time, too, the guide led us through some
very difficult parts of the mountain and about two or three o'clock in the
morning, when it was coldest, I simply could not continue and lay down
in the snow – I was unable to go on. The guide was pretty severe. He
roused me by kicking me and then sprayed some wine into my mouth from
his flask which gave me strength. I got up and continued walking.
Gradually the dawn broke and I saw the most beautiful sight in my life, an
alpine glow.

As the sun rose it threw its rays upon the high peaks. Other parts of
the mountain were still dark and it seemed that the higher peaks were bathed
in a kind of glorious pink and then in red gold, like fire. This was an
absolutely marvellous scene and somehow made me forget my tiredness.
I also saw mountain goats and an eagle. We still had several hours of
walking ahead. Then from afar we saw the frontier guards. The guide

had binoculars and ordered us to drop down on the ground and wait until the guards went away. It became exceedingly hot with the sun shining on the snow, and at about ten or eleven o'clock the guide suddenly announced, "Ahead of this next high peak lies Spain and you must now continue alone." The two Frenchmen went on ahead as they were quicker, and Gilbert and I walked more slowly behind. It was very hard to climb and after reaching the top of the mountain we first walked down but then decided to sit and try to slide gently down part of the other side. After that we ran.

We thought we had at last reached Spain. We were on the south side of the Pyrenees and it was warm in spite of there being a lot of snow. As we descended we reached a little stream and I sat on a big flat stone covered with snow and said to Gilbert, "Go and look, there are some houses over there." When he came back he said with some surprise, "Yes, this is a village, but it is Andorra and not Spain!" As we approached the village we were naturally still nervous.

In Andorra there was a nest of smugglers. Gilbert took me to an inn and the women there brought me a plate of fried potatoes and oranges. I was greatly relieved to be able to go to bed as I felt so terribly tired; I slept until the evening. Gilbert, who was between twenty and twenty-five years of age, was intelligent and energetic and discovered an Englishman in the village, a Mr Robert, whom I thought worked for British Intelligence. Gilbert already knew this although we were not able to converse with Mr Robert easily as my knowledge of English was limited. In the evening Mr Robert came to see me again and I said to him, "I am a courier from Poland and I have a password to convey to the British Consul in Barcelona." He believed me and said I should sleep in the same inn.

The next morning he arrived in a black car in the village street and from this village of Old Andorra we drove to the capital, Santa Julia. On the way we passed the two astonished Frenchmen who had left us earlier. I was in rags and completely filthy. My shoes were in tatters. Mr Robert handed me over to another person who rook me to a good hotel where I remained until the evening. Meanwhile they had bought me some local shoes made from thick plaited string called espadrilles. In the evening another guide turned up. He had been a District Officer and because he had fought against Franco knew that if caught he would be hanged.

We proceeded on foot towards the Andorran/Spanish frontier. It took us two to three hours. As we made our way down the mountain we were perpetually on the lookout for frontier guards and the situation continued to be dangerous. It was not quite so cold but snow was still thick on the ground. Gilbert kept reminding me that I was not keeping up the pace and he found me heavy to push. We faced yet another mountain to cross and the going was hard. Finally, we reached a primitive stone hut where we lit a fire and in a very simple pot cooked some scrambled eggs. There were no lights but only a holder fixed to the wall in which shavings topped with tar were burnt to give light. Afterwards I was taken up to the hay loft where I slept soundly. I remember wearing a light-coloured scarf over my head to stop the hay getting into my hair.

The guide woke us early the next morning. There were three of us. We emerged from the hut and started the descent. It was a bit foggy.

We thought, mistakenly, that we were relatively safe and far away from the enemy and foolishly spoke too loudly. Apart from this my light scarf was conspicuous. Suddenly, the guide who carried my small bag started to run. He had very long legs and got away from us very quickly. At the same moment Gilbert also left me. They had seen two guards! Naturally I also started to run as fast as I could because they were shooting and fortunately I reached a tall rock with bushes which I climbed and knelt down covering my face and hands as I had trained to do. I knew I could not go on any further as I would have been in sight of the guards who continued to fire; as it was the bullets went over my head and to either side of me.

Meanwhile, I quickly removed my headscarf. By this time the guards were standing at the foot of the cliff and were able to see Gilbert and the guide running far away in the distance and they continued to shoot at them but failed to hit them. The guards stood awhile, talked a bit and then, to my relief, walked away. I sat in a crouched position a long time and wondered what on earth to do next as I was alone without a map and practically no money. I knew only a few words of Spanish. It was still early morning and pretty cold and I began inadvertently to sneeze. Gilbert heard this noise and so was able to find me. I think, too, he returned because I was on his conscience.

The three dollars and the vital information and reports remained stitched inside my clothing. We continued to walk in the mountains searching for a village. We found a stream, but this did not run in the right direction. Then, in the afternoon, we saw from afar and below a village and an orchard of almond trees in blossom – a beautiful sight. The village appeared to be deserted as the workers were busy somewhere. We went into the first empty building – a small house – and climbed a ladder in order to hide. We did not know what to expect so we remained under the roof and waited. Later an old man appeared. I gave him my last three dollars and he handed me some cold cooked beans. He left to go into the village. We did not know if he would denounce us or what he would do. Hours later, in the evening, he returned with a very nice teacher and a donkey and the teacher brought us to his simple classroom. He also wanted me to listen to the BBC and give him news. We were unable to sleep in the classroom and he took us to his two frugal rooms where I slept deeply on a mattress.

We could not remain in this village and I asked the teacher to find a mountaineer who could make arrangements to board a train to Barcelona and report to the British Consul there. I was in a dilemma and although it was strictly forbidden to ask someone else to report to the Consul and use the password "I am a member of the Chisholm Clan" I did so. On the man's arrival at the Consulate however the receptionist and guard sent him away. He returned to us in an angry mood. The poor teacher could only advise us to take a bus ourselves from the next village, which was bigger, and he produced money for the tickets.

At 4 a.m. as the bus approached, policemen unfortunately came to inspect the passengers' papers. It was therefore impossible to proceed and we had to walk. After a mile or two, two engineers in a car gave us a lift for a very short distance. Again, the police stopped the vehicle to check the papers, as we were still near the frontier. We succeeded in getting out of the back seat and hid in a ditch. Either the police failed to see us or we were lucky and the engineers were important people – I will never know the answer – and we continued our long, long walk – 60 kilometres the first day in hot sunshine. We had had nothing to eat or drink. We saw a young girl with two slices of bread and two little salty fishes. We begged her to give these to us. I gave my fish to Gilbert, who then suffered from a frightful thirst and he had to stop and lick water from half-melted icicles.

On our way we passed through part of Catalonia where during the Spanish Civil War (1936–1939) many bridges and villages had been destroyed and lay in ruins. Some were still uninhabited, but for safety we kept to the higher part of the mountains. The Spanish police had orders to hand over to the Gestapo anyone escaping.

In the darkness, just before midnight, we found an empty house and were able to lie down in the hay. When we woke in the early light we found ourselves on the edge of a precipice and might easily have turned over and rolled down to our deaths.

As we approached Manresa we met a young boy and asked him to buy us our tickets with the money the teacher had given us. I had not been conscious of days passing, but someone reminded me that it was the 1st April, and at 6 a.m. we caught the train to Barcelona. Gilbert reported to the French Consul with the hope of joining the Free French Forces. We promised to meet at the Poste Restaurant in Toulouse after the War, but sadly I never heard from him again.

As the British Consul did not arrive before 10 a.m., I waited inside the house and admired its beauty. There was a Spanish maid on her knees washing the floor. I was absolutely filthy. The Consul had already received a telegram from London asking where Zo was. He was advised of my identity and my other name of Zofia Zofkowska, No.30030, and my password which was "I am a member of the Chisholm Clan."

After I had met the Consul and had been fitted out with clothing, I went down to the pier and there to my astonishment was one of the Polish couriers, Lipkowski. Despite his arrest at Figueras he had managed to destroy the post and messages he carried. He advised me to wait as he believed we could reach Lisbon and from there might get a lift on an aircraft to London, but I thought this waiting period might take too long.

A few days later I begged the Consul to get me away as soon as possible, and I boarded a train for Madrid. There the Polish Consul took me to a very civilised hotel where I met Czechs who had also escaped. Whilst waiting again I looked briefly round Madrid and then continued on my route to Gibraltar.

The frontier crossing from Spain to Gibraltar was naturally very well guarded because the British authorities suspected Germans and their agents of gathering any information they could about convoys, etc., and everybody was thoroughly searched. As I carried a letter from the British Consul, however, I was driven by car to Gibraltar. There I saw, for the first time, a Scotsman wearing a kilt. I waited for a few days in an hotel and one night was taken on board a troopship to share a cabin with three Englishwomen who had survived the siege of Malta, but whose nerves had been wrecked by the experience. To my great surprise each had a bottle of whisky with her.

They told me that Malta suffered heavily from air attacks during its long ordeal. [It had 3,343 alerts. By the end of 1942 over 14,000 tons of bombs had fallen upon 122 square miles of Malta and the small island of Gozo. The enemy lost over 1,000 aircraft, and in the island's defence 568 British aircraft were lost. Civilians killed or who had died of injuries numbered 1,486. More casualties would have been inflicted if a large proportion of the people had not slept in the rock caves. After the war King George VI awarded the George Cross to the island for its bravery.] We went in convoy with nineteen other ships. The troops were sleeping on different decks and there were many hundreds of Poles who had been deported to the Soviet Union in 1939 and had made their way to the Middle East via Iran, whilst others had escaped through France from the prison camp Miranda. I heard for the first time from them about the massacre at Katyń. Later, I was to hear that I had lost my brother-in-law there – he had been murdered with 12,000 other Polish officers. Some of the Poles on board were ill and needed to be given some strength and so I managed to procure a bottle of wine. We were on board for Easter and I remember attending Mass which was celebrated by a Scots chaplain. He and the British troops were overjoyed to hear the Poles singing hymns loudly and with such fervour.

The route which the convoy followed was a long one and we sailed almost to mid-Atlantic. Once the German U-Boats and an aircraft tried to attack us and the ship had a near miss. We had constant boat drills. It took eight days from Gibraltar to reach Bristol.

At Bristol we docked on 1st May. All the troops disembarked and I was left alone until finally a policewomen came and took me on a train to London where, to my surprise, I was interned for two days. Then a English officer appeared who spoke Polish and he escorted me to the Rubens Hotel in Buckingham Palace Road. There, in the foyer of the hotel, I met Lipkowski again. He had managed to get to London on an aircraft from Lisbon. The last time we had met in Barcelona. I reported to the Chief of 6 Bureau (the Headquarters for Special Duties).

The information which I, and indeed all couriers, carried covered a multitude of subjects and was intended for the Polish Commander-in-Chief in London, his staff, our own Foreign Office and all relevant ministries. The information concerned:

U-Boats in the Baltic
German troop movements
V1 and V2
Auschwitz
Photographs for forged documents
Escape routes
German industry
Munitions factories
Sabotage
Information and plans of enemy aircraft and armour
The Jewish ghettos and the rising in the Warsaw ghetto
Co-operation with the Resistance in Hungary and Germany
Extermination of Poles and Jews, particularly in the parts
     annexed to the Reich.

As a courier I was not allowed to know the exact nature of the information I carried in case I was captured and subjected to torture.

There, at headquarters, I worked for two months to discuss and clear up matters concerning my mission.

From headquarters I went for a parachute course at Ringway, near Manchester, and then for further training in Scotland. I visited several stations of SOE to give lectures on the work of the Resistance. On one or two occasions I was allowed by Security to see training camps for women of the ATS (Auxiliary Territorial Service).

It was on 9 September 1943 that a Halifax aircraft took off from Tempsford in the early evening, and we had a long cold flight ahead of us. Over Denmark the plane was fired on. The route lay over Sweden, from where the plane turned and followed the line of the Vistula river. A small reception committee was waiting for our group of three. I received the signal "Go" from the dispatcher and I jumped, followed by my two companions. I was dropped in a small clearing near the woods at Podkowa Lesna, near Warsaw. I did not fall as well as I should have done and slightly hurt my heels, which made it difficult to walk for the next 45 minutes through the woods to spend the remainder of the night in a cottage there. My parachute was buried by members of the underground reception committee – occasionally (and only if it was considered safe) a parachute was smuggled away and made up into articles of clothing. What I wore was subjected to another thorough search, lest any clues of my true identity should betray me in the event of my capture.

The following is a brief description of one of the last of Elizabeth's many journeys:

January 1945. The purpose of travelling to Villingen was to leave a message there for another courier of the Resistance. I was sitting in the carriage of the train while I was carrying false documents which indicated that I came from Villingen (Rheinland). I was returning from a visit to my "husband" who was seriously wounded. I wore mourning and a veil as my "brother" had been killed on the front. On the documents I carried was a false rubber stamp (*stempel*) plus a signature.

The German police began checking passengers on the train. When they checked the papers of the woman sitting next to me, to my horror I saw that the papers showed that, by a complete coincidence, she had come from the same hospital in Villingen and, of course, her genuine papers bore a completely different rubber stamp and signature. I purposely looked tired, and this shock persuaded me to try and get some fresh air. I attempted to make my way out of the compartment before the Germans could ask me for my papers. I was interrupted by another policeman however who, fortunately, had not seen the right papers of the German woman but, of course, there was always the risk that he might compare them later.

Before the Second World War Elizabeth graduated in mathematics from Poznań University. One of her professors there was Professor Krygowski who taught the two Enigma experts – at that time they were his assistants – though Elizabeth did not know anything about their secret work.

After taking her degree she taught mathematics and joined Przysposo-
bienie Wojskowe Kobiet, a voluntary women's corps which had many
thousands of members. In September 1939 Elizabeth served in Silesia, then
at Lwow (Eastern Poland) in the Women's Battalion.

Elizabeth summarised her subsequent activities as follows:

> Autumn 1939–December 1940: organiser in underground and
> courier in Silesia.   January 1941–May 1942: courier. Warsaw –
> Berlin.
> December 1942–May 1943: courier. Warsaw–London.
> September 1943–March 1944: during this time the Gestapo
> continually arrested many members and in March Zagroda
> was largely destroyed – many were denounced and fled to
> convents 8 April–15 July 1944: hid in Szymanow Convent. The
> Reverend Mother Sapirha was a close relative of the Cardinal
> in Kraków – Jewish girls were also in hiding there.
> 15 July 1944–1 August 1944: returned to Warsaw.
> 1 August 1944: Warsaw rising.
> 2 October 1944: I was in one of the Women's Battalions.

Many thousands of women took park in the fighting while some helped to
drag the badly wounded from the street battles and from the underground
routes connecting one cellar with another. One of these low "streets" was
named after Sikorski and even had dim temporary lighting. An unknown
number were auxiliary nurses, messengers and couriers.

A parachutist named Andrzej was dropped in 1944. His young sister
Wanda, aged 19, worked as an auxiliary nurse. Both her hips were shot
away and she died of her wounds. Later Andrzej was executed.

After prolonged and bitter fighting the city fell again into German hands
and together with my colleagues we led about seventeen soldiers through
the sewers to another part of the capital. For thousands, this was their only
way out.

The acute shortages of food, water, medicines and dressings were
appalling. I can truthfully say that the only food some of us had was yeast
from a brewery which we mixed with drops of water and cooked where
and whenever possible.

Later, when I reached Kraków on 4 October 1944, I met an old
colleague – a colonel – and offered him one of the used "biscuits". He
looked at it and said, "This resembles the Sacred Host."

At the end of September as we were rounded up and marched out I
succeeded in escaping and on 2 October 1944 I arrived in Kraków via
Częstochowa.

4 October 1944 – February 1945: organiser and courier again – many
journeys to Czechoslovakia, Austria, Germany up to the borders of
Switzerland and Denmark.

My last journey was early in February 1945 when I heard the Allies' guns
on the Rhine and the Soviet guns the same day. Some of the towns I had
to visit were in flames and I took cover, mainly under steps, for protection.

From the spring of 1945 I worked as a teacher in different towns. My
mother died of skin cancer; she had been in a Gestapo prison. One of my

brothers had been murdered in Auschwitz and a beloved friend, Maria Zawodzinska, had died of tuberculosis – the majority of those I had loved had lost their lives, including my brother murdered at Katyń.

During the evening of 2 September 1951 (in the Stalin era) I was arrested in Olsztyn and later sentenced to twelve years' imprisonment. I served this in Mokotow, Fordon, Grudziadz, Bojanowo (near Rawicz). There was a wonderful feeling of unity amongst us – so many brave men and women. Finally, in February 1955, I was released after an amnesty and returned to my father. Those were hard times.

Later on I worked, and from 1965–1975 I was employed at Gdańsk University.

From 1975 until my retirement in 1978 I worked at Torun University.

The Zagroda, a division of the Home Army in Poland, had branches in many different Polish cities, among which were Kraków, Katowice and Gdańsk. It also operated in a number of European cities including Budapest, Bucharest, Berlin, Vienna and Paris, and in Denmark. As well as communication by means of couriers, Zagroda daily handled hundreds of orders, reports and items of information by radio. The radio equipment used was either sent by Britain or made locally in clandestine workshops.

Zagroda had several hundred members working for it. Emilia Malessa ("Marcysia") was the chief of Zagroda between 1939 and 1945 and Elizabeth Zawacka was her deputy between 1942 and 1945.

1. *The Southern Division* gave reports to Budapest, Constantinople, Cairo and London.
2. *The Northern Division* was responsible for reporting courier services from C-in-C to their base in Stockholm and then on to London.
3. *The Western Division* operated through Paris, Spain, Portugal and Berne in Switzerland and then enciphered messages sent to London.
4. *The Technical Division* used to reduce the coded reports to microfilm and pack them in special hiding places necessary for couriers.
5. *The Documentary and Financial Division* was responsible for preparing forged documents and currency of all European countries for the couriers.
6. *The Hiding-Places Production Division* produced furniture, toys, bags, pencils, cigarette-holders, powder compacts, pocket-glasses, cigarette lighters, notebooks and purses in which to hide microfilms carried by couriers.
7. *The Personnel Division* was responsible for selecting and training new couriers and other workers.

Zagroda couriers carried approximately 150 long reports and messages from Warsaw to London during the War. They were carried from the Chief of the Home Army in Poland to the Polish Commander-in-Chief and Polish Government-in-exile in London. Each packet of reports was copied two or three times and sent in by a separate route. Each usually took several weeks to reach London. If a courier fell into the hands of the Gestapo he or she usually managed to destroy these reports. The reports were concealed so well that the Gestapo rarely found them. For instance, when the courier Tadeusz Wesolowski was arrested and taken by the Gestapo to Berlin, he was carrying reports hidden in his cigarette lighter, and during interrogation the lighter was used to light a cigarette, but the reports were never discovered. Earlier, Tadeusz had been working in a factory in Warsaw, and the Gestapo made numerous telephone calls with their opposite numbers there to try and gain information. After brutal interrogation he survived without disclosing anything and was eventually released, still with his lighter and its secret contents.

It was very difficult to keep good couriers. Many were arrested by the Gestapo and, after torture, were murdered either in prisons or in concentration camps.

There were four types of courier:

1. Liaison couriers who took messages from early morning until the curfew from one district of Warsaw to another. There were many such couriers and they were exclusively women.
2. Short-distance couriers who travelled from Warsaw to different towns close to the General Government frontier. They were mostly women also.
3. Long-distance couriers who travelled to various European countries. These couriers were changed frequently. There were between fifty and one hundred individuals altogether. About fifty per cent were women.
4. Special emissary couriers who carried reports and messages from Warsaw to London. There were only eight such couriers during the whole War and only one woman – Elizabeth.

* * *

Within a week of Elizabeth's departure from the Station in September 1943, Diana (nicknamed "Dipsy") Portman arrived from the Special Training Station at Thame Park and shared the same room with me. Dipsy and I became the closest friends, remaining so until she was killed in 1944; she was about my age and similar in height – about five feet. Although she had a very serious side to her nature, she enjoyed life enormously, and we shared an interest in nursing, ballet and music. We also appeared to have the same sense of humour. On the wall Dipsy hung a picture of two young people standing on a river bank holding hands, with the inscription "A Moment Out of Time". She was a radio operator and also hung up a poster which showed a woman operating a wireless set, overshadowed by the figure of a German listening as she transmitted, about to pounce on her.

Though books or films about SOE often catch the tension involved in the work, they rarely recapture the dreadful fear and anguish that most of the Bods, if not all, experienced. The romance which is invariably introduced into such works seems out of place. We had those platonic friendships which people say are impossible: they do not seem to realise what such friendships really mean, nor the necessity for them.

I remember a large number of the Bods, and especially Robert. He was aged eighteen and he was a courier. He had a premonition about being captured and tortured. At the op station for several nights before being flown out to be dropped, he walked up and down this large room which held a contour map of Poland. One evening when the others had gone to sleep I asked him to tell me what was on his mind. Everything came pouring out and I said I was sure he would not be thought of as a coward if he did not wish to go, and explained this to the briefing officers. He was racked by the situation, but after thinking it through concluded that never in any circumstances could he let his colleagues down. Alas, Robert's premonition came true.

About 332 Bods went through the stations while we were with them, which meant over 300 "Goodbyes", and a questioning of all accepted values. In the heightened awareness of life and death, it was quality and not quantity that counted; in the final analysis, faith, loyalty, courage and truth were all that mattered.

It has been said that I was born with some instinct, a sort of sixth sense, which made me especially sensitive to atmosphere. I noticed with particular vividness how extremely responsive the Bods were, and as a general rule how cheerful. During the War, when strict discipline had to be maintained, I found that they were able to keep up a wonderful relationship both with each other and with the FANYs to many of whom they used to give some complimentary nickname. All of us undoubtedly were the better for having been together and exchanging thoughts, whether about the fundamentals of life or about personal or confidential matters.

The Resistance, of which the Bods formed so essential a part, was a situation unlike any other. Yet, in the years to come, when in the presence of those who suffered some misfortune or terminal illness, I was to have the same kind of feeling, as if there were a common identity between the two. With them, too, the moment of saying farewell has always moved me deeply.

The Bods used to remark how strange it felt to be in an English country garden one day and Oslo, The Hague, Warsaw or Prague the next. I remember particularly the ops station near Watton-at-Stone where a wall of the main room was covered with a massive contour map of Poland, while on the other walls hung mementoes from some of the groups – a collar, a jacket, a shirt, each bearing its owner's code-name. From whatever country they came, these men and women had great optimism, although some said they might marry unhappily or be diagnosed as suffering from cancer, or become alcoholics. "Better to die now than that," they thought. The Bods were referred to as the "silent parachutists" and later their maxim was: "We were unknown then, we shall remain unknown now."

I remember often listening at night to groups of parachutists as they talked in a simple but profound way about life: the mistakes that had been made, and what they believed could be done with peace when it came. In a very real sense the FANYs shared the fears, and the joys, of the men and women who were about to return to their native countries in such hazardous circumstances.

I began then to think of ways in which the qualities they possessed – tolerance, faith, courage, humour and gaiety – might be perpetuated. I thought that instead of trying to remember all those who died fighting in the far-flung corners of the earth or in prison camps by means of a plaque or monument, one should go out and provide assistance and comfort to those who are sick and in need, wherever they might be, regardless of nationality or religion, creating in this way a "Living Memorial" to the dead.

5

Service Overseas

IN 1943, WHEN AIRCRAFT losses became heavier, especially on the route across Denmark and the Baltic Sea to Poland and Czechoslovakia, it was decided to transfer one of the Special Duties Squadrons to North Africa and later to Italy.

We were then operating from an ops and holding station in Buckinghamshire, and the aircraft were taking off from Tempsford in Bedfordshire.

Before leaving for North Africa we drove some of the Bods to Tempsford one afternoon at short notice and, after rechecking everything, we escorted them aboard the two aircraft. Dipsy Portman was one of the FANYs with me and we stood together on a log on the edge of the runway as the Halifaxes took off. Dipsy turned to me and said: "I suppose people in the future will never believe what the Bods are going into. If ever a film is made about them it must include Tchaikovksy's Piano Concerto in B Flat Minor." In the first aircraft Richard was standing with the midgunner's turret open, his fair hair blowing in the breeze as he waved goodbye and the aircraft taxied down the runway.

On the aircraft with Richard was Zdzislaw Peszke (code-name *Kaszmir*), a radio operator. He was surrounded by the Gestapo while operating later in Poland and swallowed his poison pill to avoid capture and interrogation.

The second Halifax carrying three other young Bods was shot down near Kalisz. They were eventually reburied in Poznań cemetery. Their names were Ryszard, Wladyslaw and Kazimierz.

All five men had already survived deportation from Poland to Siberia before they arrived in Britain. Richard was later arrested and spent the rest of the War in Dachau.

When we were told who had been chosen to go overseas there was great but subdued excitement. We were instructed to check over our uniforms, including the greatcoats (which had a double line of buttons fanning out from the waist to the shoulders, scarlet lining and deep cuffs). We believed these greatcoats and battledress would ultimately be needed for the victory parade if we reached Warsaw and Prague. We were briefed in the greatest secrecy about a vague but possible plan to break through the Danube gap in an attempt to get ahead of the Red Army, but this sounded both impractical and unrealistic as the Americans trusted Stalin and the Communists more than their other Allies.

This attitude was borne out at Casablanca in January 1943, at Tehran in November/December 1943, at Yalta in February 1945 and at Potsdam in July/August 1945.

We were allowed to write to our mothers to say we would be going away, but we were not permitted to give any clue as to where we were going or how we were travelling. We also had a week's leave, which went by very quickly. At that time I was able to endure great physical tiredness and I would compensate for this by sleeping for up to twenty hours at a time when on a normal forty-eight or occasional seventy-two hours' leave. I could imagine no better feeling than going to bed realising I could sleep on, and my mother used to spoil me by bringing breakfast up to me. My family, whom I hardly saw, rarely or ever asked questions, but Mama was perturbed. She had consulted the mothers of Dipsy and another friend, Pammy, who suggested that we should have our last tea at the Berkeley or some such place in London.

The nature of our work meant that we had to have a cover story and this was all the more necessary in North Africa, because the authorities knew we would be in close contact with other servicemen and women. We were told we were to wear the Polish eagle on our FANY uniforms, even though we were also partly attached to the Czech Section. The Poles were delighted to provide the eagles for us. I remember Dipsy saying: "Just think if we had been allowed to wear the national emblems of the other Bods – Dutch, Belgium, Danish, Norwegian!" Neither of us had ever served with the French Section.

Dipsy had received part of her Radio Telegraphy training at Thame Park and later we met at Grendon Underwood, a signals station near Oxford, where we slept in bare unheated Nissen huts. It was a dreary place surrounded by barbed wire and fierce dogs to guard it. I believe it has since been converted into a prison. We both decided at holding station No 20 to leave farewell letters to our mothers. Mine I put in a box marked "S.R." inside a container specially made by a Bod. We also decided to preserve our notes and the other small souvenirs given to us by the Bods we had known. I suppose because we realised we were never likely to meet them again; the different Bods and their various missions were very vividly present in our minds during those last nights in Britain. I remember that Dipsy and I talked to one another very late at night in the bathroom with the taps running, which we considered to be the safest place. We recalled the different people and their ops, remembering especially those who had been dropped more than once.

We also tried to count the number of SOE stations and made a very rough guess of about sixty. Years later in June 1992, Gervase Cowell wrote: "There is no substantive list in the SOE record of the many establishments in the UK which were used during its life time."

He reached after a lot of research the number of seventy seven, but concluded this was certainly not a comprehensive coverage.

In London we saw one or two FANYs who had been serving with Polish Division in Scotland and had worn the shoulder flash Poland on their uniforms since 1940. Naturally, they considered themselves part of the Polish Army and they expressed surprise on seeing our eagle, not knowing that we belonged to Special Operations Executive.

On enlisting, the FANYs bought their uniforms, new or secondhand. A kitbag, a sleeping ("flea") bag and a canvas bag containing a gas mask were part of the equipment. The mask and a knife had to be carried at all times. One issue of khaki drill (KD, as it was known), consisting of light-weight battledress, was free. Regulations were strict and after a certain date in spring, KD had to be worn with the sleeves rolled up above the elbow. The FANYs who were being posted abroad stocked up with boot polish and soap and were given an extra allowance of coupons to buy items of uniform. We were billeted in London opposite the FANY Headquarters, which were in the Vicarage of St Paul's, Knightsbridge. Our billet was high up in a draughty room in the Alexandra Hotel, which had already been damaged in the Blitz. Later, after the War, a memorial plaque to the FANYs who had died was unveiled by HRH Princess Alice of Athlone on the wall of St Paul's Church, in the presence of Field-Marshal The Earl Wavell.

My mother came to London the day before we were due to embark. We prayed together in St Paul's Church and then I saw Mama into a taxi at Hyde Park at the start of her journey back to Thurlow. As the taxi pulled away she leaned out of the window and said: "Please come back to see us before you leave to work in Prague and Poland for years." Clearly, my mother already had an intuition of the course my life was to take and I hoped the taxi driver would not repeat her words if he had heard them. Much water was to pass under the bridge before we saw each other again very briefly in 1945.

Dipsy and I enjoyed going to Floris in Jermyn Street and having a free spray of scent; then we listened in a Bond Street record shop to Rachmaninov's "Rhapsody on a Theme of Paganini", to Brahms' Violin Concerto and to "Softly Awakes My Heart" from *Samson and Delilah*. These were treats to be packed in on what was almost our last day.

After embarking at Addison Road station we few FANYs travelled overnight in a heavily blacked-out train which appeared to stop at every station, making the journey seem endless, before finally reaching Liverpool. In the docks we waited hours in a damp warehouse while embarkation onto the troopship proceeded, and it was afternoon before we trudged up the gangplank carrying our kitbags and packs worn on our backs. We were allocated our berths with four other girls in a cabin which, before the War, had accommodated only one or perhaps two passengers.

A company of the Rifle Brigade who were also on board wondered who we were. Our cover stories must have sounded weak, for they expressed surprise at what they were told and asked us awkward questions about our past service and where we had been. From the adjoining cabin very early one morning we heard a message tapped in morse code on the cabin bulkheads, which we were of course able to decipher. One of the messages, which concerned us personally, was as follows: "We are commandos and suspect that you do similar work."

As the troopship joined the assembling convoy off Scotland, the sight of the Clyde in the misty and mellow atmosphere made a vivid impression. It was to remain in my memory for a long time.

For some of the hundreds on board the troopship the feeling of optimism and cheerful good humour remained throughout the extended voyage to North Africa; but overcrowding, particularly for the unfortunate troops below deck, and for others who were sleeping on the stairs, aggravated the tremendous feeling of boredom, broken only by regular boat drills and occasional enemy attacks on the convoy. Three ships were lost. The crew often talked about the thousands of servicemen who, from 1940, had been obliged to spend weeks on troopships sailing round the Cape to join the Eighth Army because the Mediterranean was closed to convoys, and of others who had had equally boring and monotonous or dangerous weeks at sea.

When I think of that time now I think of Rupert Brooke's poem:

Fragment

I strayed about the deck, an hour, to-night
Under a cloudy moonless sky; and peeped
In at the windows, watched my friends at table,
Or playing cards, or standing in the doorway,
Or coming out into the darkness. Still
No one could see me.

I would have thought of them
– Heedless, within a week of battle – in pity,
Pride in their strength and in the weight and firmness
And link'd beauty of bodies, and pity that
This gay machine of splendour I'd soon be broken
Thought little of, pashed, scattered. . . .

Only, always,
I could but see them – against the lamplight – pass
Like coloured shadows, thinner than filmy glass,
Slight bubbles, fainter than the wave's faint light,
That broke to phosphorus out in the night,
Perishing things and strange ghosts – soon to die
To other ghosts – this one, or that, or I.

During the voyage we had time for reflection and for discussing, always on deck and away from the others, our hopes of linking up across the Adriatic Sea with the Yugoslav partisans and of ultimately breaking through Slovenia into the Danube valley and beyond. Later, we heard about a special commando force which might be used in such an operation.

Our temporary FANY Commanding Officer was a formidable figure. She never lost the opportunity to lecture us to refuse any offer of help regardless of the circumstances. When we disembarked in Algiers, she told us to march very well indeed, to the standard of the famous foot-guards* as taught too by the FANY, through the docks to our billet carrying our kitbag, gas mask and sleeping bag on our shoulders and our pack on our back.

The billet turned out to be a pension of doubtful repute, and during our first night there some Americans of the First Army had an orgy of drinking and were sick on the stairs. We helped to clear up the mess. We were made very uncomfortable by the intensely cold nights which succeeded the brilliant sunshine of the days. Amongst the local population there was a general distrust of the French, a shortage of food, and great poverty.

Some of my friends joined FANYs posted to the west of Algiers – Inter-Services Signals Unit 6, as the Unit was called – which was concerned with building up and organising the Resistance in Southern France and Corsica, and the jargon of sabotage was on their lips. Joannie Cutting remained behind while Muffet Panting (who had lost her parents in the Far East in Japanese camps and her husband and brother in other theatres of the War) was subsequently parachuted into Corsica. Later on, Dipsy Portman and Bar Legge travelled overland on a troop train which broke down and the acting CO told them to leave the train and give their seats to the Polish Bods, who expressed great indignation. They found some bread and toasted it at the end of bayonets round a camp fire and got water from the engine to brew up with their tea-sugar-dried-milk cube.

Together with two or three others I flew to Tunis in a Liberator, the crew of which was from the Special Duties Squadron, captained by Wing-Commander S. Krol. Amid all the squalor, the beauty of the sunrise and sunset was breathtaking and I was reminded of the descriptions given in letters from friends who had fought in the campaigns across the 2,000 miles of desert. These people, who had struggled in the desert, wrote short, descriptive, but censored, letters of the contrast between the bitter fighting and their brief leaves back in Cairo. Sadly, most of these notes, sometimes accompanied by poems, have been lost. But this I found from a tank commander, a radioed last message: "We have been attacked and are on fire . . . please . . . send remembrances to our families at home. Sunray." And this from a friend, about Jeremy who died of his wounds: "I hope he felt God's presence when he lay unbefriended in the desert groaning and writhing in pain." And from another, this moving stanza:

> We heard beyond the desert night
> the murmur of the fields we knew,
> and our swift souls with one delight
> like homing swallows northward flew.

*The Grenadiers, Coldstream, Scots and Irish Guards.

One colleague wrote:

> The desert was its own world. Silence broken by the noise of trucks or
> tanks or a carrier and by guns and planes. But when they stopped you
> could hear the silence. Until the mess tins clanked for brew-up or the
> banging in of tent pegs or stanchions for barbed wire.
>
> The sand rippled, little flurries of wind caught it. But the great
> movements came with the hot Khamseen, the desert wind, that blew for
> days, pillars of sand across the desert, blotting out light and pinning men
> and machines to the ground, the sand gritting men's eyelids, lining their
> faces, gritting the food, percolating into every crevice and cranny, the
> all-pervading sand.
>
> The sun-beaten desert stretched flat and far but not endlessly, the distant
> horizon broken by ridges and escarpment, whilst in between came the
> sunken wadis, the dried watercourses and areas of soft sand to trap one's
> truck. Splotches of bush decorated slopes. The occasional palm tree rose in
> the distance. An oasis would be rare. To the north more palm trees and
> then the Mediterranean itself glinting in the sun and alongside the main
> east-west route, a ribbon of road, that descended in zig-zags through the
> steep passes. By day, heat! by night, cold! But at night, too, the white blaze
> of stars from end to end of the heavens. There the Milky Way looked milky.
> And in all this space two armies met. They set up their camps, dug little
> trenches, erected signs, laid out 'phone lines – so much to be reclaimed by
> the desert within weeks of departure. The troops shared all this empty land
> with the few bedouins who popped up from nowhere, trading pigeon-sized
> eggs from unseen hens for mashed tea leaves and foul, issue cigarettes.
>
> But the true inhabitants of the sand were the flies. The eternal flies!
> Millions and millions of flies! Stinging flies, too! And when the wind blew
> from the Quattara Depression, uncovering the bodies, a world of flies
> swarmed with the smell.

A poem written by Sydney Maiden, "Epitaph for a Grave in Libya",
expresses the feelings of the numbers who were killed or died of their
wounds.

> Beneath this sand from War's alarms,
> He lies who was not bred to carry arms.
> One of a host prepared in haste learned
> The soldier's trade while for his own he yearned.
> Thus, swift apprenticed, of his best he gave
> Till, meeting Death, he found this desert grave;
> Far from his home and all he held most dear,
> His heart in England but his valour here.

My friends also knew what hunger meant – not infrequently they had only
eaten a ship's biscuit, rock hard by the afternoon. Their water ration
consisted of one pint per day – more if they were lucky – for drinking,
washing and shaving.

During my stay in Tunis the Town Major offered me a bath, and two prisoners of war from the Afrika Korps heated and carried the water. They told me they were convinced that Germany would win the War. There was no bolt on the bathroom door and I put a box in front of it to keep it shut, but while I was having a good soak the door opened and a soldier from the Eighth Army appeared with a look of amazement on his face. "Cor!" he said, "I thought I was in Blighty again!"

Another occasion on which a bath was possible was in the former headquarters of General von Arnim.

We were billeted on the outskirts of Tunis, where the Arabs were very short of food and existed in absolute squalor. We suffered severely from mosquito bites, and once when the Unit was to be inspected by the Commander-in-Chief I was unable to be present as the swelling from the bites was so ugly and acute. It was on that night that I was surprised by friends bursting into the shelled room I was sharing carrying loaded revolvers. They rushed over to the low wall opening where a local Arab, whom they had noticed on their way into the billet, was climbing the wall with a knife between his teeth and was about to swoop into the room. I was sitting on an upturned empty ammunition case with just the light of a flickering candle in the room and I was quite unaware of his presence. If my friends had not arrived at that time I might have had to fight off the Arab.

Our hand-picked group of four FANYs now travelled on to Italy, for there had been only two or three flights from Tunisia to Poland and Czechoslovakia. Conditions in Italy were rough. In one place, at a farm we called "Tara" (from *Gone with the Wind*), of course there was naturally no heating and the only electricity was generated by a wind vane. Sheep and goats occupied the ground floor and we were billeted upstairs. My kitbag had been lost and the Poles unselfishly offered a blanket, which they nailed onto orange boxes to serve as a bed. When possible, they also put up where they could pieces of canvas sheeting to give partial privacy for the loo, a hole we had dug in the ground, before moving on again to another hidden place.

One of our Commanding Officers, Colonel Trevor Roper-Caldbeck, wrote of that time:

> At first I was not altogether happy at the thought of having women in that situation, but the four who came as an advance guard were superb. Their courage, cheerfulness and guts in the face of every obstacle amazed me, and I cannot speak too highly of the way they tackled any task.

A British Naval Commander seconded to our Section had a different approach. He said: "Well, if you want to risk your bloody neck, don't expect anybody to be there to fall back on."

The Germans had told the local people in Italy various horror tales of what would happen to them when the Allies landed, but the Italians' fear was tempered with astonishment at seeing a girl in trousers and battledress and a man in a kilt (which they called a "skirt"). Some villages seemed deserted, for the inhabitants had shut themselves up in their small and often poverty-stricken dwellings and were waiting anxiously to see what was going to happen.

The intense cold and wind, especially during the winter of 1943 with temperatures falling to minus 20°C or lower, were unforgettable. Our only occasional heating was from a round charcoal brazier, and if it burned all night the fumes became lethal. We thought we would never be warm again and, at night, we occasionally lay awake dreaming about a hot bath and clean sheets. Tents were blown down and one worked in a continuous blizzard. The Italians considered it the worst winter for forty years. But naturally we came to terms with it, as did others. One of the air crew gave me his spare flying suit, and I remember using it at night, as well as my sleeping bag. Any old bottles we found, we filled with hot water, when obtainable. These served as "hot water bottles" but if the bottles cracked during the night the cold and ice in the morning were terrible. Everything froze and the blizzards were blinding. The diesel in the trucks froze, so engines had to be switched on and turned over every twenty minutes.

I found a letter from this winter time which brought back memories of those long cold nights. "You must have had an appalling journey. We heard you had left before dawn and my fears were all confirmed. We were under three feet of snow and it snowed hard all Tuesday. We are ghostly figures moving about in snowsuits and snowshoes." (The FANYs had abandoned wearing ties and caps and replaced them many months before with informal scarves and balaclava helmets and indeed anything that would keep out the cold.)

There were long tedious drives through blizzards in the mountains, with Italians begging for rations (bully beef, hard biscuits, margarine) or left-over food. Troops sat on the back of the 15-cwt truck discouraging children from stealing the kit. Worst of all were places where bridges had been blown up by the Germans and the Royal Engineers had been given no time in which to erect a Bailey Bridge, so we faced driving onto narrow planks of wood (in winter rutted with snow and ice), praying one would reach the other end and not suffer the fate of truck that had skidded and fallen far down the ravine onto mines.

In Naples a terrible typhus epidemic raged, caused by dreadful living conditions, and this cost the lives of many adults and children. Food was so difficult to obtain and the black market was rife everywhere. A bottle of cooking oil cost the equivalent of a month's wages – for those fortunate enough to have any money or something to barter. Often people queued to fill any containers they could with water.

Italian partisans became active. I quote from Gervase Cowell:

No 1 Special Force, known also as MARYLAND, arrived from North Africa in October 1943 and later its HQ at Monopoli, near Bari. It was conceived only as an operational out-station, not a directing HQ and was designed as a more convenient launching point for operations into many destinations besides Italy, but in practice it proved to be the local reference point for practically all Italian operations. A tactical HQ went forward with 5th Army through Rome and up to Florence and was responsible for all the work of close collaboration with the Partisans in the field.

In April 1945 SOE's No. 1 Special Force estimated that the partisans took over 40,000 German and Fascist prisoners and liberated over 100 towns. But for the death of each German at least ten Italians were killed and, as elsewhere in Europe, they were strung up from trees, lamp-posts and balconies. One cluster of villages named Marzabatta literally disappeared from the map after two SS companies herded their 1,830 inhabitants into a church and massacred them. In all approximately 44,720 partisans, and 52 members of SOE lost their lives. There were also 9,980 civilians killed in reprisals. Many crimes in other parts of the country were committed. The horrendous and heroic landing by the Allies at Salerno and later Anzio cost the lives of many young soldiers.

It was a winter of discontent. Churchill's warning against "crawling up the leg of Italy like a harvest bug" proved unhappily prophetic. For the Army there was slow, bitter and tedious fighting. The Germans were firmly entrenched in the mountains and few of the Allies understood the long drawn-out strategy they were forced to follow in the perpetual flogging, slogging trudge northwards to Rome and further. It had not been expected that the conquest of Italy would be so laborious and slow; indeed, it was to have been completed by 1 June 1944. I wrote a note to Dipsy: "My God, are we ever going to get there? Let's pray things will be all right. Aren't we lucky to be taking part?"

The following is a prayer Dipsy and I always used:

> Teach us, Good Lord, to serve thee as Thou deservest:
> To strive and not to count the cost;
> To fight and not to heed the wounds;
> To toil and not to seek for rest;
> To labour and not to ask for any reward
> Save that of knowing that we do Thy Will.
>
> St Ignatius Loyola

Eventually the bitter winter began to give way to spring. The frozen snow, rutted and packed hard on the mountain tracks and roads, began to grow grey with mud.

Casualties since the landings had been very heavy indeed. The topography of the country with its succession of ravines, swamps and mountain ranges offered the Germans excellent natural defences. No sooner had the Allies, fighting so hard for every yard, driven the enemy over one mountain range than they were met with yet another to reduce.

We heard that General Alexander's Army was very cosmopolitan and besides the British included New Zealand, Canadian, Indian and South

African Divisions as well as the Free French, 12,000 Moroccan *goumiers* and the Polish Divisions, though these were under strength. The Poles became famous for the bitterly fought battle of Monte Cassino where 281 of their officers were lost and a third of their other ranks, totalling 3,503 men, were killed or missing. In addition, there was the Fifth Army. Their gallantry was superb. On the memorial in the Polish War cemetery which stands on the slopes of the hill known as Point 913, there is the following inscription:

> We Polish soldiers
> For our freedom and yours
> Have given our souls to God
> Our bodies to the soil of Italy
> And our hearts to Poland.

Alexander and other far-sighted and wise commanders realised that if only the extremely hard-won battles in Italy could be followed through then a break-out into Central Europe was still possible.

In *Cassino – Portrait of a Battle,* Fred Majdalany writes of what happened next:

> And now the Fifth and Eighth Armies, flushed with success and sweeping forward on an irresistible flood tide of victory, were poised to finish the job – to complete the rout of the enemy and compel abandonment of the Italian front altogether, or at least heavy reinforcement from a central reserve that could no longer spare it.
>
> But this was not to be. A crowning act of strategic folly was at hand. As a final irony, the Allied Armies in Italy were to be deprived of total victory at precisely the moment when it seemed at last to be within their grasp.
>
> Alexander had 28 divisions chasing 21 German, of which more than a third had been reduced to impotence. The chase was in full cry and there was no reason why the broken armies of Kesselring should not be driven back to the Alps. With the Normandy landing now well established it was the perfect moment for a knock-out blow in Italy that could have taken the Allies to the frontiers of Central Europe, the end to which Winston Churchill's far-sighted strategy had been aimed from the very beginning of the Mediterranean campaigns . . .
>
> The Allied commanders in Italy might from time to time have had their clashes of temperament and their differences of opinion in matters of tactical detail. But now, as never before, there was passionate unanimity. With one voice the American and British commanders protested against the folly of weakening their armies at the very moment when total victory as at last within their reach. Desperately Alexander pleaded for the retention of the forces that he had brought to the brink of a final triumph that would make up for all the disappointment and sacrifice that had gone before:
>
> "I cannot over-emphasize my conviction that if my tried and experienced commanders and troops are taken away for operations elsewhere we shall certainly miss a golden opportunity of scoring a really decisive victory and

we shall never be able to reap the full benefits of the efforts and gains we have made during the past few weeks. I feel strongly that it is of the greatest importance not to let go the chance that has been so hardly won."

Alexander was supported up to the hilt by Churchill in this urgent plea to be allowed to retain his full strength to finish the task so auspiciously begun. But the American Chiefs of Staff were adamant. The invasion of Southern France must go through. And so, at the height of its victorious pursuit, the Fifth Army had to withdraw seven of its best divisions – three American, four French – for the new operation.

At first the Germans were incredulous, suspecting some new and subtle deception. Then, grateful for this unexpected stroke of luck, they put new heart into the delaying tactics at which they had became so expert. By the summer's end they had established themselves on yet another mountain barrier, the Gothic Line, south of the Po. For the Allies it seemed a poor reward for the long winter heartbreak of Cassino and the great offensive with which Alexander had brought it to an end. [It was a poor reward, too, for all the other innumerable battles fought since the invasion of Italy, some of which resembled the terrible trench warfare of the First World War.]

The pattern of the Italian campaign was now complete. It had started, owing to the lack of interest of Washington, as a secondary campaign. This had led, with the inevitability of Greek tragedy, to the climactic deadlock of Cassino.

I quote from Professor Gilbert:

> Alexander was eager to continue his attack northward through Italy; General Maitland Wilson, commanding the British Forces in the Middle East, was keen to carry out an amphibious landing at the head of the Adriatic, and strike eastward, first to Zagreb, then towards Austria and the Danube. Churchill and the British Chiefs of Staff pressed Roosevelt and the American Chiefs for an amphibious landing at the head of the Adriatic. On 28 June their view seemed to be reinforced by a top-secret German naval signal, sent early that day and decrypted at Bletchley the same morning; a directive from Hitler himself which made it clear that he intended to hold the Apennines at all cost. "And now we have the most marvellous information," Brooke noted in his diary, "indicating clearly the importance Hitler attaches to northern Italy." "It would be a grave strategic error", Brooke, Portal and Cunningham telegraphed to the American Chiefs of Staff later that day, "not to take advantage of destroying the German forces at present in Italy and the drawing further reserves on to the front".
>
> That day Churchill telegraphed to Roosevelt to remind him of "how you spoke to me at Teheran about Istria". He also sent Roosevelt a copy of the decrypted German naval signal. But on the following day Roosevelt rejected the Adriatic plan, telling Churchill that for "purely political consideration" in the United States he would never survive "even a slight setback" in Normandy if it became known "that fairly large forces had been diverted to the Balkans". Churchill hastened to point out that the new plan had nothing to do with the Balkans. At the Teheran Conference "you

emphasised to me the possibilities of a move eastward when Italy was conquered, and specifically mentioned Istria. No one involved in these discussions has ever thought of moving armies into the Balkans; but Istria and Trieste in Italy are strategic and political positions, which you saw yourself very clearly might exercise profound and widespread reactions, especially now after the Russian advances."

Roosevelt proposed putting the dispute to Stalin. Churchill was against this, pointing out that on a "long-term political view" Stalin might well prefer the British and Americans to do their fighting in France "and that East, Middle and Southern Europe should fall naturally into his control."

Churchill decided to go to see Roosevelt to put the Adriatic plan to him in person. On 30 June he gave orders for both his flying boat and his Lancaster bomber to be made ready for a flight across the Atlantic. But Roosevelt had made up his mind; the South of France landing would go ahead, and Alexander's army in Italy must therefore be reduced in strength. "What can I do Mr President," Churchill telegraphed on 1 July, "when your Chiefs of Staff insist on casting aside our Italian offensive campaign, with all its dazzling possibilities, relieving Hitler of all his anxieties in the Po basin (vide Boniface), and when we are to see the integral life of this campaign drained off into the Rhone Valley in the belief that it will in several months carry effective help to Eisenhower so far away in the north?" Churchill added, "I am sure that if we could have met, as I so frequently proposed, we should have reached a happy agreement."

Roosevelt would not change his mind, Churchill and the British Chiefs of Staff, and their two senior military commanders in the Mediterranean, were forced to abandon their preferred strategy. Alexander would not be allowed to exploit a known German weakness, and a classic opportunity. It was a low ebb in the Anglo-American Wartime relationship.

The decision that an invasion of southern France should follow the Normandy landings had been taken at the Tehran conference the previous year. To quote General Mark Clark, Commander of the fifth US Army in Italy and later American High Commissioner in Austria:

A campaign that might have changed the whole history of relations between the western world and the Soviet Union was permitted to fade away, not into nothing, but into much less than it could have been . . . Not alone in my opinion, but in the opinion of a number of experts who were close to the problem, the weakening of the campaign in Italy in order to invade Southern France, instead of pushing on into the Balkans, was one of the outstanding political mistakes of the War . . . Stalin knew exactly what he wanted in a political as well as a military way; and the thing he wanted most was to keep us out of the Balkans . . . It is easy to see, therefore, why Stalin favoured ANVIL at Tehran . . . but I could never see why as conditions changed and as the War situation changed, the United States and Britain failed to sit down and take another look at the over-all picture . . . There was a question that the Balkans were strongly in the British minds, but . . . the American top-level planners were not interested . . . I later came to understand, in Austria, the tre- mendous advantages that we had lost by our failure to press on into the

Balkans . . . Had we been there before the Red Army, not only would the collapse of Germany have come sooner, but the influence of Soviet Russia would have been drastically reduced. Thus, the great opportunity for the advance into Central Europe, and everything which would have followed from this, was lost.

* * *

The aircraft flying from Italy to southern Poland used three main routes: the first crossed Lake Balaton in Hungary and passed west of Budapest and over the Tatra mountains, the distance to Kraków close to 750 miles, then to Warsaw nearly 900. The second route was slightly further east, via Kotar in Yugoslavia, east of Budapest and into Poland east of the Tatras. The third lay still further east via Albania, a distance of 684 miles. For the crews it was dangerous, as weather conditions were often very bad and visibility down to nil – especially over the mountains – and there were always the night fighters and the flak to contend with.

The courage and enterprise of the Polish Resistance and of the Bods parachuted in to help them were responsible for the discovery in 1942 of the German V1 and V2 rocket installations and launching pads at Peenemunde. As a result of the information the Poles supplied, a bombing raid was carried out, the success of which set back the development of these rockets by many months.

I quote from Gervase Cowell:

> When the rocket factories were no longer safe the Germans developed a complex of tunnels deep in the Harz mountains, by Nordhausen. These had been mined for ammonia. It was in these tunnels where the prisoners were kept, never emerging, while they hewed their way forward, breathing the poisonous dust, licking the dribbling condensation which was their only water and dying in three weeks at the rate of 100 a day.
>
> It was not death, but labour, that was the purpose of Dora, yet the relentless brutality of that labour brought death as readily as any extermination camp. When the tunnels were finished and work could begin on the V1 and V2, the 11,000 prisoners were moved to sheds above ground, where hundreds more regularly had the open-air luxury of being hoisted by the crane-load onto the gallows by the parade ground. As Werner von Braun walked unconcernedly by, back to his neat villa each night, perhaps he did not then imagine how adroitly he would pass from this obscene qualification to future adulation in America's space programme, or how, to ease that transition, the story of Dora would be long concealed.
>
> Also within a few days of the aerial attack by the Royal Air Force on Peenemunde the Germans decided to move the rocket station to the south-east of Poland – beyond the limits of air attack. A small village called Blizna, near Pustkow, was chosen. Its population had earlier been forcibly evacuated. But the Germans underestimated the activities of the Home Army who, as Churchill mentioned, "had their eyes open".
>
> It was to Blizna in 1941 that thousands of Russian prisoners of war had been brought and Nazi concentration camps created. Most of the prisoners

became victims of typhoid. They were used as slaves to build roads,
railways and huge underground caves (bunkers) and then a launching pad.
Reports were sent by the Home Army to London by radio, and also by
microfilm carried by couriers, to tell of what was happening in the area. In
November/December 1943 soldiers of the Home Army reported:
    (1) that firing had started.
    (2) that large cylinders of "frozen air" had arrived at Blizna.
    A close watch was kept on the places where the rocket components
fell after firing. It was imperative for the Poles to search for and salvage
whatever parts they found. Their efforts were finally rewarded when an
almost complete V2 was located in a river bed. Two professors of science,
J. Groszkowski and M. Struszyński, examined the rocket under most
dangerous conditions in Warsaw. If they or anyone connected with them
had been discovered, the worst possible consequences would have been
inevitable.

Undoubtedly, an unknown number of people in Britain owe their lives to
the discovery by the Poles of the rocket installations, and to the information about the construction of the rockets which they were able to obtain
and pass back to Britain. If the RAF bombing raid had not delayed their
developments, these rockets would certainly have been launched against
Britain much sooner than they were and in much greater numbers, resulting
in appalling casualties.

The V1 attacks commenced a few days after the Allied invasion of
Normandy began in June 1944. In the early autumn of the year these
attacks were reinforced by V2 rockets launched mainly from Dutch bases.
This long-distance bombardment ceased on 27 March 1945 when the
1,050th and last rocket landed in Orpington, Kent.

The V1 (*Vergeltungswaffe Eins* – Revenge Weapon No. 1) was 25 feet
long and carried nearly one ton of explosive. In Britain the V1s killed 6,184
civilians and seriously injured 17,981. The V2s killed 2,754.

The details of the rockets were sent out by radio cipher or by courier.
A few of the couriers and some of the precious technical documents on the
rockets were brought out of Poland at night by an unarmed Dakota from
334 Squadron, fitted with two extra fuel tanks, in an Operation called
Bridge 3/Wildhorn. This was the third attempt. The Dakota flew to Motyl
near Tarnow from Italy – a long and perilous mission, dependent upon very
good weather conditions to enable the pilot, Flight Lieutenant S.G.
Culliford from New Zealand, and the navigator, Captain Kazimierz Szrajer,
to find the landing area. Every detail of the Operation had to be planned
and timed down to the last minute, for speed was essential if the aircraft
was to land, load its passengers and cargo, and take off before the enemy
arrived. Because of the very real risk of the enemy locating the landing
area – the sound of the aircraft passing overhead was certain to alert every
German patrol in the vicinity – the pilot had to be ready to take off at
a moment's notice. The passengers would therefore board the Dakota
according to a pre-arranged order of priority, to ensure that those with the

most vital information would not be the ones left behind if the aircraft had to leave before everyone was aboard.

The Dakota was to bring out of Poland a sack containing all the drawings and technical details of the rockets, as well as several of the Bods who had information which was of vital importance to the Allies. The sack took priority over the passengers and was to be brought back to Britain at all costs.

The mission almost met with disaster. The aircraft's take-off from Motyl was delayed by eighty minutes because the landing ground was too small and soft. The Dakota was off-loaded in an attempt to reduce weight, and it was even thought that as a last resort it would have to be destroyed by fire, but further frantic efforts to place wooden planks under the wheels were successful. Against all odds the aircraft eventually returned to base where it landed without brakes because the crew, believing that the brakes were jammed, had cut the connecting cables and drained off the brake fluid. The composure and courage of all those participating were the more remarkable in view of the great danger and tension which characterised the whole Operation.

One parachutist, a good friend of mine, Wladyslaw, had been dropped in Poland in April 1944 and played his part in the many places where he worked as a radio/telegraphist. He was constantly in peril and escaped after being arrested twice. During Operation Bridge 3/Wildhorn he transmitted messages and told me later:

> I had a bad experience owing to a thunderstorm with lightning and thus there was no power or contact with Headquarters Brindisi (Italy), but the local people managed to reconnect the electricity with great difficulty.
>
> As always, I was in danger of being detected and remember two German Storch aircraft flying round and round. Frankly, I was rather terrified and thought the Germans would locate my transmitter. The noise which the reception committee and others from the Home Army made was bad – although the Germans were in retreat, one never knew what might happen.
>
> After the Dakota's second approach and landing, lights had to be used. I was about half a mile away during the landing, off-loading and reloading.
>
> I sent the first transmission back to Headquarters after the Dakota finally took off. I was helped during this operation by a girl courier, Krystyna, aged nineteen.
>
> We were all linked together in a chain. Naturally, there was very strict security. Only two or three people knew what the operation was about for fear of arrest and torture. I knew the navigator of the Dakota, Captain Kazimierz Szrajer, from my previous squadron.
>
> Preparations were made for a further Operation Bridge 4, to collect more parachutists and escaping prisoners of war, but for various reasons this operation had to be abandoned.
>
> Within a week I had reached Warsaw and I was a Radio Operator during the Rising.

Wladyslaw evaded capture after this Operation and continued as a radio operator in touch with Stanmore and Brindisi, the two signals stations which were run by the Poles and to which only two or three of us were allowed entrance. Quite understandably, the Poles had deep suspicion that if they did not have complete charge of their signals stations the British would pass on information to the Soviets.

Wladyslaw was arrested in 1945 by the Russian KGB together with Adam, another parachutist who was a friend of mine, and Krystyna, the girl courier. They were sentenced to death in Moscow but by a miracle Wladyslaw and Adam were returned to Łódź prison in Poland from where they succeeded in escaping to Britain, hidden in the coal hole of a small Swedish ship. Alas, Krystyna was never seen or heard of again.

* * *

Sometimes in Italy the British and Yugoslav Bods attached to Tito's military mission came up to the hillside hideouts and talked. They discussed Tito and the way he was uniting the people in the areas of Yugoslavia that had been liberated. Rougher than the Poles, the Yugoslavs were ferocious fighters; like the Poles, they were motivated by patriotism and nationalism and took appalling risks. Wounded partisans, men and women, came to the Adriatic coast; there was a great number of women amongst the partisans, and they enjoyed complete equality with the men. They came from bitter, savage mountain country. Some had gangrene – I had already seen poverty and want, but I was now to witness even greater suffering. Yet still there was courage and laughter and friendship, and the stimulation of new sights and sounds. A friend Geoffrey in the Rifle Brigade wrote:

> I am not at all happy about you. You seem to be working much too hard and much too long. Has J. mentioned the local Fauna? There are masses of small finches and warblers here. Greenfinches and goldfinches are frequently to be seen. I saw some siskins a few days ago, more wagtails, more tits, many types of larks, hoopoe, bee-eaters, practically every known type of hawk and buzzard and several types of eagles, and even ravens have appeared since I have been here. There is a quaint little animal called a wingill or wugill – a cross between a badger and a polecat – which lives in the sand and sometimes shows itself. Jackals live round about in the hills and I often hear them at night.

I replied:

> Your letter reminded me of the sort of things that we too are seeing and meeting with. Among the many things which used to be described in letters from the desert were the cold nights and the quite unbelievably glorious sunsets and sunrises. They make up for an awful lot of other things, and I wonder in what other countries one sees such exquisite skies. Perhaps in Asia. And I wonder too whether we shall find them in the other lands that perhaps eventually we may reach. The birds we are more than conscious of. I wish I had time to go into greater detail,

as you have. Certainly the jackals at night make quite a noise, don't they?

The pressure, you know, has been with us really ever since the beginning and isn't all that bad. It's a challenge which we may not only enjoy, but would expect. What is far more important, is the gaiety and laughter, the singing, and even, at odd moments, the dancing. The stories, too, and discussions held on many different subjects . . . and, above all, there's so much else in this life that we are now experiencing, the faith which I can't really properly describe, and never will be able to, the courage, the songs that we have been taught, and the endless discussions and talks on such a variety of subjects. It is as good almost as being in a sort of university lecture room, but in a more relaxed atmosphere and hearing it all from much younger people. I wish you were part of it and could listen with us, but doubtless you have occasions too in trenches and on mountainsides, on muletracks, in the back of trucks. It probably even reminds you of the poop deck and watching phosphorous out into the night, in convoy, and many other things.

Geoffrey Sparrow of the 10th Battalion the Rifle Brigade was awarded the Military Cross for conspicuous gallantry, leadership and devotion to duty near Faella on 30 July, 1944.

Lieutenant Sparrow was in the leading platoon of a company ordered to occupy a vital feature. On reaching the first of the three crests which constituted the feature, his platoon came under heavy shell and machine-gun fire, and at the time found themselves involved in an extensive anti-personnel minefield.

Lieutenant Sparrow went forward alone, under fire and in view of the enemy, and showed the utmost skill in the use of ground and the very highest degree of personal courage and determination.

He personally cleared a lane 150 yards long through the minefield, in the process neutralising a large number of mines and booby-traps. A patrol passed safely through the gap, but 250 yards farther on ran into another minefield, all the patrol becoming casualties. He went out again, picked up a badly wounded N.C.O. and, still under fire and after neutralising yet a further number of booby-traps on the way, carried the wounded man back to the safety of our own lines.

Through Italy and the hard treacherous way north, every yard was defended by the Germans. Travelling through the country, the signs of inequality between rich and poor impressed and shocked me. From Naples to Rome to Florence and beyond we saw heartbreaking poverty, and on occasions we had a strange feeling that we were amongst neither friends nor enemies. I remember, too, in late May 1944, driving up Highway 6 past a village bombed mistakenly by American planes, which had killed a number of Allied soldiers. The unburied bodies lay swollen and black in the sun and we could smell the sickly scent of death, as always there were swarms of flies by day and rats came to eat at night.

We reached Rome just after the Liberation on 4 June and enjoyed the luxury of a bath and sleeping between sheets in a proper bed – an incredible sensation. I was serving with No. 1 Special Force and another FANY and myself had been given a room in the Hotel Eden. We were amazed at this because even after the landings at Anzio it was rumoured that the Americans had decided which hotels to commandeer when they reached Rome. Amid all the hustle and excitement there was a look of surprise upon the faces of those standing in the hall we entered. Our Commanding Officer was in his kilt and we were both battledress. Having lost my kitbag shortly after arrival in Italy I had with me only a worn Army blanket which contained a change of uniform, a tin "used for many purposes", a precious piece of soap and my original small soft pram pillow which miraculously remains with me today. The contents of this blanket spilled out onto the marble floor while the orchestra played palm court music in the background.

We had parked the three-ton truck outside the Hotel, ready to leave forty-eight hours later. When the Bods in SOE whom we had to drive back to the mountains were being loaded we turned round and saw General Alexander waiting patiently in his staff car behind our vehicle which was blocking his way. He gave us a delightful smile, and many years later, while attending a Royal Academy dinner, I saw the Field Marshal again. This time he came over and spoke to me as he had noticed the Italian campaign medal among the miniatures I was wearing. It was an unforgettable moment to hear such a great person speak about his thoughts of those years, and when he said "Do you think we ever met?" I summoned the courage to mention the time when, in error, another FANY and I had parked the three-tonner in front of his staff car after the Liberation of Rome. He smiled and said, "I am glad you have told me and I would not have minded at all, especially as you were serving with the Poles who were some of the best soldiers I ever had the opportunity of commanding."

In Rome we had an audience with the Pope; there were great crowds, and much singing and excitement in the blazing sunshine – even dancing in the streets. A friend, Tim, aged twenty-one, an officer in the 10th Battalion Rifle Brigade, had a day's sick leave, and I was allowed to meet him; together we walked up to a village, explored churches and heard the Italians singing "Caro Nome" – Home to our Mountain, and other extracts from Verdi's operas. We listened, too, to the birds and talked about the value of faith. As Tim left, I had a strong feeling that this would be our last meeting, and he was in fact killed on 26 July.

The following note came to me from Geoffrey, a brother officer:

> We were doing one of those beastly night marches and a dawn attack, and Tim was in the company on my left. I believe "high-ups" thought that the particular hills were unoccupied, but as usual they were wrong. Anyway, Tim's company ran into German machine-guns and heavy machine-gun fire. His platoon was sent round to the right towards us to get behind them, and got lost in the valley. After a lot of trouble, both convoys got on to their objectives and established the position, but nothing was heard of

Tim's platoon which, it later transpired, had gone too far to the right – in fact, they met some Germans on our right. Unfortunately Tim was leading. They heard some movement ahead of them. They challenged and the reply was "Italiani" which was followed by a burst of Schmeisser killing Tim, very badly wounding his corporal and just missing his platoon sergeant. Later we found Tim's body where he fell. Mercifully he had been killed outright and could not have known anything about it . . .

"I believe so much," Dipsy wrote afterwards to me, "in not letting one's personal tragedies affect work or other people's lives; in knowing how those who have gone before would so hate one to mourn and not for the better things in the world. But it's so hard to laugh and forget, even for five minutes – 'Better by far you should smile and forget, than that you should remember and be sad' – but I think one does both."

Neither of us ever became accustomed to death.

* * *

I have always found it difficult to describe my feelings. On rare occasions (one of which was in Naples), despite the typhus epidemic, we heard the operas *La Bohème* and *La Traviata*, the latter sung in Rome under the stars in an improvised opera house. I remember, too, the beauty of the mountains in spring, the first sunshine and our intense relief when the snows started to melt.

I wrote to a friend ". . . Don't you think we are witnessing such contrasts of ugliness and beauty, the latter including the music, art and wild flowers amidst countless other things which we shall miss when we pass on into Eternity. You or I may possibly still be here on earth when the present struggle finally ends and the next stage of our life, which will certainly include relief work, begins. Each of us has a time limit on earth and so it is up to us to make the most of our lives while we are here. It is sad how many millions of people die without leaving any trace of themselves behind. So many true stories, and particularly heroic ones, are never recorded, but the legacies of great artists and writers of music remain and *their* works are handed down from one generation to another giving immense joy to millions."

* * *

In Poland, untold acts of heroism occurred daily as the arrests and executions continued. Some people were arrested on suspicion, some were betrayed. Others were arrested in round-ups in the streets when whole blocks were sealed off or villages surrounded. There were frequent public executions, and no less than 15,000 people were shot in different parts of the City of Warsaw. Similar arrests and executions were occurring throughout the country.

SS Brigadier-General Kutschera was a symbol of this terror and crime. In January 1944, plans were made to assassinate him. Bronislaw, aged twenty, was ordered to organise the assassination.   Kutschera lived in Aleja Roz and whenever he left his house it was always in a well-guarded car. His daily departure at 9 a.m. was always punctual, and he normally went round the corner to his headquarters at 23 Ujazdowski Avenue, which, naturally, was also heavily guarded. The attempt to assassinate Kutschera could only take place over this short route, which was constantly patrolled. The first attempt was to have been made on Friday, 28 January 1944, but as Kutschera did not leave his home that day it was called off.

Shortly afterwards, on Tuesday, 1 February, the patrol in Aleja Roz signalled that Kutschera was in his car. Bronislaw took off his hat as a signal to the young soldiers of the Home Army at the tram stop and they took out their pistols. A car driven by a soldier of the Home Army was also signalled and it entered the street at speed across Kutschera's route. As the General drove into the gateway of his headquarters, Bronislaw opened fire and members of the Home Army exchanged shots with the Germans positioned in the building and neighbouring houses. Kutschera's ADC was badly wounded and later died. One guard was also killed. Kutschera was found dead on the floor of the car. Three members of the Home Army, including Bronislaw, had been hit, but they managed to withdraw with their wounded and, despite coming under heavy fire from the Germans, they all got away.

Two members, "Sokol" (Kazimierz Sott) and "Juno" (Zbigniew Gesicki) were escaping in their seriously damaged car when they were ambushed by the Germans on the Kierbedzia Bridge and, having run out of ammunition and their only grenade, they jumped into the river Vistula. The Germans fired on them from the bridge and the river banks and they soon disappeared under the water.

Bronislaw died on the morning of 4 February and another of his colleagues died two days later. Fourteen members of the Home Army, including three young women, had taken part.

During the summer of 1944 sorties into Poland continued – and the losses continued too. There were also 169 sorties to Yugoslavia and northern Italy. Though the surviving crews were weary, they were always ready to volunteer for further duties. When the Warsaw Rising started during the afternoon of 1 August 1944, there was dismay and also concern as to how help could be given. Night-flying by moonlight to special dropping zones had proved difficult enough, but now the crews were faced with the need for dropping from a low altitude large quantities of arms, food and medical supplies on Warsaw, which was encircled by fires and hidden by smoke, with sectors constantly changing hands. The aircraft had to contend with harassment by German fighter planes and anti-aircraft defences throughout the long journey, as well as over the dropping zones. British, Polish and South African losses were appalling. There was only one USAF mission to Warsaw on 18 September 1944 when 107 Flying Fortresses belonging to 13 Bomb Wing of the 3rd Air Division of the 8th Air Force flew from Britain and dropped their supplies. The majority of the containers fell into German hands.

> We who are left, how shall we look again
> Happily on the sun, nor feel the rain,
> Without remembering how they who went
> ungrudgingly, and spent
> Their lives for us, loved too the sun and rain.
> A bird among the rain-wet lilac sings –
> But we, how shall we turn to little things
> And listen to the birds, and winds and streams
> Made holy by their dreams
> Nor feel the heartbreak in the heart of things?
>
> W. W. Gibson

I wrote to Dipsy:

> You once said my feelings on death and eternal life were well clarified. This I question. But what I have no doubt about is the ghastly frustration and hopelessness which face us whenever there are moments to think. The mere fact of so many people being killed hourly in the desert, in the jungle, in submarines, in the mountains, being shot down, in concentration and extermination camps or in Gestapo headquarters or prisons – they are all suffering untold hell for something which each believes in or hopes for. It's silly to boast about idealism. War is too bloody for an individual suddenly to become a hero – or to say good and brave things when he's tortured or dying. It's more likely to bring out the opposite – but each of us has to try.

Molly, another of my friends, was serving with the YMCA up in the line on the Senio river with the divisional machine gunners of the Sixth London Division. During my visit to her, mortar bombs were lobbed over and the Germans were very visible. It reminded me yet again of the smell of death and the whistle of shells from 88mm guns in other places on the way. I had to get a lift to Senio and back, and on the way the truck stopped for the Tommies to "brew-up" on a spirit stove, using their rations of dried milk and tea prepared as a soluble cube. Noticing that I too carried my mug on my battledress, one Tommy said, "Watch out there that enamel isn't too chipped, lassie, and never borrow one, for it's VD you can get from this."

The characteristics of the men of different nations were very evident, especially under stress of tiredness. I recall one incident. There was a long convoy slowly climbing up and hugging the mountain road on one side while the truck that I was travelling in (probably contrary to orders) was coming down the other side of the road. Within minutes I realised from the driver's behaviour, his language and his manner of driving that he was "bomb happy". I persuaded him to stop and allow me to take over the driving. Mines had not been cleared from the road and there were signs along the edge, "Beware of the Verges", with the usual unprintable sign or message underneath.

It is difficult for anyone who did not serve in Italy to realise the contrasts between the bitter cold in the long winters and the fierce burning heat of summer. I vividly recall the roughness and parched rocky country and the olive groves and the wood from the trees there which could not be burnt; the bright blue skies and no twilights; skin turning from red to brown, then peeling; swarms of flies and mosquitoes; the uneasy political situation and general unrest and the "after tomorrow" attitude, particularly in the south.

*   *   *

Dipsy received special permission to marry a pilot serving in the Special Duties Lysander Squadron whom we had both known and admired for some time. The marriage was very short, for both were killed near Florence and buried on the banks of the Arno. It seemed almost impossible to bear this life without Dipsy who had, until then, shared my feelings about death in the fullest sense, and I kept thinking it must be somebody else and that I could go and discuss it all with her still. We all attended a short service, the mimosa alive in its tin vase bearing the promise of spring and life.

That night, in the dim light from the hurricane lamp, I found Dipsy's battledress on the camp bed, her compass, her spare army boots, Lyall's *Languages of Europe,* her well-worn English/Polish textbook and dictionary and her hairbrush which smelled of Chanel No. 5. On a scrap of paper I found the words: "When Thou hast a sorrow, tell it not to thine arrow, but tell it to the saddle bow and ride thee singing forth."

Into my mind came this poem, of which we had been so fond:

> Look for me in England
> On each oak and swan
> When I am gone,
> Pay the tribute of my glance
> As if by chance
> My shadow on the water stirred
> The real surface with your own
> Look on bud and leaf and bird
> Not for yourself alone.
>
> Hear for me in England
> The music of the shires
> By memory's fires
> The whisper of the flame
> Engraves your name.
> Listen to the bells which spell
> That name where echoes peal and stray
> Beyond the valley and the fell
> To us who are away.

Touch for me in England
Bark of elm and yew
The morning dew
Hands in your lap shall be
Cradles for me
Your fingers on the pen reach out
Through words to mine, that trace
On sands and on the seas about
As if in braille your face.

Weeks later from Dipsy's father, Brigadier Portman, I received the following letter:

This is to send you my warmest thanks for all you have done for us, for your letters and your friendship for Diana. Your letters were the helpful and sympathising sort I wanted to have from Diana's comrades, and you managed to convey so much I longed to know, which no one else could have; you made me very happy and almost cheerful.

You were a jolly good friend to Diana and those you both served with and for. What a merry team you were; there can never have been such a unit in any other wars. I am afraid she never got my last letters, as scarcely any letters got through.

I am terribly proud too that part of my old team, the London 56th Division (Black Cats) have done so well.

Yours very gratefully,
G.P.

Dipsy's farewell letter to her mother, which she had left in a sealed cake tin, was opened by Mrs Portman in my presence when I came back briefly in 1945; it was very touching and read as follows:

My darling Mummy,

Please open the contents of this box, which will probably appear to you a collection of strange and apparently meaningless rubbish, but to one of my friends who had a similar collection they are all things of great sentimental value. They may perhaps give some clue to the object for which so many Bods worked and of which one must never disclose an inkling: "There is no excuse and no mercy". A strange and poignant org [organisation] as we called it.

You may imagine the appalling constraint and international atmosphere we lived in, and always "goodbye" . . . so very much here today and gone tomorrow, but it was for these Bods, their amazing courage and wonderful gratitude for the comparatively small share we were privileged to have in being with them and perhaps helping that we always endeavoured to give of our best, not only because we felt out of a sense of duty, respect or admiration, but because we tried in some small way to make up for all they had suffered and lost and were going to face, whatever race they were, and to try and give them a good and lasting impression of England and her people – that they could also realise how deeply we felt their cause as well as our own and that they should see what a decent English girl could be. We set a tremendously high standard for ourselves which we struggled, although often tired, to keep up. Never to say "No" to anything they asked us to do for them and how many of them have gone out of this world never to meet us afterwards again, in some outlandish spot in one of their countries. Of all these people, I feel most for the gallant and delightful Poles, and I should like at least £100 of my small amount of pocket money to go to their relief fund. What more can I say? I cannot begin to really write what I feel for my heart is full and the small hours of the morning draw on. Simply this – thank you for Everything accept this and "not what might have been". "One crowded hour of glorious life is better than an age without a name,"

Diana

Much later, when Dipsy's parents and I were discussing a headstone for the grave of their daughter and son-in-law, I suggested inscribing the lines: "Lovely and pleasant in their lives, and in death they were not divided."

* * *

After hostilities ceased the work with Special Operations Executive came to an end and the next phase of my life began.

Please refer to Appendices for further information on Air Supply Sources to the Polish Home Army, Nazi Concentration Camps, Casualties of the First and Second World War.

6

Recall to Life

Because of you we will be glad and gay,
Remembering you we will be brave and strong;
And hail the advent of each dangerous day,
And meet the last adventure with a song.

And, as you proudly gave your jewelled gift,
We'll give our lesser offering with a smile,
Nor falter on that path where, all too swift,
You led the way and leapt the golden stile.

Whether new paths, new heights to climb you find,
Or gallop through the unfooted asphodel,
We know you know we shall not lag behind,
Nor halt to waste a moment on a fear;
And you will speed us onward with a cheer,
And wave beyond the stars that all is well.

MAURICE BARING

Amongst the hardships and difficulties of the life we were leading, memories of books and poetry meant a great deal to us. Maurice Baring's poem "To Julian Grenfell", written in memory of the poet who was killed in the First World War, was one of my favourites, for it seemed to epitomise the spirit of those who, a generation later, were fighting yet another World War.

For the majority of the public the full terror of life in occupied Europe was only to be known after the Liberation, but in SOE we had received first-hand accounts day by day and later, as we proceeded across Europe, we were to see for ourselves the suffering that these atrocities had caused. It was a corroboration of everything that those who had entered or left these territories earlier had reported – incredible and sickening. Moreover, it involved many people whom we had known and cared about deeply, people who had been lost and not heard of again, caught or betrayed, taken to prison and herded off in cattle trucks to forced labour or, more usually, extermination and concentration camps.

Since the 1930s when I listened to stories from escaped Jews and others and heard well-informed people discussing Nazism, I had continued to be amazed that so few of the real facts of the Nazis' ideology and of their racial persecution were known to the public in Britain, the Commonwealth and the rest of the free world. Since 1933 a number of Germans, including the well-known theologian, Dietrich Bonhoeffer, and other courageous individuals, as well as members of the Opposition parties, had tried their best to inform us all – *long* before war became inevitable – but their warning voices had been silenced or ignored. It is a pity that so few people outside Germany read Hitler's speeches, especially when he stated that even if he could not conquer he would drag the rest of the world down to destruction with him.

As I mentioned in Chapter Two, there was no doubt in my mind that a lot of people knew before the War (and this was confirmed to me through my service with Special Operations Executive later on), that there was a cover-up in the highest ranks of the Foreign Office and the BBC as regards anti-Semitism. They suppressed news about Germany's attempts to exterminate European Jews, Slavs and gypsies and many millions of others. This evidence is contained in documents from BBC archives and Government papers at the Public Records Office.

By the permission of Jacques Delarue, author of the *History of the Gestapo** I quote:

> Between January 1st and August 25th 1944, the date of the last despatch, 326 convoys left France, not including the departments of the Upper Rhine, Lower Rhine, and the Moselle. Convoys consisted of anything up to 2,000 persons. The rise in the number of convoys throws a light on the continuous stepping up to Nazi repression: three convoys in 1940, 19 in 1941, 104 in 1942 (the seizure of power by the Gestapo in Paris is immediately apparent in the figures), 257 in 1943. In France about 250,000 persons were deported of whom only 35,000 returned, indelibly marked by their experience. At Dachau the barracks, which held 300–400 persons in 1942, housed 1,000 in 1943 and 3,000 or more at the beginning of 1945.
>
> The Dutch hold the sad distinction in Western Europe of having the smallest percentage of deportees to return, out of 126,000 deportees 11,000 only were repatriated.
>
> When the Gestapo thought that they had extorted everything possible from a prisoner of any age group, he was often transferred to a deportation convoy.
>
> This frequently meant a slow death sentence through forced labour, sickness and ill-treatment. The transport was carried out in closed and sealed cattle trucks, frequently lasting a minimum of three or four days and nights or *many* more according to the distance and country of origin. There were 100 to 120 persons per truck, deprived of air, food and water and any facilities. The convoys arriving at Buchenwald and Dachau often numbered twenty-five per cent dead or more.
>
> Once the survivors reached their destination the camp commandant was allowed to use his own initiative.
>
> At the beginning of September 1944, a group of forty-seven British, American and Dutch airmen, who had baled out after their machines had

*Macdonald, 1964.

been shot down during raids on Germany, arrived at Mauthausen. They had been condemned to death after more than eighteen months detention, having tried to escape. Instead of having them shot on the spot, the camp commandant sent them to Mauthausen where they met with an atrocious death.

There was a gigantic basin, one of many into which one descended by a staircase roughly hewn in the stone, consisting of eighty-six steps. The forty seven, bare-footed and clothed only in a shirt and shorts, were laden with stones weighing fifty to seventy-five pounds which they had to carry on their backs or in their arms to the top of the steps under a hail of truncheon blows and kicks. As soon as they had deposited their burden at the top, they had to descend at the double and fetch a slightly heavier stone than before. By the first evening twenty-one of them were dead. The remaining twenty-six were subjected to the same torture on the following day. Not a single one remained alive by the evening of the second day. Thousands of others somehow managed to survive. Mauthausen, Güsen, Flossenburg and Grossrosen were notorious for their stone quarries.

During the War, on 31 May 1942, Bonhoeffer and his friend, Pastor Schönfeld (Secretary of the Ecumenical Council in Geneva), met George Bell, the Bishop of Chichester, at Sigtuna in Sweden. Bonhoeffer managed to make the journey to Sweden through the help of his friends in the German Foreign Office. Speaking for the German Resistance, Bonhoeffer asked whether, if they succeeded in overthrowing Hitler and his regime, the British Government would give some assurance of a willingness to negotiate peace. On his return, the Bishop put the proposition to Anthony Eden who consulted Churchill, but the overture was rejected. With the benefit of hindsight one might well feel that this was a tragic mistake.

The "official" conspiracy of silence which descended from the time the Nazis seized power up to the "discovery" of Belsen and other equally notorious camps has always seemed to me inexplicable. Throughout the War years the Polish Home Army had sent out *repeated* warnings and detailed reports to London about mass arrests of their citizens as well as full reports of terrible atrocities throughout Poland (the part annexed to the German Reich and the central part of the Country called "General Government" by the Nazis). As a poignant reminder there are now signposts all over Poland which lead to those infamous places.

One of the many people who wrote such reports was Major Witold Pilecki (who was also known under the pseudonym of Tomasz Serefski). He was an agriculturalist and a reserve officer in the cavalry Regiment. Major Pilecki fought against the invading German Army in September 1939 and then joined the Polish Home Army. On 19 September 1940 he allowed himself to be rounded up during street arrests in Zoliborz (a suburb of Warsaw) and was transported in a cattle truck to Auschwitz as prisoner no. 4859. He did this deliberately so that he could report back to the Polish underground and the free world on the conditions and horrors he witnessed in the Camp. On 27 April 1943 the Major made a miraculous escape and was able to make his report. He continued to take an active part in the underground and fought in the Warsaw Rising when he was taken prisoner. On being liberated from Murnau, Bavaria, in 1945, Major Pilecki was repatriated to Poland. In 1947, during the Stalin era, he was arrested, and on 15 May 1948 he was sentenced to death by a military court. He was one of the countless victims.

If the public and those engaged in the War had been told the truth earlier, would it not have enabled them to understand better the true nature of the monstrous evil we were fighting against? I can find no adequate words to explain my feelings on this subject.

Walter Rosenberg, who later changed his name to Rudolf Vrba, was another who tried to expose the German atrocities. He had been transported to Birkenau in June 1942 when he was aged nineteen. He worked in the special clothing and clearing *Kommando* called "Kanada" by the prisoners. Human hair was made into material; bones of the victims were made into soap; human skin and skulls were made into lamp shades. The twenty-two Kanada barracks were so called because, to the prisoners, that country epitomised wealth and the barracks received the "wealth" of thousands of victims, which was transported to the Reich or to Banks in Switzerland. This included gold extracted from prisoners' teeth after death. All garments, personal belongings, including jewellery and currency of any description and from all nationalities, were sorted by prisoners like himself after each transport had arrived. Following the regaining of their sovereignty in 1949, the Germans arranged for this source of accumulated wealth to be transferred back to their Banks and this contributed towards their "economic miracle".

This system was used in all the main Nazi concentration camps and prisoners who were professional jewellers, artists, art historians, bankers, accountants, dentists, doctors, surgeons, watchmakers, textile merchants and many, many other professions and trades besides, had their lives lengthened because the SS insisted upon every item taken from the dead and indeed from all prisoners on arrival at the prisons and camps being removed.

It was a premeditated and gigantic operation. Special trains left with the loot to be stored mainly in Swiss banks and in a few other neutral countries. The Nazis used diplomatic bags and indeed all imaginable means to take these stolen valuables to Switzerland.

Scrupulous records were kept daily of everything with copies sent to the main huge office buildings in Berlin. A few friends of mine who had managed to survive showed me lists and indeed I found with them a few US dollars tramped into the ground near the place in the infamous Kanada barracks where the sorting was done.

This operation was organised in addition to the art treasures and sacred objects from art galleries, churches, castles, palaces and millions of individual houses and homes in occupied countries looted by the Nazis throughout Europe.

I wrote about this subject *long* before this information became public, I now quote from an article which appeared in *The Times* of 11 September 1996:

Gold has proved to be the most intractable legacy of the Second World War. More than 50 years after Hitler's defeat, Governments, refugees and holocaust victims' families are still waiting for their share of the $84 million held in British and American banks.

Efforts to trace the missing ingots and return them to their rightful owners have been frustrated by greed, confusion and legal wrangles. But the main problem has been the nature of the metal itself: the jewellery, coins, heirlooms and Jewish sacred objects plundered all over Europe from families imprisoned or exterminated were all sent to a central smithy, melted down and turned into ingots whose provenance can never be established.

Yesterday the Foreign Office responded to the growing concern over the gold and suspicion that intelligence documents had been held back by releasing a summary of the Government's role in tracing the Nazi gold and the attempt to compensate the victims of Nazi looting.

Two main difficulties, both during and after the War, had haunted all efforts to reach a just settlement: how to prevent the Germans sending their ill-gotten loot abroad – principally to Switzerland; and how to persuade the neutral countries that received tons of processed gold from Germany to pay back the money after 1945.

Allied monitoring of Nazi gold began before the War. By September 1939, German holdings had swollen by some $97 million worth of gold from Austria, Czechoslovakia and Danzig. The Reichsbank maintained that it had reserves in 1939 of $71 million, the same figure as in 1937; the Bank of England considered the true figure to be nearer $111 million.

But the War proved costly for Germany. Reserves were so depleted that Germany had defaulted on loans and exhausted its credit and almost all trade had to be on a barter basis. The War could be financed only by systematic plunder – of state treasuries, especially $223 million of Belgian gold, $193 million from Holland and $24 million from Hungary, and of personal assets, particularly those of the Jews. Britain estimated in 1945 that Germany had plundered $550 million – almost certainly an underestimate.

German used its gold to buy raw materials and vital foreign currency. The main route was via Switzerland, but other neutral countries – Portugal and Sweden and, to a lesser extent, Spain and Turkey – also received German gold.

The Allies tried to monitor the sums to provide evidence of plundering, but the Reichsbank sent out ingots that had been reprocessed and back-dated to a period before the War.

Banking records confiscated after the War show the elaborate deception. Booty seized by the Wehrmacht was sent directly to the Reich's Treasury; that seized by the SS was handled exclusively through the Reichsbank, where it was received into a holding account in the name of "Melmer" and its value transferred after assessment to an account in the name of "Max Heiliger".

Dr Puhl, of the Reichsbank, admitted under interrogation in 1945 that all gold was melted down to conceal its origins; much was sent abroad. Britain estimated that by March 1943 Germany had sold more gold than it had held in 1939.

Britain and America were unsure how to put pressure on the Swiss not to accept the gold. Switzerland, entirely surrounded by the Axis powers, could not be coerced. Any outright embargo on Switzerland would also prevent the Allies from obtaining the Swiss francs they needed. Instead, Britain and America issued in January 1943 a declaration in which they reserved their rights "to declare invalid any transfers of, or dealings with, property, rights and interests . . . which are, or have been, situated in the territories which have come under the occupation or control, direct or indirect, of the Governments with which they are at war."

The warning was political; the Treasury had doubts. The Bank of England thought it would simply drive the Germans into more elaborate deceptions to conceal their looting of Europe. But the Government decided that the neutrals must be told bluntly that if they accepted gold from Germany they would be liable to "claims under the terms of the inter-Allied declaration."

The Bank of England also said it would pay no interest or dividends to anyone living in Sweden or Switzerland until those two countries declared that their gold holdings were "free from enemy taint".

The Treasury was reluctant, but Mr Cobbold of the Bank of England told the Swiss Embassy in London that he could rely on his country having "the maximum amount of trouble" after the War.

The problem, as the Allies later discovered, was that this was a bluff. The Swiss, realising the way the War was going, belatedly said that they would not accept any gold from anyone in German-occupied territory and in December 1944 blocked all Hungarian, Slovak and Croatian accounts in Switzerland. But the end of hostilities revealed the Allied weakness; they had no legal way to compel the Swiss to hand over the gold.

With all the other neutral states, the Swiss claimed that such a demand violated their neutral status. They agreed, after being urged on moral grounds, to begin talks. The Americans believed the Swiss held $200 million worth of Nazi gold. At first they denied all knowledge, but when talks became heated Mr A. Hirs, their chief negotiator, let slip that Swiss banks had $500 million.

Finally, in May 1946, they agreed to a one-off payment of 250 million Swiss francs in gold to the Federal Reserve Bank in New York. The Allies, angry but impotent, decided this was the best deal on offer and waived all further claims against the Swiss. The Swiss later made a further ex-gratia payment of 121.5 million Swiss francs. But they kept, in the end, about seven-eighths of all the German gold deposited.

The New York sum formed the basis of the Allied Tripartite Gold Commission. The hunt was also on for gold hidden in Germany. The occupation forces found a hoard worth about £54 million in a salt mine in Merkersm but reckoned it was only a fifth of all German Gold. The Americans found several other hoards in their zone and an informant also revealed a cache amassed by von Ribbentrop, the Nazi Foreign Minister, which was guarded by the German Foreign Office.

All the gold was gathered together in Frankfurt, then sent to London and New York for safekeeping pending distribution. The problem then was to decide how to give it back. Britain argued that all rightful owners should get back their goods, but most of the gold had been melted down and was untraceable. Instead, the Americans suggested that it should be distributed in proportion to the claims by those countries that had lost gold. This formula was accepted: payment would be compensation rather than restitution.

Dozens of obstacles have held up payment. The main one is that the sums claimed far exceed the gold found; the Bank of England estimated in 1945 that just over half the amount was available. The other problem has been individual restitution, especially to the relatives of families killed in the War.

The other main difficulty had been calculating the value of what remains. The prices were all worked out in exchange rates of 1945 and 1947. Distribution has also been complicated by the issue of Albanian gold. This entirely extraneous question arose after Britain, which held gold in trust, refused to return it until the Albanians offered compensation for a British warship sunk in 1946.

That issue dragged on for more than 40 years; an agreement was reached only five years ago and it was only last week that the Albanian parliament ratified the deal. For the first time since 1945, the way is now open to to pay the Nazis' victims compensation.

and from the leading article, again from *The Times*, "Tainted Gold":

The Foreign Office report on Nazi gold is a fascinating account of greed, deception and double-dealing half a century ago. It does not admit to any British conspiracy to hide ill-gotten ingots in the Bank of England. But it does point to an almost unconscionable delay in overcoming the legal and bureaucratic obstacles that stood between the Nazis's victims, or their heirs and representatives, and the money plundered from them to fund Hitler's war machine.

More damningly, it points to the outrageous refusal by Switzerland, by far the largest benificiary of German gold exports, to hand over more that a fraction of the huge sum of booty hidden in Swiss vaults. The issue is certainly one which the Swiss, with their tidy habit of hiding away past embarrassments, want to forget. Malcolm Rifkind should have told them bluntly during his visit that their behaviour has been immoral, selfish and unworthy of a democratic nation. He should have demanded that they step up their half-hearted response to regular inquiries by Holocaust victims.

The Foreign Office report, drawn from documents already declassified, is a crisp and well-compiled historical survey. It highlights, with the help of historical distance, the two awkward issues the Allies had to face in their relations with the neutral countries both during and after the War. How could they limit the economic dealings between Nazi Germany and countries such as Sweden and Switzerland without infringing their neutral status? And what legal instrument could they use after Hitler's defeat to ensure restitution of the gold to its rightful owners?

Britain's Ministry of Economic Warfare knew that Switzerland, and to a lesser extent Sweden and Portugal, were vital sources of foreign currency, which Berlin bought with gold seized from Jewish and other families and businesses and melted down. It favoured a tough approach to the Swiss, warning them that they would have to answer to the Allies if they continued accepting gold seized from occupied Europe. The Bank of England, however, was more circumspect. It recognised that the gold was impossible to trace, that sanctions against the Swiss would backfire – the Allies also needed Swiss francs – and that the gold's owners would be almost impossible to trace later.

So it turned out. The Swiss, who heeded Allied warnings only late in the War, denied at their first encounter with postWar negotiators that they had any looted gold. The lie was quickly detected. But when the miserly payment of 250 million Swiss francs was agreed, they were left approximately seven-eighths of the Nazis' gold still in their vaults.

For the past 50 years, various groups have attempted to appeal to the Swiss conscience. Such a commodity appears to be in short supply in Zurich. The arbiters of Swiss banking secrecy rebuffed all attempts by survivors, Jewish groups and American congressional committees to reveal the full extent of their Wartime gains. But repeated accusations that the Swiss have been laundering the money of crooks, drug-dealers and dictators as well as the Nazis have begun to have effect. Banking secrecy is not the steel door it once was. The Swiss have accepted that their banks have no business living off the proceeds of crime, and in many cases now co-operate with international investigators.

That makes it all the more worrying that they have refused to open all the files on their Wartime dealings. Repaying today's full value of the presumed gold holdings would indeed be very expensive. But if Switzerland slowly inching out of its self-imposed international isolation, really wants to make amends for its ambiguous Wartime behaviour, it should give free rein to the new commission of experts who will look into the dealings with Nazi Germany. Britain, as a member of the Tripartite Gold Commission, has a residual responsibility here. Mr Rifkind's talks with Flavio Cotti, his opposite number, would carry more weight if the Foreign Secretary could also announce that the British Government had found an appropriate home for its own holdings of Nazi gold forthwith.

* * *

The sheer size of Auschwitz is often forgotten or not known. The Camp, which was divided into Auschwitz 1 (main Camp) and Auschwitz 2 (Birkenau) plus auxiliary camps attached to each of them, covered in all forty square kilometres. In Auschwitz one there were twenty-eight prison blocks and one crematorium; in Birkenau 250 blocks and four crematoria and there were forty prison blocks attached to the auxiliary camps.

The prisoners arrived at Birkenau in sealed cattle trucks. If they were selected for slave labour they were stripped, forcibly shaved and put under the showers by the SS who hounded them with whips and dogs. If they were declared unfit for work they were gassed within a very short time of their arrival. Vrba learnt from prisoners of the preparations the SS were making to step up the rate of the killing.

Meanwhile, Alfred Wetzler, another young Slovak Jew, who was born on 10 May 1918 at Trnava, Slovakia, was arrested on 13 April 1942. He was transported to Auschwitz in the spring of the same year.

Wetzler and Vrba met and jointly planned to escape. They made contact with a secret international Resistance group inside Auschwitz. Their purpose was to alert the outside world about the daily mass murders in the concentration camps and of the fate awaiting the remainder of the Jews in Hungary whom the SS referred to as the "Hungarian salami".

As a prisoner Alfred Wetzler worked as a registrar in different parts of Birkenau, including the crematoria and mortuaries. He met some of those in the *Sonderkommando,* a special unit of prisoners whose duties were to clear the corpses from gas chambers and to transport them to the crematoria. Every few months this unit was also gassed and replaced by other prisoners.

On 7 April 1944, a couple of hours before the evening roll call in Birkenau, Wetzler and Vrba were hidden by their colleagues in a specially prepared hideout which a number of prisoners had helped build during their work on an extension to the Camp. It took the outward form of a large pile of planks of wood and was in the outer perimeter of the Camp. The area in which the hideout was made was called "Mexico" by the prisoners, and the ground round the pile was soaked with petrol and tobacco clandestinely obtained by the prisoners. This was to prevent the guard dogs from sniffing out the escapers.

The alarm was given at about 6 p.m. during evening roll call when the two numbers were missing. Vrba and Wetzler waited for three days and nights while a huge search was carried out. On the first day signals were despatched by the SS to different parts of occupied Poland and the Reich, including Berlin. It was almost a miracle that on the fourth day the Germans wrongly assumed that the prisoners had got away and consequently the guards were withdrawn from the outer perimeter of the Camp.

On 10 April at 9 p.m. the two men crept out of their hiding place and succeeded in escaping without being spotted by the sentries in the outer watchtowers. Though they did not carry a map, compass or have any local contacts, they had been given a rough sketch of the route by a nineteen-year-old Polish boy, Pavel Gulba, prisoner No. 7699. They also each carried a razor with which they intended to kill themselves if captured. The two men reached the mountains and, in spite of being fired on by a German patrol, they crossed the Polish-Slovak frontier safely. On reaching Skalite, a distance of 140 kilometres from the Camp eleven nights later, they fell asleep, completely exhausted, under a tree in the garden of a villager called Andrej Canecky. On discovering them, Andrej took the men into his cottage and after washing their feet he gave them his own bed in which to rest. Andrej advised them that there were still some Jewish doctors in the area who had been exempt from deportation because of the scarcity of doctors in Slovakia. This exemption had covered the doctors' wives and children, but not other members of their families who had been taken away by the Germans. One such doctor was Dr Pollak in Cadca, and Andrej advised Vrba and Wetzler that if they could wait until the next morning they could catch the train to that town on the pretext of taking some pigs to market. So, dressed as peasants, they left for Cadca the following day and on arrival made their way to Dr Pollak's house. Vrba immediately recognised the doctor as the same man he had met at the time of his own deportation in June 1942 and he had the terrible task of telling him that his parents, brothers and sisters had all died in the Camp. With the help of Dr Pollak and some of his friends they were able to continue their train journey to Zilina the next day, still dressed as peasants, and contact was made there with Erwin Steiner and Oskar Krasnansky, who encouraged them to compile their terrible indictment.

The report they composed consisted of about fifty typed pages. The information it contained had been collected by Wetzler with great bravery and unbelievable difficulty. He personally typed eighteen copies. It included an immense amount of detail about Auschwitz, the Resistance movement that existed there; a list of different transports from all parts of Europe; the methods used in the camps to kill the prisoners; a plan of Auschwitz and Birkenau with the crematoria, also a list of well-known political prisoners and many names of the SS in the camps.

One copy was handed to a delegate of the International Red Cross and another to the Papal Nuncio in Slovakia, Monsignor Giuseppe Burzio, who was reputed to be anti-Nazi and who was asked to pass it onto the Pope. Additional copies were forwarded to the War Cabinet in London, to Rabbi Weissmandel, to the Free French Radio in Algeria and to the American Board of Jews. Alas, despite their gallantry and the appalling information which these two brave prisoners had the courage to assemble and translate, no effective action was taken; indeed the SS continued to build two more gas chambers and the fate of a further 750,000 Hungarian Jews was sealed. As a well-known European said to me, "Supposing their efforts had not been in vain, where would the 750,000 Jews have been allowed to settle?

Some years ago Wetzler gave me a synopsis of his report and I now quote the foreword:

> Two young Slovak Jews – whose names will not be disclosed for the time being in the interest of their own safety – have been fortunate enough to escape after spending two years in the concentration camps of BIRKENAU, AUSCHWITZ and LUBLIN–MAJDANEK, where they had been deported in 1942 from SLOVAKIA.
>
> One of them was sent on 13 April, 1942 from the assembly camp of SERED directly to AUSCHWITZ and then to BIRKENAU, while the other was sent from the camp of NOVAKY to LUBLIN on 14 June, 1942 and, after a short stay there, transferred to AUSCHWITZ and, later, to BIRKENAU.
>
> The following report does not contain everything these two men experienced during their captivity, but only what one or both together

underwent, heard, or experienced at first hand. No individual impressions or judgments are recorded and nothing passed on from hearsay.

The report starts with the story of the young Jew who was removed from SERED. The account of his experiences in BIRKENAU begins at the time the second Jew arrived there and is, therefore, based on the statements of both. Then follows the individual narrative of the second Jew who was sent from NOVAKY to LUBLIN and from there to AUSCHWITZ.

The declarations tally with all the trustworthy yet fragmentary reports hitherto received, and the dates given with regard to transports to various camps agree with the official records. These statements can, therefore, be considered as entirely credible.

After the War ended Alfred Wetzler married Etela, a young woman born in 1925 who had survived Birkenau, they lived in Bratislava. Their daughter, Tanya, is mentioned in Chapter 17 – Stagenhoe. After the Communists seized power in 1948 he lost his job in a library. Alfred died as a result of his sufferings and because perhaps he knew he had failed to prevent the huge Hungarian transports of countless prisoners doomed for extermination. I naturally continue to visit his widow and daughter.

In all, 667 men and women escaped from Auschwitz and of these 270 were certainly recaptured. Many of the prisoners who succeeded in escaping joined the Home Army and Partisans, and no records are available to prove whether they were killed or survived. Some years ago the Auschwitz Museum was successful in tracing the names of eighty escapees living in Poland.

Another friend of mine, Tadeusz Szymanski, was in the first Polish transport to Auschwitz 1, the main Camp, in June 1940. After the War he became one of the first curators of the Auschwitz Museum and still lives there in one of the SS blocks within the main Camp. Mr Szymanski, who has given his life to the heart-rending search for, and the documenting of, the Auschwitz children, has made these comments:

> I was, and still am, rather embittered as both RAF and US aircraft flew over and took aerial photographs. I personally think that if some attempt had been made to bomb both the gas chambers and crematoria (particularly the former) this would have made the Germans stop, even temporarily, from continuing the mass murder. We knew that if railway lines had been bombed they could have been repaired and, of course, diversions could have be found by the Germans. We often discussed this moral obligation of the Allies and were frankly dismayed at their apparent lack of concern.
>
> Despite the fact that many thought they had been abandoned by the world others, in some incredible way, even imagined the great pressures placed on the Allies and that the aircraft had to concentrate on bombing German industry.

The reasons for not attempting to bomb Auschwitz were set out in a letter dated 15 January 1941 from Air-Marshal Sir Richard Peirse to General K. Sosnkowski, who had sent the Air Marshal a plan of action for Auschwitz:

High Wycombe, Bucks.

Strictly Confidential   15 January 1941

Dear General,

    I have considered very carefully all aspects of the proposal put forward by Captain Zamoyski in his letter of 4 January 1941 regarding an air attack on the concentration camp at Auschwitz and have also discussed this proposal with Sir Charles Portal.

We both decided, with regret, that a successful attack on Auschwitz cannot be carried out in practice. There are two main reasons. Firstly, our bombing forces have as their principal task attacks on industrial centres, as we consider that we shall probably accelerate the crisis in Germany's war industry in the current year. For that, it is essential to take advantage of every opportunity to attack the chosen targets with all the forces at our disposal. The atmospheric conditions which would allow us to attack targets in Poland are exactly the same as those which make possible attacks on major targets in Germany. Secondly, we know from our experience that sporadic attacks on targets such as Auschwitz would probably not bring about the expected result such as damaging the barbed wire fences or ammunition stocks so as to make it possible for the inmates to escape. Air bombing of that kind would require enormous precision not to cause serious losses among the inmates.

I am sincerely sorry to have to send you this kind of answer but I know you will understand the reasons and the fact that only a precise concentration of our bombing forces on major objectives will prove effective in the struggle against our common enemy.

Yours sincerely
Richard Peirse

It is interesting, too, to note that at a special Zionist conference held at the Baltimore Hotel, New York, on 9 May 1942, Dr Nahum Goldmann warned his colleagues then that it was possible that no more than two to three million Jews would survive in Europe by the end of the War as against a pre-War total of eight million. In October 1944 he made a request to the United States War Department for the camps to be bombed but was advised to approach the British representative on the Allied High Command, General Dill, as any decision as to the targets of bombardments in Europe was in the hands of the British.

With some difficulty Goldmann managed to obtain an interview with General Dill. Their talk he recalled in a letter to Martin Gilbert, dated 27 February 1980, and reproduced in Gilbert's book *Auschwitz and the Allies* (published by Michael Joseph/Rainbird in 1981), was both unforgettable and depressing, and he added:

General Dill took from the start a completely negative attitude. His argument was that bombing the camps would result in the death of thousands of prisoners.

I replied to him that they were destined to be gassed anyhow and explained that the idea to bomb the death camps had been suggested to us by the Jewish Underground in Poland, with whom we were in a certain contact through the Polish Government in exile in London, which regularly conveyed messages from the Jewish Nazi victims to us – mainly Rabbi Stephen Wise and myself – via the American State Department.

General Dill thereupon revealed his real motivation, by declaring that the British had to save bombs for military targets and that the only salvation for the Jews would be for the Allies to win the War.

I answered that the few dozen bombs needed to strike the death camps would not influence the outcome of the War and pointed out that the Royal Air Force was regularly bombing the I.G. Farben factories, a few miles' distance from Auschwitz.

At the end of our talk, which lasted over an hour, I accused General Dill and his colleagues of lack of human understanding for the terrible tragedy of the extermination camps. He regarded it as discourteous of me to be so outspoken in my criticism.

From the end of May until 26 December, 194 aerial photographs were taken by reconnaissance planes and a force of bombers that flew over Monowitz (an auxiliary slave labour camp of Auschwitz and only four kilometres from the main Camp). Monowitz was also the site of the I.G. Farben synthetic oil and rubber plant and for this reason it was bombed on 20 August, 13 September, 17 October and 29 November, 1944.

The treatment of prisoners of *all* ages among the twenty-five nationalities in the camps was uniformly barbaric; but the Jews, the gypsies and the Slav races were singled out for a very special savagery.

In all, more than four million defenceless human beings died in Auschwitz and Birkenau alone, of whom one million were children.

Confronted as they were by the horrors of the camps they liberated in their advance across Europe, the Allied armies had to help internees there as best they could. Although this was only part of our work, what we underwent there made an indelible impression on us; and even after so many years many of us find it quite impossible to describe what we saw. When I am asked to talk about the experiences of the men and women I knew who fought in the Resistance during the War, or to describe the scenes I subsequently witnessed myself, I find that my voice breaks as the memories come back to my mind. I also feel that I owe it to those men, women and children no longer here to speak for themselves to depict those scenes as they really were; yet I know that I am not equal to the task. I wonder, too, whether the reader could believe that what I am describing truly happened; and so perhaps I may fall back on an extract taken from a doctor's diary, written at the time.

The late Dr Michael Hargrave, formerly in practice at Wootton Bassett, was one of the medical students from London hospitals who went to Belsen ten days after the liberation of the Camp to do what they could for its victims. He gave permission for the following extract to be published from his diary:

Brigadier Glynn-Hughes, RAMC, Senior Medical Officer, 2nd Army, gave us an account of how, when conditions got completely out of hand in Belsen, the Germans decided to pass on the baby to us and so they asked us to take over the Camp. We agreed, providing that we also had an area round the Camp and that the bridges over a nearby river were left intact. This the Germans refused to do, and so it was decided to fight for the bridges, but it was agreed that there should be no firing into or out of the area round the Camp which they were going to give up. This worked in practice, although a few shells did land in the area. There was no actual fighting in the area, though the Germans did not completely evacuate it.

From the German sources it was learnt that the political (Waffen) SS were in charge of the Camp and they handed over to us on 13 April at 1200 hours, leaving only administrative officers and introducing Wehrmacht (Army) guards.

Brigadier Glynn-Hughes was the first of our people to enter the Camp and he was followed by one battery of anti-tank soldiers consisting of 120 men.

That evening there was a riot over a potato dump. Some German guards fired at internees who were trying to get some of the potatoes. Several internees were killed. Glynn-Hughes told Kramer (the Camp's Nazi Commandant) that if there was any more shooting he would have one SS guard shot for every internee shot. There was no more shooting from the Germans. But what struck him most forcibly was that neither Kramer nor the German doctor responsible for health in the Camp was in the least ashamed about the Camp. He made them bury bodies, but all the time they maintained an air of dumb insolence.

Typhus was raging in Camp I. Inside the huts conditions were appalling: the dead and the living were lying together. Brigadier Glynn-Hughes personally counted twenty women living in an area of 30 square feet, whereas a soldier never, under any conditions, gets less than 45 square feet living space. There were piles of dead everywhere in the open, accumulated in a fortnight because the crematorium had broken down. Women were leaning against these piles of dead to eat their food.

There were about 10,000 dead lying around in the open, and the British soldiers hastened the death of about 1,000 more by giving them chocolates and their own rations. Seventeen thousand people died during March. Since the Camp's liberation, 23,000 had died.

The death rate in Camp I had now fallen from 500 a day to about 90–100 a day. There was no typhus in Camp II and its inhabitants were fairly fit.

One striking thing we noticed was the Camp smell. This was a hot humid smell mixed up with the smell of burning boots, dirty clothing and faeces. Once smelt, never forgotten. We eventually came into the Women's Lager (Camp) where the smell increased in intensity.

Hut 224 was painted the usual pink colour with the Red Cross which the Germans had the nerve to paint on each hut. We went into the hut and were almost knocked back by the smell, but we went on into one of the two main rooms. There were no beds whatsoever and in this one room there were about 200 people lying on the floor. In some cases they wore a few tattered rags and in others they wore no clothes at all. They were huddled together. In many cases one blanket had to cover three people. The floor was covered in faeces and soaked in urine, and the people lying on the floor were in just the same state as they all had extremely severe diarrhoea and were all too weak to move.

Next to each person was a tin can or old mug and various small pieces of bread which they were carefully hoarding up, this latter lying on the floor, and when they felt like it they took a bite out of it, irrespective of what it had been lying in. Their hair, hands, faces and feet were all covered in a mixture of dry faeces and dirt. At least three-quarters of them had hacking coughs and the other quarter were just lying there. Here and there a dead person could be seen between two living ones who took no notice of her at all and just went on eating, coughing or just lying, and these were all women whose ages varied from 15–30.

We had a look at one or two patients and they were quite literally just a mass of skin and bones with sunken eyes which had a completely vacant look. They all had bites and severe scabies and some had terrible ulcers and bed-sores the size of small saucers, with no dressings on them at all.

To my relief I found that on Monday, Hut 210 had been cleaned out by the Hungarians and equipped with double-tier bunks. There was a young Polish woman doctor in charge of it and under her were six Polish women nurses. One of the nurses spoke quite good English.

The floor of the hut was clean and the hut was divided into seven rooms. In one of these lived the doctor and nurses and the others were divided up into wards, and these wards were used for typhus, post-typhus and advanced tuberculosis. There were about forty people to each room and they were lying two to a bunk, i.e. four to each double-tiered bunk, which was hopeless over-crowding. I learned that there were about 260 people in the hut and that every single one, including the doctor, had either had typhus or was having it now.

After supper, an RAMC Lieut-Colonel gave us a talk on the clinical aspects of typhus: it was very good and much appreciated. He was interrupted in the middle to say that the Germans opposite the 21st Army Group had surrendered (hence V.E. Day). All very pleased.

Saturday May 5th

I went up to the office and asked Mrs. Crossthwaite if there were any huts without any students in them. She said there were plenty. I was given Hut 217 and decided I was definitely needed there. It was smaller than the others – 30 yards x 7 yards – but it contained about 460 women. It was easily the most crowded hut I had yet seen. It was composed of one single large room with people lying, sitting and standing and standing all round the walls and also in the centre of the hut: most of the people who were very sick were lying opposite the door and along the right wall of the hut. They were lying in roughly three rows, but were all packed together head to foot, so that there was absolutely no room whatsoever between the rows.

George Woodwark showed me round Hut 216, and it certainly was the worst. In many places whole sections of the floor were missing and you squelched down into earth and God only knows what else. It was hopelessly overcrowded and faeces were even more abundant than in the other huts. George said they had pulled several bodies out from under what floorboards were left, and I could quite believe it. Was jolly glad to get out into fresh air again.

One of the most impressive things about the Camp was a pile of boots which the Germans had taken off the victims before cremating them. I don't know how many years it had taken to build up this pile, but it was about 20 yards long by about 6 yards across and about 12 feet high. The shoes at the bottom were squashed as flat as paper, so you can imagine how many thousand pairs of shoes were there, and each pair had once had an owner. Though the Germans may have destroyed all the records of this Camp, this pile of boots and shoes provided more mute but absolutely damning evidence of the number of people who had died in this camp before the British arrived, for we did not add the shoes of the 23,000 whom we buried.

This is an account of only *one* Camp, and by no means the worst. Belsen, which was built only in 1943, was not listed as an extermination camp, as for instance Treblinka where it was estimated that a minimum of 800,000–1,200,000 men, women and children died. Today there are fewer than forty survivors from Treblinka. Indeed, no book or film can recreate the unmitigated suffering.

To quote from the late Lord Russell of Liverpool, who was the deputy Judge Advocate General at the Nuremberg trials:

As the visitor passed through these places and surveyed the scene of so much suffering and tragedy, the stench of rotting bodies and the smell of burning flesh seemed to rise to his nostrils, and as he came into the clean fresh air and raised his eyes towards the heavens to clear away this haunting vision of evil, what did he see? Nailed to a pole on the crematorium roof, a little rustic nesting box for wild birds, placed there by some schizophrenic SS man.

Then and then only was it possible to understand why the nation which gave the world Goethe and Beethoven, Schiller and Schubert, gave it also Auschwitz, Buchenwald, Ravensbrück and Dachau.

All over Europe, but especially in the Central and Eastern parts, thousands of prisoners had been taken out on death marches as the Allied armies advanced. In some camps, evacuated early in 1944, the sick were left behind, but in others thousands upon thousands of them, prisoners of war included, too weak and ill to walk, were force-marched until they dropped and then shot and left by the roadside.

Each individual prisoner, regardless of age, had his or her own story of suffering. For all it is a memory that remains for ever. Though many wars have been waged since 1945 in different parts of the world and terrible oppression of one sort or another goes on, no comparison can be made with the calculated, deliberate and *official* extermination policy of the Nazis.

In her book *A Thread in the Tapestry*, Sarah Churchill quotes a remark her father, Winston, made to her one night near the end of the War: "I do not suppose that at any moment in history has the agony of the world been so great or widespread. Tonight the sun goes down on more suffering than ever before in the world."

Of the many individuals with whom I have worked, it is almost impossible to single out anybody, but I will mention here very briefly Zofia Chlewicka. The Germans murdered her husband in October 1939 and she herself worked in the Polish Resistance until she was arrested on 15 December 1942 and taken during the night to the infamous prison at Pawiak in Warsaw. She was eventually transported to the extermination camp at Majdanek, right on the main road leading out of the city of Lublin, which claimed 400,000 victims. This is how she described to me one of her experiences:

Amongst the constant transports (prisoners in cattle trucks) arriving in Majdanek from different parts of Europe, there were those bearing survivors of the Warsaw Ghetto Uprising in April 1943. I was working at that time as a nurse in Field 5 – Majdanek was divided up into five different fields and each contained 20 huts. Sinister parallel fences of electrified barbed wire surrounded each field and again the whole complex, and made a terrible impression on any passer-by. At the beginning of September of the same year we were transferred to Field 1. On 3 November, after the early morning roll-call the blocks were locked (*Blocksperre*). Double lines of SS men and women encircled the Camp and reinforcements stood in the watchtowers. From the top bunks we looked out of the very narrow high windows and saw double lines, column after column of Jews who were being marched along the long road outside Majdanek and on the perimeter to beyond the crematorium.

No less than 18,000 people were shot during the course of that day. We all lived from hand to mouth, day to day, never knowing when the next batch of us might not be selected for the gas chambers. This was true even of the prisoners allowed to work as doctors and nurses in the Revier (hospital), though without any of the drugs and proper facilities. And indeed, at 4 p.m. on that day of massacre some SS men came to the Revier to seize our Jewish physicians and nurses. An appalling scene followed as we made pathetic attempts to protect them by giving them our own ragged white coats in the vain hope that they might be spared as essential medical staff. One of the nurses, Helena (widow of a doctor), a very fair-haired young women, came up to me and shook my hand. In the tumult she said quietly: "Before I die, I want as one human being to another amongst thousands, to thank you and to say how I valued our working together as friends to comfort the sick and each other, regardless or our nationalities or religious beliefs."

During the second swoop the same afternoon the SS returned drunk and roared about, wrenching an odd thin blanket away from the sick and dying, and the night was bitterly cold. I asked one of the SS men when our doctors and nurses would return. He shouted at me: "Never".

At the height of this uproar I saw a young 14-year-old girl silhouetted in the wide doorway of the block. She was slim and beautiful in spite of

having suffered from spotted fever: she had been alone ever since her family
died. Turning to me she asked in a calm voice "Do I look very pale?"
Trying to comfort her, I said "No, but why do you ask?" "I am glad," she
replied, "because I do not want them to see that I am frightened." Then
she was taken away by the SS and the Alsatian dogs.

Of the children in just one of the thousands of camps was written:

> One of us
> Will teach these children how to sing again,
> To write on paper with a pencil,
> To do sums and multiply:
> One of us
> Is sure to survive.

These words were written by Dr Karel Fleischmann in Terezin
(Theresienstadt), an old town in Czechoslovakia which was in part a
"transit-ghetto" for Jews awaiting extermination and in part a terrible
concentration camp in which 77,297 victims are known to have died. There
is no register of the number of Jews who passed through the ghetto. The
other part of the town is surrounded by a moat and in Napoleonic times
it had been used as a fort. In these buildings the Germans kept prisoners –
of many different nationalities and creeds – in barbaric conditions, often in
cells with little or no light.

After graduating from secondary school and medical college Dr
Fleischmann became a specialist in dermatology in Ceske Budejovic,
Czechoslovakia. He devoted his free time to art and also wrote prose and
verse.

In April 1942 Karel Fleischmann was deported to Terezin where he
worked as a doctor. Most of his pictures and two volumes of his poetry
were preserved, thanks to the Resistance groups in the camps. In October
1944 he and his wife were transferred to Auschwitz where both perished in
the gas chambers.

Some of the Camp prisoners met death in tragic circumstances just before
Liberation. The Nazis were making a last desperate effort to get rid of
tens of thousands of internees from such camps as Sachsenhausen and
Ravensbrück – some were driven to death in forced marches, while others
were transported hundreds of miles in cattle trucks towards the Baltic coast
with the intention of drowning them there en masse. Some prisoners from
Neuengamme Concentration Camp near Hamburg were marched to
Lübeck and then loaded onto the *Cap Arcona,* a 10,000-ton merchantman,
and two other smaller vessels, *Thielbeck* and *Deutschland.* The *Cap Arcona*
was crammed with 4,700 people including Russian prisoners of war,
Yugoslav partisans, members of the French, Belgian and Norwegian underground movements and a number of German anti-Nazis who had survived
ten or more years in Hitler's camps. Earlier the ships had been observed by
the Royal Air Force; what the RAF did not know was that the vessels

were laden with camp prisoners, not with fleeing Nazis. Major Vaseili Bukreyev, head of the underground Resistance organisation in Neuengamme Concentration Camp, described what happened:

> As the Allied troops drew near the camp, we planned a rising. I was elected leader. Our plan misfired. On April 24th the camp was evacuated and we were marched to Lubeck, and there loaded on to various vessels.
>
> On board the *Cap Arcona* we planned to seize the ship. We organised a group of former sailors. Not far from out vessel lay a number of barges. They were loaded with prisoners from Stutthof (near Gdańsk) concentration camp. In the harbour lay German U-boats.
>
> During the night of 2 May we heard two huge explosions and frightful screams. The U-boats had torpedoed the barges laden with prisoners. Then on 3 May RAF rocket-firing Typhoons attacked the *Cap Arcona* and the vessel went up in flames and sank in shallow water.
>
> I jumped overboard and then clambered back aboard along the anchor chain. The survivors were only those who got back on the ship. Those who tried to swim ashore were shot from German boats and by U-boat cadets who lined the shore.
>
> How many people were killed that day in Neustadt bay? Probably 8,000. I waited on the scorching skeleton of *Cap Arcona*. In the evening a ship came alongside and announced that Canadian troops had reached Neustadt. A boat took us ashore. I was appointed officer-in-charge of repatriation and remained in Neustadt until August 1945.

In the afternoon of 3 May the British Liberation Army rushed ambulances to the scene and ferried those who reached the shore to the local hospital where they had to overcome opposition to get them admitted.

The "Canadians" who were reported to have occupied Neustadt were in fact troops of the British 11th Armoured Division. They did all they could for the surviving prisoners, their allies. Major Bukreyev, who took charge of the survivors, was given British battledress; others had to make do with requisitioned civilian clothes, or even with captured German naval uniforms. A few days later at an official ceremony a British squad fired a volley over the graves of those whose bodies had been washed up, and a bugle sounded the Last Post. On the shore some 9,000 people are buried in a mass grave. This grave is preserved, and on its stone the twenty-two nationalities of the dead are recorded. The British officer whose job it was to care for the living and honour the dead was Captain Pratt of the British 11th Armoured Division.

I was later to come to know some of these survivors very well when I visited and helped nurse them in the hospitals. One of them had lost the use of his right hand, had suffered severe burns and his sight had been affected during the bombing. While in a state of semi-coma he repeatedly asked for his only son, Christopher. One day some Allied soldiers stationed with a Brigade at Schleswig-Holstein were talking about this survivor and of how he had cried out for his beloved son. Someone heard them mention the name Christopher and wondered whether he himself might be the man they were referring to. He was! This led to a very moving reunion. Afterwards when his father reached England he wrote this letter:

> Dear Miss Ryder,
>   I just want to share my joy on reaching Britain. It has helped me more than all the medical treatment. Thank you for your compassion and kindness – for all that you did for so many of us. Hope to see you soon.
>
>   George

From the window of one of the offices in which I worked I could see the hull of the *Thielbeck* which was sunk approximately one mile offshore. In the late 1940s a French team brought her to the surface. They found many bodies. Some were identified by the metal disc which they wore. Mummification of a few bodies had occurred because the people had been so tightly crammed in, which had prevented total decomposition. It was a grim and tragic story, made worse by the fact that the *Thielbeck* has been put back into service.

Many years ago Ministers of the State of Schleswig-Holstein and local authorities agreed to a camping place with scores of caravans and ice-cream stalls to be sited on this same shore, *very* near the memorial . . .

Each year on the anniversary of their liberation, pilgrimages are made to the main camps by survivors from the majority of European countries who have their own clubs and associations. There are also international committees for most of the main camps with well-known chairpersons. These committees are responsible for creating memorials and museums to remember the sacrifices and heroism of those who suffered and died and to teach the present and future generations. The pilgrimages are deeply moving and create a strong feeling of friendship and fraternity, and the bonds which hold them together will never be broken.

In Poland each association holds a monthly meeting in its cities and towns. The meeting is not only a reunion but a gathering at which social and medical problems are discussed and decisions made on the best way to help each other. Many survivors have written and published their own books but, alas, few have been translated into English.

* * *

On 8 May 1945 the War in Europe was over at last. For those now returned from the battlefields, especially to devastated countries, the huge task of reconstruction was waiting. Those who fell have never been better commemorated than in some lines translated by J. Maxwell Edmonds, written on the British War Memorial to the Fourteenth Army at Kohima in Assam:

> When you go home
> Tell them of us and say
> For your tomorrow
> We gave our today

In countless parts of Europe there were very many whose "tomorrow" did not bring the fruits for which they had suffered and fought.

One of the most tragic events of the War was the forced repatriation of Soviet prisoners at the insistence of Stalin. I myself was witness to part of this tragedy in the course of my relief work; but, before recording these memories, I can do no better than to quote from Professor Martin Gilbert's account of how the decision to return these prisoners came about. In his book *In Search of Churchill,** Professor Gilbert writes:

> . . . Six months before [the conference at] Yalta [in 1945], Anthony Eden had argued in the War Cabinet in support of sending back to the Soviet Union the 1,500 former Soviet Citizens, all of whom had fought alongside the Germans, and then been held as prisoners-of-war in Britain. During the discussion that followed, Churchill said that the ambivalent position of these prisoners, as former allies of Germany, should be shown in the most "extenuating" light and, if possible, their return delayed. Four days later Churchill wrote to Eden: "Even if we are somewhat compromised, all the apparatus of delay must be used. I think these men were tried beyond their strength."
>
> In October 1944, in Moscow, Churchill told Stalin that Britain was sending back 11,000 ex Soviet prisoners-of-war, who had been captured in the West since the Normandy landings as the German military units in which they were serving had surrendered. But he pointed out to Stalin the difficulty of separating those who had fought for the Germans willingly, and those who had been forced to fight. Nevertheless, he agreed to Stalin's insistence that all captured men be sent back. When, a week later, the British Embassy in Moscow raised various procedural matters, Churchill minuted: "Are we not making unnecessary difficulties? It seems to me we work up fights about matters already conceded in principle. I thought we had arranged to send all the Russians back to Russia?"
>
> . . . Churchill went from Egypt to Yalta by plane. While he was on the journey, the War Cabinet discussed, in his absence, a Soviet proposal that any reciprocal agreement to cover "the repatriation of prisoners-of-war" "should be extended to all liberated Soviet and British subjects". The War Cabinet accepted this Soviet proposal. This meant that any Soviet citizen who was liberated in western Europe, not merely those who had fought in the German ranks or aided in some way the German policy of persecution, should be "repatriated" to the Soviet Union.
>
> Churchill took no part in this considerable widening of the repatriation agreement. Those who did included Clement Attlee, who took the chair at the meeting, and Ernest Bevin, later, as Labour's Foreign Secretary, to ensure that the agreement was carried out in its wider form.
>
> Reaching Yalta, Churchill was shown a minute by Patrick Dean [a civil servant] setting out the basic agreement. It was a reciprocal one. Several thousand British and American prisoners-of-war, liberated by the Red Army in German camps in the east, were to be repatriated to Britain and the United States. Soviet citizens captured by the advancing Western Allies

* *In Search of Churchill: A Historian's Journey*, Martin Gilbert, London, Harper Collins, 1994.

while serving in the German ranks were to be repatriated to the Soviet
Union. Churchill made no comment on the substance of the agreement.

The minutes of the discussion later that day, 10 February 1945, show the
two leaders in discussion on the issue: "The Prime Minister spoke of
the embarrassment caused us by the large number of Russian prisoners
in the west. We had about 100,000 who had already been transported
home, and 7,000 more would leave this month. He wanted to know the
Marshal's wishes about the rest. Marshal Stalin hoped that they would be
sent to Russia as quickly as possible". Stalin went on to ask, in the words
of the official note-taker, that those who were to be repatriated "should not
be ill-treated and that they should be segregated from the Germans." Stalin
added, "The Soviet Government looked upon all of them as Soviet citizens.
He asked that there should be no attempt to induce any of them to refuse
repatriation. Those who had agreed to fight for the Germans could be dealt
with on their return to Russia."

Churchill then told Stalin "that we were anxious that these prisoners
should be repatriated, and the only difficulty arose from the lack of
shipping space. As regards segregating them from the Germans this was
difficult in the first instance, but 'as soon as they were sorted out, they
would be kept separate.'" Turning to the aspect of the issue that most
concerned the British public, Churchill asked Stalin how many British
prisoners the Red Army had released during its advance. He begged for
good treatment for them: every mother in England was anxious about the
fate of her prisoner sons.

Still worried about the situation of the British prisoners, Churchill told
Stalin that "we wanted to send liaison officers to the Red Army to look
after our men". Stalin agreed. He had got what he wanted with no dispute.
Thus was concluded what was to become one of the most controversial
issues of the Yalta Agreement, the return to the Soviet Union of tens of
thousands of men, some of whom had fought actively in the German ranks
and some of whom had not; but the majority of whom were subjected on
their return to the most rigorous punishment. One author, Nikolai Tolstoy,
has estimated that twenty per cent of all those repatriated, including those
under the Yalta Repatriation Agreement, were sentenced either to death or
to twenty-five years penal servitude in labour camps; that a further twenty
per cent were given labour-camp sentences of between five and ten years;
that perhaps fifteen per cent were sent as conscript labourers to various
areas devastated by the War; and that up to twenty per cent were allowed
to return to their homes.

Stalin had been insistent at Yalta that no harm should come to the
captured men while they were still in British or American custody. His
insistence rings hollow today. Learning two months later that many of
the British prisoners-of-war liberated from German camps, but still in the
Soviet Union, were being subjected to harsh treatment by their Soviet
liberators, Churchill telegraphed to Stalin: "There is no subject on which
the British nation is more sensitive than on the fate of our prisoners in
German hands and their speedy deliverance from captivity and restoration
to their own country. I should be very much obliged if you would give the
matter your personal attention, as I am sure you would wish to do your

best for our men, as I can promise you we are doing for your men as they come into control along the Rhine."

Professor Gilbert concluded: "It was the ill-treatment of British prisoners-of-war by the Soviets, not the possible fate of Soviet citizens being repatriated, that dominated the British agenda".*

During the course of my relief work I found myself among a number of Soviet ex-prisoners-of-war and others of all ages, some of whom had seen their villages or towns looted, burned or destroyed. These people had lost everything. Many were sick and still suffering with typhus and tuberculosis. Neither the Nazis, nor the Soviets, had observed the terms of the Geneva Convention in regard to their treatment of their Soviet prisoners, and had treated them abominably. Out of a total of 13,000 Soviet prisoners taken to Auschwitz Concentration Camp, only ninety two were still alive when the Camp was liberated.

In 1945 these Soviet prisoners pleaded to have the opportunity to enjoy a new life in another country, removed from the past. Thousands of them had already experienced the worst years of Communist rule in the Soviet Union, including famine and Stalin's reign of terror, and they were terrified of what awaited them if they returned. The Allies had decided, however, on Stalin's insistence, that all of them should be repatriated.

The scenes of tragedy and sheer horror which followed in the hospitals and camps as this decision was implemented defy description. These prisoners, who had fought for their country and been captured by the Germans, had already received horrific treatment at the hands of their captors. Unfortunately, all these prisoners were regarded as traitors by Stalin merely because they had been taken prisoner.

It is estimated that Stalin and the KGB murdered 40 million Russians.

All this is even more ironic as I quote now from a personal letter from Professor Gilbert:

> . . . A minute ago I came across this enclosed, which I hasten to send you: an early repatriation document (French, not Russians).
>
> On 27 June 1940 Churchill made plans to sent about 20,000 French troops then in Britain to French North Africa, then under Vichy.
>
> In his instruction, he included the sentence:
>
> *Care must be taken that no officer or man is sent back into French jurisdiction against his will*

The late Lord Boothby regarded Yalta as one of "the greatest tragedies of the twentieth century". He called it a shameful episode – worse than Munich because, not only did we betray Czechoslovakia but Poland,

Personal Note: The politicians and the other principal participants at the Casablanca, Tehran and Yalta Conferences acceded to Stalin's wishes in regard to the repatriation of Soviet prisoners of war and they disregarded the likely fate of those who had fought honourably on the Allies' side. Thus, they ignored, too, in my opinion, the plight of the future generations who were to be born in the countries that remained shackled by the Communist system.

for whom we had gone to war, and every country in Central and Eastern Europe.

While working for a short time in one camp, I was responsible for the welfare of Soviet prisoners who had fought against the Germans as members of the Red Army or as partisans: (Count Nikolai Tolstoy records that no fewer than 8,000 joined the French Resistance, and that the Soviet authorities themselves claimed that these men inflicted 3,500 casualties on the Germans).* Many of these men pleaded with me and with a Russian social worker named Ludmilla (whom, fortunately, we managed to keep hidden and who later emigrated to the USA), to do everything in our power to protect and to hide them, as they knew well that, if repatriated, they faced execution or exile to Siberian camps. The dilemma was appalling and there seemed to be no one to whom one could appeal. For a very few of these prisoners we were able to change their names and forge false documents, carefully but with great speed, giving them a new identity and nationality, but time was against me. I myself drove them by night, hidden in an ambulance, to nearby hospitals and camps where they could mingle unrecognised with people of other nationalities. But first I had to dodge the British Military Police, praying that the prisoners would not be discovered in any search. It was hard and dangerous work, and was made more diffi- cult because they did not speak the language of the country written on their false papers.

As prisoners realised that repatriation was inevitable, some of them, with all hope gone, resorted to desperate measures. I well remember entering a wooden hut which contained a long trough with taps at intervals where people washed themselves and their clothes. It was a dark, dismal place. Hanging there were the bodies of several prisoners who had committed suicide. Their limp bodies were blessed by a Russian Orthodox priest, the late Father George, who in due course came to live in London. I remember, also, the sight of other prisoners, filled with grief too deep for tears, being herded onto trains. The memories of those awful days are heart-rending.

Anthony Eden, Tom Brimelow and Ernest Bevin lacked all compassion when dealing with the Russian repatriation, and he later wrote in reply to a letter from Lord Selborne, at that time Minister for Economic Warfare (I quote): "if these men do not go back to Russia, where can they go?"

Brigadier R. Firebrace, the liaison officer between The Mission and the War Office wrote a plaintive letter to Christopher Warner at the Foreign Office:

> You have given me a most unpleasant task as, with few exceptions, the men, whether claiming Soviet or Polish nationality, protest violently at being sent back to the Soviet Union or even to their homes in Poland. A large number insisted on giving reasons for their wishes not to go back and related with wealth of detail their experiences in the Soviet Union or in Poland after the entry of the Red Army. There was one long story of

* *Victims of Yalta*, Nikolai Tolstoy, Hodder & Stoughton, 1977.

shootings, arrests, ill-treatment and deportation of families. They stated that they did not want to return to a land where these things were allowed and where a man had no rights. There were cases of Kulaks' [private farmers] sons who had been chased from pillar to post and one young man stated that he had been in prison from the age of twelve until released to join the Red Army. Most of them said that they preferred death to returning to the Soviet Union and some even invited the British to shoot them in preference to handing them over. I have never in my like seen such human misery or such despair.

Thousands upon thousands was repatriated by ship and trucks or cattle wagons either to be executed immediately or interred long years in labour camps, where intense cold, hunger and disease made life an unending hell.

Probably some 400,000 Russians were forcibly repatriated and most had an appalling death. I quote from Lord Bethell's book:* "And as for these wretched prisoners, it was not suggested that Stalin would punish them on mass, by the million? Such an idea seemed absurd." Those who did not meet and try to comfort these Russians could not or did not want to hear this horrendous and shocking story.

British troops, many hardened by years of fighting in the 8th Army in the desert followed by Sicily and Italy were sickened by the tasks they faced. An English officer wrote (again I quote from Lord Bethell's book):

"You might have been in a hell of a battle during the day, you might have captured a position, but when the prisoners started coming in you didn't just cut them down. You'd be much more likely to give the man a cigarette. After all, he'd given himself up and that was the end of it." He was horrified to think that men who had surrendered voluntarily and who had been accepted as prisoners-of-war were being sent to their deaths. The idea was unsoldier-like.

Such feelings were held even more strongly by the soldiers whose unpleasant duty it was to escort the trains into Soviet territory. One unit which did this in the early days was the 2nd Battalion, London Irish Rifles. The Battalion's Commanding Officer, Lieutenant-Colonel (later Major-General) H.E.N. Bredin, remembers receiving orders that all Russian prisoners were to be repatriated and being surprised at how vehemently these men protested that their return to the Soviet Union was impossible. At first his men were irritated by the frantic complaints and the wild stories of what was likely to happen. He recalls some of his men telling the Cossacks not to be silly and not to exaggerate. Bredin says: "The dear old British soldier at that time could not believe that such things were likely to happen. But then our men went to Russia as guards on trains, and it wasn't until the first troop came back that we heard that prisoners were being taken away and shot." Bredin did not himself see such incidents but, he says,

I spoke to people who had seen prisoners being shot and I think there was clear evidence that shootings took place. Anyway, my men were quite sure of it and we heard enough about it to be sure that it was

*The Last Secret, Nicholas Bethell, Andre Deutsch, 1974.

not the sort of thing that we ought to be having a hand in. We also got reports that there were suicides on the trains, people jumping off or cutting their throats with bits of broken windowpane. A fairly serious situation arose with the soldiers very nearly getting to a point of saying, "Sorry, sir, we won't obey your orders. We will not take these men to where they are just being mown down without any sort of trial."

The London Irish was a seasoned, hardened regiment. There were 300 men in Bredin's battalion who held the Africa Star and 200 who had twice been wounded in battle. It was most unusual for such men to make representations to their commanding officer in this way. Bredin cannot remember it happened at any other time during the War. "They'd seen plenty of carnage during the War, but this was one thing they would not put up with," he says. He consulted his subordinate officers, who confirmed the seriousness of the problem, as well as a few of the German officers, now prisoners-of-war, who had commanded Cossack units. He particularly remembers one of the latter, who spoke perfect English, telling him before repatriation began, "I don't know if you realise it, but these Cossacks will be cold meat as soon as they're off your train."

On 20 February, the Pope Pius XII published an allocution protesting against "the repatriation of men against their will and the refusal of the right of asylum". Senior Vatican officials told American reporters that the Yalta policy was "a betrayal of the morality and ideas for which the Allies fought" and "against humanity and justice". The Vatican claimed to possess information that when the Russians arrived home "only too often they end up in Siberia." Many of these Russians had fought for the Germans, the Vatican admitted, but "whether they did or did not, they are treated alike." This information was correct.

Some Polish friends of mine who had been imprisoned in Ravensbrück Concentration Camp were horrified when they were "liberated" by the Red Army to see Soviet women and girl prisoners forcibly separated from them and taken away by their fellow countrymen.

For at least sixteen years after the War no Russian survivor attended our annual pilgrimage to Ravensbrück (apart from those who had been in the Red Army). One year, therefore, my friends and I were greatly surprised to see three or four Russian women whom they remembered as prisoners in the Camp, but these women completely ignored us. The following year these women again attended the pilgrimage and this time my friends managed to meet them in secret. It was then they learned that the Russian women had been forcibly transported to Soviet prisons and concentration camps. The brief discussion my friends had with these Soviet ex-prisoners was very poignant; they said that they had never forgotten the friendships they had made in Ravensbrück nor all they had learned from other prisoners, especially about God, which had helped to give them the strength of will and the determination to remain alive in their further terrible years of captivity and isolation after the War.

Occasionally, my duties included escorting Russian repatriation officers, and on one of these excursions the officer, who belonged to one of the Soviet Military Missions, attended a meeting held in a huge vaulted cellar in the barrack. Only a table divided the officer and myself from the people he was addressing, who included Estonians, Latvians, Lithuanians, and Poles from eastern Poland. On hearing that they would receive a safe passage home they took the officer to task about the millions who had been deported and had disappeared. On receiving no satisfactory explanation, their fury erupted into uproar and, if it had not been for a window with loose grating behind us which provided a means of escape he would most certainly have been lynched. As it was, his vehicle was overturned and burned. Such was the feeling of bitterness in that camp as in many others in regard to forced repatriation.

There were known to a few of us small, secret billets or hiding places where a few surviving members of the Russian aristocracy, and intellectuals from the Baltic States, were in hiding. To these people I tried to take what rations I could scrounge and to give them some moral support. One afternoon, after mounting a dark staircase, in dire need of repair, I knocked softly on the door of the hiding place of the last Lithuanian Prime Minister. Inside, I could hear continuous sobbing. On giving my name, the door was opened an inch or two and the Prime Minister's wife told me that her husband had been kidnapped by the KGB a few hours earlier. She was distraught with grief and despair, knowing well the fate that awaited him and that he would never be heard of again; this, unfortunately, proved to be the case.

The Poles who were repatriated after fighting with the Allies in the West were all known to the KGB and were blacklisted. Huge numbers of men, women and children who had been members of the Home Army (AK) were also blacklisted. Many who were repatriated from Britain were arrested as soon as they arrived at a Polish port. Others, who were searching among the ruins of Poland's towns and cities in the hope of getting news of the whereabouts of their families, were also arrested. The majority, when news reached them of the fate that had befallen comrades on their return home, had rapidly to change their names and to carry false documents – as they had in the War – and even then they were in constant fear of arrest and were compelled to keep on the move.

Some Poles who worked with me in relief teams simply vanished – at one moment I would be working with them examining patients and helping to provide relief (some medicine or a little food from our meagre supplies) only to turn round and find that someone had disappeared and was never likely to be seen or heard of again. Although people had thought they were "safe" living under the new identity given to them in their forged documents, and had succeeded in evading arrest, incidents like this and the sudden arrests continued up to the time of Stalin's death in 1953.

None of us who had any connection with the Polish Section of SOE during the War were safe in Poland and I was tipped off in 1949–50 that it was foolish and dangerous to remain in Poland despite my altered identity. It is estimated – though not substantiated – that a minimum of 50,000 Poles disappeared between 1945 and 1953. Most of those who had been in prisons made notorious by cruelty and torture during the War were sentenced by the Soviet authorities to terms of terrible imprisonment ranging from eight to fifteen years, where cruelty knew no bounds.

*   *   *

I was twenty-two then, but knew what dehumanisation was: I had seen what happened to people when everything, even their hair, was taken from them, and their minds and bodies subjugated until some could only crawl on all fours or lie in silence.

After the War ended the German Government introduced compensation laws for those who had survived the Nazi extermination and concentration camps. Very many survivors did not apply as the offer was £15 for each month they had spent there and the humiliation of answering often impertinent questions put to them in the courts brought back too many harrowing memories. This also applied to the few War crimes courts. My Mama worked tirelessly in her efforts to help the survivors and gathered over 20,000 signatures from people all over Britain showing their indignation at the Germans' attitude. She was also well aware that the Japanese offered meagre compensation, and were unwilling and refused to apologise, or acknowledge their crimes, or to inform and educate any of their people or children.

A friend in SOE who served both in Europe and the Far East was cruelly killed by the Japanese; eventually his decapitated body was found.

His parents later had this engraved on his headstone:

> Write on the stone no word of sadness,
> Only the gladness due,
> That we, who asked the most of living,
> Knew how to give it too

and another friend, Julian Tennyson:

> Morning he knew and Spring,
> And the promise of life,
> But never high noon or the fulfilment
> But having great gifts he gave – gladly

Years later I had long conversations with Father Rorke SJ who came to say Mass at Christmas here at Headquarters. He was a prisoner-of-war of the Japanese and said that during all his ordeals and after the War he prayed hard and constantly to bring himself as a Christian to forgive but *never* to forget. Father's voice broke and he sobbed as he told me about the atrocities and the scale of the appalling suffering.

He spoke too, of the thousands and thousands of women and children who were treated with indescribable cruelty in Malaysia, Indonesia and elsewhere – dying in terrible conditions of starvation and of diseases such as beri beri, typhoid and dysentery. Most have no known grave or memorial.

It is only now after all these years that documents in the Public Record Office at Kew have been published, and we see how the Japanese War criminals were let off so leniently.

A young twenty-five-year-old, Lieutenant-Colonel Pat Spooner, was responsible for locating War criminals, first in Indonesia, then in Burma and, finally, in charge of all Britain's War crimes investigation teams in the Far East. With a team of British officers and any number of British, Dutch, Indian, and other assistants, his units debriefed released prisoners, or at least those not in such bad shape that they had to be immediately repatriated. They toured remote villages for witnesses and created and stored the paperwork the burgeoning exercise produced.

The main problem was actually tracking down the suspects. There was no lack of evidence of the crimes, but the Japs had been on the move for two or three years. Some were dead, some had returned to Japan. Several of the Kempeitai, the notorious secret police, had managed to escape by masquerading as Red Cross workers.

Western witnesses, many of whom were very ill, were often unable to distinguish between their torturers. Nevertheless, over the ensuing two years, systems were worked out that eventually led to the prosecution of 889 criminals in more than 300 trials.

Mr Spooner's experiences give him a peculiar insight into Japanese atrocities. He saw their results at first hand, and yet had to develop the detachment required of a professional investigator. He said:

> "One became extraordinarily immune to these stories of atrocities. Some were truly horrific. I never really knew why they carried out water torture, where they piped water into people's stomachs and jumped on them.
> "The worst I think they did was using prisoners as bayonet practice. That, for me, was the depth of depravity."

Mr Spooner supports those who desire compensation for the wrongs they suffered and said he would find it hard to forgive the many crimes committed. Now he feels that the most important thing the Japanese could do by way of reparation is to teach their children the truth about their country's War record. He feels that the young generation do now have a realisation that something was radically wrong with their elders' generation.

No one mentioned the outcome of his work. He was aware that a halt had been called to the trials in 1948, leaving possibly 100,000 suspects free to leave prison, including 9,000 in British custody. Soon afterwards those convicted were released, to the amazement of many. As Mr Spooner commented:

"All the efforts that we made to bring some, only a small proportion,
of those who committed War crimes to justice, well it just makes me
incandescent.

"The American administration in Japan were understandably concerned
that the Japanese would get drawn into the Communist camp, but you can
understand the feelings of those of us who worked there, in what were very,
very difficult conditions, to bring these people to justice."

Hundreds of convicted Japanese War criminals were freed early by British
and Allied Governments after intense Japanese lobbying, according to
research unveiled in 1996. Of almost 800 Japanese convicted by British War
crimes courts, 220 were executed. But documents show that the remainder,
including many involved in the torture and murder of prisoners, were
released within eleven years.

On the 50th Anniversary to commemorate VJ (Victory over Japan) far
more publicity was given to this. The fifty-years ban had been lifted, which
enabled writers and those involved to know the truth about the attitude of
the American and British Governments.

Recent media attention and the previous Prime Minister, John Major's,
visit to Japan, prompted many enquiries and indeed further represention
to Government for recompense in the form of additional compensation.
Since the emotive period during the PM's visit, both media and Far East
Prisoner of War (FEPOW) correspondence has waned. However, it is
perhaps advisable to be armed with relevant current information should the
subject of compensation for FEPOW's become a focus again.

The question of compensation was settled in the 1951 Treaty of Peace
with Japan, following which the Allied Powers accepted that the Japanese
had fully discharged their obligations.

In the Treaty, Japan agreed to pay reparations to the Allied States
(including the UK) for "damage and suffering caused by it during the War".
The UK received a sum of £3,005,321. The British Government decided to
share this among former Far Eastern prisoners of war, or their dependants,
and civilians held by the Japanese, or their dependants, who made claims
to the Government. The Japanese Government also undertook to compensate "members of the armed forces of the Allied Powers who suffered undue
hardships while prisoners of war of Japan". A sum of £4.5 million was
paid, of which the UK's share came to £1,636,281. A further £174,871 was
contributed by the Thai Government in respect of the Burma–Siam railway.
These sums were also made available to former Far Eastern prisoners of
war and their dependents.

The total received by the UK for compensation was therefore £4,816,473.
The compensation was paid to claimants in instalments between 1952 and
1956. Approximately 50,000 former Far Eastern prisoners of war, or their
dependants, received the equivalent of £76.50 each. About 8,800 former
civilian internees, or their dependants, received the equivalent of £48.50
each. The level of compensation was less than the Government would have

wished for, but at the time the British Government and the other Allied States did not wish to repeat the mistakes of the Versailles Treaty with Germany at the end of the First World War.

Successive British Governments have taken the view that the Treaty obligations which were entered into in 1951 preclude any further formal approach to the Japanese Government on this issue. The Government is very much aware that many of those who were prisoners of the Japanese remain bitter about their experiences and the level of compensation that they received. During the Japanese Prime Minister's visit to London in 1992, the Prime Minister drew the attention of Mr Miyazawa to the concern some people in Britain still feel about this particular subject. The Japanese Government have also made occasional expressions of regret on the issue.

The Allies should have insisted that *both* the German and the Japanese Governments paid compensation *within the shortest possible time. Alas, the Allies totally failed to do this.*

More than 3,000 veterans have died in the last two years alone, as the compensation battle has slowly ground a path through British apathy and Japanese stubborness.

I now have permission to quote from *The Times*, Monday, 21 August, 1995:

HONOUR DUE

THE LAST GREAT LINE UNDER THE GREATEST WAR

With yesterday's church parades and sunset ceremonies, Britain finally honoured the veterans of its victory over Japan. And as the old soldiers marched away behind their flags down the Mall, and at services from Wick to Belfast, the United Kingdom once again worked its peculiarly intuitive but disciplined magic of solemn commemoration, ceremonial and celebration.

There has been recrimination and bitterness in recent weeks. Cries of anger have mingled with calls for compensation to create a sense that this was a War that would never end while its fighters lived. These veterans were, in fact, never wholly without honour. As they marched for their day in the sun, the clink of their VCs, George Crosses, and other medals for high gallantry and endurance above and beyond the call of modern imagination proved that. The Burma Road and the Chindits, Kohima and Imphal, were already written on the national roll of honour beside the Battle and Alamein, Waterloo and Agincourt. But this weekend they were formally and fully unveiled.

The men and women of the Burma campaign, and other theatres in the Pacific War, have always taken a perverse pride in their epithet as "forgotten army". By the time they were demobbed and came home in 1946, Britain had moved onto the new challenges of the postWar world and wanted to forget the horrors that were still so fresh. But the pride of the old soldiers has demanded proper public honour for their bravery and sufferings and open homage to those of their comrades who died. Yesterday and on Saturday they received that due.

At beating the retreat and lowering of the Commonwealth Flags on Horse Guards Parade last Night, the Queen spoke for all her peoples when she recalled the qualities that brought them through those terrible years: "The courage, the comradeship and, above all, the sense of common purpose. They are still with us, and we must cherish them, for they have served us well down the centuries."

The Duke of Edinburgh, too, caught the spirit of this last and greatest church parade, when he decided to march with the veterans of the Burma Star because he wanted to give the salute rather than receive it. At the drumhead at Wick, the Queen Mother, whose brother in the Black Watch was killed in the 1914–18 War, embodied the pride and sacrifice of the astonishing mixture of tribal loyalties that go to make up Britishness. After the Last Post and two minutes silence, in which even the traffic of London fell quiet, the throaty roar of the Lancaster bomber aimed as straight as a pathfinder down the Mall recovered the lost world of fifty years ago more powerfully than words. The million poppies it dropped were halo for the veterans before a carpet for the crowds.

For celebration there were fireworks over the Thames, visible and audible from the outermost suburbs. And the pipes and drums and steel bands. And the marching of the less celebrated heroes, the Bevin Boys and the Women's Land Army, the fire brigades, the Home Guard and the Girl Guides. And then those old trucks and the jeeps, the great British eccentric parades, and all the antique engines of the War that helped to win the victory.

So the nation formally honoured its veterans. But the chief honour was done by the veterans themselves, boys grown old men whose fierest and finest hour came fifty years ago. There will never be such a parade of pride and honour, remembrance and celebration of comrades, again. Prophets see no future War that will last as long or engage so many people. This weekend drew the last great line under the greatest era and gave due honour to worthy pride and inconsolable grief."

It is now time again to ask whether the same urgent sense of unity, purpose and ability to work, that had carried us through to victory in War, could be continued in peacetime, lest we should fail the generations who have died or the children who would be born in the years to come. We who remain must always be responsible for their future.

PART THREE
Post-War Relief Work

7

After a Famous Victory

IN 1942 I HAD volunteered to do relief work in Poland and elsewhere in Europe when I could be released from SOE duties. Thus, after the War, I found myself in the ruins of Poland and also for a very short time in Normandy.

In 1945 the conditions of – and for – relief work in the battle areas of Europe were very difficult. Communications were in a state of chaos, and everywhere was to be seen the material wreckage of total war. With colleagues, I continued to work through whole regions which proved that with calculated destructiveness man can far out-do any earthquake.

The relief units, severally and collectively, were financed by *Amis Volontaires Français* (AVF). They were tiny in relation to the problems challenging them. One of the first units was assigned to operate over the worst devastated areas of Normandy.

Few knew of, or gave credit to, the Poles who fought with such valour on all fronts (except the Far East), including Normandy and far beyond, right into Germany.

Their 1st Armoured Division, formed by General Maczek,* was composed of soldiers who, after defending their own country, escaped by many different routes from Poland to fight before the fall of France. The survivors later escaped again to land in Britain and to defend the coast of Scotland in 1940 in the event of a German invasion.

On 7 August 1944, two months after the Allied invasion of Normandy, the Germans launched a counter-attack in the direction of Avranches, in the hope of destroying the Armies which had broken out of the beach head. Suddenly aware of their danger, the German forces (some 70,000) tried to disengage and force a way back through the remaining outlets.

On 15 August General Maczek's tanks crossed the river Dives at two points north-east of Falaise and went on to cut one of the three remaining German escape routes. There followed an inferno of death and destruction as the enemy tried to hammer a way through the sector held by the Poles, and the Allies launched salvo after salvo of bombs and shells onto the German Seventh Army's men, tanks, guns and vehicles.

* General Maczek was unable to repatriate in 1945 as his home in Lwow had been given to the Soviet Union, and he remained in Scotland, but received no pension from the British and worked as a part-time barman.

Though other Allied units, principally the 2nd Canadian Corps, were approaching as fast as possible, the Poles were virtually isolated as the 1st Adolph Hitler and 12th SS Hitlerjugend Divisions, fighting with the desperation of the doomed, launched repeated attacks. As tank fought tank at close range and men engaged in hand-to-hand struggles, the Poles were running short of food and ammunition and their wounded could not be evacuated. Not until 21 August was the pressure relieved. *The Daily Telegraph* correspondent, H.D. Ziman, writing on the day, described the battle:

> The entire German force, with supporting infantry, bore down on the Poles, who were temporarily out of touch with their allies on either flank.
> The Poles stood their ground. Compelled to face about – for the enemy force had approached them in their rear as well – and with both their flanks exposed, they fought back all day against the Germans, who emerged in wave after wave from the cover provided by the forest of Gouffen.
> After six days of dogged fighting the Poles had taken 5,000 prisoners, including a general and 140 officers. In the Falaise "pocket" as a whole, the German losses amounted to 50,000 prisoners, 10,000 dead, and the equipment of an entire army.

* * *

From the devastation of Normandy we later were told to go into the Pas de Calais, Belgium and beyond, as might be necessary. We were to bring urgently needed succour to all who required it, regardless of age or condition, and to help all those suffering from hunger, disease, distress and strain.

General de Gaulle had given his blessing to the small unit to which I was attached – a rare occurrence, for he did not allow France, because of her pride, to accept help from the United Nations Relief and Rehabilitation Administration (UNRRA).

I was told to collect a lorry in London loaded with paraffin lamps and stoves, supplies of benzyl benzoate for the treatment of scabies, drugs for tuberculosis and typhoid, syringes, blankets and pillows. And with all this on board, the lorry broke down in Vauxhall Bridge Road. A most untypical London taxi driver stuck his head out of his cab window as he passed, not to offer assistance but to suggest, rather luridly, that the lorry was past helping. However, with the aid of passers-by, I pushed it into the gutter, got out the tools, replaced the sparking plugs, cleaned the carburettor and the petrol pump, and was soon off again.

Then I crossed to Dieppe, to find that there was nobody to meet me. No map was available and petrol was scarce, but I had been given vague directions to go to "the hospital near the Cathedral in Rouen". I reached the ruins of the City in darkness and asked the way from a Frenchman, who replied wryly, "There once were several hospitals". He directed me to one of the few that had not been destroyed. There, to my relief, I found the other workers. They, too, had been dispatched from England with the sketchiest of briefs, and after a stormy Channel crossing in a tank-carrying craft, had landed well off their routes.

From the first moment when I decided to do relief work I had wished to work with the people of the country, under the guidance of the ministries and local authorities; the experience which lay before me is one which I shall never forget or cease to be thankful for.

The members of the teams were usually divided into groups of two and billeted in the simplest accommodation, thus sharing the conditions of the local population. Rouen was only the first of many widely dispersed bases for the unit's mission, and my memory is of an almost continuous succession of very testing road journeys, some short, some long, so varied in their destinations and nature that to attempt to describe them would be very difficult indeed. Yet isolated memories live very vividly in my mind, amongst them driving by night in strange, ruined towns with no street-lighting; and after a while learning how to navigate by smell – the different smells of open sewers, choked drains, decomposing bodies not yet recovered from the ruin. The ruins themselves became memorable and useful as landmarks or signposts as did the relics of a street lamp, of a charred wall, of a sagging roof truss, or the shell of a church or a tall fragment of spire. Rightly, even amidst these conditions the French police insisted upon us passing a driving test and fitting direction lights high up on the vehicle. Consequently, when we had to adjust or replace them, it proved quite difficult. During the driving tests we could be directed by the instructors to drive any type of vehicle up to 15 tons, regardless of the fact that we might not be acquainted with its make, and also to prove we could to keep it under control on special skid pads. As a FANY, I had to do all the maintenance on the vehicles I drove.

In a pencilled letter home I wrote:

> St Lo has been 75% destroyed and Caen, after enduring 73 days of bombardment and fighting, has been reduced to ruins, but Bayeux Cathedral, with its glorious stained glass windows, is undamaged.
>
> From 4th June up to the end of August 1944 there were 37,000 Allied dead. I am reminded of the French poet who wrote ". . . sad sobs of Autumn." I feel, indeed, among those who have given their young lives for us to cherish Freedom.

Tuberculosis was widespread, and efforts to bring it under control were high on the unit's list of priorities. But the menace of other epidemics was also great; we were trying to cope with over twenty diseases, including cholera. This was partly because diseases that were less familiar, and for which the available antidotes were little known by the general population, had come with the survivors from concentration camps, in particular, typhus, typhoid, and associated illnesses.

All around, the bodies of the dead still lying beneath the ruins were a potential source of infection, especially cholera. As almost everywhere in Europe, local authorities organised groups to search for them, and one naturally helped in this macabre but essential operation. When possible, we wore masks over our faces and just hoped that the dirt and dust would keep out of our eyes.

My colleague was a nurse. The two of us were based in what remained of a General Hospital near Villers Bocage – in the lush country which had been the scene of prolonged and fierce fighting, totally unsuitable for tank warfare. A thin partition divided our extremely small room, where we could just get in two camp beds and an upturned box for a table, from that of the obstetrician, and we were often disturbed at night by nursing nuns who came to his door to announce an imminent birth. Details of the girl or woman in labour were given in rapid French, but often the obstetrician was very tired and loath to get up, understandably enough, as he was sometimes called up nine or ten times in one night. The nuns would then appeal to the nurse and me to persuade him to come. If he had already fallen asleep again, we would try to rouse him tactfully, and if we did not succeed, we would go back to the nuns to offer our assistance. Due to the terrible conditions the mothers-to-be experienced during pregnancy, some miscarried their babies. To see a tiny stillborn baby filled us all with sadness and reminded me of the ghastly experiments I had seen elsewhere when the Nazis had aborted babies for medical experiments. The theatre sister, named Agnes, I remember, had a beautiful face and a very remarkable serenity.

Before the devastation, the Hospital had its own Psychiatric Department, but this had been moved to the block where the obstetrician, my companion and I were accommodated. So, in addition to the pleas of the nuns to the obstetrician, there were distractions from psychiatric patients. One, nicknamed "Shaky Saul", was also suffering from Parkinson's disease and was for ever coming to our window, with his friend "Leering Laurie", asking for *megots* (cigarette ends).There was a shortage of ambulances, and one night, when an emergency call came and there was no one else to help, I took Saul and Laurie as stretcher bearers. I remember having to go up a long flight of stairs in the dark with no electricity to find the patient, and the consequent difficulty of getting her down to safety in their inexperienced hands without the stretcher being tilted.

Another nurse I worked with was Elizabeth O'Neill. Betty, as she was known, was born in Australia of Irish parents. She trained in Melbourne and worked in Paris at the American Hospital before the War. During the occupation she was arrested but got away, and immediately started organising false papers in order to evade arrest by the Gestapo. She was highly qualified and a skilled midwife. Some of her knowledge she passed onto me and I enjoyed working with her. She wrote later:

> I think you will remember those beautifully knitted things, including babies' and small children's clothes which I had not seen in Britain for years. Anyway, it was all marvellous and the heaps of syringes and surgical supplies which you and I had to sort out and label, to say nothing of the enormous containers of Benzol and Benzoate which we used to swab down

from head to foot the myriads of scabies infected children. Their feet were
so dirty that they had to be bound up in turpentine-soaked bandages for a
while before they could be washed. Poor little things! they only had disin-
fected hovels or places to return to. In spite of it all, as we set out early
each morning it seemed a new and wonderful experience meeting so many
splendid people.

Years later, I received the following from "B", another friend:

I think you should mention Betty's feelings on the importance of giving
instructions – in a very clear practical way (in French, of course) – to
prevent the spread of infectious diseases; to boil water and never ignore any
sign of infection in a wound; to instruct mums on pre-natal care, more
especially as their living conditions are so awful.

After leaving relief work in 1946 Betty was asked to return to the American
Hospital in Paris, and in 1950 she accepted the post of Nursing Superior
there, where she remained until her retirement in 1967 when she went to
live in Limerick.

On the 20 October 1994, I received the following letter from a niece of "B":

Sadly I am writing to let you know that my aunt, Bertha Cass ("B") has
passed away very peacefully at the age of 103. Her mind was very active
and lucid to the end and when she spoke of her nursing career she always
mentioned the time she spent with you, the mobile units and the children
in the ruins.

I shall miss her as I visited her on a weekly basis for many years.

I have asked for donations in her memory to be sent to you, so these
should reach you in due course.

I trust you are keeping fit and well,

Kind regards
Patricia Woodhouse (Mrs)

A friend in Britain sent me an advertisement from *The Times* which read:
"Can anyone visit the wayside grave of my son?" It gave a rough location,
and I was able to do this. We kept a list of early temporary burial places as
well as of graves in Allied cemeteries. I received a moving note back from
the mother telling me that she had known others who had visited the slums
in the Leeds area before the War, and had been indirectly connected with
my family.

On call with the women of the Croix Rouge (Red Cross) I drove a mobile
clinic. In convoy the girls tended to drive fast, regardless of the potholes,
and the locker doors at the back of the converted 5-ton truck, previously
used in the Blitz on London, used to fly open until I secured them more
firmly. Their leader was strict, and once rightly reprimanded me for not
wearing the uniform correctly. I realised that it was not complete, as I was
not wearing a forage cap and, having always taken a pride in my uniform
(in all, I wore it for over twenty years), I felt ashamed and readily agreed
that no uniform is complete without its appropriate headgear.

Morale was very high, and this was important, for conditions were harsh. Amongst the memories I recall is sharing the roughest accommodation with eight girls of the Croix Rouge: we slept and ate in a stable, and washed at a tap in the yard, and there was only an earth closet which offered no privacy.

Ambulance calls were organised on a rota system, but some of the girls were not as disciplined as one or two of us thought desirable, particularly given the demands on their time. One night a call came and the girl whose turn it was to go out did not have her ambulance parked by the exit at the back of the narrow yard. At that moment another girl, who was sleeping in the rear of the van I used, lit a paraffin stove to warm up some cold tea, having come in late. In the darkness and the excitement of trying to get the ambulances reversed, the stove upset and the flames spread. We ran from the doss room to the pump in the yard only to find there was no water. However, between us we succeeded in extinguishing the fire by using the water in a jerry can which I always kept in reserve and by applying an old blanket to smother the flames.

There were always dejected queues of adults and children to be vaccinated, and queues of sick people waiting for injections. We had to search for water and then carry it back in buckets or in whatever was available. We also had to disinfect groups of people standing in the ruins or in the middle of open fields and to dip children like sheep before they were sent to improvised or already overcrowded hospitals.

We got absolutely sodden through with perspiration and rain. Our uniforms clung to us and we could even feel them shrinking. We had squelchy boots and filthy socks. We wondered whether they would ever dry out. Could we ever become free of dirt and lice, and shine again as clean people?

In all the places and hospitals to which the unit was attached we heard the same story of suffering that could have been prevented or at least eased if only the right drugs had been available, if only the appropriate instruments had been at hand. Amongst our basic kit we carried: plaster of Paris dressings; slings; bandages; splints; stethoscope; rubber sheets; rings; sphygmomanometer; opthalmoscope; auriscope; thermometer; enemas; catheters; intravenous drips; blood transfusion sets; sterilising kit, including tablets (formalin etc.); oxygen cylinders and masks. I would stress that there were no plastic materials, so all glass, metal and rubber had to be re-sterilized after use. In cases of cholera, sheets had to be hung out after being dipped in carbolic acid.

When there are too few beds available it is always very hard to decide between the rival claims of a terminal patient and those of an "acute" case for whom treatment, if an accurate diagnosis were to be made, might prove effective. It is harder still where proper facilities for diagnosis are lacking. "If only we could get hold of a microscope we could do blood tests . . . if only we had a lab!"

At Caen, the beautiful mediaeval town that had been almost razed to the ground, there were some nights when we had to sleep in a brothel. It was in Caen that I admired the gesture of a girl in her twenties, whose husband had been killed. A group of German prisoners had been detailed to help clear a small section of the debris. They told the girl they had little food and kept begging her to give them some, and she brought them her own small ration of bread, which they accepted. I did not admire the prisoners, who received parcels from the International Red Cross and had better rations than many of the French. Later, in Lübeck, and in various other parts of Europe, I again saw the very people whom the Nazis had most tortured and humiliated offering food to German prisoners of war, and many German soldiers told me that during the campaign in Russia it was from Russians, and Poles too, that the German POWs had received help, in spite of their own indescribable suffering.

We soon developed a liking for the dehydrated bananas and powdered milk (sent out from England by Headquarters) and swapped our allowance of Camembert cheese for croissants. But often we ate potatoes while on the rounds, served on rare occasions in a chateau, on a separate plate as a main dish. There was also, occasionally, the limited luxury of a long French loaf to pull at. We used to make up menus and dream of what we would best like to eat. An important morale booster was a hairset for eight cigarettes. There was no shampoo, so very poor quality soap was used, and hair had to be dried in front of the open door of the oven. As in Poland, parts of Holland and other occupied countries, hairpins were scarce and if any were dropped they were always picked up from the floor. On a shop counter there was the occasional glimpse of a bottle of Dior or Chanel perfume, selling at an exorbitant price. However, sometimes a kind assistant would let me sniff at an empty bottle.

There were nights when sleep was not possible, but we got into a rhythm of work and when tiredness seemed about to take over we often found a "second wind". I remember snoozing on my feet.

During this period, for a very short while, I made one of my attempts to keep a diary. It survives on a few dog-eared scraps of restaurant paper. This extract is typical:

> Long loaves, berets, clogs and black pinafores. Shawled figures through the market. Garbage tins, potholes and mud. Fat men eating cabbage and labourers drinking Calvados. Women in widows' clothes with sallow complexions, hair piled high. The clip-clop of sabots on the cobbled courtyard. Cupboards with costly cosmetics. The subdued voice of a woman offering forbidden goods. Selfish farmers, oblivious to want and despair. Black market butter and Camembert cheese, hake and crab sold on filthy barrows, hours wasted in idle chatter. Gesticulations and hand-shaking: "Ca va bien?" The prevalence of the bourgeois.
>
> Fleas in the beds and tins of DDT. Water frozen in the jug and a threadbare carpet. Reckless drivers, oblivious of danger. Covered carts hogging the road, overcrowded hovels. Milk given out in shelled barns

to crowds of curious children. Swastikas scrawled on buildings; slogans written overnight on walls. Germans detonating mines. Straw mattresses and small boys vomiting; the smell of vaccine. Tussles with corsets to get them undone. The smooth touch of benzyl on scabied skin. Cognac on lumps of sugar. Doctors, unshaven and distraught. Flacons in canvas bags and bubbling test tubes. Overcrowded rooms with windows closed and the squalls and screams of babies. The girls of the Croix Rouge in limp, creased aprons. Truckloads of the Boche driving to the docks. The noise and dirt of cranes moving. Field grey uniforms and gaunt faces under peaked caps. Familiar divisional signs on rusted armoured cars. The remains of dead bodies in burnt out tanks.

Midnight Mass in a martyred church. Bells tolling from battered belfries. Old chateaux and the sound of owls at night in overgrown gardens. A flying bomb site almost obliterated by nature. The expanse of solitary grass and rows and rows of little regimental crosses stretching beyond the eye's comprehension: Pte J.C. Hawkins, 1st Black Watch, X KIA 17.6.44.

The mocked defiance of a German 88 mm still hidden in its camouflage. The strange, sad, shocked silence of these scenes by moonlight. Derelict landing craft. Seagulls crying. Torn clothing on barbed wire. Green mounds in mine-fields marking the place of the dead. POWs digging graves and lowering shrouds on stretchers. Notices that hang drunkenly from broken hinges in unexpected places: "Out of Bounds", "Water not drinkable", "Rear HQ – DR's entrance", "Canadian Signals on Left", "Rauchen Verboten" (Smoking Forbidden).

The remains of twisted girders and the quiet solemnity of Bayeux Cathedral. The gracious movement of nuns in the cloisters chanting their prayers and psalms like bees buzzing on a summer evening.

Official meetings in flag-draped halls. Rats gnawing beneath floorboards. Cattle trucks marked "pour 20 hommes", human export for the Reich. Concentration camp survivors wearing dirty striped jackets . . .

On the outskirts of Falaise the road was littered with evidence of the German retreat – smashed tanks and useless, twisted ammunition. In the middle of it was a flattened Mosquito which had been shot down, the painted nickname *Just Jam* glared in the sunlight on its side. A woman living in part of a small, damp cellar said: "We'd seen the writing on the wall, but we never thought it would come to this."

There were people all over the country living like her in corners of cellars and in very bad conditions. She symbolised millions of men, women and children in many countries who, despite their circumstances, retained a supreme sense of courage and humour.

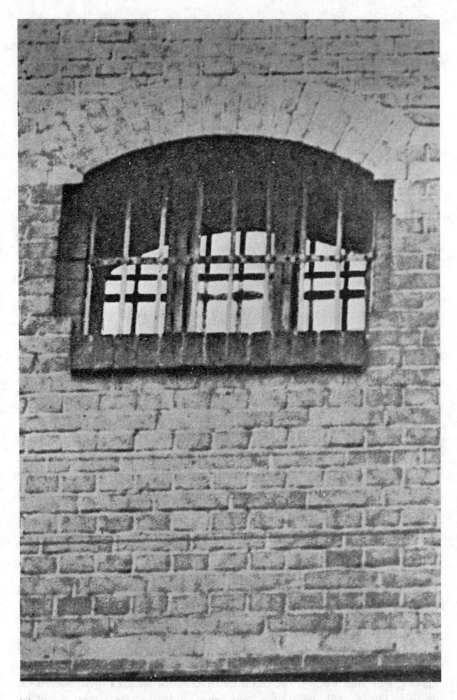

The spirit cannot die – in no circumstances, under no torment, despite whatever calumnies, in no bleak places.

FRANZ MARC

8

The Boys

THE CHAOS CAUSED BY the destruction and breakdown of all services and communications at the end of the War in Europe left thousands of citizens with a total lack of purpose and resulted in some of them taking to crime. Many of those who took to crime were Poles, due to the numbers who had been uprooted and treated most cruelly. Others came from Albania, Czechoslovakia, Estonia, Hungary, Latvia, Lithuania, Rumania, the Soviet Union and Yugoslavia. Most of them were young. Over the years I have visited and "adopted" some 1,400 of them and to me they have become known as "the Boys". One of my most vivid recollections was seeing a young Jewish boy of fifteen, an orphan, being handcuffed and marched off to prison. This was a situation which had not been foreseen by UNRRA or other relief agencies, and they had no trained workers to deal with it. There were, of course, some officials who took an interest in the local prisons, but they had to follow the rules laid down by their organisations, and these were primarily concerned with the immediate relief of human suffering, the visiting of hospitals and helping with repatriation.

I first started prison visiting in France in 1945 when I was a member of *Amis Volontaires Français (AVF)*. The great need for such visiting was quickly apparent, particularly in Germany, where I obtained permission from the penal authorities to enter the prisons. I made out a card for each Boy I visited, and completed a form which I had drawn up. In addition, I kept notes in my ring book, and these were subsequently transferred to the file held in my office. A card index system was also kept in the office, containing as many details as possible.

By 1950–51, following the handing back of authority to the Germans, I had files on Boys in 130 prisons, which were kept in old secondhand filing cabinets. The files were distinguished by colours indicating the different States in which the prisons were situated – for example, Baden Wurtemberg had blue files; Hamburg, Schleswig-Holstein and Bremen had yellow ones. When visiting a prison, my procedure was to ask for the card index of *all* prisoners and then go through every name – sometimes as many as 800 – making sure that I had those of all non-Germans, which I then entered on my list. Those cards bearing a "red rider" indicated Boys who might be released. Occasionally, I was given the opportunity as well of going through old files and the card index boxes which covered the whole period 1933 onwards. This gave one ample evidence about the way the penal system was administered by the Nazis. Many German prisons had their own printed form which was completed for each prisoner held on remand. A copy was forwarded to my office, thus informing me immediately of new prisoners.

It was poignant to see sometimes on these prisoners' cards that the entry against "Previous Prison" read "Buchenwald", "Nordhausen", "Mauthausen" or some other concentration camp. I realised that these prisoners, in an alien country and many hundreds of miles from their own families, would have no one to visit them if I did not do so. Thus, I felt that I could become a link – perhaps a vital one – between the prisoner and his family and the outside world.

I was very hard-pressed to keep pace with correspondence, visiting, and the work in general, which included the sick in central and southern Europe. The driving seemed interminable. I owe a deep debt of gratitude to the conscientious, hard-working and loyal secretaries of different nationalities who coped in different places with innumerable queries, problems and letters whilst I was away. This work was covered despite the appalling lack of telephones and disrupted lines. Telegrams were cheap and relatively dependable, mail also had to be relied upon and included the use of couriers.

Before I visited the different prisons, the files were selected by my secretaries and packed into cases on the rear seat of the vehicle I drove. My briefcase and picnic basket were in the front. It was vital to enter a prison with the right files, and when on long drives today I often think of the many stops I made by the roadside to take out the relevant files and check through all the details thoroughly, as the prison authorities expected me to present them with a list of the Boys I hoped to see and, on occasions, to discuss a case with them. These files were equally important and necessary when visiting the *Staatsanwalt* (public prosecutor).

A comprehensive dossier was made out by the Germans from the time the Boy was arrested. Usually I had permission to go through these individual dossiers too, but they contained so many pages that I rarely had time to take down much of the contents as I could not write shorthand and there were no photocopying facilities. Frequently the information was biased. The fact that I could not retain a copy of the dossier was a grave disadvantage, especially when it came to discussing the charges with the Boy concerned. A few of the public prosecutors intended to be helpful and would lend me a copy of the indictment, but this too extended to many pages in German legal language and I was expected to do my best to absorb and advise the Boy accordingly. During the period of the Allied Courts, a Boy was occasionally helped by a defence lawyer of his own nationality. Later, under German law, he was entitled to the advice of a German lawyer, but sometimes one just did not appear. If he did, he was often of little assistance or showed no interest in the case. There were lawyers too who would only take the case if they were promised payment for their services. I had always filed from front to back, but the German method was in the reverse order, with the latest letter or report at the front.

From hundreds of cases I clearly recall one entry on a form:

> *Reason for arrest during the War:*
> The Accused was not in possession of a *Kennkarte* (identity card)
> *Punishment:*
> Transported to Auschwitz

Many Boys were involved in black marketeering or possession of firearms. In the chaotic state in Europe during the postWar era, almost every other person was similarly involved in one way or another, some to scrounge a living, whilst others bartered rations to receive otherwise unobtainable commodities. Food was used as barter because currencies were valueless.

It was little wonder that among the flotsam of Europe and the thousands of homeless, uprooted people, there were inevitably some who broke the law. I was always amazed at the small percentage, considering their desperate plight and the conditions under which they existed. Some Boys lived in cellars; some were sick and in overcrowded hospitals; while others existed in miserable huts. Free food rations were available, but inadequate.

In my experience, the lawless behaviour of the Boys could nearly always be attributed to the atrocious conditions during the War and the chaos of its aftermath. Hunger was a prime factor. There were many who raided local farms for food and clothing. They usually operated in small groups, and sometimes – although this was not always intended – shooting occurred. Reactions varied. There was one German farmer who, despite having had twelve members of his family killed during such raids, came forward many years later and offered to do anything he could to help the Boys who had not been executed. He understood their terrible plight only too well.

There were also Boys who, having lost families, friends and possessions in the War, were at the end of their tether and decided to take personal revenge. Often it was known that former members of the Gestapo, the SS who were not on the list of War criminals for whom search warrants had been issued, were living in the neighbourhood; then some of the Boys would decide to take the law into their own hands and execute them.

There was a third group who, in the boredom which followed the excitement of the Liberation, and from lack of work and the discipline of routine, drifted into the underworld of the camps or hospitals. They were often accused of "black marketeering" or of comparatively petty crimes, but the sentences they received, if caught, were savage.

I tried everything within my power to reason and plead with the authorities on behalf of the Boys in prison. Once sentence had been passed, even if it had only been partly served, the prisoners knew they had no hope of ever being allowed to start life afresh in another country.

In the British Zone, Military Courts had been hastily set up in some areas, but they had not been adequately briefed about the background and

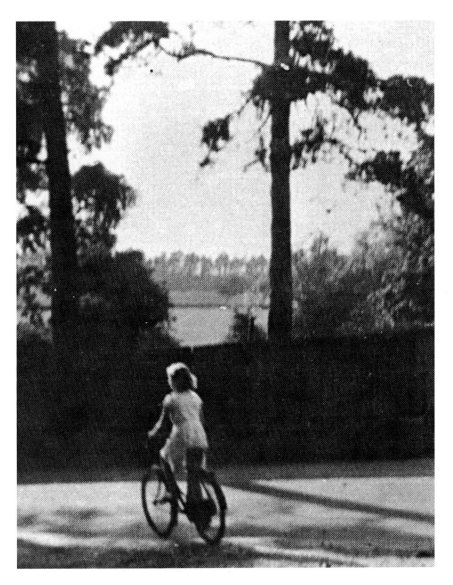

Sue Ryder – Childhood at Thurlow

Mama – Mrs Mabel Elizabeth Ryder

ABOVE Part of The Street, Little Thurlow

BELOW Little Bridge Street, Leeds – from Lydia Street

ABOVE In contact with Europe – FANY wireless operators with SOE

LEFT Display cabinet in the Sue Ryder Museum with map depicting dropping zones in Poland (top left-hand corner). Also on the left-hand side are items given by Bods to this museum. Other items include parachute, dagger, pistol, poison tablet, forged identity card and transistor used/carried by SOE Bods

BELOW Bod's (Agent's) AMK III transceiver, morse key and headset

ABOVE Elizabeth Zawacka Watson ("Zo")

BELOW Prisoner in Mauthausen Extermination Camp, Austria, on his way to the gallows accompanied by the members of the camp orchestra who were forced to play by the SS

ABOVE Child prisoner number 60308, Auschwitz. (Over one million children and three million adults died there.)

BELOW, LEFT Zofia Szachowicz, prisoner number 10111, Ravensbrück. Zofia was previously imprisoned for work in the Resistance in Radom, Kielce and Czestochowa. After being selected for execution on 29 April 1943 she sat at a bare table and shared crusts of bread with her companions, to whom she said: "There are thirteen of us here – it is like the Last Supper." RIGHT Jerzy Karwat, executed in Auschwitz at the age of 18

ABOVE Interior of one of the 110 barracks at Majdanek Extermination Camp.
From two to five prisoners "slept" in one bunk

BELOW Have you no heart? Victims on the way to the Gas Chambers, Auschwitz

ABOVE Victims. An SS photograph

BELOW Ruins of St Martin's Church, Piwna Street, Warsaw

ABOVE Ruins in the old city, Gdańsk

BELOW The same street rebuilt, with St Mary's cathedral in the background

LEFT The head of the Madonna and the rosary were made secretly from bread which had been saved by two Polish women prisoners from their tiny rations. They were given to Sue Ryder after the war. They are now in the Foundation's Museum

BELOW Group-Captain Cheshire greeting his wife, Lady Ryder, and daughter Gigi at Felixtowe in January 1982, on their return from Poland

RIGHT Georg Baecker, one of the Boys

BELOW Poland 1945 – women clearing rubble with their bare hands

ABOVE Lady Ryder and Professor Podowski (Pod), a very old friend, on the occasion of their both being awarded Honorary Citizenship by the Lord Mayor of Warsaw

BELOW Professor Eleanora Reicher

ABOVE Keith, the Foundation's foreman/builder, with Sue Ryder on the roof of an extension to one of the Sue Ryder Homes in Poland

BELOW The Sue Ryder Homes in Konstancin, Poland

One of the many pilgrimages to the shrine of the Black Madonna of Czestochowa

ABOVE Horses pulling the lorry out of a snowdrift in Poland

BELOW Sue Ryder with one of her lorries

circumstances of the Boys who came up before them. As a result they meted out sentences which were out of all proportion to the crimes. For armed robbery, or for being in unlawful possession of firearms, sentences varying from ten to thirty years were passed.

The Military Courts were succeeded by Control Commission Courts, whose personnel were often either ignorant or prejudiced. There were, of course, exceptions; some of the judges to whom I spoke, after hearing of the circumstances in which the homeless Boys were living and the tragedy of their lives, understood how they had come to fall foul of the law, and took account of it.

For the Boys who had not committed crimes, there were many problems to be coped with if they were not to be driven to crime. The greatest problem was preventing them from brewing "Bimber" – a crude drink, sometimes with a methylated spirits base, and sufficiently potent to blind or even kill. There were gatherings which the Boys referred to as "parties", to which I was often invited. I did not refuse, but explained to them that I was not going to be persuaded to drink "Bimber" as I did not enjoy the concoction!

It was useful to go to the gatherings. For instance, I might hear of a plan for a raid later that night, and could then say to them: "Look, there are better things in life than going out raiding. All is not really lost, and if we manage to keep our heads and our sense of humour, one day we may again see a more normal life." Sometimes when the "Bimber" had not already got too great a hold on them they would drop the plan. But whether they did or not, it meant my staying until very late to keep an eye on the Boys to prevent them from getting blind drunk, though some of them would inevitably succumb. I remember especially the ones who retained their dignity and sense of humour and helped to carry the helpless ones to their beds. In spite of all the squalor, the great thing that came through was the humour and the singing.

In the early days just after the War ended the Allied Courts sat at numerous places within their own zones of occupation. The non-German prisoners were scattered throughout the different zones. During 1946–7 it was decided to concentrate the non-German prisoners in the British Zone at Schleswig, Hamburg, Altona, Werl and Hamelin – a considerable area. Generally drives between prisons in different parts of Germany were made overnight, but sometimes, if not able to finish my visits at one prison in the course of a day, I had to remain overnight in the vicinity of the prison and resume visiting next day. This meant that I had to try and find food and accommodation for the night; more often than not unsuccessfully. In the areas of Germany where there were existing hospitals, camps and canteens, however bad the overcrowding was – and there were some with a total lack of privacy – I always met colleagues who would find me a bed or a mattress and share with me their meagre rations. Occasionally friends in the British Army of the Rhine, including Major-General H.R.B. Foote VC and his wife, Annette, offered me most welcome hospitality and the luxury of a bath.

But in other areas, finding food and accommodation was a great problem. Enquiries at local pubs frequently brought an uninterested or negative reply, and this meant that I would have nowhere to wash or sleep or to write up my notes. Thus the cab of my vehicle became my mobile home.

Every year the SS and former members of the Gestapo hold reunions, usually in the time of the Shooting Feasts, widely celebrated in Germany but especially in Bavaria.

These were horrendous events which inevitably I became a witness to, because once they were aware of my vehicle and its different number plate, they threatened me. On other occasions if I had found a bed in a pub (there being no other place to stay for even a few hours), I was woken and threatened by these and other thugs.

From the Danish frontier to the Austrian frontier is about 1,000 kilometres. I came to know the routes to almost every prison in Western Germany and this involved me in driving thousands and thousands of kilometres. The Germans were famous for their *Umleitungen* (diversions) on the road and these, together with the many frustrating hours lost because of some of the warders' dilatory behaviour, added to the work very considerably.

I can clearly recall the monotony, broken only by shouts of abuse, clanging keys intermingled with strong language, day after day, night after night, with only a glimpse of the sky through bars to remind one of the universe. From countless, almost daily insults, fortunately only a few remain in my memory, but the noises, smells and arrogant behaviour of many of the prison directors, warders and other officials are never likely to be forgotten, however hard I try. Practically all the prisons had accommodated both political and other prisoners during the Nazi era from 1933 to 1945, and because of the appalling deeds and horrific cruelty meted out in these prisons, a dreadful atmosphere continued to prevail. In a German court if a person was sentenced to life imprisonment it meant exactly that. Sometimes the court even sentenced a prisoner to "double life". From my own recollections the first prisoners who had their sentences commuted were Germans.

At Werl, the non-German prisoners were held in one wing of the prison and came under the British Governor who was also responsible for German prisoners. The Governor and some of the British warders were greatly respected by the prisoners, who referred to them as their "father" or "uncle". In the same prison were a few German War criminals, some of the *Kapos* (camp foremen) and some women who had served in the SS. This concentration of different types of prisoners in one place made for a very difficult situation needing careful handling. The tension was increased by the attitude of the former SS women, who were allowed to sit outside their cells knitting; whenever I had occasion to pass them on my way to visit other prisoners they would use foul language and shout insults at me. What I can never forget is their lack of repentance. One of the German staff who held a high position at Hamelin prison was known to have been a former member of the SS, and over the years I had to deal with him a lot.

Alex, one of the prisoners, was a typical victim. Like many Russians, he might have been an astute scholar if he had been given the chance, and he had a warm-hearted nature. I first met him in Czechoslovakia where he was being hidden. Alex had fought in the Red Army and had taken part in the greatest tank battle of the War at Kursk. His Wartime experiences, which he was loath to talk about, were of great interest, but after the Red Army had entered Poland he fell in love and became engaged to a pretty Polish girl. Sadly, this was discovered by the Soviet authorities and he was arrested and court-martialled. Knowing he faced execution he decided to escape.

First he was hidden by Poles and then by Czechs. To reach the West he had to cross the frontier into West Germany. By this time he had changed his name, but he had no ration card. Luck ran out on him and he was discovered hiding, after stealing food. He was sentenced to three years' imprisonment for theft.

In a cell at Hamelin, one afternoon, Alex told me he had witnessed the exhumation by the Germans of SS criminals who had been sentenced to death by British Military Courts; among them were the thirteen SS guards who had been hanged by Albert Pierrepoint, the British official executioner, on 13 December 1945. These included:

Josef Kramer, aged thirty-nine, infamous in Auschwitz and the last Commandant of Bergen Belsen.

Irma Grese, aged twenty one, the woman with the whip and the dog, who was responsible for thirty or more deaths a day.

Elisabeth Volkenrath, who was notorious for selecting prisoners to be killed.

Juana Bormann, who had habitually set her wolfhounds on prisoners to tear them to pieces.

Dr Fritz Klein, who had killed prisoners by hypodermic injections and sent thousands of others in tipper-type lorries to the gas chambers in Auschwitz.

Military honours were then given to these criminals on reburial. The story later appeared in British newspapers and aroused considerable controversy.

After Alex's release he dreamed of reaching Britain and a colleague offered him work in this country but, alas, on the eve of his departure he was insulted by a German and panicked and went over into East Germany. He found work there in a garage as a mechanic for several months, but he was re-arrested – as he had dreaded – after approximately six months of "freedom" and sentenced to eight years' solitary confinement in one of the worst prisons. He survived this, but realised that he would never see his sister in Russia again. He was fluent in English, and this was one of the many letters he wrote to me from prison:

> I know that you are always like a knight errant on the move and under pressure of much work, but I hope that in spite of all this you will not mind me trespassing with these lines upon your precious time. Now several years have passed since I had the honour of your acquaintanceship, and when I consider the bygone years, the circumstances, our correspondence and everything else, then I really don't know how to thank you for the pains which you took in our connection. Then you were the only person who through all these years of bitterness and despair did her best to alleviate fears and worries.
>
> In your last letter you were apologising for the bad spelling of greetings on the Christmas card in my language. My dearest Sister, it absolutely doesn't matter how you spelt them – the main point is that you meant it, and this was indeed lovely of you, and believe me it gave me great pleasure. You wrote in your previous letters, after giving me money for the wireless, that it gives you great pleasure to think of me tuning to the BBC and other stations. And if you knew how much I do enjoy this, then I'm sure it would give you still more pleasure.
>
> Sometimes it makes my head ache because of disturbances, but all the same it helps to pass the time, and above all it is a tutor! Well, now, I want to come to our last talk, when you said that I must do something (or appeal) for myself. May I beg you to come here in all haste whenever possible with reference to this request. Meanwhile, with my best wishes, and special thanks for your lovely Christmas card.

Wladyslaw, a Pole who had been sentenced to life imprisonment by the US military court, was also encouraged to learn English and made rapid progress through his diligence and enthusiasm. From his many letters I quote the following:

> I thank you very much for your letter of 22 August and am delighted that, on your meaning, my knowledge of English makes progress.
>
> For my long silence I beg your pardon. It was again lack of time. The week after receiving your letter we had an electrical welding course. And lest the manufacture of our workshop should not be neglected, we have had to work a fortnight long till eight in the evening. The time remaining to us, before light is turned off, was generally long enough to wash oneself and go to bed in order to be fresh and fit for a new day's work.
>
> Mr. Hagan's answer to my letter, that I shall have to serve my "good time" is just the same that I was afraid of. But I don't care much about it; the last nineteen months will soon be over and I shall have my liberty again. What does make me much more care as all the other, is the banishment and the uncertainty whether I can get rid of it. I must know it certainly in order to prepare myself for another country, in case that I should be compelled to leave Germany instantly after my dismissal.

I am glad that we shall discuss all this facts at your next visit, and am especially thankful for your readiness to help me whatever decision I would have made.

I take comfort in the quotation from Macbeth by Shakespeare. "Come what come may, time and the hour runs through the roughest day." And hoping for a better future, I remain yours respectively,

Wladyslaw

Eventually, and after great difficulty, I obtained his release. He was repatriated to Warsaw and succeeded in working as a waiter at the Grand Hotel there. Later, he married a teacher and their daughter studied law. She came to stay as a volunteer at the Foundation's Home and Headquarters in 1980.

Jan's story, another Pole, like millions of others, is particularly tragic. Up to September 1939, he lived with his parents in the eastern part of Poland and attended elementary and secondary schools. He was parted from his family as a result of the occupation of Poland both by the Germans and the Russians and, at the age of nineteen, he was arrested by the Gestapo, tortured and deported in sealed cattle trucks to Buchenwald Concentration/Death Camp. He was badly beaten and worked in appalling conditions, which affected his eyesight. In spite of this Jan managed to survive and was liberated by the American Army in the early part of May 1945.

Though he was still very weak from his terrible experience, after a short time he managed to recover sufficiently to join the Labour Service Company which was used by the American Army for guarding barracks. Alas, this period of freedom was too short.

Jan and a number of other Poles – in search of vengeance – committed serious criminal offences. The American Military Court sentenced him and his colleagues to death. This was not all unusual and at least fifty young non-Germans, who had experience similar to Jan's, were sentenced to death for killing former SS personnel or simply stealing food. At that time the Americans arranged for a number of former Nazi scientists to enter the United States, where their expertise in the development of long-range rockets was highly valued.

After nearly two years in the death block in Landsberg in Bavaria, where the cell was lit by day and night, his sentence was eventually, and through a great struggle on my side, commuted to life in confinement. He was transported with a large number of other Poles, from the infamous prison at Landsberg to the equally infamous Straubing.

In 1960, Jan was released at last, but at that time there was high unemployment in Germany and it was very difficult for him to get work and to find somewhere to live. He was, in fact, homeless and took refuge in so-called hostels, but was only allowed to stay one or two nights there.

He was completely bewildered, not only by the world in which he found himself, and especially the materialism which he encountered for the first time in his life. This bewilderment and disorientation led a German psychiatrist to declare that he was unfit to live as an ordinary person. As a result of this he was sent to a psychiatric hospital.

After thirty years of mistreatment he was finally released and work was found for him by a German friend, Hannes Kramer.

Jan cannot return to Poland because that part of the country he came from was handed over to the Soviets at the Yalta Conference; nor does he know what has happened to his family. He believes they were deported to Siberia.

Jan is not entitled to any State pension, so through this same German colleague of mine who befriends him, we send him a small amount of money each month to buy essentials.

What of his future? He has none really. He still has a faith and hopes that he will enjoy better health for whatever sort of life lies ahead of him.

Another of the Boys, who was taken to Auschwitz in his teens, was sentenced to death after the Liberation by a US Military Court. He was charged with two or three other Boys with stealing food, in the course of which a German farmer had been killed. Several gangs were operating in the district at the time and the Boys always maintained their innocence of this crime. After approximately two years the sentence was commuted to life imprisonment.

During the years I was fighting this Boy's case, he received an *Aufenthalsverbot* from the Federal Republic which ordered him to leave the country, even though he was still in prison! This meant that many years later, when eventually I got him released, he could not register with the police or obtain the documents for legal residence in Germany. I had to keep him hidden and fed, so he was therefore forced to travel around in the van with me and even had to sleep in it for fear of being re-arrested. After a extremely hard struggle I finally won the battle, but only on condition that I got him out of the country. This I did and he settled in Britain where later he married and earned his living as a commercial artist. In one of his letters to me he wrote:

> When I went back on holiday to the place I originally lived in Warsaw, near the statue of Copernicus and the Church of the Holy Cross, memories came back to me of what had happened there in 1939. I saw the dead all around me on the street and a dead horse which I had to cut up for people who were starving and hiding in the cellars. It was then that I realised that it was not possible for me to return and live there, for every street brought back memories of horror and disaster.
>
> Z B

Father W. Wnuk, a priest from Poland who had been a prisoner in Dachau for many years, was appointed chaplain at Werl, where he continued faithfully in his work with one assistant until approximately 1951. Once he said to me, "I am almost at breaking point, having prepared thirty young non-German prisoners and given them the Last Sacrament before the death sentences were carried out." To Boys who were under sentence of death and to whom I knew that faith meant a lot, I handed out the prayer by Cardinal Newman called "A Meditation". I had learned from both camp survivors and the sick that God gives people special grace and strength to forgive, to overcome adversity and to win confidence:

A MEDITATION

God has created me to do Him some definite service; He has committed some work to me which He has not committed to another. I have my mission – I may never know it in this life, but I shall be told it in the next.

I am a link in a chain, a bond of connection between persons. He has not created me for nought. I shall do good, I shall do His work. I shall be an angel of Peace, a preacher of truth in my own place *while not intending it* – if I do but keep His Commandments.

There I will trust Him. Whatever, wherever, I am, I can never be thrown away. If I am in sickness, my sickness may serve Him. He does nothing in vain. He knows what He is about. He may take away my friends. He may throw me among strangers. He may make me feel desolate, make my spirit sink, hide my future from me – still He knows what He is about.

An eighteen-year old Boy left the following letter for me:

I am leaving this letter with my companion, for you to remember us. Please if you get the chance have the courage to read this letter to our friends. May I ask you to try and find my father who, as you know, has been missing since the Gestapo took him, and give him a copy too. I beg you not to let this letter out of your hands, and to say goodbye to everyone. Much as I would like to do so myself, it isn't possible, and I hope to be forgiven.

We are taking leave of you for ever and of our beloved country. In a few short hours we shall be taken to the place of execution. Let us hope that somewhere there will be understanding for what we have done at this early age and in exile. We must die at the hands of our Allies for shooting the SS who killed all our families. We fought in the same cause, but this and the things which followed are all forgotten. We are leaving this world after receiving Extreme Unction from Father C.

Four Boys signed the letter before being taken out to face a British firing squad.

In another prison I had to break the news to a Boy that his death sentence had been commuted to life imprisonment. He looked at me and said, "So this means that all the days of my life will be in prison . . ."

Although I had never had the opportunity of studying it, law had always interested me. Later on, when the Allied Courts had handed over jurisdiction to the Germans, it became a necessity to grasp as much as possible of German criminal law, and I was instructed, usually during the discussion of cases, by German lawyers (Rechtanwälte). Up to the early part of 1949 the Legal Department of the British Control Commission, whose Headquarters was at Hereford, with branches in different parts of the British Zone in

Germany, were extremely co-operative. They knew of the difficulty of trying to rehabilitate those whose sentences had been commuted. Many were repatriated to central and eastern Europe, but there were those who had lost not only their families but their homes too, because the villages or towns in which they had lived had been destroyed.

One afternoon, during a lengthy discussion, the British lawyer at Kiel with whom I worked suggested that under a German law passed on 9 April 1920, prison sentences should be deleted from the Central Criminal Register (*Strafregister*) in Berlin. (On 11 May 1937 the law on passport-foreigner-police-registration and deportation was passed; this was followed on 1 October 1938 by an Order governing the deportation of undesirable foreigners. This in turn was followed on 28 April 1965 by the "Foreigners' Law" (*Bundesgesetzblatt*, Part I, page 507) which came into force on 1 October 1965.) We both felt that if we were able to get some sentences deleted from the Register (after the appropriate applications had been made and due consideration given), it would enable the people concerned to be considered by the immigration authorities and perhaps to start a new life in a country overseas. We pursued this objective and were sometimes successful. The Australian and New Zealand immigration authorities proved to be particularly helpful in accepting immigrants whose sentences I had managed to get deleted. The British Army also proved responsive, and offered civilian jobs to some of the Boys. Production work in prison undoubtedly prepared prisoners for work and life outside. It is an immense pleasure and relief for me to see those who – despite all the odds – have succeeded in getting jobs as waiters and shopkeepers (often as a result of learning English and other languages while in prison). Some of them, too, developed a great interest in painting, pigeon-racing, boating or fishing.

There are so many cases which I would like to include in this book, and from the many hundreds it is exceedingly difficult to single out even a few. My task has been made all the more difficult as explained later on, in Chapter 8, because the majority of the original files were destroyed when the first Home at Frankfurt-am-Main was burnt down. However, the following accounts may, I hope, illustrate what some of the Boys endured.

* * *

G.B. was finally repatriated after years of negotiation with both the German and Yugoslav authorities. He was arrested on 30 December 1946 and sentenced to death on 5 June 1947 by a US Military Court at Munich. This sentence was commuted to life imprisonment on 30 March 1949. On 24 February 1953 G.B. was sentenced to concurrent life imprisonment plus ten years penitentiary by a German Court. The saga of trying to get a prisoner serving a life sentence returned to his country of origin was incredibly slow and fraught with frustrations. G.B. was repatriated on 18 January 1976 and was admitted to a psychiatric clinic in Zagreb, Croatia, where he received at long last treatment from Dr K. Brzak, a consultant psychiatrist.

When he saw G.B. he was shocked by his state of health. He felt he had been reduced to the status of an animal and was surprised he had survived such a length of time in prison. Not surprisingly, G.B. died of heart failure less than a year after his repatriation.

In spite of the fact that he had been under sentence of death, this simple, quiet Boy accepted his fate until one day when he was in the queue waiting to buy a small amount of extra food with his meagre prison earnings he broke down. I was not surprised to learn that he had cracked under the physical and mental duress. He was then put into solitary confinement and treated with grave suspicion. He was refused any form of work and he deteriorated to such an extent that when I visited him in the so-called prison hospital he was unwashed and unshaven and was crawling about on all fours. He was also refused food and did his best to obtain tobacco which he then stuffed up his nose. For months one could not have a normal conversation with him, and it was only after exerting great patience and insisting with the German authorities that I alone must try and reason with him, in the company of another Boy whom he trusted, that I could get him to sign his name in order to make efforts towards his repatriation. His hand hardly stopped trembling.

* * *

F.C. was born on 4 October 1918. He attended primary and secondary schools and had hopes of finishing his apprenticeship to a builder.

After the Nazi invasion and occupation of Poland he joined the Resistance as a saboteur, but was arrested on 6 January 1942 and beaten by the Gestapo in Nowy Sacz prison. From there he was transferred with sixty other prisoners to the large and infamous Montelupi prison in Kraków, where he survived four months of interrogation. Twice he was put up against the execution wall. From Montelupi, F.C. was transported with about sixty other men in cattle trucks to Auschwitz-Birkenau. On being off-loaded he and the other prisoners were ringed by SS men and women, and the Commandant greeted them with the words, "Here your only escape is through the chimneys" – i.e. the crematorium.

Conditions were indescribable. He was attached to a *Kommando* which worked knee-deep in water clearing the swampy ground to extend the Camp.

F.C. had typhus. He volunteered for the *Sonderkommando* (special work group) in the faint hope of getting better conditions, but instead he had to clear the gas chambers and heap the bodies onto carts leading to the crematoria. On average, every prisoner in this work group had a life-expectancy of only three months.

F.C. met a doctor in the Camp who knew his elder brother, and the doctor secretly advised him first to investigate which SS men were "good" and less bloodthirsty than the others, and then in their presence to hurt his own leg. F.C. obeyed and put his leg under the wheel of the cart on which he transported corpses. He was admitted to the *Revier* (so-called hospital block) where the same kind-hearted doctor tried not to treat the wound but rather to keep it in an infected state. It was the only way to keep him in the *Revier* as long as possible. But the *Revier* became so overcrowded that there were regular selections for the gas chambers. Fortunately, in spite of the danger, the doctor was able to come to F.C.'s help again and, advised him to exchange the cotton striped garments of a dead person (which bore the number of this dead man) with his own. In this way he was saved, and did not return to the *Sonderkommando*.

In November 1943 F.C. was transferred to Ravensbrück – a camp for women and children. There he worked on building air-raid shelters for the Germans.

In January 1945 he was taken to Sachsenhausen (one of the original Camps established in 1933). Towards the end of April he was taken out on one of the death marches. He eventually arrived in the woods near Schwerin, where during the last seven days before the Liberation thousands of prisoners died of hunger and disease.

When he was liberated by the US Army on 2 May 1945, he weighed 37 kilograms (6 stone). He slowly recovered in an improvised hospital and eventually landed up in Lübeck, where living conditions were very bad. He resorted to looking for, and selling, scrap metal, which at that time was unlawful. For this a British Military Court sentenced him to three years' imprisonment in 1946. His sentence was later commuted, but he was refused permission to return to the local barracks (used as a transit and repatriation camp). This meant that he received no rations and could be re-arrested at any time for having no fixed abode or valid documents. Little wonder that he had reached desperation point and wept when he came to see me in my office in Neustadt. While queues of other distracted and distraught people waited outside, messages calling for help kept coming in from block leaders and also from others at the hospital. There were never enough hours to try and cope.

I took courage and called on the Commanding Officer of the 15/19th King's Hussars, who introduced me to a large and jovial quartermaster who offered F.C. a job as storeman! As he entered the storeroom in his gym shoes (which had been sent over from friends in Britain), his eyes were alight with joy and relief.

Later on, I got his sentence deleted from the Central Criminal Register and persuaded the Australian immigration authorities to accept him. He sailed for Melbourne on 2 March 1951 in the Norwegian ship *Skanbryn*. It was on this ship that he met a girl from Poland who was to become his future wife. On arrival in Melbourne he was sent to a temporary transit camp at Bonegilla in the state of Victoria. There he was responsible for all fire extinguishers. The accommodation in the tin huts got warm very quickly during the summer months. He worked there for three years for £8 a week, and after the first two years he was able to pay back his fare of

£90. In 1953 he was married and the couple moved to a suburb of Melbourne. They bought an old wooden bungalow which they renovated and improved, and later they brought some land on which they built their present house. It is modest, but very clean with a lovely garden. In Melbourne he worked first in a wool mill, then in a paint factory, and for twenty-three years he has been employed as a machine operator in a metal factory, and now he lives in happy retirement.

* * *

The following is an example of the sort of notes I copied in German in the prisons:

> M.T. Father a Shoemaker. Single child. Seven years primary school. Deported at the age of sixteen to hard labour in Austria. 1942 arrested, as he had listened illegally to the BBC Overseas Service.
>
> 1944–45 in Flossenburg Concentration Camp. After Liberation moved to Muhldorf.
>
> 1947 – possession of arms. Sentenced to five years by US Military Court. No information or news from parents in Poland. No fixed abode. Unemployed. Catholic. An alert and active man. Mentally alive. Believes he has been sentenced unjustly. Refuses to accept sentence. Is an obstinate fighter. Expresses distrust and offers resistance against their reasonable judgment. Stubborn, independent.
>
> 1. Active perpetrator by inclination.
> 2. By fighting against the sentence is difficult, negative and produces false accusations.
> 3. Is transferred from the cobblers' workshop to paper works because of rebellious behaviour. Difficult. Marked as an escapee.

* * *

International areas in whatever country have their own history of crime and prostitution. The infamous Reeperbahn in Hamburg was no exception, even when the rest of the City was in ruins. At a time when black marketing was rife and currency had no value it was a breeding ground for vice.

A young sailor from a Polish ship became involved in a brawl and was accused by the Germans of carrying a pistol. He should never have left the ship and was a victim of circumstance. One of the *Staatsanwälte* asked me to investigate after I had pleaded with him that this young sailor should be allowed to proceed back to Poland. This led me into searching for the prostitute who had accused the sailor. Though I had been in many red-light areas in my life, I was, to say the least, slightly aghast at the size of this particular one and the number of similar incidents reported daily. The area defied all description. This made me all the more determined to get the young Pole away. My main problem was to persuade the captain to wait for the boy. This involved detaining the ship whilst I endeavoured to get the charge dropped. I finally succeeded in doing this, but not before I had received full and untruthful abuse in the most lurid language from various prostitutes.

In several ports, ships which had been sunk, and subsequently raised, were inhabited by the homeless as a last resort. The heavy smell of sea water did not exclude the smell of rust, decay and the overwhelming stench of dead fish. At night it was particularly gruesome.

In the smaller French Zone I found that there were fewer homeless amongst the non-Germans and, consequently, that the French Courts were not faced with the same large number of cases. Moreover, as France herself had been occupied, it was easier for the French authorities to understand the Boys' situation and to handle it. They carried out very few death sentences and were quick to realise that it was often necessary to commute sentences, rather than let the prisoners linger indefinitely in gaol. The French concentrated their relatively small numbers on non-German prisoners at Wittlich, where they also had a few of the German War criminals whom they had arrested. Again it seemed to me most unfortunate that these two types of prisoners should be housed under the same roof. I have a distressing recollection of parcels weighing five or seven kilos being brought in for the War criminals by their relatives, while non-Germans had no one except myself to visit them or to fend for them.

So far as the American Zone was concerned, their Military and Civilian Courts were as harsh as the British towards the non-German prisoners, or definitely harsher; and I was shocked to find that, having been sentenced to death, a number of the condemned Boys had to wait anything up to two years before they were executed or had their sentences commuted to life imprisonment.

In a certain prison, which was one of the largest in the whole of West Germany, there was a block which was openly referred to as the "death block". On one occasion, an American officer strode into this block brandishing a loaded revolver. This incensed the prisoners and almost caused a mutiny.

In some of the prisons where the Americans held non-German prisoners, their bureaucratic attitude and marked lack of compassion created a tense atmosphere. I vividly remember waiting to be admitted into the presence of an American official whose signature was needed on the list of prisoners I wished to visit. I spent hours in the office of his German secretary, and all the time could hear him talking in his own office; but I had to be patient and pretend not to worry about the passing of valuable hours – at least it gave me a chance to write up my notes. When eventually I was allowed in, I found him with his feet on the desk and had to listen to unfriendly remarks about the dubious value of my work and presence in the prisons. Finally, however, I collected my signed list and started off on the long drive to the prison. Another time I succeeded in getting my list signed by the American penal officer only to find, on arriving at the prison, that he had rung up to say that my presence there was not desirable. As I did not wish to disappoint the Boys who had been looking forward to my visit, I made myself as pleasant as possible to the German warders at the outer and inner gates and asked to be shown to the Director's office. Whilst I was not very optimistic about the outcome of the interview, as I suspected him of being in complete agreement with the American officer, I thought it at least worth a try. I then discovered that it was the Director himself who had received the phone call. After much persuasion, he agreed that I could see some prisoners, but only those whose cases came before the German Courts. I argued that it was equally important that the American Court Cases should be visited, especially as they had been told the date on which I would be arriving; but he was adamant in his refusal.

Undeterred, I returned to my vehicle and, in the loo of a local garage, changed into my old relief-worker's uniform. I then re-entered the prison and made my way back to the Director's office. The sight of my uniform seemed to have the desired effect and he let me through.

This type of obstruction happened on another occasion: having collected my list of prisoners, duly signed by an American official, I drove to the next prison on my list only to find that I was refused permission to visit. Again, the prison Director was in collusion with the American authorities and he removed the files from the table. Then he ordered me out under the guard of an armed warder and I was marched off to the gate with a loaded rifle pointed at my back.

I decided that the time had come to ask for an explanation so, hoping Providence would tell me what to say, I drove back to the American official's office – a distance of over sixty miles. He was taken aback at seeing me. Politely but firmly I asked for a full explanation and said if he wouldn't give it to me I should go straight to the British press with my story. This was bluff because to contact the Press would have proved very difficult indeed. I told him I did not consider that this was the right way to behave to a person who was trying to do something positive amongst men who had lost all hope, were totally disillusioned, and who, if further provoked, would become very much worse. I added "Unfortunately I have never worked in your country, but I am sure that what is happening to me is not representative of the American attitude. One is already up against all possible odds; either we co-operate or we decide to differ, but you should not say one thing to me in the office and then, when I am on the road, go back on it. If I have given you reason for complaint, please say so; I would rather you were frank with me." His answer was that he did not consider it necessary for the non-Germans to be visited or to receive any form of welfare.

It was essential never to prejudice the Boys' situation and so, whilst maintaining a firm attitude, I had to proceed with great coolness. Whether it was in the hospitals, the prisons or the *Pass-Stelle* (identity card and passport office), or with the police, the authorities or the *Staatsanwälte*, I hope I made an honest attempt not to react to provocation or indignation. I did my best to restrain my feelings, otherwise there would have been a complete breakdown of any working relationship and no hope of reconciliation. After all, the authorities did not have to accept me.

On another occasion the American penal officer rudely shouted, "Why don't you British get your own gaol at Werl in order before you come here!" This particular American *eventually* came to realise that I meant to carry out my work conscientiously, and that I was not prepared to accept his bullying behaviour.

One day, approaching despair, I felt obliged to remark on this to the Head of the Penal Department at Bad Godesberg, Richard Hagen, an American official whom I held in high regard. He himself was deeply affected by the injustice and told me, just before he left his post, that he had had to obey instructions from Washington, which required him to give preference to the release and rehabilitation of War criminals. He was very objective, tried against impossible odds to improve conditions, and made every attempt to persuade his colleagues to see the true situation; but in many cases he failed.

In order to review the sentences of non-German prisoners, the Mixed Clemency Board was formed, which held regular meetings at the main prisons to consider – and usually reject – the appeals made by these prisoners. In addition, the penal officers themselves were given authority to decide appeals. Many of the German officials and warders had welcomed me from the start, looking upon my work as constructive and recognising it as a bridge between prisoners and the world outside. Some were even courageous enough to do their best to see that local conditions were eased for the victims; others followed the line laid down by the Americans.

The following letter is one of many received by Georg Baecker and other Boys between May 1950 and November 1963 refusing commutation of sentence:

OFFICE OF THE UNITED STATES
HIGH COMMISSIONER FOR GERMANY
THE HICOG CLEMENCY BOARD

Munich, Germany
210 Tegernseerlandstr.
30 November, 1950.

Mr Georg Baecker,
c/o Warden, Straubing Prison
Straubing, Germany.

Subject: Panel Action, BA453.

Dear Sir:

Panel No 55 of the HICOG Clemency Board has considered your application for commutation of sentence, dated 21 Apr 1950, and advises that your application has been denied.

Very truly yours,
Saul Moskowitz
Chairman, Panel No 55

In my meetings with the prisoners all I could hope to do was to listen patiently, hour after hour, to men of different nationalities – each one pouring out his troubles, grief, bewilderment and grievances. I tried to take a bit of the sting out of the situation. I thought at the time – and still do now, in retrospect – that both the best and worst in human nature were exposed in those circumstances, and that tolerance and optimism were the qualities to which we needed to cling. It was not uncommon to have to visit between thirty and forty prisoners a day, but to each I tried to give as much time as possible.

The lack of adequate food during the years after 1945 – and well on into the '50s – often gave rise to problems. These, ironically, led to hunger strikes, and during the course of one such strike, I remember the Boys saying to me, "We cannot sleep or think – even isolation in the cells doesn't affect us so much as hunger." One day, a group of Poles who had received life sentences made contact with each other and planned the following night (at midnight) to start howling together as loudly as possible. The plan was duly carried out. The *Nachtwache* (night warders) became apprehensive, and the town was greatly alarmed.

The result was *Bestrafung* (punishment) by the Director, who sentenced them to three days in the "bunker" (underground cells). However, he did say that if they agreed never to howl again, he would increase their food (at least for a month) by 150 grams of bread and about two potatoes (boiled in their jackets). This had a calming effect, and it was a better solution than some practised elsewhere.

Hardly any women were arrested or charged, but one who had originated from the Baltic countries remains in my memory. She could not face being repatriated because she had lost her family, and tried to emigrate to the United States, but her application was rejected as she had a young mentally handicapped child. In despair she drowned the child one evening in a stream. Her remorse was pitiful. My visits to that prison brought me again into contact with several of the female staff warders who had served Hitler's Third Reich as members of the SS.

Although it was not until 1949 that West Germany regained her sovereignty, the French, the British and American authorities handed over judicial and penal powers to the Germans in 1948. Thus, the Boys were handed back, as far as they were concerned, to their old enemies, and it seemed to them that the Allies had deserted them.

At that time the non-German prisoners in the French Zone were kept in more than twenty small prisons scattered throughout the State of Rhineland-Pfalz. This made the work much more onerous, since it increased both the number of places to be visited and the distances that had to be covered.

At one place, the Director, who had a notorious record as a High Court Judge in Poland during the Nazi occupation, used to send for me on nearly every visit. "Is it the English social worker?" I would hear him say. He enjoyed the sound of his own voice, which was shrill and piercing. He also delighted in telling me that none of the Boys could be rehabilitated. "Culture ends at the frontier of Germany," was one of his favourite expressions.

One afternoon in January he insisted on seeing me alone in one of the cells. He proceeded to shriek at me because a parcel – allowed only at Christmas – which I had brought in for a Russian prisoner (and which I had requested should be forwarded to another prison as the Boy had been temporarily transferred there) had failed to reach him. The Boy had therefore made a complaint. "I consider that you should be locked up and kept in this cell for your part in this plot," he shouted, his face close to mine, bloated with rage.

I attempted to explain that there was no question of a plot, but simply a matter of trying to trace the parcel to which the Boy was rightly entitled under the Christmas regulations. However, this did not pacify him, and he continued to rant and rave and to take sides with one or more of his warders, who were always reminding me that the British started the War, and of the wicked injustice of the trials at Nuremberg "when German Generals were hanged". I kept calm and looked bored, and his rage eventually abated (after about an hour).

I wrote on a Foundation Christmas Card a greeting for each Boy in his own language.

Each state in West Germany produced its own stringent regulations about parcels for prisoners, and I was provided with an official list from each prison of what I was allowed to give the Boys. This included details of the contents, shape and weight of each parcel. Regulations had to be rigidly conformed with. Normally, for the German prisoners, each parcel was opened and searched, but happily for me, many prisons decided that I was trustworthy enough to bring in and distribute the parcels myself. Unfortunately, there were others whose staff behaved arrogantly, as I have said earlier, and the officials would seize my parcels and cut through the string and wrapping paper and then place these with the contents on the scales. I well remember the Director of a prison in Hamburg who had duelling scars on his face. His behaviour was almost explosive at times; one day he cut open the oranges I had taken saying he was searching for notes! I told him I had neither the time nor the inclination to think of such silly things.

In Werl prison, I remember attending a conference one day with the authorities to decide whether a small Christmas candle could be included in my parcels to prisoners. The meeting lasted well over an hour!

In another prison, an official hectored me at length for including some nuts which, again, I was told were a great danger as they could have concealed little notes or perhaps money!

Amongst the endless difficulties which I experienced was one which began when the Lutheran pastor at Werl beckoned me into a cell. He told me that one of the most dangerous things ever to bring into the prison was the Bible. After a long and dreary explanation, he persisted in trying to convince me that people could write messages between the lines in the Bible despite the closely printed text. I told him I found all of this very hard to accept and that Bibles or prayer books which I brought in were completely free of any such messages. "Ah," he said, "how can you be so certain that these have only been in your hands."

Although homosexuality amongst the German prisoners proved a problem, it was happily not the case amongst the Boys. Kasjan, who was later repatriated, was in a cell with two Germans, one of whom was a homosexual who managed to smuggle in extra clothing and dressed himself as a woman. Kasjan's existence was made even more difficult by a murderer who had been caught after some years and who had earned the nickname of "the moonlight *Autobahn* murderer". Kasjan insisted that I got him transferred. This proved exceedingly difficult.

After the Nuremberg trials, and when I was still continuing to visit and work in the remand prison at Nuremberg, which was near the court house and the prison in Zellenstrasse where only a few of the many major War criminals had been held, the chief warder came to me one day full of importance and said he wanted to take me on a secret mission. I was extremely preoccupied at the time and thought that he had a serious matter to discuss with me about one of the Boys. To my surprise he led me to the cell where Goering had committed suicide with a concealed phial of potassium cyanide. The chief warder's whole attitude was one of awe and he clearly revered the place. Although I had been before, he then insisted upon walking me to the part where some prisoners were executed, and I had to listen to a long dissertation about the wickedness of the War crimes trials.

I remember one of the many warders in Lingen who had a habit of studying the family trees of aristocratic families in Europe. He thought I could help him by filling in information he needed on family trees of the British nobility. I had to be polite, but this sort of interruption took up precious time, especially as my knowledge was scant, and I advised him to obtain a copy of Debrett.

Lingen was a *Zuchthaus* – a convict prison. A prisoner sentenced to a *Zuchthaus* received harder treatment than those sentenced to a *Gefängnis* (ordinary prison). After being released, they automatically forfeited certain rights such as a driving licence. Attached to the convict prisons were the different *Aussenkommandos* (auxiliary camps) on the peat moors and included Esterwegen and Papenburg – the former one of the first concentration camps to be established in 1935. On one of my many visits to the Boys, a warder who felt isolated on the moors told me gruesome stories of what had happened to the prisoners there. He described the way they were disposed of, and took me to a burial ground, but he was loath to think that I should pass on this information for others to know of his knowledge and connections.

In the winters we used to huddle in the hut around a solitary stove with a long chimney attached. The fuel burnt was of course peat. This part of Germany, Lower Saxony, was in those days referred to as "Siberia".

In another prison there was a room referred to as the "Museum", the walls of which were lined with objects which prisoners had swallowed, including large spoons, forks, and so on. One of the warders never understood why I did not enjoy visiting this place, especially as one of the Boys who was my responsibility had, in moments of desperation, also swallowed various objects. Although this Boy proved exceptionally difficult in confinement and used to stutter and talk at length in a most excitable manner, he was eventually rehabilitated and a part of the cottage at Grossburgwedel near Hanover, which the Foundation built for him, became a model of simple comfort. He took great pride in his aquarium, and there was not a thing out of place in his new home. Furthermore, he worked well, but had one lapse at Christmas. He stupidly took a shirt from one of the big stores in a local city. That night he confessed to me and I had to tell him that I thought it was both unnecessary and foolish.

He replied, "Well, they have robbed me of my family and everything else, do you not think I can take a shirt off them?" At that moment the local German police arrived, and after a very lengthy and involved discussion with them alone, I was able to persuade them not to prosecute the Boy. I then handed the shirt back to them.

In Borgermoor the warders followed the custom, as elsewhere, of inviting me to their Christmas party. As a result of too much drink it was not unusual for them to get on their chairs in the smoke-filled hut and sing in a raucous manner, "We are marching against England". I had no option but to listen and hope that eventually a cell would be offered me to sleep in. It was also an area known for bad fog and mists. One year my mother accompanied me, but could only sit outside the prison. Afterwards we found a remote pub to stay at, and after sleeping fitfully with feather quilts to cover us – which she used to refer to as "balloons" and which constantly slipped off the bed – we found, on rising, that the water in the jug was frozen.

In a smaller remand prison was Henryk who had been arrested with his family at the age of twelve because they had listened to BBC broadcasts and distributed underground pamphlets in Poland. He often used to tell me the story of the Gestapo surrounding his house and of his family's frantic efforts to hide the radio. He was tortured indescribably and lost his father and mother. Henryk, although often tearful, nevertheless helped to boost the morale of the other Boys. The head warder was co-operative and always pleasant. Moreover, he seemed to have some feeling and sympathy for the Boys.

Two other Boys, both called Josef, had become psychiatric cases. One, before his trial, made up his mind never to speak. There were only occasional moments throughout the twenty years I visited him when he said a word, otherwise he would shake his head or simply nod, according to how the conversation went. But to Henryk he disclosed, in whispers, part of his ordeal. He once attempted to escape and was found ten days later half-frozen in the snow and brought back to prison. Eventually he was released. Henryk, too, finally was discharged, but died in a road accident.

The other Josef was confined to his cell and his allotted task was to glue paper bags together – an extremely monotonous job, especially as a "norm" (about 200) had to be completed every day. Henryk used to accompany me to Josef's cell. He always sat with his back to us, and we would stand there trying to make some sort of conversation with him and attempting to draw him out. I eventually arranged his release and he worked from the Foundation's Home, getting up every morning at four o'clock. He was well thought of in his job where he worked extremely hard. For the first few years after returning to the Foundation's Home late every evening he used to help us with the washing up after supper and filling the stoves with oil in the various rooms. He had a huge appetite and drank plenty of milk. Later, unfortunately, he took to drinking beer instead of milk. He was usually withdrawn and did not participate in what was going on. One day he was found dead in his room from heart failure.

In another prison in Germany, although the Director always proved correct and polite towards me, he nevertheless, for some unknown reason, thought is was his duty to read from the files of prisoners endless notes about their behaviour. As I had, on average, between thirty-five and forty-two prisoners to see, this custom not only wasted valuable time, but became exceedingly monotonous. We were interrupted by warders coming in with reports, saluting both before and after presenting these. The notes were never short, and they had been composed by a psychiatrist who considered every one of the Boys irredeemable and appeared to delight in writing frightful, long-winded sentences about their sins. As he scarcely knew the Boys, much of what he wrote was untruthful.

One day, a Boy who was known by me for his patience, was called in before the Director after being sentenced by a US Court. He had written a letter to his family after they had been traced in which he requested that they write to him and, if possible, send him some food for Christmas. The Director had strongly reprimanded him for this action, whereupon the Boy seized a table lamp, which was switched on, and hit the Director over the head with it. All hell was then let loose, the siren was turned out, and I was sent for immediately. The Boy was sentenced to twenty-eight days' punishment in an underground cell. I attempted to restore calm and assured the Director that the Boy had no intention of killing him. Fortunately, in the end, I got the Boy repatriated after many miserable years spent in prison.

In the same prison all the Boys were allowed to meet together to allow me to distribute parcels and then to sing carols; a general discussion followed. A few of the warders considered that this was a terrible risk and exclaimed, "It could be a great plan to escape or even lead to a mutiny". They then added, "But Miss Ryder does not believe this, and she has a very calming influence".

In one prison the *Oberpolizei-Inspektor* (Chief of the Police Section in the prison) collected material on sailing ships. He took his hobby very seriously. He seemed quite unaware of taking up my time and would ask me whenever we met to provide him with information on sailing ships through the ages. Sometimes it meant searching or writing to Britain for the information, but when I was able to present this to him his attitude to the Boys showed a marked improvement.

In Fuhlsbuttel – a complex which consisted of three separate prisons – some of the Germans who had been members of the *early* Resistance movement against the Nazis during the 1930s, had been horribly tortured. The cells which the Gestapo had used for torturing and interrogating prisoners, and others in which prisoners had awaited execution or transportation to concentration camps, were grim reminders of the regime which the prisoners had striven to inform the world about. As dissenters, they had stood up against the Nazi authorities with incredible moral courage, but to no avail. Many others were later sentenced to death after the plot to assassinate Hitler on 20 July 1944, and were hanged on piano wire from beef hooks.

One evening in Altona, as I was crossing the yard on leaving the prison, a warder fired shots at a cell window and fatally wounded one of the Boys. His only reason for doing so was because he saw the Boy looking through the bars and incorrectly assumed that he was attempting to escape, though there was no proof of this.

The cell to which I returned was bespattered with blood and the young Boy was dying there in a pool of it. It was indeed a difficult situation and only the reasonable attitude of the German Governor prevented a mutiny. I was asked by him to go round to each of the Boys in turn and try to persuade them not to attempt to take reprisals against the prison staff.

Several months later, in May, a Boy named Richard, together with another one (both were in their teens), actually succeeded in escaping by filing through the bars of their cell and tying their threadbare blankets together into a long rope which they lowered to the ground at night. Having succeeded in getting over the exceedingly high wall (one sprained his ankle in the rubble in the road), they then made their way to a repatriation camp where they hid. Two days later, they contacted me and asked me to provide them with enough food to proceed on their long and precarious journeys back to their homes in Czechoslovakia and Poland. I warned them of the dangers, especially as both the British Military Police and the Germans were, by coincidence, already searching the area. Within an hour of persuading them to get out the whole place was cordoned off. The main reason for this search was because a leading British official adviser had been killed in Vlotho. The ringleader of the gang, a Silesian German, was caught, brought to trial and sentenced to death, but was afterwards reprieved.

Once they had reached their homes and found, to their astonishment, that their few remaining relatives and friends were there, they wrote post-cards (which took weeks to reach us) to both the Director of the prison, whom they had respect for, and to me, to say that they had arrived back safely. Richard had originally been arrested at the age of ten and had lost no less than fourteen members of his family.

The wearisomeness of prison life cannot be imagined by those who have never experienced it. The loneliness, too, is terrible. Indeed, in my own small way I felt something of it, especially because in some parts of Germany there was no one in between prisons with whom I could share my thoughts and the pressures. I used to stand or sit for hours in the narrow confines of the cells and stare up at the sky through the high windows and their bars, and I could not help thinking how unfair it was that so few of the very many thousands of SS thugs were ever caught or punished for all the terror and wickedness they had wrought.

Alas, those who were not witnesses to the atrocities were inclined to say, "Oh, forget them, they can't all be bad." This unlimited injustice was probably the hardest to bear and share with the Boys, perhaps even more than their lack of liberty. We did not feel bitterness, only a deep resentment and astonishment that others should forget "a grief too deep for tears". Attendance at Mass, whenever possible, sustained me and gave me strength to try and cope with the situation.

I was in the remand prison at Frankfurt Hammelgasse, a building since demolished, when the infamous Nazi, Wilhelm Burger, who was arrested in Schleswig-Holstein, arrived and was treated to a programme of carols by the German Prison officers.

A Lithuanian Boy held in custody was gifted in languages and spoke German fluently. He mixed with the prisoners awaiting special trials in the German Courts, who were held for crimes committed in Auschwitz. He was reliable enough to inform me of the bribery that went on and also how these remand prisoners were allowed to mix and therefore how they knew prior to the trial exactly what each was going to say.

* * *

It is important to remember the huge numbers of the SS and Gestapo who, with the help of the Americans, escaped to the United States and South America.

In an attempt to locate a few of the many millions of Nazis who got away, specialised British teams (members of the Intelligence Service) were organised in secret by April 1945. There were four main teams oper-ating and usually six men to each team. The matter was considered very seriously by the British and required confirmation of bone-fide evidence for subsequent presentation to the Tribunal in Nuremberg.

A close colleague of mine, Airey Neave, Lieutenant-Colonel British Crimes Executive and late Commissioner for Criminal Organisation in

Germany, served the indictments on the few Nazis captured and tried. He had the task of collecting information from each team "leader" and to accurately collate it suitable for presentation to the Tribunal.

It was soon realised that there was a major leak in security arrangements, and to their dismay, they realised the Americans were using the old German international network where very many senior Nazis sheltered. This knowledge made their mounting frustration all the worse. An official complaint was sent to the Government in London about how the Americans had set up their own method of "spiriting" known war criminals away to the USA.

Of the many hundreds of cases dealt with, records show that only sixteen senior Nazis were charged at Nuremberg and hanged. Six were sentenced to long terms of imprisonment but many of these sentences were commuted.

In the words of my colleague, Terry Blatch, "we had personal knowledge of the arrest of Himmler (who was later fed poison in his cell to avoid trial) and also of the case of Dr Mengele (whose speciality was to experiment on twins in Auschwitz) – we just missed him in Hamburg a day after the American Network had got him away to South America.

I quote from Guido Zembsch-Schreve on the subject of Werner von Braun, whose work developing the rocket-fired V1 and V2's at Peenemunde, was explained in Chapter 5:

The Americans arrived at Nordhausen on 11 April 1943 when Dora had been evacuated of all but a hundred or so prisoners. The region, under the Yalta Agreement, was to pass under Russian control on 17 June 1945, together with all equipment and personnel. The Americans, nevertheless, unilaterally removed the rockets they found there as well as a large quantity of documents. Meanwhile, Dornberger, von Braun and five other senior scientists had taken refuge in a hostel near the village of Oberjoch in the Tyrol, where they awaited the arrival of the Americans. Since the Americans had occupied the village, but had not thought to climb up to the hostel, the Germans had to make the first move and sent down the young Magnus von Braun to make contact. He was well received and it was arranged that the group should present themselves on the following day. The news of the reception the group had received spread to others and some 300 workers were approached by von Braun and the Americans to persuade them to go to America, although not all agreed. The problem of getting them to America was a delicate one. The British wanted Dornberger for trial as a War criminal and many feared that the Germans would represent a danger rather than a prize for the American programme.

A first group of seven, led by von Braun, were taken secretly to Boston, arriving on 29 September 1945, then Washington, and finally to El Paso on the Mexican frontier. They were followed on 2nd December by forty-five others. By February 1946 there were 111. They were on 14th March installed at Fort Bliss, where one of the DORA rockets was launched on 28 June 1946.

On 30th October 1946 Truman made the first public announcement of the presence of the German scientists. Their status was not regularised until the end of 1946, when they were taken back to the Mexican border, crossed into Mexico and returned to complete immigration formalities which were accomplished in hours, as opposed to the usual months.

There were also schemes set up by the British to recruit labour into Britain. Amongst those from the Baltic countries were Germans, including former members of the SS, whom I saw with my own eyes.

Among the reasons for calling at yet another transit camp called "Transmitter" was the opportunity it gave to trace missing persons. It also lay on the route to Neuengamme, a former Nazi concentration camp on the outskirts of Hamburg. The British were criticised by other nationalities for using Neuengamme as a prison (after 1945), where a few of the non-German Boys were held.

I called at a small room in one of the huts referred to as a surgery, where a friend of mine, a Lithuanian nurse who had lost all of her family, was working. She told me about a Volkdeutsch doctor who burnt out the tattoo from under the left armpit of the SS men. The tattoo consisted of the SS sign, individual's blood group and the registration number of *Reichsicherheits-Hauptamt* (SS Headquarters). While I was there in the surgery, the doctor continued his work.

The SS had no need to think they would be properly screened or be medically examined. The only reason for refusing somebody a place on the British Labour Scheme was if he or she suffered from tuberculosis. Many hundreds were accepted.

*   *   *

Every German prison has a sad association. After the overthrow of the Weimar Republic the political prisoners were confined with the criminals. In the prisons I visited I was not infrequently asked to provide medical assistance for the War criminals, which included trying to find unprocurable medicines. After a particularly gruelling day in Hamburg, I came back to where I was billeted to find a list of messages and a note from the penal section asking me to provide worm powder for a notorious woman *Kapo* (camp foreman) who was awaiting trial. Later she was extradited to Poland to stand trial for crimes committed in Auschwitz and other camps.

It was necessary for me to attend the War Crimes Courts (and, on occasions, to console the witnesses, themselves survivors), the Military and later the Control Commission Courts, and after 1950, the German Courts. These experiences I have endeavoured to wipe out from my memory, as not only were they gruelling; but the accused (in the case of Boys) stood very little chance of being acquitted. Sometimes I would see the judge before proceedings started and explain to him as best I could something of their circumstances. For the most part, however, it was a matter of just sitting in Court hoping to give some measure of encouragement and support by the mere fact of being there in person. I remember returning to my billet one night to find that a close friend, Vicki, had pinned on my pillow Reinhold Niebuhr's prayer:

God grant me the Serenity
to accept the things I cannot change
Courage to change the things I can
and Wisdom to know the difference.

On several occasions, when visiting the prisons, I was locked in and the warder would say after night had fallen, "I had forgotten about you, there was too much to do."

Owing to the number of Boys in some of the prisons, and the problems and time it took to deal with them – often from 7.30 a.m until 6 p.m. – I was obliged to remain in the prison all day on my visits. I was rarely offered food or even the use of a loo. More than once when I asked for the latter I was told by the warders that they had no place for a woman! My pretext for leaving the prison in order to find a loo was to go out to fill up my vehicle with diesel or check it for oil, or to say that I had to go to the post office, but as the latter closed between the hours of 1 and 3 p.m. (depending upon the part of Germany one was in, and according to the local regua- tions) I was usually reminded that there was no sense in going out then. Once I was escorted along the cell corridors to use a bucket!

Before the appointment of social workers in Bavaria the prison chaplains were supposed to be responsible for the welfare of the prisoners. Some of these chaplains and, indeed, all the warders and Directors for many years after the War ended, still referred to the prisoners by number, and I was constantly scolded for calling them by their names.

In Niedersachsen (lower Saxony), one Boy whose parents had been killed in front of him refused to follow the prison regulation. On my different visits he used to be dragged into the Director's office by no less than four warders. Though the Director himself had been a member of the Nazi party and was a very keen shot, he believed in letting me talk to this Boy to try and cool his temper and take him back to his cell unescorted by any warder.

Twice, when I was pleading for the release of a Polish Boy who had been unjustly taken into custody, and for whom I had borrowed money to pay his train-fare back to his wife in Scotland (he had served as a young soldier with the Polish First Armoured Division), I became giddy for lack of nour- ishment. It was a great relief when the Boy was ordered to be released, but I was shocked when I was told that I had been given only a few hours by the court to get the Boy out, not only of the remand prison, but the country itself. The only train left at midday. The scene that met me on my arrival at the bureau was chaotic. There was only one over-worked assistant who suffered from a bad blink and was being continually pestered by telephone calls. After what seemed an interminable time, I was finally attended to, and I was just able to put the Boy on the train. Later, he wrote me an exceed- ingly kind note which he published in a British magazine called *Titbits*, expressing his appreciation for being released and repatriated.

I remember, too, other occasions when, after spending hours trying to comfort those awaiting execution, I had to ask to go out into the *Hof* (exercise yard) for a few minutes to breathe the fresh air.

Later on, two British soldiers were imprisoned after coming up before the German Courts on charges of manslaughter and murder. Although they were isolated from other non-German prisoners, they quite soon adopted the same attitude to the harshness of prison life. They spoke virtually no German, and they knew that the Deputy Director of the prison in which they were being held had a very good knowledge of English. They therefore expected that when he sent for them they could converse in their native tongue. He refused to allow this, however, and told me that it was not proper for them to speak English, and he would only converse with them in German. He was normally a very reasonable person and had a high regard for our borstal system, which he had studied and visited officially. Moreover he was one of the few who, on two or three occasions, had invited me into his house for a meal. I appealed to the two British Boys to learn more German, which they subsequently did. Both were eventually repatriated. One was found a job as a long-distance lorry driver and the other, who was especially talented, became an electrician: later, he developed a great religious fervour.

The Deputy's superior was a notorious former member of the Nazi party, known for his outbursts of bad temper and his weakness for drink. Early one morning he sent for me and shouted: "You have written to my Deputy. As he is absent I will make myself liable to punishment if I open the envelope." I explained that there was nothing personal in the letter and I had written it out of courtesy, not wishing to trouble the Director. He refused to open it and asked me for the copy which, fortunately, I had in the file with me. A little later he found me in one of the cells, and reminded me of the bad days at Werl, when he had been there on the staff with the British Governor and warders whom he considered to be not only nitwits but softies. He went on to say: "No doubt you think as they did, that by being tolerant to a prisoner you may get respect and the best out of him." I utterly refuted this, and in a harsh penetrating voice he reminded me of an incident in Werl when the Governor had given one of the Boys a cigarette. "Never in my life, and particularly in the golden days of the Third Reich, could we believe that such a thing would be possible," he exclaimed. I asked him if he was displeased with my efforts in his prison. To my great surprise, he did not answer.

Later, a Hungarian prisoner committed suicide there.

There was an American Court Case where the Boy concerned implored me to buy him a trumpet and then earned himself a place in the prison orchestra. The Director of this prison was a retired, Army colonel. He was polite and respected, and also proved co-operative. The Boy decided to celebrate his forthcoming repatriation, after approximately twelve years in prison, by playing the then-popular tune "I'll be with you in Apple Blossom Time", and the samba "Cherry Pink and Apple Blossom White" on New

Year's Eve. The music resounded around the prison to the delight and surprise of some of the inmates, but not the warders.

One morning, in more recent years, whilst working inside one of the prisons, I was called to the telephone to be told by the warder at the entrance that there was an English woman sitting there to whom he referred to as a *Dirne* (tart). He said that she did not speak German and he had enough to do without having to deal with problems of this kind, especially as the prison was for men only. After some persuasion, he allowed me to speak to her on the telephone, and a very clear, well-spoken English voice said, "Oh, thank goodness you are here – I saw your vehicle outside with your rosemary sign on it; my two daughters supported you whilst they were at St Mary's School, Wantage. We are expecting you to come and see us. I do not know why I am locked up as I was looking for a stud farm. Can you prevail upon the warders to let me out?" I asked if she had shown her identity card to the Germans, and she said that this had made no immediate impression. I thereupon spoke to the warder again and explained to him that he was greatly mistaken to think that this lady was a *Dirne*. She was, in fact, the wife of a British Army general and should be released immediately and allowed to proceed to the stud farm. To her relief, he agreed. When I told the Boys they were extremely indignant, though amused!

There were complications in another prison where the Director allowed certain prisoners, who had particularly good records of behaviour, to keep budgerigars. These, inevitably, posed problems because, although they were all meant to be male budgerigars, one or two were female, and to the delight of the Boys they laid eggs, and so the budgerigar population increased! The Boys expected me not only to get them repatriated but to arrange for their budgerigars to leave with them!

The regular visits to the 130 prisons were an experience I would never regret. Tiredness, frustration and sorrow were there for much of the time but there were individual Directors, warders and officials who, although they did not have to do so, went out of their way to be welcoming and co-operative. Often at the outer gate a familiar voice would greet me, "Ah, Frau Ryder is here!" Some of them recognised my difficulties and predicament, even though by off-loading their own problems they perhaps took up valuable time; and if others were uncouth or ate their sandwiches and drank their coffee in front of me while I had not eaten for hours – well, one came to terms with it.

The joy of being released, and particularly the additional delight of knowing that they could be repatriated, was indescribable for the Boys. Whenever time allowed, they would ask me to take them to a cafe where they insisted on treating me to a cup of decent coffee and a cake. From their limited savings they also wanted to buy a watch or some other present, if they had someone to go back to. Using the gifts of clothing donated to my Foundation, together with what they had received from the prison authorities (except in the early days when clothing was scarce and the latter could not provide any), they were determined to look as smart as possible and so keep their self-respect.

The struggle to get Boys released sometimes took many, many years. In March 1970 on arrival at Browina in Poland after most difficult and long drives in the snow in *Joshua*, my van, I was greeted with an unexpected and urgent message from Carol Brookes who had worked with the Foundation as "foreign office" secretary. She had managed to get through on the telephone and left a message that Airey Neave (a Councillor of the Foundation) had approached Chancellor Willy Brandt during his official visit to London about the plight of the Boys still in prison. Both Airey Neave and Willy Brandt asked us to prepare lists of those Boys whose sentences appeared to us particularly harsh, to enable Willy Brandt to see what he could do to convince the States (for it was their responsibility and not the Federal Government's) to commute some sentences. Consequently, priority lists were prepared and it was left to Dr Per Fischer, who worked in the Chancellery at Bonn, to help me put pressure on the authorities in the different States. Often this was deeply resented. Willy Brandt asked to be kept informed and owing to his influence some of the Boys were ultimately released.

*   *   *

In 1952 I was able to found the first Home for the Boys. This was thanks to the persistence of Ministerialrat Professor-Doktor Albert Krebs, Doctor of Philosophy, social worker and then Governor of Untermassfeld prison, Thuringia, until 1933, when he was dismissed by the Nazis. Between 1945 and 1965 he was in charge of the penal section in the State of Hessen, and Honorary Professor of Criminology at Marburg Universtiy. He is also well known for his writings.

One of my first meetings with Professor Krebs was in a prison, when he expressed concern for the safety of my life and reminded me that a woman visitor had been murdered in a borstal. Later, he realised the necessity of this work, and gave his full backing to prison visiting when he attended conferences with the Heads of the States' penal authorities, and asked me to accompany him.

I remember one memorable day when, on completion of his official rounds of Deeburg and Darmstadt prisons, he accompanied me in the car on the remainder of my visits. Later we drew up by the side of a country road and talked. It was on the top of a hill overlooking fields which stretched away in the distance. I shall never forget his advice and comforting words. Both on this occasion and others when the Professor had accompanied me round some of the prisons in Lower Saxony he stressed that however hard the road, and whatever the odds, I should never feel discouraged. He went on: "There is a greater power working and guiding you – nothing is wasted, not frustrations nor time nor ideas which do not materialise."

Professor Krebs became one of my closest colleagues whom, with his wife Doris, I greatly admired and respected. They gave me hospitality and a bedroom in their own house, and occasionally would invite a released prisoner to visit them. It was Professor Krebs who helped find an empty hut on the outskirts of Frankfurt-am-Main, which was converted into a Home and a small office for non-German prisoners released into the chaos of those years. One Sunday, however, when I was on the road, the Boys hung their washing too near the stove, and within an hour their Home was burned down. Their main concern had been to try to rescue hundreds of valuable dossiers and files that I kept there, but unfortunately the majority of these were lost.

After this disappointment, Professor Krebs suggested that a disused prison at Bad Nauheim, a fashionable spa, could be converted and used as a Home, and Princess Margaret of Hesse and the Rhine agreed to go and see the Mayor. It was undoubtedly due to the high respect in which she was held, the knowledge of her many activities and social work, and her strong personality, that he reluctantly agreed.

The prison building was surrounded by a high wall. Naturally enough, the idea of a Home for discharged non-German prisoners was disliked by the local residents, but at least it met, for a while, the great need for accommodation for Boys who had literally nowhere to go. Many were at the end of their tether – jobless, without identification cards or birth certificates. Some were awaiting repatriation, hopeful of finding their families. It was my task, together with the warden, to attempt to get jobs for them, even though in those days jobs in Germany were at a premium.

Bad Nauheim was not ideal for the Boys. It was too far out of Frankfurt and meant that they had to get up at 3 a.m. to reach their place of work. Moreover, they were incensed at seeing the high standard of living of the local population. They had been the victims, and now the people who had caused such misery were reaping the benefits denied them. Some argued that they did not consider it a crime to force open a car door and take the contents.

One of the Boys there, called Kazy, a Lithuanian, had lost his parents who were deported from Lithuania to Siberia by the Soviets in 1940; he had been left in hiding until he was found and forced to join the Red Army. He was taken prisoner of war by the Germans in 1943 and transported to Sachsenhausen Concentration Camp with thousands of other Russian POWs. He was selected for medical experiments, survived, but was mentally and physically affected. In 1946 he stole food and was sentenced by the US Court to four years or more for theft. After endless pleas I got his sentence commuted to three years and he was one of the Boys who came to live in this Foundation's Home at Bad Nauheim, converted from a prison.

I had to restrain the former German warden and his wife from reciting at great length and in detail the horrendous events which had occurred there between 1934–45. The Polish Housefather found Kazy work in the market at Frankfurt-am-Main while we both tried to obtain a *Reisepass* (passport) for him.

Very early one morning the German police appeared and said they had come to arrest Kazy for a murder committed in Frankfurt during the night. The Housefather calmly explained he was in fact living with them in the Home but they refused to listen and he was handcuffed and pushed down the stairs into a police van. Nearly a year later, on 30 August 1958, Kazy was sentenced to life imprisonment.

In Butzbach he tried twice to commit suicide, broke his arm and became mentally ill. The Director of the prison agreed he might be allowed to pick flowers from the very few in the exercise yard, to be pressed into a book and used for cards. The Police Inspector objected saying that the glue and so on, could be dangerous. However the Director agreed with me it was harmless.

After a search had been made of his cell by the wardens, they confiscated everything, including the pressed flowers and the new summer shoes I was allowed to buy him. At this point Kazy broke down . . . and confirmed again and again he would *never* sign an appeal to be released as he was innocent of the crime. I asked the wardens why they had reduced him to this state: their reply was because the flower petals looked untidy on the grey blanket of his bed. I reminded them that nothing else of course was ever allowed to be hung on the walls of any cell of any prison, and I told them that he had not done this or intended to be untidy, but they replied that matter would be brought up at the next *Straf* (punishment) Conference.

Fortunately, the Director prevented this, and allowed Kazy's only remaining items to be returned to his cell.

Both the late Pfarrer (Father) Degen, a courageous Catholic Chaplain, and later, his young successor, tried to help – unsuccessfully.

In 1992 Kazy died from cancer.

In the '50s, a small committee of German supporters was formed in Frankfurt, and after hearing about my difficulties, encouraged me to search yet again for another site to establish a Home to replace the Bad Nauheim one. After much searching a suitable property was found on the outskirts of Hanover near a small lake, but planning permission to extend the existing house was refused. Finally, a site was found at Grossburgwedel, which consisted of about two acres of ground with an existing house which then had to be renovated. We also had the problem of sitting tenants who occupied most of the house, leaving many of the volunteers who had come to help the Foundation, with little accommodation.

We soon found that there was an additional need for tuberculosis patients who, for much the same reasons as the Boys, were stranded. Funds were collected and volunteers came from sixteen different countries to build eight cottages at St Christopher's near Celle. My deep appreciation goes out to them and also to David Ennals who, at that time, was working in the United Nations Association and gave a great deal of moral and physical support. The volunteers lived simply, camping out in an attic where the snow penetrated the unfelted roof during the winter.

The whole site first had to be cleared, and several of the Boys worked alongside the volunteers and enjoyed the experience – with the exception of one who, believing that he was to be re-arrested (he had a persecution mania), took a dose of fifty aspirin tablets and then proceeded to climb the tallest pine-tree on the site. We finally persuaded him to come down and he was taken to hospital.

The volunteers worked under an experienced builder from Britain and there was a local German honorary architect, Herr Schulz, who had previously spent a short holiday with the Foundation in Britain.

A small international committee was gradually formed, and through a teacher in one of the prisons, we made contact with a man who ran a Quaker settlement. One day the honorary architect said that he had some grave suspicions about this man, which confirmed my own. It turned out that he was not a Quaker nor a deacon but a rogue. He had forged other people's signatures and broken into the desk in the house removing the last of our money for food. He then accused one of the Boys of doing this and went to the local Burgermeister (Mayor) to accuse another Boy falsely of stealing a ring.

One morning, when I went to the bank in Hanover, I was told to my amazement that there was nothing left in the account. I rang Herr Schulz who warned me that his house was surrounded by Kripo police (similar to the CID in Britain). Within minutes of my call they had cut off his phone so he was unable to communicate with anyone else, and as I left the bank to return to Wesley House (a canteen run by the Methodists for the British troops), I was met by two plain-clothes policemen who took me into custody accusing me of training spies in Britain. I spent the whole day being interrogated but refused to sign a written statement they had prepared. I told the police that they should have arrested the other person who had turned out to be a rogue. After twenty hours I was peremptorily released after being threatened and abused.

Meanwhile, one of the volunteers, Captain Gruszczyński, had also been arrested and charged with being a member of the Resistance in Poland and with fighting against the Germans. Herr Schulz and two others were threatened with arrest, but were not taken into custody.

Fortunately, Captain Gruszczyński was accustomed to the Germans' methods and knew how to defend himself. During the War he had endured innumerable Gestapo interrogations in different prisons and five extermination camps. He spoke German like a native (having been educated in Poznań). In my own case, through my Wartime training and later experience in the German Courts and prisons, I knew what to expect.

The next day I went to the bank and asked for a full explanation, but they were unable to give a satisfactory one and accepted no responsibility at all. They also introduced me to a useless lawyer.

The rogue was subsequently arrested. I went to the Chief of Police and insisted that he confiscate whatever possessions the man had, this was possible under a paragraph in German law, but the rogue was cunning and had hidden everything.

A trial took place, during which defence counsel interrupted my evidence by telling the judge that I had married a Polish officer in the War, which was totally untrue. The trial went on all day. The rogue was found guilty and sentenced to only six months' imprisonment.

I then went to see the *Generalstaatsanwalt* (Prosecutor-General) in Celle and, after a good deal of persuasion, I managed to get the trial reopened – a *most* unusual concession. This meant that we again had to go through the trauma of hearing nothing but lies and false accusations, but the rogue received a heavier sentence of twelve months and was then let off after serving one-third of this term!

The lawyer for the Foundation – who had been paid in advance – never appeared, but fortunately we had prepared our own case which we duly put together with green judicature ribbon over which we fastened large seals in red sealing wax, and this impressed the Court.

This serious setback only made us more determined than ever to ensure that the work on the eight cottages was completed, though the large house could never be wholly renovated, and it was not practicable to have central heating installed because of the expense. The house did, however, serve a very useful purpose and several hundred Boys passed through it. We were fortunate, too, that the sitting tenants left after a few months. Eventually we were able to rehouse two or three Boys in the cottages.

Sadly, the history of the settlement was not without its traumas. During a brawl one Boy was shot, and later a warden was killed by a tubercular patient who had been admitted from the psychiatric hospital against our wishes. He had accumulated an arsenal of guns and explosives which the police told me was enough to blow up the whole settlement! We had warned them about him but they took no notice until it was too late and the fatal injury had been caused.

The attitude of the authorities at the *Pass-Stelle* varied enormously. Some saw the need to issue permits so that the Boys might have a chance of finding work, security, and a new start in life, but others stubbornly refused. Some declined even to issue the essential passports and national insurance cards, without which the Boys had no official existence. A further difficulty was that, according to the law, all persons had to be registered with the police, but in order to do this it was necessary to have accommodation. This presented yet one more problem because any form of accommodation – whether in a hostel or in "digs" – was extremely difficult to obtain; the more so when the Boys had been released from prison. In several of the States it was fairly common practice to adhere to the 1938 Nazi Aliens Law (since revised by an Aliens Law passed in 1965). This decreed that undesirable aliens should leave the country. In Frankfurt, Munich,

Nuremberg and a few other cities, the *Pass-Stelle* authorities actually suggested that I should take the Boys out of Germany in the boot of my car, adding: "We feel no responsibility for them."

Here was a dilemma which clearly called for patience and coolness – on the one hand the obstinacy of officialdom, and on the other the frustration and disappointment of homeless prisoners. For Poles , Czechs and Slovaks, the nearest repatriation centres were in Berlin; but to get there they needed to cross East Germany, which they could not do without passports. No one, sadly, seemed interested at that time, and there was virtually nobody else to whom these unfortunate people could turn.

There were grim scenes in the large cities and, in particular, in the bunkers, the air-raid shelters erected in Germany before and during the War. Some of them were used as dosshouses. One, at the Ostbahnof in Frankfurt, remains vividly in my memory. Long before evening there were queues of both Germans and others trying to gain admittance for a wretched bunk bed and a bowl of soup. This was one of the many places I used to visit as often as I could, and the men – many of them very rough – were always respectful and polite and would let me go through to see the warden and his wife who were in charge. Both were members of the Salvation Army and proved helpful colleagues.

The bunker was very dimly lit by 15-watt bulbs, and had no windows. Brawls were frequent, and the language was unrepeatable. Not infrequently I would find myself trying to separate two men or two gangs who were going for each other, or having to help lift a drunk off the floor. And all the while there was the noise of the queue shuffling up to the so-called "reception" office, a kind of hatchway behind which were the ever-calm members of the Salvation Army who tried to explain that there were no bunks left and no food. Everyone had to be put out by 6 a.m., and nobody was allowed to stay for more than two nights. The unfortunate Boys had no alternative but to work unofficially in the local markets, where they were always picked up by the police for not having passports or labour permits.

As this situation was repeated throughout most of Germany's large cities, it was little wonder that the after-care of released prisoners was a never-ending struggle.

The American authorities considered that this was not their responsibility, and in the neighbourhood of Kaiserslautern (in the State of Rhineland-Pfalz), previously in the French Zone, yet another serious situation had to be dealt with. Among units attached to the US Army in France and Germany were the Labour Service companies. These consisted of civilians of various nationalities, some of whom had had very chequered careers fighting with the Foreign Legion during the War, while others were the flotsam of Europe who between 1939 and 1945 had lost their families, their homes and all their possessions. Suddenly they found themselves discharged without papers, without proof of identity, and with nowhere to go. Towards these men the US Army authorities sometimes pursued a ruthless attitude, forcing them to take to the woods. Known in the neighbourhood as the local "Mau Mau", they had to live off whatever food they could scrounge or steal.

In all my attempts to intervene with the US authorities at Heidelberg, I found only one officer who seemed to care. He made it clear that his position and career would be in jeopardy if it were known that he was ready to help, yet he was prepared to do so.

By that time there were between one and two-hundred men who were likely to take the law into their own hands; I knew that they would have to be moved out of the woods and taken somewhere, but the question was where? Eventually I arranged with the friendly American officer for Army trucks to be made available to carry the homeless away. Starting at short intervals, these were driven some hundreds of miles to the Headquarters of the Rhine Army at Bad Oeynhausen, which took a minimum of nine to ten hours. It was like running the gauntlet for there was the ever-present danger of pursuit. As for the American officer, he risked a court martial; for no American truck carrying non-United States personnel could be allowed officially to leave the American Zone. Indeed, the US Military Police – nicknamed "Snowdrops" because of their white caps and braid – were often hot on the trail.

At Kassel, a town bombed to destruction and still at that time largely in ruins, was an American hotel. Here I had to make sure that a truck was parked near my own vehicle, where I could be certain of finding and recognising it at night. I asked the Boys in it to promise that they would lie low and keep quiet while I went into the hotel to get boiling water for the flasks. This done we continued our journey, and before dawn made coffee in the woods on the outskirts of Bad Oeynhausen. It was then necessary to conduct each Boy separately to a loo, where he shaved, and afterwards take him to a British establishment where I explained the situation to an obliging British major. Eventually these Boys were gradually absorbed into the mixed service organisation attached to the British Army, and to the best of my knowledge, all made good; certainly I received some very touching notes from the Boys who had found some sort of security and a sense of belonging.

To the question that I am sometimes asked, "But wasn't your work dangerous?", I can merely answer that I was threatened only once. Quite frequently in dosshouses, cellars and attics, camps and woods, I was breaking up fights and appealing to the Boys, yet I never came across disrespect from any of the different nationalities. I was never frightened, which perhaps sounds conceited, but I know fear: I am frightened, for example, of Alsatian dogs, which remind me of the horror of Nazi camps and prisons.

The night I was threatened (some years after the immediate postWar era), I had a suspicion that one Boy was getting steadily more drunk and that he intended to commit a crime, although I was not sure whom he had chosen as his victim. He had threatened violence, both in the afternoon and that same evening. He had managed to procure more beer and liquor, and now said in a very tipsy voice that I should have got his repatriation papers through, which was true in so far as I had written repeatedly and telephoned to East Berlin, but to no avail. He was fed up and frustrated.

I talked to him for hours. We cooked supper for him separately – he refused to eat it with the others. Suddenly he left the Home. When he returned the doors were locked, but he got in through a window, staggered up the very narrow steep staircase to the attic bedroom where I was sleeping and said through the door, "Here I am, ready to bump you off." I replied that this would not lead to his immediate repatriation, and suggested that he go downstairs for some hot coffee, where I would join him. After several minutes he followed my advice and then, as I heard him go down, I walked to the warden's room where I found his wife looking very white and frightened. We locked the door. Shortly afterwards a shot was fired and bricks were thrown through the window. The Boy rushed up the attic stairs, and wrenched the door of my attic room off its hinges thinking that I was still inside.

I thought it prudent to telephone the police, only to be told that they were out on patrol and that we must wait. This we did – for forty minutes. Since the Boy was armed and very drunk and was muttering threats, the situation needed cool heads. We spoke to him through the warden's door. Eventually the local policeman arrived and, in his presence, the culprit was asked to account for his behaviour. Because of the amount of alcohol he had consumed he was unable to give any coherent reply. I asked the police, for everyone's safety, to take him to the local police station, and although the policeman was very reluctant he finally agreed, saying that they would release him at 8 a.m. next day.

When the Boy returned he had a bad hangover; I gave him black coffee and he was apologetic.

There was also the night Gregory arrived. I was working in my small office in Sandweg, Frankfurt-am-Main, on a day when there seemed to have been even more callers then usual seeking advice or assistance of one kind or another. Kenneth Brentford, who looked after the office for me, had left to return to his room in the city thinking that there would be no more visitors. When Gregory appeared he obviously had a long story to tell about what he had gone through in extermination camps and prisons. He then said he had decided to kill someone of whom he had at one time been fond. He showed me the knife and boasted that he also had a pistol. Since he was under the influence of drink, I made him some black coffee and kept him in the office until morning. I spent the whole night imploring him not to unlock the door and go off to carry out his threats. At one moment he made an attempt to get out of the window and I had to struggle with him. As the hours went by, I tried to keep him occupied by asking his help with the filing or his advice on some of the letters, thus diverting his thoughts from his plans, but the effect of the alcohol made him very aggressive. It was one of the longest nights I can remember. There was no chance of sleep because whenever my attention was turned away from him he attempted to get out. By the time I was cooking his breakfast he began in a confused way to thank me for prevailing upon him not to carry out his threats.

During this period I received an invitation to attend a dinner at General Headquarters Rhine Army, which was to be followed by a meeting to organise help for the sick and homeless. I had driven five or six hours over bad roads in a snow blizzard from an emigration resettlement camp where a handicapped and prospective emigrant had been rejected. I had to return him to the awful conditions in which he existed. With some assistance, it was necessary to carry him to his repatriation hospital. When I arrived at GHQ I was met by a couple of batmen and the General's gracious wife in her long elegant evening gown. The case containing my change of clothes, which I believed to be in the ambulance, was nowhere to be found, but a variety of hot water bottles and my original gas mask bag were taken into the house by the batmen and solemnly carried up the main staircase to my room where the contents (apple and banana skins and the remainder of our rations) were laid out on the dressing table by the German maids and the hot water bottles lined up in a row on the bed.

When the General's wife came to escort me to dinner she looked at me with some amazement, I explained that my carefully pressed uniform had inadvertently been left behind, or off-loaded with the unfortunate patient, and I had nothing to wear but what I stood up in. My hostess appeared to understand, but it was far more difficult to explain it all to the company below in their mess dress and the women in their evening finery, especially as I had to give a talk to those assembled afterwards.

Amongst those who in different ways have helped was the late Margaret, Princess of Hesse and the Rhine, who since 1955 had given practical support and abundant moral encouragement. She was a prominent member of the German Red Cross. For very many years she chaired a small German committee in Frankfurt, which did what it could to further the prison work I undertook in Hessen. In addition she generously provided overnight hospitality at her lovely house, Wolfsgarten, especially just before Christmas every year. On my arrival, regardless of the weather, she would come out to greet me with a characteristic warm embrace.

The Princess was a friend of the Foundation and countless people of all backgrounds and nationalities in many parts of the world found her compassion and advice invaluable. Her knowledge and love of music (she was an early supporter and founder of the Aldeburgh Festival and close friend of the late Benjamin Britten and of Peter Pears) was known to many; so too was her marvellous courage and sense of humour. Amongst the *many* letters and notes she wrote to me I find: "Sue dear, a sweet loving and very warm welcome to *your* Wolfsgarten. The frame is for Leonard's picture, the present for your lame ducks. Peg OX."

In 1954, Hannes Kramer, a young German social worker from Caritas, a Catholic international relief organisation, was appointed to take over visits and after-care of the Boys in Bavaria and, until he was forced to give up through ill health, he relieved me of much travelling. Hannes continues to help individually in special difficulties. He always had a very strong faith, patience, and hid in the woods because he refused as a youngster to join the Hitler Jugend.

In Hamburg, my work has been made much easier through the personal assistance of Hanna Lenz, who has devoted a great deal of time to the task of dealing with correspondence and translations, but to find someone acceptable to both the Boys and the prison authorities to take over at least part of the prison visiting has not proved possible.

In the prisons, Christmas is a particularly poignant time of the year, and I have always made a special point of visiting each of them at this period. Christmas cards and greetings were written to each Boy in his own language. Until 1974, when a different system had to be introduced, volunteers were found to make up food parcels for each Boy, which I would then distribute individually. Making up these parcels was not an easy task for, in each State, regulations as to the contents of the parcel varied. In addition, it was not always easy to ensure that the lists of Boys were complete and up to date and that no one was missed out.

In one of the large prisons in Hessen, where there were more than 800 German and non-German prisoners, the German Director invited me each year until his retirement to attend the Christmas Eve service. It was at the same time a ceremonial and a moving occasion. As the only woman present, I was invited to walk with the Director from his office down the spiral staircase from which fanned out the three wings containing the prison cells and at the bottom of which were gathered the prisoners waiting for the service to begin. By the staircase itself was the Christmas tree decorated and illuminated with plain white candles; in front of us the prison orchestra, which always included some of the Boys; and on all sides of us, gathered round the staircase, the huge crowd of prisoners, gaolers and other officials. Everyone would take part in the singing, and both the Director and the prison chaplains, in the addresses which they gave, would offer me welcome and a word of encouragement.

In another prison, in Baden-Wurtemberg, I was invited by the Director to attend Mass in the prison chapel. Amongst the Boys was another who refused to talk and insisted on everything being put in writing. Even in the chapel, where we could not see each other, we would sit exchanging notes. It seemed strange in such a setting, but somehow I think that it contributed towards his rehabilitation, for gradually I was able to win his confidence, saying that it would be much more practical if he would agree to speak; and eventually he did.

Several of the non-German prisoners who had been sentenced by the Allied Military and CCG Courts between 1945–49, and whose sentences

I was able to have commuted with great difficulty, were then released. I was able to get them identity papers and a job, but to their horror, and mine, the German police re-arrested them and charged them with the crimes the British Courts had been persuaded to let drop, and with other, invented, offences. This was totally unfair. False witnesses came forward and gave evidence, as a result of which they received double life sentences. After years of struggling against this second injustice, I finally succeeded in getting the Boys released, but they died soon afterwards, which was not surprising.

My own spirits were revived by the example of Dietrich Bonhoeffer (a leading German theologian) who himself was long in prison and made so great a sacrifice in the cause of truth and freedom. His books, especially *Letters and Papers from Prison*, and his prayer "Who am I?" are particularly inspiring.

WHO AM I?

Who am I? They often tell me
I stepped from my cell's confinement
Calmly, cheerfully, firmly
Like a squire from his country-house.

Who am I? They often tell me
I used to speak to my warders
Freely and friendly and clearly,
As though it were mine to command.

Who am I? They also tell me
I bore the days of misfortune,
Equably, smilingly, proudly,
Like one accustomed to win.
Am I really then all that which other men tell of?
Or am I only what I know of myself?
Restless and longing and sick, like a bird in a cage,
Struggling for breath, as though hands were compressing my throat,
Yearning for colours, for flowers, for the voices of birds,
Thirsting for words of kindness, for neighbourliness,
Tossing in expectation of great events,
Powerlessly trembling for friends at an infinite distance,
Weary and empty at praying, at thinking, at making,
Faint, and ready to say farewell to it all?

Who am I? This or the other?
Am I one person today and tomorrow another?
Am I both at once? A hypocrite before others,
And before myself a contemptibly woebegone weakling?
Or is something within me still like a beaten army,
Fleeing in disorder from victory already achieved?

> Who am I? They mock me, these lonely questions of mine,
> Whoever I am, Thou knowest, O God, I am Thine!

In my 1972 annual report to the Ministry of Justice in the State of Hessen, I referred to the words spoken by Winston Churchill as Home Secretary in a speech he made in the House of Commons in 1910:

> The mood and temper of the public with regard to the treatment of crime and criminals is one of the unfailing tests of the civilisation of any country. A calm, dispassionate recognition of the rights of the accused, and even convicted criminal, against the state; a constant heart-searching by all charged with the duty of punishment; a desire and an eagerness to rehabilitate ... tireless efforts towards the discovery of creative and regenerative processes.

In this age of widespread violence these words may seem difficult and too generous to accept, but the principle they lay down seems to me to be supremely important.

My prison visiting has involved a great deal of effort and taught me much. The work is complicated by the variety of bureaucratic systems operating in the different States of Germany. It would be simpler if there were a national system throughout the Federal Republic. Nobody could have been more helpful in the last few years than Dr Wagner of the German Red Cross and Herr Rechtsanwalt K. Geier.

Over the years one of the more commendable things which I have noticed is the improvement in the general standard of hygiene, which reflects the very large sums of money which have been made available for this purpose by the State Governments. In particular, this has included the provision of flush loos in cells, but regrettably regulations do not permit prisoners to eat communally, though there are a few exceptions.

It is difficult to decribe the position of the prisoner, his dilemma and the necessity for respecting the dignity of the individual and his potential contribution to society.

The care of the non-German prisoners may be divided into five aspects:

1. Actual prison visiting.
2. Visits to those released and to others who have been repatriated.
3. Appeals on behalf of others wanting to return to their countries of origin.
4. Those who cannot be repatriated and have nowhere to go.
5. After-care.

Several prisoners are recidivists, but, even so, we cannot judge them by any average yardstick. Usually they have no roots in the country of their captivity, no fixed abode other than their gaols, and have long lost touch with whatever natural home they ever had. It is difficult for the long-term prisoner to keep alive hope for the future when he is serving a "life" or a long sentence, has already been in prison for a great number of years, and has, to a large extent, lost contact with the outside world.

In general, there seem to be three different attitudes of mind among those whom I visited:

1. Those who, regardless of the odds against them remain optimistic, positive and actively interested, not only in their immediate surroundings, but also through books, newspapers, foreign languages, television and radio, in the greater horizons outside the prisons. They maintain a normal relationship with the wardens and authorities. No effort should ever be spared to offer these individuals even greater possibilities for extending their thoughts and interests. Hobbies must always be encouraged and discussed during visits. Sometimes their adaptability, even in their fifties, is remarkable.

2. There are those – probably the majority – who have mentally deteriorated and for whom society is sour and unattainable, since they have become so introverted that they have no wish to take their place in the community. They might abuse the chance if they were allowed it. Isolation and imprisonment only increase their bitterness. Only treatment and trust (two essentials, but difficult to put into practice) could perhaps restore the confidence of someone to whom almost everything is the same. I can only reiterate that in my opinion it is positively bad to confine anyone like that in a community so large, but at the same time so uniform and restrictive, that he simply cannot preserve, still less expand, his own personality. Also, regrettably, a few cannot work – they have periods of deep depression and spend their days reading; one or two occasionally paint with materials which I provide. For other prisoners, I have always found that once an opportunity has been given to them to learn a profession or trade they have almost always responded, although nowadays there is much unemployment, and this means that a percentage of the prisoners are inevitably without work after their release.

3. The not-so-hopeless or ill person who might yet become a good citizen, and who might remain "on the level", given the right opportunities while still in prison after learning a trade or working.

With regard to repatriation, judging from those who have already been repatriated, this solution seems the most logical and it is perhaps the best – at least for some – though visits to repatriated individuals cost money and involve a lot of driving, which I did myself.

The importance of after-care and of the Foundation's original small Home at St Christopher's near Celle cannot be over-stressed, nor for that matter can the problems of handling a small number of men of different nationalities, backgrounds and personalities, particularly in view of the inevitable tendency amongst a few to seek refuge in drink. Well over 300 have lived there for short or long periods, according to their state of health and ability to remain independent. Several had originally worked with the teams of volunteers from sixteen different countries who had built the cottages. Though the building itself where most of the Boys lived was ugly and very difficult to make cosy and homely, each had his own room which reflected his personality. One Boy had been completely homeless and a tramp, but later took a full-time job as an agricultural worker on a farm and his room was next door to mine in the attic. He chose to paint it in black gloss and I never got a full explanation from him as to why he had decided upon such a colour.

Right at the beginning a Boy called Josef spent his only pocket money on buying us some food when we were so short. Sadly, years later, he was re-arrested for a minor crime and was beaten to death in a prison in Nordrhein Westfalen.

In the absence of furniture we sat on logs from trees which had been felled on the site, and a British chippie with the Boys made tables. Some of the volunteers in the adjoining attic slept under part of the roof which had never been felted and a few who had beards woke up with little icicles on them.

At least 1,300 Boys have been visited regularly and assisted in a number of ways.

I am conscious that this is a long Chapter, but the reason for its length is best summed up by quoting an extract from *My Early Life* by Winston Churchill:

> . . . the days are very long. Hours crawl like paralytic centipedes. Nothing amuses you. Reading is difficult; writing impossible. Life is one long boredom from dawn till slumber. Moreover, the whole atmosphere of prison, even the most easy and best regulated prison, is odious. Companions in this kind of misfortune quarrel about trifles and get the least possible pleasure from each other's society. If you have never been under restraint before and never known what it was to be a captive, you feel a sense of constant humiliation in being confined to a narrow space. What it must mean for any man, especially an educated man, to be confined for years in a modern convict prison strains my imagination. Each day exactly like the one before with the barren ashes of wasted life behind, and all the long years of bondage stretching out ahead.

There were times when only gloom and monotony seemed our lot, but the whole experience tested our faith to the limit and I was constantly reminded of the mystery of suffering.

PENAL CODE

On 1 January 1975 a new version of the Penal Code of 1871 came into force. *Before* 1 January 1975 a distinction was made between penal servitude and imprisonment.

Paragraph 14 said: "Penal servitude is for life or for a period. The maximum time in the case of a period is fifteen years. Minimum time is for one year."

Paragraph 16 provides: "Imprisonment: Maximum time is five years. Minimum time is one day."

Since 1 January 1975 there has been provision for only one kind of imprisonment. That means there is only one kind of punishment.

Paragraph 16 says: "Duration of Imprisonment. Imprisonment is for a specified term unless the law lays down a life sentence. The maximum imprisonment is for a term of fifteen years. The minimum is one month."

*   *   *

PRISON REGULATIONS

In West Germany prison rules varied among the States. It was unusual for a prisoner to be transferred from one State to another once he had been charged and sentenced, but it was not unknown for a prisoner who had become a recidivist to be charged subsequently in another State. Consequently, he would often protest at the difference between the respective penal regulations and this would aggravate relations between himself and the prison authorities. I was sometimes asked to act as a mediator and explain to the prisoner that some States were much stricter than others. Usually a special *strafe* (punishment) conference took place, to which I was invited, on a certain day of the week, depending upon the prison. This involved the prisoner appearing before members of the prison authority to hear the charge made against him and the punishment imposed.

The following examples give an indication of the regulations that were enforced.

Punishments
1. *For minor offences* – detention in a dark cell was inflicted. "Minor offences" included: staying in bed too long; looking through the cell window; playing cards.
2. *For an attempted escape or insulting a member of the prison staff* – twenty-eight days in an underground cell with bread and water, but on every third day "normal" food, such as was issued to prisoners in the cells.

   As regards sleeping: two days without a mattress and only one blanket on a hard plank bed. On the third day a mattress alternating with no mattress at all.
3. *Correspondence*
   Outgoing. While on remand a prisoner was allowed to write one letter per week. While serving a sentence one letter a month was allowed.

   If a special letter was requested, a prisoner had to apply to the *Polizei Inspektor* (Police Inspector) and give his reasons.

   Incoming. For prisoners both on remand and already sentenced, the only letters allowed were from relatives whose names were registered at the prison. Letters from strangers or acquaintances were not allowed.
4. *Work.* While on remand, prisoners were not obliged to work. While serving penal servitude work was obligatory.

   Earnings were related to conduct, e.g. if forty-five pfs were earned in a day, as a punishment for bad conduct earnings would be reduced, say to thirty pfs per day, for the next three months.

   During the first three months a prisoner serving penal servitude could earn eighteen pfs per day. After that, thirty pfs per day, provided that the work norm was adhered to.

If the foreman approved of the prisoner he could increase his earnings fractionally, but the highest amount allowed to be earned was sixty pfs a day, no matter if a prisoner was there for two or ten years.

Fifty per cent of earnings was kept in *Rucklage* (reserve fund for use on release).

5. *Illness*. If a prisoner claimed that he felt ill and the doctor thought he was malingering, the prisoner was subject to punishment and sometimes he was forbidden to buy anything from his monthly allowance (*Hausgeld*).

6. *Privileges*. Once a month a prisoner could buy from the prison shop certain items of food, e.g. coffee, sugar, sausage, etc., plus two packets of fifty grams of tobacco and toilet articles such as toothpaste; this had to be paid for with *Hausgeld*.

7. *Exercise*. Prisoners were allowed half an hour every day.

Inevitably for anyone who becomes involved in prison visiting, to however small an extent, the question of penal reform and the prison system arises. With the necessity for capital punishment I do not and cannot agree. How to cope with murderers, hijackers, kidnappers; and those who resort to violence and robbery, is a huge problem to which no one knows the answer, but clearly these increasing and horrific outrages must be combated on an international basis in the strongest possible way.

It goes without saying that we must discharge our responsibility towards the public and recognise that there are certain seriously maladjusted individuals who, either because they are psychiatrically disturbed in some way or because they are fanatics, *must be put into a place where they can receive treatment and learn also to give something back to society*. But there are some people for whom no psychiatrist or medical treatment can do anything and one has to accept the fact that nearly all of them will be a danger for the rest of their lives. According to Dr Jan Nowak, one of the first political prisoners in the Extermination Camp of Majdanek, who later continued to read medicine and became a practising physician and psychiatrist, there are individuals born with a criminal gene who have an unmistakable tendency to commit certain types of crime, among which are those involving sexual perversions. Experience has shown that therapy and medical treatment often have very little effect in curing these tendencies. As time goes by this should improve but I feel an offender has to be kept segregated from the rest of society according to the defect of his character. Support and counselling is required ideally on a one-to-one basis.

Personally, I do not believe in allowing such people to be at liberty in society because they can constitute a danger or potential danger; but we must be realistic and understand that simply locking up a person out of the way does not always provide a solution. Is not the provision of more treatment, more productive work, more social workers and more psychiatrists part of the answer? But this is the ideal and so very far from practicable in the foreseeable future or even beyond – indeed, the frightening crime rate continues to grow. Prisons become desperately overcrowded and in some there is little or no work. Alas, a percentage of prisoners simply refuse to co-operate and instead they plan their next crime. The ignorance of the public on this matter is still profound, but since the first edition of this autobiography, the Neighbourhood Watch Scheme has been introduced and several million people, I believe, follow the Crime Watch programme on BBC 1, helping to make people more aware.

Unjustified violence begets violence, and in principle I am against arming the police except in cases and situations where this is patently necessary; it brings to my mind riot situations in which each side becomes trigger happy. In Britain, all Forces have some police who are specially trained in the use of firearms and operate in what are called *armed response units*, which are mobile and provide full-time area coverage by crews which get directions and instructions by car radio. Armed robberies provide most demands but crews are available for all duties so long as they remain available for "armed response", and treat this as a priority. A police officer is permitted to use his firearm only as a last resort in self defence of himself, or somebody else whom he has a duty to protect, and then in the most clearly defined circumstances.

An increase in the severity of the punishment does not necessarily produce results. I think the police are put in an extremely invidious position. But the norms are wide and varied, so it is extremely difficult and indeed wrong to pass judgment. On questions of morality where this touches the conduct of the police, it is also important that one does not apply a double standard. With armed robbers, however, one should be extremely firm. If *ever* a sound scheme could be worked out whereby the offenders be made to pay a part of their earnings to the victim or his family this, in itself, would not only give some slight form of compensation, but such a scheme would give the offenders a better sense of their responsibility to society. One should try to make them conscious of the evil they have committed. We know that some choose crime to avoid work. Also, because of the desperate overcrowding, many prisoners come back into society the worse for having been in contact with other offenders, for they may well have learnt other crimes from them rather than have been educated into better ways. We should make *every* possible effort to persuade people to accept better moral standards, which would, in turn, serve to protect society. *We should also never cease to teach the young respect for their fellow men, to know the meaning of right and wrong and to discipline themselves.* Since so much depends on the environment in which they grow up and live, our determination must be to build and if necessary rebuild the communities, physical and metaphorical, that once engendered a sense of harmony and sharing a common interest.

Throughout the years since 1945 when I started visiting the Boys, the deepest impression has been made upon me by the fortitude they have shown. Although they have been through the most appalling suffering and difficulties, many of them managed in some incredible way to remain almost unaffected by this. One of the Boys, who had been in Belsen and various other camps, said to me: "You know, people can get used to anything if they have no alternative." To the present day there remain the most remarkable courtesy and good manners amongst the Boys. On their side the Boys regard me as their "sister" – I am of their generation – and to some of them I am even "Mum"!

PART FOUR

The Spirit of Optimism

9

A Corner of Suffolk

THROUGH ALL THE YEARS of relief and social work, including nursing, I continued to be reminded everywhere of the Bods in SOE and of the desire which had arisen in me of perpetuating their spirit of optimism, courage and sacrifice – and that of their people too – by founding a Living Memorial. I wanted to commemorate the millions lost in both World Wars by providing relief from suffering and insecurity of all kinds through personal contact and service, restoring dignity to the humiliated, irrespective of age, sex, race or religion. By these means I hoped to contribute towards the building of a better world, one in which peace might be established, however hard the struggle and endless disillusionments.

After I had for some years worked with and for international relief units in Europe, they withdrew – the Red Cross in 1949, because of heavy commitments elsewhere, and the Guide International Service in 1951, when they had exhausted their funds. I continued the work on my own. It never occurred to me to give up. Everything in my childhood, and my experiences during the War, seemed to lead to this inevitable decision. Those were very difficult days, with no funds and no certainty of any support. I shared the frugal life of those who faced uncertainty, sickness and disappointment most of the time, and they told me that they felt I was one of them.

At this stage I was working in different countries and my activities, both during and after relief work, consisted largely of prison and hospital visiting, the provision of medical aid and the Holiday Scheme for people who were ill or suffering. I hoped to establish Homes in Britain and in different parts of the world.

The work I was doing in the prisons and hospitals of Europe grew so quickly that by the time I returned to England on short leave in 1951–2 I had decided that it was necessary to form a small committee and to register the Living Memorial with the Charity Commissioners. After discussing the germ of the idea with people I knew, and in particular with my mother, the Sue Ryder Foundation as it is today was born.

After my father's death in 1942 our family home at Thurlow, together with the land, alas, had to be sold. My mother remained in the Village with her many varied activities, and War work, until 1946, when she moved to the Village of Cavendish twelve miles away. The wrench of leaving the community at Thurlow with all its memories was very great and we found it extremely sad not to be able to stay there. I continue to miss its beauty and the friendship shown by the people.

The house to which my mother came to make her new home was originally a farmhouse and contained five bedrooms. It is reputed to be over 300 years old and has some beautiful Tudor bricks and timber beams, but it was very damp and without heating except for coal fires in a few rooms. Originally there had been fifty acres attached, but when my mother moved there the garden consisted of two acres.

My mother continued to lead a full and very busy life, and parallel to this she offered me every kind of encouragement and strength. She had always been heart-and-soul behind me when in 1945 I first started relief and social work; and later when the international organisations withdrew, she was as convinced as I that the rest of my life should be devoted to the relief of suffering. Despite rationing, which lasted until 1954, she sent me food parcels for distribution in the different countries where I worked. Moreover, she gave talks in a wide area, having a great gift for public speaking, and thereby the work – part of which she had seen during visits to the Continent – gradually became known in Britain. It was through her friends and contacts that the first postal orders had come in. One of our earliest supporters preferred to remain anonymous, sending regularly 5/- postal orders and 10/- notes with a written message, such as "From a Suffolk housewife".

Searches for a suitable property in Britain went on for months, and my original hope of trying to find a large property, preferably within striking distance of London and easily accessible to people coming to the Foundation from many parts of the British Isles, was thwarted. This plan would have entitled the Foundation to an improvement grant and also a grant from the Historic Buildings Council. Certain houses (all listed buildings, Grades 1 and 2) which would have been eminently suitable were snatched away, lost to greedy property developers and, to my dismay, demolished. West Suffolk was not geographically ideal, but two suitable properties were empty at the time. One was Rushbrooke Hall, near Bury St Edmund's, which was demolished. The other was Coldham Hall, Lawshall, which I *just* missed. It was sold for £4,850 and had eighteen bedrooms, two chapels and priest holes. Several of its lovely main rooms were panelled. It is sad to relate but it is true, and perhaps not well known by the public, that 712 country houses in Britain were demolished, gutted or fell into ruin between the years 1945 and 1975.

In 1953, the Foundation having been established with the help of a small legacy, credit from the bank and much optimism, I had no alternative but to buy the house in Cavendish where my mother was living to serve as the Headquarters of the Foundation and as a Home. My mother herself later moved to a smaller house in the lovely Village of Clare, but she continued to help with the running of the house here and in the building up of the Foundation. Without her constant encouragement my tasks would have been twice as difficult; she worked tirelessly for the Foundation until she became handicapped at the age of eighty-five, by which time she was living in a bungalow here in the grounds of HQ. Apart from countless other activities, she ran the clothing stores at the Home, writing hundreds of letters of acknowledgment by hand. She was also a well-known speaker and gave talks far and wide nearly every evening.

The Home is an important part of the simple Headquarters here. It was originally registered to cater for forty-one physically handicapped individuals, but, even though there was a long waiting list, due to bureaucracy on the part of the Health Authorities, and at their insistence the number was reduced to thirty-one, and an extra sluice put in, in spite of the fact that residents were fully ambulant and well able to use normal toilet facilities near their rooms.

These individuals come from different parts of Britain and are looked after by a matron, three full-time and four part-time Registered General Nurses, and one enrolled nurse, assisted by care assistants and volunteers. These residents/patients (affectionately called "the Bods" in memory of the Bods of SOE) live together in the community; before they came here many of them were living on their own, unable to cope with life through loneliness or lack of care; others were blocking hospital beds, and they came to the Foundation through applications made on their behalf by social workers, physicians and local authorities in Britain. From the beginning we have had close ties with the Bods, living as a family.

When a person died here it was a privilege to lay them out with help from a member of the nursing staff. We naturally tidied up their room too. We left a lighted candle and flowers, and moved the individual to rest in the chapel after the undertaker arrived.

Alas the new bureaucratic system no longer permits us to carry on this tradition.

There were many people who helped in those early days and continued to do so as the work expanded. Of all these unselfish and generous individuals it is very hard to single out anyone specifically, but I feel I must mention the name of Harold Ince, the Honorary Treasurer. He and his wife, Dorothy, both lived in the Village – she was a graduate of Girton College, Cambridge, and an enthusiastic producer of plays performed by the Dramatic Society. Dorothy was a dominant figure and believed in Mama's ability to read through plays quickly, so that it was not uncommon for her to send Harold to my mother well after 11 p.m. with a variety of plays and the request that she make her decision by the next morning!

Members of the cast rehearsed relentlessly. Although Mama had little time, she enjoyed acting and threw herself into a play whenever an occasion permitted.

Harold Ince was a keen musician, sang in local choirs, served for over forty years on the parochial church council, and was very active in many other aspects of village life. He had his own tailor's shop in Clare. As Honorary Treasurer of this Home for twenty-two years he will always be remembered by the staff and Bods with love and great affection. No one could have been a more loyal or devoted worker, never sparing himself during evenings or weekends. He will also be remembered by countless people for his punctilious work and determination to gain the maximum discount on every transaction. Often while burning the midnight oil I would say, "Oh Harold, do stop work and rest," and his reply to me would be "How can I? This is the public's money and I must find the threepence which does not tally with my accounts." Nobody was spared! Late one evening he came up to our room bearing an envelope marked "Urgent". On opening it I found a note from him and attached was a sketch of the village cemetery. He was asking me to mark our joint plot by the morning! Moreover, he believed that we should make a block booking so that eventually all the Bods and staff should be buried together. Harold even approached newcomers to the Foundation, including young people, and to their astonishment asked them to choose and pay for a plot!

"Has that lunch been earned?" he would ask me sternly, eyeing a visitor at the table, "or shall I charge her for it?" His death, as the result of a road accident in January 1975, was a severe blow to the Foundation and a great sadness to me personally. Harold Ince was a very long-standing and faithful friend.

At the thanksgiving service in St Mary's Church, Cavendish, the Reverend C. Storrs-Fox paid a moving tribute to the memory of a man who will long be remembered by us all as a very special person:

> When he saw what he believed to be the right course of action he was prepared to go through with it. He undoubtedly trod on many corns, for he could be very brusque at times and very obstinate. All who knew him experienced those disconcerting moments when, before a conversation had ended (or so we thought), he would suddenly turn his back and walk away. But such idiosyncrasies, and others like them, had also an endearing quality, and made us aware that we were dealing with a real "character"; and of these there are too few around nowadays. (I do hope that we shall still keep some of our personal quirks and oddities of temperament in heaven; otherwise we shall hardly recognise one another.)
>
> No account of his life would be complete without mentioning his deep and active love of music. "The man that hath not music in himself, nor is not moved with concord of sweet sounds, is fit for treasons, stratagems and spoils . . . Let no such man be trusted," wrote Shakespeare, and I think Harold might have echoed his words.
>
> When I heard the news of his death, my first thought was, "How sad that a road accident should bring an end such a life of service to Church and Community and, through the Sue Ryder Home, to the victims of 'man's inhumanity to man'." But then I thought, "How much better this is than a gradual dissolution of mental and physical powers." And I remember the last sentence of his last letter to me: "I pray that 1975 may be the year of my release."
>
> His prayer has been granted. He has his release: freedom from the bondage and burdens and frailties of this earthly life. The freedom of

heaven. In our traditional symbolism of heaven, music has a large place. So surely we may think of Harold's fine bass resounding in the heavenly Hallelujahs, his voice and ear fully restored, nay, perfected.

I am so glad that we have sung the hymn, "Jesus, these eyes have never seen that radiant form of thine." It was one of Harold's favourites. In the last verse it points us to a still more glorious prospect:

> "When death these mortal eyes shall seal
> And still this throbbing heart,
> The rending Veil shall thee reveal
> All glorious as thou art."

This puts into verse the sure and certain hope of the fulfilment of that wonderful work of promise in the last chapter of the Bible: "They shall see his face"; the face of the Lord himself.

So, as we pray the traditional prayer – "Rest eternal grant him, O Lord", – it is (to adapt a prayer of Father Benson) for that rest which remaineth to the people of God, where nevertheless they rest not day or night from his perfect service.

The building in this Village was plainly far too small for our purposes at the outset; in addition it had no central heating, and the pre-War Esse stove (brought from the stillroom in the Hall at Thurlow) badly needed to be replaced. Nevertheless, the house was furnished with the help of a friend who owned quantities of dilapidated second-hand and antique furniture (which had to be renovated), and volunteers wrote in from many parts of Britain and abroad offering their services. Soon we were being helped by a large number of people, including nurses, carpenters, several part-time Secretaries and two Honorary Treasurers. When I was not otherwise occupied, I enjoyed taking my turn at cooking, scrubbing and nursing, for I found it relaxing as a change from coping with office work. Everyone worked together as a team, and knowing how short funds were, many people insisted on paying for their keep.

No sooner had the house been acquired by the Foundation than the first groups of patients arrived. Able-bodied patients took great delight in helping with the gardening and with the decoration and conversion of the house. In those days the kitchen was the heart of the Home, possibly because of its central position and its warmth. It was the gathering place for everyone, both at mealtimes and in the evening when, in addition to typing, discussions with patients and staff took place there. These lines of Edna Jacques come to mind:

> I like old houses that are weather-stained
> Whose doorsteps sag beneath the weight of years;
> Old walls that echo back with softened tone
> The laughter that we knew, the sounds of tears . . .
> Old homes that breath of peace and quiet hours
> That we in happy dream may see again . . .

The following was written by a person who used to live here:

Dear Sue Ryder,

It is indeed good of you to have acknowledged my small contribution personally. I greatly appreciate it.

You say you have often wondered about the people who have enjoyed living in the house where I lived in the past and which you have now converted. You have chosen the right word – houses, I think, have an atmosphere and even though I was only in my teens when I lived there, I was aware that it was a happy house.

In the 1800s a Mr. and Mrs. Green lived there. At the end of century Sarah Carverley, an old-fashioned family nurse, came to look after Mrs. Green, who was in failing health. Before that Sarah Carverley had looked after Frances Hildler Havergal, the hymn writer – some of whose hymns are still sung.

When Mrs. Green died, Miss Carverley rented the house from the Misses Garrett at £25 per annum and set up a home for people in straightened circumstances, also those in need of convalescence from the Mission field. Further more, she took in people for country holidays. She charged £1.1.0. or £1.5.0. In 1913 steak was 8d per 1b, eggs 1/- per score, a large loaf – 2 lbs for fourpence h'penny. She was able to make ends meet. The Congregational minister, Mr. Jones, also lived there as he was a bachelor.

When Miss Carverley was finding that she could not keep on because of her age, an aunt of mine suggested that they (my parents) should take over. My father was a Congregational missionary in the South Seas (Samoa) and had to retire early because of ill-health; so the Hawkers moved in in 1914 for three years.

The house, which had been a farmhouse, had no plumbing, but we did have a septic tank. The lighting was by oil lamps and candles. We had a knife boy who came every day to clean the knives on an emery board. The lamps had to be cleaned and filled every day. Winter was very cold and we had a good wood fire in the dining room and drawing room. We often had to break the ice in our water jugs. We had a hip bath in front of the fire and carried cans of hot water upstairs. It really was quite pleasant in front of the blazing fire.

On Sunday afternoons the family, including those who had come to convalesce, gathered in the drawing room to sing hymns before tea. The furniture was Victorian; there was a good grand piano.

I remember particularly the old yew hedge when I was sixteen and wanted to find a place to read; and as a child in New Zealand I had often climbed up such a tree and lain in the yew hedge in the garden. Unfortunately the yew hedge in your present home had not been cut properly and was rather thin in the middle and I was considerably heavier than when I was eleven years of age; and I went right though and found difficulty in getting out at the bottom!

The oval lawn was used for croquet and was also used by the missionary ladies.

On the orchard side there were walnut and mulberry trees. We made mulberry wine and pickled walnuts. The fishpond (near the old farm), later named the lake, was full of fish, including roach, with an old pike to keep down the numbers. The orchard was let to the butcher who kept sheep and ducks in it.

One summer holiday a younger cousin came to stay with us. We were put in what was called the fourth bedroom overlooking the lake. It had a large press just inside the door, with a mahogany bed and dark curtains. My cousin remarked "this is a ghostly room". Two or three nights later, she clutched me and said, "Look"; a diaphanous shape came through the window through the room and out of the other window. My father told me it was just mist floating in the moonlight, and a lady next day said there was no ghost in such a happy house, that it must have been an angel; so this room was known as the wispy angel bedroom.

It has been fun for me to remember the days of over fifty years ago, I am getting old now and suffer from rheumatism. I married a grammar school-master and now lead a quiet life. May God bless you and all who continue to live in what was my old home.

H.M.

Nobody coming here since this, the first Foundation Home in Britain, was started in the early '50s, could ever have imagined the extremely hard daily struggles that had gone on both to convert the house to make it habitable for sick people, and to restore the building by revealing the original timbers, the beautiful Tudor bricks, the chimney-breasts and fine oak dresser – all of which had been covered by countless layers of wallpaper and painted in dreadful green. Nothing had been spared this colour. During the evening, volunteers stripped this paintwork with wire brushes and sandpaper – it took hours. We even had to use a blow lamp. We worked in pairs or groups, often singing, and the day ended after a welcome "cuppa" when we felt physically exhausted but happy to see the result of our labours.

In the early 1950s the greenhouse was taken down and moved elsewhere and a wing added to provide more accommodation for the residents. The wooden lean-to garage became the general office, in which six of us worked until the second extension was added. It is a pity that no photographs were taken to show the extent of these additions. A local builder in the village, Mr Rice (a real craftsman), helped greatly in the early days. He had the reputation of sending in his bills years later.

Over the past forty-three years five wings have been added to provide extra rooms to enable more patients to be admitted and so share this Home with us.

In 1975–6 a further phase, nicknamed "The Dream", was planned to give more downstairs bedroom accommodation, to create a better and larger kitchen and communal dining/sitting room (called the "Golden Room"), and also extra sluices and a large laundry and drying room. The only place left for this particular and large extension was the original kitchen garden which was prone to flooding, and therefore very special foundations (including a ring beam) were essential before erection was possible. The building had to be raised to a certain height to ensure that if flooding should occur no water could enter.

Happily, this particular extension coincided with the Job Creation Programme and thus the Foundation was given the opportunity of finding nine tradesmen and labourers who otherwise would have been unemployed, and their wages, plus ten per cent of the building materials, were paid for under this programme.

The second kitchen garden had to be converted into a car park in order that the front drive should be kept clear and not cluttered with vehicles. It also enabled ambulances to enter and the public to walk peaceably in front of the front elevation.

The Foundation was also fortunate to obtain the assistance of the Royal Engineers who built two bridges across the stream. These were called the Harding Bridges because it was through my friendship with the late Field-Marshal Lord Harding and his late wife Mary that he prevailed upon the War Office and GOC Eastern Command to allow the Royal Engineers to build the bridges as part of an exercise.

It is no exaggeration to say that every nook and cranny of the original building was always used. At one time we cooked and ate communally round the kitchen table in two shifts, and Hilary Phayre (my personal secretary) commented with her merry laugh, "This really is a gobble and go!" From there, to the relief of the voluntary cooks, the volunteers moved into a small but lovely little room which had originally been the pantry and larder, covered also in brown and green paint before being converted. Different volunteers over the years wrote rhymes and ballads and these were hung on the wall there. Perhaps the congestion around the small tables added to the informality at mealtimes.

During the first few years the Home was a place of curiosity and callers dropped in, especially on Sundays, often bringing clothes and gifts with them. On one particular evening as supper was being prepared, no fewer than four coachloads of visitors arrived to be shown round. When they stopped to admire the supper, I asked whether they wanted any refreshment and was slightly taken aback when they gladly accepted the invitation. There was a shortage of crockery and cutlery but, by frequent washing up, the problem was overcome.

Visitors are often surprised by the informality and atmosphere of the Home, and though it is not easy to run because of its low doorways and unexpected corners, one is aware of its history and of the many people through the centuries who have lived here. It was a convalescent home for missionaries in the last century, and a charming description has been given of them going out for walks on Sundays with their parasols. Today, on each door of the rooms and offices there is a plaque with the name of a flower representing the colour of the room. Our bedroom (nicknamed the wispy angel room) is called Dawn and my two offices, Forget-me-not and Red Room.

The national press took a great interest, and in 1956, much to my embarrassment and surprise, I was confronted by the television programme *This is Your Life*, of which I had never heard. I was told afterwards that I was the fifth "victim". Although I have a personal dislike of publicity, it is, however, most useful to focus attention upon the needs of large sections of the community, both here and abroad. Thousands of letters, accompanied by donations, came in. Here are two:

> I send you £10 for having nearly walked off Eamonn Andrews' Show. I know you remained for your people's sake. I am like la mule du pape, late but sure! You shall have more (as a little boy told me) when I got summink I'll give you summink.
>
> L.D.

> Once upon a time, many years ago, when you were one of the first people to appear on "This is Your Life" I drove over to the Sue Ryder Home in Suffolk to find little candles burning in the windows, waiting to welcome those who were coming. This sight touched me deeply and the atmosphere was special, living, warm and good. You were away and for so many years have travelled very far indeed and, if I may say so, achieved a lot. The sight of the candles with the Christmas spirit will remain in my memory.
>
> R.E.

The original chapel was made by converting and enlarging the box-room and garden shed, and oak pews were made in commemoration of particular individuals. The oak itself was donated by a company in Bury St Edmund's and the pews made up by a carpenter in the Village and others by the Foundation's tradesmen. In time we hope to get more pews of the same design for the chapel. The main altar is of Cornish rock and extremely solid and heavy. It was given by a supporter in Cornwall. The oak beams were donated by the boys of St Joseph's Reformatory near Peterborough from their pocket money. The holy water stoop was given by a priest and nursing nuns of a religious order from the former Yugoslavia. The candlesticks were carved by hand by one of the Home's supporters.

On the right-hand side of the chapel there is a small room with a statue of Our Lady where people can retire to say their prayers in more privacy if they wish. In here, at Christmas, we have a tree illuminated with plain white electric candles and a small simple crib hand-made by Poles who served in Fighter Command from 1939–45. On 24 December every year a bouquet of flowers is sent anonymously from Liverpool with the message, "In loving memory". The altar bell, dated 1669, was found on a battlefield during the First World War. Over the years the original chapel had to be enlarged to hold the large congregation attending Mass on Sundays and holy days of obligation.

Mass is said in the chapel every Sunday by the resident chaplain or by the priests from the Augustinian Priory at Clare. Priests who are themselves survivors of the Dachau Concentration Camp come to stay at the Home. On Tuesdays the rector comes over to celebrate Holy Communion and to visit those unable to attend. For years, Christmas Midnight Mass was said by the late Father Rorke, SJ, who was a prisoner of war of the Japanese.

Despite lack of funds, in 1990 a new chapel was designed by Brian Muggleton as the roof of the old one was beyond repair. This is larger than the original chapel but still remains very prayerful. There is a small Lady Chapel adjoining the high altar, which is dedicated to Our Lady of Jasna Góra at Częstochowa in Poland.

There is also a copy of 'Our Lady of Vilna', a painting from Vilna (Vilnus) in Lithuania. The original was painted by an unknown artist, probably between 1620 and 1630, and set into a wall over one of the gateways of the Carmelite Monastery. No one passing by the gateway can fail to see the painting, and people can always be seen kneeling in prayer before it in the street. In spite of the risk of persecution by invaders throughout the centuries, the picture has remained an object of profound veneration. A small chapel is built on one side of the gateway, and the Madonna is adored not only by Catholics but by members of the Orthodox Church. It remains to this day a popular place of pilgrimage, and leads into a principal street of the City. Before 1943, Vilna belonged to Poland but it was ceded to Lithuania at the Yalta Conference. Lithuania, which had been occupied since 1939 successively by the Nazis and the Soviets, was subsequently annexed to the Soviet Union, but regained its independence in 1989.

Three prayers hang inside the chapel here at Headquarters; the first was found on a scrap of paper near the body of a dead child in Ravensbrück:

> O Lord, remember not only the men and women of goodwill, but also those of ill-will. But do not only remember all the suffering they have inflicted on us, remember also the fruits we bought thanks to this suffering, our comradeship, our loyalty, our humility, the courage, the generosity, the greatness of heart which has grown out of all this, and when they come to judgment, let all the fruits that we have borne be their forgiveness.
>
> Give us, Lord, a humble, quiet, peaceable, patient, tender and charitable mind, and in all our thoughts, words and deeds a taste of the Holy Spirit. Give us, Lord, a lively faith, a firm hope, a fervent charity, a love of you. Take from us all lukewarmness in meditation, dullness in prayer. Give us fervour and delight in thinking of your grace, your tender compassion towards me. The things that we pray for good Lord, give us grace to labour for: through Jesus Christ our Lord.

The following prayer my husband and I composed together in 1958:

> O most Holy Face of Jesus, who in Thy bitter passion looked down with such mercy from the cross for the salvation of the world, look today upon us all, poor sinners. Grant peace and eternal rest to all the departed, but especially to the millions known and unknown who died as prisoners in many lands, victims of the hatred and cruelty of man. May the example of their suffering and courage draw us closer to Thee through Thine own Agony and Passion, and thus strengthen us in our desire to serve Thee

in the sick, the unwanted and the dying wherever we may find them. Give us the Grace so to spend ourselves for those who are still alive, that we may prove most truly that we have not forgotten those who have died.

Bless us continually with the awareness of Thy presence; give us humility, gentleness and unselfishness in all our work for Thee; dispose our hearts never to refuse what Thou askest through Thy inspirations and commandments. Compass us about with Thy holy angels and grant that at the hour of our death they may lead us to Thee in the splendour of eternity. *Amen*.

Usque Ad Mortem – Unto Death

To Thee, O my God
Who art infinite Love
Yet who hast called us to be perfect, even as
Thou art perfect:
Who so loved the World,
That Thou didst give us
Thine only begotten Son,
And who hast thereby given
Thine all, Thine everything:
Who emptied Thyself of Thy Glory,
And become obedient unto death
Even the death of the Cross,
For us;
To Thee;
We surrender our all, our everything,
To be consumed by the unquenchable fire of Thy Love:
We desire to love Thee even as Thy own Mother loved Thee,
To be generous as Thou only art generous,
To give our all to Thee as Thou givest Thine to us:
Thou hast called us, O Lord, and we have found Thee
In the poor, the unwanted, and the suffering,
And there we will serve Thee unto death.

Near my kneeler is a photograph of a crucifix sketched by an unknown prisoner on a wall of the underground death cells in the dreaded Block II of the main Extermination Camp of Auschwitz.

When the Home began here, and for several years after, this Village had a railway station and a regular service of trains on the branch line from Cambridge via Sudbury to junctions with the main London line at Marks Tey and Colchester. This, of course, was most useful and the sudden, permanent closure of the branch line in 1967, due to Dr Beeching's determination to cut the railways throughout Britain to 10,000 miles, was a cruel blow to the Home, and to many of its patients, supporters and visitors, and to the general population of the Stour Valley who were deprived of the ability to move easily out of their towns and villages. The number of vehicles on the roads has increased to an appalling level and thus both the number of serious injuries and mortalities are very high. Alas, too, the bus services have become far less frequent.

There have been various crises and emergencies in the Village over the years, such as the flood of 1968 when the Stour rose and filled the house with water to a height of eighteen inches, causing some hundreds of pounds worth of damage. Thanks to the initiative of the staff and Bods and the help of the local fire brigade, the most handicapped were quickly rescued and taken upstairs, although the lights were out. Within thirty minutes the firemen had also managed to remove to safety all the card indexes and most of the furniture. They did this under the most difficult conditions by the light of lanterns and torches. Regrettably we lost ten beautiful regional costumes from different countries which were in an oak chest. After the tide of water had subsided a lot of mud was left behind. There was a further threat of flooding after heavy rains in the autumn of 1974. Nevertheless the house has continued to serve as Headquarters of the Foundation, and over the years further extensions have been added to provide more accommodation for patients and staff.

At present the building at Headquarters harbours the offices of my Assistants, including my Senior Personal Assistants, five Secretaries, the Covenants Treasurer and his Assistant, the Financial Director. Visits are received regularly from my many Assistants. There is also a wing which contains all the Accounts Section for the Foundation. Altogether about twenty-eight people work at Headquarters, some of whom regularly visit Sue Ryder Homes elsewhere. And of course there are also very many volunteers.

Over the years I have been served most loyally by several Personal Assistants. It is difficult to single out individuals but there are two who must be mentioned. Paul Lewin was my Senior Legal Assistant until a few months after my husband's death. He worked closely with me for ten years, and became a full-time Minister of the Catholic Church. He is greatly missed.

On 12 May 1995, I lost my Senior Personal Secretary of many years. As June Backler was deeply concerned with this autobiography, I may be allowed to write the following:

June joined the Foundation in 1972. After leaving school, she worked in the Tax Office in Sudbury and then with a firm of solicitors. This experience was to prove invaluable when she came to work with us at HQ, as amongst all her other work, she coped with legacies.

June expected and did work long hours, and for many years this included lots of Saturdays too. She was happy to travel to HQ by bus from Sudbury where she lived, or to be collected at 6 a.m. (not every day!) to keep pace with the piles of letters which found their way to her wire tray. She had excellent shorthand, and was devoted to her manual typewriter which must have turned out many millions of words. Her filing proved immaculate!

Everybody in the various offices at HQ knew when June was present. She was kind, firm, strong-willed and outspoken and a little awe-inspiring to those who did not understand her somewhat quick temper . . . which soon subsided. She was a perfectionist and looked for perfection in others.

Working and living together for more than twenty years, and more latterly in the Red Room sharing our thoughts, feelings and experiences – we lost our beloved husbands within ten days of each other in 1992 – created a friendship which is hard to describe. Above all I should express my gratitude to June for her invaluable assistance with the first edition of this autobiography. On occasions, we dictated Chapters on trains (much to the surprise of fellow passengers), or wherever and whenever we could. We never lost an opportunity to bring the work forward.

June had been diagnosed with cancer twenty-six years before. She had surgery, radiotherapy and in the last months more chemotherapy. Her absence from HQ grew longer but we had very frank talks about the disease. In April she said: "Go away on your long drives to the work overseas and I will be here to cope – I am determined to hang on through this summer." She asked me then outright whether she might live so long, and I had to be truthful, so we took leave of each other in the chapel.

Her family told me that the Foundation proved June's lifeline. We all remember her reliability, her staunch faith, her courage in her illness, her laughter and enjoyment of life, and her knowledge and love of music.

June had a most supportive family – three daughters and a son. We offer them our prayers and deepest sympathy.

May I add: "Thank you, June, for being a very loyal member of the Foundation's team, and for the example you gave me of your stoic courage."

The team here have grown ever closer together – many have served long years for the Foundation in their service at HQ – and I want to try and express my appreciation to them all.

In addition to the resident and non-resident Secretaries, very valuable assistance with the office work is given voluntarily by the "weekend" Secretaries who travel from London or far further afield to help in whichever way they are needed. A blessed quiet occasionally falls upon the house from about one o'clock on Saturday afternoon and lasts through Sunday. Although on many weekends I know I am not likely to remain entirely undisturbed, the knowledge that perpetual phone calls will not interrupt my train of thought is a heavenly balm. We have found that far more correspondence can be dealt with early in the morning or late in the evening when the offices are quieter.

The following are two from many letters received from several Secretaries who gave two weeks of their time to the Foundation:

Please accept my offer to come in to work, as needed, as my contribution to the work you do. As a Buddhist, I look upon my small part as my "thank you" for all the good things in life I have – such as a loving husband, a nice home, and after all you can only wear one dress at a time and you eat just so many meals in a day!

S.

I am writing to thank you for having me to stay with you. The last fortnight has been an enlightening one for me: first, because it has given me insight into the work and the *needs* of the Foundation, and secondly because the work you asked me to do has given back to me a great deal of self-confidence (which has not been one of my most prominent talents). I am very glad to have been able to give you a hand: please be assured that I will continue to support you and the Foundation in every way I can.

My husband was delighted to meet you. We will both feel personally included in your work, now. I am sure that our prayers will be heard, and that the needs of the Foundation will be met. It has been a privilege to meet you and to work a little while for you. You will always be included in my prayers – especially when you go upon your journeys.

Please accept the enclosed – just a token offering towards my keep for the fourteen days.

Yours very sincerely in Christ,
J.B.

And from a Dutch volunteer:

Dear Lady Ryder,

You gave me a home when I needed it. You gave me a place to work and at the same time I could sort out my life, for the first time all alone.

I want to express my gratitude and warm feelings.

May you get all the help and love needed and may God be with you.

For more than eighteen years volunteers also helped with the cooking, working in pairs according to a daily rota (which at one time numbered over thirty strong) and preparing lunch for everyone in the Home. Sheelagh Crawford and Honor Penton organised the rota and proved amazing supporters, as were the voluntary cooks. Some brought delicious dishes with them even though a number of these volunteers had long distances to drive here.

Very much of the work done for the Foundation is voluntary, and paid members of staff work for the smallest wage they can so that only a small percentage of the money received by the Foundation is spent on administrative costs. The service of the late Mrs Edna Swan, who was Chairman of the Home Support Group, for many years, was incalculable.

Of several thousand young volunteers from Britain and overseas who have worked here during the past forty years, many went on to read medicine, train as social workers or enter a nursing school. Several trained as nurses at Guy's Hospital and other hospitals in London and elsewhere.

Some volunteers and Assistants have later taken Holy Orders or joined a religious congregation. A lot come prior to university, and their presence and fresh approach to caring for and being with the Bods is most encouraging.

Ideally, volunteers are needed during the months of October to May; unfortunately the Foundation cannot accept many of the large numbers who apply to help in the summer (referred to within the Foundation as the "migration of birds") from about fifteen different countries.

We have always struggled to keep up the beauty of the garden, so were very pleased when Brian arrived in 1995, a highly qualified and very gifted Head Gardener. Already he has made many improvements. The influx of volunteers, especially in the summer months was, both a blessing and a trial, depending upon their knowledge of gardening. One year we decided to divide up the Finns, Portuguese, Spaniards and Poles in such a way that they were unable to converse with one another. You needed eyes in the back of your head to ensure that they had not stopped weeding to practise their English on one another. The Foundation's gardeners and tradesmen have over many years added to the garden such features as the small bridge and summerhouse at the end of the lake. We are always delighted to receive bulbs and herbaceous plants and gifts for the greenhouse.

In the wing of the main house there is a place packed to the ceiling with gifts made and given by the patients and voluntary helpers, including items ready to go to the Sue Ryder Shops. Wherever possible, both in Britain and abroad, work therapy is encouraged among the residents and children in the Homes. Items such as trays, stools, and knitwear are made by the patients and sold to raise funds for the running of the Homes. There were at one time nearly 1,000 voluntary helpers who knitted cardigans for the patients of all ages. In other rooms and wherever space can be found, there are sacks of goods which have been emptied, sorted, rebagged and labelled, according to the Sue Ryder Shop they are destined for.

There are the clothing stores (nicknamed "Mecca" and "The Ark"), which for many years were looked after by my mother and her friends, working in the then unheated storerooms and keeping meticulous note of the thousands of items donated.

Unknown to Mama or to the helpers, somebody once put a notice in a woman's magazine announcing that the Foundation would welcome wedding dresses, and there was an incredible influx. One of the Boys, referred to in Chapter 8, who was helping Mama, had yearned in vain to be married; so for him it was particularly distressing to be surrounded by nearly 400 dresses and veils (some accompanied by bridesmaid's dresses too). The situation was almost too much for him. Nobody who had not witnessed this amazing scene could imagine how the limited floor space of the store was transformed by those hundreds of wedding dresses of every style and material. We felt we had one of the biggest bridal stores in the country with no space for display!

In the midst of this a worried mother wrote to say that in her enthusiasm, after reading the notice, she had posted her daughter's wedding dress and please could we now send it back. She described it as being made from wild silk with a tulle veil and sprigs of orange blossom. For hours Mama and the Boy searched, selected and sent off various wedding dresses nearest to the description, but to no avail. So Mama finally hoped that a small gift would help to smooth things out.

Today the work of handling the daily arrival of parcels and gifts is done by concentration camp survivors and by young voluntary helpers who come from Poland and Czechoslovakia, for periods of six to twelve months. They work very hard indeed in an honorary capacity dealing with many tons of clothing and other items which arrive from different parts of Britain.

Here I would like to include a profile of one of those volunteers that appeared in our *Remembrance 1995* annual magazine:

Pani Josefina Kvetuse Libenska, a founder member of the Foundation's Support Group in the Czech Republic, tells of her life in the former Czechoslovakia and her current work for the Foundation in Prague. For the past three years Pani Josepfina has made annual visits to the Foundation's Headquarters in Britain to help with the work in this country.

PANI (MRS) JOSEPFINA KVETUSE LIBENSKA

I was born in Ostrava on 3 November 1924 and attended a grammar school in Prague. Later, I hoped to enter the medical school of the Charles University (founded in the fourteenth century by King Charles IV), but I was not accepted owing to the Communist coup in the Spring of 1948 . . . so my great hopes were dashed. I became a secretary in a office where I could practise my knowledge of foreign languages: English, French and a little German. Then, on the 22 March 1951, I was arrested on the street by the Secret Police and accused of activities against the State. They interrogated me in Prague-Bartolmejska prison, and also in the notorious Pankrac prison (used too by the Nazis during the German occupation March 1939 – May 1945). I was blindfolded before being taken to the interrogation and placed in solitary confinement for one year before being sentenced to sixteen years for high treason. I cannot describe my feelings or the conditions.

I was a prisoner in Juhlava, Ceska Lipa, Pardubice – a special prison for about one thousand women of different ages. Nuns stripped of their habits were also prisoners and I referred to their cell as the Vatican. I had to work one of three shifts and was obliged to use heavy cloth to make uniforms which were sent to the Soviet Union. The worst prison was perhaps in Zeliezovce, Slovakia, where I became very weak due to the hard work on the land with no machinery and through lack of food.

Finally, I was released in 1960, a so-called amnesty – actually, a release with conditions, and I was also under surveillance from the Police for many years. I had no civil rights for several years and was not allowed to work in an office but only in a store for heavy machinery. Officially I had to remain a labourer.

My daughter, Barbara, was born in 1961, but I only had a short maternity leave. However, gradually my life improved, but our short-lived time of hope, the Prague Spring, ended in August 1968 when the Soviet Army invaded and occupied my country.

I retired in 1980 but continued to work in offices to augment my pension. I had made a few friends in the different prisons but they died young and so I only met the survivors at funerals.

In 1989, I saw President Havel released from prison and experienced the Velvet Revolution.

I had always prayed hard but secretly and some girls in the prisons made a Rosary from bread, as was done during Nazi occupation. I belong to the Sue Ryder Prayer Group in Prague. We also meet for Mass every Monday in the Church of St Mary of the Snow in the centre of the city. I am helping Tom Noel, Lady Ryder's representative in the Czech Republic and other volunteers. We prepare and work for the bazaars and twice I joined the young people clearing up the debris outside the future Sue Ryder Home, Michle Court in Prague.

This is my third visit to the Foundation's Headquarters, I enjoy coming and consider this place to be my second home.

After waiting many years, my daughter gave birth to Filip Václav on 27 September 1994, so I am now a grandmother!

Pani Josepfina wrote to me in one of her letters: "Lord, we pray not for a lighter load but for a stronger back to carry our load. Amen."

Pani Josepfina is only one of many volunteers to participate in this operation, and not many people can imagine what is involved for the helpers. They include professional dressmakers, especially Sabina Granuszewska, an expert dressmaker who was arrested by the Soviets, forced into their Army, and as a nurse at the front saw indescribable suffering and barbarities for hundreds and hundreds of kilometres right up to Berlin. She was repatriated to the ruins of her country Poland in 1945.

All these volunteers helped to sort, wash, iron and repair the contents of hundreds of black sacks, day in, day out. I and my late husband, too, took our share in helping in this operation. Leonard coped with the more delicate laundry in our own washing machine whenever he could on a Sunday afternoon. One of the Area Managers also comes down once a month to spend a whole weekend assisting. These sacks when re-sorted and bagged up are destined for fifteen or more of the upmarket Sue Ryder Shops in London, and are delivered there every fortnight by the Foundation's van from Headquarters. Other Area Organisers also call to sort and assist in various ways.

Other clothing, books, bric-a-brac and so on, are sent to Regions where new shops are being opened and supplies may not be sufficient at the beginning. In addition thousands of sacks are prepared for distribution to those in such need overseas.

Ideally, the Foundation requires an aircraft hangar. Sadly there is a dire lack of space left in the grounds here and, for a number of reasons, the distribution has to be done from Headquarters. The sorting of gifts is carried out in all Regions, but not on such a large scale.

Many people are surprised to learn that "Harrods" exists at HQ. This is the mail order store, which has been in place for over forty years, and dispatches items featured in the Gift Catalogue.

"Harrods" was organised by the late Hilda Herbert, who was a perfectionist; and she was assisted by Margaret Boreham, who has worked here for twenty-four years. In addition to the despatch of items ordered from the Gift Catalogue, "standard" goods are also sent out to some of the Sue Ryder Shops and Sue Ryder Support Groups and it is where stock is held for the Gift Shop attached to the Foundation's Museum. "Harrods" holds a vast range of gifts from Sue Ryder crested goods, for example, badges, key fobs, pens, thimbles, and so on, to more expensive and upmarket items.

At "Harrods", it often seems to be Christmas all year round! Early in January, a senior representive from the Medici Society visits to show dozens of cards for the Catalogue for the coming year – other members of HQ staff are called upon to help with the selection. It is always difficult to determine what the general public will wish to buy and this task calls for experience and judgement of the current public taste.

Following the selection of cards, comes the equally difficult task of choosing gifts. Thanks to the efforts of Margaret Hibbard, samples are sought after throughout the year. In addition to her work as Regional Manager for the Sue Ryder Shops in the South West, she visits the various gift fairs to seek out possible items for inclusion in the Catalogue. These items, of course, have to be light, easy to pack so they will travel safely through the post, eye-catching so they will stand out in the Catalogue, and available at an affordable price for the customer.

Once the selection has been made, attention is paid to all the finer details of specifications, delivery requirements, the placement of orders, and, of course, the compilation of the Gift Catalogue itself.

The Gift Catalogue is despatched to 59,000 supporters, together with *Remembrance*, and is also distributed throughout the Sue Ryder Shops. Soon after the despatch in September, orders start arriving.

By this time willing and invaluable volunteers have been chosen to help with despatching the orders. Often these are young people taking a year out between school and university and they are able to obtain a good insight into the workings of part of the Foundation's fundraising strategy.

Many people often ask why goods in the Gift Catalogue are not sold in all the Sue Ryder Shops. Unfortunately, it would be impracticable to have the necessary stock available and such a system would also take away sales from the mail order, which we feel is a particularly useful service for many people, especially those who are housebound.

"Harrods", the Sue Ryder Gift Shops and Coffee Shops come under the umbrella of the Sue Ryder Remembrance Company, which is the trading arm of the Foundation set up some thirty years ago. The Remembrance Company – unlike the Charity itself – is legally empowered to make a profit on trading, and these profits form a vital part of the funds which support the international work of the Foundation. The contribution of "Harrods at HQ" is itself a very important and much valued element in the whole essential fundraising process.

Many people ask why the Headquarters of this small Foundation should be part of the Home itself. The advantages far outweigh the disadvantages. The residents have felt a part of our lives and whatever has been going on throughout the Foundation. Many have contributed by helping to sort trading stamps, keep records, or assist in the garden; one of the residents, Mr Edwin, acted as the chapel's Sacristan for several years. It is an honour to be under the same roof with them, and one is reminded every time we meet in the corridors, dining room or in their bedrooms that we are part of the same family. Moreover, if we are together under the same roof we complement each other. The residents are nursed here until death calls them, and to be with them then is a great privilege.

It is hard to single out anyone from the many residents who have lived with us, or who are with us now, for all in their own way have contributed to the community, however sick they were. Their characters and personalities would be hard to describe, but I cannot resist mentioning a few names.

Bill Fryer, aged sixty-six, used to work as a warehouseman in a paint store before his accident. He was a keen punter and always enjoyed watching racing on television. Moreover he was an expert on form. Both the auxiliary nurses and volunteers were introduced to his hobby and telephone calls to the local bookie made on the public phone box were frequently heard. Bill, when lucky, was generous, and would give a donation to the Foundation.

Major Michael Drakeford, in his early seventies, lived alone. He had a small cottage near Canterbury in Kent, and suffered from bulbar palsy (a condition in which that part of the spinal cord within the skull is affected). He had been advised by his doctor to live in a community, and the following letter showed his wish to retain as much of his independence as possible. He wrote:

> I want to find a Home in which I can participate a bit and contribute to, and also to carry on with my cooking (everything has to go through the liquidiser). I do not just want to be looked after until I die. I want to be part of the Home I live in and feel I *belong* there.

We replied to his letter and he then wrote to us again:

> Your letter has completely removed my dread of the future. The Foundation has already met two of my immediate needs. It has given me hope for the future . . . It has also given me an ideal and an aim to work for in my declining years.

As a result of these letters, Major Drakeford came to stay with us for two or three weeks every year until he died.

Another Bod is C.D. who was admitted to the Sue Ryder Home here at Headquarters at the end of 1979. She was diagnosed as suffering with motor neurone disease and also from cerebral atrophy, dysphagia and dysphasia (difficulty in swallowing and difficulty in speaking coherently). C.D. had been employed by the Greater London Council as a social secretary all her working life. She has travelled to many parts of the world with – and to visit – her many friends. Her last visit was to America. C.D. has led a full and active life and writes me delightful letters – and frank notes – on various topics which I find most helpful.

Two sisters, Margaret and Dorothy Gregory, both had strong characters. They had lived together in the Home Counties and were indignant at being told by a social worker that they could no longer cope on their own and therefore would have to move. They suggested to her that they would find an alternative place themselves.

Margaret trained at the London Hospital, Whitechapel, and had firm ideas of how nurses and auxiliaries should work and maintain a high standard. She became a Catholic, while her sister, Dorothy, who lost her sight, was a strong Methodist. Dorothy bore her final illness with great dignity and died of cancer while we were praying in her room.

Edward was our Librarian. He had created and built the chapel at the Concentration Camp at Flossenburg, which was started in May 1938. The Village of Flossenburg is not far from Nuremberg and the frontier with Czechoslovakia. Its granite quarries where prisoners worked were notorious.

There were over 100 auxiliary camps attached to Flossenburg, many of them a great distance from the main Camp, but all in or very near villages, towns and cities; and it is estimated that one third of these auxiliary camps – some of them holding up to 5,000 persons – were occupied by female prisoners. A considerable proportion of some 100,000 prisoners registered from 1938 to 1945 was assigned to these auxiliary camps. Epidemics, such as typhus fever and typhoid killed large numbers. At this Camp, Soviet prisoners of war were neither registered nor documented. It is estimated that people of twenty-four different nationalities were imprisoned in this Camp, and that at least 74,000 died there. After preparing for a visit from Bishop (later Cardinal) Rubin, Edward told me, "Now my work is done and I want to die"; he did die ten days later.

Then there was Bubie whose room looked out over the pond and God's garden, as he described it. He did the glazing of the prints for the photographic section and kept a record as well of all envelopes he addressed to new people who wrote in for information about the Foundation. In the evenings he enjoyed playing the piano. His mind was an encyclopaedia and his merry remarks about "fantastic news", "a marvellous meal" could be heard in different parts of the building. When I came in from long drives

he would say to me: "Now do go and soak yourself in a warm bath." Bubie
died of tuberculosis and chronic rheumatoid arthritis after great pain,
which he bore nobly.

Having a very small percentage of psychiatrically disturbed individuals
means that even more time must be given to listening to and discussing
their ideas, complaints and problems. We remember, too, at Headquarters,
the individuals from various parts of Britain who have turned up unexpectedly, including the alcoholics, drug addicts and the woman who had
been a nurse, but had suffered a breakdown, and sat counting the blades of
grass on the lawn.

It is important that the handicapped should be integrated into the
community and not relegated to a shadowy half-world where they have no
interests or occupations apart from their ailments and the television. Being
handicapped, after all, does not disqualify one as a human being, but
merely necessitates acquiring "a new technique of living", as we call it.

Perhaps one might add a word of advice to all well-meaning people who
come into contact with the handicapped. Although it may seem to be an act
of kindness, never complete a sentence for someone who is slow of speech,
or attempt to do anything for a handicapped person which he is capable of
doing himself, albeit much more slowly. This is a small point, but of great
importance to people who are trying to lead normal lives.

We are fortunate to live in the midst of the Village and thus feel a part of
whatever else is going on. The Home is easily accessible and the ambulant
Bods enjoy doing their own shopping and going for walks. The wheelchair Bods, too, enjoy going out into the Village and, therefore, do not feel
isolated or cut off.

In the past, many builders and tradesmen lived and worked here, some
of whom applied their skills to the maintenance of this Home, while others
went forth from here to work in different parts of the world. At times there
were several tradesmen with the same names and so nicknames were given.
Many, too, have left particular memories as a result of their hard work. For
instance, "Long John" restored the rosewood piano by stripping and
french-polishing it. Several of the tradesmen remain in contact and call in.

As is always the case in life, there are differences of opinion and temperament, but to the outsider it is perhaps surprising to see how naturally, easily
and enjoyably the residents, the staff, the tradesmen and volunteers –
usually about 300 a year, of many nationalities and age groups – come to
terms with one another, the routine, the handicapped, and with whatever
they can make of life in this corner of Suffolk.

*　*　*

From the very beginning, after the Foundation's Home and Headquarters
had been established, thousands of visitors and supporters "dropped in" or
made appointments to come. During most of the first years, groups of
various sizes had been guided through the Home and given the opportunity

of seeing as much as possible. My colleagues and I always made a point of showing them the chapel at the end, where I tried to explain as much as I could about the work of the Foundation and invited them to ask questions. In spite of this, apart from the fact that we never had enough guides, especially when groups arrived unexpectedly and members of the staff were busy with other duties, the visits inevitably created problems and also caused considerable inconvenience to Bods in the Home. Some enjoyed visitors, but there is a difference between people coming to see and talk with patients, and strangers intruding unintentionally upon their privacy.

I remember in particular one evening at about 9.45 when the volunteer on the switchboard buzzed me to say that a coachload of visitors had arrived. They were not entered in the diary or in the appointments file. I came down to greet them in the chapel and politely expressed some surprise at their arrival at that late hour, whereupon the leader explained: "Oh, we are out on a mystery tour." This was not the first or the last of such unexpected groups.

One member of a group of visitors was once heard to remark about me: "Yes, I think it's a good eighty years since the event – pity she's dead." Another turned to her companion and said, "I hope you've enjoyed yourself?" "Yes," came the reply, "but *where* are we?"

It was not unusual for them to be confused as to whether my husband or I were even married. I would hear them say, "Oh you mean that man Cheddar, well he has nothing to do with Sue Ryder, she helped to start Dr Barnardos and helped to exterminate smallpox in South Wales!"

Partly as a result of all these visitors I conceived the idea of a Museum at Headquarters which would not only house items of historical value, but also provide a dramatic visual introduction to what the Foundation had set out to achieve and the conditions which existed in the countries where I worked.

In the late 1960s these rather vague ideas crystallised in the form of a definite plan for the Museum building. Although I wanted the Museum primarily to serve as a tribute to those whose suffering and courage brought the Foundation into being, the Council of the Foundation specially requested that it should be extended to show how I felt drawn to undertake the work.

The only piece of ground available for the site of the Museum was in the front of the Home, near the gates.

On the site was a small herbaceous border and a rather shabby shed built with breeze blocks and left unrendered. This was levelled and some of the hard core used for the foundations of the new building which our own tradesmen laid.

Because of the small area of the site – and the limited funds available – we were obliged to revise the original plan for a somewhat larger building. This meant that the displays and tableaux in the Museum would have to be on a much smaller scale than I had originally intended, and that I could not attempt to include tableaux on many aspects of the work which seemed to merit it.

While the drawings were being prepared by one of the Foundation's architects, the task of appealing for building materials and equipment began. The construction of the Museum was put out to tender, but the quotations received were far in excess of what we could afford. At this point, out of the blue and to my immense surprise and joy, a most generous anonymous cheque arrived one morning in the post. Buoyed up by this, we went ahead using our own tradesmen and labourers, who were later joined by others from the Job Creation Programme.

Certain companies which had been especially generous to the Foundation in the past came to my rescue again with gifts of building materials and some even sent their own people, including two or three directors, to help with the construction at weekends.

Among the companies to respond, one wrote in their trade magazine as follows:

> Recently Redland Tiles answered a request for help from the Sue Ryder Foundation with all the aid they could muster. Not only did the chairman and managing director, David Lyon, consider it a worthwhile charity to support; he also believed that tiling a roof would give the representatives who did it a greater insight into the technical problems connected with the product they sell.
>
> The enthusiasm which the Founder and her staff put into the running and equipping of their Homes somehow comes across in the many letters sent to the companies like Redland asking for help. Many give materials or let the Foundation have supplies at cost.

Owing to the splendid help we received, both in labour and in materials, the pace of construction was good and we were able to keep to schedule.

The walls of the interior were to be white and the floor red ceramic (to signify sacrifice). Blue hessian was chosen to line the exterior and white felt the interior of the display cases.

The Museum was linked by a long room to the bungalow in which my mother had lived, and her small drawing room and dining room, together with the long room, were converted into a place for visitors to enjoy light refreshments. In an adjoining room we created a gift shop and a second refreshment room.

Once the carcase of the building had been rendered, unexpected gifts and large quantities of furniture rolled in. One day I said to Pani (Mrs) Mita, a volunteer from Poland helping in the clothing store, "What are we to do, because we have no other storage place in which to sort out and repair the furniture that will be needed once the extension is ready?" She replied, "Pray harder and God will come to our rescue".

There seemed to be an ever-increasing flow of furniture of all descriptions, and thanks to a local farmer and his foreman, we were able to label it all with coloured tags. The colours varied according to what had to be done with the furniture, for some was damaged and had to be repaired; some was suitable for immediate use; other items were perfect but had to be kept back for future extensions. These last were all taken away by tractor and stored for a few months, but the whole procedure entailed a lot of hard work which was quite separate from the more obvious tasks associated with the construction of the Museum.

People visiting the Museum for the first time in later years might find it hard to imagine the meticulous planning involved in gathering the great variety of exhibits from so many different drawers and boxes, then sorting, labelling and putting them into their proper categories (uniforms, items of equipment, handicrafts, photographs – the latter mounted by two supporters and volunteers from Christchurch, New Zealand, Harvey and Katrine Brown, who came over especially and gave up their holiday in Britain to assist). The choice of appropriate quotations and the hand-printing of these and the many captions also took long hours of careful labour, and for this I am indebted to one of my former Secretaries, Anne James.

When work first started on the Museum the road ahead looked very long and difficult, but as we progressed a clear pattern emerged and we were all drawn into the excitement and satisfaction of creating the Museum.

Without the volunteers from Poland who humped trunks and boxes and helped in a thousand other ways, little would have been achieved. Every available table, including the garden furniture, was carried into the Museum and the exhibits were temporarily stacked upon them. Then we had to concentrate on the huge but exciting task of assembling in turn the contents of each display case. A professional window-dresser gave me good advice and assistance – he drove down from Norfolk when he could.

Tadeusz Szymanski, one of the curators of the Auschwitz Museum, accompanied by Pani Eva Gorecka from Poland, helped me plan the layout of the Museum. Later, invaluable advice and considerable help were received from the Imperial War Museum, who had expressed interest in the project and had kindly loaned us an AMK III transceiver which was needed to complete one exhibit.

The following is the Foundation's decription of the completed Museum:

> The Museum has something for everyone. It is fascinating and colourful; it is of immense historical interest; it is harrowing, saddening and thought-provoking; and at the same time it points to the human spirit rising triumphant. It should become a focal point of interest not only for Suffolk but for counties and countries very much further away.

Inside the entrance there are notices about the Museum and the Foundation, including the Foundation's rosemary Logo:

> This Museum was conceived by Sue Ryder as a tribute to those whose suffering and courage brought her Foundation into being. At the special

request of the Council of the Sue Ryder Foundation, it has been extended
to show how she herself felt drawn to undertake this work.

The Sue Ryder Foundation was established in 1952 with the intention –
as expressed by the Founder – that in offering help and hope to those
in need, it should also serve as a Living Memorial to the victims of war
and those who continue to suffer from persecution and racial intolerance.

This small Museum attempts to tell the story of the various influences
on the remarkable life of the Founder; the past and present work of the
Foundation; and its hopes for the years that lie ahead. It is a story of
the triumph of the human spirit.

Opposite this is an enlarged photograph of Dawn with the following quotation from 'The Gardener' by Rabindranath Tagore:

> Dawn sleeps on the shadowy hill
> The stars hold their breath counting the hours.

Each Section of the Museum tries to portray a particular theme. I searched
for suitable quotations which could be matched to the tableaux on the items
displayed.

The opening tableau is a facsimile of my mother's room. It includes many
of her small personal treasures. Her prie-dieu and the desk bearing all the
signs of ceaseless endeavour are included, together with a bookcase with
a few of her favourite books and prayers.

The dairy tableau shows the various utensils which we used when I was
a child.

There is a tableau depicting a trench scene in the First World War and
adjacent to it are items sent in by supporters whose relatives fought in,
and in some cases, lost their lives in that War. In all, 908,371 British and
Empire soldiers died on the various fronts in the War. Sargent's immortal
painting "Gassed" is displayed, together with Siegfried Sassoon's poignant
words which express the sorrow and grief depicted:

> Do you remember that hour of din before the attack – and the anger, the
> blind compassion that seized and shook you then as you peered at
> the doomed and haggard faces of your men? Do you remember the
> stretcher-cases lurching back with tired eyes and lolling heads – those ashen
> grey masks of the lads who once were keen and kind and gay? Have you
> forgotten yet? . . . Look up, and swear by the green of the Spring that you'll
> never forget.

Further on, photographs bear witness to the slums in the north of England
which we visited regularly.

The displays which concern SOE and the FANY, and the terrible
slaughter in the concentration camps, show original uniforms and letters.

The tableau of a scene in an improvised "hospital" in which I worked
(a small space cleared amidst acres of ruins) brought the following words
to mind:

> Can I see another's woe
> And not be in sorrow too?
> Can I see another's grief
> And not seek for kind relief?

William Blake

One of the aspects of the Museum that I particularly tried to emphasise was the miracle of rebuilding from the unimaginable scale of ruin and devastation.

> Build it well, whate'er you do
> Build it straight and strong and true;
> Build it clear and high and broad:
> Build it for the eye of God.

F.M.M. January 1898

With two exceptions, *no* photographs were officially allowed to be taken in the prisons I visited, so the Section on the Boys had to be limited to a map showing the great distances between prisons, one of the card indexes and a few of the Boy's handicrafts.

When creating this Museum it was vital to convey the incredible willpower that existed, and continues to exist, amongst those who lost everything; and so we moved from the horrors of war and imprisonment to the beauty of the world of the Resurrection. Carvings, paintings, sculptures, brilliantly coloured woven hangings and cloths, exquisitely dressed dolls – all these things delight the eye in a riot of colour and charm. Tragedy may underlie the beauty, however – the dolls were made by children with rheumatoid arthritis, the superb galleon was carved by a young handicapped man and given to me with gratitude by the community – but the tragedy perhaps even enhances the beauty. From Africa, Poland, Yugoslavia, Czechoslovakia, India, and from *many* other countries besides, artefacts are shown which demonstrate the richness and diversity of each country's traditions. A simple but lovely white woven plastic bag was made by a twenty-two year old paraplegic boy who had to lie on his back in a very small low hut until he died.

As if by a miracle, the Museum's display was almost transformed into exhibits of exceptional handiwork, reflecting the courage and talents of the afflicted as well as their folk art and culture. We became utterly absorbed in arranging the cases as we wanted to share in the awareness of the human spirit's victory over what had appeared to be hopeless adversity.

> All that loveliness which passes through men's minds into their skilful, suffering hands comes from that supreme loveliness.
>
> St Augustine

There is, however, a sobering postscript to the Third World Section – a scene in which a mother and child are "living" in a reed-roofed hut, too low to stand upright in, whilst beyond in the street outside homeless figures wrapped in threadbare blankets are sprawled on the open roadway. They exist on less than 700 calories a day, while an average person in Britain is fortunate enough to receive over 3,000. This scene tries to bring before the visitor the hideous reality of the starving and impoverished nations places before all today. It is one that *cannot* be ignored.

In stark contrast to this scene there follows a representation of a typical resident's room in one of the Homes.

After more photographs showing the work of the Foundation today, there is a corner in which are reproductions of the famous artist, Wita Stwocz, depicting the fourteenth-century reredos in St Mary' Church, Kraków, and a statue of Our Lady modelled by a handicapped sculptress who has been confined to a wheelchair since the age of fifteen.

The visitor can also read the Beatitudes and a few prayers. There is time to pause and reflect on the misery and horror that greed and evil inflict, the courage and faith of the individual, the urgent work that awaits us daily, and the knowledge that strength can only come from God.

> Rejoice in hope
> Patient in tribulation
> And constant in prayer

We kept aiming for a D-Day – before the Foundation officially heard that Her Majesty Queen Elizabeth the Queen Mother could come – and at the announcement of Pope John Paul II's election in October 1978, we felt the doors could be opened for a preview on the Sunday of his coronation.

It was on a day in November 1978 that the late Sir Martin Gilliat, Private Secretary to the Queen Mother, told me in confidence that Her Majesty had accepted the invitation to open the Foundation's Museum at Headquarters, on 27 April 1979.

The weeks beforehand preparing for the great event in April included both joy and tribulation. The pressures grew steadily, and at one time, despite pre-dawn attacks on the problems, we wondered whether we would ever complete the outstanding inventory of things to be done. The very bad winter weather – deep snow and frost, followed by no less than three floods – had soaked the garden around the Museum building and added to our fear that all might not go according to the carefully conceived plan.

My Assistants and the Foundation's staff and volunteers took the main responsibility for all arrangements as I returned from working in Australia only a few days beforehand.

An action list was drawn up so that those concerned knew exactly what they were required to do, but as the day came closer the inevitable interruptions grew worse, with a steady stream of callers and reporters from the press, television and radio.

But when 27 April 1979 finally arrived, we discovered – perhaps to our own surprise – that all the many different pieces of the puzzle had somehow fallen correctly into place. We had to labour against the clock and it was only by a lot of hard team work – with many last-minute adjustments – that we were ready for the day. For the official part of the ceremony, members of the Foundation's Council, supporters, friends and Bods from the Homes in Britain and overseas gradually assembled and waited with mounting excitement in the main drive outside the Home and Museum. So conscious of security were the original Bods of SOE that they locked themselves in a room with the plainclothes officers of Special Branch until they were assured of their identities.

Earlier the sky had been overcast, but the sun came out to greet the Queen Mother who arrived at 3.15 p.m. in a helicopter of the Queen's Flight which landed on the Village green. Crowds, including schoolchildren, surrounded the car and then she drove slowly down the Village street to the gates of the Home where she was received by the Foundation's late Chairman, Mr H.N. Sporborg, who presented members of the Council. As she walked along the drive, the Queen Mother graciously stopped to speak to different people and to the Guides and Scouts who formed a guard of honour. She was presented with a posy by Helena Kuszell, a wheelchair sculptress from Warsaw, before mounting the steps outside the Museum to unveil a plaque carved in stone by a twenty-one year old mason, David Williams.

After the Chairman of the Foundation, Mr Sporborg's welcome, the Queen Mother said in her opening speech:

> I am so glad to be here today on an occasion of especial significance for the Sue Ryder Foundation.
>
> This Museum, established with so much care and devotion at The Sue Ryder Home, will be not only a lasting memorial to those who gave their lives in two Wars but also a tangible record of the history and origins of the Foundation – its past and present work, and its hopes for the future. Hopes which are expressed so clearly in the words of its Charter: 'To render personal service to those in need and give affection to those who are unloved, regardless of age, race or creed, part of the Family of Man.'
>
> In a most vivid way this Museum reminds us of the human needs which exist in Britain and throughout the world today. We can see here both the struggle and the ultimate triumph of the human spirit in the face of adversity.
>
> It now gives me great pleasure to declare open the Sue Ryder Museum.

Once the Museum had been declared open by the Queen Mother the church bells were due to start ringing. A Girl Guide was stationed in a bedroom on the first floor of the house overlooking the Museum and in full view of the Village green, where a runner had been placed to cross to the church on receipt of a signal from her to let the bellringers know to start their peal. But, as so often happens, all the best plans go astray and the bells began pealing before Her Majesty had declared the Museum open. The rector ran to the church steeple in an attempt to reach the bellringers, but found the door locked and was obliged to run back to the Rectory for the key.

In the meantime, the policeman at the gate was asked, "Can you get a message to the church tower?" whereupon he said to a colleague through his walkie talkie, "Stop those bloody bells!"

When my turn came to reply to the Queen Mother's opening speech I said:

> On behalf of all those connected with my Foundation, and most especially our friends and helpers who are over here from Poland, Belgium and other countries, I would like to try and say how deeply grateful we are for the honour that Your Majesty has so graciously paid us in coming to our small Headquarters and Museum in the midst of your very many commitments.
>
> This Museum has been made possible through the generosity of many individuals and companies who have donated building materials and their time. May I take this occasion to express our warmest appreciation and gratitude to them for their contributions. I know the fact that Your Majesty has taken the trouble to come so far to perform the Opening Ceremony means a very great deal to them, as it does to me personally and all those with whom I work.
>
> If I may be permitted to say this, it has been my dream and hope over many years that one day this Home might be graced by Your Majesty's presence, and I say thank you with all my heart for your great kindness in being here and the enormous encouragement which your presence gives us to renew our commitments for the future.

Prayers of dedication were spoken by the then Bishop of St Edmundsbury and Ipswich, the Rt Rev. John Waine, and by the Roman Catholic Bishop of East Anglia, the Rt Rev. Alan Clark.

When Bishop Waine saw the Queen Mother at Snape Maltings a day or so later she told him how much she had enjoyed the occasion and went on to say that she had particularly appreciated the blessing by the two Bishops at the end. Bishop Waine asked if she thought it had been effective, to which her reply was, "I thought that it was positively double-strength!".

Inside the Museum, the Queen Mother was introduced to individuals who had a particular affiliation to members of SOE, concentration camp survivors or the handicapped. It was difficult for Her Majesty to absorb everything and she turned to me on several occasions and said, "How I wish I could stay longer."

When the Queen Mother came to sign the visitors' book there was a slight hitch as the small drop-leaf table it was on collapsed, but Her Majesty proved quite equal to the occasion, and with her pen poised in one hand neatly caught the book with the other. Looking up she said, "I haven't panicked, have I?"

The royal party walked out of the Gift Shop and coffee room and were introduced to more individuals on the way. They then took tea in a huge marquee on the main lawn. The person who served Her Majesty at table was absolutely thrilled. As a young boy he had lost his parents and family. They had been killed in a particularly brutal way by the Nazis, and in 1945 he had taken his own retribution against a fifty-five year old SS man and had been sentenced to death; later the sentence was commuted to life imprisonment. I had visited him throughout those dark years and I was given the opportunity to offer him a job and a new life – he became a professional waiter. As he said to me both before and afterwards, "I could never have imagined that I would ever have the privilege to serve tea and wait on the Queen Mother." He wore his special blue velvet suit for the occasion.

From the marquee the Queen Mother walked through part of the garden to be introduced by the Chairman of the House Committee to the Home itself where she met individual residents who live here, some of whom presented her with gifts they had made themselves. Her Majesty was visibly touched. On entering the drawing office, which was then used by three young Foundation architects, Her Majesty exclaimed, "Whoever works in here? I have never seen such an untidy room!" They had been working up to the last hour helping with preparations and never expected the royal visitor to call at this office! The Queen Mother ended her walkabout in the Home by seeing the chapel where Ian Wilson stood in his habit of the Augustinian Order.

The hours had passed too quickly and as Her Majesty came out of the front door to get into her car with her Lady-in-Waiting, Elizabeth Basset, the Poles who were staying on the Holiday Scheme and volunteers from Poland spontaneously broke into singing Sto Lat: "One hundred years, one hundred years, may you live for a hundred years."

The Queen Mother left at about 5.30 p.m. after driving slowly back to the Village green, and we watched her helicopter disappearing into the evening sky. As Mr Sporborg predicted in his speech of welcome, the Queen Mother had performed the ceremony in her own inimitable style.

The Queen Mother's interest in everybody and everything was very touching and gave us all the greatest encouragement and delight. I was reminded of how the late Norman Hartnell summed up her qualities: "Her beauty and charm," he said "are timeless. She is unique."

Later, in 1991, Josef, the Boy in the blue velvet suit who waited on the Queen Mother when she opened the Foundation's Museum, wrote to me:

The British Authorities have made me a very, very precious Christmas present and I swear by Almighty God that I will be a faithful British citizen and bear true allegiance to Her Majesty Queen Elizabeth the Second, her heirs and successors according to law. What a honour and what a beautiful moment it has made in my life and in the life of my wife too! I am very grateful and you can be sure very, very proud. My dream has been fulfilled and it is such a marvellous feeling.

Twenty-eight Christmases ago I was nobody with nothing but a stay in this lovely country for more than a fortnight. Today, I am a very proud and grateful citizen of this magnificent nation and its most generous people.

* * *

When I am at Headquarters the day begins early. I usually wake up just before 4.30 a.m., and after washing, dressing and brushing my hair I make a cup of coffee and listen to the BBC's World Service at 5 a.m. and then say the Morning Office. These prayers take about thirty minutes. I then start going through my ring book, in which I have written and numbered outstanding work for action, and make further notes. Each matter is numbered and comes under a heading, "Action – Musts – Date". Work left undone from the previous day I ring in red. Often it is not possible, however long I work, to cope with everything and the work therefore has to be carried forward, so this also includes re-sorting mail into priorities.

I consider the still hours of the morning as God's hours and I therefore like to visit the chapel to pray and to light votive candles. At 6.25 a.m. I like to listen to Prayer for the Day. When the Home has a resident Chaplain daily Mass is said at 5.30 p.m. If I stay with sisters of religious congregations certain parts of the day are devoted to prayer and meditation, however busy they may be. I admire them greatly, especially the vows they take of Poverty and Obedience. Although I do not appear to be as disciplined as I should be, I do endeavour to keep to a routine, with frequent pauses for meditation in the chapel and prayers and readings at night.

Since I left off wearing uniform I have bought my clothes from the Foundation's Shops. Fashion is unimportant to me, but I like a neat appearance and for this reason I always try to keep my hair short. I also feel more comfortable in loose, long-length dresses and coats. Out of necessity I have to work in the office for certain periods, but I like best to work in the field and would prefer to spend far more of my life among the poor and unloved. Though the hours are naturally much longer in the field and the conditions sometimes most trying, it is easier than the mental tiredness I experience in facing a barrage of unending paperwork, telephone calls and interruptions.

The furniture in the office where I work was donated by friends and supporters, as indeed were all things at Headquarters and the home here. Much of it came in a dilapidated state and needed renovation, with the exception of a small rosewood table given to me by my mother.

On the desk among the letters, files and ring books are trays marked "Pending", "Urgent", "Building", "Social Workers" and "Personal Secretaries". There are also a few gifts and mementos that I have received over the last thirty-five years. Other gifts are kept in our bedroom, including pictures of Our Lady and of St Francis, made out of corn, which were given to me by the Minister of Culture in Poland. Indeed, this room holds several small treasured gifts, some of them the donors' only possessions. I always find it exceedingly difficult to accept such presents, but each gift reminds me of the giver and of all that he or she did and meant; moreover, refusal would have upset them greatly.

The "Foreign Office" Secretaries (experienced volunteers who come over from Poland) deal with a lot of correspondence and all manner of enquiries and requests. These people are also responsible for co-ordinating the domiciliary care work carried out by the Foundation's voluntary social workers in Poland, Czechoslovakia and other countries. Meticulous records are kept, especially the card indexes and the filing of forms and reports completed by the social workers after each visit.

The Secretaries also have had to ensure that all documentation was done when sending supplies to Poland. These were sent out by the Foundation every few weeks in returning empty juggernauts. Everything was distributed by our Honorary Social Workers and Doctors and also through the church, which had an excellent and efficient organisation working in all dioceses and parishes, thus ensuring that the goods go direct to those most in need, but this has been temporarily stopped by the present Government in Poland which is very sad. The sorting, packing, weighing and loading of food, medicines and tons of clothing by volunteers continues seven days a week at Headquarters.

The morning mail is usually delivered at about 7 a.m. The earlier it is delivered to Headquarters the better, for it all has to be opened, date-stamped and sorted into priorities. My Secretaries and I set a deadline for completing the distribution by 8.45 a.m. At this time I prepare my breakfast in the tiny kitchenette in the narrow passage by my bedroom. I eat very simply and enjoy cereals only.

Back in the office I try not to be interrupted before eleven o'clock in order to get as much dictation done as possible. The first post goes out at 9.45 a.m. and there is great activity in the different offices to get as much correspondence as possible cleared by then.

A volunteer on the switchboard comes on duty at 6 a.m. and hands over to one who works at 9 a.m. The same volunteer or another takes over from 5 p.m. to 10 p.m. She is asked to cope with messages and defend us from interruptions as much as possible. I personally dislike the telephone, although it is good at times when one wants to reach someone quickly. Often the gist of a call could well have been committed to paper instead of the operator having to put down everything in the message book. For this reason the Foundation's telephone number is not given on its writing paper. The fax machine is in constant use and far more practical, cheaper and to the point.

At 10 p.m. the telephone, which is manned continuously, is at last switched through to the nurses on night duty and to our room, but even this does not mean the end of the working day. Tradesmen on one of the sites in Poland once rang up at 11.30 p.m. to say that the window frames had not arrived, and I remember another occasion, having been several weeks on the road and trying to get an early night, being awakened at 10.40 p.m. by the Chairman of one of my husband's Homes in Ireland with the news that the Home had been burnt down; patients and staff were fortunately safe. On one occasion an enthusiastic supporter in Canada has also phoned, not realising that it was 2 a.m. in Britain. I remember, too, a person ringing up at eleven o'clock one night just to "have a chat"! My husband was not amused.

The pressure of correspondence is unrelenting and a morning mail of two hundred letters or more is the norm. The post covers a variety of subjects, so that many hours of each day are devoted the dictation of correspondence and other matters. These are dealt with by very willing Secretaries and Assistants who are literally my left and right hands. We work as a team. Every letter received is acknowledged personally when I am at Headquarters, or by the Secretaries and Assistants when I am absent, so those who say "Please treat this clothing or postal order as an anonymous gift" earn our particular gratitude.

The day always seems to gallop, especially if I have to leave correspondence to attend meetings, and often it is only after the 4.30 p.m. post has gone out that my colleagues and I try to find second wind and have time for discussions. This is followed by evening mass, when a resident or visiting Chaplain is here.

Much of an average day is also occupied by discussions with colleagues and particularly with members of the Foundation's Council on whom I depend for advice, guidance and decisions. I also like to relax, when I can, with members of the staff and discuss a wide variety of problems with them, and I try always to be accessible to every one of them. There are all kinds of official visitors to be received and much of my time is devoted to talks with medical and social workers, local authorities, builders and architects, members of the Foundation's Support Groups and others. In addition, each year there are, on average, 200 meetings to be attended and talks to be given on the work of the Foundation, all of which entail a great deal of time and long hours of driving. Naturally, there are talks representatives in each region of the country. On one occasion when a message to this effect was telephoned to the organiser, a bold voice exclaimed "When I ask for the organ-grinder I don't expect the monkey!"

Part of each year is spent abroad. Every year varies according to requests and commitments. I keep in close contact with the various Homes, domiciliary teams, support groups and the 500 Sue Ryder Shops in Britain, though unfortunately it is never possible for me to spend as much time with them as I should like; it is always a joy to visit them and I only wish that I could do so more often.

In relationship with other people, consideration and warmth have both meant a great deal to me at all times. Coming from Yorkshire, I believe in being frank but without hurting a person's feelings, if this is possible; I try to remember that there are always two or more sides to a problem. Having lived and worked with people from all walks of life – central Europeans in particular – I have noticed and appreciated their etiquette and pleasant manners; they would think it over-familiar to use a person's first name until requested or permitted to do so, and then only when they have got to know that person extremely well, and they act with a courtesy which has never failed to make a deep impression on me. Being surrounded by members of the Foundation's family whom we have the privilege to serve and live with here, I am always conscious of the courage with which they face each new day; and I understand why some of them feel bitter, frightened and disillusioned.

* * *

On one side of the garden at Headquarters is "Mulberries", the bungalow where my mother came to live in 1967 with Miss Bainbridge, who had been with her over forty years and cared for her until she died here on 14 February 1974.

All through her long life, spent mostly in Yorkshire and Suffolk, with many visits abroad, countless people looked upon Mama as their friend. Her interests were wide and various, and her impulse was always to give. She took part wholeheartedly in the life of the local community and gave freely of her time to help people. For many years she was a magistrate, besides which she served on over thirty committees and had the ability to make each member feel that he or she was wanted so that all worked together as a team. She was gay and cheerful, often told jokes about herself and was never pompous or touchy. Inwardly serene and happy, her smile won people's hearts. Few seem to have left so beloved a memory.

Mama's sense of humour was infectious. She had a store of very amusing stories, and in almost every situation in life she could see the funny side. We should have persisted in a more determined way to get her to write down some of her experiences but, alas, she did not and most of them have faded from my mind. There is one, however, I remember her chuckling about long years afterwards.

Some friends had rented a house in Suffolk and invited many people to a garden party. Although Mama disliked some aspects of such occasions, she so enjoyed meeting people that she accepted the invitation. I think at the back of her mind she wondered, too, if there might be some guests with whom she would have things in common and who could be persuaded to become involved in helping others.

A moat surrounded this historic property, and an old boat ferried guests over to see different parts of the beautiful garden. On this particular afternoon, the boat sprang a leak and soon the passengers were soaked – the men in their tail suits and the women in long dresses, which is what they wore on such occasions in those days. A distracted French governess who lived with the family kept repeating, first in French and then in English, "All dis happens 'ere quanstantly, quanstantly . . ." In the end the boat stayed afloat just long enough for its passengers to be rescued. Guests – some annoyed, others amused – reached the safety of the bank with their shoes and clothing soaked. In the house, efforts were made round the old kitchen stove to dry the dresses and trousers on horse rails, while the host and hostess, who were clearly embarrassed by the whole incident, tried to find enough of their own dry clothes to go around. Happily, Mama had stayed safely on dry land!

Without Mama's wisdom, constant encouragement and active participation, it is difficult to imagine the Foundation ever having been consolidated or expanded. I could consult her at any time and, in spite of all her other activities, she was always available to guide me and to help me cope with the correspondence, meetings and various problems. She would often pass onto me quotations applicable to the moment or remind me of prayers, such as the following, which I find among my papers:

> What can I wish on this your birthday morning
> Save that the Friend, the faithful and the true
> In his great Love all earthly love transcending,
> Be near today to bless and comfort you
> And with his smile make glad the day now dawning.
> Chasing the shadows from life's darkest place
> God's perfect Peace your heart and mind enfolding
> Till in his joy you see Him face to face.

And another passage, that I also found among papers:

> There are seasons when we have to leave the path and go home – go into retirement, into solitude, into seeming uselessness. And the hardest part of these moments is just the sense of having missed our destiny. We have been shunted from the path, we have been made to lie down; and it seems to us as if God had no further place for us beneath the circle of the sun. What a comfort at such moments are these words of the ancient psalmist – "Thou compassest my path and my lying down!"
>
> They tell us that the quiescent hour be a divine hour, that the seeming useless moment may be full of God. They tell us that the greatest day of our life may be the day after we have quitted the path – the day of our prostration, our pain, our weariness.
>
> They tell us that the places where we are forced to lie down may be God's green pastures, that the coming to quiet water may be God's own leading. The hour which our soul is rejecting may be the hour when the Kingdom has come.
>
> "Thou compassest my lying down" G. Matheson. Psalm 139-3 Jesus leadeth them – apart by themselves – and He was transfigured before them. Mark 9-2

For as long as I can remember her, Mama seemed to have an instinct for instant recognition of the moment when somebody was most in want of companionship or of solitude. This gift, and her use of it, naturally endeared her to people and the Bods at the Home. She would perceive and respond equally to their need of someone to rejoice with them in their joys or to share quietly in their sorrows, or simply to give them by her company the reassurance and encouragement that their perplexities craved for. Mama would herself prepare special dishes for them, pick strawberries, invite them for meals, or accompany them to flower festivals and concerts. They loved her for her gaiety and the interest they shared in so many subjects but, above all, for her compassion, her affection, and her respect for them as human beings.

Once Lord Monyihan, the famous surgeon at Leeds, with whom she served on various committees, said to her, "I envy you your faith".

Mama said to me when she was dying: "Always pray hard: prayer is the source of life, share it, remember to give *time* to God everywhere and the importance of silence – solitude."

It would be impossible to quote from all the hundreds of letters and cables received before and after her death, but the following may sum up their feelings:

> I shall always picture her as a luminous and lovely person, full of fun and energy. She was the leader and guide of our group and, however late or early, your mother found out what we liked most, and those who were unwell she would care for and look after. When she was driving or accompanying us she would often sing. We loved, too, to hear her playing the piano. Please feel we will stand by you, realising that it was she who laid the foundation-stone of your work. Her activity will always remain a clear signpost, not only to you but to countless others who enjoyed her friendship and love.

10

Partnership

IN FEBRUARY 1955, LEONARD Cheshire invited me to visit his new home for the handicapped at Ampthill and I arrived at the wrong gate – the one locked in the park. I was tempted to turn back home. It was a cold bleak day, and as I had a kidney infection I did not have much inclination to go on, but I felt it would be rude not to keep the appointment. The journey along familiar roads had brought back memories of Wartime days and nights at Tempsford Station – the blackouts, the signals, the changing huts, the briefings, driving the Bods to the aircraft, watching the take-off and waiting for the crews to return.

I had not heard of Leonard Cheshire. Neither of us knew about the other's work. Having been immersed in Special Operations Executive and later in relief work, much of the time overseas, I was out of touch.

Originally he had won fame as a bomber pilot, and I quote from his citation in the *London Gazette* of 8 September 1944 for the award of the Victoria Cross:

Wing Commander Geoffrey Leonard Cheshire, VC, DSO, DFC
Royal Air Force Volunteer Reserve
No. 617 Squadron

This officer began his operational career in June, 1940. Against strongly defended targets he soon displayed the courage and determination of an exceptional leader. He was always ready to accept extra risks to ensure success. Defying the formidable Ruhr defences, he frequently released his bombs from below 2,000 ft. Over Cologne in November, 1940, a shell burst inside his aircraft blowing out one side and starting a fire; undeterred, he went on to bomb his target. About this time, he carried out a number of convoy patrols in addition to his bombing missions.

At the end of his first tour of operational duty in January, 1941, he immediately volunteered for a second. Again, he pressed home his attacks with the utmost gallantry. Berlin, Bremen Cologne, Duisberg, Essen and Kiel were among the heavily defended targets which he attacked. When he was posted for instructional duties in January, 1942, he undertook four more operational missions.

He started a third operational tour in August, 1942, when he was given command of a squadron. He led the squadron with outstanding skill on a number of missions before being appointed in March, 1943, as a station commander.

In October, 1943, he undertook a fourth operational tour, relinquishing the rank of Group Captain at his own request so that he could again take part in operations. He immediately set to work as the pioneer of a new method of marking enemy targets involving very low flying. In June, 1944, when marking a target in the harbour at Le Havre in broad daylight and without cloud cover, he dived well below the range of the light batteries before releasing his marker-bombs, and he came very near to being destroyed by the strong barrage which concentrated on him.

During his fourth tour which ended in July, 1944, Wing-Commander Cheshire led his squadron personally on every occasion always undertaking the most dangerous and difficult task of marking the target alone from a low level in the face of strong defence.

Wing-Commander Cheshire's cold and calculated acceptance of risks is exemplified by his conduct in an attack on Munich in April, 1944. This was an experimental attack to test out the new method of target marking at low level against a heavily defended target situated deep in Reich territory. Munich was selected, at Wing-Commander Cheshire's request, because of the formidable nature of its light anti-aircraft and searchlight defences. He was obliged to follow, in bad weather, a direct route which took him over the defences of Augsburg and thereafter he was continuously under fire. As he reached the target, flares were being released by our high-flying aircraft. He was illuminated from above and below. All guns within range opened fire on him. Diving to 700 ft. he dropped his markers with great precision and began to climb away. So blinding were the searchlights that he almost lost control. He then flew over the city at 1,000 ft., to assess the accuracy of his work and direct other aircraft. His own was badly hit by shell fragments but he continued to fly over the target area until he was satisfied that he had done all in his power to ensure success. Eventually, when he set course for base, the task of disengaging himself from the defences proved even more hazardous than the approach. For a full twelve minutes after leaving the target area he was under withering fire but he came safely through.

Wing-Commander Cheshire has now completed a total of 100 missions. In four years of fighting against the bitterest opposition he has maintained a record of outstanding personal achievement, placing himself invariably in the forefront of the battle. What he did in the Munich operation was typical of the careful planning, brilliant execution and contempt for danger which has established for Wing-Commander Cheshire a reputation second to none in Bomber Command.

The raid on Munich destroyed several Nazi party buildings, including the Gestapo Headquarters at the Wittelbascher Palais. My husband's predilection for low-level marking was now unquestioned by his superiors. He once told me that after the Munich operation his aircraft returned to base with only ten or fifteen minutes worth of fuel left in the extra tanks fitted.

On 10 September 1944, Leonard, now a Group Captain again, left England bound for India, on posting to the Eastern Air Command Head-quarters at Calcutta; but by the end of the year he had been moved to the USA where he joined the British Joint Staff Mission in Washington, ostensibly to study tactical developments. Here he was selected to act as a British observer with Sir William Penney for the second atom bomb raid by the United States Air Force against Japan, and in late July was sent to Guam, then Tinian Island, base for the B-29 Boeing Superfortresses tasked with this historic mission.

In summer 1945, her sea power shattered and her industry crumbling under almost continuous aerial bombardment, Japan faced inevitable military defeat. However, the Japanese Government was dominated by the military, to whom defeat was unthinkable. The closer the War approached Japan, they argued, the more the advantage would swing in their favour, and the final decisive battle on their home shores would bring victory, "even if it cost a million men". The people had been duped into believing that Japan was invincible, and preservation of the "national essence" demanded nothing less than a fight to the last man.

With the exception of Admirals Leahy and King, the Americans had given up hope of ending the War through the blockade and the already devastating bomber offensive, and were assembling a force of five-million men for the invasion of Japan. But the Japanese military had amply demonstrated the casualties they could inflict on invading forces and the lengths to which they would go rather than surrender. On Okinawa they had made the schoolchildren walk over the minefields in front of their Army, and had forced many hundred civilians to commit hara-kiri rather than surrender. They had proved themselves even more merciless to their POWs (including civilians), the remaining 300,000 of whom were to be executed the moment the Allied offensive to recapture south-east Asia opened. An anxious War Department estimated that victory over Japan would cost a further year's bitter fighting and three-million lives or more.

The alternative was the atomic bomb, the first of which was to be ready for testing in mid-July. Amongst the few who knew of it – so few that it has been called the best-kept secret of the War – it had aroused intense and conflicting emotions. On the one hand they saw in it a means of enforcing surrender without the fearsome prospect of all-out war on Japanese soil; on the other they were deeply concerned about the implications of using such a weapon. The Interim Committee set up by President Truman to examine the arguments for and against, recommended, after much heartsearching, that it be used, on the grounds that it would end the War in the shortest possible time and with the minimum loss of life. First, however, the Japanese were to be warned of the destructive power that America now possessed, in the hope that they could be persuaded to surrender.

The difficulty was how to present the ultimatum in terms that would satisfy Allied War aims and at the same time make it easier for the Japanese to accept. The Americans were prepared to safeguard the personal position of the Emperor, but not the Imperial system which had helped the military dictatorship into power. They were aware of the small peace faction in Japan and by 18 July, when the Potsdam Conference opened, they knew that Togo, the Foreign Minister, had instructed the Japanese Ambassador in Moscow to seek Soviet mediation for favourable peace terms. But they also knew that ultimate power lay with the military leaders, and that to them surrender in any form was unacceptable: the term did not even exist in the military dictionary.

On 17 July, the day before Potsdam, the bomb was successfully tested, and on 27 July the Potsdam Declaration containing the finally agreed text of the surrender appeal was broadcast. It warned that Japan faced "prompt and utter destruction" unless she accepted unconditional surrender, but went on to offer hope for the future in terms indicating that something less than unconditional was being required. Togo recognised this and urged that it be treated with "the utmost circumspection", but the military would have nothing to do with it, and it was their voice that carried. At 4 p.m. the elderly Prime Minister, Admiral Suzuki, announced to the press: "We must kill it with silence," an unfortunate phrase suggesting an element of contempt. The Americans could only conclude, correctly as it turned out, that the military clique was still in control, and orders were given to prepare for the first atomic attack. Only two bombs existed.

Truman's directive was that the bomb was to be dropped only in good visibility and against a major military target surrounded by buildings. General Spaatz, Commander of the Pacific Air Force, who had been entrusted with the detailed planning, chose Hiroshima, Kokura, Niigata and Nagasaki, and warned all four cities they would be bombed. He was ready by 4 August, but bad weather caused a delay of two days to a take-off time of 02.45 on the 6th from the small island of Tinian. A few hours previously four B-29s loaded with conventional bombs had crashed at the end of the uncomfortably short runways, and as an insurance Captain William Parsons achieved the remarkable feat of arming the atomic bomb after the aircraft was airborne.

The nuclear age opened with nine days of high drama. Russia hastily brought forward her declaration of war against Japan, and on 8 August attacked Manchuria, to add huge territorial gains to those already gratuitously promised to it in East Asia by the Western Allies at Yalta.

Returning from Potsdam on the cruiser *Augusta*, Truman told the world that an atomic bomb had been dropped and warned that unless Japan surrendered she would suffer "a rain of ruin from the air the like of which has never been seen on this earth".

In Tokyo, Togo argued for acceptance of the ultimatum and, through the good offices of Marquis Kido, the Lord Privy Seal, won the moral support of the Emperor. But War Minister Anami on behalf of the military firmly rejected it and ensured that the people were not told that an atomic bomb had been used. Despite the further shock of the Soviet entry into the War, the Japanese Supreme Command had made up its mind that victory could still be wrested out of defeat on the beaches of Japan, and plans for the mobilisation of four-million civilians were accelerated.

Bad weather was now closing in on Japan and, with the Met Office predicting the last foreseeable day of good visibility as 9 August, the Americans concluded that to delay using the only remaining bomb until perhaps September would only strengthen the hand of the military. Kokura was designated as the primary target, but poor visibility forced the pilot to divert to the secondary, Nagasaki, and only on his second run did the cloud clear sufficiently for the bomb to be dropped. Even so it missed the aiming point by two miles.

Nagasaki brought to a head the clash between the powerful militarists in Japan and the fragile, but steadily growing, peace faction. After eleven hours of heated debate the Cabinet could reach no agreement, and when the Imperial Conference that followed was similarly deadlocked, the Prime Minister took the extraordinary step of requesting the Emperor to make his wishes known. Without hesitation, but visibly moved, he said that he desired an end to the War: "The time has come when we must bear the unbearable." For the Emperor to intervene directly in a political decision was unprecedented, and his words shattered most of his hearers. With the added clause, "so long as nothing prejudices the prerogatives of the Emperor", the capitulation document was signed and despatched through slow-moving diplomatic channels to Washington. But the Japanese military chiefs, who felt betrayed and bitter, forced the Cabinet to issue a compromise statement to the press that made no mention of surrender. Back in the War Ministry they declared to the assembled officers that regardless of the political decision the troops must be ordered to continue fighting. While rumours began to circulate that a third atomic bomb would soon be dropped on Tokyo, a group of angry officers led by Major Hatanaka began plotting a military coup.

The American reply, received on the evening of the 12th, was not as bad as feared: it left some ambiguity about the Emperor, but stated that the future form of the Government would be "in accordance with the freely expressed will of the people". The Emperor unreservedly accepted it, but the military did not, and for another thirty-six hours the outcome lay in the balance. Hatanaka failed to win over the Chiefs of Staff, but was not disciplined for his action. The Emperor resisted the military's pressure to reverse his decision, but could not weaken their fanatical resolve to die to the last man rather than surrender. Finally it was Marquis Kido, now under threat of death and confined to the palace, who tilted the scales by winning over first Suzuki and then Anami.

By the morning of the 14th Allied leaflets had dropped on Tokyo giving the full text of the Japanese Government's acceptance of Potsdam and the American reply. The hitherto secret negotiations were now in the open, and in consternation Kido and Suzuki urged the Emperor to command that an Imperial Conference be convened. This time his words carried, and the

Emperor personally recorded an Imperial rescript, which was then locked away in the palace safe to be broadcast to the nation the following day. On hearing of this Hatanaka launched his attempted coup. He shot the Commanding Officer of the Konoye division and tricked the garrison into sealing off the palace while he searched for the recording in order to destroy it. He never found it, and at dawn the General Officer Commanding Eastern Army entered the palace and ordered the troops out.

At noon on the 15th the Emperor's recording was broadcast to an awed public, many of them listening on their knees. The Emperor had made specific reference to the bomb, thereby inducing a subtle but dramatic change of heart in the military, as the 65,000 prisoners of war who had managed to survive, many of whom had already been forced to dig their own graves, will each testify. No army can fight the atomic bomb, the military leaders were able to say, and because it was not to a human enemy that they were surrendering, they could lay down their arms with honour in the best interests of the human race. Neither the shooting of their prisoners, nor the personal act of suicide which the Army code demanded of all its officers and men was any longer necessary.

Much more publicity continues to be given to the victims of Hiroshima and Nagasaki than is given to the slow agony of those who died of exhaustion, disease and hunger, both in Burma, and in other parts of that vast area which the Japanese invaded and occupied and where they showed no mercy or regard for human life.

The following statistics from the Imperial War Museum of casualties in the Far Eastern theatre December 1941 – September 1945, speak for themselves:

Allied prisoners of war		175,000
Civilian internees		125,000
Allied casualties:	Dead	177,682
	Wounded	252,627
Reliable figures of civilian deaths in captivity not available.		
Estimated total number of Chinese soldiers killed during the Sino-Japanese War (1937-45)		1,300,000
	Wounded	1,938,000
Estimated Chinese civilian casualties		5,800,000

Of the various branches of the British Armed Services, Bomber Command of the Royal Air Force suffered one of the highest casualty rates of the Second World War. In all, in the War against Germany, the Royal Air Force lost:

Killed	66,080
Missing	5,404
Prisoners of war	9,727

Within this total Bomber Command alone lost 55,573 aircrew.

For Leonard Cheshire the next few years of civilian life were years of idealistic ventures and schemes, and of searching for the answers to imponderable questions. Still a young man, barely thirty years of age, he had spent his formative years first in the atmosphere of an undergraduate's existence and then, in complete and sudden contrast, in the swiftly maturing company of death and destruction on a scale which outstripped logic and meaning – where total responsibility for other men's lives and futures had been thrust upon his youthful shoulders without preamble. He had been left a large empty Victorian house at Le Court near Liss in Hampshire by an aunt, but it lacked all amenities. There he camped out wondering what to do until one day a telephone call came from the matron of a local hospital asking him to take in Arthur Dykes, a former serviceman diagnosed with cancer who had nowhere to go and was blocking a hospital bed. Leonard accepted him and soon found there were many others who were in a similar plight, and thus the first Home to bear his name was started.

In 1952 Leonard became ill and tuberculosis was diagnosed. In the next two years he underwent four operations (two-stage thora) at Midhurst Sanatorium, courageously facing sickness and pain. During this time he was obliged to delegate to local committees the task of running his four existing Homes, which involved some difficulty for he was reluctant to delegate – but actually it gave him greater freedom of movement and opened up avenues of expansion which otherwise he would not have had. He had splendid encouragement from his late father, the international jurist Professor G. C. Cheshire.

At Ampthill that afternoon he talked to me about his work and showed me over the house. Both of us were totally involved in our own work and animated by it. I told him a little about my small international Foundation and about the residents, and I explained briefly to him the aims of the Living Memorial. This was new to him, but it was clear that both of us worked and built up our respective Foundations without funds and on faith. Apparently, after this meeting, Leonard said he had a feeling he had met someone with whom he had an affinity. "I could not define it," he said to others, and added, "but it made a vivid impression on me."

We had established our respective organisations long before meeting each other; the Foundation on the one hand and the Cheshire Homes on the other hand had each developed its own positive and distinctive character and individuality. The work done by the two charities also differed, yet complemented, the other. The Cheshire Homes were intended mainly for the physically handicapped, including the young, whereas this Foundation cares for the sick and handicapped of all age groups, whereas this Foundation cares for the sick and handicapped of all age groups, and specialises with patients diagnosed with cancer, Huntingdon's Disease and other neurological diseases. In addition the Foundation operated a Holiday Scheme for survivors of the Gestapo prisons, Nazi concentration camps and also those captured by the Soviet Secret Police and who had survived the infamous labour camps throughout the vast areas of the Soviet Union.

The Foundation also had Domiciliary Care Teams and Bereavement Counsellors. In some countries specialised psychotherapists and social workers visit individuals in need and the handicapped. Prison visiting and after care has already been written in Chapter 8. Each organisation had, however, been established for the relief of suffering, and to that extent their general purpose was the same. Later I became a Trustee of the Cheshire Homes and for years attended the long, lively and happy Trustee meetings on Saturdays at Leonard's office in Market Mews (now in Maunsel Street) in London, giving whatever encouragement I could to the handful of Trustees about taking on more properties and opening new Homes. In the early days there were grave decisions for us to make. Leonard had became a Councillor of my own Foundation.

Thereafter we met at intervals at Staunton Harold in Leicestershire where two or three survivors came with me on brief visits to help restore this large and lovely house. Leonard also accompanied me on a few of my drives to the Continent, but it was in India that we really got to know each other, ultimately getting married there in April 1959.

In 1957 I went to India for the first time, arriving from Moscow where I had gone for further discussions concerning the repatriation of Russians still in German prisons. While in Moscow, to my surprise, I was permitted to walk alone, though naturally under close surveillance. On one memorable visit, I was invited out to supper in a restaurant by a Russian doctor who spoke English fluently, and we were joined by a friend of his from Smolensk. After supper, when it was dark, they asked me to accompany them to a room near an Orthodox Church as they wanted me to listen to them reciting the Lord's Prayer in English and to correct them if necessary. It was a very moving occasion and showed the extent of their faith and courage.

When friends attached to the British Embassy where there in Moscow, they most kindly invited me to stay with them. I was not permitted to stay with a Russian family (although there were several invitations), as this was strictly forbidden by the Communist system. On two occasions, I was obliged to stay in a cheap hotel where, for breakfast, a slice of ham and a roll were weighed separately on a very old-fashioned scales, with a queue before and after me!

* * *

I later flew on via Tashkent in a Russian plane, seeing the beauty of a part of the Himalayas, and landing in Delhi.

Leonard met me at the airport and together we travelled through the country by train and bus, often suffering considerable discomfort in the heat, but getting to know at least some of the individuals among the anonymous millions. I was deeply impressed by the vastness of India with its teeming masses of people and its many different languages. The poverty and suffering haunted me and what I saw was often appalling, but I grew to admire the way in which the people put up with their sufferings and with the dreadful natural calamities that so often ruin their lives; I admired, too, their willingness to share even the little they had; their friendliness and helpfulness to others; and their attempts to improve their situation.

The Indian Army, with its splendid tradition of service, will always be remembered with pride. The soldiers who served were all volunteers and in the two World Wars they suffered the highest rate of casualties of any Commonwealth nation. In the 1914–18 War 64,449 men were killed, and in the 1939–45 War they lost 24,338 men.

Together we visited the various Homes Leonard Cheshire had founded in India with the Indians, who made themselves responsible for raising the money either to convert a building or on occasions to construct a new one. This they did independently of outside support and were responsible too for raising the funds and covering the maintenance of the Homes. Later we travelled in Ezekiel, a second-hand ambulance bought in Malaysia and shipped to Calcutta, where it was renovated and serviced voluntarily by the Indian Army. Taking it in turns to drive, we covered several thousands of miles to Jamshedpur, Burnpur, Allahabad, Lucknow, Agra, Delhi and finally to Dehra Dun. Travelling rough, we appreciated the hospitality which was warmly offered by the locals and friends wherever we went.

Near the City of Dehra Dun in Uttar Pradesh we found a site of some thirty acres which seemed to us suitable for a joint venture. This site had been offered to Leonard by the Government of Uttar Pradesh, and the two of us visited it together, bicycling there across the dried-out bed of the Rispana river. Here we determined we would create a centre which in time would care for many different kinds of people in need – mentally handicapped children, spastic children, healthy children whose parents, because of illness or poverty, could not care for them, and cases of leprosy. It was to be named "Raphael" after the archangel of healing.

In 1958 we founded the Ryder-Cheshire Mission for the relief of suffering and this enabled us to initiate projects which, for one reason or another, did not fall within the scope of our respective Foundations.

In February 1959 Leonard Cheshire and I became engaged. This was a step we had to think about very seriously. The work had meant my life, and nothing I felt should or could change this. How in the future could one combine both marriage and work? This posed a grave question. Moreover, even in normal circumstances, marriage inevitably brings great responsibilities – I had always felt that it was a gamble. Furthermore, the implications are so serious that it is wiser to remain single and work than to run the risk of an unhappy marriage. Comparatively few people prepare themselves for or are equal to sharing literally everything.

Before any announcement was made, the following note, signed by both of us, was sent to colleagues, supporters and friends of both Foundations:

Before the news should become public, we want to let you know personally that we are engaged, and plan to get married in the near future, quietly and abroad. In doing so we assure you that our sole aim is still the good of the work and to help those who are sick or in need, whoever and wherever they may be, but that together we feel strengthened and better equipped for all that lies ahead. During the last few years, as we have gradually seen and appreciated each other's work, we have come to realise not only how many opportunities of giving assistance were missed, but also how much remains to be done. We believe that with God's grace we can now help each other cope more adequately than we have in the past, and wherever the work may take us we always look forward to keeping in personal touch with each of you. We do hope that our intention will receive your approval and that you will give us your blessing.

We were married by Cardinal Valerian Gracias on 5 April 1959 in his private chapel in Bombay which, in 1966, Pope Paul used during the Eucharistic Congress. It was a very simple wedding, as we meant it to be, attended only by a handful of close friends, and took place after my return to India from working in Poland and Czechoslovakia.

After taking part, in the humid heat, in the reception given by local supporters and patients at the Cheshire Bethlehem Home on the outskirts of Bombay, we left on the thirty-six hours train journey back to Raphael at Dehra Dun where we took part in modest celebrations with the staff and patients.

The demands made on us were to be as heavy after our marriage as before, but in future we would be able to bear much of the burden together. Significantly enough, our married life began with a joint undertaking, a tour of Australia and New Zealand, where we were to give talks on our work in India and elsewhere, and to raise funds for it.

Before leaving, however, we tried – despite the intense heat – to spend three days peacefully together in a simple hut on the banks of the river Jamna, cooking over a camp fire and drawing water from the river, seeing the everyday life of India continuing in the distance – the boats passing on the water, the people washing themselves and their clothes – and hearing at night the beat of drums in the neighbouring village. But even here our solitude did not remain undisturbed for long: on the second day we were awakened by the noise of 300 children who had arrived on an outing, and soon also an Indian family of six came to take up residence in the small hut where we were staying.

From India we flew to Singapore to visit the local Cheshire Home near Changi, and from there to Sydney to begin our first arduous tour of Australia and New Zealand. To our astonishment, the acting Prime Minister of Australia, Sir John McEwen, lent us his house and the use of his den and car. Then we returned to Britain to the Foundation's Headquarters at Cavendish. Here we had our base in one room of the house. In this room we lived and worked, our children were born there and it became their nursery, and today the same room still forms part of our home. Several years after our marriage an adjoining room became available, which is used as an office/study. Our children, Jeromy, born in 1960, and Elizabeth, born in 1962, had a small bedroom each near our room.

Both Jeromy and Elizabeth were delivered by the local district nurse, Sister Collins, assisted by Miss Knapp; they were midwives of the old school, whom I respected and liked, and they also used to enthral me with tales of their experiences. I was able, and anyway preferred, to keep working normally until a few hours before the children were born, and shortly afterwards responded to the cables and correspondence. One Support Group who had planned their annual general meeting expected me to attend this in any case. There was great rejoicing throughout the Home when the births were announced. The joy of having a newborn child in our midst created a new happiness, especially to those who had lost families or had been denied them. The children were christened in the chapel at Headquarters in ceremonies attended by the residents, relatives and friends.

For seven years after the birth of the children, Catherine McGrath, a State Enrolled Nurse from Cork, helped us to look after them. Kitty, as she was known, tried to ensure that the one-room home did not become, in her words, "a transit room or rather like a main railway station". Kitty remained a close friend until her death in 1987.

Jeromy, and Elizabeth, we hope, have grown up as part of a family which comprises not only us but also everyone else – whether volunteers or Staff – for whom Cavendish is "home", and at no stage in their lives have they or the residents felt different or separated from each other. It was delightful on Saturday afternoons or summer evenings to hear them playing games in the garden with volunteers and members of staff. It gave them an aware-ness of other people's needs and taught them at the same time that the sick and handicapped are human beings with the same feelings, hopes and fears as theirs, differing only in the fact that they have to adapt themselves to living with their disability. Like us, both children are extremely sensitive and feel very deeply about people. It was whilst driving in the truck with me in Poland that Gigi (Elizabeth) said: "I've been thinking so much about the Bods and what they put up with – it is amazing how some have survived."

One of the essential tasks which divided my husband and myself was the work of our respective Foundations, which occupied much of our time and entailed long journeys, separating us from each other and from the children, who have now grown up. We disliked these separations intensely, but we tried to accept them. Sometimes we met as one or the other of us was arriving or departing. During the course of each year, either my husband or I were often away working at our respective Foundation Homes or attending fund-raising events, public meetings, and so on. I might also be visiting the Sue Ryder Shops. We always aimed to be together more often, as we greatly looked forward to the few opportunities of sharing each other's thoughts, joys and problems. We had to allocate time to go through our diaries for months ahead to plan our proposed itineraries, and it was impossible to accept a great number of the varied invitations received.

Each of us coped with our own packing, I always followed and ticked lists, although we helped each other, and both of us felt the pressure of always getting through as much work as possible before departing. We were grateful for the way our Assistants tried to protect us from constant interruptions before we left but we each sensed a great relief on finally getting away. We were fully aware the heavy schedules facing us but in no way could we ever let people down and, therefore, we had to snatch as much rest as we could en route to our destinations.

We always enjoyed being together and felt delighted when we travelled together too. Quite often, when we flew, the Captain would invite us onto the flight deck where we spoke to the crew and talked about the aircraft. We met with great courtesy and help from so many airlines, and I mention especially New Zealand Airlines, Qantas, Air India and British Airways. On leaving a country we always tried to write our thankyou letters immediately.

We enjoyed the contrast of working in the field and if necessary, washing in a bucket, with staying in a Royal Suite in an Embassy or at Government House. The welcoming love and support we received from so many people was always immensely encouraging and gave us a special joy.

I remember one function we attended together was in aid of a Cheshire Home, to which we had both been invited by a prominent member of the judiciary. It was an occasion in the early 1960s when my husband had been given a Mini car, which we both drove. Before reaching the outskirts of the town where the engagement was planned, we thought we should stop by the roadside and tidy up, but we could not find Leonard's jacket – he had left it in the hallway before leaving home. This was a risky thing to do as articles left there were usually earmarked for the clothing store and, sure enough, the volunteers, quite rightly, collected it up and left it in the store ready for selection for the Foundation's Shops. A quick telephone call to Headquarters confirmed that it had been found there. The day was warm, and my husband had the choice of inspecting the guard of honour either in his shirt sleeves or in a very darned pullover. On arrival we found that a friendly but curious local crowd had gathered, leaving us feeling more than a little embarrassed. The band struck up, and just before the inspection was due to begin I asked the manager of the ballroom – who was helping to organise the occasion – whether he could lend my husband a suitable jacket. To my amazement he took out of his cupboard in the office a pale pink jacket with gold-coloured buttons, exclaiming. "Isn't it lucky that my spare one is here!" Lost for words, I volunteered as tactfully as possible that it was both too large and not my husband's colour, but nothing daunted the manager's enthusiasm. The reception committee, a few of whose members were not aware of what had happened, were plainly aghast at what they evidently imagined to be Leonard's own taste in jackets. They were also puzzled by the fact that he had on an identical one to that worn by the manager. We proceeded inside to meet a large number of supporters, serenaded by the blare of a revolving electric organ in a large room lit by different coloured lights. From the low ceiling of the room there dangled huge, garish, imitation birds which seemed to hover precariously just above our heads.

Another occasion I recall with amusement was when we went to see a property which was for lease by a local council to either of our Foundations. The house was shuttered up and, in fact, had dry rot. The caretaker seemed a little eccentric and at one point on the round of the house – at the top of the stairs – I remember we asked him where he had served during the War. "In the Air Force," he said, and we then asked whether it had been with Bomber or Fighter Command or Coastal Command, to which he replied, "Well, you know nothing about it to ask me such a silly question!"

There are many things which united my husband and myself, and which we held in common. The chief amongst these was the faith we shared. We both love Britain and the Monarchy and were delighted to be called patriotic, and we believed that by its own particular nature Britain had an opportunity to set a moral example to the world. We also believed strongly in the British Commonwealth of Nations. These views I still hold and always will.

Prayer meant a great deal to both of us and I found amongst my husband's letters one written in 1990 to a Community Tutor; a part of it reads as follows:

> As to your specific question, the total time to allot, each day divides itself into various forms of prayer. First is the more formal liturgical prayer, that is to say Mass and the Divine Office. I make it a habit to go to Mass each day, but if this is not possible, then I use my own Missal and read through the Mass privately. Intercessory prayer I regard as very important and I like to try and "visit" in imagination each of our Homes and the different projects and individuals with whom I am concerned. I do not linger on any one of them, still less enter into a dialogue, so to speak. My intention is to place myself consciously in the presence of God and then invite each Home or person in turn to sit quietly before Him. I find that this makes me feel much closer to those I am remembering, deepens my affection or love for them and actually gives me strength. The prayer of quiet is something apart and distinct from all the others. I set aside a period in the morning and a period in the evening, where possible three quarters of an hour each. Finally, there are devotions such as the Rosary or the Stations of the Cross.
>
> Obviously one should attempt to be praying in a different kind of way throughout the day, raising one's mind briefly to God and little rules such as saying the briefest of prayers each time the telephone rings, or one enters a room and so on, can help form the habit. Scripture seems to call us to watch as well as to pray and seems to imply a difference between them. Watchfulness I look upon as being alert and open both for the promptings of the Holy Spirit and for the needs of one's neighbour.

In spite of the immense joy and comfort that the media bring to millions of lonely and sick people and the insight it gives them to many different subjects which otherwise would be unknown to them, we deplored the unnecessary emphasis made on so much violence and ill-will. All too little attention was and still is paid to the constructive work being done by so many people. As The late Reverend Agnellus Andrew, OFM, Bishop of Numana, has said:

> I speak particularly of radio and television which make their way into almost every home. In fact, the radio or TV set has become almost another member of the family – often the most articulate and vocal. In some countries, radio and television are entirely subordinated to the political demands of the State: in others, they are hardly less dominated by commercial motives and are bent to serve the consumer society. In other countries there is a high concept of public service and the media are designed to inform, to educate, and to entertain. But almost everywhere, because of trends in contemporary society, there are grave dangers of worldliness, of underlying false assumptions and false aims, of triviality, of constant stimulation, and very often exploitation of sex, pornography and violence. It is a sad commentary that often the most violent programmes are the News.
>
> In bygone days our forefathers went out to the theatre as the result of deliberate choice: they went out for entertainment, for drama, for music, for debate, for discussion, (or they invited others into their homes). Now, all this invades our homes and, alas, many of our people have a passive attitude, exercising no discrimination or choice, but letting radio and television drip over them, entirely passively. This is particularly dangerous with children – some parents even use the television as a baby-sitter, keeping the children occupied and quiet while they go on with other things. False opinions gain easy entrance: false attitudes are easily created: and although research costing millions of dollars still refuses a definite answer on the effects of radio and television, there can be no doubt that over the days and over the years the minds and hearts, the opinions and attitudes of our people are affected.

Top communicators who set the media agenda are often prejudiced against Christian religion. A distinctive characteristic of the media élite is its secular outlook. A study on quality television in five countries including Britain showed that religion, as a category, is almost *totally* neglected in prime-time programming in all five countries.

It seems to be a growing habit in this country to criticise or denigrate any person, group or association which is trying to maintain standards. Consequently, we are bombarded by negativity and scandal which the majority of people certainly do not want to hear, even if it were true. I firmly believe that the constant intrusion into people's private lives is wholly wrong. Each person's private life should be protected; and if the media are unwilling to check or restrain themselves, they will, sadly in my opinion, have to be checked by law.

We shared the conviction that one beneficial effect of both World Wars was the national unity of purpose – sadly defused since 1945 but still latent under the surface.

Richard Dunning, a close colleague and supporter, bought the infamous Lochnagar Crater from a French Farmer and there is a pilgrimage each year to commemorate 1 July 1916, the first tangible day of the Battle of the Somme. Each year more and more pilgrims come and in Richard's words:

> It feels increasingly that strong bonds of fellowship and "family" that Lochnagar continues to generate is a powerful echo of the unique comradship found in the battered trenches of 1916.
>
> This morning, each poppy petal scattered, each small cross planted represents a life unfulfilled and countless hopes unrealised.
>
> I think Locknagar can give us a glimpse into that terrible day eighty years ago and a unique opportunity to reflect on what their lives might have been – and what ours are yet to be.
>
> If we who are here today can return inspired and recharged by the qualities of those who remain then Lochnagar will have been worthwhile.
>
> Amidst the clamour of the world, this single, simple piece of ground can continue to give inspiration to us all in such a special way.
>
> Today, while we remember the tragedy and suffering of those events let us also celebrate the legacy of friendship and fellowship that embraces all who visit Lochnagar.
>
> > Thank you
> > Richard Dunning

Both Leonard and myself both felt strongly and wished that the two minutes' silence could be revived throughout the country. The silence, which is still observed at the Cenotaph ceremony, was introduced in 1919 and was observed by the whole country until a few years after the Second World War when someone in Whitehall decided it was no longer practical.

In essence our reason for wanting the return of the two minutes' silence was to honour the dead and at the same time to remind people of the precious nature of peace. Peace is very fragile, chiefly because there is so much injustice in the world, and particularly the injustice of mass poverty and starvation. If we do not make up our minds, individually and as a nation, to do something about this injustice, there is a real danger of the world breaking down into chaos. To prevent this catastrophe, strength and discipline and the courage of our convictions, both as individuals and as a country, are essential.

Leonard and I naturally shared each other's problems and frequently these were talked over during the brief time we spent together at meals, though even this was often interrupted by telephone calls. We ate in a tiny dining area we created on the landing. My husband had to keep to a very strict diet, and this proved especially difficult when he was travelling. He was also a light sleeper and did not always feel physically strong. Indeed for many years he frequently felt really tired and inevitably perhaps a lot of people expected too much of him. Despite pleas from his doctors, they took no notice. It used to take Leonard more than five years to visit all of his Homes, and even this proved difficult, especially with all social and official occasions he felt bound to attend. Whenever we were apart on our separate journeys, we wrote and left notes for each other. We tried very hard to remain in close contact.

Leonard also had sprue – a diarrhoea caused by malabsorption, involving bacteria: this caused pain, cramp and colon irritation, so stools were passed frequently. On his many visits overseas, he quickly developed an infection, especially a chill, because of his history of TB, and often he became very ill. I insisted that he travelled with suitable antibiotics.

Leonard was diagnosed much later on with skin cancer on his head and face, sadly the result of not trying hard enough to protect himself in the hot sun.

During the last two or three years of his life, on the advice of David Lean, Leonard used a typewriter, but he quickly progressed to a word processor for all the wide variety of his written work. He was meticulous about preparing his talks and after writing out the theme, he would memorise what he intended to say in an astonishing way. If he found writing a taxing business, he was also very good at it – with a real gift for the telling phrase. I had *always* begged him to write his own autobiography, because however good another writer is, that person can never imagine or know what went on in Leonard's mind. To my sorrow he wrote other books but never *his* autobiography.

Neither of us drank or smoked. We enjoyed very simple food and looked forward to the rare occasions when we could enjoy listening together to pre-War and Wartime melodies on tapes, including famous dance bands. On the radio, one of our favourite programmes was "Your Hundred Best Tunes" which was introduced by Alan Keith at 9 p.m. on Sunday. Leonard often taped these programmes for me so that I could play them in the car or lorry during the long drives in Britain and overseas. They gave me great joy. Although we seldom had the opportunity to watch television, we particularly enjoyed programmes on nature, historic places and architecture, as well as "Face the Music," "Upstairs, Downstairs", and "Nanny". On occasions, I like to listen to talks describing gardens and Italian opera, and to "Songs of Praise".

We also tried to follow football and I remember vividly the suspense before England won the World Cup in 1966, and the moment when Bobby Charlton rolled down his socks.

In general, we disliked social events and talkative people. But Leonard always enjoyed the reunions of the Victoria Cross and George Cross Association, and I had the honour of accompanying him when I could. He also liked to attend the reunions with the survivors of the 617 Squadron and other Squadrons which he had commanded in the RAF.

On my side, I tried to attend the very small annual reunions in London of Polish Parachutists who had served in the Polish Section of Special

Operations Executive, and also the reunions of the Czech Parachutists survivors, who after the Communist Coup in 1948 suffered in different prisons for fifteen years or more. They were only recognised and rehabilitated after the release of Havel, a most distinguished Dissident, who himself was imprisoned for nine years before becoming President of the Czech Republic in 1989.

After very many years I still continue to attend the large annual pilgrimages of survivors to the Concentration Camps of Auschwitz, Mauthausen, Buchenwald, Sachsenhausen, Ravensbrück and Neuengamme, and other equally notorious camps. The lifelong comradeship among the survivors of these Camps, who came from some thirty to forty different nations, was heartwarming, and extremely poignant. And so Leonard and I, each in our own way, were blessed to be part of many, and such unique occasions.

My husband loved tennis, and played I believe, very well, and as frequently as he could find the time, especially for health reasons. If I could choose, I would like to read more, listen to music, walk a great deal and enjoy nature, the smell of the soil, the changing skies. I like to meditate and pray in silence – surely an essential part of life.

As regards food, I enjoy fish and vegetables. Baked apples, butter, decaffeinated coffee and apple juice are also things I like to eat and drink. Meringues, eclairs and melons are rare treats. I can only digest a little at a time and therefore prefer to "nibble". Also I am on a diet and rarely eat supper except fruit, especially strawberries.

The pleasure of a private loo, a bath, or indeed water, are all things which having had to do without for years, I will always consider a luxury.

Another thing we held in common was a strong sense of humour, but it took a different form in each of us. My husband was given to gentle leg-pulling, especially with strangers, invariably accompanied with a deadpan expression, while I see the humorous side in most serious situations and enjoy gently mimicking people I have met; I also call places by nicknames. On occasions I have been known in the past to dress up very quickly in order to play a practical joke on unsuspecting members of the Foundation, and I keep a folder, which is not shown to anyone, of past letters and notes I have made up as job applications.

We always tried to watch the end of the last night of the Proms, to share the enthusiasm and patriotism of the huge audience. The experience was always exhilarating and, though Leonard did not share my love of music, he showed a greater interest as the years passed in our marriage.

My husband was very domesticated – he too disliked untidiness and kept his papers and letters in orderly piles, using a dictaphone for dictation. He was apt to be forgetful and not keep memoranda of things to be done. I can only work by keeping a detailed record of actions/musts to be done every day and these notes are kept securely in my ring-books in date order.

A start is made in August each year on sending out over 4,000 Christmas cards. These are all signed and some have personal messages, too. Boxes are provided for the different countries and we work from long computerised lists giving details of individuals.

Later, my husband would hang the many we received from one end of his study to the other in as many rows as possible so that they appeared to form a false ceiling. As we looked at them they brought back many memories of people and places.

Often Leonard, like me, had been without money as he had no private source of income but had to manage on the small RAF pension (which included a disability allowance because he was a TB patient). He washed up and cleaned well and was always willing to wash our clothing at night; he was a splendid partner in sharing chores whether on the long journeys we sometimes shared together or in our bedroom and office at Headquarters.

One dissimilarity between us I would mention was that I believe in rising between 4.30 and 5.00 each morning, whereas my husband preferred to make a later start. One, therefore, was an owl, while the other was a thrush!

As Mother Teresa told us years ago in Calcutta, marriage would mean more sacrifices, but we would be the better for it. Sharing problems made all the difference to both of us. Our feelings are best expressed in the following prayer we composed together in 1958:

USQUE AD MORTEM
(unto death)

To thee, O my God,
Who art infinite Love
Yet Who Hast called us to be perfect,
    even as Thou art perfect:
Who so loved the World,
That Thou didst give us Thine only
    begotten Son,
And who has thereby given Thine all,
    Thine everything:
Who emptied Thyself of Thy Glory,
And became obedient unto death,
Even the death of the Cross,
For us;
To Thee.
We surrender our all, our everything,
To be consumed by the unquenchable
    fire of Thy Love:
We desire to love Thee even as Thy
    own Mother loved Thee,

To be generous as Thou only art
generous,
To give our all to Thee as Thou givest
Thine to us:
Thou hast called us, O Lord, and we
have found Thee
In the poor, the unwanted, and the
suffering,
And there we will serve Thee,
Unto death.

                                                                 Amen

Early in 1988 Leonard had a vision of forming a world-wide memorial fund
for disaster relief – a vision I shared. He recognised that he had been blessed
to survive the Second World War and he was always conscious, therefore,
of the debt he owed to those who did not. The fund was launched by
Leonard at a service in the chapel of Christ's Hospital School in Sussex,
where he gave a talk on Remembrance Sunday of that year.

During this century 100 million lives have been lost as a direct result of
wars; two-thirds of those lives were civilian. The number alone of these
dead – appalling though it is – says nothing of the value of each life; only
when a face and a name is known of the dead does the enormity of the loss
become apparent. Leonard and I wished to remember them by raising a
fund world-wide and using the interest on the money to give immediate
succour and relief to anyone suffering as a result of war or natural disaster.
As the capital would never be spent, the fund would be a permanent memorial to the 100 million dead. Thus was born the aim of the fund – "for every
life lost, a life saved".

The logo of the fund is a red whistle symbolising the whistle blast which
sent thousands upon thousands of men "over the top" from their trenches
and into the face of the enemy in the First World War.

The international concept of the fund was very dear to our hearts and we
both hope that it will gradually spread and flourish throughout the world.
Already in India, as in Britain, the cause has been taken up and there is a
strong committee and helpers.

With so many calls being made today upon the generosity of the people
of Britain one is reluctant to add to them. Nevertheless, fund-raising
concerts are now being organised regularly, and many schools have undertaken sponsored walks along a stretch of eighteen miles of the Somme
battlefield of the First World War, to raise money for the fund.

Leonard was raised to the peerage on 15 June 1991. He chose as his title
Baron Cheshire of Woodhall in the County of Lincolnshire. When
discussing what place-name he might choose I suggested Woodhall in
Lincolnshire because that was where Leonard had flown from on so many
operations during the War. He took his seat on 24 July 1991 sponsored by
Baron Moore of Wolvercote, a close friend of both of us, and by myself.

I believe we were one of the few couples to sit at the same time in the House of Lords and both of us took our seats on the Cross-Benches. We shared a profound interest in the work for handicapped children and adults, the developing world, the unborn child and the rejection of euthanasia and Sunday trading. We both tried to urge the United Nations to be more effective in maintaining law and order in the world and in safeguarding everywhere the rights and dignity of the individual. Leonard and I felt that on these issues we would be more effective working together.

In his maiden speech in the House on 16 October 1991, made in the course of a debate on defence, Leonard said:

> My Lords, I feel that I cannot start my maiden speech without acknowledging the honour that I feel at being among you. For twelve years I watched my wife Sue Ryder make space in what I thought was already a totally full life in order to attend the debates, study the papers and prepare her speech. The warmth with which she spoke of the quality of the debates and the courtesy that she received is at least an encouragement. When she told me that her maiden speech was the easiest that she had ever made, I cannot say that that gave me great encouragement.
>
> But as I stand here I am conscious that we ourselves stand at a critical threshold of world history. The century that we are now leaving must rate as one of the most momentous that the world has ever seen. Never have so many men, women and children been killed in war as in this century: never has state-organised tyranny so violated human dignity. Even the existence of civilisation itself has been threatened by the confrontation between two nuclear superpowers. Now, as we move through the closing years, nearly everything has changed. There is opening up a hope of a safer and better future and one that more conforms to the dignity of the individual. But whether we achieve that will depend on us. It will depend on governments primarily but also on every single person in his private capacity. So it is with the thought of what has happened in the past that I make my comments.
>
> I look first at the mistakes. In 1914 there was euphoria in the nation. From on high there was the statement that the War would last for only a few weeks. It was said that it would end before the autumn leaves fell. Well, the leaves did fall, regiment upon regiment of them. They were not autumn leaves but green, spring leaves in the full vigour of first youth. By the time it was all over 25 million had died across the reaches of the warring countries. One would have thought that we had learnt our lesson. But we were thrown to the other end of the spectrum. There was fear of war, and disarmament and appeasement were the cries of the day. When Chamberlain took off from Croydon in 1938 it is reported that he looked down on the suburban houses and said, "If I fail in my mission these will be destroyed by bombing". But when he came in to land at Munich he did not look down – or so it is reported – at Dachau, which was then in its fifth year of carrying out Hitler's oppressive extermination programme, and consider that issue.
>
> I say that in no sense of criticism because for the most part, with some very notable exceptions, the nation thought the same. I say it because

I think that we tend to be short-term and not long-term thinkers. Although as an air-force man I do not like looking at other services, we do not have a crow's nest looking out at the distant horizon. We are concerned with the immediate. Much of what I have heard in the debate today is focused on the change in the perceived immediate threat.

The world has changed. The nature of war has undoubtedly changed, but human nature has not. Men of violence will still stalk the world. There is still greed for wealth and lust for power. I can see the possibility of new, strong ideological forces gathering, linked to national ambition. Technology not only gives the great state immense destructive power and high precision capability; it is going to give increasingly great power to the undercover terrorist. We do not know what lies ahead. No generation has ever before faced such an unknown, uncharted future. Therefore, I ask that we think deeply and carefully and do not jump too quickly.

I want to look at something which has not been discussed – that is to say, the full role of the Armed Forces. What the police force is on the national scene, the Armed Forces are on the international scene. There is as yet no world army, so our own Armed Forces have to perform that role. We think of them as purely meeting external aggression, but we should start thinking of them as the keepers of law and order in the whole human family. That is not my own personal first thought, because others have said it.

The United Nations is built on the sovereignty of the individual state. If there is one issue that all 165 members or whatever it is will agree on it is the necessity to respect that. But the human individual also has a sovereignty, and that sovereignty needs to be respected. If it is grossly violated in a nation either through the regime's active fault or because it cannot be bothered, then the United Nations should have the authority and the teeth to go in and do something. I realise that that is a step-by-step process but we should move towards it. If we are to move towards it we have to have Armed Forces that are capable of implementing it.

The policeman not only stops crime and keeps law and order but he helps people under certain circumstances. Now, as we sit here, Somalia is in civil strife. Only ten or twenty per cent of the food and aid convoys going there are getting through. I believe that there should be armed soldiers in blue United Nations berets escorting them and guaranteeing to the host country and to the donors that the aid is going exactly where it is needed and nowhere else, and not being diverted into the black market.

The Armed Forces have a role to play in disaster relief which nobody else can play. They are organised and disciplined; they have communications, rapid deployment, medical and construction units and so on. They should be used more and more. We should move towards the day when there is a United Nations disaster relief force or capability. When nations are asked for a specific unit for a particular disaster, given availability, it should be sent. That means that those countries with disaster relief expertise in the military should pass that expertise onto smaller countries. Then the world would have a disaster relief capability which is far more effective and cost-effective than what we have today. Also, we need better intelligence – undercover work. I heard it said today that the initiative lies with the aggressor. If that is so it is because we lack the intelligence. We should know; we should be prepared; we should be stalking the aggressor, ready to stop him.

Only those who have served in the Armed Forces, particularly in war, know the value of tradition. When one joins one's first squadron, regiment or ship, one is a little frightened in war. But then one realises that one is walking a road that other men before you have walked. In a sense, one is in their shoes. One knows that one has to try and live up to the example they set. I am saying that the Armed Forces have a far greater role to play in the future good of mankind than we may think at present. I hope that we shall not let that opportunity go. I thank your Lordships for the courtesy of listening to my maiden speech.

Viscount Whitelaw, who spoke after Leonard, paid him the most handsome tribute in the following words:

My Lords, I have had many great privileges in my comparatively short time in your Lordships House, including that period when I had the great honour of being its Leader, but I do not think that I could possibly have a greater privilege than that which has been given to me this afternoon to thank and congratulate the noble Lord, Lord Cheshire, on a really remarkable maiden speech.

It is very rare that one is given the chance to congratulate someone who one knows in one's heart is one of the really great men of our generation in peace and in war. We cannot be more grateful that the noble Lord has come to our House and will take part in our debate. The noble Lord said it was an honour for him to be here. I can only say to him in return that it is a very great honour for all of us to have him here. We are deeply grateful for what he said. It would be fair to say that from the number of people who have listened to the noble Lord's speech we shall be very anxious indeed to hear him again at the earliest possible opportunity. Following him I can make only the rather mundane comment that to make one's speech now is a very humbling experience indeed. I feel suitably humble in seeking to do so.

For a long time I had been seriously worried about Leonards's health and in *Remembrance 1992* I wrote the following article:

Since the summer of 1991, my husband's health has given reason for great concern. He had major surgery in 1952–53 for Tuberculosis. He also has Coeliac disease and skin cancer. In mid-February 1992 he was diagnosed with Motor Neurone disease, which means that he has a neurological condition which is affecting the nerve supply to all voluntary muscles throughout the body. There is no surgical or medical treatment for this disease. He has terrible cramps, is extremely breathless and dehydrated, and his mouth is always so sore due to a complete lack of saliva. At night, twitching and cramps are at their worst. Now, too, he finds swallowing a great problem.

This disease, which is causing his health to deteriorate rapidly, has at the same time given us, I hope, an even stronger faith. Because I have the privilege of caring for him and nursing him at Headquarters, I am ever conscious of not being able to carry out my normal programme of visits and travels at this time.

I am reminded of the following words from 2 *Corinthians* 4:8, 16–18:

> We are hard pressed on every side, but not crushed; perplexed, but not in despair; struck down, but not destroyed . . . therefore we do not lose heart. Though outwardly we are wasting away, inwardly we are being renewed day by day, for our momentary troubles are achieving for us an eternal glory . . . so we fix our eyes not on what is seen, for what is seen is temporary, but what is unseen is eternal.

I am greatly sustained by my Assistants and the volunteers, especially those from Poland and the Czech Republic whose example I have always tried to follow because they have endured indescribable suffering, both from the Nazi and Soviet systems, and yet have retained their faith and shown superb courage, and this has continued all the time.

Please do not write especially, but we will *greatly* value and count upon your prayers.

In May 1992 my husband expressed a wish to pay a last visit overseas and we were extremely fortunate to receive from British Airways two free first-class tickets. Without these we could not have afforded the journey. It was decided that we should pay a short visit to India to see the leprosy patients, some of the ten million people with tuberculosis, the destitute children, the mentally handicapped and others. By receiving special leave from work Jeromy and Gigi were able to join us.

Thanks to Virendra Singh and others in the Indian Foundation, they kindly arranged for us to stay quietly and rest in the Orian Hotel for a few nights, before proceeding by helicopter to the joint Ryder/Cheshire Centre in Raphael. The poignancy of this, Leonard's last visit, proves indescribable and so too were the welcomes and farewells.

The temperature in Delhi and Dehra Dun was well over 100°F, but then I am used to this, and indeed to the many diseases.

Paul Freeman, the producer, and David Puttnam, one of the Directors of Anglia Television, accompanied us and we were joined in India by a film crew. A video film of our visit was made entitled "An Indian Summer" and this was shown on Anglia Television in September 1992. At the end of this Leonard spoke the following words:

> Heaven is a place of peace
> This world, by contrast, is a battlefield
> I just want to remain on this battlefield
> I want to remain with my family
> and those I love, and do what
> little I can to help those in need.
>   (Leonard Cheshire)

Leonard's last public appearance was in London on Sunday, 31 May 1992, when, following a moving service the Queen Mother unveiled the statue of Sir Arthur Harris outside St. Clement Dane's Church in the Strand, the crowds cheered him as I pushed him in his wheelchair. After the ceremony a close friend of mine went to see the statue and she wrote to me:

> There were three things which stood out on this occasion. There was a simple wreath of flowers, saying "From your friends, the people of Holland"; a beautiful bouquet of flowers with a simple note attached reading "But for you, I, as an English Jew, would have been sent to the gas chambers"; and last, but not least, another bouquet of flowers bearing the label: "From everyone in the East End".

Later, on Thursday 9 July 1992, we were both invited by the Queen to a reception at Buckingham Palace for members of the Order of Merit. This was to be Leonard's last journey to London and, afterwards, he made a brief visit to the House of Lords; he was totally exhausted by the time he reached home.

It had been clear for some time that Leonard's life was slowly ebbing away. He and I always read the breviary and prayers together, but towards the end he could absorb only short sentences, and we prayed especially to Our Lady during the night when Leonard found it impossible to sleep. When Leonard asked me to put his breviary (from which he said his Divine Office each day) in the little bookcase at the end of the Easter cycle, he said: "This reminds me of putting away my Log Book in 1945 at the end of the War."

Almost to the end Leonard took delight in dropping crumbs of bread on to the small ledge outside our window where many birds from the garden would come to sing. Resting on his special bed in the bedroom he also loved to look at the magnolia tree and see the buds blossom; so, although terribly weak, he remained alert and retained his love of nature.

For weeks before his death and while he still retained some strength, he continued to sort his personal papers. He also dictated to me notes about the present and future of his own Foundation, and the way he wanted the work to proceed. It was a great pity these thoughts were not recorded in writing, especially as afterwards, although I had been a Trustee of his Foundation since the mid-1950s, it proved difficult to pass these wishes on in the way he asked me to, and to see them implemented.

Leonard also dictated *Last Thoughts*, edited by Father Reginald Fuller with a foreword by Alan C. Clark, Bishop Emeritus of East Anglia, I now quote the Foreword:

> It is only rarely that even close friends are allowed to enter into the prayer-filled thoughts of a dying man of the calibre of Leonard Cheshire. Father Reginald Fuller has in the following precious pages put together these thoughts taken down in writing on different occasions by those who were "with Leonard" in the last months of his life. He has carried out a difficult task. So many people who enjoyed the company and friendship of Leonard

will feel privileged to read of his prayerful search and his "finding" of the ways of God.

Of those with him in his last illness none was closer than Sue (Lady Ryder of Warsaw) who, as wife and confidante, as well as nurse, was particularly united with him in that sacred part of his life – his going forth to God. He died at their home in Cavendish, Suffolk, known as the Sue Ryder Home, where they had spent all their married life when not travelling abroad on behalf of their respective Foundations.

Leonard, as is well-known, suffered from motor neurone disease and in spite of the stress involved spoke of the truth as he experienced it. His "conclusions" were hard-won which makes this booklet all the more valuable to those who, one way or another, knew him and enjoyed this friendship.

What follows then is a record of some of Leonard's deeply held convictions which, even in the period of his sharply declining health, he wished to share with others. The title "Last Thoughts . . ." though exact, can hardly convey an impression of the profound intensity of his faith and spiritual experience. But the record here given is sufficient to reveal something of the mind and heart of a unique "soul" full of grace and truth. One is overwhelmed by the greatness of his friendship with Christ at the centre of his being.

Our thanks to Sue, his wife, to Father Reginald Fuller and all those who took part in making these "verba ipsissima" of Leonard Cheshire available to us.

By mid-summer Leonard weighed less than six stone. He had hardly any flesh left on him, yet he managed to say: "I am offering up my suffering and small discomforts so that your work will consolidate and grow, with more funds and people to help you. I pray, too, that you will keep our small family of International Foundations together." During the last weeks of his life I can truthfully say that he was in great distress. He could not lie on his left side owing to the fact that he only had one lung. If he lay on his right side the muscles contracted and earache proved extremely painful. It was painful, too, for him to lie on his back owing to the fact that his spine was very sore because of the flesh that had wasted away and also because of surgery he had received when he had had tuberculosis. Mercifully, though, he had no bed sores, due to the constant attention which I tried to give him, together with the nursing staff who offered to come up if we wanted them to help. Leonard bore his suffering courageously, and nursing him was, indeed, a great privilege. During the last months and especially every evening, we always continued to say our prayers together. At the end Leonard could only listen to me reciting a few short lines from prayers every few hours. These included the following:

"If you can have some share in the suffering of Christ, be glad, because you will enjoy a much greater gladness when his glory is revealed."

"Simon Peter said, 'Lord, to whom shall we go? You have the words of eternal life; we believe and we know that you are the Christ, the son of God'."

IN REMEMBRANCE AND MEMORANDUM.

During the last night Leonard's pulse became hectic, and he died from heart failure on 31 July 1992. It was my privilege with Sister Ann Gentry to lay him out and surround him with candles and flowers. The sense of loss and the grief I feel for him, however, will never leave me.

Tributes were paid to him throughout the world. Anyone who had known my husband would have appreciated the quiet dignity with which he conducted himself, and it was his wish that his Requiem Mass should be simple and dignified and be held in the chapel at Headquarters which he loved so dearly. Later on, a more formal Mass of Memorial was held in London. The Requiem Mass was celebrated on 10 August 1992. On his own instructions invitations were restricted to my husband's and my families and to members of staff and volunteers chosen by my husband before he died.

We were privileged to have in attendance Father Walsh OSB, Secretary of the Diocesan Liturgical Commission, and members of the choir of St Edmunds Church, Bury St Edmunds, and the Mass was concelebrated by the Bishop, the Right Reverend Alan Clark DD, Father Kevin Doheny who had worked closely with both of us on overseas projects, Fathers Barry Clifford and Patrick Killian from Clare Priory.

The hymns chosen were some of our favourites – "All Creatures of Our God and King", "O Love That Will Not Let Me Go", "Blest Are the Pure in Heart", and the second reading was from St Paul's First Letter to the Corinthians, which was read by my youngest brother, Stephen Ryder –

> If I speak with the tongues of men and of angels, but have not love, I am become as sounding brass or a clanging cymbal. And if I have the gift of prophecy, and comprehend all mysteries and all knowledge; and if I have all faith, so as to displace mountains, but have not love, I am nothing. And if I bestow in doles all my goods, and if I deliver my body to the flames, but have not love, it profiteth me nothing.
>
> Love is patient, is kind; love envieth not, is not pretentious, is not puffed up, behaveth not amiss, seeketh not her own, is not provoked, regardeth not evil, rejoiceth not over wickedness, but rejoiceth with the truth; beareth all things, believeth all things, hopeth all things, endureth all things.
>
> Love faileth never; whereas prophesyings, they shall have an end; tongues, they shall cease; knowledge, it shall have an end. For we know in part, and we prophesy in part; but when the perfect is come, what is in part shall have an end. When I was a child, I spoke as a child, I felt as a child, I thought as a child; now that I am become a man, I have made an end of childish ways. For now we see in a mirror, obscurely; but then face to face. Now I know in part; then shall I know fully, even as I have been fully known. So there abide faith, hope, love, these three, but the greatest of these is Love.

The Mass itself was sung in Gregorian chant and, by coincidence, Marie Therese Cunningham, a soprano, who had supported me in the early days of my work, was singing with the choir. She sang Schubert's *Ave Maria* during the Preparation of the Gifts and this was followed by our friends from Poland singing one of their familiar hymns, *Jezusa Ukrytego* (Jesus concealed).

Afterwards, the burial took place in the Village cemetery across the green from the Home.

Both during Leonard's long illness and afterwards I received constant enquiries from the Press. Following his death I received more than 3,000 wonderful letters, cards, faxes, telephone messages and calls; each was acknowledged personally. My Assistants and Secretaries coped magnificently with all of this and they were joined by Eileen, a weekend Secretary, and two sisters, Susan and Angela, who worked day and night as volunteers replying to each communication. It has been difficult to select a few from the many messages I received, but I hope that the following will stand for all:

Mother Teresa of the Missionaries of Charity in Calcutta wrote –

> I have heard of the death of Lord Cheshire who went home to God on 31 July.
> Let the thought of his going home to God, to Him who loved him first fill you with the certainty that he is watching over you and is closer to you now than ever before.
> I assure you of my prayers for the eternal repose of his soul and for you and your family.
> God bless you.

The Prime Minister, the Right Honourable John Major, MP, said in his letter –

> Dear Sue,
>   Norma and I were very sad indeed to hear of Leonard's death.
> He was a great man, a man of wisdom and fortitude and a thoroughly decent human being. Together, you and he touched directly the lives of thousands of people and gave them hope and encouragement . . .

From a Wartime friend, Geoffrey Sparrow, who served in the Rifle Brigade – a few of whose letters written then have been reproduced in Chapter 5 – came the following letter –

> I believe great men never die, they become their own chapter in the book of the History of the Nation. The obituary in *The Daily Telegraph* said it all and one is left gasping that one man could have made such an impact on the lives of others – a giant in War and equally so in Peacetime.
>   . . . I can think of no more wonderful legacy than to leave what Leonard and, ultimately, you will have left to posterity. The names of Cheshire and Ryder will live on in the generations to come – an inspiration for all who seek to serve others less fortunate, lacking care and attention in their own countries and danger of being forgotten as the years pass by. The world loves you, and I, as one very humble and long time friend, feel I can write to you in this way and put a few rather uncollated thoughts on paper. Others, no doubt world-wide, will have overwhelmed you with

similar letters. Please don't reply; just think back to those long-past days when you were a young girl in the FANY and I a young boy in the Rifle Brigade; I realised then that you were a very special person. I often think of our 'voyage' on board a troopship to North Africa, and with gratitude for our subsequent friendship.

Another long-time friend wrote –

> . . . You had both been in our thoughts and prayers since we received your letter telling us of Leonard's distressing illness, and when we heard of his death our immediate reaction was "How wonderful that he is now in Heaven with his Resurrection Body and with no more suffering and without any pain.

Next, I quote from a letter I received from all the residents in one of my husband's Homes; it was signed by each of them and read –

> As residents of a wonderful Cheshire Home, we are all so grateful that due to G.C. (as Leonard was known to so many people) "our lives are very fulfilled in spite of being handicapped. We want you to know how much we admire and respect G.C. and the unique contribution you have both made to Humanity.

I feel that my husband would have treasured especially this tribute from the people to whom he devoted his life as it sums up all he wished for and worked to achieve for the handicapped.

Many people sent me beautiful prayers; one, by Archbishop Benson, reads –

> O God, to me who am left to mourn his departure, grant that I may not sorrow as one without hope for my beloved who sleeps in Thee; but as always remembering his courage, and the love that united us on earth, I may begin again with new courage to serve Thee more fervently who art the only source of true love and true fortitude; that, when I have passed a few more days in this valley of tears and this shadow of death, supported by Thy rod and staff, I may see him face to face, in those pastures and beside those waters of comfort, where I believe he already walks with Thee. O Shepherd of the sheep, have pity upon this soul of mine.

Another passage, which is attributed to Robert Louis Stevenson, is also very lovely –

> To have lived in the light of that splendid life, that beautiful, bountiful being – only to see it, from one moment to the other, converted into a fable as strange and romantic as one of his own, a thing that has been and has ended, is an anguish into which no one can enter with you fully and of which no one can drain the cup for you. You are nearest to pain, because you were nearest to the joy and the pride.

The Right Honourable Lord Callaghan of Cardiff, KG, in sending me a copy of the tribute he wrote to Leonard in the *House of Lords Magazine* – extracts of which I set out below – wrote:

Dear Sue,

> . . . You will miss Leonard this Christmas but I know you have all the courage in the world to carry on, as well of course as the work to which you are dedicated.

Part of Lord Callaghan's tribute reads –

> He met and married Sue Ryder, a kindred spirit, whose dedicated work for the survivors of the Nazi concentration camps, together with her other international relief work, complemented his own efforts. Her strength of character settled his own uncertainties and together they began their joint efforts by launching their first overseas venture in India. Thereafter, their aspirations grew and together, against all the odds, they established an astonishing number of Homes throughout the world.
>
> He and Lady Ryder of Warsaw, a Baroness in her own right, had hoped to work effectively together in the Lords in pursuit of their joint cause of caring for the handicapped and sick of all ages at home and overseas, and it is a tragedy that he was able to make only one more speech before his death.
>
> All her friends and many who knew her only through her work, send our affection and sorrow at the ending of her partnership with a very great man, and salute her courage in continuing with the tasks they were jointly pledged to.

The great Memorial Mass was attended by some 1,700 people. It was held in Westminster Cathedral on the 25th September 1992 in the presence of His Eminence Cardinal Basil Hume, Bishop Alan Clark and eleven priests. My husband's medals were carried in the procession by two former members of the Royal Air Force who had served with him in 617 Squadron as a pilot and a member of ground crew respectively. The Cardinal gave the homily. At the conclusion of the Prayer of the Faithful, I read again the prayer *Usque ad Mortem* (Unto Death) which Leonard and I had composed in 1958 and which is set out on page 278. The tributes paid to my husband that day will be with me and members of my family for the rest of our lives. Both Odette Hallowes GC, her husband and Her Royal Highness, Princess Margaret of Hesse and the Rhein sat in the same pew. They had been wonderful supportive friends for years and especially during and after the long months of Leonard's illness. I was also so touched by their constant telephone calls and beautiful flowers and plants they sent.

The arrangements for this Mass were drawn up by four of my closest Secretaries/Assistants at Headquarters, with the help of members of the Cathedral staff. We kept the same hymns as for the Requiem Mass with the addition of the one which used to be sung at every Remembrance Day ceremony, "O Valiant Hearts". Mozart's *Ave Verum* followed and was sung during Holy Communion.

O Valiant Hearts, who to your glory came
Through dust of conflict and through battleflame,
Tranquil you lie, your knightly virtue proved,
Your memory hallowed in the Land you loved.

Proudly you gathered, rank on rank to war,
As you had heard God's message from afar;
All you had hoped for, all you had, you gave
To save Mankind – yourselves you scorned to save.

Splendid you passed, the great surrender made,
Into the light that nevermore shall fade;
Deep your contentment in that blest abode,
Who wait the last trumpet-call of God.

Long years ago, as earth lay dark and still
Rose a loud cry upon a lonely hill,
While in the frailty of our human clay
Christ, our Redeemer, passed the self-same way.

Still stands His Cross from that dread hour to this,
Like some bright star above the dark abyss;
Still, through the veil, the Victor's pitying eyes
Look down to bless our lesser Calvaries.

These were His servants, in His steps they trod,
Following through death the martyr'd Son of God:
Victor He rose; victorious too shall rise
They who have drunk His cup of Sacrifice.

O risen Lord, O Shepherd of our Dead,
Whose Cross has bought them and whose Staff has led –
In glorious hope their proud and sorrowing Land
Commits her Children to Thy gracious hand.

(Words by Sir John S. Arkwright)

In her message to the people of Britain and the Commonwealth on Christmas Day 1992, Her Majesty the Queen referred to Leonard in the following terms –

Curiously enough, it was a sad event which did as much as anything in 1992 to help me put my own worries into perspective. Just before he died, Leonard Cheshire came to see us with his fellow members of the Order of Merit. By then, he was suffering from a long drawn out and terminal illness. He bore this with all the fortitude and cheerfulness to be expected of a holder of the Victoria Cross. However, what struck me more forcibly than his physical courage was the fact that he made no reference to his own illness, but only to his hopes and plans to make life better for others. He embodied the message in these well-known lines: 'kindness in another's trouble, courage in one's own.'

One of his Cheshire Homes for people with disabilities is not far from this house [Sandringham, Norfolk]. I have visited others all over the Commonwealth and I have seen at first hand the remarkable results of his, and his wife's, determination to put Christ's teaching to practical effect. Perhaps this shining example of what a human being can achieve in a lifetime of dedication can inspire in the rest of us a belief in our own capacity to help others.

Such talents and indomitable spirit are not given to all of us. But if we can sometimes lift our eyes from our own problems, and focus on those of others, it will be at least a step in the right direction and Christmas is a good time to take it. I hope that his example will continue to inspire us all in the years ahead.

After such a close and harmonious partnership and friendship which lasted for nearly forty years, it is impossible to describe how greatly I miss Leonard's companionship.

There was so much to share with him, to talk over, to search for solutions and to plan for the future. We depended upon each other's advice. We rarely disagreed, and when this did happen we dropped the subject and would go and pray in our bedroom or in the chapel. And that night we would ask each other forgiveness in our prayers together.

I remember these words: "Whenever I look I see him and whoever I am with he is there" (source unknown).

When Leonard died I was reminded of what St Bonaventure wrote:

> Be not afflicted
> In Heaven
> I think of you,
> I love you
> and, as in life,
> I am still
> with you.

11

India

THERE ARE SOUNDS, SIGHTS and smells which instantly bring a country or place to the mind. Within the confines of a few pages one can recapture only a few impressionistic memories to illustrate the immensity and diversity of India.

I think of overcrowded trains; cooking in the carriages; steaming heat rising from the ground; bitterly cold nights; people sleeping on pavements; scraggy dogs scrounging for scraps amongst the garbage; the sound of waves lapping on the shore; the grace of women carrying water or bricks on their heads, combing or plaiting their long sleek hair, winding brilliant saris round their bodies; the greeting *namastes* with folded hands; the jingling and jangling of horse-drawn tongas; twinkling lights; changing a wheel by candlelight on the road; ticklish warmth of 90°F; notices at Delhi airport – *In case of any grievance contact the Assistant Collector. No anonymous complaints*; the savour of chapaties cooked over a simple fire; the tooting of hooters; relief at the caress of water and rain; thronged and raucous bazaars; maize, rice, bananas; swarming flies, occasional mosquito nets; the chirping of crickets or cicadas at night; the haze rising everywhere at sunset from innumerable family fires; ubiquitous and penetrating dust; tropical storms; the shouts of children; staggering loads carried or pulled by men, women or emaciated buffaloes; holy men in silent meditation; innumerable migratory birds in the hill stations; minahs with their cheeky chatter; spontaneous *salaams* from all and sundry; the powerful scents of frangipani blossoms and bright marigold garlands; the disciplined bearing of the men and women of the Indian Services; the strong and prevailing smell of curry and spices; the howling of the jackals by night; the stark contrast between the human ant-heaps of bustling cities and the fatalistic calm which broods over hard-working villages; camels plodding on the wayside; the delicious taste of succulent mangoes and refreshing papaya; eternal snow on the distant Himalayas in their lonely majesty, in contrast to the littleness and transience of men.

Two endemic problems which in India affect us directly are the continual movement of people from the country to the cities and towns. Many uproot themselves or drift away from the country because of the poor soil conditions or lack of water, or because their tiny plots of land cannot support them, and they vainly hope by moving to find work in the city.

It is tragic to discover whole families or even whole village communities who have done this, only to find themselves living on the pavements or in shocking huts unfit for human habitation. Intense heat makes such an existence almost unbearable, and it is particularly awful to witness the exhaustion of the sick, most of whom know that there is no relief. During the rainy season (if the monsoon does not fail) the huts are frequently washed away.

* * *

Before the construction of a simple airstrip, there were two ways of approaching Dehra Dun – by train chugging through the long night from Delhi, or along a dusty road. The road runs fairly direct for 150 miles through villages and the cantonment towns of Meerut and Roorkee before climbing and twisting into the forest-clad Siwaliks. From these the road drops into a broad plateau and so into the city of Dehra Dun.

To find the Ryder-Cheshire Centre one must leave the City and, on its outskirts, cross the dry bed of the Rispana river. Just beyond the river, against the blue haze of the Himalayan foothills, one sees through the sal trees a group of white buildings. This is Raphael: the Centre consists of a village for people with burnt-out leprosy; a Home for severely mentally handicapped children and adults; a day-centre for mentally handicapped and deaf children; the Little White House for children whose parents are suffering from leprosy; a school for these and other children; a physio-therapy unit; and a small hospital with two separate wings – one for general care of physically handicapped patients, the other for treatment of tuber-culosis. The function of the hospital is supplemented and extended by two Mobile TB Units, which work from the Centre in the area around Dehra Dun. At night the glittering lights of Mussoorie, a famous hill station, watch over the Centre from the mountain ridge just to the north.

The Centre stands 2,000 feet above sea level on a site of twenty-four acres of forest land on the outskirts of Dehra Dun – a large town in the foothills of the Himalayas 150 miles north of Delhi. It was made available by the Indian Forestry Department and was leased to Raphael by the State Government of Uttar Pradesh on the recommendation of the late Jawaharlal Nehru, the first Prime Minister of independent India. Seasonal temperatures range from the boiling heat of summer to a short cold winter. The monsoon rains occur between June and August. The scenery, which stretches for hundreds of miles, is magnificent in its grandeur, and on the twisting roads one meets various hill people – they have fine faces and are always friendly – with their herds of goats and buffaloes. On one of our drives up these very twisty mountain roads, my husband and I stopped the jeep and my husband asked a woman, who was walking towards us with a very straight back and carrying a huge stack of hay on her head, whether we might take her photograph. She replied in Hindi, "Yes, you may, if it is going to be a good photograph."

For us, the establishment of the Centre in 1958 was a big project, all the more ambitious because we had no money to invest in building. Undeterred, however, we decided to make an immediate start. With volunteers, including a few of the leprosy patients, we started to clear the site of bushes and undergrowth with just sharp knives. It was hard work, especially in the heat. Then, three tents, lent by the Indian Army, were erected and, in these, physically handicapped children were soon being cared for by two nurses who had come from Britain, together with local ayahs (nannies) and a cook.

Not long afterwards Ava Dhar, the widow of an Indian civil servant, offered her services as Secretary-Administrator, in which capacity she stayed on at the new settlement until forced, through ill-health, to retire. Ava Dhar was a remarkable person. Shy and reserved, she had the ability to create beauty in the simple surroundings. Before she started her long working day she would go out to collect wild flowers with which to decorate the office. An admirer of Pandit Nehru, she was liberal-minded and often spoke warmly of the positive contributions which Britain had made to her country in the past – in particular, the judiciary, the civil administration and the railway system. She shared with me an interest in medicine and history, and a love of poetry. For many years she had worked with the Red Cross.

Ava Dhar was a quiet administrator, and if at the start she sometimes lay awake at night wondering whether there was going to be enough money at the end of the month to pay the wages and the bills, she quickly adopted the view held by us that financial security is not to be achieved at the expense of refusing admission to the Centre to applicants for whom such refusal would mean certain death. She always believed whole-heartedly that Raphael must not be just a shelter in which those who cannot fend for themselves may be protected, but that its objective must be to offer a new life and a sense of purpose to those who previously had none.

Sadly, in 1966 Ava Dhar was diagnosed with cancer and had to give up her work. In a letter written after she left and shortly before her death she says:

> It was a terrible wrench to leave Raphael in this way. I had a long, last look to bid farewell. The children, patients and sisters and the leprosy patients were standing together along the bank waving until we were out of sight. It was a heart-breaking moment.

In her simple sari Ava Dhar had for many years been a lovely and reassuring presence at Raphael. Barbara Lewis, an Australian who had worked with her, wrote:

> To those for whom she worked, the individuals both at the Centre and nearby, to those who came to her in their distress and learned of her extra-ordinary compassion, this loss must seem irreparable. She was a serene figure dressed in white [the sign of being a widow]. Each morning she calmly washed her hair after the buckets of water had been filled up during the night. She had great sensitivity and anticipated our moves. Before going to sleep, as part of her ritual, she read passages from both the Gita [the

Holy Book of Hindus] and the Bible. She was an extremely well-read woman. Ava initiated me into India. She taught me that you can always laugh with the Indians, but not at them.

I have a mental picture of Ava warming her long fingers and hands over the charcoal fire in the winter. She wore a Kashmir shawl over her sari. She always thought well of everybody and had great understanding and sympathy for the poor. There were very few who worked like her and believed that money would come, but she fully realised the difficulties of raising *dibs* (funds), especially from the children and those who could hardly afford to give.

Some people think that volunteering is an escape, but this is never true in the Foundation. Ava tried to cope. When I talk to people who are not only thousands of miles away but have little imagination, I ask them to imagine twelve million extra people pouring into Sydney (population three million), then an extra ten million over-nighting. A friend in Australia asked, "Why didn't they prepare for this influx?" To this and questions about apathy I reply, "Well, yes, I agree some are apathetic, but then who would not be existing on a subsistence diet, and where has all our hurry got us in this life?"

As the "Village" of Raphael grew, it was run by a Governing Council, and one of its distinguished Chairmen was Lieutenant-General S. P. Bhatia. He was Director-General of the Armed Forces Medical Services in 1960–62. On his retirement from the services he became the Government of India's first Commissioner of Family Planning.

"Shiv", as he was known, died on 21 March 1980, and to those of us who knew him his loss is irreplaceable. A close friend wrote the following obituary:

> With a gentleness and a peacefulness that was characteristic of his personality and of his life, Shiv moved quietly and unobtrusively out of this and into a new dimension.
>
> He was so persuaded, perhaps through his calling, of the needs of human beings that he never questioned the obligation to respond willingly and quietly to the call of his fellow men, whether that call was a cry of pain; or a whisper; or the unuttered call – the most insistent of all because it is the call of one heart to another.
>
> In both his private and his public life he reacted with conviction and with persistence to pleas for help in those particular areas in which he was convinced he was most competent to contribute. Shiv was dignified in his posture and carriage and gracious in his manner and attitude; his righteous indignation when roused was tempered only by his tolerance. He was a doctor and a soldier, distinguished as both, but, above all, he was a gentleman in the ancient and proper meaning of the word.
>
> Qedrwl (L. W. Leybourne Callaghan)

Another of the qualities for which Shiv is remembered was his delightful sense of humour and store of good jokes. It was good to look forward to listening to him after a long day's work. He had an infinite amount of time on rounds for the patients and I could listen to his knowledge of medicine for hours.

Shiv was succeeded as Director-General of the Armed Forces Medical Services by Lieutenant-General R. S. Hoon. He was one of India's most eminent medical doctors. After his retirement in 1977 he was Secretary-General of the Indian Red Cross for two years. During his active career as a doctor he invented a number of biomedical instruments and apparatus and was honoured on several occasions by the Indian Government and various private bodies. He succeeded General Bhatia as Chairman of Raphael's General Council and died while still at his post, in 1982. He brought to his work at the Centre not only his skill as a doctor but a quiet, unassuming good humour and a capacity for hard work which immediately won him the love and respect of everyone with whom he came in contact.

Major-General B. N. Bhandari succeeded General Hoon and he too had an equally distinguished medical career. He qualified as a doctor in England in 1930, and after his return to India he, too, joined the Armed Forces Medical Services. He retired in 1964 and afterwards held a number of important civilian posts.

In 1973, Major-General Ranbir Bakhshi and his wife Shobha, who is herself a doctor, settled in Dehra Dun. The following year "Rummy", as he is known, was invited to join the General Council of Raphael and in 1975 he became Director of the Centre. Rummy brought to the post of Director not only his military flair for administration but also a real and deep-rooted concern for the welfare and happiness of everyone who lives at Raphael. His regard for them is returned in full measure, and the sight of his tall figure surrounded by small children on his daily rounds is familiar to every visitor to the Centre. He has now officially retired as Director and has become Chairman of our Council. His successors were Colonel Rege and Brigadier Harshpati who, in turn, have brought their own knowledge and abilities to look after Raphael.

Raphael receives some grants in India from individuals, organisations and the Government, but it depends mainly upon donations and sponsorship fees collected in Australia, New Zealand and Britain, including the proceeds from two Sue Ryder Shops. Currently, it costs about £310 a year to keep and nurse each resident.

Each of the various constituent units which make up the Village has a part to play in the general community. It is, in fact, a working experiment in a Village of very different people, with the large numbers broken down into manageable groups. Above all, it is a human experiment and, as such, despite everyone's best endeavours, progress is not without its share of difficulties. Many at Raphael feel, however, that they have found a place to which they belong in a world which had largely rejected them; what is more, through the links with their friends abroad who support them, they can now feel they are part of an international community.

*   *   *

    Bless this little heart . . . that has won the kiss of
       heaven for our earth.
    . . . He has not learned to despise the dust, and to
       hanker after gold.
    Clasp him to your heart and bless him.

Tagore

The Little White House is so named after a Polish folk song. The building was made possible by the generosity of two sisters in New Zealand. Here we have seventy healthy boys and girls whose parents cannot look after them because of poverty or illness. Whereas the progress of malaria has been largely arrested, thanks to the World Health Organisation and other agencies, cholera and typhus are, unfortunately, still prevalent, though far more in other continents and places in the World. A few of the children at the Little White House are orphans. Some were brought by relatives who walked for miles to reach the Centre. Often, when the children first arrive, they are shy and sad, never having had the opportunity of playing with a toy or knowing where their next meal was coming from. These children are educated in the primary school on the site and near the Home up to fifth standard. For higher education they attend schools in Dehra Dun and the older girls live in a boarding school there. The emphasis is on vocational training for all children in keeping with their abilities. The girls are trained in general nursing or Special Education and the boys are trained to join defence forces or factories as technical hands. In bringing them up, the staff aim first and foremost to show them that they are loved, and to ensure that they are equipped to cope with life when they are grown up. In preparing the normal, healthy children of leprosy patients for their eventual place in society beyond the Centre, realism dictates the decision to allow them to live separately from their parents, but with regular visits. Apart from these children, there are others who may have been abandoned or who come from very deprived homes. A few are children of parents with active tuberculosis.

To be at Raphael is to share in the fullest sense in the daily lives of the individuals living there. When we stayed at the Centre we also had the opportunity of listening to them and exchanging ideas and thoughts. The children always greeted us by saying, "Hello Mummy, hello Daddy." They enjoy and respond to the opportunity of being educated, and it is delightful to hear what each of them plans to do in the future; even the five-year olds eagerly join in a discussion about learning a trade or profession. Their wishes, like those of all children, are diverse and most probably cannot be fulfilled, but it is wonderful for both the sponsors and ourselves to see them grow and become useful members of society, like Rajender or Krishna.

Rajender was born in 1962 and admitted to the Little White House in 1968, shortly after his mother's death. His father was then living in a leprosy colony at Jagadri, Haryana State, suffering from tuberculosis as well as leprosy. Rajender's brother and two sisters were also admitted to the Little White House at the end of 1968 because their father was no longer able to care for them. He died in 1970.

During his school years, Rajender studied hard and also took a great interest in sports. He was helpful in the Little White House and took responsibility for his younger brother and sisters. In 1979 he was taken into a Sikh family in Chandigarh, who wished to adopt him. In 1980 however, he returned to Raphael. The separation had proved hard, not only for him but also for his younger brother and sisters. In 1981 he joined the Comet bulb factory in Dehra Dun and is still happily employed there.

Krishna's parents both suffered from leprosy and lived in the Nalapani colony, not far from Raphael. She was taken into the Little White House in 1967. Two years later, her mother was also admitted to the Foundation's Centre where she died a few days later in the tuberculosis unit. She left behind her a two-week old baby, Rohit, who also had to be admitted to the Little White House. The remaining brother, Sarvan, came some months later when his father, who was blind, could not look after him.

When Krishna first came to the Centre she was very shy and seemed reluctant to play with the other children. She did not find her studies easy, but nevertheless worked hard. Initially her concern for her two younger brothers affected her studies. Her particular interests were music and sports. She was a lovely looking girl, even-tempered with a calm attitude towards life. One of her greatest thrills, which is still shared by the other children today, was participating in the production of concerts, which included mime, acting, dancing and singing.

In 1979 she and four other Little White House girls were accepted for training at the nurses' school at a hospital in Nainital. In that same year, Krishna (in a class of forty girls) came first in her exams and was accepted as a first-year student. Later on, Krishna met a young man from a Hindu family in Nainital and both of them asked the Director's permission to get married. Krishna is very happy in her married life, and in November 1981 she gave birth to twin boys.

Since the Little White House was conceived and built, over 200 boys and girls have been admitted and have benefited from the care, attention and security they have received. Each has been sponsored by a far-away family, school or individual in New Zealand or Australia. These sponsors have followed the progress of their adopted child from the time of his or her arrival to the moment when the child's education and vocational training is completed, before going out into the world. Each year the sponsors are sent news and a photograph.

The poverty from which these children emerged was so shocking that it is all the more amazing to watch each child develop and adapt in his or her own individual way. We have spent some of the happiest moments with these children who have become so affectionate and loving. Only a few have played truant and have had to leave the Centre.

On Founder's Day (5 April), and on other occasions, the children, together with the Housemother and teachers at the Little White House, are responsible for organising a concert to which outside visitors are invited. The audience sit together and include patients from the Foundation's hospital nearby. They give an amazing variety of songs, dances and mime, and for them these entertainments are often the highlight of the year. They help to make their own costumes from the simplest clothing and resources, and preparations begin weeks beforehand.

Everybody contributes to the concert, including the leprosy patients, and for years, Junoo, who had lost her hands and part of her feet, danced too. Their performances are a humbling experience and put our own lives into perspective. They show, too, how the most destitute in society can both shine and triumph over adversity if they are given the opportunity to do so.

At dusk, after the concert and tea, when ice-cream and sweets are provided as a very great treat to the children, little twinkling candles are lit on the verges of the paths and in the small and simple chapel. Dancing starts in the leprosy colony by the bonfire where we join them, and the patients there sing to the beat of their drums.

Another time for celebrating is during the Holi Hindu Festival, which dates back to ancient times. The children take great delight in sprinkling different coloured powders over everyone's head and clothes. I finished up looking like a punk! Pop music is also popular and some of the older children organised a pop festival, when jiving went on until two in the morning! It was great fun for all, and everyone who had the energy joined in.

* * *

The Ava Vihar (Ava's Garden) Unit, which cares for the mentally handicapped, has patients whose ages range from eleven to sixty-five years old, many of them severely retarded and in need of specialised medical care. Many of the children have been abandoned or have parents who, because of their deprived circumstances, can no longer cope. The need for such care as can be given at Raphael is huge in India, and the aim has been to seek the resources necessary to separate those who are capable of responding to treatment from the others who, sadly, are not.

This has been of paramount importance because of the very wide range of disabilities among the young patients. This is the Unit which has the longest waiting list. Its present capacity is for sixty, but we hope it will grow to accommodate 120. In time we intend not only to increase the accommodation but also to classify the patients according to their particular needs and so provide better care.

Pamela Breslin, the Australian teacher who started the school for these patients, arrived in 1960. She needed faith, patience and skill; with the minimum of facilities she was able to evoke a response from a few children and to introduce calm and discipline into their lives. She taught them to identify colours; she helped them to cut out patterns, to recognise nursery rhymes and to sing simple songs. When she left, she was succeeded by Indian teachers and volunteers from different countries. One Indian, a fully qualified work therapist, has taught the children and adults to make a variety of crafts, including beautiful candles which are sold in aid of the work.

The patients' disabilities and backgrounds vary considerably. There is a deaf and dumb patient who, although mentally retarded, has learnt that some people can be kind. Another patient, who is blind, can hear music in the wind. Then there is a Muslim girl who had had to mother two other children: she was found begging in the street, demented as a result of ill treatment, but she is now one of our regular helpers. One little boy stumbled in by himself with nothing to identify him but the name of the Ryder-Cheshire Centre scrawled on a piece of paper pinned to his shirt.

Among the different volunteers from countries overseas was Sarah Taylor, who went to work in Ava Vihar in 1982. Afterwards she wrote:

Munna was found in a wicker basket on a train at an Indian railway station. Daljeet was left on the doorstep of an English couple living in Dehra Dun. Elizabeth, half Chinese, half American, was found wandering the streets of Rishikesh, a holy Hindu town at the source of the Ganges. All of them are mentally handicapped and are only three of the fascinating people with whom I spent my summer.

In June I went to Raphael. As a volunteer I paid my own air fare, but was given free board and lodgings in return for my work.

I had been brought up in India and thought that the memories of my childhood would make my time there less surprising, but right from the beginning I was fascinated and amazed by Raphael and India.

Raphael's true value is that it accepts only people who are truly destitute with nowhere else to go. All of them, including Munna, Daljeet and Elizabeth, were brought to Raphael by people who found them wandering. A boy called Subash, for example, contracted a fever while his mother carried him on her back out of Muslim Pakistan into Hindu India. By the time she got him to a doctor he had suffered permanent brain damage. His mother heard about Ava Vihar and brought him here.

Each day was a revelation to me. There was a rough schedule, but the unexpected always governed.

One morning two patients and I headed down to the leprosy colony, a series of small houses, to chat with these people who spent their days tending their chickens, collecting firewood, squatting under trees smoking hookahs and trying to cope with their daily lives.

With the encouragement of an amused woman I was invited to try the hookah. Coughing and spluttering, I said "Bidis, bidis!" meaning "Cigarettes are better." My small group from Ava Vihar stood around in rapturous enthusiasm and had to be dissuaded from trying the hookah themselves.

Before I went to Raphael, I had been working in Britain with the mentally handicapped and had become used to the generous provision made for them in this country. Raphael, however, is funded entirely by donations, and as such is critically poor. The equipment we used was all handmade – jigsaw puzzles, rough-hewn beads, glue made of flour and water, old magazines given by the people in town, computer paper donated by the Army based in Dehra Dun. I learnt, too, that expensive equipment and articles are not as necessary as love and compassion. In spite of not having the generous reserves available in this country, the people in Ava Vihar find a reality within which to live. Raphael and Ava Vihar provide them with their reality, the people who work there provide them with love.

I particularly remember Rajender who was in his early teens and had arrived in a state of shock with serious heart failure; he was near death. He came from a remote village in the Himalayas. After walking several miles he was brought down by bus over rough roads and then by scooter to Raphael. On arrival he was examined by Dr Verma in the dispensary. Raj was terrified at the sight of a hypodermic needle. The first day, while I was working with other patients who were trying to console him as he wept, I asked what he would like. Raj very touchingly produced a crumpled one rupee note – which was all the money he had ever possessed – and quietly asked me to buy him a tangerine. I said, "Raj, this is your home now and you are a member of our family here. There is no need to pay for this tangerine." He looked at me with deep-set eyes and thanked me in Hindi through the nurse attending him, adding: "For the first time in my life I have a bed to sleep on and I know that if I am hungry or thirsty I will receive food and water."

Throughout the years, I cherish memories of an orderly crowd of patients, trying to fend off the flies, waiting quietly outside on the verandah of the dispensary. Each comes into the room in turn while Dr Verma and, later, his successor, makes his diagnosis and writes up notes in his book. The first thirty need their dirty bandages removed to clean their ulcers and have fresh dressings and bandages applied. The compounder and I used to work together but, sadly, he died and his work has been taken over by Dr Gupta. Others have aches and pains, infected eyes and wasted nerve tissues; small children are heard crying in the background. This goes on until 1 p.m. before a break, and then on to the outpatients. Afterwards, other patients are seen at the hospital.

*   *   *

"I cried because I had no shoes, until I saw the man who had no feet."
Spanish proverb

The leprosy unit at the Centre cares for 120 burnt-out cases; this means that the disease has been arrested and the patients are not infectious, but as a rule they are suffering from severe mutilation. Some have lost their fingers, some their toes, and if they have stumps left these are devoid of sensation.

Others have lost their eyesight or suffered some other severe disability. Injections are administered and drugs given under the supervision of a medical adviser, while a medical orderly treats the patients' hands and feet which are often badly ulcerated. Loss of sensation in their hands makes it difficult for these people to learn trades which will enable them to be independent.

There is a workshop for those with leprosy who weave sufficient cotton cloth to provide two sets of clothes for each resident, sufficient sheeting material for bed sheets, and towelling material to provide towels for all in Raphael. Some of them work as tailors making clothes and linen and some as cobblers to stitch shoes for deformed feet. The leprosy patients also provide the manpower to take care of plumbing, drinking water, the maintenance of electric fittings and repairs to wooden fixtures and furniture. Others undertake all kinds of errands and small jobs to ensure the smooth running of Raphael.

The leprosy unit consists of eight small, single-storey cottages, where each couple or family have their own simple room and a verandah on which they can cook their meals. There is also a dispensary. Many of these people were originally reduced to begging as they had no means of employment. Some came from the mountainous area of Tehri-Garhwal in the foothills of the Himalayas, having left their families in search of treatment.

On 14 January 1981, at the start of the International Year of Disabled People, Viscount Mersey spoke in the House of Lords about the scourge of leprosy. The following is an excerpt from his speech:

> Leprosy is the biggest single cause of disability in the Third World – and that includes damage from the motor-car; it is greater than even that. There is forty per cent disability normally among untreated leprosy patients and four out of five patients never get treated – perhaps 20 million people. Yet ironically, the disability can be avoided and the disease can be cured. So why the huge number? I think that again one must return to this problem of the label. The man with leprosy is not a man, he is a leper. The word "leper" is swamped in emotion. People may regard it with loathing, with hatred, with fear, or, if one is lucky, with compassion and pity.
>
> Built into this swamp of emotion are several misconceptions about the disease, which I believe are quite important. I should like quickly to mention three of them. The first is simply that leprosy is unclean. This is not so. It is in no way associated with filth, squalor or promiscuity. It is caused by a bacillus, *Mycobacterium leprae*, which is similar to that which causes tuberculosis. It is true that poor people are more prone to catch it. This, in the Third World, is just a reflection on their living conditions; they are so crowded together that cross infection is more likely. The second misconception is this business of leprosy being highly contagious: that if you shake hands with a leper, you have got the disease. That is not so. It is in the *Guinness Book of Records* as being the least communicable of all communicable diseases; and rightly so. Recently, leprologists have discovered that the main route of infection is not by touch at all; it is simply droplet infection by coughing and sneezing, the same as with the common cold.

The third misconception is this business of fingers and toes dropping off in this disease. They do not, but leprosy causes anaesthesia and that is serious. It causes a numbness in the hands and the feet: and numb hands and feet are easily damaged by hundreds of daily tasks. Cooking, for instance. The first sign that a sufferer will have that he has burnt his hand will be the smell of burning flesh. If he does nothing about that burn – and he might well not – it will become septic, it will ulcerate and, if he continues to cook week after week, year in, year out, he will get a mass of infection on his hand, so bad that the hand will disintegrate. Feet (with which, at least, you do not cook) are a worse problem because many people in the Third World cannot afford shoes. Those with numb feet can walk over the sharpest, possibly toxic, surfaces and do not feel anything. One Indian leprologist said that the chief pain of leprosy is the lack of it.

Of course, it is much better to treat the disease before all this anaesthesia sets in. Leprosy is curable. The first effective drug, which was DDS, came into use just after the Second World War. It was hailed as a miracle, though rather a slow one. It took some three years on average to cure the patients. Lately – and this is rather less good news – the bacillus has become resistant to the drug. But there are new drugs, Rifampicin and Lamprine, to name two of them.

I am happy to say that a British Leprosy Control project in Southern Malawi has worked to a huge extent. Of the 14,500 original sufferers, 12,000 have now been discharged free of leprosy. The remaining 2,500 are still on a small maintenance dose. This is an outpatients' scheme based on Land Rovers visiting every infected village every week. Badly disfigured people are taken to hospital and not to a leper colony. That is a thing of the past. The vast majority of patients take their tablets from the Land Rovers and carry on working, leading their normal lives. This British project, which is presided over by the noble Viscount, Lord Boyd, has now moved to the north of that country. Leprosy now in Southern Malawi is such a small problem that the local Ministry of Health has been able to assimilate it into their overall health programme. I would say that Dr Hastings Banda has been commendably realistic about his country's leprosy problems. He let the experts in; and the problem is well on the way to being solved. Southern Malawi has lost its ball and chain. However, I do not believe that the Malawi method is relevant to, say, the Indian sub-continent. I calculate that at least 3,000 Land Rovers would be needed in India for the weekly visits.

What is needed to fight leprosy on a world-wide scale is a drug so powerful that it will cure the disease with one shot or perhaps two and, of course, a vaccine. Another breakthrough is needed: the ability to cultivate this bacillus in a test tube – in a broth as it is termed. Then it will be possible to mass-produce vaccine cheaply. With regard to that breakthrough, I can only say that I detect a note of guarded optimism emanating from the Medical Research Institute at Mill Hill. I can only hope that in the next ten years this will be done. When it is, then surely the world leprosy problem will start to be solved by vaccination. Then, and only then, will this colossal and largely unnecessary cause of Third World disability be removed and the source of the stigma will go too. That is in the future.

For the present, I can do no more than wish every doctor working on this disease in every part of the world every success.

It is believed that 3,200,000 people in India suffer from leprosy out of an estimated 10,800,000 in the world.

What is being done at Raphael is a single *very* small attempt to deal with this terrible illness, but it is hoped that it may make its contribution towards inspiring and convincing others. Many people may think of the victims as permanent derelicts dependent upon charity, but it is entirely fair to say that most of them prefer the dignity of work which gives independence. In the context of our task the words "aid" and "charity" have become devalued by misuse and prejudice. In a neighbouring leprosy colony with which we often exchange visits, social workers from Europe have proved in the last twenty years that even the most deformed leprosy patients are willing and able to produce textiles for export.

An important factor in the concept of Raphael as an international centre is the presence of overseas volunteers. From Raphael's inception, these volunteers have given invaluable service in specialist fields such as physiotherapy, occupational therapy and areas of trained nursing, working in close co-operation with their Indian colleagues. The volunteers have come from many countries, including especially Britain, Ireland, Australia and New Zealand. Without their contribution, the progress Raphael has made since it began as a collection of tents by the Rispana river would not have happened. Their commitment is as vital now as it ever was and will continue to be so in the foreseeable future.

Today, Raphael is housed in modern concrete buildings (valued at £2,000,000) built with donations collected by supporters in Australia, New Zealand and Britain, and through the proceeds of Sue Ryder Shops.

* * *

The problems of tuberculosis in India are numerous and especially tragic. It is estimated that there are now some 10,000,000 cases out of which nearly 2,500,000 are infectious. But the disease is now both preventable and curable *if* diagnosed early enough . . . and a regular systematic follow up carried out preferably with a social worker too.

Tuberculosis is an infectious disease caused by a germ called *Mycobacterium tuberculosis*. It can affect any part of the human body, but commonly attacks the lungs (pulmonary tuberculosis), lymph glands (glandular tuberculosis), bones and joints (tubercular osteomyelitis and arthritis). Besides these, the central nervous system, skin, genito-urinary tract, internal organs (e.g. liver, spleen, intestines) can also be affected, usually as a spread from a focus in the lungs or glands. Of all these, disease of the lungs is most frequent and the only manifestion that is infectious.

From archaeological discoveries, it has come to be believed with a fair amount of certainty that tuberculosis was a scourge as far back as 5,000 BC. Although with present-day chemotherapy, it is possible to cure almost all patients of tuberculosis, in actual service programmes in India, the results fall considerably short of that, possibly because many patients drop out of treatment, even if requisite drugs are made available free of cost. Sociological studies carried out by prestigious research centres in India have shown that the reasons for "drop outs" in urban areas are ignorance, inadequate motivation, and clash between the working hours of the patients and official clinics. In the rural areas, apart from ignorance and lack of motivation and facilities of follow-up, the main problem is the long distance between the patient's dwelling and the nearest Health Centre leading to loss of working hours (and wages) and expenditure on repeated visits to collect drugs. It is thus logical that if good treatment is provided free of cost at a convenient time as near the residence of the patient as possible, patient's compliance will be much better. Tuberculosis projects of the Ryder-Cheshire Foundation are based on this philosophy.

One of the many who came to Raphael in 1959 was Baisakhi. She had badly deformed hands and feet and poor eyesight. She always enjoyed, despite her handicaps, a happy disposition, and she liked being in charge of the workshop. During the past few years she has worked as an ayah in our hospital and she insists upon receiving only rations, accommodation, drugs and twenty rupees per month. When Anne Young (now Boyd), an Australian nurse, who had previously worked at Raphael for seven years before taking a specialised tuberculosis course in London, started visiting the poor in the area surrounding the Centre and then opened a clinic at Tehri, Baisakhi volunteered to be her Assistant. They were complementary to each other. Anne, having learnt Hindi, thoroughly enjoyed the company of Baisakhi. They were fearless travellers, going on public buses for miles and miles into the hills, visiting people in isolated villages who were too weak and sick to get to hospital. Not infrequently there are landslides, when transport has to be abandoned. There is now a jeep, plus a converted van, which are invaluable, particularly as the travelling is still tough. When they reached the patients many were in an advanced state of tuberculosis and then very little could be done. Whenever I was at Raphael, I enjoyed accompanying Anne and Baisakhi. We walked for miles between villages where we always received a warm and moving welcome. Naturally trying to get through queues of patients was hard, but far worse to diagnose a patient with an inoperable cancer or other disease and have no medication. We slept on occasions in a small hut and saw the beautiful sunsets and sunrises of the Himalayas with its snow-capped mountains.

But as this work develops we hope to be more effective to these men, women and children, either by giving them treatment in one of the mobile clinics with very simple domiciliary care, or, as we had previously been doing, by attempting to get them to the hospital at Raphael. The majority of villages around Dehra Dun receive regular visits from one of the teams, whilst the other one concentrates on the lower foothills of the Himalayas.

The clinic at Tehri is a journey of seven-and-a-half hours by bus or five hours by jeep from Dehra Dun. On arrival Anne and her companions would have a thorough wash and then decide on a practical order of precedence for patients, trying to see first those who had been waiting longest, or who seemed particularly ill, or who had to return quickly to work. We always had and followed a routine for examining each patient: weight, temperature, pulse, blood pressure, respiration, lung capacity, sputum, erythrocyte sedimentation rate, haemoglobin, etc. Then would come the treatment by free supplies of isoniazid and thiacetazone tablets, or BCG vaccine, or whatever was available and necessary. All this added up to a heavy day's work, and afterwards they would sometimes go onto another clinic at Dhanolti.

In 1982, Margaret Baddiley, previously the Foundation's Honorary Nurse Adviser in Britain and overseas, wrote:

> Each year something in the region of 12,000 sufferers from tuberculosis in the United Provinces, assisted by a spouse or relative, expend their last bit of energy in undertaking the very long walk – which can take up to several days – to seek help from the Ryder-Cheshire Centre Raphael on the outskirts of Dehra Dun. All these sufferers need food, and drugs which can cure tuberculosis. Some of these who are seriously ill need rest and nursing care. A few who need nursing care the most are admitted to the twenty-six-bed tuberculosis ward, but all are given the requisite chemotherapy free of cost.
>
> The sufferers, knowing that only the more seriously ill can be admitted to the ward, frequently leave their arrival at Raphael too late. It is indeed a very sad picture to watch these unfortunate human beings, including many children and young people, struggling along the last half-mile – needing to rest every few yards.
>
> What can we do? We think that prevention of the increasing spread of tubercle infection is vital. Hundreds of people with tuberculosis-infected lungs huddle together with their families or neighbours for warmth in their tiny huts sealed against the cold nights. Inevitably lumps of tubercle-containing sputum are carelessly ejected, and so the spread of infection grows.
>
> The dedicated workers at Raphael struggle to offer treatment, but at the same time are attempting to organise a progressive programme of prevention. This will include a health education programme, followed by a methodical screening test of all people at risk. The essentials of preventing infection like covering the mouth while coughing and proper collection and disposal of sputum are demonstrated repeatedly.
>
> The Ryder-Cheshire Centre in Dehra Dun has a fine Director who is able to recruit locally professional staff – doctor, nurse, laboratory technician, record keeper and health teacher who will work in parts of this whole region with a mobile laboratory. Those people found to have a positive reaction are started on treatment immediately. Children and some adults are offered vaccination against the disease.
>
> A most generous gift of £20,000 from Holland has made possible the

purchase of a vehicle, but more support and encouragement is needed to
assist the workers at Raphael in their mammoth task of trying to alleviate
further suffering from tuberculosis for some of the thousands in this huge
and hilly area.

Mobile Tuberculosis Units were set up primarily on the initiative of myself
with the full backing of my husband and in consultation with the General
Council at Raphael, Indian tuberculosis experts and the Indian Ministry
of Health.

The objectives are:

(i) to survey the designated areas village by village to identify people
suffering from tuberculosis;

(ii) to provide free diagnostic service almost at the patients' doorsteps.

(iii) to initiate and follow through a full course of treatment;

(iv) to provide hospitalisation at Raphael's tuberculosis hospital, where
necessary;

(v) to provide health education to the communities in question.

The people who benefit from the Project are villagers whose chief
occupation is subsistence farming. Without the service provided by the
Mobile Unit very few would receive timely diagnosis and treatment for
the illness and no health education because of Governmental health centres
being usually far off and the inconvenience and expenditure involved in
visiting these centres periodically for a long time.

Towards the end of 1983, as a result of the gift referred to by Margaret
Baddiley, a mobile medical team was launched at Raphael to continue the
work begun by Anne Boyd. With the use of a specially modified Land Rover
a small team led by a doctor visits villages which lie around the town of
Dehra Dun and the foothills of the Himalayas, and identifies and treats
people of all age groups who suffer from tuberculosis, making full notes on
their dreadful living conditions. In 1991 the SOIR-IM (Sweden) agreed to
fund and maintain another mobile team.

There are ten Centres in the valley which are visited once a month by the
doctor to examine old and new patients and issue the medicines for
the following month.

It has quickly become apparent that many more such mobile teams would
be needed if all the needy patients are to be given effective service from an
easily accessible centre.

The Delhi Urban Project – The Project started its operation on 1 October
1989 and its objective was to provide a good diagnostic and treatment
service, absolutely free, to the under-served population of slum colonies at
the periphery of the City, virtually on their doorsteps and at a convenient
time. A team consisting of a specialist doctor, laboratory technician and two
health visitors was constituted and a van was provided. The population of
the selected slum were exposed to intensive health education with the help
of film, cassettes and talks. The health visitors then visited the slum in the

evening by which time the workers usually return home. The symptomatics attended on the pre-informed date and they were examined by the doctor who collected a sputum specimen. Those found positive were put on treatment at the next visit whilst negatives were kept under observation, until the diagnosis was arrived at. If an X-ray examination is required the patients are carried to the X-ray centre and brought back to their dwellings; this service is provided at no cost to them. The treatment region is the best standard Short Course. The van visits each slum once a week or fortnightly, depending on the number of patients, and these are issued with a two-week supply of drugs if they are needed. If the patient defaults, his house is visited then and there by the health visitor to retrieve the defaulter. New slums are taken up when the symptomatics of the previous slum have all been attended to.

The team now caters for nine slums with a population of about 200,000. When the Project was started, it was expected that the drugs for free distribution will be made available by the Government and within its resources the RCF will be able to cater for a bigger population. However, since the Government supply of drugs has not materialised, the Project has stopped taking up more slums till additional resources and another team become available.

The results, as expected, vary, but some are very good. All patients take treatment regularly and those who complete the stipulated duration of treatment are almost cured. The "drop out" rate, though more than that of Dehra Dun Project, is much less than that in the official clinics in Delhi; and this is because of the higher percentage of "floating population" of a big metropolitan city in general and the slums in particular.

There are three further vans operating full time in Delhi and these concentrate upon the slum areas. It is estimated that there are 24,000 positive sputum carriers of tuberculosis in that vast City alone. Ideally, I would like to concentrate upon setting up more mobile preventive teams with their own vans.

The Dehra Dun Rural Project – Raphael had been running a TB Clinic for domiciliary treatment of tuberculosis supplemented by twenty-six beds for simple indoor treatment of very ill patients. In 1984 it was decided to extend its service to rural population. A team consisting of a doctor, a laboratory technician and para-medical health visitors was constituted and a van was provided. A compact block of villages was demarcated and each of these villages was visited by the team. The essentials of the programme was explained and health education on TB imparted to the population. The health visitor then visited every house in the village to identify the symptomatics, collected and examined their sputum on the spot. They were then seen by the doctor and sputum-positive patients were put on treatment whilst sputum negatives were kept under observation. X-rays were arranged, where necessary, on subsidised rates. The team stayed in the village till all the symptoms were dealt with. The villages were grouped in sixteen lots; one from each lot was designated as a "Nodal Centre" which we visit once a month. The patients from all the villages of a lot come and collect their drugs on pre-informed dates and times from the Nodal Centre. On average they have to travel a distance of three to five kilometres. The reputation of the service is such that patients from other villages not covered by the original survey, and those who have developed symptoms subsequently in the surveyed villages, attend the Nodal Centres voluntarily. All patients are given free drugs, according the best Short Course Chemotherapy regime.

A cohort analysis of patients diagnosed and put on treatment in 1993 will show the acceptability and contribution of this service. Of all TB patients, forty per cent were sputum positives. Eighty per cent completed the treatment regularly and were cured, seven per cent died (mostly due to far advanced disease, within a few days of starting treatment); two per cent migrated and only twelve per cent were "drop outs" (as compared to more than sixty per cent in rural areas under the National Programme). Encouraged by this result, the 'Disaster Relief Fund' has started similar projects in rural areas of Sikkim, Gujarat and Himachael Pradesh.

The Conclusion – According to the international world TB specialist Dr Pamra, fifteen medical mobile clinics are required to make real progress in Delhi. The present team is working in eleven areas covering 166,500 population. The working of the Dehra Dun and Delhi Projects has shown that the philosophy on which these are based is correct. They have to relieve some people although they cannot entirely solve the TB problem in India. As the Government cannot adopt these measures for the whole country, voluntary organisations, of whom there is no dearth, should emulate the Ryder-Cheshire Foundation and take up similar projects in their area of operation.

Owing to the potential size of the Centre and the needs, we did not feel it fair to leave all the fund-raising to the Indians; the more so as there is a local Home in Dehra Dun as well. Consequently, during our first tour of Australia and New Zealand, we asked for support from these countries. This aim has been achieved in no small measure due to the interest and generosity of countless people, including very many school children, who become sponsors of individual children or adults at Raphael and thus feel a special responsibility for them, receiving in turn reports and photographs to keep in touch.

These sponsors are joined by others who are willing to undertake raising funds for the approach road known as The Causeway, the greatly needed tubewell (which we hope may overcome the acute shortage of water) and extensions to the Little White House and other Units. The tubewell was gifted by Col SP Wahi, the Chairman of Oil & Natural Gas Commission with its HQ in Delhi in 1989 (Col Wahi was a Gentleman Cadet in the Indian Military Academy in 1950, when Major-General Ranbir Bakhshi was the Chief Instructor). The tubewell started to provide water in abundance to Raphael from February 1993. During the past fifteen years, selected nurses, occupational and speech therapists and physiotherapists have come – mainly from Australia and New Zealand – usually for a period of two months or more. Each volunteer working at Raphael is provided with free lodging and linen, besides a fully equipped mess, which is manned by trained cooks who prepare and serve meals to them. The work of these overseas staff in the different Units complements that of the Indian staff. We have also had nursing sisters from Spain.

The team personnel at Raphael consists of :

1. Director
2. Medical Superintendent
3. Matron and four nurses
4. Two laboratory technicians
5. Dispenser
6. Compunder
7. Administrative staff
8. Housemother and Houseparents
9. Six full teachers for the Primary School
10. Ayahs and ward boys
11. Cooks, washerman, night chaykidars, drivers
12. Specialist staff for Vocational and Educational Training
13. Education Psychologist in Ava Vihar and Primary School
    There is training in Ava Vihar (paid by the Central Government)

In 1961, on the Feast of Divali (the Festival of Lights), the late Prime Minister, Pandit Nehru, visited Raphael, and to welcome him the pathway to the Centre was lit by dozens of flickering lamps. I was impressed by the personalities of both the late Mr Nehru and his sister, the late Madam Vijay Lakshmi Pandit. After her extremely long and distinguished career in the Diplomatic Service she retired to live in Dehra Dun. Madam Pandit became a patron of the Centre and a stimulating visitor to it. I could listen to her for hours as she was a wonderful conversationalist and a woman with real humility and a great sense of humour, too.

A bi-monthly report gives me, wherever I may be, a vivid account of the growth and consolidation in India of the Ryder-Cheshire Mission for the Relief of Suffering. The term "Mission" has been used deliberately in connection with the Centre because it comes from the Latin word *missio* which means "sending". It was chosen to stress to those who participate in the work that they must look on themselves as being "sent" to those who are in need. On advice, and although we both felt reluctant, the word "Mission" was altered to "Foundation".

This Centre is not the only enterprise in India with which the Foundation is associated. In Madras in the south of India there is also a Ryder-Cheshire Foundation Centre called Gabriel.

Gabriel is a little haven of peace off a busy main road and is situated in Manapakkam on the outskirts of Madras, just past St Thomas' Mount.

In the surrounding area are many young people who are physically handicapped through cerebral palsy or through having suffered from leprosy or poliomyelitis. Because of their handicap and the stigma that attaches to them, they find it difficult to get work. So it was that in 1967 the Ryder-Cheshire Mission entered into an agreement with the Archbishop of Madras/Mylapore who allowed them to use a piece of ground next to his church for a vocational training centre.

Two training courses were instituted – printing and a fitter's course. The old printing machine is rather like an old warhorse, producing no elegant computer printouts, but it keeps turning out well-presented work to fulfil commissions from local businesses. The fitter's course has developed over the years. Since 1989 it has been recognised by the State Government of Tamil Nadu and supported financially by them. It is a two-year course for a minimum of fifteen handicapped young men between the ages of fifteen and thirty years who have reached Grade 8 in their general education. The training is both theoretical and practical, for which they go out to work in local factories. A really positive aspect of Gabriel's work is that none of the handicapped youngsters have any problem in finding work when they leave.

Gabriel attracted some local support. The Chairman, Mr Raghavachari, a retired member of the Indian Civil Service, and his colleagues at the Madras Guild of Service, are planning an expansion of the number of trainees and of the types of courses, to include new areas such as tailoring – an ever-present need in India.

The Indian Committee which is responsible for the running of this Centre also raises its own funds: as well as receiving individual donations they organise functions of one kind or another, including concerts, sales and parties.

At the time of writing, Gabriel is undergoing fundamental change. In 1995, the Catholic Church in Madras decided to re-claim the land it had originally given to allow Gabriel's construction. The Centre was left to find new accommodation. The present intention is to move to existing buildings beside the K. K. Nagar Hospital in the City – and later, perhaps, if funds become available, to construct a new, purpose-built Gabriel on a different site. In the meantime, the nature of the training offered will be revised to reflect more accurately the skills which are most in demand today in Madras.

*   *   *

The Ryder-Cheshire Foundation is also associated with Seva Nilayam – which means House of Service. It is a clinic and farm set up in Madurai District, South India, in 1963, by Dora Scarlett, a remarkable English woman who settled in Southern India in 1958 at the age of fifty-three years. After four years working in and around Madras she moved, with an Indian farmer and his family, many miles south west to the Village of Aundipatti. It lies in a poor rural valley, fifty miles west of the Town of Madurai, in the foothills of the Western Ghats.

Seva Nilayam began as a group of mud and wattle huts from which Dora Scarlett and an Indian assistant started to dispense simple medicines to local villagers who had no access to Government health services.

A series of volunteers – many of them nurses – from Britain, the United States and Australia soon arrived, and a retired Indian doctor provided the medical expertise. In 1968, a proper clinic building was constructed for the project by OXFAM.

Since then, the scope of Seva Nilayam has widened year by year. It is now a registered charitable Society and treats more than 200 patients a day for a wide variety of illnesses. There is a tuberculosis programme and a programme of mother-and-baby care. It has developed a reputation for treating successfully a number of different and common skin complaints. There is accommodation for some twelve in-patients.

In 1991, the Council of Seva Nilayam – at Dora Scarlett's suggestion – invited us to bring the Ryder-Cheshire Foundation (which already ran several similar projects in India) into partnership with Seva Nilayam – especially in order to develop the scope of the tuberculosis programme. This invitation arrived at a time when Leonard and I were determined to expand the Ryder-Cheshire Foundation's offensive in India against the appalling incidence of tuberculosis in that country.

A formal Agreement was drawn up and the Project is now known as Seva Nilayam *in association* with the Ryder-Cheshire Foundation.

As a first step in the development of its own tuberculosis programme, the Ryder-Cheshire Foundation obtained a most generous grant of £15,000 from the Overseas Aid Committee of the States of Jersey. This money allowed the appointment of a Director and the construction of a house and office for him and his family; the purchase of the Centre's first vehicle; and the construction of a larger, better-equipped in-patient facility.

An expansion programme was drawn up by the Director and Council of Seva Nilayam, following a second visit by the Ryder-Cheshire Foundation's Projects Officer at the end of 1992. The total cost of this programme was Rs.442,800 (about £10,000), and, among other things, it has made possible the establishment of nine mini-clinics in villages around the Centre. In 1997 these have now been restyled into Community Development Centres, reflecting their changed nature from being treatment clinics to being centres for health.

In the main clinic 15,267 patients were treated during the year up to March 1997, an increase of 2,780. Of these seventy-six per cent came from outside the area which is a ten per cent reduction from the previous year. It seems that these people spend considerable time and money to visit Seva Nilayam, partly because of its reputation and the faith they have in it, and partly to confirm a diagnosis and treatment prescribed by their own doctor, whom they may not trust. The aim is to discourage out of the area patients in favour of local people. The main problem remains skin diseases but the injections of B complex, used largely as a placebo, have been phased out. There is a lot of heart disease but without an ECG machine little investigation can be done.

567 patients were admitted during the year of whom just over half came from the area. The majority suffered from skin disease.

The joint tuberculosis scheme between Seva Nilayam, Arogya Agam and Vasantham, covering the whole of the Aundipatti Taluk, supported by a fifty per cent grant from the Overseas Development Authority and backed by free drugs from the Indian Government, is progressing well. Areas of geographical overlap have been sorted out and the policies rationalised so that the three Centres are now all treating patients who are either sputum or X-ray positive. During the year, Seva Nilayam treated 311 patients of whom fifty-two per cent completed their treatment successfully and were cured and a further forty-four per cent were still under treatment. In the four months since the new TB Ward opened, forty-seven patients (all from the Project area) have been admitted to the ten beds available, with an average stay of twenty days.

We now have two skilled and knowledgeable staff nurses as well as two nursing assistants and four trainees.

Thanks to all the good work and development, Seva Nilavam, which has always had a high reputation, is becoming much more widely known.

*   *   *

I just wish that those people, near and far, who criticise or make light of the efforts of people in India to help those in need could come with me to see for themselves what it is like. The sheer size of the sub-continent, the physical differences of climate and soil, can in themselves cause many desperate material problems from which we in more temperate climes are protected. I wonder whether these critics would do as well if they found themselves in a similar situation, and whether they would show the same patience and endurance.

As in many other developing countries, extended family ties in India remain strong. The Indians show a willingness to help themselves and to strive towards self-sufficiency. Of course it is true that there is passiveness and fatalism, but where there are people to organise and take the lead, results can be seen. Whatever may be thought of the Indians' civil hospitals and their very low standards, their military hospitals would be a credit to any nation. The solution of the country's problems lies with the younger generation. With idealism, far more organisation and enthusiasm, a great deal could be accomplished and more improvement brought about despite the extremely serious population explosion with all its consequences, including lawlessness.

The rationing system in India is a legacy of the Second World War period. It has been continued in a modified form after Indian Independence declared on the 15 August 1947. It is applicable to all the States in the Indian Union including Union territories.

The rationing system was really meant to help the citizens of low income group by providing four basic necessities of daily use at subsidised rates. In actual practice, there is no monetary limit laid down to determine entitlement for this concession. In other words the not so poor can also get rations at sudsidised rates. This system is currently under review, and a more targeted approach with the aim of benefiting the real poor is under preparation and will shortly be presented as a Bill to the Government.

The prices that are fixed by the authorities vary according to the market rates and the production situation. These are substantially less in the Fair Price shop centres than on the open market. Every individual wishing to benefit by this scheme has to apply to the District Supply Officer on a prescribed form. Apart from the information required in the form, proof of age and address must be given.

Adults and children over five count as one unit and children over five count as half a unit. The quota for a unit is as follows:

> 10 kg . . . . wheat flour or wheat germ
> 10 kg . . . . rice
> 900 gms – 1kg . . . . sugar
> 10 litres . . . . kerosene oil
> (only 5 litres to those owning gas stoves)

Alas too, like so many countries, India too has changed for many reasons. There is a more noticeable and widening, indeed huge gap, between the "haves" and "have nots". The wealthy, I refer especially to the new rich, who are, as elsewhere, loath to part with their riches. What a difference this would make to millions of people.

It remains an extremely serious problem how to address, approach or reach out and involve "the new rich". As elsewhere, the majority are ignorant or remain uncommitted and indifferent. Fortunately, the older families retain their social conscience and do a lot to relieve suffering and the poverty.

Pope Paul VI's visit in 1966 caused immense interest. He was the first Pope to visit that country and dense crowds packed the long route from the airport to the Cardinal's residence when he arrived in Bombay. Each night during his week's visit to India my husband and I attended Mass which was celebrated in a huge open space with the high altar set in the middle. The majority of the congregation were non-Christians. They were deeply devout, and when the Pope came to bless the sick no one could have failed to have been extremely moved by the compassion shown on his deeply lined face. Kneeling next to me was a man with a very young spastic son and I saw him weep as he received the Holy Father's blessing. (I was wearing a large medallion of Our Lady of Jasna Góra which the Pope also blessed as he paused over us.)

To my great surprise the following was written by a volunteer after a much later visit to India in 1955:

In the last week of March, we were pleasantly surprised when a message was received to say that Lady Ryder was visiting Raphael in April and would be spending the Easter Week with us. Everyone at Raphael was delighted. Lady Ryder arrived here on 11 April and left for Delhi on the 16th. As usual, she spent a lot of time with the residents and the TB patients, giving peace and joy to all. A special meeting of the Council Members was held on 15 April followed by an entertainment programme organised by the residents of Raphael. Lady Ryder recorded the following in our visitor's book:

> Thank you so much for the truly wonderful morning and warm welcome. Daddy and I shared everything here since 1958 but I felt his presence all the time, and wherever I went you made me, as always, feel completely at home. If only I could explain the pleasure, the encouragement and inspiration you continue to give me. Also the feeling of close friendships as we are indeed members of one large family and must always remember those who are waiting and suffering.
>
> Every visit is full of memories of every kind, mostly with those who have lived and worked here and those who bear their pain and disability or problems with such courage – and those who have died.
>
> As always, one of the lasting memories is the concert, so beautifully prepared and performed – full of music, singing and dancing.
>
> I am overwhelmed by your lovely presents, garlands and flowers. I am extremely sorry and sad to leave, but you know, I hope, that each of you is in my prayers and thoughts every day and night wherever I go.
>
> With love, heartfelt thanks and prayers. Mummy.
> God bless you.

The compassion and dedication of Lady Ryder which I saw when I met her, I would like to imbibe and function in my capacity keeping these qualities in view. (This is a personal tribute from a volunteer working at Raphael.)

Sue Ann Bruhn, an Australian volunteer, recorded her observations during the course of the visit as:

On Tuesday, 11 April, Raphael was abuzz with people primping and preening the grounds and waiting in great anticipation for the arrival of Sue Ryder, Baroness Ryder of Warsaw, one of the two Founders and a frequent and faithful visitor to Raphael. We heard so much about this most remarkable woman, and could tell from the genuine excitement seen in the eyes of residents, teachers, staff and visitors that she is indeed someone special.

By 10.30 a.m. the drums of the leprosy patients started to beat and we knew that she had arrived. We saw a very emotional welcome given by all with garlands of marigolds hung round her neck as she embraced her old friends with deep and true affection. This continued to be the tone of welcome as she made her way to each unit of Raphael.

I caught my first glimpse of Lady Ryder when she came to greet the residents of Ava Vihar. I was surprised at how small in stature she is but soon learnt that in every other way this woman is a true powerhouse; although her stay with us is short, not one moment is wasted; her schedule is tight and during her time she will include in her programme inspection and talks to each patient and member of staff in the TB hospital and the outpatients. She spent a whole day working with the Mobile TB Team and visited Ava Vihar, where the mentally handicapped are cared for mainly by the volunteers and Indian staff, Shiv Sadan (the leprosy cottages), the RADC Day Centre Chronic Ward and attended a General Council Meeting. All the other time is used visiting the Chapel, talking with her old friends and also managing to chat with the volunteers about their perceptions of Raphael.

Not one aspect of the daily running of this place is left unquestioned, and with great energy and compassion, Lady Ryder really takes the time to talk and listen to those around her.

Over the last week I have seen Lady Ryder working with patience and seemingly endless energy. I have had the opportunity to speak with her and find her to be a woman of true strength and determination yet she is calm, gentle and at times surprised us with her twinkling eyes and sense of humour. I believe that Lady Ryder leads us all by example.

We are all drawn to work, live and visit for a variety of reasons; how special it must be to come and see the fruit of your labour.

Lady Ryder is not motivated by whim or fancy, her principles are grounded in a strong belief that we share this world, and in turn share the responsibilities of care for each other.

My time at Raphael has been made just so much more special and valued and I will not soon forget meeting such a person.

While more could and should be done by the wealthy countries for the underdeveloped ones – of which India presents one of the greatest challenges – I believe that the contribution of the West should not be exclusively financial. What our Foundation seeks to do is to render personal service, and so to show the people we are trying to help how they can help themselves. If the dangerous gulf between the rich and poor nations is ever to be bridged, it is not just a question of spreading the world's wealth more evenly; the quality of life in the developing nations must also be improved, but this can best be done on a very personal level by individuals directly involving themselves, even though this may be at distance. In our small way this is what we hope to achieve, but we realise that our effort is painfully small in relation to the immensity of the task.

The average visitor or tourist, understandably, is not only appalled but confused by the experience and shocked by the sights which meet him. What I have mentioned in these pages is our own personal experience, which must in turn be related and harnessed to the good will and determination not only of the Indians but of humanity elsewhere. If we all despair, then nothing can be done, but to quote a Chinese proverb: "It is better to light one candle than to curse the darkness."

Australia

GIRL GATHERING ROSES

Earth's roses never can possess
The meaning we would have them share:
They merely stain the summer air
With promise of a fruitfulness
JAMES MCAULEY

SHORTLY AFTER OUR MARRIAGE my husband and I were invited to
give talks to a wide range of organisations and schools in several States in
Australia. This was the first public task we shared together, and it gave us
an insight into what was to lie ahead for us in the years to come, both there
and in other countries.

On arrival in Sydney late at night we found that we had been booked
into a large hotel (since demolished). Next morning, after walking to
the Cathedral for Mass, we returned to find the Press waiting in force
to interview us, while our breakfast grew cold on the tray.

Afterwards I asked for the hotel bill and was shocked to realise that we
did not have enough money on us to pay it. I therefore had to go and
explain to the Manager who seemed, not surprisingly, slightly taken aback,
but the wonderful fact is that in thirty-eight years of such journeys we had
never been required to pay for our lodgings.

The first visit led later to the formation of autonomous Ryder-Cheshire
Foundations in each Australian State except the Northern Territory and
Tasmania, several of them being incorporated societies in their own right.
There is an Association of these Foundations which holds biannual meet-
ings and has a National President, Liaison Officer and Secretary to handle
matters best dealt with on a joint basis.

The Foundation accepted responsibility to help our work in the Third
World, particularly at Raphael. The main thrust is to raise the funds to meet
Raphael's annual budget. This is done by a number of different – and often
ingenious – methods, the most important of which involves arranging the
sponsorship of every man, woman and child for whom Raphael provides care.

Since the first visit to Australia which my husband and I made in April
1959, many thousands of people have responded to the needs which
Raphael seeks to meet. Their selfless generosity has allowed, first, the
consolidation of the original work there, and gradually in recent years,
the expansion of the scope of the Centre.

Mr Justice J.F. Nagle, was our first Federal Chairman (1971–August 1975). He was succeeded by Dame Mary Daly, and on her retirement in July 1977, Mr Peter Alexander took office until April 1980 when the then National Chairman, Dame Justice Roma Mitchell, a greatly respected Judge of the Supreme Court, succeeded him. She was known as an outstanding Chairman of the Human Rights Committee and became Governor of South Australia. Dame Roma is the first woman to hold such high office in Australia and resides at Government House, Adelaide. She remains a close friend. Dame Roma's drive, tact and determination are well matched by her successor, Air-Marshal John Newham AC (Retd), who is greatly welcomed everywhere as National Chairman. Their main responsibility has been to co-ordinate support for Raphael, and one remembers with a deep sense of gratitude the efforts of countless thousands, especially children and pensioners, who often sponsor a child or leprosy patient at the cost of considerable self-sacrifice. There was one woman, I remember, who went out to work in order to take on this commitment. This is but one example of the extraordinary generosity and desire to help that we have found in Australia.

Australians are well known for their hospitality and many open their homes for you. This culture dates back from a time when hotels and eating places were very few and far between, and often not very good. Many people were, and are not well off, so staying in hotels is a luxury. The total area of Australia is 2,967,909 square miles and the present population is approaching eighteen million, so the Australians are accustomed to vast distances.

Only the wealthy own private planes. Air services are widely used by business and private people, mainly to save time, as it is certainly the most efficient and fastest way to cover the huge distances and there is a remarkably comprehensive network of air services weaving here and there across the country.

Small branch-line train services have been closed over the past twenty years, and train travel is less common anyway. Intercity train services are being restored for commuters and main line Interstate services are still available. The famous Indian-Pacific train now takes two-and-a-half days to make the trip across Australia, from Perth to Sydney.

Travel by coach and car gained popularity as roads and facilities for travellers improved. Most people use cars, in fact the ratio of cars per person is among the highest in the world. Journeys are, however, long and tedious and can be very hot by European standards. Petrol is actually available at wayside roadhouses or in the "outback" at the stations (huge sheep farms) without much difficulty. However, travellers do need to think ahead regarding both petrol and water supplies if they move off the main highways or journey into the centre of the country. People get stranded and die of exposure or thirst, even today, travelling into the outback without taking adequate precautions.

* * *

Throughout Australia there are small memorials in every town, however small, where services are held on Anzac Day (25 April) which is a national holiday throughout Australia. Schools have a broadcast on the 24 April and lay a wreath on their local memorial and the flag pole in the school yard. It chiefly commemorates the campaign against the Turks at Gallipoli in 1915 when the Australia and New Zealand Army Corps suffered enormous losses and showed heroism and courage which have gone down in history. Anzac Day honours these and other ex-servicemen and women from both World Wars and other wars. The day begins in many towns and cities with the Dawn service, sometimes on a hill or mountain facing east. It is attended in Canberra by the Governor-General and by the Governor in each State and in New Zealand by the Governor-General. The tramp of the ex-servicemen and women as they march through the grey, pre-dawn light is a very moving experience. After the service, wreaths are laid at the cenotaph, followed by the Last Post. After the wreaths have been laid the cenotaph is full of colour and the scent of chrysanthemums fills the air. The Last Post is followed by the two-minutes' silence. Somewhere during the service the poems "In Flanders Fields" and "For the Fallen" are usually quoted. The whole day is too poignant to describe and I admire the Australians for this remembrance and respect for those who gave their lives, however many years have gone by since the two World Wars. Furthermore new emigrants become deeply involved in Anzac Day too.

On 11 November the Remembrance Day commemoration ceremony takes place, for it was on this day that the Armistice, which ended the First World War, was signed in 1918. There is no holiday on this day, but throughout Australia the two minutes' silence is still observed. On the Shrine of Remembrance in Melbourne are engraved the following words by Rudyard Kipling:

> So long as memory, valour, and faith endure,
> let these stones witness, through the years to come,
> How once there was a people fenced secure
> Behind great waters girdling a far home.
>
> Their own and their land's youth ran side by side
> Heedless and headlong as their unyoked seas -
> Lavish o'er all, and set in stubborn pride
> Of judgment, nurtured by accepted peace.
>
> Thus, suddenly, war took them – seas and skies
> Joined with the earth for slaughter. In a breath
> They, scoffing at all talk of sacrifice,
> Gave themselves without idle words to death.

Thronging as cities throng to watch a game
Or their own herds move southward with the year,
Secretly, swiftly, from their ports they came,
So that before half earth had heard their name
Half earth had learned to speak of them with fear;

Then they returned to their desired land -
The kindly cities and plains where they were bred -
Having revealed their nation in earth's sight
So long as sacrifice and honour stand,
And their own sun at the hushed hour shall light
The shrine of these their dead!

In Canberra the Australian War Memorial ranks high amongst the great national monuments of the world for the grandeur of its architecture, the beauty of its setting, and the manner in which its many exhibits tell their historic story. It houses a magnificent art collection, including a library of priceless material and the world-famous Hall of Memory with its six-million-piece mosaic and the roll of honour of those who have died.

In the words of one of the many school teachers who bring children to the Memorial each year; "It is truly remarkable that such a vast and almost incredibly wonderful display connected with war has been put together without a hint of the slightest glorification of war as such. All Australians can be proud of this unique achievement."

Apart from the galleries and the most moving pictures painted by War artists there are sixty-eight dioramas (originally called picture models) covering most theatres of both World Wars, and those in Korea and Vietnam. They show vividly the mud of a Somme winter, the sand and endless desert of Sinai and Palestine, and the jungle of New Guinea. They range in size from 9 metres by 7.5 metres to 1.3 metres by 1 metre.

* * *

At Singleton, New South Wales, a dedicated Ryder-Cheshire worker, Mrs Anne Boyd, has established a small Home for the physically handicapped, which is still known by its original name "Locksley". The Centre enables the residents to develop independence in a special environment. It also provides "Respite Care" where self-help skills can be learnt, and a break given to the family of the handicapped member.

As a young nurse, Anne had previously worked as a volunteer at the Ryder-Cheshire Centre in India, where she later established a Mobile Clinic to assist the sick in the lower Himalayas.

In 1988 Anne's story was included in a book *Unsung Heroes and Heroines of Australia*.

The Singleton Home was "officially opened" on 30 November 1985. "Open Day" extended over the whole weekend so the town could see the house before residents arrived (and featured a pottery exhibition by a woman who started the first Singleton Preschool in the house). The first resident moved in on 28 January 1986.

Committee selection was based on Ryder-Cheshire guidelines and criteria of Government department providing subsidy. Though extensive renovations were required, Locksley's old house atmosphere and space, wide doorways, verandahs and spacious yard with rear access were all added attractions for ramping and wheelchair access.

Twenty-six physically handicapped people between nineteen and seventy years of age were accepted for visits which ranged from three days to seven years. Six were long-term residents and twenty were there for respite care.

Increasing utilisation (in terms of user numbers), whilst at the same time retaining existing constructive patterns, is important. To this end a survey questionnaire was handed to each user for more feedback. It is also hoped to increase the use of the facility for respite care, and to this end, a live-in caretaker has been appointed. Beatriz comes from Colombia and, with husband, Umberto, and children Samin and Sabina, residents are more like an extension of the family.

Residents at this Ryder-Cheshire Home, Singleton, pay rent, currently $40 per week for permanent residents. ($10 per night and $50 per week for short-term.) Residents provide their own food and home care, and pay for electricity. The House Committee pays telephone rental and service fees on the pay-phone, as well as water and garbage rates, and maintenance of the house. Service clubs and ambulance drivers provide firewood. The garden was planned, organised and supervised by Tony Arnold (a former quadriplegic resident) using (as his "hands") Corrective Services community service hours. An award-winner in Singleton's annual garden competition, it continues to be beautifully maintained by the caretaker family.

The first Ryder-Cheshire Home to open in Australia, however, was at Ivanhoe, a suburb of Melbourne, Victoria. It was created in this way. While I was in Melbourne I inquired about patients diagnosed as suffering with cancer, and during visits to the Peter McCallum Clinic I had discussions with Dr Cyril Minty and his team about the number of patients treated for this disease. It soon became evident that the problem of such patients blocking acute hospital beds was very much on the minds of the staff of the Clinic.

The matter was discussed with members of the Ryder-Cheshire Council in Melbourne, and in 1978 they started to search for a property. A subcommittee was formed to co-ordinate the search and finally, after successful negotiation with the Returned Servicemen's League, two large adjoining properties were leased, at a cost of $22,000 per annum, which have a total of thirty-five rooms, and now a further nine rooms in an adjoining new house purpose-built and owned by the Ryder-Cheshire Victoria Foundation. They have acquired from the Returned Servicemen's League first option to buy the two original buildings should they decide to sell.

There are six family rooms and the rest have two beds and kitchen facilities and are comfortably furnished. The new building has en suite toilet facilities providing accommodation for cancer, epilepsy and other patients, mostly from the State of Victoria, but many from interstate or even over-seas. Some of them have to travel hundreds of miles for treatment at the Peter McCallum Clinic and other hospitals in Melbourne.

The first patients were admitted in September 1980, and Ivanhoe was formally opened by my husband when he visited Australia as a guest of the Royal Australian Air Force. Ministers from the local churches blessed the Home. Mrs Mary Walta, the mother of nine children, one of whom died of cancer, and formerly a prime worker in the Foundation's Support Group at Geelong, and originally with Ballarat, became the Housemother and Mr Anton Van Lith became Housefather. Like Mrs Walta, he is of Dutch origin and he understands some of the needs as he lost his beloved wife through cancer in 1976. In the words of Mary Walta:

> The way we are running this Home on a voluntary basis impresses many people, and I think that is the reason why so many support us. Our Caring Friends Support has increased from $7,000 to $20,000 donations over the years. There are no grants from the State, but many groups and organi-sations have taken on the responsibility of raising funds in a variety of ways.
>
> The amount originally charged per patient was $10.00 per night, although if people were not able to pay, then any cost is waived. In 1995 the charge was increased to $20 per night for some patients who receive financial reimbursement but remains at $10 for others.
>
> Within the Home there is also a boutique. A great number of people take their gifts there, and in one month alone $1,200 was raised by the sale of these goods.

When the Dutch Community could no longer find people to work as Houseparents at the Ryder-Cheshire Home, Ivanhoe, it was suggested to the Committee to approach the Conference of Major Superiors of Religious Orders, asking them to circulate the job description about Houseparents amongst anyone they knew – either religious or lay people.

Several Sisters responded and were interviewed, and Sister Catherine Harper, Sister of the Order of St Joseph and Sister Mary Myers of the Brigidine Order, were offered and accepted the work. They naturally had to consult with their Provincial before accepting, and explained that the work interested them most "because it is caring for many people and especially those suffering in mind and body". Sister Catherine was later replaced by Sister Vendramina and then Sister Declan. In 1996 the Houseparents were Sister Patricia Giles, Sister Declan and June Gorey.

So the high standard of care and compassion is being sustained in each House by a religious sister who is experienced in counselling; they are not paid but do receive expenses. They are responsible to the Ryder-Cheshire Victorian Homes Foundation Committee Chaired by Don Sinclair. This is a separate Foundation to the Ryder-Cheshire Foundation (Victoria) supporting Raphael. The Home is financed through the fees charged, donations, sundry fund-raising events and a monthly coffee morning.

The Home is clearly meeting a great need and is a place of comfort and support for patients and their families at times of great stress. An estimated 6,000 – 6,500 patients and carers pass through the Clinic and hospital each year and at the Ryder-Cheshire Victorian Homes, Ivanhoe, it is estimated that 5,500 of these patients stay each year, including 150 epilepsy patients.

The following are extracts from some of the letters received from patients and their families:

> . . . I still think myself very fortunate to have stayed at Ryder-Cheshire and to have had your help and support.

> . . . We want to thank you most sincerely for the care we received at Ryder-Cheshire. Everything is so clean and comfortable and welcoming which was appreciated in 'our' state of health.

> . . . I dreaded coming to Melbourne, but the homely surroundings and thoughtful care I was met with took all my fears (and my family's) away.

Of the number who have been admitted, one patient came from far away – Warrnambool. He was recovering from surgery and his wife was able to remain with him. Their children were grown up and married and were living in distant States, and as the father was far too weak to go home they and their families were invited to stay at the Home. To quote Mary Walta again: "So I invited them all here – thirteen adults and nine children. We put up extra mattresses. It was a very happy weekend and one which everybody will remember." The father died a month later.

People come to us from all sorts of places. A Fijian couple arrived in Sydney with little money. Because they had to wait for a flight to Melbourne, they spent much of their money on accommodation. When they arrived in Melbourne they found it necessary to stay for four weeks instead of the relatively short time they had been advised. They rented a house, but this was beyond their means and they were distressed until their admission to the Ryder-Cheshire Home was arranged.

One man who stayed with us came from Nauru Island. He had accompanied a severely injured relative who was unable to speak English, and was required not only for support but to serve as an interpreter for his relative. He stayed with us for several weeks.

Another family stayed with us for four weeks. The husband, aged twenty-six years, was out of work and suffering from testicular cancer. He and his wife had four children whose ages ranged from five weeks to six years. At first they had insufficient means to feed themselves or pay the charge for accommodation. We were able to arrange for various agencies to help them.

The mother of a child suffering from leukaemia wrote to her local newspaper describing her experiences. When her son first developed leukaemia he was very ill and became an in-patient at the Royal Children's Hospital. She and her husband could not afford to stay in Melbourne and be with him. They had to return to their home which was over 100 miles away. They visited him as often as they could and each journey was a nightmare, because they did not know if their son would still be alive when they arrived in Melbourne. He recovered, and his remission lasted several years. Unfortunately, his leukaemia returned and again he had to stay in hospital. This time his mother stayed in the Ryder-Cheshire Home and was able to visit him every day. It was she who gave the Home the name "The Home Away from Home".

In 1992 "Eddy", from Western Australia, came with his parents to stay with us in order to have tests and hopefully surgery, at nearby Austin Hospital. Eddy has cerebral palsy which has also brought on very severe epileptic fits. Much to the delight of everyone, Eddy had an operation which reduced the severity and number of epileptic fits. The parents stayed with us and Eddy also for a couple of nights before and after operations. Eddy has improved tremendously and is now a smiling boy, and even talking much better.

Liz came to the Ryder-Cheshire Home in 1993 to have radiotherapy after a brain tumour. She brought along with her, her six-weeks old beautiful daughter. Liz was very brave – her husband would drive down some Friday nights to be with her for the weekend and would leave on Sunday afternoon. She has come back once when her daughter was eighteen-months old and even more beautiful. Her reports since have been excellent. On a card sent to us she said, "Many thanks for your wonderful support during my stay".

In April 1992, after huge fund-raising efforts, an adjoining building of ten self-contained units was officially opened by Air-Marshal John Newham AC, and blessed by Ministers of the local churches.

My deepest appreciation goes out to those who spend weeks and sometimes months preparing for my visits to Australia; especially for the meticulous care taken in planning each itinerary, which usually lasts for seven weeks. Because of the vast distances, I prefer to start the day early there. I always try to set aside time after a talk for questions. With young children I ask them to relax and feel free to wriggle. The carefully thought-out questions show the interest and concern the people feel for the "have-nots" although it is sometimes difficult for the "haves" to imagine the needs of the less fortunate, whether nearby or thousands of miles away. I refer especially to those in the large cities of Australia. In the country areas there is a marked equality in the standard of living and, generally speaking, the same applies in New Zealand too. The landscapes, especially on the coast, the flowers and the bird life, are spectacularly beautiful in both countries and always a source of great pleasure to me.

I am always amazed by the interest of the news media, and at almost every place included in the itinerary one is interviewed and filmed. The Press seem genuinely concerned for the work and display a lively interest in one's way of life. On one occasion they interviewed me through the door of a room, which could not be opened because both its handles had come off!

I find schools and universities most stimulating, and they give me great hope for the future chiefly because of the penetrating questions asked by the young people. When time allows, I prefer a frank discussion about the world's problems, poverty and the subject of disability. In the country areas people may be a little more removed from the difficulties in the Third World. In the last ten years farmers have suffered much hardship because of the changing world-market situation particularly wheat and wool, as well as wrestling with the elements themselves – flood, drought, all sorts of insect plagues wiping out their crops, and so on. Because of their isolation in many areas they do support each other a lot, and are always raising money for projects to help each other. However, once alerted to the needs of their overseas neighbours they rally to help in an extraordinary way.

I am very often asked by nine-and ten-year olds: "Why can't these poor people come to our country where we have such a lot of space and food?" Others want to go out to Third World countries and do something.

At a school near Canberra where many of the children were immigrants, the local Chairman of the Foundation mentioned in his introduction that it cost ten dollars an hour to keep Raphael going in those days. Two young girls promptly came forward and offered their lunch money: "This is all we have for today, but please use it to keep Raphael running for two minutes." This example of real generosity is only one of hundreds my husband and I have experienced during visits to schools and other organisations there.

It is a paradox of our time that we have a "generation of concern" growing up in a world dominated at almost every level of society by the disease of materialism and greed. Hence, I am convinced we have a right and obligation to make sure that the concerned, including the youngest of them, know exactly what our problems are among the neglected, impoverished, sick and handicapped, and how concern for them can be expressed in positive action. Too often hospitals, for instance, are unfamiliar areas and the people living there unreal, so that the artificial divisions between the sick and those leading "normal lives" persist in quite an unnecessary way.

"Your summons," writes a friend in Australia and former Bod in SOE, "is a summons to seek and face the facts, to deny ourselves, to dedicate ourselves, to be there with those who are suffering. It is a challenge to all the young who find life insipid."

I do not believe the young want to be ostriches shielded by sterile sand from uncomfortable perception of other people's sufferings. Often, alas, the eager are thwarted because they lack the required education, or fail their examinations for the careers on which they have set their hearts. Young people with a really genuine vocation should not be denied a chance to fulfil it simply because they cannot attain the heights of academic achievements. Britain has lost generations who are frustrated, disappointed and disillusioned. If we continue to fail in trying to offer them – at an early age – practical trades and opportunities, the situation will become steadily worse.

There is a great need for more regular and recognised schemes to harness this urge into useful, satisfying channels with the participants following practical courses of instruction. Perhaps this scheme could become international. Practical jobs are of vital importance in any community. Routine work, like making beds, scrubbing, washing up and peeling potatoes is of just as great value as the more high-powered duties. As George Herbert said "Who sweeps a room, as for Thy laws, Makes that and the action fine". Most important of all is tender, loving care.

The following is a fairly typical day in my itineraries Down Under:

8.00 a.m.	Radio call in.
9.00 a.m.	Mass at Nazareth House. Meet individuals and staff afterwards.
11.30 a.m.	Attend Fair at Junior School, Ballarat and Clarendon College to raise funds for their adoptee boy Mohammed Ashan.
	Talk to children.
	Judge best decorated bicycles (forty to fifty) and head-gear.
12 noon	Visit Queen's Grammar School, Ballarat.
12.15 p.m.	Interview, ABC Regional News.
	Lunch at School.
1.00 p.m.	Junior School of Ballarat and Queen's Anglican Grammar. (Children running their own "Bina Day" to raise funds for baby Bina, born to leprosy parents at Raphael.) Bina is now fourteen years old and still sponsored by these children. Give talks to small groups of children.
1.30 p.m.	Wendouree Primary School. Meet staff.
1.45 p.m.	Talk to children (separate groups).
2.15 p.m.	Television.
2.15 p.m.	Depart for Austin McCallum School and McCallum House Workshop for Intellectually Disabled Adults.
3.25 p.m.	Work and correspondence with voluntary Secretary.
3.50 p.m.	Interview with the *Courier*.
5.20 p.m.	Peplow House (overnight shelter for homeless men).
7.00 p.m.	Call on Bishop Ronald Mulkearns.
7.15 p.m.	Return to Park View.
7.30–11.00 p.m.	Informal meal with Committee.

Most days in Australia and New Zealand, I give between four and seven talks, sometimes as many as nine, followed by questions. There was one school, I remember, with a headmistress who would not allow classes to mix, and on arrival I was told that I would be required to give two separate talks with a break of only three minutes between them! On a recent visit, very young children begged their teachers to allow them to remain behind long after it was time to go home so as to continue their questions. I remember, too, a wonderful boy of seven years who was sitting on the floor of his classroom. When I asked, "How do you think we should show to the world the suffering of others and persuade them to help?" he replied, "Well, we must do everything we can and *persevere*. Each of us will give up our lunch money to help those people for as many days as you want."

Two of the most moving nights were spent with the devoted teams of St Vincent de Paul in two of Australia's large cities where there are terrible problems amongst the homeless and derelicts. These individuals are visited wherever they can be found in the late evening and, if necessary, all night too, when a van goes out with a team of volunteers – including young people, some from universities – carrying hot soup, sandwiches and, above all, the companionship of those who care. There are literally thousands of unemployed and homeless people, many through no fault of their own.

Each month the Treasurer received an envelope, gummed up all round and containing $12 for Raphael. It always had a stamp from the Australian Antarctic Territory and an indecipherable postmark. No amount of enquiry could find out where or who it came from. This continued for many years. One month the envelope also contained a scrap of paper on which was written "Pray for me". It was the last such envelope ever received.

In March 1991, I opened the Ryder-Cheshire Home in the grounds of the Royal Perth Rehabilitation Hospital in Shenton Park, seven kilometres from the City of Perth. One of the prime movers behind this new Home was Mrs Barbara Seabrook. The Home provides low-cost, home-like accommodation in Perth where a person from miles away in the country may stay while undergoing treatment that does not require hospitalisation or nursing care. A carer may also stay with the person having treatment, or support an in-patient at a nearby hospital.

In its first three years of operation, the Home has seen 7,100 total days stayed or "heads on pillows", representing an increase in occupation to eighty-three per cent in 1993 and a mean duration of stay of 7.3 days in the same year.

The success of this Home has demonstrated the increasing need for this type of community support. Now a Lotteries Commission Grant, together with generous fund-raising support by the Rotary Club of Hollywood, and funds raised by the Foundation will enable additions to be made to the House to provide private accommodation for the Housemother as well as improvement to toilets, bathrooms and communal facilities for the guests and increase of four to five beds.

No Chapter, purporting to deal with Australia, would be complete without some reference to sport.

Admittedly, for many of us in England, our only first-hand exposure to Australian sporting prowess is watching Test Matches – for me, not always the most enjoyable of sporting experiences!

Others have heard the recurring myth of the number of women nurses – all in spotless white uniforms – to be seen playing lawn bowls, under the hot Australian sun. A few may be nurses, but all are simply wearing the official uniform of the Lawn Bowls Association.

However, it was quite salutary for me to see at first hand on my early visits to Australia the amount of sporting facilities available there – even in small isolated communities.

These facilities are not only in intensive use at weekends, but also during the week, especially for evening meetings and competitions. As in other parts of the world, golf is played early and late, well and badly – light permitting!

Obviously, I have no statistical data on this, but I believe that the competitive energy and sense of fair play brought out by this devotion to sport spills over into many other aspects of Australian life. It has been seen by me in their concern for the well-being of others less fortunate, and in the determination which they bring to the successful launching and completion of aid projects.

On the lighter side I may perhaps be permitted to remember a funny occasion which occurred very many years ago.

Most regrettably, I have never kept a regular personal diary, but amongst my notes I find that I scribbled a description of the following incident whilst staying at one of the Government Houses.

I had had a gruelling day with seven talks and engagements, and at intervals I was relieved to be able to return to my suite for a quick wash and refreshing soft drink. The attache was always aware of my comings and goings and had the habit of coming to the door of the suite to remind me that I had exactly three or four minutes before starting again.

On one occasion whilst I was reading welcome letters from home, he announced that Her Excellency wanted me to come as soon as possible to join her in the huge green drawing room, to which he then escorted me. There, to my amazement, were boxes of hats spread out over the carpet. "So now you can be the model as well as me, for I have to make different choices," Her Excellency announced without preamble. "I was told you have ten minutes to spare."

Without wishing to appear ungracious, I suggested that I was not the right person to advise on hats, and almost admitted that the three I possessed were bought at a fête or Sue Ryder Shop, but Her Excellency insisted. So, for the first and last time in my life, one variety after another of garden party hats, hats worn at race meetings and other sporting events, hats in all shapes, sizes and decoration were placed in quick succession upon my unwilling head, accompanied by a running commentary on their respective merits from Her Excellency!

As in all countries, one grows attached to both the people and the different regions, and perhaps I may be allowed to mention the work undertaken by supporters in Perth and my memories of arrivals and departures there, whether in bright sunshine or at night, which remains so vivid.

Talks too, given outside – sometimes under the stars – created memories which have never faded.

In each State the Foundation is honoured by having the Governor as a patron, and formalities at Government House are naturally taken very seriously. In the midst of rather a strenuous itinerary it is most refreshing to be offered hospitality and to enjoy the beauty of their splendid gardens.

Western Australia alas, is the only State where two or three shops for the Ryder-Cheshire Foundation have been founded. During the past forty or more years, many thousands of people elsewhere in Britain and other countries now actually say, "Oh! I buy my clothes from Sue Ryder." They are posh, elegant, worn with pride, knowing that the proceeds are used to relieve human suffering. Each volunteer and customer benefits from getting to know the other and giving service to their community.

I still feel very strongly that if only an experienced person from the retail trade can be found in Australia, upmarket shops bearing our names or mine could be started and flourish, thus ensuring continuity for fund-raising, and attracting entirely new customers and supporters, as has happened so successfully in Britain and other countries. A Trading Team would work closely with Support Group , but not cause them any extra work and pursue their odjective of trading . . . which is most lucrative.

It is envisaged that more Ryder-Cheshire Homes will be established in Australia as the need arises and finance can be raised, but the construction of these Homes will never diminish – and indeed will only increase – the concern of new people to continue support of the Ryder-Cheshire Centre at Raphael in Northern India.

13

New Zealand

If your whare* is warm, people will come to it.
Traditional Maori proverb

BOTH MY HUSBAND AND I had contacts in New Zealand – he through service with bomber crews and my own from a few of those who had survived SOE and also from members of relief teams who had worked with me in Europe. Between them, these kind people arranged the itineraries for our early visits.

New Zealand covers more that 100,000 square miles and is approximately the size of the British Isles. The population is 3.5 million and there has been a marked upsurge in immigration to this country.

It is fertile land with a gentle climate and is one of the great food-producing countries of the world despite its relatively small size. The economy until recent times was substantially reliant upon grasslands and farming production but today its base is broadening considerably. In order of importance, the economic welfare of the country is underpinned by the exports of sheep meats and beef, dairy products, wood products, fruit and vegetables and wool, aluminium and fish. Tourism is now one of New Zealand's biggest foreign exchange earners.

The energy crisis of the early 1970s forced New Zealand to step up its search for indigenous fuels and other sources of energy. It has large resources of natural gas in the Maui gas field and an abundance of cheap hydro-electricity derived from its alpine lakes and fast-flowing rivers; in addition, oil is being found in small quantities but at an increasing level each year.

The population is centred on the two main Islands, divided by a costly and sometimes hostile area of water, Cook Strait. Bird and animal life receives a high degree of protection and many of the great natural forests are being preserved for posterity as national reserves.

The standard of living in New Zealand would by world standards have to be described as high: sixty per cent of the people own their own homes and their own piece of ground. Traditionally New Zealand is an egalitarian society and racial tensions between Maori and European are kept at fairly low levels, though there are significant differences. The Maori people are a proud and magnificent race of Polynesians who have a great love of the land and have served New Zealand in times of war with great distinction and dedication. They were recognised, particularly in the Second World War, as

* whare = house (in Maori).

one of the world's elite fighting corps in the desert and in Italy. History records that the Maori Battalion performed feats of great heroism and the battle for the Cassino railway station is a legend in Maoridom.

The Maori have become a people of two cultures, and have preserved in the national life of New Zealand a warmth and colour which is most distinctive. In their communal and tribal gatherings, the exchange of chants, songs and dances preserves for posterity the heroic history of their race.

The colonisation of New Zealand led to many battles over the possession of land, whose right of ownership the Maori fought fiercely to retain. Great leaders emerged amongst the tribes. Peace came painfully and through much tribulation. The intelligence of the Maori was soon proved by those who entered the professions. Sir Maui Pomare, a doctor of medicine, was knighted for his work as the first Maori Minister for Health in the Government before the First World War and there have been many since who have occupied high positions in Government, the armed services, business and the wider community.

In recent years, the validity has been re-affirmed of the Treaty of Waitangi, by which the Maori chiefs ceded New Zealand to Queen Victoria in 1840. Substantial progress has been made in righting past injustices to Maori, notably restoration of inshore fishing rights and compensation of the Waikato-Tainui people for the confiscation of 1.2 million acres of land on a false pretext in 1863. Even this rate of progress has been insufficient for some Maori activists so that various forms of protest action have become part of the New Zealand scene. Fortunately this is being met generally with restraint as cooler heads work towards fuller settlement.

The oil crisis of 1973 coupled with a series of unwise economic and financial decisions by the Government in the following decade brought the economy to the brink of collapse with an escalating burden of national debt. A new Government in 1984 introduced a series of drastic changes which led to a strengthening of the national economy in the next ten years. Accompanying this has been a big change in health, education and housing policies. One effect of this, as perceived by many people, is that "the rich are getting richer and the poor are getting poorer" so that New Zealand's remarkably egalitarian society may be a thing of the past before long. Another significant change, decided at a referendum in 1993, is in the method of electing Members of Parliament from "first past the post" (as in Britain) to a form of proportional representation. Since this means a substantial shift in power within the electorate, dynamic changes in society in New Zealand may be expected to continue.

Few countries can equal the spectacular beauty of New Zealand's mountains and coastline. In many places the green fields and grazing land with their herds of cattle and flocks of sheep remind one of the lovelier parts of rural Britain.

One of the most striking features of the country is the individuality of the people's homes and the pride taken in their baking (especially their pavlovas, a rich meringue cake) and also their gardens. Their warm hospitality and generosity are so marked wherever we go and characterise the New Zealand people.

Our itineraries in this country are similar to those for Australia. They are invariably mixed and include many schools and organisations. One derives great pleasure from responding to the generosity of the Kiwis and we endeavour to reach as many people as possible and show them our appreciation for all their help and encouragement.

My husband and I felt very privileged to receive several traditional Maori welcomes on our visits to New Zealand. The ceremony is generally split up into five parts and is as follows:

> *Wero* – challenge by a warrior as visitors enter the *marae* (courtyard)
> *Karanga* – a call of welcome chanted by one or more of the women
> *Powhiri* – an action song of welcome by the hosts
> *Mihi* – speech of welcome
> *Hongi* – the pressing of noses

The guests are challenged, usually by a single warrior bearing a short, sometimes carved, rod, in lieu of the challenge spear (*taiaha*). The challenger goes through the intricate mincing movements of the *wero*, brandishing his *taiaha*, but always taking care to ensure that the tongue of the weapon does not point directly at the visitors. When the warrior retires, the ancient ceremony of chasing him is symbolised by one of the visitors picking up the rod and moving forward to the *marae*, where the women still stand clutching their short branches and performing the *powhiri*.

We also enjoyed a traditional Maori feast called the *Hangi* where the food is cooked in the ground (meat, vegetables, fish and poultry can be cooked in this way). It is very hard work making the fire which involves digging a pit and lighting a wood fire inside it. The fire is brought up to a fierce heat and then flat, scrubbed stones are placed upon it. When the stones are red hot they are covered with wet mats and woven flax baskets containing the food are placed on top, everything is covered with clean sacks and then earthed in. The Maoris judge the cooking time by the smell of the food and they still use this method to cook large quantities of sea foods and shellfish which abound in New Zealand; they also cook different kinds of European food most deliciously this way.

The meal is served with warmth and humour while the enjoyment in sharing the meal is expressed in the talking and greetings, and the deference expressed towards the old by the younger members. All speak of the Maori *aroha* – the love into which each member of the tribe is drawn. Every Maori can be confident of the warmest welcome from his fellow Maoris, irrespective of his success or failure in the world, even after an absence of many years from his home. All that matters is that he is there. And this *aroha* they extend to their non-Maori friends.

* * *

Ryder-Cheshire Foundations were established in the 1960s in Auckland, Christchurch (Canterbury), New Plymouth (Taranaki) and Wellington and incorporated in due course and support groups were started in some other Centres. The purpose of these Foundations is to provide support for Raphael, the Ryder-Cheshire International Centre at Dehra Dun, India. By agreement with the Australian Foundations, the New Zealand Foundations maintain Raphael for three months each year and the Australians for nine.

The New Zealand Foundations appointed a National President and Liaison Officer in 1981. Mr Owen Hannigan and Mrs Grace Finlayson were the first holders of these offices. The *Ryder-Cheshire Chronicle*, published by the Canterbury Foundation, became the national newsletter.

The Foundation in Auckland was honoured to have the late Air-Chief-Marshal Sir Keith Park as its first President. Sir Keith, himself a New Zealander, was seconded to the Royal Flying Corps in 1917 from the Royal Field Artillery and by April 1940 he was Air-Vice-Marshal, commanding No. II Group, upon which fell the brunt of the fighting in the Battle of Britain. Later he served with great distinction in several other theatres of the War and retired from the Royal Air Force as an Air-Chief-Marshal in December 1946. His quiet but determined approach was largely responsible for the formation and subsequent progress of the Foundation in Auckland. I always remember his tall dignified figure and deep-set thoughtful blue eyes.

The late Charles Upham, first Patron of the Canterbury Foundation, was another wonderful person. The only combatant soldier to be awarded the Victoria Cross twice for bravery, was one of only three double VC holders in the history of the decoration.

When the Germans invaded Greece in April 1941, Upham, by then a Platoon Commander and a Second Lieutenant, went with his Unit as part of the force which was put into the country to try to repel them. After British and Commonwealth forces were hustled out of Greece by the advancing Germans, he was among 28,000 British, Greek, Australian and New Zealand soldiers who were dumped on Crete with orders from Churchill to hold the Island at all costs.

In a New Zealand force, under its pugnacious and skilful Commander, General Bernard Freyburg VC, Upham won his first VC on Crete in May 1941, commanding a platoon in the battle for Marleme airfield. During the course of an advance of 3,000 yards his platoon was held up three times. Carrying a bag of grenades (his favourite weapon), Upham first attacked a German machine-gun nest, killing eight paratroopers, then destroyed another which had been set up in a house. Finally he crawled to within fifteen yards of a Bofors anti-aircraft gun before knocking it out.

When the advance had been completed he helped carry a wounded man to safety in full view of the enemy, and then ran half a mile under fire to save a company from being cut off. Two Germans who tried to stop him were killed.

The next day Upham was wounded in the shoulder by a mortar burst and hit in the foot by a bullet. Undeterred, he continued fighting and, with his arm in a sling he proceeded to draw enemy fire and enable their gun positions to be spotted.

With his unwounded arm he propped his rifle in the fork of a tree and killed two approaching Germans; the second was so close he fell on the muzzle of Upham's rifle.

During the retreat from Crete, Upham succumbed to dysentery and could not eat properly. The effect of this and his wounds made him look like a walking skeleton, his Commanding Officer noted. Nevertheless he found the strength to climb the side of a 600 foot-deep ravine and use a Bren gun on a group of advancing Germans.

At a range of 500 yards he killed twenty-two out of fifty. His subsequent VC citation recorded that he had "performed a series of remarkable exploits, showing outstanding leadership, tactical skill and utter indifference to danger".

Even under the hottest fire, Upham never wore a steel helmet, explaining that he could never find one to fit him.

His second VC was earned on 15 July 1942, when the New Zealanders were concluding a desperate defence of the Ruweisat ridge in the 1st Battle of Alamein. Upham ran forward through a position swept by machine-gun fire and lobbed grenades into a truck full of German soldiers.

When it become urgently necessary to take information to advance units which had become separated, Upham took a Jeep on which a captured German machine-gun was mounted and drove it through the enemy position.

At one point the vehicle became bogged down in the sand, so Upham coolly ordered some nearby Italian soldiers to push, though they were somewhat surprised to be given an order by the enemy, Upham's expression left them in no doubt that he should be obeyed.

By now Upham had been wounded, but not badly enough to prevent him leading an attack on an enemy strong point, all the occupants of which were then bayonetted. He was shot in the elbow, and his arm was broken. The New Zealanders were surrounded and outnumbered, but Upham carried on directing fire until he was wounded in the legs and could no longer walk.

Taken prisoner, he proved such a difficult customer that on 1944 he was confined in Colditz castle, where he remained for the rest of the War. His comments on Nazis were always sulphurous.

For his actions at Ruweisat he was awarded a Bar to his VC. His citation noted that "his complete indifference to danger and his personal bravery have become a byword in the whole of the New Zealand Expeditionary Force".

Charles Upham died on 22 November, 1994, at the age of eighty six. To the end of his life he maintained that his VCs were a recognition of the achievements of all the young New Zealanders who had fought in these conflicts, in which so many had died.

As a long-time supporter of the Canterbury Foundation, he had spoken most movingly at our meetings.

My thanks, too, go to the busy Secretaries who, at almost every place I visit in New Zealand and Australia, volunteer to take dictation and type dozens of letters for me. Joyce Petrove of New Plymouth has been Secretary of the Taranaki Foundation for many years, and Pat Mahoney in Wellington, are just two I remember.

With the commitment of the New Zealand and Australian Foundations to keep Raphael running, the Sue Ryder Foundation, with the help of many anonymous individuals, succeeded in finding the capital which enabled us to erect different parts of the settlements in India, such as the Little White House at Raphael, for children who are destitute and orphaned. Like Australia, the New Zealand Foundations have also sent excellent volunteers to serve at Raphael.

Many schools are involved in raising funds, and again it is a delight to spend time amongst the children and to hear of their wholehearted enthusiasm and concern for those who are underprivileged and do not share the standard and beauty of life which they have always known. Ever since our first visit thirty-four years ago, the subject of a Home had been the topic of conversation.

It was soon realised that facilities, particularly for the young handicapped, were very limited in New Zealand, and so the Ryder-Cheshire Foundation Manawatu was formed at Palmerston North by a group of local people concerned about lack of accommodation to allow the handicapped to live as normally as possible within the community. Many handicapped people were living permanently in hospitals, often in geriatric wards, despite their relative youth. It was very easy for these people to become institutionalised, for they are cut off from the outside world, left idle, and without friends or possessions around them. For many handicapped people, their families carry the major load in successfully keeping out of hospital-type accommodation and, for some, this is the best solution.

However, if the strain becomes too great within the family, then a breakdown can occur with considerable suffering for all concerned. The burden of providing constant care for a severely handicapped family member is not easily appreciated by those without first-hand experience of this situation.

Very dependent handicapped people need an environment where the provision of physical care and medical treatment are not allowed to dominate daily living. Their environment must be designed to help dispel feelings of uselessness, inertia and the depression inherent in physical and economic dependence. When living conditions are improved other benefits result. Self-reliance and opportunities to contribute to the lives of others restore self-respect and improves the quality of life.

Handicapped people, like everyone else, wish to live as normally as possible in the privacy of their own homes where they can plan their own lives and make their own decisions. Where disability is not severe, these aspirations are not so difficult to achieve if sufficient help is available from district nurses, home help and voluntary services. To gain the same degree of independence a severely handicapped person needs much more support. There is a need for specially adapted flats in the community for those who can manage the problems and difficulties of living alone, and for residences providing more physical help which, in some cases, could be half-way houses to an independent life.

The general aims of the Foundation, which are common to Ryder-Cheshire Homes throughout the world, can be stated as follows: we wish to establish a place of shelter, physically, and a place of encouragement, spiritually; a place in which residents and staff can acquire a sense of belonging and ownership by contributing, in any way within their capacity, to the functioning and development of the community. A place to share with others, and from which to help those less fortunate; a place in which to gain confidence and to develop interests; a place of hopeful endeavour and not of passive disinterest. We recognise that a satisfactory place to live is of fundamental importance in any attempts to build a new life from a position of serious physical disability.

The Ryder-Cheshire Foundation Manawatu is attempting to give physically handicapped people, including the severely handicapped, a life of maximum independence, responsibility and freedom of choice in a group of houses built in Te Awe Awe Street, Palmerston North. Some factors which are important in achieving this aim are the location of the site, architectural design, tenancy arrangements and management organisation. Relationships between residents, care-staff and the management committee play a critical part in the success of the venture. One effective way to promote friendship and co-operation is for both residents and staff to participate in management and admissions decisions. Residents manage their own money and pay for rent, heating and telephone, as control over money is an important factor in choosing one's own way of life. Admissions are made without reference to race, colour or creed, but are related to the degree of need and the ability of a handicapped person to benefit from the opportunities which the houses offer for a positive and purposeful way of life. The development of this project arose from the concern of a group of Christians.

In all, there is accommodation for thirty-three people with different degrees of disability. There are two eight-bedroomed houses and two five-bedroomed houses, in all of which a high level of care is provided, including the provision of night care. All meals are provided in the eight-bedroomed houses, but residents in the five-bed houses cater for themselves with some assistance from carers.

For those able to live more independently, three smaller houses are provided, one three-bedroomed and two two-bedroomed. One of these is the most recent addition to the complex, opened at the end of 1994.

From all houses there is easy access via covered ways to the central offices and the recreation room, which serves as a focus for social and community activities. As well as being open to all the residents, it serves as a day-centre for handicapped people living elsewhere.

The location of the houses was an important factor in the Foundation's objective to provide a better place to live for those who are physically restricted. Residents in the houses are able to go to local shops on their own and the central position of the land acquired for the development encourages contact between the handicapped people and the rest of the community.

Opportunities exist for learning new skills and for the development of crafts and other hobbies. Close contact is kept with agencies who seek to improve the employment opportunities available for physically handicapped people. The accommodation provided is a key factor in allowing some residents to obtain further education or training. The emphasis is on total rehabilitation, so that some who come to live in the houses will later go out to an independent life in the community. Those who are unable to do this are entitled to look upon the residence as their home for the rest of their lives.

The first residents moved in on 10 October 1983 and further units have been occupied progressively. Interest in and awareness of the complex have increased tremendously in the host City of Palmerston North, local firms offering discounts without being asked and many offers of voluntary help being received. The Home was officially opened on 3 March 1984. The following extracts are from an account of the opening ceremony published in the *Ryder-Cheshire Chronicle* that month:

> The opening ceremony was held in the community hall of the complex which was full. Mr Murray Gray, Chairman of the Ryder-Cheshire Foundation (Manawatu), introduced the speakers and apologised for the absence of the Minister of Health. The Mayor of Palmerston North, Mr Brian Elwood, a supporter of the Foundation, said that this was a significant day in the life of the city and was evidence of the concern of its citizens for handicapped people. It was also the first official visit of their Excellencies the Governor-General and Lady Beattie. The Minister of Social Welfare, Mr Venn Young, praised the chance of an independent life which the project offered the handicapped. He said that the local Members of Parliament, Mr Michael Cox and Mr Trevor De Cleene, had been assiduous in their representations on behalf of the Homes. There was to be a special additional benefit of $65 per week – in addition to their social security and disability allowances – for the residents of the eight-bed home for the first year as well as a special grant of $10,000 for this year only, to help meet the operating costs of the Home. Mr Young also mentioned the suspensory loans available to allow handicapped people to enter business.
>
> Sir David Beattie and Lady Beattie, who had travelled from Auckland

with Mr Owen Hannigan and Mrs Joyce Hannigan, congratulated the Government on its support of a new form of health funding. He then unveiled a commemorative plaque. Mr Hannigan, in his speech, drew attention to the work of the other Ryder-Cheshire Foundations and of the Leonard Cheshire and Sue Ryder Homes throughout the world.

The available space at Palmerston North has now been filled. The actual cost of the building proved to be more that the original estimate of $1,259,000. Approval of a Government subsidy of $887,000 (eighty per cent of building costs) was received on 8 October 1981, subject to the Foundation raising their share before building began. The site, being Crown Land, was purchased from the Government.

One of the former residents of the Home, Sara Georgeson, is a woman with a purpose, and in the June 1984 *Newsletter*, published by the Centre for University Extramural Studies in Palmerston North, the following article appeared:

Have you ever wondered whether you could still study if you were severely handicapped? Twenty-two year old Sara Georgeson is wheelchair-bound and a very successful Massey student.

Sara has congenital amelia – a rare condition which results in the absence of all four limbs. Until recently, she lived at the Pukeora Home for the Disabled in the Hawkes Bay. She received her primary and secondary education through the Wellington Correspondence School, passed five subjects in School Certificate and was accredited University Entrance. At the age of eighteen Sara could see two paths before her: a sheltered workshop at Pukeora or further education. She chose university study but the specialist residential care that she requires was not available at any university hostel in New Zealand, nor did her family live in a university town. CUES (Centre for University Extramural Studies) provided the solution – she could study extramurally from Massey and continue to live at Pukeora. In 1980 Sara enrolled in her first two papers.

"The first year I didn't really understand what university study was all about," said Sara. "I only attended one of the voluntary vacation courses and had a rather disorganised approach to my studies. Consequently, I failed one paper and got an 'R' pass in the other. But I learned some valuable lessons – attendance at vacation courses was essential for me and two papers were not enough to keep me at my studies in the kind of disciplined regular way that is needed. So in 1981 I took three papers and passed the lot, proving to myself and everyone else that I *could do it!*"

By the end of 1982 Sara had passed five 100 level and two 200 level papers. She had made her goal the Bachelor of Social Work degree with the eventual aim of entering the work force as a social worker. Last year she took the two 100 level Sociology papers and the first year Social Work paper. Then in October 1983 the Ryder-Cheshire Foundation opened its Residential Homes for the Disabled in Palmerson North. At the beginning of the year Sara shifted in and was to enrol as an internal student at Massey.

Although she found the first two months as an internal student very tiring, she adjusted and thoroughly enjoyed campus life.

ABOVE: Young mentally handicapped patients taking part in a concert at Raphael, India

BELOW: Sunday visiting. Rupsi, a leprosy mum, greeting her daughter Sampati, who was being educated at The Little White House, Raphael

LEFT Lady Ryder with sick children in the Czech Republic

BELOW One of the Foundation's many TB patients being examined by Dr Verma at the Ryder-Cheshire Centre, Raphael

RIGHT Ethiopia, 1985, during the airlift. In this sea of suffering an example of dignity, patience and humility was shown by the victims

BELOW Lady Ryder and Lord Cheshire on what was to be his last visit to India

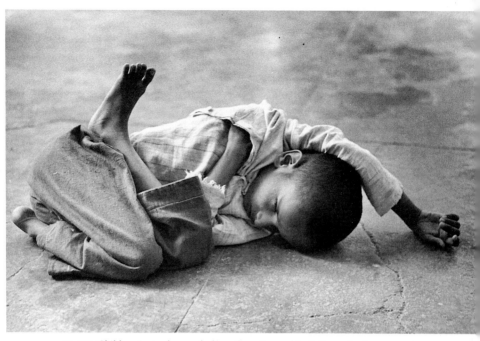

ABOVE Child patient who symbolizes those in need in India and other countries

BELOW Dr Robert Rawat and Lady Ryder with the Foundation's mobile clinic discussing what medication may be available for an overwhelming number of TB patients, North India

ABOVE A group of children waiting to meet Lady Ryder and Lord Cheshire. Many had been destitute before living and being educated at Raphael

RIGHT A leprosy patient at Raphael

ABOVE Leprosy patient – one of three
and a half million in India

ABOVE Leprosy patient in Raphael

BELOW Kazembe Juwesi during rehabilitation work in Malawi

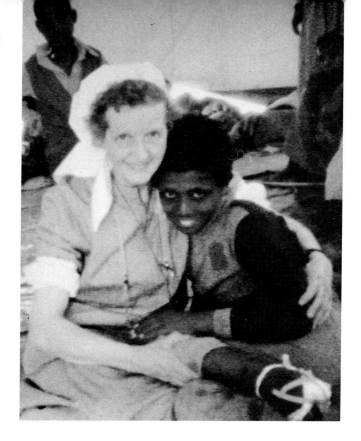

BELOW Lady Ryder with Sister Gabriel standing near an RAF Hercules mercy aircraft
which flew them into the famine areas of Ethiopia. Behind them an Aeroflot plane
used to carry Ethiopian children out of their homeland

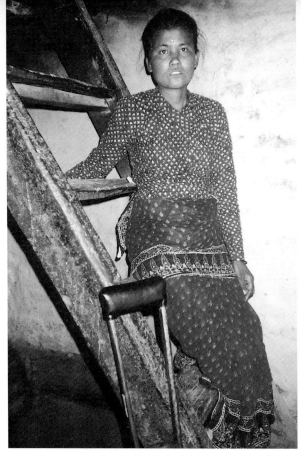

ABOVE Isyuri Chetri who died with cancer, in Nepal,
was provided with wool to knit and sell jumpers
to buy her food and medication

BELOW The Diocesan School for Girls, Auckland

ABOVE Rossmini College, Takapuna, New Zealand, with pupils from the Westlake and Dargaville Schools and Rangitoto College who also give great support to the Foundation

BELOW Sue Ryder enjoying a ride on a haycart at a Fair held by pupils/supporters from the Junior School and Queens Anglican Grammar School, Ballarat, Victoria, Australia

ABOVE Pupils at the Genazzano Catholic School, Melbourne, who have over the years raised substantial funds for the Foundation with their voluntary work

BELOW Dr Kraus, Federal Minister of Health, Yugoslavia, with Sue Ryder deciding on areas to be surveyed for future Foundation Homes and Hospitals during the post-war era

ABOVE Bolesia (nicknamed "Sunshine"), a young patient with
rheumatoid arthritis who died at the age of 16

BELOW Lady Ryder with a baby born in one of the
Foundation Homes in the former Yugoslavia

A patient in the Sue Ryder Home in Zyrardow, Poland, showing
his Auschwitz prison number tattoo

ABOVE Malgosia – still in her twenties and in spite of her terminal illness painted a beautiful picture on silk for the Foundation

BELOW Zofia Siodos. Biopsy of this extensive ulceration showed cancer of the adeno carcinoma fungating type. The only treatment was to keep this patient as comfortable as possible, applying regular dressings and relieving her pain

ABOVE Zofia, in the workshop of the Sue Ryder Homes in Konstancin. Many of the tea towels and other Foundation gifts are designed by the girls there

BELOW The workshop at Konstancin

Sister Monika and Sue Ryder at Travnik in Bosnia

LEFT A Polish woman, living in extreme poverty in the Ukraine, suffering with rheumatoid arthritis

LEFT A patient in one of the Foundation's Palliative Care Homes in Poland

Two more years of internal study saw completion of Sara's BSW. She was also thrilled when Margaret Biggs, a multiple sclerosis sufferer, who is also confined to a wheelchair, had her BA degree conferred at this year's May graduation ceremonies.

Sara completed her Bachelor of Social Work degree in 1986, and worked for two years co-ordinating a training programme for social workers dealing with incest and sexual abuse. In 1988 she took a job as a social worker for the Crippled Children's Society, where she worked for three years before moving to her present job. At the moment she is a tutor at the Manawatu Polytechnic, teaching towards the Certificate in Teaching People with Disabilities.

Sara left the Ryder-Cheshire Home in 1987, and has been living independently since then.

A group, led by Dr A. P. Snell of the Waikato Hospital in Hamilton initiated the Ryder-Cheshire Foundation Waikato with the objective of establishing a Ryder-Cheshire Home in Hamilton. The first House was formally opened by a Patron, Sir Ross Jansen, on 28 March 1992. A past National President of the New Zealand Foundations, Pat Moore wrote about it to me:

> I went to Hamilton for the opening of the first Home there today; it was attended by supporters from several organisations and the residents played a leading part in a simple official ceremony and the saying of prayers.
>
> The Home is quite lovely; beautifully built and planned with the needs of wheelchair residents in mind. Apart from a few settling down problems the residents seemed very happy. Our greatest good fortune is that we have two more plots of land adjacent to the Home and can begin planning two independent Homes very soon. They will eventually be surrounded by lovely lawns and gardens. Many of the people I met recalled Leonard's last visit and your earlier joint visit to Hamilton and spoke of you both. I reminded them that the Home they have now opened under the Ryder-Cheshire name brings them firmly into an international family and that our responsibility for the care of handicapped people is the same wherever they may live.

The House is purpose-built for the needs of people with disabilities using wheelchairs, on one of the three sections given to the Foundation by Waikato Area Health Board. The Foundation continues to operate it. Five residents are supported by a part-time carer but manage their own affairs and the running of the house. All residents are involved with the management committee in decisions relating to operation of the Home and are very happy and satisfied with their situation.

Changes in national policy for health services have twice interrupted planning to build two more Houses on the Foundation's adjacent sections. The Waikato Trust believes the real need in the area is for accommodation for people with severe disabilities requiring full-time support and care. The Trust is vigorously pursuing new alternatives. Its members received much help and encouragement from a visit by Patsy Wright-Warren, CBE, Projects Officer for the Ryder-Cheshire Foundation in the United Kingdom; yet more evidence of the strength we derive from our international associations.

The founding of Ryder-Cheshire Homes makes the work and needs, both there and in other countries overseas, better known, and introduces people to a world they cannot imagine. Furthermore, it gives young people an opportunity to offer personal service. The Governor-General is a patron of the Ryder-Cheshire Foundations in New Zealand and the Manawatu community is very aptly known as "A place to Live".

The supporters in New Zealand remain deeply committed to the task of funding Raphael, the Ryder-Cheshire Centre in India – and many personal links are forged by visits to Raphael – especially by volunteers who continue to offer their services there as they have done for many years.

PART FIVE

Building a New Life

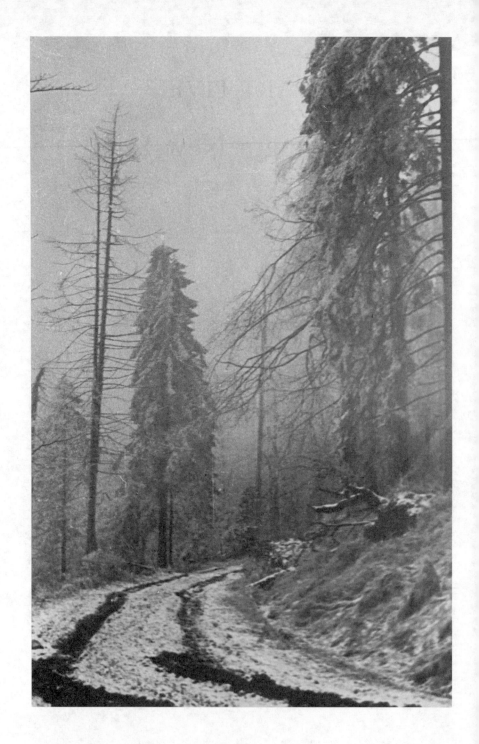

A typical winter's road in Central and Southern Europe.

14

Greetings on Frontiers

"GEE, THAT MUST BE exciting," someone once exclaimed when he heard that my work involves travelling: "Do you fly everywhere?" or "Do have a lovely trip", an expression I rather dislike. The answer to whether I fly everywhere is generally no, except in certain large countries where distances are very great, or in cases when the only quick way of reaching my destination is to travel by air. Years ago one had long waits, overcrowding, stopovers for refuelling and rapid changes of time and climate. In the course of my travels I have experienced tropical storms and emergency landings. People who fly these days cannot imagine what it used to be like, yet they still find it very tiring.

I never cease to be amazed by the enormous network and organisation of so many different airlines, which is a world of its own. Occasionally I receive the rare treat of being "upgraded" and then it is absolutely wonderful and a great relief to be able to stretch out and be looked after, indeed it is a holiday. I have always been spared the feeling of jet-lag and once abroad and away from the telephone and other interruptions I usually feel free to work and sleep. I only wish the excessive food left over could feed the hungry; in my humble opinion it is immoral that the airline authorities maintain that all the food may be contaminated. So all food not used on flight is, as I have seen, taken off the aircraft and dumped , whereas it could feed hundreds of people. On one particular flight, encouraged by the steward and cabin crew, I went round to the astonished passengers and asked them if they would kindly consider keeping some of the dishes untouched to feed the hungry at the next stopover. Many agreed.

In an average year I drive approximately 50,000 miles to the Homes, new properties and official engagements in Britain, as well as driving to and in the other countries where the Foundation works. I make regular visits to various countries in different Continents. I try to visit Australia and New Zealand as regularly as I can, about every three to four years according to my schedule in other countries, and my husband used to come with me whenever possible. To go straight into a meeting and give a talk after having driven or travelled by air for twenty-four hours calls for considerable stamina. At the Foundation's Headquarters in Suffolk one day it was amusing to hear two visitors ask, "When are you next leaving on safari?"

The warmth of the welcome awaiting me wherever I go, especially in the schools and among young people, compensates for fatigue, and one is always heartened by the generosity and good will one encounters.

Visits abroad include not only countries in which the Foundation already works, but also those in which the authorities and people have learnt of the work we do and invite me, or other representatives of the Foundation, to discuss with them ways in which we can co-operate in caring for the sick and handicapped.

The major part of a tour of Central and Eastern Europe, on the other hand, will be spent visiting all the Foundation's Homes in Poland and former Yugoslavia, and attending meetings to discuss the existing Homes and hospitals and to plan the founding of new ones or the renovation of others. Several suggested sites for new Homes will be visited, and where possible, a few will be chosen. These visits take place every year to eighteen months and each one lasts for about six weeks to two months.

Renovation and building work is planned at least two to five years ahead, according to priorities in the area, the funds that are available locally and the plans of the people themselves. Whenever I work (with a few exceptions) the local authorities are responsible for the providing staff, giving grants for the day-to-day running, and the provision of food and medical supplies, the Foundation being responsible for maintenance, renovation and the building of extensions. Unlike Britain, local autonomy is aimed for, as the Homes, Centres, Domiciliary Care Teams and Mobile Medical Clinics clearly have to be administered locally.

Another important aspect of the Foundation's work is the assistance given in the homes of individuals who are sick or handicapped or in any kind of need, by providing medication, wheelchairs, walking aids, hoists or any other special equipment which enable such people to be looked after at home rather than in hospital and to live a more normal life, retaining or achieving a large measure of independence. For those recommended by our social workers, nurses and physicians as being in financial need because of sickness or other misfortune, the Foundation tries to provide a small grant in some countries, and food and clothing is also distributed. I spend as much time as possible with the social workers, physicians and nurses and go on the rounds with them.

In Germany the Foundation's principal work of prison-visiting and aftercare has already been described in Chapter 8.

Inevitably, there is much work to be done and always will be, and these long journeys are accordingly a vital necessity, enabling me to keep in contact with all aspects of the Foundation's work, to help extend it, and to bring it to the attention of those who are not aware of what we do. Outsiders sometimes envy me for being able to do so much travelling, imagining my travels to be some extended form of holiday, but they would soon realise their mistake if they could see what is really involved. Not only is my schedule everywhere taken up almost entirely by very vital meetings and discussions concerning the Foundation, but often – as on visits to the Continent – I drive myself and great distances have to be covered.

Driving between one Home and another in Poland or in Yugoslavia can mean some 300 to 700 miles. In addition, the weather can often be very bad. In winters there are blinding blizzards with snow and ice on the road and sleeting rain; the side and rear windows of the Land Rover and other vehicles fog up, and it is difficult even to see the wipers on the windscreen. In the cold one's hands within hours become chapped and the nails break; fortunately the cream specially prepared and made by a very handicapped artist-friend in Plsen has a most soothing effect. In summer the heat can be intense and the dust very troublesome; sometimes one sticks to the seat as one drives.

I have to plan every day and night of the itinerary with great precision with all who are involved, paying meticulous attention to detail, for unless I do this I am unable to fit into the time available the large volume of work awaiting me in these countries. Furthermore, the itinerary has to be synchronised with the availability of ministers, local authorities, social workers and others with whom we work so closely. It is probably true to say that the weeks preceeding these journeys are the most strenuous and intensive part of the year.

I do not know how to describe the awful pressures which build up a long time before I leave for the work in different parts of Britain, and especially when I go further afield overseas. I prefer during the preceding weeks to get to bed by 10 p.m. and to rise early, at 3 or 4 a.m., and thus concentrate in complete silence on sorting and clearing trayloads of correspondence.

I draw up two "Must Lists". The first one itemises action to be taken before leaving; the second one lists what I need to take with me. In drawing these up I always refer to my old lists in previous ring books and items on both lists are checked off one by one. These days are perhaps the most tiring of all as lists inevitably grow longer, and the pace and urgency of the work which has to be got through is unremitting. An hourly programme is written up for all essential work which has to be done.

We are always grateful when we do not have interruptions as there are many matters to attend to including recent mail and appointments for the months ahead. In the past there were also meetings with builders, engineers and contractors to ensure that all necessary building materials were on site. In countries such as Poland, it is essential to get the carcass up and clad with brick during the good weather between April and the end of September, so that internal work can proceed during the long and severe winter months. Nowadays these meetings are handled by Brian Muggleton the Senior Architect.

In past years we have also been busy packing very large lorries. Later on we used *Joshua*, the two-ton van given to the Foundation anonymously; afterwards we had Land Rovers. The gathering together of equipment, materials, wheelchairs and gifts is a major task, for the loading has to be done in such a way that things needed first on the journey are packed into the vehicle so that at each place we are able to find the relevant goods immediately and not waste time unloading and reloading. Lists are typed in triplicate in different languages. I have little space for my clothes – usually one suitcase marked "Personal" and an overnight bag – but I take certain supplies of food (according to my diet) and fuel so that I can be independent and make hot drinks during the long night or early morning drives.

Apart from this there used to be the correspondence with embassies of the countries concerned about passports and visas for the builders' tradesmen – plumbers, bricklayers, decorators, carpenters, electricians and floorlayers – who made up the teams going out to renovate existing Homes abroad or to erect new ones. While some of the tradesmen worked only on the renovation and restoration of the Foundation's properties in Britain, others come to one of the British Homes first for us to get to know each other, and after assisting us for two to three months they proceed overseas. They learn of the work from advertisements placed by the Foundation in trade journals, and most of them joined because they feel this is a practical way of doing something worthwhile and assisting others by using their own trade and experience.

Now, before I leave, pictures form in my mind of what lies ahead: the long drives; talks with patients, doctors, social workers, consultants, engineers, architects and others; their cultures and traditions. When I leave home I feel perhaps a little hesitant and the first few miles of the way pass in silence but then there is a warm welcome at Dover or Felixstowe aboard the P&O Ferries, formerly the Townsend Car Ferries, and the sight once more of familiar and friendly faces.

During all these years I have driven many different vehicles on my journeys. Later, because I had to convey people and goods, lorries were necessary: sometimes these have been called after the prophets, including *Job, Daniel, Ezekiel* and *Elijah*. The vehicles are thus named because it makes them more "alive" and they seem to become part of one's life. Once I get into the cab the vehicle becomes personal to me: driving reminds me of riding, of getting into the saddle and staying there. It is essential to keep the inside of the cab clean daily so I also carry a small hand brush and some cleaning cloths.

When I used the large three- five- and ten-ton lorries, there were two side lockers which were locked but not sealed by Customs, so that access to the tool and food boxes proved easy. Inside the cab, opposite the driving seat, I kept the jack and wheel-brace, and in a net above my head an extra pair of driving gloves, scarf, dark glasses and a second-hand warm cap. Behind the gear lever on the left was an extra container which held a bottle of fruit juice, cups, tissues and thermoses. Other supplies included things such as powdered coffee, butterscotch, Polo Mints, butter and cheese, and a sponge bag. When I stopped for refreshment I used either the top of the engine or the adjoining seat as a table.

In the past, motorways were very limited in number indeed, and therefore all the earlier travel was done over inferior road surfaces, including dirt tracks and cobbles. Most of the vehicles only had canvas flaps instead of doors. Heaters were unheard of and so were anti-freeze and de-icer. One had to unwind the windscreen if visibility became bad. Only in more recent years have I had the comfort of a well-sprung vehicle, and I can never get over having the luxury of a heater. People sound surprised to hear that I automatically switch to driving on the right at the port of arrival on the Continent. I have driven probably more overseas and thus it comes naturally.

On these journeys I have on occasions had to try and cope with various mechanical problems, and I am grateful for what I was taught in the FANY. In 1952 I also worked briefly at Rootes' well-known service centre in London, to gain more knowledge and to refresh my memory on the main-tenance of vehicles. I firmly believe that before drivers receive their licences they should be instructed on the necessity of maintaining and servicing the vehicle regularly; they should be told more graphically of the dangers to themselves and others of driving aggressively, and of the results, with possible multiple injury and disablement for the rest of their lives. As a doctor put it, it is the biggest epidemic of our time, but it will not be cured until the patient realises he is sick.

Quite a number of women were still employed at Rootes when I was there and were considered as assets and equals; indeed, their language and humour equalled the men's. We were attired in boiler suits and carried a tool box. On admittance each vehicle received a job card which had to be followed strictly. Time was allocated for *every* part of the work. In those days the chargehand was very strict and if we omitted to use the wing covers or were seen dawdling he used strong language. Once the work was finished the vehicle was driven to the inspection area, and if the inspectors were displeased it came back until the job was done to their complete satisfaction. As in the FANY, the engines were cleaned down and painted over with paraffin so that literally no dirt or dust could be found.

My journeys are planned so that most of the driving is done at night. I prefer this because hours can be saved avoiding the appalling volume of daytime traffic, particularly on the autobahns and motorways of Western Europe, and the huge juggernaut lorries, the roar and speed of which are horrible; in summer it is also cooler. I have seen so very many terrible and macabre accidents that I prefer to drive steadily. I remember on one of the many nights when conditions were atrocious seeing huge articulated lorries with extra trailers as long as the lorries themselves being spread-eagled over the road. One lorry driver said to me, "Now we start the hard part of the year again".

For the first twelve to fifteen years after the War there were endless diversions on the roads, principally in countries which had been devastated and where so much clearance of rubble and rebuilding was going on. These diversions were often not properly signposted, which added to the difficulties of the drives. On coming to new motorways even today often no signs are given and those that are there appear only at the last minute. Consequently, one has to be as sure as possible of one's bearings, which frequently involves making quick decisions. In winter, snow and ice cover the signs. The curves of many hills, roads and motorways stretching ahead are familar to me, often remembered in connection with some particular journey – usually one made in bad weather. When I get tired I *always* stop and pull in for a rest, keeping the engine running in very cold weather, and when I want to sleep I lock both doors and stretch out across the engine or the seat with my old soft pram pillow behind my head and take care to be well wrapped up.

At the end of each night's journey I note the distance, the route, weather conditions, and the time it has taken. I have always noted and filed these details of the journeys. Necessity has obliged me to drive at all times of the year and in all weathers, and this information has proved most useful, as I know whether I am behind or ahead of schedule, whatever the conditions.

Living out of a suitcase and always carrying files, boxes and drawings with me has been a part of my life for so long that it is a wonderful feeling to reach a place where I know I shall stay more than two nights. Nevertheless, out of long habit, I automatically return my night clothes to the overnight bag whether or not there are any drawers or cupboards (and usually there are none). Being able to stretch out, to wash and get the dirt off, and then luxuriate in a hot bath, not having to get up early or answer the telephone – these are very rare treats. Letters and messages, however, are with me all the time, awaiting me at every stop, and have to be answered whenever and wherever possible.

It has been my custom for many years to keep a daily journal in a ring book which I write up before I go to sleep each night. This can be quite a difficult task at the end of a particularly long day but I have always found that having a record at a later date is well worth the time and effort involved.

Offers of help with driving from drivers holding a clean licence have come in, but I prefer to drive myself while abroad because, in particular, I know the routes, and do not like to take responsibility for another person in this way; furthermore, I am then free to stop and rest and to start very early in the morning before dawn breaks. Another main reason is that accommodation everywhere is extremely cramped. Moreover these drives provide some of the rare occasions when I can find quietness and solitude away from the telephone and other distractions. There is time for meditation and prayer, which I find absolutely necessary. On the quieter roads it is like a spiritual retreat: one can admire the flowers, trees and birds, and I like especially watching the sky, the starlit nights, the sunrises and sunsets.

When the Foundation operated in Greece (prior to the Colonels' coup in 1967) there were the long drives to the villages and towns there. I also travelled on the overcrowded car ferries to Crete, where at night I would climb up onto a cupboard on deck and go to sleep listening to the dashing and lapping of the waves against the ship's side and wake to see the sun glistening upon the sea.

During these long journeys one is aware all the time of the number of people who are waiting for assistance, of the great gaps in the existing services and the many we never reach. The volume of requests for help is very great, and one can become exhausted or perhaps it is better to say frustrated, longing for dibs (funds) and for people to realise that suffering *could* be relieved if only the funds were available. After a day filled with discussion, meetings, difficulties, frustrations, greetings and farewells, it is essential to find solitude for awhile.

Whenever I stop for brief breaks – preferably in a wood to listen to the birds and to enjoy nature – I brew up decaffeinated coffee or drink apple juice and write up my notes, but all too soon it is necessary to continue my journey in order to keep to the tight itineraries.

My constant criss-crossing of frontiers has taught many of the Customs authorities to recognise the Foundation's familiar blue vehicles. Usually I have no trouble with the frontier authorites – indeed, I am generally greeted with kindness and good humour – but it does depend upon the particular officials who happen to be on duty on any given night. If the man in charge knows me, then there is no need to produce the *laissez passer* document (which is in five languages) – I am waved through. Occasionally, however, a bored or difficult official examines the *laissez passer* and goes round the sealed lorry with his torch.

Years ago, because of thick fog, I was late for a rendezvous at 2 a.m. at the frontier post at Aachen. The son of Dr Wagner, an old friend and senior official of the German Red Cross, had waited with a letter for me from his father; but believing that I had decided to return to Belgium until the fog had cleared, he left the letter with the Customs authorities and went home. On arrival at the frontier post I presented a letter of introduction from the German Ambassador to Britain, but the officials refused to accept it. Confronted by five men, I tried to strengthen my position by saying: "Well, to prove to you whom I represent, here is a letter from the Red Cross, this one which you have just handed to me, in addition to the letter I have just shown you from your Ambassador." They denied, however, all knowledge of the fact that Dr Wagner's son had been waiting for me, and demanded DM20 for the transit of *Liebesgaben* (gift parcels or comforts). An unnecessary and time-wasting argument followed, which lasted for nearly two hours, but finally the point was won by my bluffing and saying: "Look it up in your *Gesetz-Liebesgaben*, and under such-and-such a paragraph you will find that *Liebesgaben* may be taken through free of charge." On another occasion, an official complained: "This is an ambulance, yet there are no patients in it." I replied, "When it is full of walking aids, wheelchairs, and everything?" On another occasion the authorities wanted me to count the number of clout and twist nails, not to mention raisins.

At Waidhaus on the German-Czech frontier, near Flossenburg (where Pastor Dietrich Bonhoeffer was hanged on 9 April 1945), I invariably meet with courtesy from the Germans, before I go through a stretch of no-man's-land and on to meet the friendly Czechs waiting at the frontier post on a steep hill. They offer the use of their loo and give me boiling water for the thermos. One night, however, when I was accompanied by Ann Batt of the *Daily Express* we found Czech officials on duty whom I did not know. They told me that a new regulation had been made, and that for any vehicle of two tons and over in weight, tax had to be paid. I asked them for their co-operation, but they explained that the authorities to whom they had to refer had gone home. They gave up their office to us and we stretched out on chairs with the border officials' thick coats over us, for it was very cold, despite the stove in the room, and dozed until Prague could be consulted at 6 a.m. Officials there confirmed that we might proceed. On arrival in Prague, the legal adviser at the British Embassy who had contacts in the right quarter obtained a special certificate, as has been issued every year since, which enabled me to travel into Czechoslovakia freely and without paying tax.

In 1989, Czechoslovakia's freedom was at last attained through the people's great courage, patience and faith. Their hero, President Havel, was released from nine years in different prisons, so they have no problems – except queues of vehicles, waiting for hours while the understaffed officials try to cope with checking everyone's passports.

On each journey to Plsen I attend Mass at the Cathedral of St Bartholomew, the grandiose building founded in 1292 and built of sandstone. In a niche above the tabernacle over the high altar stands a graceful statue of the Holy Madonna which dates probably from the time of Charles IV of Bohemia (1346–78). Here, in this City too, there are welcomes from many people. One of them was the late Mr Ota Musika, who was handicapped as a result of his suffering at the hands of the Germans, and often in great pain. He used to take great enjoyment in fishing and painting. He wrote to a supporter:

> Sue Ryder has accepted me among her big "family" and whenever she comes to Plsen she visits us, always ready to help in any possible way. I am very thankful and pray for her health every day.

On the many journeys through Czechoslovakia, the women who often serve on the petrol pumps have got to know me, and spontaneously offer me the use of their loo. Members of the Czech and Slovak Armies, too, have helped me to find street numbers or to empty diesel from the jerry can into the tank.

Often I spend a night or more in Prague, an historic City of great beauty, known as "the City of a hundred spires" and "the golden City". Of Prague the poet, Frantisek Kosic, wrote: "She has always been a symbol of dignity, tenderness and mystery, a real mother to her sons, whose hearts are deeply imprinted with her suffering. She has also been a witness to their greatest glory and joy."

A member of the Czech Government used to ask me to a working breakfast at which he discussed the problems of the handicapped. He himself had been a prisoner in the Terezin (Theresienstadt)* Concentration Camp and would say to me; "I agree that Terezin must remain in the past. We forgive, although we do not forget. I always remember that the Germans gave birth to Beethoven and Goethe. He called to mind Goethe's *Es Liebt die Welt*:

> The world loves to denigrate the glorious
> and to drag what is sublime into the mire.
> But don't be afraid, there are still noble
> hearts which glow for what is true and glorious.

In various parts of Czechoslovakia I visit the housebound and try to provide wheelchairs and hoists and other aids. The following is one example from many letters received:

I received your letter with joy. Thank you very much for writing and coming again.

For those who will be subscribing towards the cost of my longed-for wheelchair, they may be interested to hear that I was born on 9 February 1947. When I left elementary school I was unable to obtain entrance to the commercial school despite the fact that I had a good record, so I became a motor mechanic's apprentice and attended courses. Sport I enjoyed and to my surprise I even received the odd medal. Unfortunately when jumping off a springboard at the swimming pool I broke my neck and am therefore a paraplegic. The consultants and nurses gave me hope to live. I gradually began to move my hands and after being in hospital was sent on a rehabilitation course. There in Marinbad my dad visited me every afternoon, he travelled by train and returned home late at night. Dad worked in the nationalised petrol department. He was unable to sleep during this time (nine months) but dozed during the train journeys. As a handicapped person I was then moved to another rehabilitation unit, but there my dad could only visit twice a week on his moped. Each way took six to seven hours.

From August 1963 I have been at home and have been looked after by my mum. She gave up her job. I loved my dad a lot and we understood each other very well. It is only a small part of their sacrifice that I write about. Dad died suddenly in October 1978 – a terrible blow to us both. My mum won't leave me, but I must confess that I am very unhappy about my future. Naturally, I prefer to be as independent as possible, but I cannot get a job and, as you know, there are several steps up to our small flat and whenever I want to go out I am dependent upon my friends to lift me down and up again. I am hopeful that the Ministry will provide me with a hoist – in fact, I am now ninety per cent certain that I shall receive one.

---

*In Theresienstadt Concentration Camp, which was completely separate from the ghetto for the Jews in the town, there were 140,000 prisoners of whom 11,000 were children of many nationalities.

Later he wrote:

> I want to thank you from the bottom of my heart for the arrival of the wheelchair. I sent the Customs Authorities the doctor's certificate and a friend went to Prague to collect the chair. I am delighted with this, so much so I cannot begin to describe my feelings in words. It is sensational, the type I dreamed about when my father was alive.
>
> My dear Lady, I am deeply grateful to you. I trust you will visit us soon when you are next in Czechoslovakia. It has been a long winter. I haven't been out since my father died, that is almost 900 days.
>
> Now, with the help of the wheelchair you sent me and a good friend I shall be able, on a warm day, to get out into the open air and see something of the countryside.

It is hard to single out individuals for special mention but one of the many who has shown great strength in adversity was the late Alice Komlos who became blind. When she was a teenager she stayed with a family in Sheffield and became almost bilingual; she looks back on those days with affection. Later, she married and lived in Budapest. Her husband disappeared during the War and has never been heard of since. She was forced to work as an interpreter and her struggle for survival both during and after the War is quite remarkable. Throughout those years she remained an avid reader and tutor of English. Her brother-in-law was arrested, together with her nephew, and both were liberated in 1945 from Belsen. The nephew, Stefan, had been so badly beaten by the Nazis that later he became an epileptic and, though he had worked before the War as a textile merchant, he never recovered his health and became totally dependent on his mother after his father died. After her death his Aunt Alice had to look after him until he died, though she was then in her early eighties. Their existence, confined within the four walls of their room, was pathetic. Each morning they would listen to the BBC World Service as a link with England, and I was one of their few visitors.

I would like to mention the friendship I have always enjoyed with both the Czechs and Slovaks. Until the Nazi occupation of the country in March 1939, Czechoslovakia was one of the most politically and technologically advanced states in Europe. In November 1989, after fifty-one years of cruel domination – first by the Germans and then by the Soviets – the country peacefully regained its freedom. The unrestrained joy of the huge crowds was wonderful to see as they applauded Václav Havel, their new President, who as a dissident spent nine years in a Communist prison, and Alexander Dubček – a hero of an earlier time.

The Communists confiscated 6,000 beautiful buildings, including countless exquisite churches. Many became slums, either through neglect or because they were used as stores. The Prague Heritage Fund created by HRH Prince Charles and Václav Havel (both the original owners, and the Religious have been offered their properties back) are now extremely short of funds to carry out the essential work of restoration.

Alas bureaucracy slows down the whole process of restitution therefore frustration is inevitable.

The Czechs are keen that the Foundation converts as many as possible of the suitable buildings into Sue Ryder Homes for the thousands of sick and handicapped children and adults who are in need. Work has been started on one historic building in a poor part of Prague and the Foundation fully realises its responsibilities both towards these people and to the buildings neglected for decades.

In 1948 I was in Prague during the Communist coup when Jan Masaryk was murdered by being thrown out of an upper floor window.

In August 1968, two days after the Red Army invaded Czechoslovakia, I drove my lorry over the Polish border into that country – one of the very, very few to be allowed to do so. I was accompanied by Hilary Phayre, one of my Personal Assistants. The scenes that greeted us were indescribable. Within hours of the invasion the Slovaks and Czechs had barricaded the road around each town and city and erased names on every street sign. They had also destroyed or turned the signposts round. Slogans were written in Russian, pinned to trees, bridges and written on the roads: "*Russians go back to the Soviet Union*".

The power was cut off each night. It was like sitting on a tinder box, such was the atmosphere! We expected fighting to break out at any moment. The Soviets were removing watches, clocks, and anything else they could from their victims on the streets. These, whom they had invaded, were climbing on the tanks telling them to go home.

On the outskirts of Olomouc I stopped to sleep because of sheer fatigue. Hilary was sleeping in the back of the lorry and I was slumped over the steering wheel when at 5 a.m., I was abruptly awakened by Russian soldiers, who thumped on the window with their rifles. In my limited Russian I told them to go away and to my astonishment and theirs, they did just that, and fortunately did not ask to see what I had in the back of the lorry. We were carrying wheelchairs, crutches and so on, to housebound patients in their homes. It was vital to keep up our visits and share this ghastly experience with them. Russians were swarming about like flies and their heavy armour was everywhere – even a moment's privacy in the woods proved a problem!

One of us always had to stay with the lorry while the other carried or humped one of the gifts to the waiting and long-suffering patients.

Perhaps one of the most horrendous sights was the vast ring of the Soviet Army surrounding the outskirts of Prague on the hillsides. We did not really expect to get through this but by a miracle we succeeded in doing so after only waiting a few hours.

We stopped to express our feelings with friends in Prague. One Anna Frankova wrote a note and slipped this into my bag. It read:

> Each of us knows you will never desert us or cease to pray. May God give
> us all strength to increase our Faith.

In 1969 I was very near to Wenceslas Square to witness Jan Palac's suicide. This student set himself on fire and later I met Dr Jaroslaba Mozerova who treated him before he died. The whole city was in mourning and on the day of his funeral huge crowds filled the streets and were everywhere.

Due to the steady stream of people bearing flowers and lighted candles to his grave, the State Secret Police removed his body from the cemetery to an unknown place. He was not reburied until 1989.

Jan Palac's death was followed by another student, Jan Zajic, who also set himself on fire in Wenceslas Square. Both these young people died in protest of the Soviet Union invasion and occupation.

In 1993, to the dismay of many admirers of the Czechoslovak people, the country formally separated into its constituent parts of Slovakia and the Czech Republic.

These journeys through Europe are memorable not only because of the friendliness and hospitality of the majority of the people I meet, but also because of the intense interest shown by the people of Central Europe in English literature and history. It is not at all unusual to be asked at two in the morning in any town, city or village there to expound upon the *Canterbury Tales*, to describe Oxford, or to explain the meaning of expressions such as "the back of beyond", "being at a loose end" or "somewhat the worse for wear". It is sometimes far from easy to get over to the inquirer in simple terms the significance of such expressions – particularly at that hour of the morning! On many occasions I am asked to explain technical terms which appear in English books in the possession of some of the people I meet. There was one occasion when I was asked by a specialist engineer to explain a highly technical term contained in a book about the stresses involved in bridge-building, a subject which fascinated me, but about which, unfortunately, I knew little.

The Foundation has been given a 99-year lease on an eighteenth-century university cloister in a peaceful corner of Prague. However, just a mile or two from the Home, the poverty and needs, especially of older people on pensions, are evident in the "third category" housing without running water. Privatisation of the health-care system has meant deprivation of basic care for those who need it most.

As well as reconstructing the Home, we are aiming to assist with domiciliary care, especially for people with cancer, and the 600 who have Huntington's disease. Most of the latter live with their families or are resident in inadequately staffed mental illness wards, with little attention given to the special needs of themselves and their families. At least thirty beds are also urgently needed to provide palliative care for those who have undergone radiotherapy. At present, there are only 123 beds for a City of 1.4 million inhabitants. There should be at least 170, or many more.

The small Foundation Council and its supporters, including International and Czech Companies, have raised well over £400,000 towards the Sue

Ryder Home at Michle Court. There has been a great variety of ways in which this money has been raised, and I can only mention a few here. A Fashion Show was held in the Liechtenstein Palace and was a show of the designs by young Czech designers, using professional models. There was also a show of Sue Ryder second-hand, upmarket clothes, again modelled by professionals.

Then there was Europe's first-ever one-day cricket tournament, sponsored by a British Company. This was followed by a treasure hunt in which all car drivers dressed as musketeers searching for the crown jewels. Each car that entered had a driver and co-pilot and paid £500 to take part in a one-day clue hunt in the countryside. At the end of the day their average distance covered was seventy-five miles. Local companies again donated prizes to the winners. This treasure hunt proved to be a great success with the Press.

Another great success was Prague's first-ever pantomine, a sell-out on both nights with nearly 600 tickets sold! Members of the expat community wrote, produced, directed, and acted in *Cinderella*. Memorable new characters were Daninoff, the Russian Butler, and Bad Penny and Bad Smell, the SSB (State Security Service). Fortunately everything ended happily ever after. The final Saturday night was so packed a rather worried-looking theatre employee said "I don't know whether the balcony will hold up, we haven't used it since World War II (May 1945)".

This fund-raising has built up much support and good-will to enable the Foundation to thrive in that part of Europe.

Training is a very important aspect of all our services here, since nurses receive no State further education and, although very dedicated, even under extreme pressure, are not trained to provide some necessary treatment.

After fifty years of moral oppression, there are encouraging signs of faith in dignity and love: groups of doctors tackling ethical issues that have become blurred over two generations, as well as an encouraging response from volunteers and officials to the Sue Ryder Foundation. Many Czechs and Slovaks have volunteered for work in Britain and have helped us on their return – among them are enthusiastic students and also Pani Josepfina and Pani Eda, who cheerfully tackle any task. Above all, the dedicated and devout Novak family from Zvahov provide the example for the young team in Prague, which has to cope with suffocating red tape.

Many years will be needed to restore values that have been neglected for decades, and our own efforts are a small part of a wider determination to help on the part of many dedicated people.

* * *

One of the most wonderful things about these journeys is the kindness and hospitality of other people, both known and unknown. Total strangers have often invited me into their room and given me a warm and wonderful welcome, and many times after Mass a priest has invited me to breakfast with him and has given me the opportunity of having a good wash. One kind host woke up the local grocer at 4 a.m. to provide extra ingredients for a meal, which included chicken soup and noodles, in spite of my protestations. In the days when there was hardly anything to eat, they would offer me their only piece of bread or their last drop of coffee. In the presence of such incredibly warm and generous hospitality one felt very humble. Nothing was too much trouble. When there were not enough beds, they would be shared, and on many occasions people have offered me the use of their own bed. I can still hear the familiar voices of women friends on the routes awakening me in English with the words, "Darling, it's time now".

I can always rest assured that people, particularly in Central, Eastern and Southern Europe, will go to great lengths to give personal assistance regardless of the weather conditions. One night during one of the longest and worst winters in Poland, when the snow was unusually heavy with drifts several feet high, a tractor was sent out to tow the lorry because the last two miles of the road leading to the Home I was making for were blocked and ridged with frozen snow; I remember particularly the glow of the rear lights on the tractor and the chugging of the engine in the dark. The driver was young and did not seem to appreciate the danger of the lorry overturning and at one point called out to me: "Come on, you can only die once!" On the return journey after two days at the Home, the tractor was replaced by two horses.

At Kudowa, the Polish-Czechoslovak frontier crossing, I was sometimes offered hot coffee when this was available. On another occasion, at the border post at Cieszyn, when the frontier formalities were over and before I climbed back into the lorry, the Polish customs and passport officials (a woman and several men) came to kiss me goodbye and hand me some tulips. At this, the Czech Customs and passport officials said: "Although we haven't any flowers for you, you know that you have our hearts." They waved me farewell as I drove off on another stage of the long journey over the bridge linking the two countries, with the gushing river below and the water gleaming in the moonlight.

I remember, too, an experience at about midnight in the centre of the historic City of Olomouc where some experts on pollution were attending a conference. They were strolling in the streets and deeply engaged in conversation. When they saw me in the lorry *Joshua* they asked me to join them; I found their company enchanting as they expounded on the fascinating beauty of rare butterflies and plants, and for a while we were lost in discussion about nature and far removed from man and his problems.

One Czech professor had such happy memories of Cambridge that details and individual histories of the colleges were vivid in his memory. He added, "I know I would not be allowed to return there but I live on these memories and they help to keep me sane".

In winter the avenues of hard, snow-laden fir trees are particularly lovely. The tapes on the cassette recorder give me great pleasure and companionship as I drive on my way, and I think about my husband and family and look forward to hearing from them. I am reminded of notes and letters which were often given me, or left for me by Mama, before such journeys in the past, and the following I have always carried with me:

Child of My love, fear not the unknown morrow,
Dread not the new demand life makes of thee;
Thy ignorance doth hold no cause for sorrow
Since what thou knowest not is known to Me.

Thou canst not see today the hidden meaning
Of My command, but thou the light shalt gain;
Walk on in faith, upon My promise leaning,
And as thou goest all shall be made plain.

One step thou seest – then go forward boldly,
One step is far enough for faith to see;
Take that, and thy next duty shall be told thee,
For step by step thy Lord is leading thee.

Stand not in fear, thy adversaries counting,
Dare every peril, save to disobey;
Thou shalt march on, all obstacles surmounting,
For I, the Strong, will open up the way.

Wherefore go gladly to the task assigned thee,
having My promise, needing nothing more
Than just to know, where'ere the future find thee,
In all thy journeying I go before.

                                        Frank J. Exley

People have asked me what mileage I have covered in my life. I have never kept a true record, but on average, I have driven over 40,000 miles a year; and as I have driven since I was sixteen years of age, this amounts to quite a large figure.

I have described only a few of my journeys. Since 1989 the frontiers have been opened, but depending upon the time of year there are now often extremely long queues waiting to cross from one country to another. During this waiting time it is a relief to notice the absence of watchtowers, Alsatian dogs, huge minefields and barbed-wire fencing.

After miles and miles of travel, it is a real pleasure and relief to cross the Belgian frontier and, until her retirement, to be assured on the telephone by the friendly and cheerful voice of Mrs Eva Johnston at the Car Ferries at Zeebrugge that, regardless of how busy they were, a place would be reserved for my vehicle and that I could also be assured of a cabin with hot water and the chance of a deep sleep. Fortunately for me, nowadays, the P&O European Ferries offer the same hospitality and kindness. I also enjoy a bag of hot chips on my way back to England, and I can never forget what it feels like to see the lights in the docks at Zeebrugge, and more recently the vast Europort at Rotterdam; to be welcomed on board the freight ferry and to reach Headquarters again, sometimes in the still of night as the church clock strikes three. I remember how wonderful it was to be welcomed by Leonard, when he was not on his travels. I have vivid, indelible memories, too, of driving through the early hours of the morning, hearing the dawn chorus through green lanes and quiet villages, reflecting on the past weeks and the hospitality, and recalling the kindness and the courage of the children and adults who, in spite of so many difficulties and disappointments, have expressed such great warmth, affection and fortitude.

15

Poland – Ruins and Rebuilding

These are the times which try men's souls.

Thomas Paine (1776)

I

I FEEL I BELONG to Poland. This colourful country, so often misunderstood, known to comparatively few and because of its geographical position subjected through its long history to attacks from its more powerful neighbours, is one with which I have been closely associated for over forty years. With its tradition of folklore and strongly marked regional culture, Poland, thanks to the fierce spirit of independence of its people, has never lost its resilience and determination to resist, despite frequent invasions and several partitions.

Here are the dates between 1794–1921 of the Polish Uprisings:

1794: the Kościuszko led Insurrection against the Russians.
1830: the November Insurrection which led to the Russo-Polish War of 1831.
1848: Wielkopolska Rising against the Prussians.
1863: the January Rising against the Russians, crushed in 1864.
1918–19: Wielkopolska Rising against the Germans.
1919: First Silesian Rising against the Germans.
1920: Second Silesian Rising against the Germans.
1921: Third Silesian Rising against the Germans.

Later Uprisings are described in previous Chapters. It has emerged as one of the most interesting countries in Europe.

At the end of the First World War (1918), Poland gained her Independence, only to be immediately invaded by the Bolsheviks during the Russian Revolution. In August 1920 Poland defeated the Red Army in the decisive Battle for Warsaw on the river Vistula and drove the Red Army back to Russia.

It was invaded again in September 1939 by the German and Soviet Armies, and the country was divided into three parts. The Germans incorporated the western part of Poland into the Reich and the Soviet Union annexed the eastern region. Poles were deported in huge numbers by both the Germans and the Russians, and the Germans replaced the Poles with many of their own people. Between 1939 and 1945 it lost six million of its citizens, and a very high percentage of its wealth and physical assets.

The central part of Poland was occupied by German forces and named the General Government. The Governor General was Hitler's former notorious lawyer, Reichsminister Hans Frank, who unleashed a reign of terror. He lived in the famous and beautiful Wawel Castle in Kraków, previously the seat of Polish kings. Frank was later convicted at Nuremberg and hanged for his part in the Nazi activities in Poland. He was one of the very few Nazis to be hanged.

The central and north-western part of the country is a broad plain; the north-east has an undulating landscape dotted with many small lakes; and in the South stretch the Carpathian and Tatra mountains, range upon range for over 800 miles.

Nothing impressed me more in Poland than the tremendous determination of the Poles to clear hundreds of acres of ruin and devastation and construct new cities, towns and villages. They were built with extraordinary devotion and skill, under the greatest difficulties, by men and women who had steadfastly refused to accept defeat. Of all the many triumphs which I witnessed in the wreckage of Europe, this will to build a new life for their children made the deepest impression on me.

Without outside financial assistance and equipment for the first few years, the task of rebuilding proved even more daunting – so huge and never-ending efforts were made to collect money. The Allies (British and American) at the Yalta Conference allowed the Soviets to set up a Soviet-style Government in Lublin in the eastern part of Poland near the Russian frontier during the summer of 1944, and so this money was collected in from some of the following ways:

1. Vast quantities of Lublin Government red zlotys (Polish currency) were printed in the Soviet Union until the Poles were allowed to print their own currency in 1946–7.
2. The black market was rife and farmers brought in produce on foot or in a horse and cart – if they still owned one – and traded this for zlotys.
3. Special postage stamps were issued and sold.
4. Bricks recovered by hand from the mountains of rubble were sold. It must be remembered that thousands of people were starving and obliged to eat horses. Therefore, the clearing of the rubble and rebuilding seemed all the more miraculous.

The actual clearing of these areas of rubble not only in Warsaw but in all other major cities and towns (only three were spared from destruction) began early in 1945. Thousands of mines had to be cleared, too, and many engineers and others were killed or injured in this work.

There were special conservation groups and both Cardinal Hlond and later Cardinal Wyszyński formed RADA (Prymasowska Rada Odbudowy Kosciolow) which functioned for thirty years.

After Stalin's death in 1953, the political situation improved and funds from patriotic Poles in other countries of the world were collected and helped enormously.

Two industrial companies in Poland itself undertook to rebuild two famous Palaces. The Ministry of Culture and Arts too helped in every possible way. There was a sense of great pride, devotion and determination. The initial work was done with the bare hands of those (including many of the young), who suffered from shortages and privations of every kind. Much of the labour was carried out by teams of volunteers, and everyone, irrespective of age and status, took part. The devastation was daunting in its immensity, but at the same time challenging in the opportunities it provided. I was reminded of the words written by Charles Kingsley:

> Thank God every morning when you get up that you have something to do that day which must be done, whether you like it or not. Being forced to work and forced to do your best will breed in you temperance and self-control, diligence and strength of will, cheerfulness and content and a hundred virtues which the idle will never know.

Professor Jan Zachwatowicz was the chief architect responsible for the reconstruction of the whole of Warsaw. In this City alone some 710 out of a total of 800 important historical buildings were reduced to rubble. They have been patiently and lovingly reconstructed in every detail, whether the style was Gothic, Renaissance, Baroque or neo-Classical, including the sculptures, relief work, mural paintings, fixtures and decorations. Fortunately, complete sketches and inventories of every valuable building were preserved in hiding or in foreign archives. In some cases an old church or palace was restored according to its original design with later accretions omitted, so that the reconstructed Old City (*Stare Miasto*) now looks more like its original self as the nineteenth- and twentieth-century houses were not rebuilt. An up-to-date and most striking example of such reconstruction is the rebuilding, in every detail, of the Royal Castle, under the supervision of the late Professor Stanisław Lorentz and his team.

Of all the reconstructed buildings in Warsaw, the Royal Castle is the largest and most impressive. Originally a Renaissance building standing on mediaeval foundations, it had undergone many repairs and alterations in the course of the centuries before the Second World War.

Jerzy Lileyko in his book *A Companion Guide to the Royal Castle of Warsaw* gives the following description:

> It is possible that there were two fortified residential complexes on the site of the present Castle as early as the fourteenth Century – Curia Minor (the small court) and Curia Major (the large court). In the fifteenth Century a monumental Gothic building was erected, called The Large House, as the first ducal residence on the Vistula escarpment (preserved until 1744).
>
> Then, in the sixteenth Century, The Large House was transformed into the Sejm Parliamentary Building. This transformation of The Large House into the Parliament (Sejm) deserves our attention as, for the first time in Poland, and doubtless in Europe, an attempt had been made to construct a building which was intended exclusively for parliamentary use. It is interesting to note that until 1611 Warsaw was the seat of the Sejm (Parliament) but Kraków was the capital, and the Kings had to make constant journeys

to Warsaw. It was Sigismund III who transferred the Royal Residence to Warsaw (1596).

Plans for an enlarged Warsaw Castle were drawn up by the Court Designer, Giovanni Trevano. King Sigismund III's son, Lidislaus, built a monument in memory of his father, and until today the Column of Sigismund is one of the most prominent landmarks in Warsaw. The Castle interior acquired rich decorations in all rooms, including the Marble Room, and many historical and beautiful paintings; also numerous tapestries.

In 1637 a new theatre was built within the Castle and an Italian opera was transported to Poland as early as the 1630s and 40s. Shakespeare's plays were presented, which is an indication of the high standard of culture at the Royal Court.

In 1764–95 Stanisław August Poniatowski, the last Polish King and a famous patron of the arts, planned to rebuild the Castle completely, but very few of his plans were carried out.

After the partition of Poland, Warsaw came under Russian domination and the Royal Castle was downgraded to the role of a governor's residence and the Royal Library was converted into barracks.

After the recovery of Independence the Castle became a palatial building, and in 1926 the permanent residence of the President of the Polish Republic.

On the 13 September 1939 the Castle became the object of mass shelling. At the same time, St John's Cathedral nearby was set on fire. Heroic efforts were made by the Mayor of the City, Stefan Starzyński, who sent teams of architects and fire engines. They tried against all odds and under constant aerial bombardment to save (and later hide) the works of art. The Bacciarelli ceiling representing "The Dissolution of Chaos" was completely destroyed. Some of the rescuers were wounded or killed by artillery fire.

Professor Stanisław Lorentz, Director of the National Museum, and his team, which included Jadwiga Przeworska (murdered in the Ghetto in 1942), led other teams, including Boy Scouts and hundreds of others.

Once the German Forces had broken through the fierce resistance and reached the City of Warsaw, they started a systematic looting of the Castle. Hitler sent a telegram to the infamous Governor Frank, who wrote: "The Fuhrer . . . has approved . . . destruction of the Royal Castle in Warsaw and the decision not to rebuild the city."

The tasks still facing Professor Gieysztor and Dr Morszkawski are truly awe inspiring. Both were completely dedicated to their work.

The Throne Room, Chambers of Parliament, the Chapel, Ballroom and many more rooms were completed between 1971 and 1984.

Professor Gieysztor, during a visit to London, attended a session in the House of Lords to witness protocol and study the seating arrangements, etc. This would be of help to him in planning the restoration of the Parliamentary Rooms in the Castle.

I have always felt overwhelmed at each stage of this huge building reconstruction and by the amazing degree of perfection given to every item, including the period furniture.

To visit the Old City in Warsaw now is a most poignant experience. It is floodlit at night and only pedestrians and horse-drawn carriages are permitted, the clip-clop of hooves adding to the old-world atmosphere as young and old stroll through the squares and streets.

Similar restoration has taken place in Gdańsk, Wroclaw, Bialystok, Poznań, Szczecin and all other ruined cities with results of which the Poles are justly proud.

In this Chapter it would be unfair not to pay ample tribute to the remarkable resurgence of the arts in Poland. The theatres are blossoming, some films receive international fame, and here I would like to mention the dance group Mazowsze, which has become famous. It was established in 1948 by two distinguished artists, the musician, Tadeusz Sygietyński, and his wife, Mira Ziminska. They had always been fascinated by the melodies' rhythms, the intricate dance figures and extremely colourful costumes of their country, and their aim in founding the Mazowsze was to bring to the stage the traditional dances and songs of Poland, perfected over generations. To select the first members of the company, the Sygietyńskis toured the villages of Poland and auditioned more than 5,000 boys and girls. No song or dance was subsequently incorporated into the Mazowsze programme unless it met with the approval of the performers. In recent years the company has toured the world on several occasions and has been widely acclaimed as one of the world's finest ensembles. The Ballet Slask Ensemble has also acquired international fame.

The other aspect of Poland which moved me profoundly is its strong religious life. Since 966, when it first received the faith, Poland has been a deeply religious country; the Catholic Church, with its tradition and teaching, cementing and uplifting the people throughout those long centuries of oppression and struggle, and linking them to the millions of Catholics throughout the world.

Between 1939–45 the Germans destroyed some 912 churches and cathedrals throughout Poland. Of these 871 were lately rebuilt, with funds from various sources, which included contributions from individual Polish citizens, subsidies from the Polish Government's Department of Arts and Monuments, and gifts from foreign Foundations. The number of new churches being built now total 834.

We do not know the exact number of cases where the Communists refused permission to build, but this did not normally deter the parish priests. Building took place very quickly at night, despite the constant threat of arrest. The whole village or small town turned out to help on the site under strong lights. Rings of men, women and children surrounded and protected them.

Where there are Polish minorities in the Ukraine and White Russia, they have restored existing churches. These were used by the Nazis for grain stores, cinemas, sport halls and so on, and later by the Soviets as Atheist Museums. Some were completely filled to the roof with salt, which the Poles removed with hand-made wooden spades and wheelbarrows. The restoration was remarkable.

Today there are approximately 14,653 churches and cathedrals throughout Poland. They are always open, filled with the strong scent of incense and usually with many worshippers coming and going. In the larger churches and certainly all those in populated areas, as many as ten Masses are said or sung on a Sunday, with great crowds of people attending and thousands walking to church dressed in their best clothes, some in regional costumes – the young girls looking very cheerful with bright bows or ribbons in their hair. On weekdays, Mass is also well attended, and people on their way to work will call in for Holy Communion, or on their way back stop for Benediction – a custom that is still preserved in Poland.

The Poles are not only romantic, they are intensely aware of their long historic traditions and they are renowned for their hospitality. As so many of their customs are unknown outside their country, I would like to record some of them here. Naturally, these customs vary slightly from one part of the country to the other, but basically they originate from centuries of tradition and are based upon Christian festivals.

Following the Feast of All Saints on 1 November is All Souls Day. Both are national holidays. On the Feast of All Souls it is quite normal for people to travel long distances by train or bus and walk miles to cemeteries in towns and villages to visit their families' or friends' graves, on which they place flowers and candles and then pray. By nightfall the cemeteries are ablaze with candles and *znicze* (night lights) are left to commemorate the dead.

The period of Advent in late November and December is strictly observed as a preparation for Christmas. *Roraty* – a daily Mass – is said, which all children too are expected to attend. They make and carry colourful lamps. Before the War this Mass was always held at 6 a.m., but nowadays it is held in the evening, and the sight of the congregation walking to and from church has a special meaning.

Even during the years of economic recovery and relatively fair standards of living in the 1960s, I cannot remember being conscious of materialism at this time of the year. Naturally, there was, and still is, an air of expectancy and excitement, especially amongst children; but not the bursting opulence and even vulgar evidence of trade by, alas, many people in the wealthy countries, some of whom buy for the sake of buying. So, for the Poles, Christmas is the most festive holiday in Poland next to Easter. Everywhere in Poland the customs of Christmas are practised in the way I had learnt from the Poles in SOE, as described in Chapter 4.

Long ago in monasteries Christmas Eve supper consisted of twelve simple courses, one for each Apostle. The meal (for the majority) begins with red *barszcz* made from beetroot, together with *uszka* (a kind of ravioli with mushrooms), followed by herrings (two kinds – either in oil or pickled). There are one, two or even three kinds of fish, usually including carp which in previous years was not expensive or considered a luxury in Poland. It is either boiled and served with a sauce, or fried. *Compote* (stewed fruit) made from dried fruit (mainly prunes and apricots) is also served. Different cakes are eaten, principally poppy-seed cake, as masses of poppies are grown by the poorer people in the country areas, and honey cake (*piernik*).

For children, Christmas Eve is considered the most lovely evening of the year on which the magic of fairy tale becomes real for a few hours in the lights of the Christmas tree, under which loving hands have placed whatever modest gift they can afford. A wide variety of carols is also sung. Then everybody walks through the snow to Midnight Mass (*Pasterka*). The Infant Jesus is placed in the crib in the "manger". The churches have packed congregations and the Mass is long as it is sung, and everyone again joins in the singing of numerous beautiful carols. Everybody is ready for sleep in the early hours of 25 December, which is spent with the family some of whom again attend Mass.

*   *   *

My memories of Lent in Poland remind me of fasting in my childhood, especially on Ash Wednesday and Good Friday. The religious ceremonies are very long and solemn and the congregations so large that the people spill outside the church into the surrounding areas. The priests always used to distribute Holy Communion when the person was kneeling, however dense the crowd. Although exceptions have been made in recent years and people can now receive the Host while standing, the former practice is normally adhered to. A linen cloth is draped over the Communion rail and this is thrown over the communicants' hands before Communion is given.

After the Mass of the last Supper on Maundy Thursday evening the Blessed Sacrament is carried in procession to the Altar of Repose (*Chodzic no groby*). This is different in every church and people walk from one church to the other to pray at these altars.

I find it extremely difficult to describe the ethereal beauty of the Altars of Repose. The figure of our crucified Lord lies on the altar and there is exposition of the Blessed Sacrament. All around this area there is a mass of flowers of every kind and colour, intermingled with beautiful pot plants. Usually a spotlight shines down on this incredible scene of adoration with thousands of children and people in fervent prayer. To me it feels like being very near Heaven.

On Easter Saturday the food is prepared for Easter Sunday and is taken to be blessed with holy water by the priest. The Easter Vigil, which begins at sundown, lasts for several hours, and again thousands swell the numbers of the congregations everywhere.

On Easter Sunday, the family enjoys a combined breakfast/lunch, but before this, hard-boiled eggs which have been handpainted in different designs and colours (*pisanki*) are cut and shared with special greetings. The

Easter meal consists of ham and sausages, salads, and different kinds of cakes, the most famous being *babki* and *mazurki*.

In the months of May (*Maj*) and October (*Pazdziernik*) special devotion is paid to Our Lady. One cannot help being struck by the fervour and concentration with which people pray, and it is noticeable, too, how many young men and women there are in the congregation. The many wayside shrines are decorated with flowers and ribbons; groups of people can be seen praying together or saying the rosary, even by torchlight as the daylight fades. Then at the end of May and beginning of June hundreds of small boys and girls, the former in dark suits, the latter in long white dresses and veils and with wreaths in their hair, walk through the villages and towns to receive their first Communion, each holding a candle.

Pilgrimages are popular, particularly among young people, including children, and the shrine of the famous Black Madonna at Częstochowa has a constant stream of pilgrims. Literally a million or more pilgrims travel *hundreds* of miles on foot, especially before and after the Feast of the Assumption of Our Lady on 15 August. (In Britain it used to be called Our Lady's Day of the Harvest). The majority of churches from all over the country are represented by people and priests from their parishes.

Over one million came too during the Pope's visit when he stayed for two days. The exquisite and world-famous painting of the Black Madonna hangs in the monastery of Jasna Góra (the bright mountain), which is set on the topmost height of the Kraków-Częstochowa Jura in Poland. The painting is on wood, and it is thought to have been part of the booty seized from Ruthenia by the Duke of Opole in 1384. It is clear that even at that time the painting was considered a priceless relic, and was regarded with the greatest reverence. After its transfer to Jasna Góra the devotion to Our Lady of Częstochowa grew up around it, and made the monastery a rich and flourishing centre of pilgrimage. According to legend, the painting was originally made by St Luke the Evangelist from the table top on which the Holy Family used to work and eat at Nazareth.

In 1430 the monastery was sacrilegiously attacked during Holy Week by Hussites from across the Bohemian and Moravian border. The painting was deliberately slashed by swords and sabres and terribly damaged. After the attack it was taken to Kraków where it was painstakingly restored with a care and devotion previously unknown in medieval Poland. The two slashes which can still be seen across the Madonna's cheek were left untouched to remind people of the infamous attack.

The painting itself now hangs above the altar in the Chapel of Our Lady at Jasna Góra.

Yvonne Kent, a close friend and supporter, sent me a wonderful account of her pilgrimage to the Black Madonna, in Poland.

> As many as 13,900 people took part in the pilgrimage from Warsaw, in seventeen groups. The sub-group, in which I walked, totalled 400, mostly young people, under twenty. We had three priests and three seminarians

accompanying us and the theme was the Eucharist and its meaning as a gift of God.

You can imagine that I was rather nervous about going as I did not know what to expect. Not knowing a soul did not help my confidence either but I knew that Someone would be watching over me and helping me.

The first day started at 6.30 a.m. with Mass at St. Anna's. After that, we all assembled behind our signs. Each group had a set of four loudspeakers which were mounted on frames and carried by the pilgrims, so that the priest and the singing could be heard by everyone as we walked along. The streets of Warsaw were lined with well-wishers and the balconies full of people giving encouragement, all visibly moved as we passed by. It was a humbling experience to be part of such bubbling enthusiasm. At each start, we sang Godzinki (prayers before the first Mass of the day to Our Lady) then, after the first break, the rosary was said and everyone's intentions were read out, the Sue Ryder Foundation being mine. At midday, we always observed the Angelus. At other times, the priests talked on various themes such as the Eucharist, the meaning of our feelings and the importance of love and prayer. Any gaps in the day were spent in singing hymns to Our Lady. Mass was celebrated every day, at different times, in the open air.

We walked an average of 30 km. a day, and the framework of prayer and instruction helped us reflect on our faith. It was so nice to have so much time for God, to concentrate on the real meaning of life and to escape from trivialities.

We spent our breaks either in fields or small villages. The local people were most generous, giving us apples, compote and even soup whenever we stopped for a lunch break. In the evenings, most pilgrims slept in tents while others made do with hay in a stable. The evening Appell was one of the high points, partly as we knew we had managed to get through another day but also because our priests were excellent musicians and animators, who generated a lovely atmosphere for evening prayers and songs of praise. We were usually asleep by 9.30 p.m.

We rose between 4 and 5.30 each morning but this was not difficult after our early night. The Polish countryside, at crack of dawn, is breathtaking, with fabulous sunrises and morning mists but it was very cold, first thing.

On some days we managed to get lost on the remote forest paths and the 30 km were more like 37 km! Some stretches of the walk were quite tough and the weather was very hot, during the day, so we had to gather more strength by reminding ourselves of our goal. I was lucky that my feet did not suffer from blisters, but was very glad to give them a rest each evening.

The final day was very moving. As you approach Częstochowa you walk up the Przeprosna Gora (a Hill of Forgiveness), where you have a final examination of your conscience. During the last break, before entering Częstochowa, the group says its thank-yous and farewells. You are also encouraged to ask forgiveness of your "brothers and sisters" for any times you may have wronged them during the journey. It may sound a bit strange but that, too, was moving and you really felt part of God's family.

Entering Częstochowa was an extremely emotional experience as the crowds of pilgrims and well-wishers were incredible. We made very slow progress and it was wonderful to soak in the atmosphere. Our group was led to Matka Boska (the Chapel of Our Lady) by a young couple who had married during the pilgrimage, so there were frequent outbursts of "Stolat" (May you live for a hundred years).

We were able to spend very little time before the picture of Black Madonna but, as the basilica was open all night, I was able to go back later in the evening and spend time there. Again, the crowds were enormous, some people spending all night in prayer. Five older ladies were very kind to me and took me under their wing. They were well prepared as they had been there many times.

This pilgrimage attracts people from all walks of life, mainly women though. One of the recurring themes is how our society tends to confuse love with sex, a message the Pope delivered to Denver, Colorado, and one that Cardinal Glemp made at Mass recently.

I send these memories to Sue Ryder (my second Mum) as I would like to share with her the positive and uplifting thoughts I had, and, especially, as I felt her presence with me on the walk.

At Whitsun (*Zielone Swiatki*) the churches are decorated with myrtle and many flowers. As always, it is impossible to get into the church unless one arrives early.

From 6 a.m. on the Feast of Corpus Christi a simple rug, tapestry or blanket is draped outside almost every window with pictures of Our Lady of Częstochowa and the local Madonna, and these are decorated with candles and flowers. Since 1979 a picture of Pope John Paul II is also included. It is the celebration of Christ's gift to us in the Eucharist of His own body and blood. It is a time when many look back and remember their first Holy Communion: a time perhaps to recall all that it meant to us then and has meant ever since. Each town and village looks extremely colourful, and after Mass a very long procession starts at 10 a.m. Hundreds of people and children walk slowly through the village or main streets of the town or city. It is a public holiday. A canopy is held over the head of the priest carrying the Blessed Sacrament, and behind at intervals four altars are carried representing the saints of the gospels, Matthew, Mark, Luke, and John. Each altar faces north, south, east or west. Young girls scatter rose petals in front of the procession.

From the Thursday in Whitsun week to the next, a procession circles the outside of the church daily. On the last day members of the congregation arrive with a small wreath made from greenery which is blessed and then hung up in their homes. Many different regional costumes are worn, and the town of Lowicz is particularly famous for its costume.

On 21 August 1974 a policeman approaching Piotrkow Kujawski in the district of Wloclawek saw a dazzling light over the Village church and he reported this to his superiors and his mother, a practising Catholic. On 3 May 1975 an estimated crowd of 15,000 people walked or rode on horses or bicycles to Piotrkow Kujawski. Many of them saw Our Lady during that night. She appeared for one, two, or three minutes in different places over the church, and in front of Our Lady's statue of the Black Madonna of Częstochowa at the door and the Lourdes statue at the gate.

In the following years, beginning on 21/22 April and usually up to the end of the month, she appears, not every night, but frequently after 11 p.m. and occasionally during the very early hours of the morning. In the parish of Piotrkow Kujawski about fifty per cent of the parishioners have seen Our Lady.

A friend of mine told me the following story:

> In May 1975 my wife and I heard a lot about Our Lady appearing over the church at Piotrkow Kujawski. After some discussion with three friends, we decided one evening to take them with us in our small car. We drove for about an hour and then were stopped approximately eight kilometres (five miles) from Piotrkow Kujawski by the police who explained that there were such crowds that we had to park and walk the rest of the way. There were hundreds of people on the road. One of our friends was sceptical, but we prayed as we walked – it was a fine and lovely night.
>
> At about 11 p.m. while we were standing outside the church amidst the great crowds, a dazzling white light and the figure of Our Lady in blue appeared with her arms and hands outstretched. The experience was indescribable and I waited – this vision lasted perhaps three to four minutes and we were left with an incredible feeling.
>
> A few nights later we returned again and saw the same figure. Professors from Gdańsk and Warsaw were there and said it was an unforgettable experience which proved that Our Lady continued as Queen of our country. We all wondered if she had appeared to calm and warn us of the forthcoming dangers.

Another friend of mine once shared a sanatorium room with the mother of the policeman. She said that her son thought at first when he saw the bright light over the church from afar that it might be a fire. He therefore called the fire engine, but the firemen found no sign of any such fire.

The church at Piotrkow Kujawski dates from the fourteenth century; the interior was later changed to the Baroque style and a chapel added. During the War it was closed by the Germans and became a store. Eight priests from the neighbourhood were shot in a nearby field. The present priest, Father F. Olczyk, was arrested, taken to the Gestapo prison in Szczeglen and from there he was transported by cattle truck to Sachsenhausen on 29 August 1940. He was later transferred to Dachau – Prisoner No. 22335 – and survived despite all his suffering and hard labour until the Liberation on 29 April 1945.

Although in the postWar years the Church has been under State surveillance – indeed the late Cardinal Wyszyński was imprisoned from September 1953 to October 1956 – it would be unfair to overlook the help which the Church has received in its rebuilding programme. Equally, it would be wrong to underestimate the amount of voluntary assistance and fervour which ordinary people have given to the rebuilding of hundreds of churches.

Warsaw had a garrison church dedicated to Our Lady, and it is safe to say that Poland had more Party members who attended Mass and had the children baptised and married in church than any other Communist country. Although the State did not give religious instruction, children were allowed to be given it by priests. In this way Christianity was imbibed by the younger generation and this is why young people make up a large proportion of the congregations.

It is indeed remarkable that, despite the influx of many rural Poles into the new industrial centres, this important demographic and social change has not led to any falling off in church attendance. It would be unrealistic, however, to ignore the very grave shortages of churches in the new housing areas. Efforts are being made to try and remedy this. In Warsaw fourteen new churches were recently built, in addition to more than thirty-four reconstructed from ruins. Twenty-one are being built now. A further 2,200 are being constructed throughout Poland and the seminaries are filled with 5,000 student priests.

II

No one can imagine how hard the Poles have had to struggle during the past fifty years: on the left bank of the City of Warsaw there was scarcely a single undamaged building. Warsaw suffered as did no other European capital. Heavily attacked by air in September 1939, it experienced two further tragedies in the course of the War. The first was the destruction by the Germans of the Warsaw ghetto, the district inhabited by Jews, whose numbers were monstrously swollen as Jews from other parts of Poland crowded into its narrow confines. Every inhabitant of the ghetto had been murdered or deported by the end of April 1943. Ghettos for Jews were established in all main cities and towns in Poland. Jews were rounded up to exist (or die) in intolerable conditions before being transported to extermination camps.

The area of the Warsaw ghetto covered 840 acres and the following is a description from the book *The German New Order in Poland* by Poland's Departments of State and Public Institutions, published by Hutchinson, London, 1942:

> In April 1940 the Nazis confined 450,000 Jews to a small area of Warsaw. An 8 ft high concrete wall was erected all round the area and any Jew who tried to escape was automatically shot. The same fate awaited any Pole who tried to help.
>
> Living conditions defied all description – there was practically no food, water or living space, and an average of six to ten people were confined to one room.
>
> On 16 November of that year the ghetto of Warsaw was closed without any warning. Supplies of food to the ghetto were stopped. The German

police confiscated the food carried to the ghetto by the Poles and also the food transported by Poles in tram cars passing through the ghetto.

Conditions in other ghettos resembled those in the Warsaw ghetto. Moreover, they were deprived of gardens, parks, green squares and open spaces. The ghetto formed a district unparalleled as to density of population, and thus will undoubtedly become a site of extreme human suffering.

Kazimierz Iranek-Osmecki, a member of the Polish Home Army and Second-in-Command to General Bor-Komorowski, wrote graphically in his book, *He Who Saves One Life,* of the heroic suffering of the Jewish population throughout Poland. The following is an extract:

> The Polish Home Army on 18 October 1940 published the following statement:
>
>> They are snatched from the streets, dragged out of their "beds" to work . . . The Warsaw ghetto takes on the dimensions of a gigantic crime . . . over 400,000 people are being condemned with all the consequences of unavoidable epidemics and a slow death from hunger, and they are left to the mercy of ruthless SS thugs.

The only way left on getting food in was by smuggling. Philip Friendman tells how the smuggling operation in the Łódź ghetto was organised:

> A Christian bakery owner in Brzeziny near Łódź produced bread beyond his allotted quota and sent this priceless commodity to the ghettos. Both the baking of this bread and smuggling of food to the ghettos were considered crimes. The baker enlisted the co-operation of children, who carried the bread to specially designated spots near the reservation wall where they were met by messengers who took the precious cargo inside for distribution. Generous Christians on the outside provided the ghetto, in the same manner, with fat and meat.

In Warsaw alone nourishment for several hundred thousand people had to be provided, while in the whole of Poland it reached over a million. Moreover, the country was being robbed and exploited by the Nazis, and food was scarce everywhere and, of course, for all the Poles, too.

Władysław Szpilman gives a description of how this system worked:

> The afternoon hours were the most propitious for smuggling. The guards, tired by the morning's work and satisfied with their gain, were less vigilant in the afternoon, occupied more with the counting of their profits. In the gates and windows of houses situated along the walls, anxious faces appeared and disappeared, waiting for the rumble of approaching carts or the tinkle of a tram. From time to time the rumble on the other side of the wall became louder, and when a cart passed close to the walls, sacks and parcels were flung over the wall, whistled signals were heard, people lurking in the gates of houses rushed from their hiding, snatched their booty and rushed back again. For a few minutes the streets were quiet again, but the apparent calm was full of tension, expectation, mysterious whisperings. On days when the guards intensified their activity the rumble of approaching carts was accompanied by shots, while, instead of sacks,

hand grenades came pelting over the walls, exploding with loud bangs and scraping plaster off the walls of houses.

The walls of the ghetto were not along all their length in immediate contact with the road surface. Spaced at certain intervals they had oblong openings at ground level, through which water from the Aryan part of the road tricked into gutters placed along Jewish sidewalks. These openings were also used for smuggling by children.

Tiny, dark creatures came rushing on little legs thin as matches, scared eyes glancing right and left, feeble paws dragging through the opening bundles often much larger than the smuggler himself. Once the goods were smuggled through, the children picked them up on their backs, bent double under the load, stumbling, veins throbbing in their temples and mouths gasping for breath, and scattered all over the place like frightened mice. Their work was as dangerous, even to the risk of life, as that of adult smugglers . . .

However, the feeding of the ghetto did not depend solely on such smuggling. The sacks and parcels smuggled over the walls mostly contained gifts from the Polish community to the poorest Jews.

The "resettlement" was also described by Bernard Goldstein:

The terror generated by the deportations paralysed the will, and frightful sounds of the merciless hunt corroded the mind. The unnatural noises were always with us – the shouting, whistling and shooting of the pursuers, the screams of the shrieking protests of their families, the whimpering and moaning of the bereaved after the cyclone had destroyed their little world and passed onto the next house or the next street.

The same scenes occurred day after day. From seven in the morning until six in the evening there were raids, blockades, shooting in the street, death marches on the Umschlagplatz. Some bit and clawed and fought back at their captors. Some went meekly, stupidly, their insane eyes glazed in merciful incomprehension.

At eight o'clock one morning we heard the wild rush of heavy boots accompanied by shooting, shouts and screaming: pandemonium again . . . They were at my door. I was caught off guard with no place to hide."

Those days also saw an act of unexampled shame. On 5 August 1942, by German order, the orphanage run by Dr Janusz Korczak was "resettled".

In spite of the terrible conditions in the ghetto, Korczak managed to gather together a group of orphans, saving them from death, from hunger, and epidemics. Thanks to his long experience, his self-sacrifice, and his heroic efforts, he managed to create in the orphanage an atmosphere in striking contrast to the nightmarish conditions outside. The orphanage was an island in a sea of despair, an oasis of peace in a maelstrom of terror.

When the order about the "resettlement" of the orphanage reached him, Korczak tried to have its execution postponed. In Nazi madness, however, there was no room for pity, least of all for children. Nor was there any consideration for a person like Korczak. The postponement was not to be. The entire orphanage had to report to the embarkation point.

The scene of the embarkation of the orphanage is described by an eye-witness, Nachum Remba:

> A packed throng of people moved on, driven by whips . . . Korczak walked at the head of the procession. No! I shall never forget this scene. This was not a march to the wagons, this was an organised protest against banditry! In contrast to the packed crowd which went like cattle to the slaughter . . . all the children were formed in fours with Korczak at their head. He was looking up as he held two children by their hands and led the procession singing . . . Even the Auxiliary Police stood at attention and saluted. When the Germans saw Korczak they asked: "Who is this man?"

The daily procedure of the embarkation point is described in *Smiere miasta (Death of a Town)* by Szpilman, published by Opracowal J Waldorff:

> The embarkation point was at the extremity of the ghetto . . . It was enormous, oval in shape, surrounded in parts by buildings and in part by fencing . . . Corpses lay there, of people killed yesterday for some misdemeanour, of perhaps for attempting to escape. Among some bodies of men there was one of a young woman and two of young girls with their heads completely smashed.
>
> From time to time lorries drove up to the gates of the square, and herds of people destined to be 'resettled' were crowded in . . . Here and there outbursts of panic took place if a passing SS man took it into his head to shoot at someone who did not get out of the way fast enough or whose looks were not humble enough . . .
>
> "Women with children in their arms moved from group to group begging for some water, of which the embarkation point had, on purpose, been deprived by the Germans. The children's eyes were still, half closed, their heads swayed on their emaciated necks and their parched mouths were open like those of little fishes abandoned by fishermen on the shore . . .

In a matter of three years most of the Jewish population in the ghetto had been transported in cattle trucks to Treblinka, Majdanek and Auschwitz. Furthermore, unavoidable epidemics, executions and starvation had reduced the population by 1943 to 60,000. This small group, knowing their fate and what they could expect from the Nazis, decided not to die without fighting back.

The Jewish forces had in their ranks a minute number of heavy machine-guns, a small number of light machine-guns and tommy guns (with a very limited supply of ammunition), and a considerable number of pistols of various types, as well as a large quantity of hand grenades, incendiary bottles and explosives.

The German forces were commanded by SS Brigadeführer and Major General of the Police, Jürgen Stroop. Two days before, he had been transferred from Lwow where he had commanded the police and the SS and now appointed to the command of the SS and police of the Warsaw district. As a well tried and experienced hand at such tasks, he had been brought to Warsaw to destroy the ghetto with infantry, artillery, armour and a battalion of engineers.

In addition, incendiary bombs were dropped by German aircraft engulfing the whole district in flames and burning the doomed occupants alive.

The hopelessness of those in the West who tried to save the Jews in Poland was apotheosised by the suicide of Szmul Zygielbojm, the representative of the Bund in the Polish National Council. Before his death, Zygielbojm wrote these words in a letter destined for the Polish President and the Polish Prime Minister:

> The responsibility for the crime of exterminating the entire Jewish people in Poland falls primarily on the perpetrators, but indirectly it also weighs on the whole of humanity. The people and Governments of the Allied Nations have up till this day failed to rise to any concrete act to put an end to this crime. By passively looking on this murder of millions of defenceless and ill-treated women, men and children, they have come to share in the guilt.
>
> I cannot remain silent and I cannot remain alive while the remnants of the Jewish people in Poland, whose representative I am, are dying.
>
> My comrades in the Warsaw ghetto died, up in arms, in a last heroic stand. It was not given to me to die as they did or to die with them. But I belong with them; I belong to their mass graves.

In the words of an eye-witness and participant, Symcha Ratajzer:

> . . . And suddenly it seems to me that we are very weak. What can we do against a well-equipped army, against tanks, armoured cars, having only a revolver in one's fist, or at best a hand grenade. Still, we were not disheartened. We are waiting for out executioners to settle our accounts with them.

Although individual members continued to fight, the organisation as a whole was losing strength. The casualties, the lack of ammunition, water and food, the loss of the bunkers (underground shelters), the exhaustion, and the heat of the fires all had their effect on the resilience of the defenders.

As Jewish Resistance decreased, the Germans intensified their cleaning-out operation. Fighters and Jews who did not fight were captured and sent to the embarkation point. Every few days trains would leave for Treblinka.

When the Germans discovered that some of the Jews were reaching the Aryan side either through the sewers or through tunnels under the walls, they set up extremely strict controls in the zone adjacent to the ghetto. When escaping Jews were discovered, special units kept on the alert were dispatched to capture them. If the Jews were armed, they fought the Germans on the Aryan side too. Ironically, many Jews who had managed to escape alive from the ghetto lost their lives on the other side of its walls.

The fighting went on from 21 April to 7 May. As soon as the battle in the Warsaw ghetto began, the Polish Authorities notified to London. General Sikorski in his radio address of 5 May, 1943, said:

> The Nazi executioners, using methods already known to us, on 19 April, at 4 a.m., began to liquidate the remnants of the Warsaw ghetto, where some tens of thousands of Jews still survived. Having closed all the exits, they invaded it with armoured cars and light tanks so as to kill off,

using machine guns, the remaining men, women and children. The Jewish population, driven to desperation, put up a heroic armed resistance. From that time on the fight has continued.

I ask my countrymen to give all the help and shelter to those being murdered, and at the same time, before all humanity, which has for too long been silent, I condemn all these crimes.

Poland has often been accused of being anti-Semitic, but it is only right for the reader and public to know that there was a special section of the Home Army (Polish Resistance) which was solely responsible for forging papers and hiding as many Jewish people, including children and babies, as possible in order to save them from extermination. I know one brave women crippled with rheumatoid arthritis who, with nine others, saved over 2,000 children. It is impossible to estimate the number saved from the millions who were sent to the concentration camps.

The *second* tragedy was the Rising of August 1944. The SS repressed the Resisters, killing and maiming them with unimaginable ferocity. Hitler's telegram to SS and Police General von dem Bach ordered that Warsaw should be razed to the ground

. . . and nothing or nobody should be left there.

I now quote from the *Canberra Times* (13 August 1994) and the *Australian* (1 August 1994) written by "Zub", a close friend with whom I had worked whilst serving with the Polish Section of SOE:

About 7 p.m. on 13 August, 1944, I stood at the end of the metal runway of the Campo Cassale airport near Brindisi in Italy watching the last of the twenty-eight Halifax and Liberator bombers take off for Warsaw, 1,450 km away.

This was to have been the longest expedition yet undertaken to parachute containers with weapons, ammunition and medical supplies to the Polish Home Army – an underground secret formation now openly fighting to wrest control of Poland's capital city from the Germans.

The uprising had begun a fortnight earlier on August 1, as the news of the successful crossing of the Vistula river forty km south of Warsaw by a Red Army Division was reported to General Bor-Komorowski, Commander-in-Chief of the Home Army.

There were also signs of panic among the Nazi hierarchy in Warsaw, and the evacuation of several units of the Wehrmacht. It appeared that the Germans were in retreat.

Earlier, in the evening of 29 July, Moscow Radio broadcast an appeal urging the people of Warsaw to rise: "For Warsaw, which did not yield but fought on, the hour of action has arrived".

The next day another broadcast from Moscow urged the people of Warsaw "to arms . . . to attack the Germans . . . help the Red Army in its efforts to cross the Vistula".

To the Commander-in-Chief of the Home Army the situation seemed opportune to strike at the retreating Germans and hold the City while the supply of ammunition lasted. The certainty of an imminent Soviet advance across the Vistula would give the Home Army its only chance to free Warsaw and then come to terms with the might of the Red Army.

But the decision to launch the Warsaw Rising proved for the Poles the most tragic mistake in their recent history. As it turned out, the Red Army stood idle on the eastern bank of the Vistula and watched while the Rising followed its course through sixty-three days of savagery during which some 150,000 ill-armed men and women of the Home Army faced the retribution of regular Wehrmacht formations supported by the SS Viking Panzer Division, the SS-Hermann Goering Regiment, several batteries of long-range heavy artillery and three squadrons of Stuka dive-bombers.

As a result of the treacherous Soviet conduct the Rising collapsed and the fate of Warsaw, a city of one million people, was sealed: some 225,000 civilians were killed in the fighting, the losses of the Home Army exceeded 20,000 and some 550,000 men, women and children were taken to concentration camps.

Warsaw as the capital of Poland ceased to exist, and with it the flower of Polish youth, together with the remaining cadres of Polish elite who, to that point, had escaped the systematic elimination ordered by Hitler.

The Commander of the Home Army, General Bor-Komorowski, called his ill-armed and largely untrained 125,000 men and women to action on 1 August. The misunderstandings and miscalculations that accompanied this fateful decision belong to the core of Poland's tragic fate.

Apart from lack of ammunition and hand grenades (these were exhausted after four days) there were thousands of Poles who were intent upon the Rising, but some Poles miscalculated Soviet intentions.

The Red Army advanced as far as the eastern suburbs of Warsaw and stood watching the agony of the City from across the Vistula.

Stalin's evil intentions against Poland were confirmed when he refused Churchill's request that he allow landing rights in the part of Poland held by the Red Army to the British, Polish, South African, Australian, and other Commonwealth airman dropping supplies. With the exception of the one USA Air Mission on the 18 September 1944.

The last word might belong to a famous native of Poland, Joseph Conrad, who was once asked to reflect on the tragic history of the Polish uprising of 1864. He said: "We have preserved our sanity." This must be a fitting conclusion for these reflections on the events of August and September 1944 – the sixty-three days of glory and shame, wisdom and folly, achievement, failure and above all, sacrifice.

The former young Poet, K. Baczynski, who was killed during the Warsaw Rising, wrote the following:

> Before you fell
> You found time to bless the soil
> With the sign of the Cross
>
> Was it a bullet my son
> Or did your heart break?

The Warsaw Rising was planned in February 1943. Somebody once said that "if you take a handful of Polish soil and squeeze it, it will squelch with blood". The total death toll in Warsaw by 1945 was about 1,800,000, and when rebuilding began early in that year about a quarter of a million bodies were found under debris and in the sewers.*

These lines come to mind

> Went the day well?
> We died and never knew
> but honour, we died for you.

Everywhere amongst the rubble were handwritten notices, some unbearably poignant. Two may stand for hundreds:

> Am searching for my son Wladyslaw Grott who was one year five months old on 7 August 1944. In Chlodna Street a German took him away from his father and gave him to some unknown woman. The boy had fair hair, dark eyes. He was wearing two shirts, a blouse with blue and white stripes, and a dark blue sweater. Please inform Wladyslaw Grott, 51 Radzyminska Street, Apt. 9, Warsaw-Praga.

> Will buy any book, in Polish or foreign language, fairy tales. Also shoe polish, shoe laces.

An estimated eighty-five to ninety per cent of the city's buildings and services were destroyed: there was no water, no electricity, no telephone service and no transport. As the railways were not functioning there was no contact with the rest of the country. Men and women struggled to work in schools and hospitals with roofs open to the sky. Many of them walked miles to work day after day from homes that were beyond the suburbs.

The Nazis thought they had dealt Warsaw and indeed the whole country a mortal blow, but they reckoned without the spirit of the citizens: this they could never extinguish. Amidst the ruins of their beloved cities and towns the courage and determination of its people burned fiery bright. They had a passionate optimism, patriotism and lack of self-pity.

No fewer than 35,000 mines of different kinds, 17,000 unexploded bombs and 41,000 shells had to be cleared by the sappers in Warsaw, in addition to 100,000 that were later discovered. The progress of the sappers could be followed by the appearance of the words "Checked – no mines" which were scribbled in the frost on the walls of demolished or gutted houses.

III

The standard appearance and size of the flats which have been built since 1947 throughout the country, especially the high-rise flats, referred to as

---

*In Poland there are 20,000 known places of execution where over fifty people were hanged or shot. There are dozens more where fewer people were killed.

"matchboxes" or "ant-heaps" by the Poles, are usually and understandably criticised, but the outsider cannot easily appreciate the acute difficulties of obtaining the right building materials nor the pressures under which everyone continues to struggle. Landscaping and parks should be a must. They give privacy where it would otherwise be lacking, but sadly this is not the case in some areas.

The average size of a flat is very small indeed – the living room is also almost always used as a bedroom/dining room. One bedroom has to accommodate two to three children in a family (boys and girls mixed). Norms are followed, but they are very different from the building regulations in Britain. Waiting lists are enormous, and thousands wait for a small flat as long as fifteen to twenty years. Meanwhile, couples continue to share with parents and their in-laws. It is not unusual for four or five families or more to share one kitchen, loo and bathroom.

During the course of my work, friends and acquaintances who themselves were architects and engineers invited me to attend their meetings, and so I have first-hand knowledge and saw for myself the huge problems they faced. I remember the words "Warsaw Lives" scrawled in the dust on my lorry.

Fourteen miles out of Warsaw is Konstancin, a well-known health resort where, amongst the pine trees, three simple Homes built by the Foundation are scenes of much suffering, but also a great deal of courage and activity. As one opens the door one senses the warmth of the atmosphere: there is a sound of voices, laughter, noises from the workshop and the room where lessons are in progress, of feet trailing slowly along the corridor on crutches and wheelchairs being pushed. In winter the trees, loaded with snow, seem very silent and have a beauty of their own. In summer the smell of pines and grass, and the natural surroundings give a feeling of tranquillity and peace.

These Homes care for girls and young women suffering from rheumatoid arthritis and at present have fifty-six residents between the ages of ten and forty-four. Three of these may serve to represent the many hundreds who have lived there or are there still.

Krystyna was sixteen when she came to Konstancin weeping with pain, her hands and feet swollen with arthritis. She had been living with her parents in a damp dilapidated house isolated from the town and from physicians. During the six years of her stay at Konstancin she underwent full medical treatment, including gold therapy, and in the meantime received training and worked as a clerk. Her state of health improved to such an extent that several years ago she married, but she still visits the Homes regularly during the holidays with her husband and two fine young children.

Maria was diagnosed with rheumatoid arthritis when she was only ten years old. At the Institute for Rheumatic Diseases she received surgery on her hands and feet and had numerous blood transfusions; so far no great success had been achieved, but she loves living at Konstancin. She retains her keen sense of humour and works for three hours a day. For Maria, Konstancin is home indeed, as both her parents are now dead, and she has nowhere else to go.

Bolesia became ill when she was six and had been in fourteen different hospitals by the time she was admitted to Konstancin six years later. Owing to a very serious degree of decalcification, her bones were too brittle to bear her weight and she had to be supported by specially made straps. Before coming to the Home, Bolesia had been a lonely, reticent and slightly retarded child with whom it was difficult to establish contact. In the friendliness and security of Konstancin, however, she blossomed. She began to trust people and developed immensely, both psychologically and mentally, becoming the soul of the Home. We nicknamed her Sunshine. She died at the age of sixteen, but during those last years of her life she reached a maturity which was very largely due to the conditions created for her and the other young handicapped at the Foundation's Homes.

Most Homes not only look after the physical well-being of their residents, but also try to create for each individual the conditions in which they may learn, to the best of their ability, to live with their handicap. The possibility of reconstructing his or her personal life is most important to the patient and often more so than a physical cure. For many people who have been cured physically it is impossible to adjust again to the realities of everyday life, and they suffer greatly from maladjustment and depression.

The average person who goes to Konstancin is struck by the normality and independence shown by the girls. For they are all determined to lead as normal a life as possible and to do as much as they can for themselves, though several have had major surgery six or seven times and received implants. It is exceptional for anyone not to study and work at Konstancin, however handicapped, or to be thought of as different in any way from an average person. In addition to their studies they also learn to carry out extremely delicate work, including the finest embroidery. Despite their disabilities and suffering the girls are usually cheerful.

Prior to being admitted, the girls have received little education, if any at all, as no buses are available in Poland to take children to and from school and, in any case, many of the girls are too handicapped to travel. As soon as they are admitted, however, they receive medical treatment, nursing care and schooling. On completion of their studies, many have gone on to qualify as dressmakers, teachers and accountants, or to attend full courses at university where they read mathematics, economics, etc. As a result of this, and in spite of their pain and physical disabilities, many of the girls are able to earn a small salary which is related to the number of hours each is able to work in the Homes. Others, after making a complete recovery, are able to return to the community outside. Those who are chronically handicapped – and fortunately they are a minority – long for the privacy of a small flatlet within the Home or nearby; naturally this is the dream of all of them.

Since 1957, 1,044 children and girls have been admitted to Konstancin:

41   have died
48   have married and many of them have healthy children
27   have been able to move into their own flats
90   have jobs
 5   have completed the Cambridge University English Course

Every girl, depending on her interests, capabilities and disabilities, can continue her general education up to "O" or "A" level standard. Many are proficient in English and French, particularly the former. They are given every opportunity to do their own housework, including laying the table, tidying up their rooms and dressing themselves, and many enjoy cooking and indeed prepare their own breakfasts and suppers. For this purpose, a weekly rota is drawn up. Lunch, the main meal of the day, is cooked for them.

At Konstancin there is, too, a workshop which resembles a small, bright, busy factory, where the girls work in shifts making various articles which are subsequently sold by the Co-ops, who pay them a wage on the eighth day of each month. The girls are also responsible for the designing of the tea towels, platters, tea cosies, and so on. which are sold in the Foundation's shops; up to 1989 the most colourful and fascinating activity in the workshop itself was the making and dressing of dolls in Polish regional costumes. The whole process used to be completed by the girls themselves, the starting material being merely a piece of wire. Fortunately, in later years the Co-ops have supplied assembled figures for the girls to dress, which relieved them of this work. Hours are spent in creating and discussing their art and designs, the mixing and blending of colours. Both girls and staff join in. It can be truly said that they have created the design centre for many of the objects sold by the Foundation.

Alas, due to the appalling inflation, materials became too difficult and too expensive to buy, also the dolls were too expensive to sell, and so a new programme of work had to be thought out and at the present day the girls are making many other things including items of clothing.

The girls take great pride in their appearance and are frequently to be found washing and setting one another's hair at night or early in the morning before work. They have a pure unspoiled beauty, a love of life and a great sense of humour and gaiety. The kitchens are gathering places.

The longed-for extension to link both the Homes in Konstancin was completed 1992 and provides a far larger and better room for physiotherapy, extra loos, bathrooms and bedroom accommodation. Materials for this extension were provided and sent out from Britain during the summer of 1991. The Poles were responsible for all work below ground, after which the Foundation's own builder and carpenter/manager, Keith Foreman, took charge. He has worked very long hours under the most difficult climatic conditions, and throughout the following winter. In three months Keith succeeded in getting the carcass up and the whole of the large roof area felted and tiled (using slate tiles). Altogether Keith has worked for the Foundation in Poland for fifteen years. He is married to a Polish girl and they have two children. Despite every possible problem and saga, Keith always remained cheerful and had a great store of jokes. He is conversant with the Polish language and it has been a real pleasure working with him at Konstancin and on other sites, too, where, thank heaven, we have had fewer difficulties and the fullest co-operation from Polish officials.

It was a great relief to me in 1988 when Mr Jerzy Boguslawski, a qualified and experienced Polish architect in Warsaw came forward and relieved me of many of the problems that had beset the building work at Konstancin. Moreover, he carries authority and has many contacts. He is firm and will not accept anything but the highest of standards.

There have been other people who have given assistance in the supervision and building of these Homes, both at Konstancin and Gdynia Redlowo. Alina Moffett, an architect in London and the representative from Metframe Limited, once wrote the following to me:

> As you know, accommodation was provided for me at Konstancin during the working week. During this time I received excellent medical treatment and care for my own personal back problems and it was my pleasure to be accepted as "one of the family" by your girls and staff.
>
> Konstancin will always be a memorable experience for me when you consider the amount of pain and suffering that your girls have endured and their sense of humour and warmth of hospitality is unbelievable.
>
> We must also acknowledge the continuous assistance of Mr Bogusławski, a real gentleman, in maintaining site progress by ensuring our service requirements were met by the Polish contractor. Brian Muggleton's architectural skills should also be acknowledged as the new Home, both in proportion and external appearance, blends perfectly with the site environment.

Since 1989, due to the great changes in the country, building materials hitherto unobtainable can now be bought locally.

Several companies in Britain were generous in donating or selling at cost price the sanitary ware and boilers and pumps for the central heating. A large quantity of floor covering has also been given. I would like to thank the Ministers of Health and their deputies in Warsaw, and other colleagues with whom I work so closely, for their understanding and co-operation in making a very substantial grant in Polish zlotys available to pay for the installation of the main services and the wages of the few Polish tradesmen and labourers. It is immensely heartening always to count upon their unfailing assistance to cover the running costs. Furthermore, the Institute of Rheumatology, which is responsible for running these Homes with the Foundation has helped a great deal, too. The first of the two Homes to be rebuilt was officially opened on 20 January 1992 amidst great excitement. I was asked especially to be present and cut the ribbon and His Lordship, Bishop Dus, blessed each room. His Excellency the British Ambassador and his wife also attended together with many other dignitaries, friends and supporters. It was a most joyful occasion, the more so because as I write, the Polish medical services have virtually collapsed, due to lack of funds. It is, therefore, all the more heartening to see such a Home built and completed in eight months.

In addition to the hundreds of Poles who make small homemade gifts to raise funds for the Foundation, the British Embassy in Warsaw had, for many years, invited the diplomatic corps and the Poles to attend a pantomime or play in aid of the Foundation, and the Directors and staff of theatres in the City have eagerly lent costumes free of charge. In more recent years a huge fair was organised in December by the wife of the British Ambassador and she forms a committee of ladies from different embassies. They worked for months beforehand to ensure the fair's success. It was always held in the Ambassador's residence and the Polish staff give unstinted service and assistance. At the end of the day everybody felt exhausted but happy with the amazing results.

My appreciation and gratitude go out to members of the British Embassy and British Council who, for very many years, have visited the girls at Konstancin once or twice a week to give them lessons in English and to take them for outings and generally to enjoy their company and hospitality. Numerous ladies have played a vital role in keeping up the continuity of these visits.

Mrs Jean Reddaway, the wife of the former British Ambassador to Poland, Norman Reddaway, who served in Warsaw for four years, together with her friends in the diplomatic corps, worked exceedingly hard and did so much to rally support and raise urgently needed funds for the Foundation's work in Poland. Jean is a gifted artist, and before leaving Warsaw she most generously offered the many beautiful sketches and paintings which she had executed in all parts of Poland to be auctioned for the benefit of the Foundation. The following is an extract from a letter from Mrs Patricia Campbell, a member of the British Embassy:

> On behalf of Mrs Reddaway, it is with the greatest pleasure that I send you the enclosed cheque for £6,500 as a donation to your Foundation. This amount represents the proceeds from the sale by auction of Mrs Reddaway's sketches and paintings in Poland, and somehow I feel that no one was more shocked by the success of the event than Jean herself. Apart from the beauty of the exhibits, their exceptional presentation and in many instances an accompanying nostalgia, much of the credit certainly went to the auctioneer, H.E. The Italian Ambassador, Signor Profili, who impressed us all with an amazing combination of zeal and panache!
>
> A few days before the sale, about twenty of the girls from Konstancin came in to the Residence for tea and a preview of the pictures, and I have no doubt that of all the memories Mrs Reddaway took home with her to England, that particular afternoon will long remain one of the most touching and unforgettable. They truly are remarkable girls.

At Christmas and Easter the Foundation's tradesmen working in Poland were invited to spend these feasts in the Homes in Konstancin, and on Easter Monday, the old folk tradition of throwing cold water (*dyngus*) on each other from 5 a.m. onwards is carried out with great glee. New tradesmen are often caught out! When many of the girls and staff came to stay at Stagenhoe for a holiday, they received a bouquet of flowers with the message: "For all the Girls from all the Boys."

Amongst the many discussions I have had with the girls, we all agreed that from time to time it is necessary to get away from community life however well we get on with one another. Each of us has moods and moments when we enjoy other people's company, but solitude and being on one's own are essential. Elizabeth Nowakowska told me that she pulls the sheet up over her head at night and tries to communicate with God, but sometimes thoughts and problems race through her head and she remains sleepless. It is impossible to be cheerful all the time, and it is not true to say that anyone can be, with sincerity. The girls' stoic courage in the face of the pain they endure is very fragile.

All the girls at Konstancin agree that the most important thing about the Homes is that while receiving long-term medical treatment they can also study and work and they very much appreciate the opportunity to make friends, to belong to a big family and to lead a social life, which is naturally most important in helping them to overcome their disability. Outings provide great enjoyment. When Nicholas Henderson was British Ambassador in Warsaw, he and his wife, Mary, allowed the Embassy's Rolls Royce and other cars to fetch the girls for tea. The girls took great delight in this and those who travelled in the Rolls Royce used to wave to us like royalty when they drove off. Going to the opera is one of their favourite pleasures and Warsaw is famous for its opera and operetta (two theatres have been rebuilt).

Although Kraków is 200 miles away, they used to love going there, too, for it has the oldest Polish university (dating back 600 years), and the whole City, the former capital of Poland, is full of beautiful buildings, among them the Royal Castle of Wawel with its historical associations with the monarchy. It was in Karol Wojtyla's early years as a priest, when he was so involved with every form of activity in his parish, that one of the honorary social workers of the Foundation, Dr Wanda Poltawska, who was working with him, helped me off-load and carry into the Royal Castle clothing needed for those in their care.

When driving in Poland, often over distances of hundreds of miles, I am welcomed and stay in many places – mainly in the Homes and hospitals, but also countless people everywhere offer me wonderful hospitality, yet I always eventually go back to the Homes at Konstancin as my base because they are to me the equivalent of Headquarters.

A pause and a walk in the peace of the woods en route are always welcome. I love listening to the cuckoo, wood pigeons and grass hoppers and smelling the soil. Sometimes, too, I have a good sleep. After sweeping the dust or snow out of the driving cabin, I climb back in again, refreshed. Usually, the country roads in Poland are long and straight with an even surface (except in winter). Moreover, a large percentage of the population walk or use public transport – buses and trains – while children are accustomed to walk to school, even over a long distance.

Life has a far gentler pace and I like the earthy feeling. In villages or on farms, if time permits, I stop to refill my thermos and I am often offered food. There are thousands of small farms, and once a week the farmers take their produce by horse and cart to market, which is a great gathering place. Regrettably, a number of carts carry no lantern or light, so at night, or in fog or snow, particular care has to be taken. In recent years, the police have rightly become very strict with drivers.

Radar has been introduced in many areas to enforce a lower speed limit. Fines and spot-checks, which include breathalyser tests and a detailed and lengthy inspection of the vehicle, are common. This acts as a deterrent on those who drink and I personally approve of the strict enforcement of rules for safety on the roads, both in Poland and elsewhere.

In the little town of Konstancin one of the churches has an illuminated clock and cross which is a welcome sight after hours of driving. I always feel completely at ease with the girls at the Homes, and am assured of a lovely and warm reception whatever hour of the day or night I arrive. Even though I insist that they should not wait up for me, they invariably do so, and when they hear my vehicle approaching they come out to greet me and help me carry in my things. If messages need delivering one of the girls, or a member of staff, always offers to take them.

I would like to mention especially Leokadia who invariably offered to drive her car (despite the years during petrol rationing) when she is available. Leokadia was eligible for a car because of her disability. The standard of living, however, only permits a very few handicapped people to own one. Leokadia has endured fifteen operations and she is often in pain, but nevertheless she obtained her degree in mathematics at Warsaw University. For many years she has been employed by a computer firm in Warsaw. She lives alone in her own small and tidy flat (where I also stay) but frequently returns, especially at weekends, to visit Konstancin. It is a very joyful place, full of gaiety and vitality, and often in the evenings the sound of records and singing fills the Homes. Television is also popular, especially such serials and films as *The Forsyte Saga, Oliver Twist, David Copperfield, A Christmas Carol, Wuthering Heights, The Stars Look Down, Pride and Prejudice, Macbeth, The Barchester Chronicles, Anna Karenina, The Six Wives of Henry VIII, A Midsummer Night's Dream, The Hound of the Baskervilles* and *The Battle of Britain*. Football is a great favourite, for which, incidentally, the entire country comes more or less to a standstill.

The late Professor Eleanora Reicher, Head of the Institute of Rheumatic Diseases in Warsaw, was one of the people instrumental in starting the

Homes at Konstancin. In the course of my work in Poland I had often visited her Department and the Hospital and later the large newly built Institute, and Professor Reicher frequently invited me to make use of her own small flat in Polna Street as a base. She was a wise and witty person who reminded me greatly of Mama because of the similarity of their outlook on life. Indeed, when they met they found they had a lot in common. Professor Reicher had been hidden in a convent during the occupation, but she continued working as a doctor. She was outspoken and very shrewd. In her company after surgery hours the Professor often had ministers, (including the Prime Minister of the day), artists – she herself was no mean painter and writer – specialists and people from all walks of life, and there were animated and long discussions on many subjects, which I was privileged to hear. One of her friends, Cardinal S. Wyszyński, was sometimes present, as well as the late Professor Lenoch of Prague, an outstanding Rheumatologist. He, too, was a man of many talents. Professor Reicher always insisted on my having a warm meal, and her lifelong companion would, however inconvenient the time, produce stewed apples.

On returning one afternoon, I parked the vehicle in the yard, rang the bell and was astonished to see a number of people inside whom I first believed to be patients waiting to be examined by Professor Reicher. Within moments, however, it became evident that everyone who had walked through the door that day was under house arrest. We were kept there for at least thirty-six hours. There were some forty people with me in very cramped surroundings. We took it in turns to sleep on the floor and eked out whatever food we had with us. The telephone line was cut. Many jokes were told among us as we waited, but if anyone asked how long we were likely to be kept there our questions went unanswered. This was a typical instance of what went on in the post-Stalin era, as thousands of people experienced.

Professor Reicher had a quality of greatness and leadership which enabled her to handpick a staff of doctors, physiotherapists, a psychologist and teachers, the majority of them women, who were to work lovingly and faithfully at the Homes. The staff are always there, but in the background, not consciously exercising their authority. The Institute of Rheumatic Diseases, together with the Home staff, decide upon admission, maintenance, cost of food, new appointments, drugs and treatment for Konstancin.

The Foundation's first Home was in the converted prison near Bad Nauheim in Germany, but the first which we actually built ourselves was this one in Poland; and it seems particularly fitting that the foundation stone of the Living Memorial should have been laid in this way in a country which was so despoiled by the War.

A love of building has always been with me since early childhood, and I am only sorry that I have never had the opportunity of studying the subject. I was inspired by the enthusiasm of all concerned, including local authorities, architects, builders, craftsmen, and women too, who worked in the archives and on the building sites.

Traditional family ties are still strong, and most of the women, whether married or single, find it possible to follow a profession right through to retirement at the age of sixty, thanks to the willingness of grandparents and other relatives who help in sharing in the care of their families and children. In Poland, both men and women have a great variety of jobs. Poles work hard and it is unusual to get up later than five or six every morning. The women never lose their femininity and have the gift of looking attractive. They have proved to me how important it is to attempt to keep tidy and to be very disciplined in the conditions and circumstances in which we have to work.

IV

I found in my earlier relief work in the most devastated areas of Normandy and elsewhere, including Poland, that we often had no drugs to administer and nursing was absolutely basic. Our presence and attempts to keep people clean in this chaotic situation – even with an acute shortage of water – apparently gave comfort and consolation to them. Water was absolutely essential, especially for patients with typhus.

Several of the diseases could not be diagnosed and dermatologists were perplexed by unknown skin diseases which caused endless irritation and for which they had no remedy.

The memories of the so-called "hospitals" crowd in upon my mind. In some of these there were beds – always shared – but many patients were laid upon the cold floor. Many people had been so badly injured or beaten that their flesh hung like raw meat, whilst other parts of their bodies were so bruised and discoloured that they could hardly bear being touched. Scenes, screams and smells will always remain with me. Time could pass so very quickly, and then it would seem to stop still as though the situation would never get better. Typhus and typhoid cases were indiscriminately mixed together in the same area and there was often confusion amongst these cases. The majority of patients also suffered from tuberculosis. I found the following amongst my notes scribbled in pencil:

> I do not seem to be conscious of time, but of evening shadows, night with little light to work by, when groans and coughs are incessant. The dawns we look forward to after the long hours of darkness. Some dawns are grey and windswept, others too beautiful to describe. Pearls in a sea of soft blues and colours of the rainbow. I seem to be much more conscious of this beauty because of the contrast of what surrounds us. It is impossible to put into words the stenches, the special smells connected with each disease. I take comfort in smelling surgical spirit. In this bitter cold I have to keep my arms bare so that I can scrub down and take full advantage of the water. This cold fresh water revives my face and head and gives my swollen (often chapped) hands and feet new strength. I dream too of

"the cool kindliness of sheets that soon smooth away trouble" also "the benison of hot water . . ." Snatches of poems come in and out of my mind.

In this ruined country the few buildings that were left relatively undamaged were converted into schools or hospitals, so as far as our own work was concerned it was obvious that the Foundation would need to provide its own simply designed buildings for use as Homes or hospitals.

Naturally, building regulations vary according to the part of the country. The hard winter brings frost penetration to an average depth of over three feet, so obviously great care must be given to the foundations. Soil tests are essential. Clearly, too, we must always adhere to the fire regulations, and in the Foundation's standard Homes at strategic points nine-inch fire-check walls in brick are built with two-hour fire-check doors.

From the beginning, sets of drawings had to be prepared by the Foundation, translated in every detail, and the Ministers and local authorities would eventually take them to the planning stage, incorporating their own contributions: roads, electricity, sewerage, central heating and water. To eliminate lengthy and voluble site meetings it was necessary for me to ask the Minister of Building and Works, as well as the Minister of Health and Social Welfare, to allow the Foundation's set of fourteen drawings to be used officially in all parts of Poland.

With the need to accommodate improved techniques and facilities, and with improving standards of care, a typical standard Home/hospital now comprises two separate patient wings each with its own kitchen and dining room, television lounge and sitting room, together with full sanitary facilities, and with total accommodation for sixty residents mainly in two-bedded rooms but including some single and three-bedded rooms. The two main wings are connected by a central wing, containing doctors' rooms, surgeries and treatment rooms together with offices and a chapel, which faces the main entrance.

Once a site has been selected, the building materials, until 1989, were ordered in Britain, apart from local supplies of sand, cement and gravel. The reason why the Foundation had to ship out its own materials was that virtually the whole country had to be restored and there was no local material available, or else it was in such short supply as to be rationed. Furthermore, most of the soil is sandy, which adds to our problems. There is a lack of aggregate. At the beginning it was rare to get a concrete mixer, so we mixed by hand, and during the long cold winters when temperatures dropped to between minus 10–15°C we used to warm ourselves around braziers when we could get them. Because of the severity of the climate, the actual erection, once the foundations were in, could only go on between April and the end of October, when the carcass of the building had to be bricked and we could then work on the interior. The summer months are warm and the temperature is usually well over 25°C even climbing occasionally to 35°C. When we have been on building sites in hot weather the delight of washing under a pump or in a bucket is inexpressible.

The timing and pressures upon the local authorities and the Foundation to get the materials onto the site in time, the saga of the documentation, combined with the frustrations of ensuring that materials are not held up by lack of co-ordination between the supplier and the shipping company in Britain . . . these alone would fill a book. Our unbounded appreciation goes to the companies who keep their word about delivery and "D-Days", and also to the Poles and Yugoslavs for giving free freight to the Foundation's supplies.

The first company with whom I placed an order were most co-operative – they also waited until funds could be raised and provided materials at almost cost price. Their drawings were headed: "When in doubt, ask." As I was usually at least a thousand miles or more away from them and could not resort to a telephone because of cost and the lack of clarity on the line, the local engineer and myself, when faced with a number of practical problems, drew up a Snag List which was composed either into a long ELT (European Letter Telegram) or into an airmail letter which could take days to arrive.

During the first years I was on my own and had to deal with the problems of erection and renovation, shipping and the complications of dealing with bills of lading, ships' manifests, and so forth by myself. I was allowed to search the docks, when necessary with the forwarding agent, for materials despatched, and despite the clearest of shipping instructions to the companies in Britain, the materials were not always properly labelled. Incidentally, twice the dockers at Hull, on hearing what the facing bricks* were to be used for, waived their loading charges.

A colleague from a building company near Wolverhampton, who himself had once been a prisoner of war in Poland, stayed out there for six months to give me assistance with the erection of Homes in Poland. He spent much time on the telephone. In those days (the 1950s) it was a triumph to get through to Britain from Warsaw and have the line kept clear. He would go into long descriptions to his astonished colleagues in Wolverhampton about problems facing us on the sites. Fortunately, the company made themselves responsible for the telephone bill! He was a Northerner, very forthright, and before site meetings I tried to take him aside and ask him to be as tactful as possible. One building engineer whom we nicknamed "King Pin" was a constant source of annoyance. Besides making flamboyant suggestions, he insisted upon such substantial foundations for one Home for children that he was told he had missed his profession in life and should have been with the reconstruction team rebuilding the Opera House in Warsaw.

I always remember Dermot Connolly, too, an excellent chippie from Ireland, who worked for the Foundation for several years on a pocket

---

*The bricks, specially made for extremely cold climates, were difficult to find, but it became possible to supply English-made high-strength frost-resistant clay bricks suitable for the harsh climate at an economic price. The original Firm generously supplied them at £25 per 1,000 bricks. Alas, they were taken over by a far larger company.

money basis. I remember Dermot not only for his sense of humour and faith, but for his ability to work under difficult conditions, and he remains vividly in my mind wearing his carpenter's apron with his tools slotted into the numerous pockets at his waist. Whilst working on a building site in a remote area in Poland he developed a desperate longing for English chocolate and wrote a pleading, tear-jerking letter describing his feelings to one of the well-known chocolate companies in this country. The company responded, to his great delight, by sending him two or three pounds of their best product. He also hankered after English toast. When we were together at odd moments, he used to remark: "Oh, Miss Ryder, there is something special about the toast at the Foundation's Headquarters back at Cavendish." He later went on to join an expedition to the North Pole.

Building teams consisting of five or more tradesmen either travelled on their own across Europe with two relief drivers or I drove in convoy with them.

Prior to departure, there was a thorough briefing about conditions of work, the drawings and plans for the prospective Home, and what could be expected on arrival. The route was also examined in detail and full written descriptions supplied in case we lost contact with one another; points of contact along the route were also agreed on in case of breakdowns or other calamities.

One team of tradesmen was travelling on their own and, like others before them, they did not speak any German, which in many ways proved to be an advantage. Arriving at the East German frontier they followed the normal custom of off-loading the contents of the van and Land Rover, and under searchlights the tools which had been listed were counted and the contents of their suitcases, containing personal clothing and working overalls, emptied. They were also asked to count all of the clout nails! There was apparently much shouting to which they fortunately did not reply, but after a lot of time-wasting and questioning, one of the tradesmen, Charles Cioffi, felt he had had enough. He thereupon took out his bottle of holy water from Lourdes and proceeded to bless each of the frontier guards.

They were amazed, and to this day no one knows whether they understood the meaning, but the team was allowed to repack and proceed without any more ado.

One autumn we were due to relieve two members who had spent all their time from early May that year erecting one of the Foundation's 10,000-square-feet Homes. They had worked with three or four local Polish carpenters and a great tempo had been set. One of them was an architectural student, John Hughes, who, in the last year before his final examination, had returned for the second time to work voluntarily for the Foundation.

Meetings had been arranged by cable and letter with the Ministry and local authorities. Unfortunately, the van carrying the replacement tradesmen had two punctures on the Hanover- Helmstedt autobahn and as it was evening no workshop was open. After eating our supper, which we carried with us, and enjoying our brew-up in a lay-by, we tossed coins to decide whether or not to proceed across East Germany without a spare wheel. Every Foundation vehicle overseas, as a matter of principle, always carried (and continues to do so today) two spare wheels plus the basic spare parts. The luck of the toss decided that we should go on and keep to schedule. This was during the years when the whole East German border evoked memories of the Hitler era, with watchtowers, Alsatian dogs and masses of barbed wire, criss-crossed over miles of deeply laid minefields.

At the border a weasel-faced official in his peaked cap shone his torch right in our faces, trying to dazzle us as we were getting out of the van and the Land Rover. He began to go through all the various formalities of filling in forms, whilst other officials behind locked doors set their own slow pace. Eventually, clearance was given to us to proceed to Customs. According to my previous notes, we still had an hour in hand on our schedule, but faced the rest of the night driving through East Germany before crossing into Poland.

After a brief respite in the woods near Skwierzyna and again at Poznań, we drove the last seven or eight hours to the outskirts of Srem, where we arrived in the afternoon. There on the roadside one of the local authority officials, Mr Szymanski, stood and welcomed us in his best Scottish accent. He had served with the First Polish Army, and had happy memories of his stay in Scotland for four years during the War. He loved the Scots and their hospitality and, from the twinkle in his eye, I guessed there must have been one lassie to whom he had lost his heart. Mr Szymanski died before coming to Britain and re-visiting his old haunts under the Foundation's Holiday Scheme. He was a typical Pole in his ability to organise, to remember, to make innumerable jokes, to know what was needed and to do his best against the odds.

We followed his official car to a building, where I vividly remember sitting at what seemed to be an endless site meeting. About a dozen people took part, in addition to ourselves, in a long and narrow room. We produced our schedule of building materials with a copy for them to check off, and for us to chase up any consignment from Britain still lying in the docks at Gdynia.

As the carcase of the Home had to be bricked in and the roofing laid, as always a bar chart (*homonogram* in Polish) was drawn up. John, the brickie, and John Mills, an architect and team leader, were trying to be realistic and decide how many bricks could be laid in the shortest period, bearing in mind that we were working against time and were short of brickies. The nights were already cold and there was the usual threat of rain and snow.

I will never forget the sound of English and Polish voices at Srem, or the dense and heavy pall of smoke. After about four hours, tables were carried in over our heads by local girls bearing very generous portions of food for the late evening meal. Finally, at about 11 p.m. I declared that we had all best take stock of the very critical situation in the early morning after a sound sleep, and on the building site itself where the Home was being erected.

Christina, the nurse in the team, who was the fiancée of Martin, a skilled decorator, wore slacks and had short hair. The Poles, though quite accustomed to women as architects and tradeswomen, remained unconvinced that she was not a boy, so much so that the accommodation list in a small local sanatorium included her in the boys' quarters. I had been offered hospitality in the local architects' and engineers' flat and found myself without Christina. I had to send one of the tradesmen up the drainpipes to the first floor of the sanatorium to search for her, with me giving what assistance I could from the ground. A night nurse eventually appeared and Christina was retrieved and drove back with me in the Land Rover.

On the eve of his departure for work in Africa, my husband managed to get through on the telephone. I was in a very deep sleep, and my host and hostess told me during an early breakfast that they had roused me from bed, led me to the telephone close by where (so I was assured) I had given my husband a brief but very lucid description of the journey and assured him that all was well. I had absolutely no recollection of our conversation!

At Popkowice, a Village at the eastern end of the country, another saga awaited me. While carrying out surveys, I was often taken to existing Homes to visit those people on the waiting list who were living in dire circumstances. One winter's night I was on my way to a small town, accompanied by Mr Siemiradzki from the Ministry of Health and Social Welfare, a colleague with whom I had worked for years. Thick blinding blizzards had slowed down our progress in *Ezekiel*, the 10-ton lorry, and snow kept blocking the windscreen wipers. We eventually arrived at 1.30 a.m. to find the town asleep. On enquiring at the local police station, we were directed to a mediaeval country house, but in the darkness it was not easy to discern. On seeing lights we went into a building and were met by two charming and talkative bakers. The delicious smell of their baking bread and the sight of benches tempted me to accept their offer of hospitality, but Mr Siemiradzki was insistent that we should find our right destination. He considered, contrary to his normal habit of a long dissertation, that a brief resumé of the Foundation's history was enough for the curious bakers who begged us to stay with them, offering hot rolls.

We walked through the silent grounds to bang on the door of the local authority's home, converted from a fourteenth-century country house to a place for the handicapped to live in. A night porter came and led us up a long stone staircase to the nuns' quarters. We were politely told that the Sister Superior had to get dressed; it was two and a half hours before the time when the nuns rose to say their first Office of the day.

We stood under the broad, steeply vaulted ceiling and waited, and I thought longingly of the bakers' bench. Eventually, the Sister Superior appeared in her habit of the Albertynki Order and, after greeting us, gently said we were expected to go on the the Director's flat "a little way across the garden . . ." We were guided by her and the porter, and upon arrival, the Director, and indeed his whole family, rose from their beds in their two-roomed flat to greet and welcome us. Warm water was produced to enable me to have a bath, and also a meal, but I begged to be allowed simply to sleep. At 7 a.m. the first meeting was due to begin and, being punctual (despite the appalling road conditions), the local authorities arrived at 6.50 a.m.

On another occasion, many years ago, I had a meeting in an orthopaedic hospital, and as is the custom in Central Europe and in other countries on the Continent, if the rooms are heated it is very impolite not to remove one's overcoat. Mine, an inexpensive nylon one with braid (which was given to me by my husband for Christmas and called an "Eskimo"), was taken by a consultant and hung in a corridor just outside the room in which the meeting was held. When the meeting was over the others put on their coats but mine was not to be found. It was a very cold night and snowing, and everyone knew that I had to move onto my next appointment in Warsaw by the following morning. They were exceedingly embarrassed and insisted upon rousing the local Professor and the Director from their beds and alerting many of their colleagues about the situation – much to my dismay. The police were also informed, and a detective appeared wearing dark glasses and looking the part. He proceeded to take down a long statement asking me the name of my father and whether I had attended a high, lower or middle school. He also requested a detailed description of the coat – calling it *Eskimoskie futro*.

I think they all had visions of *Ezekiel* being driven off because my coat had in its pocket all the keys of the van as well as my rosary. The doctor contacted a rather voluble mechanic who had his own workshop on the outskirts of the City. He came in record time to assist me in removing the front panel of the lorry in order to install an ignition, which was done very quickly despite the snowstorm. Then we had to saw off five padlocks on the lorry, including the one on the diesel tank. At that time pad-locks were in short supply, so the various doctors set off in all directions looking for replacement padlocks from their friends. Meanwhile, I had driven to the workshop where the owner kept us warm with the help of *bigos* (a Polish speciality which consists mainly of stewed cabbage and sausage) and sips of vodka while work was in progress. Before long the owner was almost incoherent with merriment, but fortunately his appren-tice kept a clear head. On completion of the work, and bedecked in a borrowed coat which did not fit me and large gloves also lent by friends, I left for the seven-hour drive to Warsaw.

On arrival, I found that the grapevine had informed the Ministry and other people, so a stream of Poles greeted me, each carrying one or more carnations (their tradition requires an uneven number of flowers). They had come to tell me that the loss of my coat was a dishonour to their country and themselves. The following day the Prime Minister sent me a special handmade coat, lined with sheep-skin and with matching hat and gloves, which has been called after him ever since.

During the past years I have been particularly helped for short periods by Graham Hughes and his son, Chris, Peter Denton, Roy Peake, John Hughes, Jock Fraser, and the late Engineer, Josef Karzel. Engineer Karzel was a Czech by nationality and painstakingly conscientious. He would telephone me on occasions to settle queries. I remember one day up in the Christmas Card Room at Headquarters his clear voice coming through from Olsztyn (in the region of the Mazurian Lakes). He wanted my advice as to the position of the oil tank which, because of the severe climate, had to be placed underground. The whole site, as well as other sites, was so vivid in my mind that I was able (without sounding immodest) to agree to the exact location of the tank; if I had been in any doubt I would have referred to the plan which I carried in my ring book.

The bringing-in of teams of builders from abroad − by agreement with the Polish ministries − was necessary owing to the fact that there was at that time no unemployment in Poland. Consequently, masons and labourers were at a premium. These teams reinforced the local people in their work on the Foundation's Homes, and are invaluable to us in our work. Altogether over seventy tradesmen, including young architects, many of whom had come from well-known firms, volunteered for a very small amount of pocket money, and spent a minimum of six months to two or three years or more in Poland where they shared the life of the community during the time they spent on the Continent. Many of them learnt the language. Over fifty visiting tradesmen married Polish girls, the wedding celebrations lasting several days and nights in the fashion typical of the country. This was a situation one could never foresee and the ramifications were numerous and highly disconcerting, as once a programme has been drawn up every pair of hands is needed to keep it on schedule.

To be taken aside in the middle of the hard work on a building site or during the course of renovation to be told by the tradesman that he wished to marry added unexpected complications. I remember one occasion when a young British bricklayer had to get special permission from his Anglican bishop before he could marry a local Polish Catholic girl. In the midst of all the difficulties, I found myself an unofficial adviser on marriage problems to worried mums and dads in both countries.

It is wonderful that a few of these couples have returned to the Foundation's Headquarters, to remember their Silver Wedding and attend Mass here.

Unfortunately, there is always a shortage of suitably qualified experienced tradesmen. If we had more, many more new Homes and/or hospitals could be built and much additional renovation done. Of course, some of the sites are isolated, conditions difficult and the food unfamiliar to foreign helpers.

No one who has not experienced a site meeting in Poland can imagine the problems which we faced, mainly due to the difficulty of obtaining basic materials and tradesmen. There are moments or even days when the bureaucracy seems insurmountable. A soil analyst once held up the building of a simple radiotherapy centre for what seemed an interminable and wholly unnecessary time due to the anxiety about the load-bearing capacity of the sandy soil.

* * *

By the late 1980s several of the original Sue Ryder Homes had deteriorated badly after over thirty years of extremely heavy use and it had become essential to replace them as quickly and economically as possible.

At that time there were virtually no building materials available locally in Poland and a considerable amount of research was carried out into various building systems to determine how the buildings could best be rebuilt.

As a result of this research, a contract was eventually negotiated with a British company specialising in the manufacture of steel building frames and the first of the new buildings fabricated in sections in England for transport in containers to Poland. The containers carried not only the actual building frame but the whole of the materials required to complete the building and equip it.

The overriding advantage of this Metframe System, as it is known, is that it was possible to erect the buildings on prepared foundations and make it weathertight in just six weeks, from the time the components first arrived at the site. This enabled work to progress on the completion of the interior and the fitting out irrespective of the winter weather, something quite impossible with traditional construction. The building was, in fact, completed and ready for occupation in the record time of six months. This compares with one or two years for a conventional building, sometimes even longer.

Since the completion of this original building, a further four Homes have been built in Poland, using the system, although with the increasing availability of materials locally, the number of containers needed to be shipped out of England has gradually been reduced.

The actual site construction work for each of the projects was carried out by a local Polish building contractor who is only awarded the contract after strict tendering procedures by the Ministry under the training and supervision of a Contracts Manager sent out by the English company. The skill and resourcefulness of the Polish tradesmen was demonstrated in the rapid way in which they learned completely new building techniques and in the quality of the finished building.

Without the skills, experience and dedication of the Foundation's architect in Warsaw, Mr Boguslawski, it is unlikely that these recent contacts would have been completed. In addition to his work as architect, he has had to battle increasingly with bureaucracy to obtain the very many approvals necessary, as well as the many hours spent in trying to get shipments through the complicated Customs procedures. He is a most valuable member of the Foundation's team in Poland.

Humour and jokes are part and parcel of the average Pole's life, without which the people would probably not have survived as they have throughout the centuries. They are well known for their political jokes and a friend of mine has collected no less than 1,232 of them. However tense and difficult site meetings prove, when I have resorted to butterscotch, Polo Mints and even resorted to smoking one or two Sport (the equivalent of Woodbines), their resilience and ability to make jokes have usually prevailed.

One afternoon after receiving kind hospitality from a building engineer whose daughter played Chopin through part of the lunch, we reluctantly took our leave to find a site situated right out in the country along partially cobbled roads. The site was further away than was anticipated and we did not arrive until the evening. We were greeted by a person who said he knew everything about the construction of the Foundation's proposed Home. John Mills, who was accompanying me as the Foundation's surveyor/architect, and I had to try to prevail upon the man to explain that although the building to be erected was of one storey, nevertheless there was a great deal which needed to be understood. We did this against the background of the nuns singing Compline in their chapel, the service being relayed on a tannoy system. Then the cook at the local Home appeared and insisted that we should partake of homemade sausage with bread and butter. In the midst of the excitement and enthusiasm of the locals I repeatedly asked to be shown the site in order to pace it out. Finally we were led through woods, under a moonless sky, and by the light of their hurricane lamp and my torch we subsequently paced out, on a field thick with cauliflowers and rhubarb, the dimensions for our proposed 10,000-square-foot building.

I asked one of those present pertinent questions as to the availability of services and how close we were to them. He replied that the water was the best in the district and, leading me to a well, he lifted off the cover . . . under which we saw a dead rat floating. Mr Siemiradzki from the Ministry of Health and Social Welfare, and the other Poles present, gave their opinion of this rash remark in no uncertain manner, but there was laughter too. Subsequently, to give them their full credit, they cleared the entire site and laid the foundations in almost record time, but here, as on other sites, we had our difficulties with the plumbers.

Finally, when a Home is erected and completed, the lights are lit, the water flows through the taps, and the staff welcome the children or patients enabling them to relax and relieving them of their pain, then all of us who have been engaged in the work as a team know that our efforts have not been in vain. Each time a renovation is carried out, or a new Home is built, it feels like giving birth to a child.

* * *

V

Since the establishment of the Homes at Konstancin, many others have been
built by the Foundation in different parts of Poland. As everywhere, the
needs are numerous and great, but special priority is given to patients diagnosed with cancer. The Poles had already rebuilt their Cancer Institute and
were trying to establish Centres with X-ray, radium, and eventually (but
only in certain places), cobalt equipment, so the Foundation has played only
a very small part. Professor Josef Lawkowski, an oncologist to whom I am
deeply indebted for sharing with us his wide experience and advice, was
head of the Polish Cancer Institute for many years. He had the dedication
and energy to accompany me round the regions and strongly believed that
by providing a Sue Ryder Home and simple facilities, together with a proper
well-trained and experienced team from the Marie Curie Institute in
Warsaw, the Foundation could relieve a great deal of suffering. So we had
plans for Centres in Koszalin, Stettin, Fordon, Wroclaw, Poznań, Kraków,
to mention only a few of the principal cities and towns. Most sadly he died
on 26 March 1970. His successor, although a close colleague, was a surgeon
and did not get out into the field and, consequently, the Foundation's plans
were greatly thwarted; and indeed thousands of patients died without the
nursing and medical care which we would have tried to give them.

I was deeply moved by the many people with cancer whom I met during
the course of the work while on the rounds with the doctors and social
workers. I remember, for example, a bedridden woman of seventy, a terminal
case, who shared a room with her daughter and two small grandchildren:
doctors and neighbours had tried to get her admitted to six different hospitals, but none had a free bed. Then there was a former milliner, aged sixty,
who, as well as suffering with cancer, had had a nervous breakdown: she
was homeless and sleeping rough in a park in a temperature of minus 18°c.
A housewife suffering with cancer died alone because her husband, on whom
she depended, had to work in another part of the town.

The country has a tradition of voluntary workers who play a valuable
part. The problems and frustrations of individuals were exacerbated by the
political difficulties and strained relations of the postWar era. I would like
to express my recognition and appreciation of all the staff in each of the
Homes and hospitals – especially of those who are married and, therefore,
have two jobs in life, and yet try to give their loyalty and time both to their
family and to their patients. The domestic staff (*salowe*) play a more than
valuable and vital role, both on day and night duty in supporting their
seniors. Sadly, as in almost all countries, there is an acute shortage of nurses
and auxiliaries. This is almost entirely due to the low salaries which have
been paid to them ever since 1945.

Feasibility surveys are carried out continuously by the authorities and
I participate in these. I felt from the beginning that something should be

done to help the very hard-pressed authorities and people who were battling so heroically to alleviate the terrible misery. The Foundation's first very simple Home for cancer patients was built at Zyrardow, thirty miles from Warsaw; but subsequently others were built within the complex of general hospitals so that they might benefit from the facilities.

I frequently had the privilege of comforting dying patients in the Homes, some of them only in their teens or early twenties, and I recall many of them vividly. Even though we could provide no cure for them, we had the consolation of knowing that they were being looked after by people who cared about them, and that they were conscious of this. One of my Secretaries, Margaret Farmer, who accompanied me once, was a soprano. She sang at each of the Oncology Centres and Homes we visited and many patients wept with joy on hearing her lovely voice.

I must stress the extreme simplicity of these Homes, and what a contrast they are to those in Britain, where all comforts and medication are available and the ratio of nurses is far higher too. In addition to lack of equipment, there has always been an abysmal lack of drugs and medication and, I may add, of all the basic necessities required to nurse patients.

It is my custom on arrival in the lorry or Land Rover to greet the staff and patients: those who are ambulant stand in or near the doorway and passage with flowers – usually carnations – or handmade gifts. Their welcome is made all the more moving by one or two of them saying or reading a message thanking me for coming and including in their thanks those I represent. Once, in different Homes, two patients recited these lines to me from Kipling:

> I have eaten your bread and salt
> I have drunk your water and wine
> The deaths ye died I have watched beside
> And the lives that ye led were mine.

and in another Home the patients said:

> and as all Poles together may we quote from Paderewski, while presenting you with these lilies:
> Our moody, imaginative, changeable, simultaneously gay and sad, ardent and dreamy race

On each visit I give every individual gifts which include a box of soap, tights and socks, lavender water, a packet of tea or coffee and a tin of fruit, preferably peaches or apricots. These are all luxuries to them.

After being briefed on the diagnoses and prognoses by the consultants, I then go on the rounds with the Sister in charge and the consultant, talking to each individual, making notes, sitting with them and listening to their stories and their experiences. When one consultant used Latin extensively it called for even greater concentration on my part. The desperate shortage of drugs in Poland encouraged experienced pharmacists in Britain to make collections and give their services in sorting them. Drugs were all listed and marked at the outset for the appropriate hospital, Oncology Centre or Home of the Foundation in Poland. At the end of a long day the consultants, doctors and nurses there would help me off-load the heavy cartons from my lorry.

At the beginning many drugs were (and some still are) very difficult to obtain. The pharmacists in Britain collected and sorted and labelled them (entirely in their spare time). Nevertheless, it was my evening penance to spend hours with a copy of *Mims*, the monthly pharmaceutical magazine, in one hand, trying to identify and correctly allocate the drugs. The hardest part was always the sharing out of the much too slender quantities of the painkilling drugs, a situation which has been in no way alleviated. Indeed, it has become far, far worse, and it is deplorable to find oneself in the position of having literally to choose with the consultant or doctor which patient (child or adult) should benefit from our sparse supplies. It is a terrible situation and one that haunts me day and night. At Góra Kalwaria, a large pharmacy was run most efficiently by a full-time pharmacist.

It is a very humbling experience, going around, sharing the thoughts, cares and joys of patients and staff. Often the patients' endurance is heroic, while others cry as they realise they are departing this life so soon or will have to leave their young children behind. Sometimes we have a husband and wife as patients at the same time. I remember particularly a young boy with an inoperable tumour who became blind and couldn't accept the fact that he had no future. He needed a lot of companionship, and became steadily more demanding as his disease advanced.

There are always poignant moments with the patients, relieved, however, by their stoic courage and humour; when I am with them I find it almost impossible to tear myself away. There was an engineer with cancer of the lungs who kept his empty tin of New Zealand peaches because he liked to imagine who the donor was and what that country looked like. Then there was a woman whose jaw was fungative; although by profession she was a teacher and had a remarkably brave War record in the Resistance, she could only write the word "Drink". There are hundreds of others, and almost each room holds memories of individuals who have been treated, discharged and readmitted. The average mortality rate is between forty and fifty per cent. This is a cruel fact which lives with me all the time. Trying to comfort and support the bereaved relatives and friends can be very exacting too.

From notes in my ring book, written long ago, I find the following:

> We drove along roads fringed with beautiful trees, the sunlight dancing on their leaves and knew that several individuals whose last hours we had shared were meeting their Creator in indefinable beauty. Neither Maria Polanowska [one of the many honorary social workers with whom the Foundation has had the privilege of working] nor I could speak, and our silence was heavy with memories of life stories and whispered conversations. Maria said softly to me: "Their stories are too poignant to describe."

During the years of working I found that, apart from cancer patients, these were the top priorities: patients with rheumatoid arthritis (mainly young girls and women), cardiac cases, physically handicapped young married couples and single people, victims of severe accidents, the elderly hemi-plegics and retarded children. Even if we limit ourselves to working in these fields, the demands on the Foundation and all concerned are tremendous and, alas, we cannot do even a fraction of what we would like to do. In the circumstances, the best course is to rely, as before, on the ministers, the local authorities and local practitioners to tell us what they intend doing, and then to co-operate with them as best we can. They themselves have built a remarkable number of homes. Each of the twenty-two districts (*wojewodztwos*) (now forty-nine) had well-qualified staff in its Medical and Social Welfare Departments.

There are, of course, other homes caring for short-term patients who are discharged after treatment; and wider social problems, including rehabilitation, are also studied.

The vastness of the need may seem depressing, yet, as colleague and former Head of the Polish Cancer Institute, has said, "If we speak only of problems, it sounds hopeless; but it isn't. Our lives are made up of prob-lems, troubles, expectations, successes and failures. We must persevere and go forward." This is my own view. We always bear in mind the preva-lence of cancer, the needs in hospitals, the availability of beds for both acute and malignant cases, discharge facilities and domiciliary care.

Regrettably, I cannot mention all the many places, hospitals and Homes, each of which, as always in life, has its own characters, personalities, humour, squabbles and differences. Every visit gave pleasure but was also a challenge and a headache. I have found a dignity and thoughtfulness which reminds me of so many gracious people – young, middle-aged and old. The late Director Raczynski (who himself had to undergo a serious operation, performed skilfully by a woman surgeon) worked with the Order of Nursing Sisters of St Vincent de Paul at the local authority Home at Góra Kalwaria (Hill of Calvary), which is linked with the Foundation's Homes. Director Raczynski was a tall, reserved man who had had to shoulder a lot of responsibility in his life. Like others in his position, he shared with the appropriate local authorities a deep concern for trying to improve the quality of life. This is even harder as they grapple with the pressures and persistence of hundreds who want to be admitted. The would-be patients who apply are usually people who have lost everybody in their family, and are often cases requiring very heavy nursing. Some of them are quite indomitable. I remember how one patient insisted upon singing "Rule Britannia" with the final line running "Poland and Britain never, never, never will be slaves".

After going the rounds of 127 patients at the Homes at Góra Kalwaria the Sisters would say: "Do come and have some coffee" – regardless of the time of day or night. This meant a four-course meal (mainly vegetables) beautifully prepared and presented in a simple room which was their Head Sister's bedroom; canaries flitting freely about the room added an unusual touch. Our conversation would turn to the patients and the children's needs in other countries. On one occasion when we were talking about the frolics and the fun of the girls at Konstancin, Director Raczynski said: "I think their lives here at Góra Kalwaria have a different sort of expression but it is very moving, and when you hear the patients and they talk to you, there is still much life in some of them." As Rupert Brooke once wrote: "Old age is only a different kind of merriment from youth, and a wiser one."

* * *

VI

"COURAGE THEIR MEETING PLACE"

The ritual and dignity of Mass and Benediction, whether said in a simple village church or any church in a town or city are remarkable. For years, Pope John Paul II as both Bishop and later Cardinal had been part of this tradition in Poland, moving around his parishes in the diocese and involving himself in everyone's concerns. He had also undertaken long train journeys (often at night) to and from Kraków and the Catholic University at Lublin where he was a professor. In addition, having been invited to several countries overseas he was able to see for himself the many difficulties in each and also the desperate needs of the Third World. Both his talks and speeches on this subject left a great impression on those who heard them. So, as Parish Priest, Bishop and Cardinal, Karol Wojtyla had already left his mark wherever he went.

The Pope's visit to Poland in 1979 was one of the most moving experiences of my life. How does one try to describe a pilgrimage of just nine days, during which the deep and abiding faith of the Church in Poland was manifested to millions of people all over the world? (The Poles' millennium of Christianity was celebrated in 1966.)

This visit by His Holiness was symbolised both by quiet reflection and vast, jubilant crowds – each person, regardless of age, openly professing the Christian faith, exulting in the strength, charisma, dignity, patience and humour of the Pope. After hearing *Sto Lat* ("May you live for a hundred years") being sung again late one night, the Pope replied, "If you want me to live for a hundred years then please may I have some sleep".

I have many, many memories of those nine days; impressions which will remain with me as long as I live. I think of the joyful music and the reverent hush during the Masses; the attentiveness, the jubilant singing and the bursts of applause during his homilies, the happy expressions on faces lined with care, sweat and the unmistakable legacy of hard work; the joyfulness of youth; babies and children being held high on the shoulders of their parents; nuns dipping into pails of water and distributing it among the vast masses in the continuous heatwave; the patter of feet on pavements and streets by day and night; roads, with group after group of pilgrims led by priests and banners; the sound of singing; guitars playing; trains and buses disgorging their passengers; sleepy travellers, propping each other up while others lay out on the grass; the chill of the night; blistered toes; swollen feet; dust-filled sandals; talkative, excited students; young people swaying and jostling; stewards with yellow caps and armbands; the vast multitudes stretching away to the horizon; the Tatra mountains shrouded in mist; shafts of sunlight streaming through the trees; woods smelling of moss and wild strawberries; a blaze of flowers around the Curia (the simple Bishop's Palace) in Kraków; the strong murmur of evening prayers on the balconies until the early hours of the morning; confessions being heard and all-night prayer vigils; priests directing the traffic whilst police stood aside; soup kitchens organised by the various parishes with equipment sometimes lent by the Army; noisy commentators, and cameras on the wide and lofty Press stands; television crews on high towers pulling up their rope ladders; hundreds of priests distributing Holy Communion; the Pope's drives through the crowds at Nowy Targ and prolonged, torrential rain after his Mass; pilgrims walking hour after hour through the rain on roads thronged with people, some with umbrellas, others only with plastic raincoats shared between them; processions of cardinals, bishops and clergy, both before and after each Mass; the variation and height of the altars at each place; flowers strewn on the paths to the high altars; the vivid and rich variety of the regional costumes; the procession of those who were chosen to go up and present many beautiful gifts to the Pope; the Pope finally interrupting the frequent hymns, "I think I must return to my homily"; the Pope's family grave garlanded with flowers and candles in Kraków. Just beyond this grave lie 462 young Allied servicemen. The inscriptions on their gravestones speak of the sorrow of their families. (The keeper of the cemetery confided to me beforehand, "I will tell you a secret – if you return here at 3.45 to 4 p.m. you will see His Holiness".)

The churches throughout the country were decorated inside and out with streamers or ribbons in the Papal colours, yellow and white, Our Lady's blue and the colours of the Polish flag; each altar a mass of flowers, and the beautiful fragrance of Madonna lilies and incense drifted amongst the packed congregations; photographs of Our Lady of Jasna Góra (the bright mountain) and the Pope in the windows, framed at night by small white lights; the ringing of the bells; the sound of the bugle call from St Mary's in Kraków echoing over the City to signal the passing of each hour, a tradition which has survived since the Tartar invasion; suntanned faces, men and women still bearing tattooed numbers on their left arms; the unforgettable moment when the Pope's helicopter landed outside Block 23 at Auschwitz-Birkenau: a woman who had been a prisoner there as a girl of seventeen crying softly; Papal flags flying from the watchtowers which had once housed armed SS guards; the high altar erected over the railway tracks where for four-and-a-half years the cattle trucks arrived, carrying their pitiful human cargoes from all over Europe, destined for the gas chambers or for slave labour; my own sense of awe and amazement on receiving one of the few tickets which allowed me to go up to the high altar at Auschwitz, and the supreme moment when, with about forty others chosen from the thousands of people present, I received Holy Communion from the Pope. From the altar I looked down on a row of survivors in their uniforms standing alongside a stone table thick with votive candles. All round this they had laid countless single carnations, and these were strewn, too, on rails of the altar. These flowers represented the martyrdom of all those who had died there. And I remember thinking that the Pope's visit to that place could only prove, absolutely and finally, that in the end good triumphs over evil.

The Pope stopped to have a more private pilgrimage in Auschwitz I, the original camp converted from brick Army barracks which had been built and used before the War by the Polish Army. There he walked down the long camp street to Block 11 – the death block – to the cells underground in which Father Kolbe, who gave his life in exchange for one of his fellow prisoners, and who has now been canonised, was murdered. The Pope laid a wreath and lit a large candle, praying on his knees in the small bare cell, alone except for a few members of his party.

Between Blocks 11 and 10 (the latter block used for the dreaded medical experiments) he laid a wreath at the execution wall and knelt in silent prayer. Then he returned on foot, past the grim blocks and beyond the perimeter of the Camp to his helicopter.

The message of his whole visit to Auschwitz and Birkenau was to show the whole world that nothing should ever be forgotten. The anonymous millions had not died in vain. God had been there, and He had sent Peter's successor to declare that the crimes were to be forgiven, but that the memories of the suffering should remain in our hearts for all time.

It seemed to me during those days that we were living in a wonderland; as though in some way we had left the world and were being prepared for Eternity. The Pope's intense fervour during prayer and at Mass was transmitted to every one of us who was there. Nothing that had happened before would, or could, diminish this ethereal experience – whether now or in the future. It was surely God's sign that he recognised the Poles, their faith, their prayers, their suffering; and one of their sons had been called to Rome to be His representative and theirs, on this earth.

Within minutes of the Pope entering the helicopter after blessing a large crowd of policemen, the heavens opened, blotting out the view of his beloved mountains at Nowy Targ. The great drops increased to torrential rain, and it seemed symbolic: tears were being shed for all that had happened, and was to come, in Poland.

*   *   *

VII

"Either our homeland will blossom in talent, work, freedom and tolerance, or it will be gripped by a frost in which all the flowers will fade," said the newspaper *Zycie Warszawy* on 6 December 1980.

Bad harvests with severe floods are only two of a multitude of reasons for the dissatisfaction felt throughout the country; and the terrible shortages, first of food, then of soap, clothing, footwear and medical supplies, made one feel that the clock had been turned back. Long and seemingly endless queues formed outside shops day and night, not only for the bare essentials of life, but also for petrol (for the small percentage of those who ran a vehicle). The situation in the hospitals became desperate and it was obvious that unless an international long-term relief operation was mounted the Poles could hardly survive.

It seemed at long last that countries which had hitherto been unaware of Poland's agony during the long five years of War, and of all her persecution, and occupations during past centuries, were gradually waking up to the plight of this gallant nation in Central Europe.

What began as a few lorries, Land Rovers and other vehicles, became small Armies bringing regular supplies to a courageous and suffering people. The first I remember seeing was in November 1980, and then there were juggernauts with registration plates from France, Belgium, Norway, Holland, Luxembourg, Denmark, Portugal, Spain, Eire, Italy, West Germany, Sweden, Switzerland and Britain which gladdened the heart and brought relief and, above all knowledge that the Poles were being remembered by so many people. It is more than difficult to choose from the huge number of letters received at Headquarters, but I would like to quote a few. Normally the Poles are givers, not receivers. From Wimborne United Reformed Church, Dorset, we received the following:

> Please could you put the enclosed cheque for £35.30 towards your Poland Fund. It is the proceeds of a special collection at our Chapel. It comes with our respect and love for all your fine work and with our prayers that you, your fellow workers and the people of Poland may be kept in the hollow of God's hand.
>
> C.B.

From Southampton:

> It might interest you to know how the enclosed £318.30 was raised. We are three small villages, just over 1,600 inhabitants. We organised a twenty-four hour vigil in the middle of one of the villages. We raised the Polish flag at 2 p.m. last Friday and, taking it in turns, it was held there for twenty-four hours. We had a carboy [large bottle] into which people could pop donations and two notices saying:
>   "twenty-four hour vigil for the Polish people"

"Please donate to the Sue Ryder Foundation"

We also distributed the enclosed explanation to passers-by. We were of course exposed to the elements and it did rain quite a bit, but that helped and it did us all a lot of good.Two Poles came out from Portsmouth and Titchfield to join us: this was very encouraging.

All good wishes for the great work you are doing.

J.B.

From Durham:

I am enclosing cheques for £309.75 and £10.25 as part of the response of my Methodist Circuit to your Food for Poland Appeal. In addition over 1,450 items of tinned goods and other non-perishable foodstuffs have been sent to the local Sue Ryder Shop from the Circuit. Every Church in this Circuit has responded in some way, and I have had donations and gifts flying at me from every angle.

B.M.M.

From Cambridgeshire:

Enclosed please find a cheque for £5 to add to your Polish Disaster Fund. We are all appalled at the conditions in Poland now, but wherever you and your helpers go the bright light on the practical expression on your Christianity brings light and hope to those to whom you minister.

E.B.

From Norfolk:

My family owes a great debt to the people of Poland who sheltered my brother and one other for three weeks in a farmhouse with the Gestapo in the other half of the house. They also helped them escape but, alas, my brother didn't "make it". What bravery those farmers showed in doing this! Forty years is a long time, but in this small way I show my eternal gratitude. I have in mind the many Polish airmen who gave their lives in the Battle of Britain.

(Enclosed £60)

S.M.

From Wales:

I am praying continually for the people of Poland – they are a shining example to the rest of the world with their unquenchable faith and their endurance of suffering. They have chosen the Way of the Cross indeed, and we must, as you say, pray for a miracle.

D.H.

The purpose of my several visits to Poland in 1980–81 was to work out there as usual, to reassure the Poles of the Foundation's continued concern and to share with them part of their experiences.

My visa was cancelled when martial law came into force during the night of 12–13 December, and just before Christmas 1981, I applied for a new visa for myself and my daughter Gigi to work in Poland, in the hope that the authorities there would consider our applications favourably. And indeed we were given *gratis* visas and also obtained transit visas from the East German authorities.

The previous months had been especially busy because, in addition to the heavy Christmas mail, the appeal for Poland was building up steadily and 19,200 letters and posters were sent out from Headquarters between August 1981 and January 1982 to churches of different denominations.

Sorting and packing of food also continued every day and well into each evening. This was coped-with at first by five volunteers from Poland, and heavy parcels containing essential items were being sent out with volunteers returning to that country. Later several more local volunteers came along.

In addition, Polish lorries returning to Poland were leaving Headquarters every fortnight filled with food and goods. For the last thirty years the Foundation has always been able to send free freight by Polish ships leaving Purfleet, Essex, for the port of Gdynia, and approximately eighty tonnes of food and essential items had been sent out in the previous year.

Among the very many generous gifts of food received at Headquarters was an extraordinary number of tea bags and tins of baked beans, followed by Christmas puddings and custard, which showed how many of the British public believed that those who were hungry could understandably be revived by cups of tea. These items are known to only a minority in Poland, and as there are frequent fuel cuts cooking the puddings presented something of a problem.

As the food arrived daily at Headquarters by car and van, having often been delivered to a local Foundation Home or Shop in the first place for forwarding, it was sorted, labelled, put into tea chests and marked appropriately. Only one kind of food was put into each chest.

With hindsight, we seemed to be given extra grace and strength, day and night, to cope with this vast influx of food and medical supplies. We did, in fact, only just manage to cope with the deluge of gifts, which continued non-stop for at least seven years.

In addition, the Foundation sent out every two months £60,000 of food, bought by a broker for the Foundation, and this was matched by a grant from the European Community. Every lorry had its own driver and escort. The latter had to report exactly what occurred at each destination and upon the scenes of poverty and pride which he witnessed. These reports were then sent to the European Community before further allocations were made. It was proof that everything reached the right hands, as lists were drawn up in every parish in every diocese in Poland and Bishop Domin, the Co-ordinator, and his team in Katowice directed the lorries coming in to wherever the supplies were most needed.

Thanks to the generosity and swift response of a garage in Guildford, a large Renault van was lent free of charge to the Foundation so that I could drive some of the food and equipment to Poland when I left at the end of December. Shell gave me free petrol coupons for Western Europe and we filled every jerry can we could carry.

Despite starting work in the early hours of the morning and other shifts taking over in the evening, we were still pressed to get the contents of the van labelled and loaded in time, and, as the hours ran out, I was informed by Felixstowe that the boat's departure time had been brought forward two hours!

I left Felixstowe for Rotterdam at 11 p.m. on 28 December on a freight ship. On disembarking, I was greeted by the kind Dutch Manager of Townsend Thoresen who expressed his deep concern for Poland and wished me luck. I then drove on for 327 miles in patchy fog conditions and over roads which had seen much snow, to the very old house of a colleague.

Next morning, when I was cleaning the van, I found that there was a puncture in the tyre on the offside wheel which had to be mended.

Gigi joined me in Hanover and we proceeded on our way to the West–East German border. At the frontier I was given forms to complete in German, and these had to be filled in at a desk placed outside in the snow. The East Germans watched us from their warm huts and came out to wipe the desk with a cloth so that the forms did not get too damp! After some one and a half hours' wait I asked if we might be allowed to proceed. Passports were eventually returned and we went onto the next control point – we had to pass through three control points in all.

The East German Customs official read the letters written in Polish and German by the Polish Consulate in London, which always included a list of contents, and then gave us curt orders to park round the back of his hut. He went on, "Now you are under my control. Everything will be taken out of this van by you." Gigi said to me: "Mum, they can't really expect us to do this without helping." I replied, "It is better not to argue and get on." There were two large tables and no sooner had we set one large carton or box on a table than he barked at us to remove it to the other one. He then turned them all out, asking questions about the contents. His obsession was to find hidden arms and ammunition, and he went to endless lengths without, or course, any success. He was deeply suspicious about my old slippers and the orthopaedic pillows made by the Sue Ryder Support Group in Layham. Each pillow was subsequently unwrapped and X-rayed on a machine which he hardly knew how to operate! He asked me to tell him the age of each blanket in which the pillow had been wrapped, where it had originated and why it was there, which I dutifully did. Afterwards, in the light of day, we noticed that the blankets all bore the label "St Mary's Hospital, Paddington – September 1939".

I also had to show him my missal (prayer book) from my overnight bag and explained that I was a believer and attended Mass. He found a typed sheet, which was a copy of a sonnet entitled "Madonna of the Cherries". I started to translate it to him but he showed his displeasure. However, I took the opportunity of explaining that this sonnet was written by one of the great Generals of the British Army in 1943, Field-Marshal Lord Wavell:

Dear Lady of the Cherries, cool serene,
Untroubled by our follies, strife and fears.
Clad in soft reds and blues and mantle green,
Your memory has been with me all these years.

Long years of battle, bitterness and waste,
Dry years of sun and dust and Eastern skies,
Hard years of ceaseless struggle, endless haste,
Fighting gainst greed for power and hate and lies.

Your red-gold hair, your slowly smiling face,
For pride in your dear son, your King of Kings,
Fruits of the kindly earth, and truth and grace,
Colour and light, and all warm lovely things -

For all that loveliness, that warmth, that light,
Blessed Madonna, I go back to fight.
                        (Northwick Park, 29 April 1943)

The official's suspicion was further raised on seeing the map and catalogue of Ford vehicles which had inadvertently been left by Mann Egerton in the left-hand pocket of the van.

Throughout all these searches, and especially while we were being ordered to carry packages of food from one table to another, he questioned me about my knowledge of German proverbs. When I said I had heard quite a number in my time he asked me to recite a few; *he* remembered this one: "Trust is good, but control is better." The Germans asked me where I had learnt their language so fluently and, as always on every single journey amongst the hundreds and hundreds I met, there were always the same questions: "How many guns and ammunition are you carrying?" The standard answer for me was: "As I am a social worker and auxiliary nurse I have no interest in such things." Once my passport had been safely handed over to the Poles, I usually turned to the Germans and said: "The last time I carried guns and ammunition was in 1945."

We did everything that was ordered of us and then we were told to reload.

Meanwhile the Polish Customs officials in their hut gave us winks and shakes of the head. At last it was their turn! When they opened the back door of the van for their inspection they jokingly remarked, "Now it is our turn to ask you to off-load!" One of them later said to me: "This is a sad evening at the end of a long year."

I bought Polish petrol coupons, but as there was no assurance that petrol could be obtained I limited the number.

We drove on for some three hours after this, but I thought it unwise to proceed further as we were very tired, although there was no curfew that night.

We reached the small Village of Bytyn at 11.20 p.m., and by sheer coincidence the local priest was standing outside his little wooden house as we drove up and welcomed us in for a warm drink. He had been a prisoner in Dachau and had undergone medical experiments there.

At midnight the church bells were rung and we were invited to sleep in a small room from where food, donated from Holland, was being distributed. The priest said how fortunate he felt, too, because a parishioner had found and given him fuel only the day before to heat his accommodation. He apologised for the late Mass at nine the next morning but, as usual, the church was crowded despite the cold.

We proceeded to Poznań to work and stay with one of the Foundation's honorary social workers who distributed food and with others visited those in need. She had been sentenced to death by the Nazis in 1943 and survived terrible beatings (which had affected her hearing), solitary confinement in a darkened cell, and many other indignities too terrible to describe.

The long, straight snow-covered and empty roads from Poznań to Warsaw stretched out before us, and apart from bridges being guarded by two soldiers, we saw little evidence of the Army, nor were we stopped and checked; but on approaching the capital, Warsaw, it was different. Control checkpoints were very evident, and we were often asked to show our passports and papers.

Martial law meant that a curfew was in force from 10 p.m. to 6 a.m.; all mail was censored; illustrated leaflets and other papers were forbidden to be published; if anyone was staying with a relative or colleague in another region before martial law came into force they had to register with the police on their return home. The Poles were not allowed to use their private vehicles, which meant that the needy and sick had to depend upon neighbours to fetch an ambulance or a doctor. Telephones had been cut. The newsreaders on the television and radio were representatives of the Army. Long food and fuel queues were evident as before, and people of all ages stood patiently for hours. It was not uncommon in queues to see children doing their homework or professional men and women attending to work brought from their offices.

I had a three-hour discussion with the then Minister of Health, Dr T. Szelachowski, a highly respected and hardworking physician from Bialystok who worked from 7 a.m. to 9 p.m. There were meetings with my old colleague and friend, Mr M. Karczewski (who from 1947 to 1989 was Head of the Social Services under the Minister).

While in Warsaw, in addition to the meetings, we visited the housebound, the handicapped, those unable to queue, and also those in the wide area of Konstancin and villages beyond. Many of the individuals were in a pitiful condition, but very proud, and they left one feeling extremely humble. As before, personal contact made it easier to try and assess what they wanted and then make up the appropriate parcels.

Permission had to be sought and given by the police to move from one town or county to another; this permission was given to us and endorsed by the Ministry of Health with whom the Foundation works.

In order to reach the north, we used the train service. This journey proved quite a saga.

We were fortunate enough to receive a couchette which we shared with another passenger. At 4.45 a.m. she woke me and asked if I had noticed that the train had been making frequent stops, but I had been sleeping too deeply to be aware of it. I then realised that it was shunting backwards and forwards, and as the light broke we saw that we had stopped over a bridge near Tczew. We were given no information. Our fellow passengers did not have any food, so we shared all our biscuits with them. Gradually one after another left the train to make their way as best they could on foot for the last fifty to sixty kilometres to their destinations. At about 1 p.m. the train drew up outside the station; the engine was then uncoupled and shunted away, leaving us sitting there in the stationary carriages. We then heard an announcement that a local train was departing for Gdańsk and we only had a few moments to get off, cross the line and throw ourselves into it. This train stopped at every station, and finally we had to disembark and walk about quarter of a mile to the main road to catch a bus. Two Poles befriended us and helped to carry the medical supplies, fruit juices, etc. which we were intent upon delivering to the Foundation's Oncology Centre. The swirling blizzard continued unabated, and after waiting some time we clambered onto a bus which was already overfilled. At each stop more people got on so that by the time we reached Gdynia it was impossible to get out because of the crush. Our two companions decided it was high time for their countrymen to be informed of our presence and the reason for our visit. To our embarrassment, a full communique was thereupon issued, and the passengers were implored to show up their country's hospitality, gratitude and respect. The driver obediently stopped the bus about a mile past the main station at Gdynia where the passengers made room for us to get off and showered us with profuse apologies and gestures of good will before we left them to walk back to the station, accompanied by our two friends.

I reminded Gigi that it was essential to walk in the soft snow on the verges as the paths had become far too slippery, but within minutes I myself had fallen on my back scattering what I was carrying! As we limped into the main station at Gdynia a woman's voice announced over the loud-speaker the arrival of the Warsaw train! We had inadvertently left the orthopaedic pillows on that train so one of our companions went up the platform to get them, only to be told by the train's attendant that a doctor had already been asking for us, that he had been handed the pillows and been informed that we had disappeared! Meanwhile, we waited below and watched seventy young sailors come in to warm their frozen limbs; two were lucky enough to be sharing six doughnuts with their colleagues.

We wanted to buy return tickets to Warsaw, but were informed that these could only be obtained after 8 p.m., which was shortly before curfew. After some discussion, it was decided that our only chance of ever reaching our destination was to request the Army and Navy to get into touch with the ambulance service, who carried a radio, and ask them to contact the Director of the General Hospital. In the meantime we were driven by some sailors in a jeep to the flat of a friend. Four of them had gone on ahead, running up the stairs, and when they rang my friend's doorbell and she saw the group of strangers her expression was one of amazement, the more so when she saw us bringing up the rear! The ambulance service eventually made contact during the night with the Director of the General Hospital, who called as early as he could to collect us.

We finally reached the Foundation's Oncology Centre at Gdynia Redlowo where, in 1981, 622 patients had been nursed after surgery and where they also received treatment, including chemotherapy and radium. A further 600 attended the Outpatients Department attached to the Centre. Although we had lost hours because of breakdowns of the trains due to the weather, we also managed to visit some other individuals in need in that area, and I was asked again by both officials and the authorities with whom I work to return and stay as long as possible.

Everywhere, despite the shortages, I found the Poles shared their meagre rations. Their gallantry is absolutely remarkable; so too is their indomitable faith. Everywhere, however, there was a noticeable silence, as if there had been a death in the National Family. The Poles no longer made jokes. There was hardly any traffic and people cried easily, while others found it difficult to explain their feelings and turned away or left off speaking in the middle of a sentence. A sense of shock and humiliation was apparent, which no words can describe.

Distribution of food and other essential items was done from lists made up by the Foundation's own voluntary social workers and physicians, together with the parish councils and other social workers. Many thousands of private parcels were also reaching people, and there was no evidence of anything being stolen or misappropriated. Distribution was done as fairly as possible and *undoubtedly* the food, soap and medical supplies which have been donated have made a considerable difference to the recipients. Naturally, it is difficult for those who have not had their pain relieved, their thirst quenched, or their grief shared, fully to grasp the significance of this help – or realise the full seriousness of the situation in the long term.

Since the introduction of food rationing in March 1981 distribution is fairer, but prices have soared by over 300 per cent and many people can no longer afford to buy food (see table)

OFFICIAL LIST OF RATIONS ALLOWED EACH MONTH – 1981-2

	Adult	Child
Meat/poultry	2.5 kg	2.5 kg
Butter	0.5 kg	0.5 kg
Margarine	0.5 kg	0.75 kg
Sugar	1.5 kg	2.0 kg

	Adult	Child
Flour	1.0 kg	1.0 kg
Sweets or coffee		
(depending on supplies)	0.1 kg	–
Chocolate	–	1 bar
Soap	1 bar	1 bar
Soap powder	0.3 kg	0.6 kg
Cereals	1.0 kg	–
Semolina	–	1.0 kg

(Quantity varied according to the region and availability)

Many of the older generation said that all of this reminded them of previous dark days in the War and the Stalin era, but there were those who felt it was inevitable and that by professing their faith the Polish people would re-emerge. The Primate, Archbishop Glemp (whom I saw and talked with) exhorted everybody, especially the young, in almost weekly pastoral letters and in overcrowded churches to remain calm and disciplined. Bishop Domin of Katowice told me, "We have had the joyful mysteries, now it is our turn to experience the sorrowful ones."

Food rationing stopped in 1990, but huge numbers of the population cannot afford the goods on sale.

We found the late Professor Cieslak, a close colleague, immersed in the biography of Lord Palmerston (borrowed from the British Council Library). He made many illuminating comments about Queen Victoria's attitude to her various Prime Ministers. Professor Cieslak's knowledge of the history of Britain was outstanding. He had been arrested with many other Professors from the University of Kraków in 1939 and miraculously survived five years of torture and suffering in Sachsenhausen Concentration Camp, near Berlin. This was one of the original camps and was established in 1936. About 200,000 prisoners of over twenty nationalities were killed there. Attached to Sachsenhausen, as to all extermination/concentration camps, were many auxiliary camps.

The patience and grace to forgive shown by the Poles has never failed to impress me – I think other people in a similar situation, especially in the bitter cold of winter or the heat of summer, would have shown anger, impatience and bitterness – especially as the queues had started before troubles came to a head in August 1980, so each day and night took its toll on people's health. Indeed, there were cases of people collapsing in the queues.

Almost our last call was back in Poznań amongst the housebound once more, and then we were ready to bath, sleep and clean out the van for the return journey.

Pani Maria, the Foundation's honorary social worker, again insisted upon sharing her rations and, as usual, we naturally brought out our grub box. The two slices of toast she made, on which we spread some butter, were

some of the most delicious we had ever eaten, accompanied by two cups
of coffee!

We were sad to leave brave Poland, but I promised to return in April.

The long drive throughout the night proved quite cold (minus 25°C). The
fluid in the thermos and buckets froze and even our briefcases containing
ring books froze onto the van floor! The fact that the van was completely
empty made it rather draughty, so we wore several layers of clothing and
Gigi sat in her sleeping bag.

In East Germany, fog and blinding snow blizzards forced us to stop and
squirt the side mirror and windows with anti-freeze. Within minutes the
East German police were telling me that I was not allowed to stop! Much
further on I was again forced to use anti-freeze, and another lot of armed
policemen immediately switched on a searchlight from their van, trying
to blind us. This action seemed rather silly, especially in such weather
conditions.

Hours later, on arrival at Bruges, then at Zeebrugge, supporters of the
Belgian Foundation told us we had been reported missing in several of
the national newspapers, including those in Britain. We were very surprised.
Later, we could only conclude that this had occurred when we were
reported missing by the guard in the Warsaw–Gdańsk train, and apparently
this news, despite martial law, had reached the Press in Britain and elsewhere. On being questioned by reporters my husband had said, "I am not
worried about them. That is my wife's scene and Poland is her second home
and she is amongst friends."

Both television and the newspaper Press turned out in force to meet and
question us at Felixstowe.

* * *

During my second and longer visit of six weeks from 9 April to 24 May
1982, wherever I went I saw many needs. It would take hours to try and
write about each of the forty places or more that I visited on those long
drives covering about 4,200 miles. From the practical point of view, the visit
could have lasted far longer; time was too short even though the days
started well before 5 a.m. and ended late. Thanks to the Minister of Health
and his colleagues, I was able to rely upon free petrol from the ambulance
stations throughout the country.

In between visits and other meetings I also had discussions with the
Deputy Minister of Health, whose grasp of the Foundation's work and
detailed problems was impressive. Meetings with the local authorities
and different hospitals were very moving because of their dire needs, which
varied considerably from one region to another.

I received every form of support and assistance from the late Bishop
Domin of Katowice. He represented the bishops in Poland and is respon-
sible for distribution of food, medical supplies and clothing sent to the
Church. This was carried out very fairly indeed through the parish priests

and the parish councils in twenty-seven dioceses. A card index and telex system is kept too.

Frequent visits to the housebound were a daily reminder that there are many people who cannot stand in the dreadful queues, which are very long and tiring, and who are either too proud to ask for help or, for a variety of reasons, fail to receive assistance. Coal, clothing and especially footwear, were desperately short.

Up to the time I left, freight lorries from many Western European countries continued to arrive at their destinations and offload, but Bishop Domin shared my concern that unless this continued in the long term, especially when the bitter weather begins, millions of Poles could be in even greater distress.

I saw and talked with 1,118 individuals, including a number of young children and teenagers, in twenty-eight Foundation Homes and Oncology Centres. My visits underlined the necessity for the Foundation to heed the pleas made by medical colleagues and to try and establish several more Oncology Centres for children, teenagers and others. There are at least two to three sites already chosen.

I also visited the sick in their sad and frequently poor accommodation. It seems hard for the Poles to have to bear their national cross as well as put up with their own particular disease or disability. I marvelled at the stoic courage, the ability to smile and pray and the gentle courtesy I received from the sick and dying (of all ages), who even found the strength to hand me beautiful flowers.

"You must be strong with the courage that comes from faith. You must be strong with the strength of faith. You must be faithful. Today more than ever you need this strength." These words were spoken by the Pope in Kraków on 22 June 1983. His second visit to his homeland gave enormous support to Poland in every way. The huge welcoming crowds seemed even larger than those which had attended each of his great Masses in 1979 but, sadly, due to the attempt on his life in Rome and the increase in terrorism in the world, nobody could take chances and instead of driving in an open Popemobile as before, his vehicle was encased in bulletproof glass to give him protection.

The Holy Father visited Warsaw, Niepokalonow, Częstochowa, Poznań, Katowice, Wrocław, Góra sw Anny, Kraków and lastly Nowa Huta.

The singing of the crowds was very moving and so, too, were his homilies. These words come from two of them:

> Poland is a special mother. Her history has not been easy, especially over the course of these last centuries. She is a mother who has suffered much and who ever suffers anew. Therefore she has a right to special love.
> Warsaw, 16 June

> Show me what you love, and I will tell you who you are.
> Częstochowa, 18 June

The Pope left us on Thursday afternoon, and on the following Saturday morning I was in the mountains with Zygmunt Kolodziejski, a concentration camp survivor of over eighty years of age who had been a prisoner of the Germans in three different concentration camps, and whose family estate was looted and burnt. Together we left his simple room which he rented in a small farmhouse in the Village of Waksmund and drove to Chochołow. We parked my car and proceeded on foot four to five kilometres up the long, climbing rough road to a very wide open triangular-shaped meadow which was bordered by woods and mountains. There, the Pope had had a private meeting with his cardinals and others. A tiny chapel stood high up on the sloping meadows. Further down, at the far end of the apex with the Slovak border on the other side of the mountains, stood a wooden guest house, part of which had been divided off and converted into a museum in memory of a Polish Olympic gold medallist – a young man – who had been killed in Auschwitz. A little further down near the rough road I talked to a young shepherd who lived in one of two huts nearby. He proudly showed me the stool on which the Pope had sat to talk with him. The place was bathed in bright sunshine and the birds were singing. It was so peaceful and lovely; Mr Kolodziejski and I were both loath to leave it. We had by chance met two or three people also out walking and mentioned the Pope's visit. They must have invented the rumour that I had attended the Pope's discussions at Chochołow because it soon became widely known both in the locality and beyond, and the girls at Konstancin were even asked whilst on retreat in the mountains as to how I had progressed with these serious meetings!

* * *

This Chapter on Poland cannot end without mention of the rise of Solidarity and the eventual overthrow of Communism.

In the late 1970s, close professional friends from different walks of life and in various parts of Poland told me about the strength of the underground movement and the changes they felt would surely come. I was very shocked, though not surprised – having witnessed the risings in 1956, 1958, 1970 and 1972 – but I had strange misgivings and a premonition that the outcome of their planning would go wrong. As 1980 dawned, it was obvious that the movement Solidarity would be born in the August of that year in the shipyards at Gdańsk. It was led by Lech Walesa, an electrician and very volatile member of the trades unions. Both during his negotiations with the then Government under Mr Gierek, and afterwards, it was apparent that many hundreds of thousands of Poles had joined Solidarity and it swept like a prairie fire throughout the country. Those of us who had been trained during the War in SOE were shocked at the lack of security at meetings, regardless of the place or situation. We were fearful of what was going on as it required only one move in the wrong direction for the Soviets to come in. We knew there were at least 60,000 Soviet troops in certain parts of Poland. They were well hidden in the woods, but their exact locations were known to all of us. I always took the precaution of not talking to anybody until I knew they had first checked their room for bugging and I preferred talking to them outside or by writing notes. It was generally thought, however, that the Russians would not use their army and overwhelm the Poles as this would have led to a bloodbath. We feared more for the political implications and that there would be a return to terror, such as we had witnessed in the Stalin era. Many of the young people expressed indignation and were loath to follow any form of advice and simply said: "Now, it is our turn."

Behind all this emotion and uneasiness was the fact that people had reached the end of their tether and felt they had nothing to lose. There was a deep conviction and belief that Communism would wane and the dark evil of that terrible tyranny would one day be extinguished. It was, indeed, one of the Pope's prayers, from the time he had been in the seminary after the War, that the Communist empire would be eclipsed. No words of mine can describe the terror and death which Communism inflicted on Poland and other countries; nor the terrible consequences they have had to suffer. It was, indeed, very similar to Nazism.

During the 1980s the Church seemed to grow even stronger and both Cardinal Glemp and Cardinal Macharski from Kraków, together with bishops and clergy, spoke out in defiant mood in their homilies, particularly on Sundays; but, at the same time, they implored the people to remain calm and look to God for their freedom.

On the night of 11 December 1980 when I was preparing to go back to Poland again, I received an anonymous telephone call from a woman. I had no idea of her name or where she was speaking from. She simply said "Please return as quickly as possible and be with us." I knew, of course, what she meant and that bad news would surely follow.

During the early hours of the following morning I awoke at about 3 o'clock to see a small picture of Our Lady of Vilna, shining in the dark, and for me that was a very significant sign that something was about to happen in Poland. It was, in fact, the night of the 12th–13th December that the main leaders of Solidarity – eleven of them – were arrested in Sopot. Hundreds more Solidarity members were arrested, and martial law was declared. With hindsight, I believe that General Wojciech Jaruzelski, who declared martial law, will be remembered with respect and as a patriot for, in my humble opinion, he saved Poland from the ghastly fate of a *coup d'état* and the Soviets taking over the country. General Jaruzelski had attended a Catholic school as a boarder in Warsaw until 1939 when he was deported from Kutno, the family estate, to Siberia where he lost two members of his family. He never found General Anders' people and was, therefore, forced to fight in the so-called "Free Polish Army" with the Russians. The reason why he wears dark glasses is because his vision was impaired by penal servitude in Siberia. He also has to wear a corset because of the treatment he received from the Russians, so he was no friend of the Soviet system.

When freedom was gained at last, in 1989, Poland was the first of all the former Communist Countries of Central and Eastern Europe to receive it; but those who were old enough knew how fragile was their newly found freedom and democracy. Virtually all the Polish professional classes, including academics, had been wiped out by the Nazis or the Soviet Communists. As a result, there were exceedingly few people with any experience of leadership and democracy who were qualified to form a Government and to give the firm leadership which was required. Unfortunately, an almost chaotic situation has resulted, and the Government is finding it extremely difficult to introduce a free and democratic society and, in particular, to change to a free-market western-style economy from a Communist one. Before there were no proper shops but since 1990 they now have many new shops, but there are still shortages. Gone are the never-ending queues. If the people have enough money they can buy anything; but over five million Poles are existing below subsistence level because of their low salaries and pensions. Medical services have collapsed and tremendous hardships exist in Poland, as well as endless problems. As I write, democracy is a fragile plant, and I believe it will take perhaps fifteen to twenty years for the country to become a true democracy under strong leaders and so take its place – as it always should have done – in Europe. It is, indeed, extremely sad that Poland is situated geographically between 80 million Germans and the massive country of Russia.

During the Pope's subsequent visits in 1986 and 1990, he had the same overwhelming receptions wherever he went, but he implored the people during his homilies and prayers at each Mass held in many different places to remember that peace was very fragile and hardship inevitable but God was more important than anything else on earth and that he knew the true meaning of living under the totalitarian systems of the Nazis and Soviets and the materialistic countries. "Never believe that the latter is right or that you should ever covet the materialistic side of life. This is all wrong."

We may never know the full extent of the contribution which our Holy Father, Pope John Paul II, made to the downfall of Communism in Russia, Eastern and Central Europe. His skills, knowledge, leadership and deeply religious life of prayer make him a unique Pope. He is reputed to have a knowledge of over thirty languages!

Alas, on all of his pilgrimages and journeys to countless countries, the Pope's itineraries have been totally exhausting. He always went beyond what was asked and as a result of the assassin's attack on him in 1982 and his bad state of health during the past six years, he is now frail and extremely tired.

* * *

I have always felt a special affection for Poland and the Poles, and visits to that country are a source of joy, no matter how many problems face us there in our work. The Poles are renowned for their hospitality, and I have many happy memories of warm welcomes. Their courtesy, too, is remarkable – though unfortunately this doesn't extend to queuing for public transport! And it is pleasant, for example, to see the male engineer on a building site kissing the hand of a female plasterer, while she is still holding a trowel with the other! The greetings, cordiality and good humour of the Poles with their many jokes and proverbs ensure that the atmosphere usually remains pleasant during discussions, however marked the differences of opinion among such strong individualists may be.

Leaving the sites and Homes in Poland after my regular visits is always a wrench, especially when I am saying goodbye to the handicapped children. On my departure, as on my arrival, all the patients and staff gather to see me off with flowers and handmade gifts, and the sincerity of their affection makes these occasions particularly poignant. I usually take some of the flowers to local churches and the rest are placed in buckets for me to bring back to Britain in my vehicle. I always hate leaving, and wish that I could spend more time with them.

A very old friend Professor Podowski and I were both honoured by the Lord Mayor of Warsaw in May 1993 when he conferred on us the Honorary Citizenship of Warsaw.

It was an extraordinary reunion, "Pod", as he was known in the Polish Section of the highly secret Special Operations Executive in the last War, had the great responsibility, with the help of special colleagues, of choosing volunteers from the Polish Services for work with the Resistance in Poland. These volunteers, later Agents, naturally had to have very special qualities. Once selected, and after arduous training, they were provided with civilian clothes, false documents and a poison tablet which we sewed into their clothing. "Pod" was with "Zub", a Briefing Officer for each Agent who left Britain, North Africa or Italy. The Agents were dropped at night during the period of the full moon into specially chosen dropping grounds in Poland where they were received by a reception committee who, too, worked under peril of capture by the Germans. The Agents, whether dropped individually or in very small groups, had to bury their parachutes immediately upon landing. They were then hidden by the reception committee until proceeding to Warsaw to confirm their final briefing as to the work they were to undertake in the Resistance. The majority of the parachutists dropped (some 332) were successful in their perilous work in the Resistance, but many were arrested, interrogated, tortured and then shot or transported to concentration or extermination camps.

"Pod" was never dropped for security reasons – he knew too much – but he made the ill-fated mistake of returning to Poland in 1948 where he worked at the Polish Polytechnic in Warsaw. Later, he was arrested, interrogated by the NKVG (Russia's Secret Police) and accused of spying for Britain, France and the United States of American. The Russians had a large number of our files, he told me, and the interrogations continued by day and night. The worst thing was being beaten, and the dreaded interrogations lasted for ten to twelve hours or longer with little or no sleep and continued sometimes for a whole month. Despite all of this, "Pod" refused to give away any information. He survived the worst and main prison, Wronki, near Poznań, and nine other prisons before his release.

Just after his release from these terrible prisons, his wife, who recognised me (although I did not know her), happened to pass a quick message to me amidst the devastation of Warsaw. Within hours the NKVG took both of us into custody and I was also interrogated and accused of being a spy against the Soviet Union.

I believe good comes out of evil, and it was wonderful to be reunited with "Pod" again on such a splendid and totally unexpected occasion. As he himself said to me: "Did you ever dream as a young member of Special Operations Executive serving with the Poles that, together with old 'Pod', you would one day receive the highest honour Warsaw can offer?"

The Poles have always been strong individualists and, sadly it has to be admitted that akin to that individualism is often a tendency to squabble. Much precious time in Poland is lost to this unfortunate national characteristic. Since regaining their freedom some of the goodness in their nature has been lost in the sense that crime has increased, materialism hitherto unknown is there and, worst of all, there are now grave differences between the newly rich and the poor. Before 1989 relatively few Poles could afford a car, but now there are far too many expensive and fast vehicles on the road and driving standards are very bad.

As the British Ambassador in Prague, Mr A.D. Brighty remarked to me, "Well, the Czechs and Poles naturally wanted to return and belong to the West, but they have bought from us a package which is both good and bad".

There is so much to be done in Poland, as elsewhere, but when I feel discouraged I remember the words of a woman doctor I met during the early days of our work there. She was lying in her small room in the last stages of tuberculosis. She suffered terribly, yet she discussed constructively and at great length the gaps and priorities in the treatment of diseases. She told me: "There are thousands of sick people and the world will always have them, but it is important that you concentrate on and cope with a few priorities. Everyone is going to ask you to provide a Home or hospital for their category of patient. In developing countries where problems of poverty, sickness and disease seem overwhelming, and in our country which has suffered such devastation, you must not be side-tracked but must concentrate on giving assistance to those whom the physicians and specialists can help by offering medical and nursing care on a short- or long-term basis. Even with limited funds you are the person to relieve the pressure on their overloaded waiting lists and to save them from having to turn away many who need to be admitted to hospital. By founding Homes, small hospitals and domicile care teams for both the acute sick and the handicapped, you are providing and releasing beds in hospitals which would be otherwise blocked. It is you we are looking to because you have dedicated your life to try and do this."

These words from the mouth of a dying person made me feel very humble and brought to my mind words scribbled on the wall of an underground cell in the infamous Gestapo Interrogation Headquarters in Aleja Szucha* in Warsaw:

> It's easy to talk about Poland
> It's harder to work for her
> Still harder to die
> And the hardest is to suffer.

* Many of the prisoners interrogated in Aleja Szucha were imprisoned in the infamous Pawiak prison in Warsaw, originally built by the Russians during the reign of Tsar Nicholas I (Romanov) for political prisoners. During the German occupation 1939–44 it contained no less than 100,000 prisoners, a huge number of which were imprisoned there under indescribable conditions. Fifty babies were born and actually survived thanks to the very strong Resistance movement in the prison and the fact that physicians and nurses, together with others who knew German, were in positions of authority. Many books have been written about Pawiak. It was destroyed in August 1944 during the Warsaw Rising and there is an excellent Museum in Warsaw which should be visited by everybody.

16

Yugoslavia

HARD TIMES

*Most of this Chapter was written for the first edition published
in 1986 before the break-up of the Country.*

EARLY ONE EVENING IN the late 1960s, while I was waiting alone in the
van for a meeting with representatives of a local authority overlooking
the Plitvica lakes, a group of tourists from Britain came strolling by and,
noticing the name on the van, stopped to tell me they were supporters of
the Foundation. Rather than spoil their holiday, I refrained from telling
them what had happened in that neighbourhood during the two World
Wars and the centuries of foreign occupation preceding them; and I felt,
too, that it would be hard for them to imagine the tragedies which had
occurred in many districts of the country. Yugoslavia attracted a large
number of tourists, but few realised the sufferings the peoples of the former
Yugoslavia have undergone, or the gaps still existing in society and the
efforts of the people themselves to meet the many needs.

They were also totally unaware that this "new" country, re-created in
1944, remained more or less united under Marshal Tito, but that it was
fraught by many problems; not least the many ethnic minorities which
threaten to become volatile, ambitious and extremely nationalistic.

It is a country of thickly wooded mountain ranges where the snow
remains on some of the highest peaks all year long, a country of lakes,
waterfalls and rivers, of winding roads offering breathtaking views, a
country of great plains where farmers reap their barley, of white beaches,
of castles built by the Crusaders, and of stone villages gathered round the
domes of their churches or the slender minarets of the mosques.

Here the Nazi invasion of 1941 caused four years of terror and suffering.
Up to twenty-five divisions, increasing to sixty, were stationed in Yugoslavia
by Germany and Italy, apart from the quisling units, and thirty-four major
concentration camps were established, as well as many smaller camps.

Amongst the worst set up by the Nazis and Ustashi (Croatian Fascists),
there was Sisak in Croatia, which was especially for thousands of children
separated from their parents, and Jasenovac, situated approximately five
kilometres off the main Zagreb–Belgrade road, where hundreds of thousands
men, women and children lost their lives, from hunger and countless
diseases, in appalling conditions. Despite what the Communists say, several
hundred Catholic priests (and nuns) died for their faith in Jasenovac,
Mauthausen (Austria) and Dachau (Germany).

The invader attempted by all possible means to break the resistance of the people. He did not succeed however, for under the leadership of the Resistance forces, Yugoslavs retreated to the forests and mountains and began to wage partisan warfare with great courage, determined to achieve the liberation of their country. It was a time of dramatic change and of many difficulties caused by the differences between various sections of the Resistance, traces of which never disappeared.

A very notable aspect of the Resistance in former Yugoslavia, and one which does not normally receive much recognition and is perhaps little known, is the partisans' medical service. Encircled by the enemy and very short of supplies, the partisans performed miracles of courage and devotion in looking after the wounded. Many of their hospitals were situated in underground shelters or caves to which a vertical shaft gave access. Down this shaft the patient was lowered, and immediately afterwards the entrance was camouflaged with tree trunks, moss, bracken, or whatever was available. In other places the wounded were taken into the houses of patriotic local families, where they would be looked after by a semi-trained nurse. Only when a fairly large area had been liberated was it possible to run open hospitals. All partisan hospitals, when located, were ruthlessly bombed by the Germans, and to seek out those that were hidden, task forces of between fifty and two hundred men dressed in partisan uniforms and accompanied by tracker dogs would be sent out.

The dangers encountered in transporting medical supplies from occupied territory to the partisan units are graphically illustrated by the account of a young partisan girl whose diary is quoted in the book *Partisan Hospitals in Yugoslavia*. The following passages are reproduced by kind permission of the author, Dr Djerdje Dragic:

> The fascist terror is rampant. The citizens of Zagreb hurry along the streets. Many faces already reflect hunger, poverty and fear. A young girl, head bowed, walks quickly down the street, her eyes always on the lookout for plainclothes policemen or fascist patrols. She has a large parcel tied with string under her arm. At last she reaches her destination. It is a shabby workers' lodging house. She enters cautiously and only when the tired face of the housewife is lit up by a smile does she relax a little and hand over the parcel. "Take good care of this," she whispers, "it contains medical materials and it should be sent as fast as possible to our men in the forest – to the partisan wounded. You see we have managed to collect a lot. Ruzica took something from the dispensary where she works; Zdenja raided her father's surgery; the hospital orderly got us a few things; I managed to buy a little in various pharmacies; and there we are."
>
> The same night the parcel travels far, far further, now carried by a brawny young worker. He has left the suburbs, and the city is behind him. Here in the forest one can breathe more freely – one can escape. Suddenly, the young man stops dead in his tracks, whistles softly, and hears an answering call from a nearby copse. This is the place of rendezvous. "The

contact is waiting," mutters the young man, and hurries towards the copse. "Halt!" echoes softly but firmly from behind a tree.

The password is whispered and the young man's heart is thumping as the thought that perhaps this is not the partisan contact but an ambush organised by the fascists or the police. If it is, his fate is sealed; there await him torture, prison, death ... But, in reply, he hears the password, "Freedom to the people." A cordial greeting is exchanged, the parcel handed over. The worker whispers to the courier "Take good care of this; it contains medicines and dressings for the patients in the Central Hospital in Petrova Gora."

The Courier now proceeds rapidly, and is already on his way through the dense forest and undergrowth. There is a point where the route passes near a German blockhouse, but there is no moonlight, and this makes matters easier. This is the thirty-seventh time that the young courier has made his way by secret paths and roads between the enemy garrisons and strong points. Every day he risks discovery by the fascists. But he is cautious, particularly this night when he is carrying a precious parcel of medicines for the wounded.

After the defeat of the Axis powers, when a National Government was established under Marshal Tito, Yugoslavia was a ravaged country: 1,700,000 people – almost one-tenth of the population – had died during the War, and there was an immense task ahead. I remember vividly the sight in countless hospitals of two patients sharing a bed lying head to foot, and even three babies in one cot while others lay closely together on the floor. This was usual in most of the republics until the early sixties. Here, as in Poland, medicines, drugs and dressings were *very* rarely available. There were thousands of adults and children with typhoid, typhus, meningitis and some with malaria; also others with appalling wounds as a result of the fighting.

I had already been working with authorities in Yugoslavia for some time when, during the late 1950s, Professor M. Andrejevic, an authority on geriatrics, drew my attention to the need to establish units in the city hospital in Belgrade. I warmly welcomed his suggestion, feeling that this was an occasion for the Foundation to carry out its primary aims – to operate in complete liaison with the local authorities and to support them in their efforts. These extremely simple Homes which were subsequently established in Belgrade for different age groups comprise two medical units and one surgical unit, together with a centre for physiotherapy and occupational therapy for patients who otherwise would be blocking hospital beds.

While these Homes were being built, others were being started in different parts of the country on the same basis as those in Poland. There was much do be done, but equally there were many problems with which to contend. Yugoslavia was a country covering more than 200,000 square miles, and although it was politically a single state, it consisted of six autonomous Republics. There are four official languages and two alphabets, and the people differ greatly in their culture, traditions and religions. Nonetheless, some of my most vivid memories are of the enthusiastic co-operation I received from the Yugoslav people – central and local authorities, doctors, nurses, social workers and engineers, and the inhabitants of the countless towns and villages where my travels brought me – and of the energy with which they have helped in the finding of suitable sites and the establishment of the Homes. In most cases the local authorities propose the site for the Home, and also introduce me to the various categories for whom they want to cater. It is always extremely difficult to make the final decision. Lengthy discussions and surveys are undertaken, but whatever group ultimately benefits from the facilities we provide I feel terrible about the others, particularly when I visit villages and towns and their existing hospitals and see the number of people who could be helped if Homes were to be erected and established for them. Many of the younger generation were killed and consequently there is a desperate need amongst the frail and elderly who cannot care for themselves. The local people, who are fully aware of their own responsibilities, use every effort to persuade us to build a Home in their area. In each of the Foundation's Homes and Hospitals in the different Republics, people whether Muslim, Catholic, Orthodox or, indeed, any denomination, were nursed and lived in harmony. I can never recall any problems except in Macedonia with the ethnic Albanians.

Whenever a Party member said to me, "You are a Catholic", I replied "Well, you are a Communist. In this work we are here together to relieve human suffering". I was often requested by the authorities to go to a Religious Congregation and ask the Mother Provincial to supply nuns – qualified nurses – to run the Foundation Homes, so I was a "bridge" between the Party and the Church – not an easy role to play!

I remember one blind woman who said, "Can you imagine what it is like to be left alone, to have nothing and no sight? If only the world could show some heart".

Invariably I am asked to join colleagues and the local dignitaries at their meal. Depending on the part of the country, the main dish may often be lamb, accompanied by plum brandy and Turkish coffee, none of which I can digest. Perseverance, enthusiasm and courtesy are general, and in the earlier days time appeared to be of little account. I remember, too, with affection, the nuns who were ready to prepare a feast at any hour of the day or night, and who always woke me at 4.30 a.m. when I was staying with them to attend Prime, the first Office of the day.

I remember driving over miles and miles of appalling road, having had no breakfast or lunch, and finally arriving late in the evening at a hut on a fish-farm deep in the woods. By that time we had even lost our sense of direction. There in the bitter cold we waited, getting still more hungry, while discussions went on as to what fish would be chosen and caught for the "evening" meal. Throughout the day I had only had coffee from my thermos and Ryvita biscuits, whilst the Yugoslavs from the different Republics who had been accompanying me in their own vehicles had existed on black Turkish coffee and plum brandy – and stayed completely sober.

The object of this exercise was to undertake exhaustive surveys in the different towns and villages and to register the housebound, the handicapped and those in need of care. This proved, as always, very interesting but equally distressing, as it meant that one saw how the poor and the needy were existing.

On another occasion several years later I was again invited by the local authorities and the Mayor to go out to supper with them. I demurred, as it was after a heavy day and I only wanted to sleep, but they were very sensitive and thought I was refusing their hospitality. I was assured that the hut, which turned out to be in a densely wooded area, was only a few miles up the road. In actual fact it transpired that we had to drive for half an hour and on arrival we found that the generator had broken down and there was no electricity. We were offered the speciality of that area which was lamb, rolled and cooked on a stick over an open fire outside. The Yugoslavs talked quite incessantly and many of them were, as is their custom, heavy smokers. Nevertheless, no matter how late the day ended they could always rise early.

At another time and place I also remember the Yugoslavs' insistence on taking me to see Shakespeare's *Macbeth* at 10.30 p.m.

Distances were so great that occasionally I would not reach the potential site until night had fallen, and thus was able to inspect it only by the beam of the car headlights. One night, as we were searching for a particular site, we came up against a bridge in the process of being constructed by the Army. The Yugoslavs insisted on climbing up on the very high concrete slabs, standing on each other's shoulders to do so. We were challenged by a sentry, who allowed us to continue when the nature of the Foundation's work was explained to him, and we proceeded to the edge of the slab in the fading light. Below us in the dusk we could hear the fast, rushing river. After some minutes the Yugoslavs were persuaded to return to the Land Rover and we continued the journey, finally locating the site after a further search on the other side of the river.

Itineraries were often very arduous, and eventually various officials insisted that stops for food and rest be included when planning the site-prospecting expeditions. I remember working with Ron Granwal (a young volunteer engineer from New Zealand) on one of the sites when the goat's cheese (with olives) which we had been given to eat on a huge chunk of bread melted in the heat of the sun.

In the early days many of the roads were merely dirt tracks and, indeed, many villages and some sites could not be reached except on foot in summer or by sleigh in winter. Once or twice I travelled by a small single-engined aircraft. I remember that air turbulence made the flight far from smooth and visibility was very poor, but the pilot was so eager that it seemed no risk was too great for him to take.

One winter when blizzards were causing havoc, it was decided that the journey would be quicker by train and that I should travel by night with a colleague and former partisan named Bosa, so we boarded a train for Athens. As it slowly started to pull out of the main station in Belgrade some talkative passengers in the corridor told us that we were on the wrong train! I was nearest to the door and decided to jump. I landed on the platform leaving a startled Bosa on the train. I then found the right one and continued the journey, meeting Bosa at some obscure place on the snow-covered line several hours later.

The Yugoslav physique is strong and at times it was an effort to keep up with what my companions proposed. We were concentrating our activities mainly in Serbia, Montenegro, Kosovo, Croatia and Macedonia, making use of every means of transport, sometimes scrambling by torchlight over overgrown boulders and, when the occasion called for it, rising at 6 a.m. for breakfast with the local Mayor and being shown around a factory and a new housing area before setting out on a day's drive.

Amongst the friends who assisted me was Olga Glogovac. Olga returned to Yugoslavia from the United States in January 1934, aged thirteen. It was a hard winter. Her father had been a miner in America and she was one of six children. In her words, "My mother was special to me, but everybody's mother is beautiful." She had helped during the Depression to feed other children. They had lived in Gebo, Wyoming, where she attended school. The reason for the family repatriating was because of the illness of her father. He suffered dreadfully from rheumatoid arthritis and became bedridden, but he gradually improved to walk with crutches and with the aid of a stick. He received no pension but with his savings earned in the US he bought a farm.

During the invasion by the Germans in 1941, Olga had just finished middle school and lived at home in Urosevac. "I really first saw the German troops in Pristina after my brother had been wounded," Olga told me. Her younger brother, Vojo, died of typhus on 6 May 1944, aged twenty, in Banica Concentration Camp.

Olga was arrested twice, on each occasion for a short time. She shared a small cell with men and women together. The former were dreadfully beaten. Onions and salt had been smuggled into the prison and the women dressed the men's wounds with these. Transports were continuously leaving to take prisoners to concentration camps in other parts of Yugoslavia and elsewhere in occupied Europe.

When released, Olga left home to join the partisans in the mountains in East Serbia. Naturally she was questioned and she told them that she spoke English. One night during the formation of a fighting column word was passed back that the girl Olga should leave and report to Staff HQ 23rd Division. After further questioning, she met the British Bods who had been dropped by parachute. They were referred to as "Fred's Group". Freddie was the radio operator and the others were Eddie and Chips. Later, they joined the 14th Corps. Olga had been trained in small arms and carried a pistol. Amongst her other work she tried to find suitable landing grounds and dropping zones for arms. She also translated verbal notes from Freddie to the Serbian partisans. They worked in a very wide area and slept in the open where conditions were exceedingly tough, especially during the bad winter of 1944.

In 1941–2 Olga organised, with others, a great campaign among the population for supplies of food, clothing, arms and medical supplies.

When I met Olga, much later on, she showed me a photograph of herself with a parachutist Bod from SOE, and so I wrote the following letter to the Special Forces Club on 21 March 1963:

> I do apologise for troubling you, but I should be most grateful for your help and advice.
>
> During my work in Yugoslavia I was asked by Mrs Olga Glogovac whether it might be possible to try and trace one or more of the members of the British Mission who served in the Zajedar, Majdanpek, Knjazevac and Trgoviste areas during the summer and autumn of 1944. Olga, as she was known to them, was the interpreter and liaison officer with the partisans at the time, attached to the 23rd Serbian Division which later on became the 14th Corps. She remembers the members of the British Mission as Captain Fred, Eddie and Chips. Mrs Glogovac has proudly shown me a few photographs taken at the time of her work with the British Mission and she still remembers the English Bods very well.
>
> I realise the difficulties entailed in trying to get in touch with any of them, but I am just wondering whether a notice in the Special Forces magazine and Club would possibly produce results?

Later I heard from Chips Jackson via the SOE Club and passed on his messages to Olga. I then wrote to him:

> It is extremely kind of you to take all the trouble to write as a result of my letter in the Special Forces magazine. Thank you very much indeed.
>
> I hope by this time that you will have heard from Olga. She did not give the appearance of needing anything when I saw her in Pristina. I think what she really would like is renewing contact with you as she spoke so warmly of the time you worked together with the Mission.
>
> There is a great deal of need in Macedonia, Bosnia and Serbia among the sick, as I am sure you will appreciate, and people like Olga have already done a great deal to improve the situation and I would so like to try and do more to support them.
>
> When I next return to Yugoslavia I shall certainly be seeing Olga and will then hear at first-hand of her surprise and delight of renewing contact with you.
>
> With kindest regards . . .

Through this coincidence, Chips helped my late husband to establish Homes in South Africa.

Another friend who up to her retirement has been a real asset to the Foundation over very many years is Dr Olga Milosevic. After reading medicine, Dr Olga specialised in gynaecology and obstetrics and practised in Belgrade for several years before the War. Her husband was a scientist. They joined the partisans in June 1941 and Dr Olga was active in smuggling medical supplies to them from the hospital where she worked in Risan. Twice she was searched by the Gestapo. She joined the High Command in 1942 and fought in the Third, Fourth and Fifth Offensives and became personal physician to Marshal Tito. She was also in charge of the medical staff at High Command. Dr Olga's worst experience was during the dreadful battle for the bridge at Jablanica in May 1943.

From January 1944 to April 1947 Dr Olga was responsible for preventative and curative medical teams. She helped, too, to organise other parts of the health service at both republican and federal level, which included maternity and children's health. Later, she became Secretary-General of the Yugoslav Red Cross and made many friends in the international field, including the late Angela Countess of Limerick, Vice-President of the British Red Cross Society.

Dr Olga was a respected and energetic person with a strong sense of humour, whose medical and nursing knowledge and wide experience are undisputed. Though a skilled diplomat, she could be equally outspoken when necessary. She was a Communist whose deep commitment dated from before the War; she came from an old intellectual family and lost both her husband and daughter in the War. A good linguist, she spoke English and German fluently, could follow some Russian and understood the language spoken in Macedonia.

I treasure many experiences shared with her, particularly those in very rough and uncomfortable conditions, and it is through her trust that I have come to know and discuss with her privately the difficult situations in the different republics, each naturally having its own particular problems and personalities.

Dr Olga made two visits to the Foundation. The first time she stayed with my mother in Clare. They loved each other and she has often told me that the fact that she was treated with such affection and made to feel so much at home gave back to her (to use her own words) "the confidence I had lost in human nature".

It is now some forty-three years or more since the establishment of the first Home in Yugoslavia and these years have seen a blossoming in the work done in the country where thousands of individuals have been treated and cared for in twenty-two Homes (at some places several of these very simple buildings are grouped together). These include one for physically handicapped children at Bansko and another for babies and children in Belgrade. As in Poland and several other countries, the Homes in former Yugoslavia are run and financed by the local authorities. A number of religious orders are responsible for the nursing.

None of the building could have been carried out without the meticulous accuracy of the clearing agents in Yugoslavia, Jugosanitariat, and I would like to pay particular tribute to the late Mr Djina Svecnjak and his colleagues in Zagreb who always had at their fingertips every item of building material, furniture, and so on that was shipped out from Britain. Their files were scrupulously kept, and whenever a Yugoslav ship docked at Rijecka, Bar or in the Yugoslav part of Salonika in Greece, Mr Svecnjak or his colleagues would be there to check off the goods with the suppliers' schedule and ship's manifest. They knew exactly what to look for. One copy of the schedule would be sent to them in advance, another to the foreman on the site, and a third retained at Headquarters in Suffolk. It was no enviable task and occasionally, to my shame, I was informed that the suppliers in Britain were not always up to the mark and there were discrepancies. It was therefore a great relief to know that we had first-class clearing agents the other end. Telephone communication between different parts of that country in those days was difficult, and Jugosanitariat would therefore send a telegram to the building site via the nearest post office to inform them of receipt, when they could expect to receive the goods, and also of any variation in the schedule/manifest.

From the twenty-two Homes and Hospitals supplied out by the Foundation I recall materials for two Homes (each required a site of 10,000 square feet) being loaded inadvertently on the same huge lorry. One of the tradesman and I worked in the intense heat, trying to sort out and mark up a vast number of roof trussles (different sizes too), windows, doors, etc. This task took us three full days.

The Yugos, including the medical staff, naturally offered to help us, but it was too complicated to explain, and with our experience, it was better that we should do this task on our own.

The enormous jigsaw puzzle of putting it all together began. The overriding target was always to get the building watertight before the onset of winter at the end of October. Once the external wall panels had all been erected, hopefully in their correct positions first time, the roof trusses could be erected allowing the roofing felt and battens to be fixed, if not the roof tiles, thus making the building weatherproof. This enabled the internal work to proceed through the winter period, in the dry if not the warm!

At Headquarters in Suffolk my main headache, after insisting that each supplier kept a D-Day, was to attempt to find out when the Yugoslav ships were due to dock. The shipping company in London was well known for its inefficiency and on visits to the Port of London the authorities always reminded me that they received no prior warning when a Yugoslav ship was likely to appear at the mouth of the Thames and require a pilot and berth!

By 1989–90 there had been great changes in Yugoslavia. The country had largely recovered from the effects of the Second World War, with signs of new prosperity in some parts, but unemployment since the late sixties has presented extremely serious problems. Over a million found jobs in Austria, Turkey and Germany as *Gastarbeiter* (guest workers), frequently doing the most menial work, but at least they were able to save most of their wages and could send a large proportion of the money earned to their families and relatives in Yugoslavia to help improve their living conditions. During the last few years, however, many Yugoslavs have been repatriated as unemployment has grown in Austria and Germany and preference has naturally been given to their own people.

There has also been a spectacular increase in the number of medical students, about half of whom are women, but, as in so many countries, relatively few after qualifying like working in isolated areas. This in itself presents a grave problem.

At first I made regular and frequent visits but now, to my regret, I am only able to visit all the Homes every two or three years, driving some seven or eight thousand miles in seven weeks. The President and authorities of each Republic kindly made themselves responsible for drawing up my itinerary for meetings, visits and generally welcoming me with their generous hospitality. Usually I entered Yugoslavia from Austria, and after a long drive through the night have the wonderful experience of seeing the dawn over the mountains; but there are other occasions when I travelled down the Hungarian road, which in winter is covered with snow and ice. Generally my rendezvous with the Yugoslavs is at Zagreb at 6.30 a.m. preceded by Mass at 6 a.m. in the Cathedral.

A typical itinerary that I remember taking before the recent troubles was:

I begin from Zagreb. One night we came upon an accident: a bus carrying a football team had overturned, having swerved right across the road before plunging into a wood, and the passengers were trapped underneath. We helped to extricate some of them who were in great pain and suffering from shock and I gave water from my thermoses to those lying by the roadside, working by torchlight in the dark. The standard of driving leaves much to be desired; initially the reason for this was because many Yugoslavs were unaccustomed to driving vehicles. Huge round wreaths made from wax and paper flowers and covered with polythene used to hang on the sides of the roads at points where people have been killed.

At Gospic, an hour's drive from the underground partisan hospital at Petrova Gora mentioned earlier, which is being preserved, the Foundation, together with the local authorities, has built two simple Homes for the handicapped of different ages, both men and women. The area was ruthlessly destroyed by the occupation forces, and I am always deeply impressed by the people's lack of bitterness and by their acceptance of suffering.

From the Republic of Croatia I usually drove onto the Republic of Montenegro where the capital town of Podgorica lies in the hollow of a flat plain. Today it can be reached by train, or an aircraft, albeit unloaded, which would not have been possible years ago.

After the usual discussions with the local authority I decided to concentrate the Foundation's efforts on relieving the situation for both patients and the Sisters of the Holy Cross (*Sestre Svetoga Kriza*) on the coast. Here, in two old stone houses, some sixty patients were accommodated in the small Village of Perast very close to the water – we could hear the lapping of the waves. These houses had very steep steps, no heating and swarms of flies in the scorching hot summer, in addition to which there were no flush loos but only one earth closet. Water had to be drawn from a well. Many of the patients were incontinent but, somehow, despite these appalling conditions, the nuns who cared for them managed to keep them clean. I cannot ever remember hearing them or the warden, Mr A. Popovic, and his small staff, grumble. Joyce Johns, a qualified occupational therapist who used to give up her holidays to help the Foundation in its early days, wrote in a report, "The difficulties at Perast remind me of descriptions of nursing in the Crimea."

The authorities and I searched for a level site in the neighbourhood – a difficult proposition, for there are many mountains and hills – and finally a beautiful site at Risan (a neighbouring village) was found with a fine view of the sea, although not level. When cleared it provided room for four Homes, a building for the laundry and, in addition, a simple house for the nuns (of whom there were originally sixteen but now only four remain) together with their own chapel. For these Homes a central heating system was designed by the Foundation's Honorary Heating Consultant and the parts were shipped out, together with nearly all the other materials for the buildings. Discussions on building problems, water pressures, plumbing, etc, continue endlessly and on almost every site everyone – whether qualified or not – joins in enthusiastically. Even today after fifty years the shortage of water still remains a problem.

The next region on my itinerary was Kosovo which borders on Albania. It has a strong community of Albanians who are volatile and cause more problems – indeed they want their own Republic! The old road used to take me over one of the highest mountains, Cakor, from where the view for miles around is of beautiful scenery. The terrain is very rocky and the road full of twists and bends with many tunnels blasted through the solid rock. Often it is quite deserted apart from the sheep grazing on the mountainside. In the autumn the flocks are driven down to the local villages because of the severity of the winter, when there is heavy snow and even snowploughs fail to clear the roads, while in summer it is extremely hot. There was also a danger of being overtaken by an overcrowded daily bus whose fast driver seemed oblivious of the horrific drops on either side of the badly surfaced and narrow road and of the many steep bends in this beautiful mountainous country. On an average I had to allow myself nine hours when driving through this area.

It is on these drives and others like them that I enjoy listening to taped music, especially "Kumbaya My Lord", which is a favourite with the local people who may accompany me. These cassette tapes were a gift to us from a film company; Leonard recorded on them music from *Your Hundred Best Tunes,* a Sunday evening BBC radio programme, and music from the Proms.

On the way to Pristina in Kosovo, part of the Republic of Serbia, besides making calls at different hospitals and having meetings and discussions with social workers, I also sometimes found myself persuaded by the locals accompanying me to divert from my route in order to see the frescoes in a mountain monastery.

At Pristina the Foundation built two Homes with the help of the local authorities, who are wholly responsible for running them. The Sisters of Mary who staff these Homes occupy one end of one of the buildings and have their own chapel. An occupational therapy room was included in this Home and colourful local craftspeople encourage the patients to do more in the way of handicrafts. The locals have a warm sense of humour and great generosity. I always sleep in the nuns' sitting/dining room next door to the chapel, and the Sister-in-Charge insists upon my having her bed, while she herself moves out into a rather crowded room with three or four other nuns. They make great preparations for me to have a bath, almost hovering over me to see that I get undressed properly! One night the warden insisted on giving me a present by booking a telephone call to my husband and our children and there was tremendous excitement when the call came through: now he and a warden at Kragujevac repeat this kind gesture on each visit.

The disabilities of the patients vary here: many of them are psychiatrically disturbed, some are fully ambulant and others are in wheelchairs. They are, whenever possible, classified in rooms and anyone who has the opportunity of having a single room enjoys it tremendously, especially those diagnosed with cancer.

According to their Rule, the Sisters observe silence during meals, while one of them reads aloud. One day when I was with them and solemn reading was in progress, two of us suddenly remembered a joke we'd been told by the patients and had such difficulty in restraining ourselves that the reading had to be abandoned.

One of the original Homes was built in the old town of Travnik in Bosnia – a place which still contains many mosques and other reminders of the centuries of Turkish occupation. There I met Sister Monika, a large, joyful member of the Order of Daughters of Divine Charity (*Kceri Bozje ljubayi*), founded in Vienna in 1868. This Order, like others, has always been admired and respected for their devotion and high standard of work against all odds. The nuns were tireless in their efforts to nurse the handi-capped – housed in most primitive conditions in an old disused Turkish school, though the workshop which the nuns and patients had created was good and produced many articles for sale. To me it was very moving to share the nuns' community life and witness the Sisters' observance of their vows of Chastity, Poverty and Obedience. Later, the Foundation built a second simple Home nearby, thus increasing the number of beds.

Sister Monika radiated warmth and affection and would hug the patients, and indeed everyone. She was held in high regard by members of the Party. Between 1941 and 1944 her family had fought with the partisans (she lost five brothers) and she had performed miracles by saving the lives of children from the Nazis. Sadly, for the last years of her life she suffered from chronic cardiac disease and respiratory failure and could only doze and never lie down. She retired to Kakanj and shared a room with two other nuns in a very simple wooden house near the church, but she could not manage to go out. Whenever I was with her she whispered breathlessly that she listened to the news on Vatican Radio and always prayed for the whole world. Sister Monika died in May 1980 and is buried in Travnik.

The sisters in Travnik used to live in their own convent with its own chapel, and some even enjoy the privacy of a single cell. After a hard day's work and while others are going off on night duty, I enjoy sitting with them in their kitchen to discuss our mutual problems. There was one young sister who studied theology. Early each morning we would walk to Mass, and I remember remarking one day how cold it was (the temperature was minus 16°C), to which the Sister replied, "Yes, it is rather chilly."

On one occasion, when there were threats of a very serious international crisis, a few of the Yugoslavs asked whether in the event of another invasion, I would go with them to the mountains as they intended to join the partisans again. The Sisters, however, had decided it was better to pray for peace and kept leading me to the chapel. After being cut off from any news for weeks we found an aerial which enabled us to use the radio and tune into the BBC in London. Instead of alarming news we heard a very English voice describing the stabling of horses at Newmarket, a Victorian play, and a calm, objective news bulletin and commentary.

From Pristina I drive down to Bitola. Now there are new roads, but in the old days it was a journey of several hours along a winding road. Bitola is almost on the Greek Frontier, and it is from Bitola that I used to go to Greece while working there. The town, which is very old, has been greatly developed with industry. In the First World War part of a French division fought here, and there is a large French cemetery, a poignant reminder of how hard the French fought; in very rough hill country some of the trenches remain.

In Bitola the Foundation has built two Homes on the site of a demolished house dating from the Turkish occupation, which lasted for nearly 400 years. The St Vincent de Paul Nursing Sisters here work in the local hospital as well as in our Homes. They and the staff, like many of their compatriots, show great warmth and love towards the patients, and are full of gaiety. One of the Sisters in fun occasionally told our fortunes by tipping the remains of a cup of Turkish coffee upside down and then reading the grains on the saucer.

The influx of tourists to the Former Yugoslavia profoundly affected much of the country and only the remote rural villages remained untouched. Living conditions there are much as they used to be, with pumps for water and earth closets. It used to be lovely to see girls and boys practising their regional dances in homemade costumes. Many of these villages are cut off during the winter and children experienced great difficulties in reaching school. There is no means of transport and they have to walk many miles each day.

At Kragujevac, one of the principal towns in Serbia, the authorities asked the Foundation to erect two Homes for the handicapped of different ages. These Homes are sited on the outskirts of the town and near to the Memorial Park (which extends to several acres) where on 21 October 1941 7,000 men, together with the boys and their master from Form V of the local school, were massacred in one day by the SS as a reprisal for partisan activities in the area.

There was healthy competition between different Homes. Before the rationing of petrol and diesel, the wardens and their staff liked to make up a convoy and join me when possible on these journeys, despite the distances.

My journeys through Yugoslavia continued up to the outbreak of the civil war in July 1991. My memories of these difficult journeys are innumerable: the lakes and waterfalls on the drive to Gospic; a lamb strapped to the back of a donkey; buses careering round corners on mountain passes; a brass band blaring at the opening of a new Home; nuns saying their Office in the chapel; a patient who lived to 113 performing a folk dance while another patient played for him on a local instrument similar to the bagpipes.

The winters I shall never forget, and the following is an extract from a letter I scribbled home:

> An ambulance had been sent out to Ivangrad, which lies in the mountains, during the late afternoon to act as my pilot for the next 150 kilometres. The roads, as I have previously mentioned, were not only like ploughed fields frozen with ice, but there were also snow drifts five to eight metres high with blinding blizzards and crosswinds. Some of the surfaces were pitted with pot holes, many very large, and it was quite difficult to keep the vehicle upright. One was fighting all the way. As usual, a long shovel enabled me to dig myself our of the drifts, but meanwhile the lorry became covered with snow as it fell so fast. Tomo, the ambulance driver, and I came across an articulated lorry which had overturned. Petrol was pouring out of its tanks and both behind and in front of the lorry buses were waiting patiently to pass, but the lorry blocked their path. Several passengers were getting on and off the buses and the whole scene, which was lit by dim headlights, is a little difficult to describe as it was dark. Tomo and I decided that our only hope was to try and clear a path on the side of mountain edge as the longer we waited the worse conditions would become. We therefore went to work with our shovels and great cheers came from the people on the buses and in the drifts when we succeeded in getting past the lorry. We were then asked to take one or two ill people from the buses in the ambulance and to inform the police of the accident. When we eventually arrived at our destination, Tomo turned to me and said to the nuns at the Home, "I have never known such a super driver" – rather nice of him, but I felt very embarrassed. I thanked him for the compliment and congratulated him, too. Tomo looked rather tired and he was revived with plum brandy!

On another drive I spent twelve hours on my own contending with gale-force winds from the Adriatic which overturned small ships and, I believe a couple of buses. Most of the way I could not open the door of my vehicle and I prayed that I would not be swept into the sea. At 10.45 p.m., after covering 547 kilometres, I arrived safely in Risan.

As in all countries where folklore survives strongly, the wanderer in former Yugoslavia may hear a variety of adages whose origins or first causes are long forgotten. One that has followed me around and remains in my mind for no reason that I can think of is:

> Don't boast in Sarajevo
> Don't ride a horse in Travnik
> Don't lie in Mostar,
> Don't sing in Banja Luka

I wouldn't dream of shocking Banja Luka!

As in some other countries where I work, the Yugoslavs used to enjoy telling political jokes.

In the Balkans, "Slava" is observed to celebrate the people's acceptance of Christianity. It is not the individual who "adopts" a patron saint on being baptised a Christian but the family, and on their particular saint's day the family gathers together and invites the local priest to their home for the blessing of a special cake and then a solemn dinner and blessing of the family. It is the responsibility of one male member of the family to ensure that this tradition continues.

Another beautiful ritual in the Balkans is the growing of wheat in a saucer of water during Advent. For those of the Orthodox faith the ceremony begins on 6 December and for Roman Catholics on the 13th, the Feast of St Lucy (her name meaning Lux-Light). It is a family preparation to welcome the Light of the World, Jesus Christ. The green wheat symbolises the Bread of Life, and on Christmas Eve candles (depicting light) are blessed, lit and placed in the middle of the growing wheat.

In collaboration with local authorities the Foundation created a Council in Yugoslavia on which wardens of our Homes sat *ex officio* as regular meetings. The appropriate federal ministry used to be represented by Miss Nevenka Novakovic, who served with the partisans. She gave me every assistance in Bosnia and later she held high positions at federal level. I found in her a staunch friend who believed in keeping in close communication with the Foundation.

There is need for more Homes and Domiciliary Care Teams, especially since the recent tragic upheavals and the Yugoslavs wish for them as much as I do. The authorities and the people themselves have done and are doing much, but we share their painful awareness that many thousands remain in need of succour which we cannot yet give them. We know, too, that even among those admitted to our Homes there are many with problems still to be tackled adequately – by medical and nursing care, or by rehabilitation, or by helping the lonely and rejected to come to terms with incurable disease or irremediable disabilities.

In July 1972 a group of twenty-four visitors from Yugoslavia came to the Sue Ryder Home, Stagenhoe, near Hitchin, Hertfordshire. Besides Miss Novakovic, the group included wardens and nuns from our Homes. They visited the Foundation's other Homes in England and several hospitals. They followed their itinerary with great enthusiasm and were tirelessly eager for first-hand acquaintance with British methods of coping with social and medical problems. From one of this party I received the following letter:

> Upon my return home to my dear city of Zagreb I would like to thank you and your colleagues for the kind welcome that I was greeted with during my stay in your really great country. My impressions were deep, but in my heart I shall always remember this journey, your great concern, and not only yours but that of collaborators, your children, the elderly and the handicapped. I keep hearing the words of the gentleman who said when we visited Papworth Industries near Cambridge on 3 August that the word "unable" was never mentioned.
>
> Thanking you, your dear children and all your friends, I now look forward to your coming visit and remain for ever grateful,
>
> D.S.

Among the many colleagues with whom I had the pleasure of working was Dr Nikola Georgievski. I first met him when he was Minister of Health in Macedonia. He later became Federal Minister before being appointed to the World Health Organisation. He was a tremendous worker with humour and determination, especially during his time in Vietnam, Cambodia and Thailand. His descriptions of the appalling living conditions of the people in those places and the lack of medical facilities and food were shocking.

The following is an extract from my report to the Council of the Foundation in Britain on my work in Yugoslavia from 15 March to 19 April 1981:

> I reached the Austro/Yugo frontier at approximately 11 p.m. on Wednesday 18 March. Unfortunately, there were well over 200 freight lorries waiting for the Customs authorities to clear first, so I was left to wait in my vehicle (there being no other place) for well over two and a half hours in the rather cold weather. An excitable customs officer, on seeing my papers, went off to report to his superior, but after being assured that the vehicle contained nothing except presents and items for the patients he apologised and let me through.
>
> I continued to Maribor, but stopped for a good sleep in the lorry on the way. At 5.30 a.m. I was awakened by the patter of hundreds of feet, this being the usual hour for those going to work. I attended Mass at 6 a.m. and the Sisters in the adjacent convent gave me the opportunity of washing, making coffee and filling my thermos.
>
> On arrival in Zagreb at 10.30 a.m. I drove straight to the Secretariat of

Health and Social Welfare (the Croatian Republic's Ministry) and was met by the Deputy Minister, Mrs Granecka and her assistants.

I was given an itinerary for Zagreb alone, which included visits to four Local Authority Homes plus an independent Home run for Jewish people and financed by the Israelis. It was interesting to see the contrast between each Home and especially the one which had been purpose-built as a sort of "hotel" for over 400 pensioners. The SRN running the nursing wing in the "hotel" was most competent and had taken a course in one of the London hospitals. There was even a bar, a hairdressing salon, a shop etc. there. This place lacked the individuality and warmth of the two others which, though dreadfully overcrowded, still retained some feeling of "home".

In addition, visits were made to individuals in need who either refused to be admitted to Homes because they wished to retain their independence against all odds, or could not be admitted due to lack of accommodation.

I was given a warm welcome and after meeting a large number of people and walking far distances in the city, a meal of delicious fish revived me. The evening continued with meetings, and I started the next day at 6 a.m. after a fifteen-minute walk to the Cathedral.

The itinerary then started again and included a long visit to the Oncology Centre where I had very frank discussions about many problems with Dr Maricic, the Director. The absence of both a hostel for those receiving treatment and coming from long distances and the lack of a long continuing care home are appalling. The Foundation tries its best to cope in the existing Homes, but it is a wholly unsatisfactory state of affairs for cancer patients.

Meanwhile, rumours had reached us that the roads leading to the Lika region were blocked, but the British Consul General was very prompt in getting a weather report on the telephone for me and agreed that things could be far worse. So, after further meetings I left the others and departed with Mrs Granecka. The 1980–81 winter had been one of the longest in many parts of Europe and a particularly severe one out there. At many places the temperatures had dropped to between minus 24 – 26°C, the road was bad and its surface was rutted with snow and packed ice and huge banks of snow rose up on either side.

I reached Gospic some five hours later.

Since the original meetings, held both with the Republican and Local Authorities to build two Foundation Homes there, there has been a great demand on the beds.

The original warden, the late Mrs Ostric (a social worker), was constantly asking me to go to Gospic and help with the building of the Homes, installation of the central heating and other services, etc. This had been an area known as the Lika Valley where the Second World War devastation of all the villages defied description. The young and old alike had lost everything. The severity of the climate added to their suffering. Marianna Ostric eventually gathered a small staff round her until her retirement.

The needs are so great that the numbers are above what we should, in fact, be accommodating, and it is estimated that a further 100 beds are required. Owing to the drastic shortage of both nursing and medical staff, however, Mrs Granecka and I both felt we could not agree to extend further here at present – though, hopefully, this would be realised in the future.

After one of those famous Yugoslav suppers, when hospitality is never spared regardless of what there is for the morrow, the staff were asked to join us for a meeting in the small and already overcrowded room, where I counted no less than nine chain smokers.

The local hospital still lacks most basic equipment and only has wards for tuberculosis, surgery, medical cases, children, obstetrics and gynaecology, with a total of 205 beds to serve a wide area. There is no laboratory and therefore sometimes the laboratories in Zagreb have to be depended on, and these are five to six hours' driving away. There is inevitably a higher infant mortality rate than elsewhere, due particularly to the towns and villages being cut off during winter.

On Sunday I eventually completed the rounds and left for Mostar (267 miles away). A surgeon and the community physician for Bosnia had already driven from Mostar to convey their Republic's greetings. They went ahead in the car through the mountainous country and I met them in Markowska for fresh fish (this had fortunately already been caught). The community physician then transferred as a passenger to my vehicle and enlarged upon the recent new Yugoslav National Health law which I found very interesting, but his enthusiasm for English grammar and idiom finally forced me to remark that English had been one of my very weakest subjects at school. It was, therefore, with some relief that we arrived at the Home in Mostar at 11.50 p.m.

The rounds in Mostar began as usual at an early hour after the arrival of the warden and the doctor. Unfortunately, there will have to be definite changes here and the psychiatric patients moved to another part of Bosnia. During the afternoon we made visits to individuals in the town, including one young man confined to a wheelchair who for years had been trying to find his own flat and had at last succeeded – a happy story! He was even planning a visit to his brother in Australia.

The doctor exercised great patience in listening to and explaining both the diagnosis and prognosis of all the others and again it proved rather a late night.

On Tuesday I left at 5.30 a.m. for Risan. The drive along the coastal road must surely be one of the loveliest in Europe and the contrast after leaving the bitter cold and snow behind was very marked. Both the present warden, Mr Stankovic, and the original warden, Mr Popovic, greeted me and took me straight to the house which the Foundation provided for the nuns responsible for the nursing, laundry and kitchen at the Home. So once more I joined their community with joy. As always, it was important to discuss problems, personalities and patients' needs and admissions etc. with the wardens and the local authorities.

The whole of this region was severely affected during the earthquakes in April 1979, which caused havoc and left many hundreds of people homeless. The Sisters told me that after coming out of chapel and while walking between the Homes they literally saw the mountains move behind them.

The local hospital, built in traditional materials, had been shattered, but the three steel-framed Foundation Homes were miraculously left intact. The fourth Foundation Home, built in more substantial materials, and which included the central heating system for the whole complex, had been damaged.

For the following three to four weeks the staff were nursing an extra 200 patients from the hospital and every available pace in the corridors, dining rooms, etc, was taken up. Here in Risan the medical classification of the individuals has been improved and there is a peace and tranquillity about the whole place which I find hard to describe. The very simple Homes are grouped together here on the same site, but the gardens, shrubs and the distant bay with the mountains behind are a truly magnificent sight. Several Sisters are responsible for each part of the community and all the residents are known by name. The ambulant ones help in the kitchen garden, laundry and with running errands/shopping, amongst other jobs. Others attempt to "carve out" a useful life with handicrafts; a few receive visits from their families or friends; others have nobody left. The Sisters struggle to keep up their standard of nursing during the long, hot summer months in temperatures of 38°–40°C but water comes on only twice a day when every available receptacle is filled.

At present this is the only Centre and Home in this Republic of Montenegro. By tradition, the family unit remains close but many are alone. The number of applicants on the waiting list is forty, but certainly there are hundreds of others whose need are as great but who are not listed. The population of this Republic is 590,000 of whom it is estimated that 65,000 are over sixty-five years of age.

It was good that the day started early to enable me to go round because only by living on the premises and sharing in the life of the people there is it possible to get an insight into the organising of the daily routine.

I slept in the Sisters' Home, and the nun in charge, Sister Ivanka, (the caller), rang her handbell at 4.30 a.m. and gently opened each of our doors to see whether we were getting up. The Office of Prime was said at 4.45 a.m. followed by Mass at five o'clock and half an hour's meditation.

6.00 a.m. – Breakfast and washing up
6.30 a.m. – Work with patients
9.00 a.m. – Break and Prayers in Chapel
9.30 a.m. – Return to work
1.30 p.m. – Prayers in chapel
2.00 p.m. – Lunch

Recreation consists of gardening and embroidery and is allowed once a week for an hour. Otherwise they do further work with patients.

6.30 p.m. – Prayers in Chapel
7.00 p.m. – Supper and washing up

The nuns off duty are expected to return to the chapel afterwards. Television in black and white (poor reception) is now allowed and so are broadcasts from Radio Vatican and elsewhere. Between 9.30–10 p.m. one is allowed to read in the dining room or in bed or to write notes.

On Friday I most reluctantly left Risan. The late Mr Stankovic and his driver followed behind me through the mountains until the road descended to the dull plain and Podgorica, the capital of this Republic.

Our meeting confirmed what had been discussed before, and we had a simple lunch in the canteen before I continued on about 240 miles to Pristina. The route was partly through high mountain roads and the road passed through well over twenty tunnels. The original dirt road took one over some of the very beautiful parts of the high mountains. Dense fog prevailed and snow blizzards held up progress.

Another Order of Nuns is responsible for the nursing at Pristina and the Sisters are energetic and tough. The individuals they are responsible for looking after still include many psychiatric patients who are withdrawn and very ill. When they come off night duty the Sisters are always cheerful, though their fatigue is obvious.

A drive of some four hours via Skopje, the capital of Macedonia, brought me to Bitola at night, and during this journey I was reminded of my previous visit in 1978 – of walks through the snow which came up over the top of my tall boots – and of a memorable journey between Pristina and Bitola when driving conditions became steadily worse; fog was a hazard for much of the time and as we proceeded further into the mountains I had grave doubts about reaching our destination safely. The car from Bitola was unroadworthy; not only was the engine in a shocking state but also the steering column. For several miles it zig zagged from side to side, and as dusk and fog came down I refused to continue.

Heavy juggernauts and unlit carts from Greece and Bulgaria were not infrequent, and as these huge lorries slithered past us they flung up and sprayed us with snow and ice. I asked Sister Ana to walk up the road and try to stop oncoming traffic while the hazard lights were switched on in my vehicle which was parked on the side of the road at a safe distance from the car in front of us. With some effort three of us pushed the lorry to the side of the road and the occupants proceeded to walk. Bitola was still some forty to fifty miles away, and the Sister afterwards told me she had been sitting with the door open most of the way before the final skid ready to make an exit!

It was a great relief and pleasure to be reunited with the Sisters of Charity in their own small convent in the town. With another Order, they are responsible for the nursing in the General Hospital, and four Sisters of Charity run the two Foundation's simple Homes at Bitola.

4.00 a.m.	– Arise
4.30 a.m.	– Office of Prime
5.00 a.m.	– Mass
5.40–6.00 a.m.	– Meditation – then to work with patients
9.00–9.30 a.m.	– Breakfast – return to work
Noon	– Angelus
1.00–1.30 p.m.	– Lunch – return to work
3.00–4.00 p.m.	– Recreation and readings
4.30–5.00 p.m.	– Meditation
6.00 p.m.	– Supper

> 7.00 p.m.   – Vespers
> 8.00–9.00 p.m. – Sisters are allowed to read, listen to the
>   radio or watch television
> 9.30 p.m.   – Retire

In this convent I had the luxury of a single room, and one morning I failed to appear before 6 o'clock knowing there was to be an Evening Mass. The nuns, on getting no reply to their knock on the door, drew their own conclusions, so when I appeared there was much laughter as they told me that on getting no reply to their loud knock they had gone to the chapel to say prayers for the repose of my soul!

One of the patients here, the late "Mr George" who, as a child, still remembers the English because he was evacuated to Britain for four years during the Great War, was very ill with chronic cardiac disease.

A lot of renovation and improvement must indeed be done in the Homes – indeed they must be rebuilt, on an excellent site recently offered to the Foundation. Nevertheless, a high standard of hygiene and nursing prevail, particularly when one remembers that a number of patients are heavy nursing cases, including cancer.

As everywhere, there is a waiting list. Many, many more could be admitted if there were beds, and the Sisters had hoped in vain for an extension.

As is customary, members of the local authority called a meeting to discuss problems, etc. I was very sorry indeed to have to move on as everybody had made me feel so welcome and at home.

The next drive took me to Bansko, which lies very close to the Greek and Bulgarian frontiers and near the Belasica mountain. The small town of Bansko is sheltered under the mountain and on the other side is Greece. In 1970 the late Dr John Apley, who was internationally known and respected as a paediatrician, worked with me in Yugoslavia and was invaluable in helping me to decide upon this site in preference to others which were offered as alternatives. Although at the time Bansko was an even smaller village, we felt it had potential and would inevitably grow, especially as it had greenhouses and natural warm springs. The local people cultivate the soil well and many vegetables and flowers are grown there. The village lies some five miles away from the small town of Strumica.

At this place sixty-three physically handicapped children (from the age of eight) live together and receive education. Many are able to complete secondary school and go on for higher educational training. Teachers come to the Home daily. The children's dream, naturally, is to become independent and eventually receive a tiny flat and find employment. This is almost impossible owing to lack of housing and jobs, even for people in a good state of health. One boy was studying law.

I was again amazed by the quality of handicrafts produced, and the girls and boys have organised their own band with the aid of the music teacher. They gave two delightful concerts singing and playing with great energy and zest. They know a lot about pop singers and groups elsewhere too. I found it deeply moving, especially as the children and young people are admitted here because of their orthopaedic and neurological disabilities:

Congenitally brittle bones

Femoral dysplosin – hip joint out of place and other deformities
of leg and foot

Progressive muscular dystrophy – congenital weakness and
wasting of muscles

Post-poliomyelitis

Cerebral palsy

Osteo-chondrodystrophy, multiple – congenital faulty bone
growth and deformities

Freidreich's ataxia – unsteady movements due to spinal cord
disease with cardiac insufficiency

One girl, as a baby, had her hands bitten off by a pig. Since she came to
live here at Bansko she has received schooling, and I never cease to be
astonished when watching her cope with fine embroidery and hearing
her sing with the band. Later she left to become a telephonist. One of her
friends, Marijan, is a tall handsome boy who seems a born leader. He hopes
to go on to do social work. At least another sixty children are known to
be waiting for admission.

As always, I was reluctant to leave these children and young people, and
on my next visit I promised to remain longer.

The route to Kragujevac covered 300 miles. Road conditions varied.
A short section was over the new *autoput* which has a toll. I then had
to drive for the last one and a half hours over a road surface which
had been broken up by frost damage and I felt as if I was driving over
a ploughed field.

The warden, Mr Kristic, one of the cooks and a couple of residents had
waited up for me. I had dreamt of sleep but they insisted on producing
supper. At this place there are two Homes, one is occupied by very heavy
nursing cases, many of whom are psychiatric patients, while the other has
a mixture of the ambulant and those confined to bed. The mortality rate
has been high in the past with a prevalence of Burger's disease.

I would like to mention two Sisters who shared a room. Both had
muscular dystrophy and their first thoughts on waking were to start their
handicrafts. They have both died, within weeks of each other. One of the
few single rooms is occupied by a retired nurse who is crippled with
rheumatoid arthritis but organises her life from her bed. She opens and
closes her pivot window with the aid of long tapes attached to it.

The officials and people remember that it was here in the First World
War that one of the famous Scottish hospitals, complete with its own
medical and nursing staff, had performed miracles in a sea of suffering, not
only for the wounded but for thousands of typhus cases. Indeed, several of
the British staff also died in this epidemic. I went with Mr Kristic to the
graves of the following:

Mabel Dearner of the Stobart Hospital, Serbian Relief Fund who
died 11 July 1915 at Kragujevac.

Doctor Elizabeth Ross of the Military Fever Hospital who died at
Kragujevac in the spring of the year 1915 during the typhus
epidemic.

> Here lies Sister Lorna Ferris of the Stobart Hospital Serbian Relief
> Fund who died 4 July 1915 at Kragujevac.

On the graves Mr Kristic laid a large bunch of red carnations tied with gold ribbon.

The Yugoslavs, as usual, had drawn up a full itinerary in Belgrade which included the following visit to the City Hospital and rounds of 130 patients in the Centre created by the Foundation, plus the Outpatients' Department. This naturally took several hours and was followed by a private and moving visit to Marshal Tito's tomb.

I would like to express my deepest gratitude to the British Ambassadors and their wives, who so kindly helped to make arrangements for my visits to the Republics and to the Federal Secretariat. They also offered me the hospitality of their Residence while in Belgrade.

They usually arranged for me to give a talk to the wives of Ambassadors representing different countries who take turns each year in forming a committee to organise an International Bazaar. The Chair changes annually. Lady Wilson, widow of the late Sir Duncan Wilson who was British Ambassador from 1964 to 1968, organised and started the committee, but since then several million dinars had been raised for the sick and handicapped of all ages in various parts of Yugoslavia. On one such occasion the Brazilian Ambassador gave a large quantity of coffee and he duly took up position at his stall just before the opening of the Bazaar, only to find to his astonishment that although most of the coffee was still on the table it had been pre-sold! The crush was so great on the day that the Chinese stall collapsed! The committee considered that more uniformed policemen were necessary for crowd control.

Children's Home: This Home is built on a site adjoining the building founded in 1938 by private donations and known as the Mother and Child Centre. In the Foundation's Home babies are admitted from birth and accepted from other Republics, although fifty-two per cent are from the City of Belgrade. There are thirty cots/beds, but at the age of three the babies are supposed to be placed elsewhere or fostered. Inevitably those with congenital disorders remain longer and each is very sick or has a disability. The bed occupancy is ninety per cent. Until recently there were two children there, both double amputees. At one end of the Home there are places for ten socially handicapped children who have either been lost in this huge city or have been abandoned.

Whilst I was visiting individuals in their own homes I went to Pancevo to see Milun Ilic, a young man of twenty-six with Tetraplegia C-56 (severely handicapped due to a spinal injury) who, despite all the odds, has taken his degree in English at Belgrade University and speaks the language fluently. He hopes and dreams to do a post-graduate course in Britain and he showed me a letter he had received from the Professor of English at Essex University, Yorick Wilks. When I remarked that the Professor's first name was rather unusual, Milun replied "Shakespeare – Hamlet – Act 5." He lay on his side in a bed in a first-floor room of a small flat, and I left, together with Inge Glisic (who helps in a voluntary capacity for those in need) feeling very humble, and was very happy to hear, later that he gained his place his place at Essex University. After he received his Degree he set up a small company in Colchester, where he lives today.

On 9 April I left for Velika (167 miles away). The Foundation's Homes there are grouped together on a site at the far end of the large village and some seven to eight miles from the historic market town of Slavonska Pozega. The site is a beautiful one with high hills behind which are woodlands. The sound of babbling brook comes from not far away. I was welcomed by Sister Nada who has worked there from the beginning.

Here there is a feeling of peace and for some a sense of purpose, because those who are ambulant help the Homes by assisting in the laundry, kitchen or garden, and with nursing, shopping, running errands, etc. Several have made their small single or double rooms look attractive and homely and there is the usual activity with handicrafts. Others who are helpless lie in overcrowded rooms, but I suppose this is better than the circumstances in which they were living before being admitted. One extension has already been built and there are plans to link the three Homes together and build, hopefully, a large community room which is greatly needed, especially for concerts and other events of that kind and also a large Chapel for Mass, private prayers and meditation.

The staff at the Homes are keen and work as a team. Their hours are very long and hard and the salaries very low. This is due to a lack of funds in the Ministries concerned.

I had to return to Bosnia earlier than expected, although mercifully I had completed the rounds of everybody at Velika. The patients were considerate enough to turn off their television sets at a reasonable hour, thus enabling me to get some sleep at night, which I really appreciated.

Sister Nada took turns with the social worker, Mrs Dvoracek, to accompany me. We were joined by a spritely ninety-year old who never tired. She enjoyed walking and standing and spoke several languages. Her only lapses were when she constantly repeated: "I worked for twenty years in Prague. I can also remember and describe to you the assassination in Sarajevo of Archduke Ferdinand of Austria and his wife."

Palm Sunday; I was due to visit a Centre at Jakese which had been set up partly through the instigation of the Secretary (Minister) of Health and Social Welfare in Bosnia, Dr Hadzi Mustafic, a psychiatrist. The place was some three hours driving from Velika and when I arrived I found about ten people waiting, including social workers and psychiatrists. There are 150–200 patients – men and women of different ages – and after assessment a fair proportion are encouraged to participate in the work undertaken in five of the workshops. About six fairly new houses had also been built each accommodating twenty-two people, the idea being that they all live together as a family. As is the common practice of the Yugoslavs, I was then taken on to the General Hospitals.

In the evening I drove on to Travnik. The standard of nursing at the Foundation's Homes remains high despite the shortage of nuns, and the patients there include those diagnosed with cancer.

After driving 225 miles to Perusic I met Dr Petrovic who shares a practice with a lady doctor. Together they have some 12–15,000 patients on their register. They cover a very wide area and during the long hard winters it has been exceedingly difficult for them to reach patients in remote villages and poor dwellings, even by sleigh. Dr Petrovic has faithfully kept to this practice over at least twenty years, and up to fairly recently was on his own. He knows practically everybody on the register and being with him always proves a very interesting experience.

I returned to Zagreb late on Wednesday evening for another meeting with Mrs Granecka. On the following day I attended further meetings and paid visits to a Children's Centre for the handicapped and to the sick in their own accommodation. The discipline of the day always enables one both to concentrate and to get round to all the matters which need attention, though obviously several more days could be spent at each place and I deeply regret that this was not possible.

In the evening of Maundy Thursday I attended High Mass in the Cathedral in the presence of the Bishop of Zagreb.

The Yugoslavs were saddened to hear of Dr John Apley's death as he had given excellent advice and was well liked, also that of Joyce Johns (whom they had nicknamed Jovanka). She had been Head of the Physiotherapy Schools in Exeter and Cardiff and had helped me for successive years. Joyce died in 1981 whilst relatively young.

In all, visits were made to the following places during my work in Yugoslavia:

Home	Number of people seen:
Bansko	63
Bitola	107
Gospic	125
Kragujevac	88
Pristina	103
Risan	273
Belgrade	145
Belgrade (babies)	40
Velika	143
Travnik	82
Mostar	72
	1,241

This figure does not include domiciliary visits, plus hospitals, etc.

When some of my friends amongst the Yugoslav Authorities heard I had become a peer they asked me why I had not chosen, in addition to Warsaw, a name of a city in their country. Then they smiled and said, "Well, to us you will always be Comrade Sue." Another added: "*Draga Sue*" – dear Sue.

The transition from conditions out there to those in Britain took a few hours for me to adjust to and, as always, I felt nostalgic and grateful for the enthusiasm, warmth and affection which the Yugoslavs expressed.

Since this Chapter was first written in 1986, the inevitable civil war broke out in July 1991. Tito had predicted this, but not in public, and had told me of his fears some years before he died. Even though a commission had been set up and a desperate attempt had been made to hold the country together by allowing the President of each Republic to hold office in turn as the Federal President for one year, this did not prevent war, it ensured it.

I had been consulted on the matter as long ago as the 1970s by the then Yugoslav Ambassador in London, who used to enjoy coming here to Headquarters in Suffolk usually on a Sunday. He was a good friend of mine, and we spent many hours discussing the fragile peace and his deep concern for the future. He told me many things in confidence and correctly predicted how hard it would be to convince the rest of Europe and the United Nations that they should intervene *before* the worst happened.

A large percentage of the former Yugoslav Army was comprised of Serbian officers and men and it is this faction which formed the Serbian Army, the third largest in Europe. For many years the Soviets and, later, the Russians, had supported the Serbian faction in the Yugoslav Army and had regularly ploughed huge quantities of armaments into Serbia. Colonel Gadaffi, too, had been sending in weapons and other material. They also have their own munitions factories. The Serbian plans for expansion and a greater Serbia had been formulated over many years by this strong clique of politicians and generals, who paid no heed to the wishes or feelings of the ordinary Serbs, many of whom did not wish to fight. Indeed, thousands of them are married to Moslems or Croats and have no desire to be part of the civil war. In 1992 the University of Belgrade was closed after many students had been conscripted into the Army against their will.

I had for years heard of the forebodings of evil and of the inevitability of this terrible catastrophe. I dreaded the bloodshed and loss of life, and the ruin of the country which would come about. All through the years from 1945 to 1990 I had striven to do what I could in all the Republics, except Slovenia (where there was a far higher standard of living) and the Vojvodina. Both the Council of the Foundation, and the wardens and staff serving the Homes – in particular the nuns – had brought about unity in their own small way, and had experienced a sense of purpose which those who have survived will never forget.

As I write this at the end of 1993 the break-up of former Yugoslavia has taken place in the worst possible way for the ordinary citizens of that region, with most of the tragedy being played out in Croatia and Bosnia, two of the successor states of the former federation. In Croatia over 300,000 people have been driven from their homes, 20,000 are dead or missing, believed dead, with many more thousands wounded and/or traumatised. In Bosnia it is impossible to calculate how many people have died – probably as many as 20,000 – over two million have been made homeless and countless numbers wounded, physically and mentally.

Furthermore roads, railways, bridges, power lines and communications have been destroyed over large areas and in Bosnia the whole economy and social infrastructure has been destroyed in many places.

Beyond the official help provided either directly by National Governments or through international organisations such as the Red Cross, the UN High

Commission for Refugees, there are dozens of NGOs (Non Governmental organistions) each having their own mandate to follow. One of the tragedies of the crisis in Bosnia is that it has eclipsed many of the chronic problems in many parts of the former Yugoslavia which have understandably continued to deteriorate. Such problems are exemplified by the situation in Macedonia.

Macedonia is the second poorest country in Europe after Albania. Its economy has collapsed, as a result of the sanctions against Serbia and the Greek blockade over the dispute about the name Macedonia. The borders with Serbia and with Greece are closed so that all freight has to be flown in, smuggled or brought overland from Bulgaria. The only external rail links were with Serbia and Greece.

The refugee population is comparatively well provided for. However, the situation is very different for certain groups such as the chronically ill, the handicapped and the elderly, having to rely on a state pension. There are 100,000 of the 200,000 old people having to live on less than $30 per month.

Almost all medicines have to be imported imposing a major strain on the foreign exchange reserves. Only fifteen per cent are manufactured locally. Much of the equipment is in a very bad state, often being more than twenty years old. A particular problem is with the radiotherapy equipment. Shortages of money are making it very difficult to pay the medical staff.

Amongst all the terrible tragedies that have occurred, that of the elderly, the very young and the handicapped is many ways the worst. These groups of people are very dependent on the communities in which they live, and in many cases that community has ceased to exist, with the able-bodied driven away or just fleeing. The problems of such people are of today – they need to be fed, clothed and sheltered, and of tomorrow – they need the healing balm of compassion and devoted care to help them recover from the traumas they have gone through. It is here hopefully where organisations such as the Sue Ryder Foundation can do an immense amount of good, on both physical and spiritual levels, and the search for the means to do that in co-operation with local people must go on.

The three Foundation's Homes in Macedonia all *urgently* require rebuilding because of such heavy use. I must also refer especially to the one at Bansko, near Strumica, for children and young people with muscular dystrophy and other handicaps. Their well-known band no longer plays, because instruments must be replaced, and the secondary school is closed because funds are lacking to pay the teachers. Ever since 1945 when I started working in this country, I understood the complexity of the political situation and the historical problems besetting the Republics. How right late Marshal Tito was to anticipate a brutal civil war and that a greater Serbia would emerge.

From the beginning, I was always blessed with freedom to work in all parts of the country and to go wherever I wanted – despite surveillance. I was taken into the confidence of local authorities and countless other people. I saw harrowing sights and an abysmal lack of hospitals with shortages of beds. Often patients had to share a bed, and cross-infection was almost inevitable as a result of this. These conditions had *always* existed and I think few of the public in this country, and elsewhere, have realised that there has always been a desperate need for more Foundation Homes and hospitals there, with the necessary equipment and basic medical requirements.

The Federal Ministers of Health and Social Welfare and their colleagues in the Republic, and indeed, countless other people, particularly those in the medical profession, had asked me to provide still more Homes and hospitals. Since I began work there, some 60,000 "in and out" patients of all age groups have been treated in the Foundation's twenty-two Homes and hospitals. As a result of the civil war four of these have either been severely damaged or destroyed.

*   *   *

Here is a report of another typical visit to the former Yugoslavia in May and June 1995. The long drives began the evening of Friday 5 May from Headquarters via Felixstowe, where I was welcomed by P&O Ferries and had the luxury of a driver's cabin with running water and loo. I took the opportunity to have a very deep sleep.

The pressures during the weeks before leaving, especially for Ruth (my Personal Assistant), were extremely tiring. However hard we tried, we never seemed able to keep to our hourly schedule of things for action. The loading by volunteers of supplies and gifts also took many hours.

Once I had departed and was back in the driving seat, I enjoyed the beautiful sunshine and, with short stops, reached Salzburg in Austria fourteen hours after leaving Zeebrugge. I was kindly offered a bed in a Convent in Salzburg for three hours and then left for Mauthausen, near Linz, where I met the large group of survivors and their children from Poland at 8.10 a.m. on Sunday morning for Mass. Those who survived usually make commemorations and pilgrimages annually in April or May – the date nearest to the Liberation of the Camp – with the exception of those of Majdanek (July 1944) and Auschwitz (January 1945). These reunions at places of such suffering are unique and touching in their dignity. Friendships are renewed and great affection and warmth is shown between the different nationalities. I marvel at their courage to return, but understand it is because they forged such friendships and solidarity in the course of their indescribable suffering.

Beautiful flowers, wreaths, posies and candles are placed wherever the survivor chooses at the time; prayers, interdenominational services and Masses are said. I take my leave reluctantly from these places, with such haunting and poignant memories.

All the main camps – except Flossenburg, where Dietrich Bonhoeffer, the famous German theologian, was hanged shortly before the War ended in

May 1945 – have formed their own international associations during the past forty years. The former prisoners endeavour to see that these places, on such hallowed ground, are properly maintained. They have created a Museum and appointed a suitable Director and guides. They also arrange for the annual commemorations in which thousands of survivors represent their countries and, to which in recent years, they bring their children and grandchildren. I witnessed this in Sachsenhausen (1933–45), and talked with a few of the two thousand Norwegians who came back again this year.

Survivors usually belong to a club or association in their own countries too, to befriend and assist any survivor in need. Many people understandably, prefer not to have any contact or to be reminded of the horrendous past, but everybody always says: "Forgive, but never forget".

Then later on to Vienna, Zagreb and the following Republics of the former Yugoslavia:

Croatia:

I am going to use here an account by a colleague who accompanied me from Vienna.

> The first Sue Ryder Home that Lady Ryder visited on her journey through the former Yugoslavia was Velika in Croatia.
>
> It was a comparatively short journey (three hours) from the capital of Croatia, Zagreb, through the autoroute which had just been reopened the week before by a military battle as it ran through Sector West, a disputed zone between the Bosnian Serbs and Croatia. There was a quiet eeriness on the motorway with almost no traffic, except from a UN outpost huddled against the side of the motorway by an abandoned filling station.
>
> Turning north from the motorway past bullet-riddled signs, destroyed houses and abandoned tanks, we drove northwards from the plains of Slavonia to the green hills which, until one week ago, had been an active war zone.
>
> Velika is a small rural town which had been famous as a health spa. The town has a long and ancient history; as if to remind you that war had always been present, high on a hill overlooking the Home is a thirteenth-century fort damaged by shellfire in 1991.
>
> The Sue Ryder Homes were built in the side of a river valley and have 139 residents and patients. Quite apart from their primary purpose of caring for the sick and handicapped, Sue Ryder Homes in this part of the world have assumed an additional role in that they shine as examples of hope and care in a country which has seen such brutality and violence in recent years.
>
> To help in this work there is Sister Nada, the Head Nurse, who started at the Homes when they were built in 1969. At the entrance to Velika, and along the corridors, hang many photographs of her, together with Lady Ryder and various Ministers and local dignitaries, taken when the Homes were being opened; Sister Nada's tall, strong presence and her warm and endearing smile, as shown in the photographs, were still there as she walked and worked among the patients.

The staff in the Home on a bright and warm spring morning were proceeding with their normal routine of ward rounds, bed changing and medical care. Words of encouragement and hope seemed to fill the rooms and wards.

The sick bay was the busiest place, as some of the rooms meant for two residents had three or even four people in them. Sister Nada explained that this was because there was such a waiting list. They found it impossible to turn people away who were in desperate need.

Despite the overcrowding and the lack of recreation rooms for the residents, the overworked staff coped well with the constant demands made on them. The staff consists of two Sisters, seven Nurses and nine Auxiliaries, working on a twenty-four hour shift. The cuts in Government support mean that the Home is unable to increase the staff or pay for the overtime and extra work that they willingly incur.

As Lady Ryder visited each person, Sister Nada talked about the need to deal with the waiting list of almost seventy people. The most pressing problem is the overcrowding and the lack of recreation rooms. A limited site for a sixty-bed extension to the Home has been identified near the sick bay. The problem is where and how to find funding during these difficult times.

The war, which has now been continuing for nearly four years, has not caused the Home at Velika to cease its work or prevent it giving hope and help when the need is greatest.

Everyone knows the desperate deprivations that people from the former Yugoslavia have suffered over the last few years and, sadly, the Sue Ryder Homes in Bosnia have themselves become casualties of the fighting there.

Sister Nada and her staff in Velika asked about the other Homes in the former Yugoslavia and while Lady Ryder was in Serbia and Montenegro, she was asked there, too, about Homes in Croatia.

The Foundation Council, which used to co-ordinate the work in each Republic, has ceased to function because of the disruptions of the war. It is not possible to telephone or communicate with Serbia, Montenegro or Bosnia. Prior to the war, the strong and energetic Chairman Nevenka Novakovic, a personal friend of Lady Ryder, drew together people of different ethnic and religious backgrounds. She always believed the Foundation blazed the trail in building Homes for the sick and handicapped.

Always in such difficult times the very poorest, the weak, the handicapped and the infirm are the most vulnerable. When more immediate needs are met in times of great emergency, long term care is often not understood or supported as it deserves to be.

The quiet and undemanding spirit of the Home at Velika, so near to the war zone, yet still fulfilling its peacetime role during a time of war, deserves the admiration and support of the whole international community."

Serbia:

I could enter only by driving through Hungary, a drive of fourteen hours instead of two and a half (when able to travel direct from Croatia to Serbia). In Belgrade, by courtesy of the Charge d'Affaires, Mr I. Roberts, I received 43 litres of fuel because no fuel stations were open. There were cars with odd-looking jars containing fuel standing on their bonnets, which were sold on the black market.

I held meetings in Belgrade, followed by a visit to the Foundation's Home for mothers and babies there. I then drove from Belgrade to Kragujevac, a journey of some three hours.

I spent one day and two nights there visiting each resident. After many years' service, the Director, Mr Kristic has been succeeded by a young man, Vesilin Mutovic, who is keen that urgent structural repairs be carried out. He also informed the Ministry of Social Policy that this Home had received no funds for food, medication and salaries since the end of March 1995. The Foundation sent a fax to UNHCR informing them of the serious situation.

At Kragujevac in Serbia, the friendly and kind Director of the Foundation's Home there, Mr Mutovic, asked if he could put a few litres of diesel in my vehicle to help me on my way to Skopje. I should have immediately but politely declined his offer knowing that fuel can only be obtained on the black market. Alas, the worst happened. I managed to drive as far as the memorial to the 7,000 people (including all children of Form V in the local school) who were shot by the SS on 21 October 1941. There, on the hard-standing car park, the Renault stopped! Within minutes a small curious group gathered round to offer advice, and I had to ask Mr Mutovic to thank them but ask them to leave. I found, through Mr Mutovic, a splendid mechanic, Tomo, and together we worked on the fuel system for five hours. It was pouring with rain, but the work and determination to get the engine running properly made us feel warm. We dismantled the filter system, emptied the fuel tank, and then both agreed that this had to be removed and completely cleaned out. The fuel which I had been given contained a mixture of water, glass and sand!

I enjoyed working with Tomo (who refused any payment) and I think this was reciprocated by him. I have always enjoyed working on engines and vehicles since my training with the FANY in the early days of World War II, and this training and experience has often proved most helpful in difficult situations.

Macedonia:
This is a land-locked country where great help is urgently required to repair and refurnish the Foundation's Home at Bansko for children and young people.

In Skopje, there are no facilities for patients in need of palliative care and others who have nowhere to stay while attending the very poorly equipped Radiotherapy Centre. A most urgent plea has long since been made to me by the Radiotherapist and Oncologist and a site has been located for a Sue Ryder Home which will serve this large Republic – this has a scattered population and 3,095 new cases of cancer diagnosed each year.

In Bitola, near the Greek frontier (which was closed), there are two simple Homes which were built in the 1960s and are now completely worn out through heavy usage. They were intended for 120 patients but, such are the pressures, many more are living and being nursed there by four devoted nurses, Sisters of Charity, and a small staff who work long hours in extremely overcrowded conditions and on very small salaries.

A beautiful site in a meadow near the hills and only five kilometres outside Bitola has been offered for a new Home which is urgently needed. We now need to find the necessary funds.

Montenegro:
At Risan, the same can be said as for Bitola. This is the only Home for the sick and handicapped in the whole of the Republic of Montenegro. There are nearly 300 patients in four separate buildings. They are greatly overcrowded and there is no segregation between the heavy nursing cases, the physically handicapped and the mentally ill. The four nuns and small number of staff work courageously on twelve-hour shifts and low salaries.

The media, and indeed many other organisations, tended to focus their attention on Bosnia (two Foundation Homes have been destroyed there too) and the tragedy being played out there. However, there are many hundreds of sick and handicapped patients in the other Republics I visited and they are rarely given any news coverage. These patients wait in silence for essential basic care and nursing assistance and, in some cases, for a purpose to live.

I reluctantly left Risan and received special permission – granted to a very few – to cross the border of Montenegro into Croatia and thus drive the long coastal road. I stayed overnight with kind friends in Split, and then with the Sisters of Charity in Ljubljana.

The distance covered during these five weeks amounted to 8,240 miles, part of it over some very bad road. There was also beautiful scenery, heavy rain, and then warm weather up to 30°C.

Living and working with the nuns of different Congregations has always seemed a privilege. Their life of Prayer, combined with long working hours (the day starts as early as 4.30 or 5 a.m.) and a very disciplined routine, made me feel how essential it is to rely upon prayer and the will of God all the time. As before during the past fifty years, I felt reluctant to leave. It would be wonderful to feel assured that more financial assistance will be forthcoming. Hours were spent calling on UN officials and in discussions with NGOs (Non-Government Organisations), in order to describe the misery they could relieve in the places mentioned here.

Olga, a close friend of mine (who had been a partisan at the age of eighteen in 1941 and later with one of the British Missions) proved, as always, a great support.

I am so grateful to the residents, staff and local authorities for the great warmth of their welcome, their affection and their uncomplaining stoicism. I felt deeply humble.

* * *

When the fighting eventually stops and some form of settlement is made, then will begin the slow and very painful process of reconciliation which most people want and all need. It will take many billions of pounds and many years of effort to repair the physical devastation which has affected large parts of Bosnia and Croatia, and it will require an effort of a will similar to that which was displayed after the Second World War. It will take even longer for the psychological wounds to heal with many traumas to be overcome. Although there are people of goodwill on all sides and countless heroic deeds of self-sacrifice shining through the darkness, so far these voices have not been heard. The extremisms which started the conflict have engendered new extremisms. These must be contained and then removed before life can gain any semblance of normality. It is difficult at present to be optimistic for the short and medium term, but eventually these conflicts will end, as they always do. At that point the common economic interests of the new nations will, one hopes, bring them to a state where they can be decent neighbours, trading and co-operating for their common good.

The brave attempt to create a union of the South Slavs has ended in terrible failure. Some thought that failure was inevitable from the beginning, but many thought otherwise and struggled for many years to achieve an idea. In the end it proved impossible to reconcile the irreconcilable, and the many successor States will rapidly have to find a *modus vivendi* with their former brothers and with the neighbours whose own interests and ambitions once helped to drive the people of the former Yugoslavia together. For some time the latter will be the easier process, but for the longer-term Croat and Serb and Bosnian and Macedonian will have to find a means to co-operate with each other, and with other ethnic minorities within their midst. This can no longer realistically be within one constitutional limit; but regional economic, cultural, environmental and other associations are inevitable in the modern world, and we can only hope and pray that eventually these will bring renewed peace and prosperity to peoples who so richly deserve them.

17

Stagenhoe, Hertfordshire

Commit your work to God.

DURING THE TIME THAT I was doing relief work on the Continent, I was deeply impressed by the sufferings I witnessed and moved by the conditions in which the sufferers were forced to exist: the lack of privacy, general overcrowding and bad living conditions, all worsened by severe winters. Many seemed, too, to face extraordinary personal tragedies and sickness. I remember a typical example, a women who for years had shared a room in a large block, separated from the others only by a blanket. She was sitting on the lower part of the bunk bed cutting one of her few dresses into shreds and saying, "I can't take any more. The noise and the misery around me all this has forced me to do it." As I witnessed scenes like this I felt increasingly the wish to give these individuals a change of environment, even if only temporary, and a holiday – something the majority of them had never enjoyed.

With the help of friends in Denmark, the Holiday Scheme was created in 1952, for the sick and the survivors of the concentration camps. The Danes were very generous with their hospitality and invited their guests to stay in their own homes for periods of up to three months while they relaxed. Although Denmark may appear on the map to be a small country, it seemed quite a large area when I helped to deliver and collect both the survivors and the sick.

The sight of large tureens of delicious soup, real coffee, butter spread liberally on rolls and varieties of bread, and fresh ham and bacon, was unforgettable after the frugal life to which we had grown accustomed.

The Danish Holiday Scheme was a short-term arrangement, but those involved felt it should be continued, though possibly in a slightly different form. Because of the distances involved and the language problems, it seemed preferable for the visitors to stay together in a group, not with individual hosts, as had been the case in Denmark. Moreover, it appeared a good idea for them to spend their holidays in a country which had been spared occupation by the Nazis and had thus remained largely unscarred.

While the Home for permanent residents was being established at Cavendish in 1953, I was therefore also looking for a suitable large house in England which could be used as a Holiday Home. This was not to prove as easy as I had hoped, partly because properties were becoming increasingly difficult to find and expensive, but also because of the type of house for which I was looking. The purpose of the Holiday Scheme was to offer the survivors the chance to forget – even if only briefly, for a minimum of three to four weeks – something of what they had endured, and to try to compensate to some extent for what they had missed. I wanted to give them the opportunity to stroll through peaceful villages and meadows, to visit art collections, enjoy outings, and above all to live in surroundings which could be conducive to happiness and peace of mind. Consequently, it was not just four walls and a roof that were needed, but a house that by virtue of its architecture and atmosphere would provide the right setting.

At that time many period houses and historic properties were lying vacant in different parts of the country, and the Historic Buildings Council were, in a number of cases, making efforts to find purchasers who would renovate and preserve them; but it is a sad fact of this postWar period that so many such houses have been lost to the nation for one reason or another. It is always easier for man to destroy than to create.

At this point my mother and her acquaintances came to the rescue by obtaining for me the lease of the empty wing of a large period house in Long Melford, Suffolk. The lease was only temporary and a great deal of hard work was needed to make the wing habitable and attractive, but once this had been done it served as a Centre for holiday groups for eleven happy years, and over 1,000 survivors stayed there. The visitors came mainly from Poland, as it is in Poland that most of the survivors of concentration camps are alive today, although their numbers diminished quickly not because of age, but due to all they had endured.

Mama especially realised how much small details can contribute towards the general effect of a welcome. She would, for example, line the drawers of the chests, dressing tables and cupboards with white paper and find gay velvet and satin coat hangers, and we made sure that the survivors had matching huckabuck bath towels and bedspreads, according to the colour of their rooms. Friends would also bring lovely flowers and pot plants. Two of the original volunteers who came frequently to give their services were Mrs Edna Gibson and Mrs Charlotte Tillman, wife of an eminent dermatologist. Charlotte was one of the best organisers and by her example she encouraged young volunteers to clean out all the rooms methodically almost every day, and in every room, including the loos, there were lovely flower arrangements done by Charlotte. She had boxes made up which carried all the cleaning and polishing materials. The whole place glistened as a result of her ability to make every nook and corner look its best. I had faithful friends who were themselves in the antiques business, and they generously gave beautiful items of furniture, which made all the difference to the appearance of the bedrooms, the drawing room and the dining room. Everything was later transferred to the Sue Ryder Home at Stagenhoe.

Dr Grace Griffiths and members of Toc H made sandwiches for the outings, and others would invite the visitors into their own homes for a few hours or for a meal. [Toc H stands for Talbot House near Ypres, and provided a place for rest and spiritual refreshment, as well as canteen facilities during the War and still does today.]

Fatigue and their own disabilities did not prevent the survivors taking a very deep interest indeed in each day's programme. Diaries were often kept, and it is moving to read years later of the different activities, people and places which afforded so much pleasure. The joy they took in small things, which for them were part of a once-in-a-lifetime visit, made those of us around them feel humble, as we ourselves were inclined to take these same things so much for granted as part of the English scene. In particular they found visits to Cambridge, with the colleges and the Backs, Oxford, London, Norwich, Windsor, Runnymede and the Chelsea Flower Show moving and enthralling. Other groups had the opportunity of visiting Devonshire, Cornwall, Manchester and Gateshead, and thus deep and lasting friendships were forged between Britain and Poland. These visits helped the survivors to forget, temporarily at least, their own terrible experiences and sufferings; but unhappily their memories were long, and it was not unusual to hear somebody walking up and down during the night or the early hours of the morning, unable to sleep, or to hear them cry out aloud in their dreams.

Birthdays and name days were always remembered on the last evening, when the helpers served supper by candlelight, and presents were exchanged.

Before the lease of this Home at Long Melford expired, over ninety estate agents had provided the Foundation with details of other properties, and some sixty were inspected, most of them in various stages of disintegration; but for one reason or another none was suitable, usually because they were too small. One house, the former home of the poet, Julian Grenfell, was discovered only as the demolition men moved in.

Many of the properties we saw have their special saga – often rich in humour, but also sad when a house was seen literally crumbling into the ground with no sign of it being repaired and saved. Sometimes this was because the owner deliberately wanted it "to come down" so that he might see the past out of sight, then build a number of modern houses for himself and other people on the same site and so make a lot of money. Alas, many of these stories are untold, and remain unknown to all but a few of the general public.

There is also a lighter side – and fortunately the following story had no connection with an historic house.

An enquiry came through the post one day from the owners of a place in Wales. I was invited to visit it, and stay the night with one of my Assistants. Although we had looked at the plans of the house and garden these were not accompanied by any description of the property. When we arrived at what we supposed to be the local town, we were informed that the "big house" was six miles away. By the time we reached the main gates the mileometer had clocked three miles, and we then drove on for a further three miles past dripping rhododendrons and azaleas, the mist getting thicker and thicker as we followed a very wide stream which ran into a lake. At last the house and mountains behind it came into view, and the lopsided notice on the front door directed us with an arrow to the side entrance. From there a middle-aged man emerged, dressed in plus fours and a boiler suit. He introduced himself simply as "the coolie" and offered to carry our baggage. We wondered who this person was and where the owner might be.

We were led up some back stairs to a nook, which in its better days had evidently been a large cupboard. The doors had been taken off and it was now an improvised kitchen. There stood a woman in her late seventies with short close-cropped hair, smoking a pipe. She was chopping up a large quantity of cabbage and stuffing this into an undersized saucepan, suitable for boiling milk in. The sight of this cabbage spilling over onto a dirty calor gas stove amazed us. "I hope you will like my special Finnish recipe for dinner tonight," she said, referring to the cabbage, into which she then scattered a cup of porridge oats. Clearly we had no choice. Turning to "the coolie" – who, we then learnt, was her husband – she said, "Well, offer them tea!" He had already put the kettle on – a kind gesture not noticed by his wife, who trumpeted: "Don't just stand there. A watched pot never boils."

The sight of this grubby stove, the unwashed sticky shelves, and the damp kitchen convinced us that we should graciously try to leave. These thoughts were soon dismissed when we were ushered into a makeshift drawing room, with a large open fire and huge logs which hissed because of the damp. Smoke billowed out. We were then informed that dinner would be served at 8 p.m. This was still two-and-a-half hours away, and it was not the sort of place conducive to work in. We put on extra pullovers and went for a walk in the sodden woods.

At 8 p.m. we met our host and hostess again, now attired respectively in a velvet smoking jacket and long dress, and sat down to eat dinner, which consisted only of the special Finnish dish served on beautiful riveted china. After the meal, still feeling hungry but having nothing left in our grub box, I took the precaution of swallowing a double dose of indigestion tablets. Our offer to clear the beautiful mahogany table and take the dishes to the kitchen was accepted and we pushed the loaded, creaking trolley down the long corridor into a large room lined with shelves of lovely china – and piles of dirty china and silver. Our hostess announced: "Oh, leave it! In this house we don't do the washing up for two or three weeks!"

When we were all seated in the drawing room, she proceeded to make jigsaw puzzles with a large fret saw, while sitting opposite her "the coolie" dutifully darned her stockings and his own socks. She was quite determined that the Foundation should lease the house, and for me it proved one of the most difficult of evenings. Each and every attempt to convince her that no staff would ever stay in the old building, because it was so isolated – and that any individuals who came would feel that they had reached the back of beyond – was flatly rejected. She then started to deplore my attitude and told her husband that she had always heard I was willing to take on any house. It was quite clear that she thought my reactions were most ungracious. She then telephoned three local supporters and to their surprise, and ours too, demanded that they should come out to the house at 9.45 that night. Fortunately for us, they also confirmed that the place was far to isolated and unsuitable for our purpose. We were then left with the rest of the night to face in the company of our affronted hostess and "the coolie" – who, of course, was the owner!

We slept between very thin pure linen sheets. Owing to the damp – the central heating had not been used for many years – I kept my sheepskin coat on!

On another occasion an invitation came in from a wealthy widow who was known to be eccentric both in her style of living and in her behaviour. There followed two memorable nights spent in the splendour of her historic house. She had an obsession both for doing petit point and for smoking from a long cigarette holder whilst she drank frequent whiskies.

I was ushered into her presence and, as we waited for the butler to announce dinner, I sat on the edge of her sofa. She turned to me and said, "Do you ever *do* anything?"

During the meal I remarked upon the lovely copy of a huge painting of the Queen by Annigoni which hung in the dining room. My hostess replied, "Oh, I think it is awful and next time she comes here I will ask her to take it away."

By the time the lease of the Suffolk house expired no alternative property had been found, and there followed some anxious months of increasingly urgent searching. Amongst those who helped to carry out surveys was John Adams, the Foundation's Honorary Architect for seventeen years – a man who shared our sense of humour and who made up practical jokes on the spur of the moment.

One afternoon, pages of stencilled prospectives arrived (chiefly concerning small houses) from a firm of estate agents, and after thumbing through them I noticed on the back page a very brief mention of Stagenhoe – a house with thirty-three bedrooms and nine acres of garden situated a few miles outside the town of Hitchin in Hertfordshire. It was almost a dream house, and though the purchase price was far beyond anything that the Foundation had ever contemplated, I felt that we must somehow try to acquire it. Beneath its coat of arms was the motto "Commit your work to God". (Proverbs 16:3.)

The history of the estate surrounding Stagenhoe can be traced back to the Domesday Book. Like similar houses in Hertfordshire it has a chequered past. The house was owned by different families; its most interesting inhabitant in 1880 was the Duchess de Modena Pomar who became the

Countess of Caithness. She took a great interest in spiritualism and wrote books on the subject. There had always been talk of a secret passage under the house at Stagenhoe to Temple Dinsley or The Bury. This was supposed to have been constructed for a priest and used as an escape route. Investigations by previous owners, including Mr Bailey Hawkins, were unsuccessful as each was driven back by foul air.

The first record we have of the manor at Stagenhoe dates from the tenth century, when it was held by "a man of King Edward", that is, Edward the Confessor. By the thirteenth century the manor was held by Simon Fitzsimon, devolving subsequently upon his heir, John de Verdun, who received permission from the Abbot of St Albans to set apart an oratory in his mansion house for the celebration of Mass. This manor house, it must be pointed out, stood not on the present site, but at a lower level about the middle of the park.

Through the female line, the estate later passed to the Pilkingtons, one of whom fought at Agincourt and another on Bosworth Field. As the latter was a supporter of King Richard, he was outlawed, and the deeds of Stagenhoe were in 1489 granted to Thomas Stanley, Earl of Derby.

The estate subsequently had a number of different owners, among them John Hale, who in 1648 demolished the old house and built a new one. When this was destroyed by fire in 1737, the owner then, Robert Hysham, erected the present mansion – originally two-storeyed – which took three years to complete. It is not known who the architect was.

In 1841 the property was sold to the Rogers family who carried out many improvements to the estate, adding a lake. When they in turn sold it to the Earl of Caithness in 1869, it consisted of 606 acres and was worth £37,000. The Earl carried out further improvements, chief among which was the addition of a third storey to the house in 1879.

After his death the estate changed hands repeatedly, one of the occupants of the house being Sir Arthur Sullivan, who rented it in 1885, while working on *The Mikado* and *The Golden Legend*, and he invited the D'Oyly Carte Opera Company to stay for the weekend. During the Second World War, it served as a maternity home for evacuees from London, and over 2,000 babies were born there; from 1948 to 1964 it was used as a boys' preparatory school.

Afterwards Stagenhoe was once more, for a brief period, privately owned; but when the Sue Ryder Foundation bought the house and nine acres of garden in July 1969 it was unoccupied and dilapidated.

The majority of the rooms in the house had to be renovated by a small group of the Foundation's tradesman and volunteers who, under the most difficult circumstances, met the deadline only days before the Home was to receive and accommodate a group of survivors and other handicapped.

The house has served two main purposes. Firstly, it fulfilled my original intention to make it a Holiday Home for sufferers coming from Poland and other areas of Europe, where the physical or psychological traumas of Nazi and Soviet occupation still oppressed them. However as their numbers or needs are diminished naturally by the march of time, the scheme is increasingly extended to young handicapped people and to others whose present circumstances or environment call for at least temporary amelioration. The Holiday Scheme, started in 1952, has benefited several thousands of adults and children and has always included others in great need who do not have an opportunity of receiving a holiday, particularly in Britain.

Secondly, The Home was registered with the North Hertfordshire Health Authority as a nursing home for forty-two patients handicapped by different diseases. It also tries to offer a short-term stay for the young, middle-aged and elderly, whose families or neighbours, for different reasons, often need respite from nursing them.

The house is very beautiful: a central hall gives access to drawing rooms, a library and a morning room, all with sash windows overlooking the terrace, lawns and fields on the west side, which sweep down to where there was formerly an artificial lake. A wide staircase leads to the upper storeys. All the rooms have large windows looking out over rolling fields of wheat and barley and the wooded hills surrounding the property. Behind the house are the remains of the stables and a series of walled gardens and orchards leading past the hothouses to the Dower House: in the days when ten gardeners were employed there, it must have been a lovely sight. It was in this beautiful garden that Her Majesty, Queen Elizabeth the Queen Mother, played as a child with the Bailey Hawkins. They especially enjoyed cricket on August Bank Holidays, with the return match at The Bury – The Bowes-Lyon's house.

Because of the delay in completing the purchase of the property, we where left with very little time in which to get the house ready for its first occupants. These were the forty-five members of a group whose holiday would have had to be cancelled but for the generosity of the Rotary Club of Weybridge, Surrey, who, on hearing of the situation, offered them hospitality and accommodation. This was only for a limited period, however; and, in order to make the long journey from Warsaw and back worthwhile it was essential to have Stagenhoe ready by the end of their stay in Weybridge, which meant that we had only ten days in which to prepare for their arrival.

It was August, the holiday season, when we were working on the house and though there had been Press reports about the acquisition of the Home and the work involved in getting it ready, not many helpers came from the district. Happily we had at that time three or four young volunteers from Yugoslavia including "Mimi" Polgar, whose nickname was acquired because of her lovely singing voice (she had twelve brothers and sisters). Czechoslovakia was represented by Tanya, a medical student from Bratislava who, after qualifying, became a paediatrician. Both her parents were in Auschwitz-Birkenau and her father, Alfred Wetzler, was one of the very few who managed to escape successfully, as described in Chapter 6.

The Polish survivors of Auschwitz and Ravensbrück who came to assist were Pani Maria Mrozek and Pani Wlada Puzanowska. Pani Wlada was married before the War to a professional soldier who, after being taken a prisoner of war by the Russians, was murdered in Katyń. She lost one brother in Neuengamme Concentration Camp, near Hamburg, and the other, a priest, in Dachau. She survived the infamous Bloody Sunday in 1939 in Bydgoszcz and was arrested on 10 March 1940. She was transported exactly one month later in a cattle-truck to the infamous Death Camp at Ravensbrück where she became Prisoner no. 3166. Pani Wlada's story deserves a Chapter to itself and, like the others, her faith and heroic behaviour are indescribable.

This small cheerful team was augmented by two English teachers, one of them (the Housemother) Dorothy Rodick Smith and the other a former member of the French Resistance who lived in this country until she died. They all immediately began work according to a schedule which had been drawn up in advance. Many of the loos did not function, parts of the electrical wiring were in an unusable condition, and the kitchen was out of action, so that the cooking had to be done on two Calor gas rings set up in the dining room.

The team included the Foundation's tradesmen who went up onto the roof to clean all the chimneys, and two carpenters who moved systematically through the house repairing sashcords and doors. For a time it was thought that no plumber would be forthcoming, but finally he arrived – at 11.00 p.m. one night.

In the first hours of work at the house everyone was absorbed in the general activity, hence it was some time before we realised with full force that Stagenhoe lies in the flight path of Luton Airport and the package-tour season was in full swing! At times the volunteers had to shout to make themselves heard. Until the office was established on the quieter side of the house, it proved somewhat difficult to make oneself heard properly on the telephone, especially when urgent calls from the Foundation's tradesmen came in from places like Prague and Warsaw, and one had to discuss technical problems with them. Then I had to turn my attention to sorting out another crisis which cropped up when we learned that the shipping company and the docks had refused to accept five lorry-loads of building materials required for the Foundation's Homes abroad. In spite of this, however, it was for me personally a happy time, even if occasionally a little hectic – partly because of the humour and spirit in which the volunteers worked, and partly because one could see the results of one's labours. A well-wisher offered some very old rugs and carpets, but these were in a somewhat shocking state and had to be hung from trees (as grass was so long on the lawns) and beaten before being cleaned and shampooed.

At one point I composed in a few moments the following letter to an imaginary Lord Throgmorton:

Thank you very much for your most welcome donation and encouraging letter about Stagenhoe. I am glad you have heard of our progress there and I am quite overwhelmed by the offer of your house at Throgmorton. Its seems to be in a lovely position by the sea and your gift of such a valuable property is indeed generous. May I ask whether you would permit our Honorary Architect and Surveyor to look around?

You mention that the roof has bad patches and that the problem of erosion on the north elevation will necessitate a full survey.

At present our hands are rather full with different aspects of this work, including the new as well as the old Homes. Throgmorton would certainly be more than large enough. It was considerate of you to tell me the number of bedrooms, etc., and if only thirty-seven out of the fifty-four were in use during the past ten years then I can believe we will face a lot of renovation. The question of wiring and installing the plumbing system to the house must, of course, be thought over very carefully. We are always short of electricians and plumbers. The patients and staff enjoy the seaside when given the opportunity of being nearby, and I am sure we will all appreciate your kindness and generosity.

I sent a copy to John Adams, and received a scribbled note in reply on which there were just two words: "Oh no!"

Then came a letter from the non-existent Lady Throgmorton:

Dear Miss Ryder,
                You will have heard by now from my husband about our dream house at Throgmorton. Oh, how my heart aches for it and you, for it is so vast and precious. Can you use it?

Amongst many things I must mention immediately are the underground cellars which lead to the cliff's edge and have a fascinating haunted story, but I will tell you about it in greater detail when you come over. Meanwhile, I expect you will be sending your loyal architects and surveyors. I know my husband expects them, and I think if they tell him of your desperate needs that he will offer one or even two of our small Reynolds. So you must explain to your architects and surveyors that they must admire the paintings and particularly the ones of the deer and of Rosemary, Duchess of Duckford (she was fifth cousin to Dickie, whom you may remember).

Forgive me for disturbing you like this – until our next meeting.
                            Yours sincerely
                            Emy Throgmorton

John Adams checked in Debrett's peerage and found no Lady Throgmorton, and when he failed to locate the area in the AA and RAC books he rang us. He took the joke very well indeed!

One morning at breakfast, Pete (the chippy) and others, asked me why the Foundation could not form its own removal and renovation team for service to the public. We refrained from carrying out this idea.

Each day seemed to bring something unexpected. News that the Foundation had purchased Stagenhoe brought an influx of commercial travellers to the door. The size and potential elegance of the house obviously made them believe that we were a wealthy organisation. The quotations they offered for various jobs matched up to this supposed wealth: the Aga cooker could, for example, be repaired for £600, and the lift restored if £1,500 could be raised. At the announcement one day that "another man has arrived to see you", I assumed that it would once more be a commercial traveller and was somewhat taken aback to find myself greeting a man dressed in black shirt and shorts. He introduced himself as Father O'Leary, a Catholic priest from a nearby parish, and he wondered whether he and his group of Venture Scouts could be of any assistance. They proved as good as their word. Father O'Leary returned immediately with his young Scouts, nine lawnmowers and scythes, and attacked the neglected lawns surrounding the house. Subsequently Father O'Leary left the area to become a missionary in Chile.

The final problem was the furniture. Local well-wishers donated a refrigerator and a sewing machine, a policeman brought a bath he had discovered on a rubbish heap, and the Foundation's Support Group in Hatfield contributed the outsize saucepans that were needed. Personal friends offered a large quantity of furniture they had collected, especially from sales, and stored this in two barns. However, one of these had been flooded and the other proved to be the home of a number of birds, so that the state of some of the furniture left much to be desired, in addition to which the furniture movers had forgotten to bring the ends and springs of the sixty-odd beds. To save additional expense a farmer offered to fetch the missing items with one of his corn lorries; but with an unusually early harvest this was not immediately available. On the very last day, therefore, with everything else that they had to do, the volunteers were faced with the task of matching up over sixty sets of bed-ends and springs, and then finding mattresses to fit the resulting frameworks. We managed to meet the deadline, however, and had twenty-four hours to spare. Then, fifteen minutes before the bus from Weybridge drew up before the front door with the survivors, a local friend arrived with a small domestic Calor gas cooker, just sufficient, with the existing two rings, to keep the temporary kitchen going until the main one had been fully renovated and the proper stove installed.

Since the arrival of the first group at Stagenhoe, 2,527 residents and others have benefited from a stay there. Individuals who wished to come applied through social workers, physicians or their own survivors' associations. Each was interviewed, and from the resulting list of recommendations – on which there might be as many as 4,000 names – a choice had to be made. The small committees in the different cities and towns of Poland found it extremely difficult to be fair. The criteria by which they decided were not strictly defined, but broadly speaking, priority was given to those whose part in the Resistance was particularly notable or who had suffered the most, whether in concentration or extermination camps, in solitary confinement or in the ghettos; due attention also being given to their present circumstances and state of health. Priority was also given to young handicapped people, and those who had suffered in some special way.

The organisation of the Holiday Scheme was placed in the hands of voluntary social workers, many of whom were women physicians who themselves had spent years in different prisons and camps and who read medicine often as a direct result of their experiences. Mr and Mrs Jan Pankowski for years worked voluntarily in running the Foundation's Holiday Scheme. They lived at 12 Miodowa Street, Warsaw, near the Ministry of Health and the Primate's residence. Their flat was up four flights of steep stairs. Sadly, they have both now died. Mr Pankowski went through terrible experiences in Mauthausen and Güsen, and suffered from chronic asthma and cardiac failure. Mr and Mrs Pankowski were later succeeded by Pani Zofia and her daughter Hania and Hanka Mierzejewska, who worked very hard during weekends and evenings both in Poland and in Britain, travelling on public transport to visit those on pending lists.

They were succeeded by Mr Tadeusz Walkowski, who had been an active member of the Resistance, and was arrested on 23 March 1940 and taken by the Gestapo for interrogation and torture in the infamous Gestapo Headquarters in Szucha Street, Warsaw. Mr Walkowski was transferred to the equally infamous and huge Pawiak prison on the 2 May 1940 and then transported in open cattle-trucks to Sachsenhausen Concentration Camp, near Berlin. His number was 23804. On 29 June 1944 he was transported to Ravensbrück – number 9501, category *Schutzhaft* (under special surveillance). Prior to Liberation he was on the long death marches to Schwerin. He had typhus and typhoid but was repatriated to the ruins of Warsaw. He was later in charge of a computer firm, and both before and after his retirement spent all his free time working voluntarily for fourteen years as the Foundation Principal Co-ordinator in Warsaw for the domiciliary work carried out, and the choice of volunteers, throughout the country.

Mr Walkowski was ably assisted by his daughter, Teresa, and by Wojtek Slaski and his father, Kazimierz, who had been a very active member of the Home Army and took part in some of the worst fighting during the Warsaw Rising. At the age of fourteen he was captured and transported to Sachsenhausen Concentration Camp in October 1944. He too died young with cancer of the lungs and heart failure on 17 May 1996. There were many other honorary social workers, physicians and nurses who work in cities and towns throughout Poland. Mr Walkowski proved outstanding and died after great suffering in May 1994.

The groups travelled by rail, receiving a special reduction in price because their number was over twenty-five. The German Red Cross boarded the train twice and provided them with refreshments during their journey through Germany, and when the group reached Bruges, the Foundation's supporters in Belgium made themselves responsible for welcoming them and showing them around. At Zeebrugge they embarked on the car ferry for Dover, where they were met by the Foundation's bus. The Immigration and Customs Authorities were informed beforehand to avoid delays, but for many the journey itself proved extremely exhausting, and often a doctor or priest accompanied the group. By the time they reached the Home in the early hours of the morning tiredness was very apparent.

One of the survivors who came over on the Holiday Scheme was Stanisława Blustein. Stanisława was very young when her mother died. She married in 1938 and was arrested in Gdynia with her husband in February 1940. Her husband was beaten to the point of death by the Gestapo and they marched her into his cell for her to witness his condition; then they finished him off in her presence by firing some shots into his already tortured body. On 10 April 1940 she was transported in cattle-trucks to Ravensbrück and became prisoner number 3075. Stanisława was in different Kommandos, building roads and doing other heavy labouring work. During her years in Ravensbrück she suffered from typhus, scarlet fever and meningitis and, while in the Revier (so-called hospital) she received an injection which prevented her from ever having children. After two months of being under filthy blankets she was smuggled out by the Resistance to another block from where she returned to do heavy work.

Stanisława was repatriated to Poland after the Liberation and for six years she worked in a children's home where an unmarried mother gave birth to a very small baby who had no fingernails. In April 1948 she adopted this child, who for years suffered from bad health. She later remarried. Her second husband had been a prisoner of war, and he died later as a result of two strokes.

In 1961, Stanisława was diagnosed as having cancer of the throat, and after some years of great suffering she died.

Another survivor of the camps was Wiesława Skutecka. She was born on 20 August 1933 in Poznań. Her father was a veterinary surgeon who, in 1943, was arrested and subsequently murdered by the Gestapo in Fort 7, a horrendous and ghastly prison/concentration camp in Poznań. On 9 August of the same year her mother was arrested and transported in a cattle-truck to Auschwitz. On 10 August, Wieslawa was arrested, together with her three brothers, and transported to the children's camp in Łódź, where she remained until the end of the War. Her brothers were transported from Łódź to Potulica in 1944 and they were all put to slave labour. The youngest boy had been separated from them in the spring. After the end of hostilities they were cared for by their aunt until their mother returned from the concentration camp. Wiesława finished her studies in 1958 and now works as a veterinary surgeon.

Paula Karwat was a remarkable person in many ways, and her example, and that of her son, Jerzy, personify the suffering of many countless others who have come over on the Holiday Scheme.

Jerzy was born on 28 August 1923. He attended school until June 1939 and passed his examination for entry to the local secondary school. In September 1939, a few days after the outbreak of the Second World War, as a boy of sixteen years of age, he joined the 20th Infantry Regiment of the Polish Army. Part of this Regiment, after being engaged in fierce fighting with the Germans, succeeded in crossing the frontier into Rumania, but at the time Jerzy was ill and had to be left behind in hospital in Wlodzimierz Wolynski.

On 20 October 1939 he returned to Kraków. There he joined the Resistance movement ZWZ (Union for Armed Struggle) and was given the pseudonyn Kazimierz Krynski.

Jerzy took part in a planned and successful attack on the German ammunition depot at Czyzny airfield on 21 May 1941. The group to which he belonged had also helped provide the Resistance with news from the BBC and a small supply of arms. During the night of 22 May, six Gestapo men came to the house to arrest him at 1 a.m. Jerzy, who had been roused from bed, was still in his pyjamas but with his pistol he shot his way out and escaped down the staircase, wounding three Germans. He himself was wounded by them in the leg, but succeeded in escaping and visited relatives, also his girl friend, where his wound was dressed and he was given clothing. They in turn also warned members of the Resistance.

In the meantime, more Germans arrived at the house and ordered everybody out. The events that followed are best described in Paula's own words:

> They arrested and took my husband away. He was also only clothed in his pyjamas. I was arrested at 3 a.m., but managed to take my husband's clothes with me. When I next saw him in the Montelupi prison in Kraków he had already been badly beaten up.
>
> During the interrogation that followed I was confronted with a man whose pseudonyn was Mikolaj. The Gestapo wanted me to say that he had brought arms to Jerzy. I absolutely denied this and also that I had had any contact with him. When I saw this prisoner (Mikolaj) he had been horribly beaten.
>
> Around the middle of June I was summoned out of my cell again for interrogation and saw my son, Jerzy, standing in the interrogation room guarded by six members of the Gestapo. I felt as though an abyss was opening underneath me, especially when the Gestapo shouted that I knew about the arms and that Jerzy worked in the Resistance. I replied that this was not true.
>
> During the next day some women prisoners approached me in secret and praised Jerzy for his courage. I discovered afterwards that they had also been confronted by my son during their interrogations by the Gestapo.
>
> On the 21 July 1941 we were awakened in the prison by a great uproar and shouts coming from the guards – some prisoners had escaped – followed by three shots from the street. The others sharing my cell were trying to stand on one another's shoulders to see what was going on out of the high window. Under the gas lamp they were horrified to see the Gestapo kicking a prisoner on the ground and we felt sure he had no chance of survival, but the Gestapo then ordered him to stand up. After struggling to do so he finally succeeded. They then handcuffed him and put chains on his legs.

As they re-entered the prison and passed our cell, the prisoner was moaning and I recognised Jerzy's cries.

At 5 a.m. I was called out of my cell. There were thirteen of us in that small cell and as I left they knelt down and prayed. The Commandant of the prison confirmed my premonitions and showed me a rope made from sheets hanging from Jerzy's cell window. He bellowed at me that this time my son had no chance of success in escaping and that he would be hanged. He also threatened that both my husband and I would be shot. I was then handed buckets of cold water and entered the cell to wash my son. As I saw the shape of what once had been a human being lying on the bare prison bed I did not recognise him. His face was swollen beyond recognition. Blood was streaming from his broken skin where he had been kicked and the wound was full of dirt from the street – his eyes resembled a pool of blood and he looked like a man who had been blinded.

I tore my blouse into pieces in order to try and wash his face. I kissed his hands which had been cut to the bone by the electrified barbed wire on top of the wall of Montelupi prison. I told him gently that we had to prepare ourselves for death, and he answered "The sooner I die the sooner Poland will be great and happy".

While I was in Jerzy's cell an older Gestapo officer of higher rank entered and examined the broken bars of the window. He also looked at the inscription scribbled by Jerzy on the wall near the window "freedom is suffering". I thought that I even saw a trace of compassion in his eyes when he looked at both of us, and after he left, the German guards shouted at us as usual and continued their threats of execution.

Later, in an old ragged coat, I was marched back to my cell. My friends remarked that my appearance reminded them of Our Lady's agony at the foot of the Cross. I tried to relate to them in whispers and in the light coming through the grid in the darkened cell I could see that Jerzy was black from the fall and the beatings. For three days and nights after that I sobbed.

The next time I saw Jerzy he was lying on the bare floor of the cell tied to the wall by an iron chain. During the intervening three days there had been constant investigations by a special board of enquiry with the aim of establishing the blame on those in authority for the broken window bars. The Prison Commandant blamed the Gestapo Chief, who in turn accused the Commandant of negligence, but whosoever's fault it was, the prisoners themselves were to be punished as the Gestapo were the masters of their life and death.

Jerzy realised this and managed to convince them that the bars had remained broken since before the outbreak of war. He even told them that the German guards passed regularly under the cell window.

For, short while the atmosphere relaxed slightly and we were allowed to receive food parcels from our friends in Kraków. I was also allowed to wash my son again and succeeded in changing his shirt which was sodden and stiff with blood.

A few days later I was marched back as though in a trance to my cell when the Commandant entered behind me. All the women gathered round me and we forgot to stand to attention, so he punished us by denying us food for three days and ordered my transfer to a darkened underground cell. The guard told me that it was Jerzy's cell that I was allocated to. I clasped my hands together in prayer and thanks. I felt so happy to be allowed to join him.

I counted our days by marking the walls of that cell. We were under constant supervision – even during the nights the guards turned on the light and observed us through a peephole in the door. We felt extremely exhausted and very hungry. Our friends collected whatever scraps of food they could and smuggled these to us and continued to pray.

Weeks later, before I was transported to Ravensbrück Concentration Camp, I returned to my cell again, still in the same old coat. They told me this time that my face was the colour of parchment and my hair had turned quite grey. I had been with Jerzy in that dark cell for seven long weeks and had hardly received anything to eat and only a tiny piece of soap with which to wash.

On 9 September 1941 I was included in a transport with my close friend Ursula Winska and seventy-six women and girls for Ravensbrück. As I left Jerzy I felt that it was the last time that we would be on earth together. Jerzy was, in fact, transported in a cattle-truck to Auschwitz where after his arrival he was executed.

Paula's husband was sent to Auschwitz, and Paula, born with the gift of premonition, knew that he would not survive. It was while she was in Ravensbrück too that her premonition of General Sikorski's tragic death in an aircraft crash off Gibraltar was confirmed.

The death of General Wladyslaw Sikorski, in an aircraft taking off from Gibraltar, came as a terrible shock. He was trusted by Churchill who regarded him as a great leader. It is also important to note that Peter Loxley, an expert on Central Europe and Senior Private Secretary to Tom Bromley who worked with Sir Alexander Cadogan and was Permanent Under-Secretary at the Foreign Office responsible for liaison with the Government organisations. Sadly Peter Loxley met a tragic death in an air crash whilst on the way to the decisive and crucial conference at Yalta.

Had they had lived, the future of Poland's history might possibly have taken a slightly better course.

* * *

Unfortunately, the Holiday Scheme came to an end in 1979 owing to lack of funds and because the whole roof of Stagenhoe had to be retiled and further and expensive fire regulations enforced. Previously six of seven groups consisting of thirty-four individuals came over from Poland each year for three or four weeks, the only limiting factor here being the availability of funds.

For members of the groups the visit to this country proved an unforgettable experience. They found it hard to leave, and we who have witnessed their warmth and affection have been moved too by the poignancy of the leave-taking, especially as they often used to sing. Each group was quite different, but as the group leader said a few words to express the feelings of his or her group, we felt each time the spirit of their courage, dignity and humour. Their gaiety and laughter have often filled the house, yet the experiences of each one of these survivors would not only reveal unlimited depths of human suffering but untold heights of selflessness and love. The gracious Georgian house, with its reminders of past wealth and privilege, provided an unexpected background for these people who had experienced such incredible hardship and suffering.

On their return to Poland they not only gave talks on their visit but also wrote most moving letters to say how much the experience meant to them. Perhaps one young girl may be allowed to speak for all those who have been enabled to visit Britain in this way. "My dear Mamusia," she wrote from Poland, addressing me affectionately as "Mother":

> Thank you very much indeed for the vacation, I will remember it till the end of my days, I did not know your country except from books and from what my father has told me. The English were so hospitable and honest and seemed to love us. I admired the neat little houses and gardens and the beautiful fields of barley. Your country has not been invaded for a thousand years. We listened to Benjamin Britten, we visited Kew Gardens, Hatfield House, Westminster Abbey, Westminster Cathedral and St Paul's Cathedral, the Colleges at Oxford and Cambridge, the Tate Gallery, the British Museum, the Wallace Collection and the National Gallery where for the first time I saw original works by Raphael, Leonardo de Vinci and Michelangelo. To us the twenty-five years since the Occupation have proved a great and wonderful challenge. We have raised entire cities from ruins, we have educated the present generations and now a few of us have had the chance to forget the pressures of life and therefore really to enjoy a holiday. The visit was like entering a fairy tale. I will not forget to pray for you.

It is the Foundation's hope that one day the Holiday Scheme will be re-opened. For this purpose another very large period property, preferably near water, will have to be found. It would have to be a special type of historic house and the purchase would depend on sufficient funds being available. The people to be cared for there would be the housebound and those who have never had a chance to travel or see places they have dreamed about. They would have the opportunity to relax in beautiful surroundings and the Scheme would not be confined to those who are able to pay.

* * *

When the House was opened it was intended that the other main use would be for short-stay physically handicapped residents, particularly to give their families a much-needed break from nursing them. Many such patients have been accommodated, but always the cry was for permanent places. Often there were pleas from those who had come for short breaks to be allowed to stay. Literally dozens of requests are received weekly for admission from general practitioners, consultants, hospitals, social workers and patients themselves, their next of kin or their neighbours; and over the years the Foundation has striven to provide more long-term beds.

During 1981–2 work was carried out at the Home to renovate and improve it, thereby increasing the number of beds available to forty. This work was supported by a local trust, and increased local fund-raising, including events organised throughout the county under the leadership of the late John Hobley, formerly Honorary Treasurer of the Home, who had known Stagenhoe since his youth. Nevertheless, the inevitable cost of additional fire precaution work has meant that the Foundation had to continue to raise funds locally to complete the work. Matron, Ann Duncombe (at the Home since 1974 and Matron since 1978), with the support of a dedicated team of staff, some of whom have worked with her for many years, do all they can to try and admit the most desperate patients, and the whole Foundation recognises their efforts and is grateful for their deep concern and personal service, which they give daily; also to the devoted nursing staff who love these patients.

In addition to those with muscular dystrophy, multiple sclerosis, Parkinson's disease and strokes, the Home nurses a number of patients with Huntington's Chorea, now usually described as Huntington's Disease. Professor C. D. Marsden describes this disease as follows:

> Huntington's Disease is an illness which, although relatively uncommon (about 6,000 cases in the UK), causes a disproportionate amount of suffering among patients and their families. It is a hereditary condition whose first definite symptoms usually begin after the peak productive years, by which time it is too late to avoid the one in two chance to each of the patient's children of contracting the disease. Besides its hereditary nature (which may be obscured in the case of early death of a parent, or of adoption of a child), the illness is characterised by the onset in middle life and gradual progression of jerky movements (chorea) and mental changes. These three features together conspire to make provision for long-term care patients a major problem as they are usually too young to come under the care of the geriatric services. Most homes for the young chronic sick do not take them because of the mental changes, and most of them end their days in the chronic wards of psychiatric hospitals, which are not equipped for dealing with patients with severe physical disabilities.
>
> The principal mental changes seen in the Disease have traditionally been labelled as dementia, but unlike the classical picture of severe memory loss combined with disorientation and loss of vocabulary and reasoning processes, the changes in Huntington's Disease are often milder and more subtle. Many patients are aware of their predicament but often incapable of communicating because of severe difficulty in articulation and phonation. For these reasons, the Foundation's Home and experience at Stagenhoe represent a most welcome breakthrough in the provision of care in a suitable environment by nursing staff interested and experienced in the condition . . .

Huntington's Disease has afflicted mankind for centuries, and many sufferers were burnt as witches in the Middle Ages. Although other writers have previously described the symptoms, the first complete account of the Disease which now bears his name was presented by George Huntington, a general practitioner in Long Island, USA, in 1872. The condition (albeit a disastrous affliction to the families concerned) remained a medical curiosity for many decades. It was known that patients dying with the disease had lost cells in the "thinking" grey matter of the cortex and also in deep structure known as the basal ganglia. The basal ganglia also constitutes the main region affected in another, much commoner, condition associated with disordered movement – Parkinson's Disease. This is a condition characterised by poverty of movement rather than the excessive movements of chorea. However, as long as the mechanisms underlying the disability in Parkinson's Disease remain unknown, this analogy was of no more than passing academic interest. In the 1950s and 1960s the role of chemical messengers in regulating communication between brain cells in the basal ganglia was discovered; and the finding that replacement of one of these messengers, dopamine, by L-Dopa tablets, could allow chairbound Parkinsonians to walk again and to lead independent lives gave birth to an explosion of research in many countries into all aspects of the chemistry and physiology of the brain – and in particular the basal ganglia.

The inverse relationship between some aspects of Parkinson's Disease and Huntington's Disease was further exemplified by the fact that L-Dopa, in excess, could produce choreiform movements, and that major tranquillising drugs could both improve chorea and worsen Parkinsonism.

The symptomatic treatment of Huntington's Chorea is still only moderately successful, and most of the drugs used either sedate patients or cause some degree of Parkinsonism, so that the potential of new drug treatments is being assessed all the time. The primary genetic cause of the condition, however, remains entirely unknown. Although Huntington's research will continue to benefit from "spin-offs" from work on other movement disorders, it is only with effective genetic counselling and further extensive research in affected patients that we will achieve the ultimate aim of eradicating the Disease or at least of arresting its progression.

Up until the middle of 1983, we really knew almost nothing about the Disease in terms of its cause. However, medical research has suddenly made a dramatic breakthrough. A group in the United States have managed to identify which part of the human hereditary material is affected in this condition. Research continued, and in March 1993, the Huntington's Disease gene was isolated, and tests are being developed which will be more accurate than in the past, giving hope at last to many affected families.

People with Huntington's Disease are often unknown in society and their plight is one of the worst. If only the Foundation had more resources and suitable large houses offered at a reasonable price we could do far more to alleviate the sufferings of these people.

The Foundation has the privilege of working with the Huntington's Disease Association. Together, we are endeavouring to improve the care of these patients and, in particular, to eradicate the stigma which once attached to sufferers. Families must no longer feel too embarrassed to tell relatives and friends that someone in the family has the Disease. Anti-social behavioural symptoms, which manifest themselves in the earlier stages of the Disease, led to families of the patient being shunned and isolated and this only added to the family's suffering. It is now accepted that regular counselling and care for the family is as important as treatment for the sufferer. Families and carers must not have feelings of guilt if they can no longer cope with the patient. The nature of this Disease necessitates the most intensive nursing care of almost all known diseases – each patient requires twenty-four hour one-to-one attention, and it is very rare that families can cope without help. It is care of this standard that the Foundation gives to its Huntington's patients, and will continue to give, relying upon the help of its generous supporters to meet the enormous costs involved.

The Huntington's Disease Association regards the Specialised Unit at Stagenhoe, and at the Sue Ryder Home, Marchmont, Scotland, and the expertise of its dedicated and compassionate staff as unequalled in Britain. The surroundings are ideal, with lovely parkland, which provides an atmosphere conducive to peace. For the patient's relatives and those who may be at risk of inheriting the Disease, Stagenhoe, with its understanding, supportive and friendly staff, can help to allay some of their fears and anxieties for the future – especially for those relatives who had feared that the only alternative to care at home was a psychiatric hospital.

Under an arrangement between the Huntington's Disease Association and the staff at Stagenhoe, staff from other Huntington's Disease Units in the country are receiving specialist training in the care of these patients. So, Stagenhoe Park, as well as providing nursing care, is also an educational centre, running various courses and lectures under the direction of a full time Clinical teacher, Mrs Jean Hayzen.

A new wing, built on the east elevation of the original house to accommodate fifteen more patients suffering from Huntington's Disease, was completed in 1987. On Sunday, 17 July 1988, Her Majesty Queen Elizabeth the Queen Mother honoured us with her presence when she opened this new wing. It was a beautiful day and, as always, Her Majesty spent longer with us than was expected. Her enchanting smile gave great encouragement to everyone, and she went to each patient and talked to members of the staff and volunteers. It was a day never to be forgotten.

Since the advent of the Community Care Act in 1993, it has been the intention that people should be cared for in their own homes as far as possible; but experience has shown that for some families at risk from Huntington's Disease, this is not always possible. Caring for a relation with this Disease when you are at risk yourself must be a very difficult and daunting task – especially when that person may have had mental and physical disabilities and often behavioural problems. The situation at home, therefore, in some circumstances, becomes impossible before the sufferer is really handicapped enough for permanent nursing care.

The pressure on beds at here, and at other Sue Ryder Homes at Ely and Marchmont, especially for patients with Huntington's Disease, is most serious.

Ideally, if only funds were available, the Foundation would like to establish a few suitable listed buildings to be converted for these brave people.

In 1992, funds donated by local organisations enabled five single rooms on the second floor of the original building to be refurbished for respite care, for which there is an ever-growing need, and an appeal continued for another extension, so great was the demand.

A new extension is opening in 1996 which is primarily a "halfway house" between living at home and being admitted for permanent nursing care. The ensuite rooms will allow for the maximum independence and privacy as is possible. A full programme of outings and activities will enable as normal a life as possible within the constraints of the disabilities of the residents.

* * *

The Sue Ryder Home at Stagenhoe is well used to all kinds of activities: for a time it had a new role as a conference centre. Since 1972 the various conferences held there have included one for sixth formers from local schools, one for the Duke of Edinburgh's Gold Award Scheme, and a meeting of Anglican bishops. But the famous old house can never have known an occasion quite like the first Ryder–Cheshire International Family Day on Wednesday, 16 April 1975. The permanent and short-stay British patients living in the historic Georgian mansion welcomed the colourful excitement of the arrival, over several days, of visitors from many countries. These guests had come not as members of the Holiday Scheme but as representatives of Sue Ryder and Leonard Cheshire Homes in all five Continents, drawn together by a very special event. It was more than a Family Day: it was rather a Family Fortnight, with a very full programme of engagements.

It all started in the summer of 1973 when my husband and I were invited to an informal lunch meeting with four or five members of the Variety Club of Great Britain. To our astonishment, they said they intended to confer their Humanitarian Award on us – the first time this had been bestowed upon a couple. We were most hesitant and reluctant to accept, but after much consideration and advice, we decided that the Award could only be accepted if those for whom we worked were the recipients. Moreover, we asked that individuals representing both Foundations should be with us for the presentation. This event took a great deal of time and organisation by both the Foundations and members of the Variety Club, and a small informal committee attended numerous meetings.

The handicapped representatives from overseas were all met at the various points of arrival and escorted to where they would be staying.

Those coming from other Homes of this Foundation in Britain all travelled great distances to be present, and shared the same accommodation with those from overseas at the Sue Ryder Home, Stagenhoe.

The opportunity of coming to Britain was so rare for the representatives from overseas that the Trustees of my husband's Foundation, and the Councillors of the Foundation that bears my name, felt that this unique occasion of meeting and mixing with one another should be of paramount importance.

We had been planning, preparing and organising for weeks beforehand, and each day brought great activity in renovating, spring cleaning and preparing the bedrooms, each of which had to have the maximum number of beds put in it. We tried hard, however, to make the rooms look welcoming with flowers and Medici prints which had been framed and hung on the walls. As the time drew near, very bad weather – with a deep cover of snow on the ground – made us apprehensive, especially as regards the visitors from overseas who would feel the cold of the English climate.

As on other occasions, nothing could have been achieved without the survivors from Poland, in particular, who, with their eagle eyes, swooped upon any dust and took down the curtains to clean them. They also swooped upon the linen loose covers and within hours these had been washed, ironed, and put back on again. An action list had been drawn up, and as each room was finished so it was ticked off and we moved onto the next. "Tosh" (Rose McIntosh, a wonderful volunteer) made up a list of guests who would occupy the rooms, but as the different nationalities arrived in groups and started to settle down, they often decided to change round. When everyone had arrived there were over 120 people staying with us. I had the advantage of sleeping on the ground floor in the passageway behind the oratory and sank thankfully into bed each night before rising early next morning.

The North Herts District Council at Letchworth provided great quantities of brilliant pot plants for the huge marquee. Jean Mumford, the Housemother at Stagengoe, and the Hitchin Flower Club, were responsible for the flower decorations on each table, and Iain (from Headquarters) did the many flower arrangements in the Home itself.

In the misty dawn of the great day, two of my Assistants who had slept in the outside flat were seen in their dressing gowns making their way over to the house to wash, shave and dress before the long day's work. Meanwhile, hairdressing had started at 4.30 a.m. by the girls from Konstancin who wanted to look their best.

Portable loos had to be cleaned out, and hardly had the tables in the huge marquee been set by 10.30 a.m. when, to our surprise, the first guests arrived. It had not occurred to us that they would turn up before noon, which was the time stated on the invitation card, nor indeed that over 100 extra people would arrive unexpectedly!

Our Chairman, Mr Sporborg, flew from Sweden the same morning and travelled on from London in a helicopter (belonging to his bank), to land on the main lawn.

Mrs Jackie Evans (who had served with Special Operations Executive during the War), and twenty-six volunteers, collected, prepared, cooked and served the lunch and tea on tables which were attractively covered with white cloths, red napkins and blue and white fluted china.

Jackie had come over weeks beforehand to talk about the menu; she always remained calm and optimistic about approaching people to provide ingredients, thus cutting the catering costs to a minimum. The day before Family Day, when the food was carried into the kitchen at Stagenhoe in huge saucepans and containers, I asked her if she was concerned about the quantity. "No," she replied, "I really believe we have enough." Later her words reminded me of the story of the feeding of the five thousand.

Canon De Haene from the Belgian Foundation said Grace in two languages: "We thank God for the food we are about to receive and remember those who have none."

Simplicity and informality were the keynote and, by the dint of Herculean efforts, costs were kept to a minimum while standards remained high. The scene in the kitchen was amazing. The mixing of the different nationalities in a completely relaxed atmosphere made it an unforgettable day. The sun was so warm that several of the guests sat outside the marquee and enjoyed the beautiful setting.

The planned entertainment underwent a sea change before it reached its audience. One of the bands of the Foot Guards had offered to play, but was unfortunately prevented from doing so; another band played instead but was over an hour late in arriving, despite the fact that they had been sent both a route and an Ordnance Survey map.

By the time the afternoon had arrived the mammoth task of clearing tables and the huge piles of washing up faced the volunteers. At that time an urgent telephone call was received by me in the office from a girl threatening to take her life. Tosh and Robert Clifton went off to try and locate her. After many anxious moments they mercifully found that she had already been admitted to hospital and, in fact, had made the call from one of the hospital's kiosks.

While they were away I remained close to the telephone and could hear the gay sound of singing coming from the marquee. The professional entertainers had not arrived and, in an impromptu way, after lunch our handicapped guests entertained everybody with songs from their own countries.

Looking out from the window, I was astonished to see a troupe of Bunny Girls, complete with rabbit tails, running out of the house along the terrace and into the marquee to sing and dance on the stage there. In the bright sunshine this was indeed an unexpected change of plan and readers may guess the reactions of many guests. Hilda Herbert, who ran the gift section in the Christmas Card Room at Headquarters, was heard to remark: "Not at 4.30 in the afternoon!" and Sister Mary Ryan in her best Irish brogue exclaimed, "They showed too much naked flesh!" This was a totally unexpected shock, especially as the late Dame Anna Neagle had offered to relieve me of the responsibility of finding a suitable group of singers. Unfortunately, this group was called away to a repertory theatre and Dame Anna believed she had found a similar group to replace them.

The Family Day at Stagenhoe also served as an eye-opener to many whose knowledge of the Foundation derived only from the local Sue Ryder Home or Shop in their particular area, or from what they had read in *Remembrance*, the Foundation's annual magazine. They mixed with patients and staff from practically every Home in Britain and overseas – amputees, Huntington's Disease cases, child patients and adults suffering from disabilities of all kinds, and they met the medical staff and supporters who cared for them. Language seemed to prove no barrier and everyone left with a far deeper insight into the nature and extent of the two Foundations' work.

Friday, 18 April, the day on which the Variety Club Award was to be made, proved extremely long for about 200 people from both Foundations.

The corridors of the Royal Festival Hall seemed claustrophobic, especially for those who sat patiently for hours in their wheelchairs during the rehearsal. The huge hall was filled by supporters and friends, while my husband and I waited in the wings.

Entertainment was laid on before the presentation, and members of the cast ran off the stage and down the ramps in their sweaty sleeveless vests into the throng waiting to be pushed up onto the stage.

A little earlier in the evening Leonard and I had been allocated a dressing room some distance from the scene, where we had a short time in which to change into our evening wear. Each time we attempted to gather our thoughts together as to what we were to say, a loud knock sounded on the door to interrupt our conversation. The messenger came with cards, telegrams or hand-written notes; flowers were also handed in. Time ran out before we had decided on the theme of what we were going to say and we were completely separated on each side of the wide stage.

Richard Attenborough and Anna Neagle gave dignified narrations. HRH Princess Margaret had graciously agreed to present the Award. She spoke to members of Leonard's Foundation and then walked over to be introduced to those who represented this Foundation.

As darkness fell and the presentation ended the rain started to pour down and it was very windy. All this added to the complications for those trying to move their wheelchairs and for the other handicapped people who, naturally, wanted to remain independent. Leonard and I joined the gathering for dinner, which was followed by further presentations and many speeches, while the representatives from this Foundation were invited to the famous and historic Guildhall, in the City, which had suffered in the Blitz. By that time they were extremely hungry and were delighted to see the simple refreshments prepared for them. A distinguished guide had been provided to give a vivid history of Guildhall. He was unaware that after such a long day they were very tired, and the translation of what he said into different languages soon began to prove an endurance test. Mother Hilary of the Brigidine Order and John Stevenson, a member of the Worshipful Company of Gardeners (who had so kindly arranged the occasion), tactfully stopped the narrative.

The first of the survivors arrived back at Stagenhoe in the early hours of the morning, to be told on arrival that the other girls and staff from Konstancin had stopped at the London Hospital at Whitechapel because one of the accompanying physicians had suffered a heart attack and was gravely ill. Happily this proved to be an exaggeration.

Amongst my many memories of the Family Fortnight is the excited chatter in bedrooms at night. On one of the last evenings a candlelit supper for 125 was followed by a sing-song by the Girl Guides from Waltham Cross. The next evening young and lovely dancers from Luton, in beautiful handmade costumes of the regions in Poland, danced and sang with us until the early hours, filling the whole Home with laughter and joy.

For the first time our guests recognised that disabilities extend beyond frontiers and that they seemed to have much in common with each other; even the problems of language barriers were overcome. As one survivor told me, "To see the black, brown and white faces mingling and joining in is a joy I could never have foreseen or contemplated."

Stagenhoe has had a long and colourful history since it first emerged in the written records of the tenth century. A return made in the Domesday Book in 1086 stated that it possessed "woodland to feed twenty swine" worth some fifty shillings in all. Nearly 900 years and many owners later, Stagenhoe was the centre of what may well have been the greatest gathering in its long history – the occasion when 500 people of many nations, many colours and many faiths were united as one great family on its sweeping lawns. What a pity the composer Sir Arthur Sullivan is no longer alive. Who knows what inspiration he might have drawn from such an extraordinary human gathering.

* * *

STAGENHOE – AND FAMILY GATHERINGS

Nine years after the Family Fortnight at Stagenhoe, an even more remarkable gathering took place, this time in Rome. In the 1983 issue of *Remembrance*, the following extract from a circular letter written by Sir Peter Ramsbotham, Chairman of the Ryder-Cheshire Mission, appeared:

> Over the past decade the Sue Ryder Foundation and the Leonard Cheshire Foundation have expanded and spread their interests and activities, especially overseas. Their international character had become increasingly significant. To reflect this development we are planning to hold the next

Family Week in 1984 outside the United Kingdom. It is proposed that we should meet in Rome for the eight days from 31 March to 7 April.

To put this proposal into effect, a Family Week Committee was set up in London with representatives of both Foundations, and the complex business of planning the week soon began. In the Former Yugoslavia, for instance, to enable participants to attend, I had to seek permission first in five or six different Republics and then at Federal level. Everywhere I received excellent co-operation. His Excellency the British Ambassador, Sir Kenneth Scott, together with members of his staff, Mr Anthony Figgis and Mr Trevor Moore (who was responsible for liaising with the Former Yugoslav Authorities, and the Foundation's representative Mrs Olga Glogvac) proved most helpful in every respect. Information on the ferry and international train services from Yugoslavia to Rome had to be sought (several of the latter began in Greece). A nun in Macedonia kindly started by offering to study the complicated railway timetables, but so many travel problems presented themselves, especially from patients, nuns and others in remote areas, that it was necessary to form a special committee to undertake the organising.

In the event, a total of 663 people from twenty-five countries, of many denominations and creeds, gathered in Rome at the end of March. Volunteers of various nationalities and denominations, including seminarians, came forward daily to help with the difficult job of loading and off-loading wheelchairs and taking small groups and individuals out to special places they wanted to visit. Their enthusiasm was infectious and their assistance invaluable. Sir Mark Heath, British Ambassador to the Holy See, and Lady Heath kindly offered hospitalty and so, too, did Lady Bridges (wife of the British Ambassador to Italy), in their lovely houses and gardens. Ralph Griffiths, a member of Sir Mark's staff, and Father Quesuel of the Holy Ghost Fathers liaised with the Pope's Private Secretary Monsignor S. Dziwisz, Monsignor D. Monduzzi, Father R. Spiazzi, OP, and others at the Vatican.

The days that followed were not without their share of difficulty and distress, especially at the beginning, when unforeseen problems arose with the carefully booked hotel accommodation. In addition, my husband became ill and had a temperature of 104 degrees, but although still unwell he was able to be present at the Special Audience.

The following accounts accurately describe what many felt. A Polish social worker wrote:

> After months of preparation, we all congregated on Platform 3 at the Central Station, Warsaw, at 10 p.m. on 29 March. Mr Tadeusz Walkowski, the Foundation's Honorary Senior Social Worker and Co-ordinator had, in addition to all his other tasks, been working towards this night ever since July 1983 when a special meeting of the Foundation's Honorary Social Workers and physicians from all parts of Poland was called.
>
> There were eight carriages on the train and the health of everyone

making the journey had been taken into consideration in allocating the top, middle and lower couchettes.

To our joy, when the train stopped at Tarvisio on the Italian frontier, an announcement was made "Transport Polonia". The Italian authorities did not consider it necessary to board the train, and we listened as another announcement was made over their tannoy system that it was a special train from Poland en route to Rome via Venice. For the majority, this was the first time they had travelled abroad, and we were all amazed when the Italians did not stamp our passports either on entering their country or leaving it.

So, we waved to them and continued on our way!

None of this would have been possible without the fullest co-operation from the Minster of Transport and Director of Railways in Poland and their colleagues with whom I had had earlier meetings. By doing this, I had an insight into the elaborate arrangements that had to be made to enable the special train to be laid on, including permission for it to travel through different countries to Rome. Thanks are due, too, to His Excellency the British Ambassador, Mr J.A.L. Morgan; His Excellency the Italian Ambassador to Poland, Mr Guglielmo Folchi, and his staff in the Visa Section; to colleagues in the Ministry of Health in Warsaw and to passport officials, and a special tribute must be paid to the Italian traffic police who were wonderful. On all excursions they assigned outriders and a police car to our convoys of coaches which enabled us to proceed through red lights and so avoid holdups – a real feat in the Rome traffic!

Pam Payne of the Sue Ryder Home, St John's, Moggerhanger, Bedfordshire, gave this account:

Never in my wildest dreams did I ever imagine that one day I would be personally blessed by His Holiness the Pope. This all came to be when I was invited to take part as a helper in the Ryder-Cheshire Family Week in Rome. It was indeed to be the holiday of a lifetime. A total of 663 people from twenty-five countries arrived in Rome, some by plane, as we did, and others by train, as the 321 people from Poland with their medical doctors, nurses and nuns who run the Sue Ryder Homes and other aspects of the Foundation's work there. Four of us came from Bedfordshire – Elsie Brown and myself, Sally McMorrow and her nurse, Sharon, from St John's, Moggerhanger.

Initial difficulties with accommodation (we were moved from an hotel in Rome to one in Ostia, 17 miles west) soon faded into the past as our international gathering got to know Rome and each other. We needed a fleet of fourteen coaches and several ambulances with a very efficient and friendly Italian police escort. The weather was mixed, the food not perfect, but who cared when we had so much love and fellowship around us.

Trips were arranged to Monte Cassino, the Catacombs at San Calisto, Assisi and Tivoli, but the most wonderful day of all was the private audience with Pope John Paul II at the Vatican. We shared it with a French Family Organisation complete with band and choir, but we all had special places at the front. How we cheered when Pope came in and the Polish

people sang Polish songs to him. Lady Ryder and Group-Captain Cheshire
sat on the stage with the Pope who gave us a talk in French, English
and Polish. He talked about suffering and the importance of faithfulness
in marriage. As an extra delight, Sue Ryder and Leonard Cheshire were
celebrating their Silver Wedding Anniversary on that same day.

The Pope then came to bless the handicapped people who were at
the very front in their wheelchairs after which, to our amazement, he
came round to all of us and we were personally blessed by him. (We
have photographs to prove it, taken unbeknown to us by official Vatican
photographers!) A truly wonderful experience captured forever.

Afterwards we wandered out in a dream into St Peter's and took part in
a Nuptial Mass to renew the wedding vows of Sue Ryder and Leonard
Cheshire. It was a remarkable service in Latin, Polish and English with
eleven priests concelebrating.

Entertainment had been arranged at our hotel each evening: either a film
show, dancing and singing by different countries, a choir from the Foreign
Agricultural Organisation singing extracts from Messiah (their leader came
from Bedford), a trio playing Brahms, informal Irish singing, finishing with
a Gala Party where Sue Ryder and her husband were presented with many
handmade gifts, as well as several cheques, for their international work,
and we had a piece of Silver Wedding cake, wine, and were given a special
souvenir mat.

As one young Polish girl said to me: "We shall never be the same again.
We have broken the barriers of nationality and creed and have been made
to value our freedom as able bodies and formed lasting friendships all over
the world. The love and compassion that flowed from Pope John Paul II to
us will continue to reach out to others."

The whole week's atmosphere can be summed up by a remark made by
an Irish priest who helped us aboard the aircraft at Rome. He said: "Isn't
the Holy Spirit lovely!"

A report from Major-General Ranbir Bakhshi, MC, Director of Raphael,
the Ryder-Cheshire Centre at Dehra Dun, had this to say:

Prior to the party's departure, it seemed as if every conceivable obstacle
had been put in the way deliberately. There were endless problems with
passports, visas, medical clearances and getting Tulsa Devi Rana's leave
of absence. Then, when all seemed overcome, there was high tension in
the last twenty-four hours when we were told that the time and place of
departure had been changed. Instead of leaving from Bombay we were to
leave from New Delhi, and it was possible that no flight reservations had
been made; furthermore, the airline objected to carrying an "epileptic"
patient! This latter dramatic twist had come about when Bijli Prasad was
inadvertently ticked off as epileptic in a "Yes or No" questionnaire!

Flying was an experience as unimaginable as going to the moon for this
group, so there was a mixture of excitement and apprehension about the
prospect of actually being in what is occasionally seen in India as a speck
in the sky – few aircraft fly over Dehra Dun. However, they all behaved like
seasoned travellers and nothing untoward happened on either journey to

Rome and back. In spite of briefings on what the interior of a plane looked like and explanations of what the knobs and levers in the plane's tiny lavatory would operate, they were fascinated by all the new gadgets and accessories they saw. They were intrigued by the way meals were served in compartment trays with food sealed in plastic cartons. (I understand some items were saved on the return journey as souvenirs to show their friends at Raphael.)The inflight movie was thoroughly enjoyed as were the earphones with channelled music playing favourite songs from Indian movies.

On arrival in Rome, our people were aghast to see such a large airport and so many big, clean-looking halls; the opening and shutting of glass doors without anyone doing so and the moving staircases.

The scheduled programme began on Sunday morning, 1 April, with a visit to St Peter's Basilica to receive the Papal Blessing. The contingent was awed by the size and magnificence of St Peter's and there and elsewhere at other places of worship they were touched by the sincerity of the devout. It was a familiar link with pilgrims at home visiting the holy sites such as Hardwar and Rishikesh near Dehra Dun. They had learned about Christianity's difficult beginnings, but seeing the Catacombs and actually walking through the tunnels where the walls contained the graves of Christians who had worshipped secretly made all they had heard seem very real. It was a pleasure and a surprise to them to learn that their English-speaking guide was a padre who had served in India not far from Dehra Dun!

There were two major excursions to the monasteries founded by St Benedict at Monte Cassino and by St Francis at Assisi. The beautiful Italian landscape was greatly admired as they drove along in their coach. Ample time was given to everyone to roam around at the stops and packed lunches were provided – even drinking water was packed in cartons. Among the crowds of tourists the girls drew some attention as they looked lovely in their colourful saris. Often Italian youngsters gathered round to have their pictures taken with them and there was always as great deal of giggling and good will from these encounters, making them wish they could speak Italian.

At Monte Cassino we stopped at the British, Allied and Commonwealth War Memorial Cemeteries where, listed on engraved marble columns, are the names of those who fell in the famous battle of Cassino, which included those who fought in the Indian Army.

Before leaving Raphael the girls had been given extra tuition in English conversation and Western-style table manners, and all were to be congratulated on the way they adapted to their surroundings and food. The men found it harder to adapt to European food than the girls and, of course, beef was taboo and they were given cheese instead, if it was on the menu. Italian ice cream got top-rating and desserts were looked forward to at each meal. Bijli was sufficiently taken with Rome to express his willingness to settle down there!

One of the outings took us to the seashore as our hotel was in the suburb of the seaside resort of Ostia. Our people had never seen the ocean and were astonished by its vastness! It was a windy day and watching the waves crashing against rocks and sending spray all over them as they stood on the pier was a thrilling experience. On another trip we saw the Forum and other important areas of Rome. They had been given a short resumé in Hindi of Italy's history and visiting some of the places mentioned made it more real to them – especially seeing the Colosseum.

A memory which is being framed for Bijli and the others is the picture of each one of them receiving the Pope's personal blessing.

The day after the audience was the last day and it ended with all of us assembling after supper in the hotel's basement for the Family Party. The Founders spoke to us and made a special point of inviting the girls and the two men to stand between them so that they could explain their background to everyone. Afterwards the couple received congratulations and presents from the group who had gathered together to felicitate them on their Silver Wedding Anniversary. The evening broke up late, but everyone was in very high spirits.

On Saturday, 7 April, homeward journeys began. Everyone had worked tirelessly and with such good humour, handling difficult situations with great skill and tact. None of us could fail to praise, nor could one not be impressed by the immense amount of thought and care which had gone into carrying out such a monumental enterprise and making it such a heart-warming and unforgettable experience.

Elizabeth Zawacka Watson, whose experiences are described in Chapter 4, came to Rome with twenty-two other surviving Polish couriers – twenty-two women and one man. She wrote:

> You cannot imagine how thankful we felt at having the opportunity of going to Italy and all the memories . . . The friendships we made; the privilege of meeting our Holy Father; the sights of the Eternal City and the many outings; the beauty of the Alps during our journey to Rome and the whole atmosphere of coming together – it was truly a great and happy occasion and an unforgettable week. On behalf of us all, please accept our heartfelt gratitude.
>
> Elizabeth

It was difficult to choose from the very large number of letters and cards received from different countries after our return home, but think the following epitomises the happiness felt:

> It really is time to write you a letter and tell you a hundred times thanks for the unforgettable days we spent together during the Family Week in Rome. I'd like to tell you that the Yugoslav group needed fifteen days to pass to let them all go back to work and to get in contact again. The girls and boys from Bansko 'phoned me first and told me that they were not able to do anything for ten days, they only talked about Rome. I also felt the same.
>
> Thank you, thank you and thank you! We all love you so much. We also are happy meeting your husband. I am sending you a photo of Mr Gordon Burrows, who helped our group so much and danced with us every night.
>
> It would be nice to meet Anthony and Gordon in Yugoslavia, as well as others.

Only some details to let you know how we felt on the Family Week. The boys from Travnik said: "Now we have to go home when we have many friends – it is too short a time." Mustafa from Bansko fell in love with a young girl from Cape Town. I myself danced and sang for the first time in seven years since I lost my husband and mother. Returning home in the train everybody said: "The best thing in Rome was that we were all the same. There was nobody with airs and graces or any hierarchy, we were really a great family."

It would be nice to be together again. My dearest Sue, I could write this letter miles long!

Olga

Lastly, a Hungarian priest, Father Polgar S.J., had this to say:

It was wonderful to receive the Holy Father's blessing, to celebrate the Mass in St Peter's and at the same time to accept in the Church's name the renewal of your marriage vows. As for the experience in the first hotel, it was just a little thorn which emphasised the beauty and the fragrance of the roses of God's graces which we received so abundantly in the Eternal City.

So many things will remain in our memories, especially the sight of the wheelchairs "dancing" to the indefatigable young people's band from Bansko in Macedonia (many of whose members suffer from muscular dystrophy). They played and sang for us every evening and usually included the very old and poignant Serbian folk song "Quiet Night". As the international gathering drew to its close, many of us danced amd sang until the early hours of the evening.

Farewells are always hard to bear and during the last evening a young handicapped girl from Portugal was found in a quiet corner of the room where she had found solitude to weep. Next day at the station, the Poles sang while loading was in progress and as the train pulled out they could still be heard singing and were waving to us from the windows until they disappeared out of sight. The British Ambassador, Lord Bridges, had come with me to wish them farewell, and he, too, seemed near to tears as they left us . . .

18

Belgium

"More is in you."

LACE MAKERS, BARGES, MOTOR boats gliding up canals, water lapping: carriages and horses, the patter of feet on cobbled streets, arched bridges, shady trees, "bicycles chained and leaning", narrow streets, shop windows tastefully dressed, groups of school children, the smell of fish, coffee and freshly baked bread; the narrow street at Christmas lit by pretty white candle bulbs; bells ringing for Mass and the tall tapered votive candles ablaze at the shrines in different churches; silhouettes of floodlit towers against the evening sky; banners draped from windows for the procession on the Feast of the Holy Blood; the historic and beautiful Burg (cradle of the City) and the market: these are my impressions of the historic City of Bruges.

This fifteenth-century City, rich in architecture, its ancient squares enwrapped so delicately in stone, is especially famous for its artists. They include the Flemish and Dutch masters, Hans Memling, Gerard David, Hugo van Goes, Jan van Eyck, Jan Britto and Jan Prevost.

When I pray before the icon of Our Lady of Perpetual Succour in the Holy Saviour's Cathedral I am given the strength I need for the long drives ahead of me to those other countries in Europe; and when I kneel before that same icon many weeks later on the return journey I feel that my pilgrimage is at an end – until the next time.

For many years groups from Poland on the Foundation's Holiday Scheme who travelled to and from their country, broke their journey at Bruges where they were always warmly welcomed.

In 1970, Douglas, an Assistant of mine, went over to Bruges to consolidate and expand the work there. Canon Piet De Haene, a champion of the Samaritans, a prominent marriage counsellor and sponsor of charities, gave him much sound advice and suggested that Douglas call on Lolly Heylen. Lolly had fled from the advancing German armies and reached the United States in 1940. She is fluent in English, French and Flemish and was therefore considered to be an ideal liaison person for the Foundation. The Heylens had five children and both Lolly and her husband, Paul, worked in their family business in Belgium before returning to the United States in 1985. Paul is a Rotarian and Lolly is a member of the Soroptimist Association.

When she first went to see the Sisters at the famous "princely Beguinage" – a mediaeval community of buildings – to consult them about the Holiday Scheme groups they had previously cared for on their way to the Foundation in Britain, Lolly was told by one of the nuns, "It is warm food that our friends from Poland need, especially after their thirty-six-hour train journey." A small family hotel on the sea front in Zeebrugge was contacted and they provided a two-course meal at cost price for the travellers, the funds being raised by the Belgians. The sheer hard work of organising and receiving eight groups (later five) in a year called for special patience and a lot of time. Spontaneous offers of help came from religious orders, and a small Support Group was formed in 1971 consisting of three ladies from Zeebrugge and three from Bruges. They undertook the hospitality of the groups and soon found more friends to help. They also organised the first gala.

Mrs Ketty Depoorter became Chairman of the Foundation's Support Group in Zeebrugge/Bruges.

The survivors from Poland were always delighted by the good humour and kindness of the Belgians which prevailed all through the years. The station-master in Bruges even delayed the international train or added extra carriages whenever necessity arose. When the groups of Poles arrived in this charming City they were usually very tired after such a long train journey but were soon revived. Many individuals gave presents and sent notes of thanks to the Belgians in token of their appreciation. Those who had never had the opportunity of a holiday or of travelling outside Poland were unanimous in voicing their joy at this wonderful experience, "so rich in memories".

The Belgians have a long history and tradition of voluntary service and from the beginning they were quick to understand the spirit of the Foundation's Charter and its conception of the International Family. They were keen, too, to establish one or more Sue Ryder Homes and Shops.

In 1971–2 the Foundation was registered as a charity in Belgium and this was the culmination of the dedicated service which had been given previously. For all the work which has been done since then my special thanks go to a very enthusiastic team of people dedicated to their fellow men.

In 1974 Professor Hendrik Brugmans became the Chairman of the National Council, formed in 1972. He was Director of the European College in Bruges. Later, he was succeeded by Fernand Nedée, President of the Banque de Paris et des Payes-Bas. Both were a tremendous driving force and full of enthusiasm. Sadly, Mr Nedée died of cancer on 3 August 1980 at the early age of fifty. By profession he was a university lecturer, and the qualities of humanity and honour – and a strong dislike of cant – which characterised him as a man also brought him great distinction as a teacher. Later, he became a leading figure in the financial circles of the country and he served as an adviser to two eminent Belgian Ministers. He was, perhaps above all, a patriot in the best sense of the term, and his love and concern for the future of his country was apparent to all who knew him.

Professor Alex Florquin succeeded him as Chairman. He was a most amiable and capable man, who was also a committee member of the of several Christian Foundations. He died in August 1991.

Another staunch supporter, to whom the Foundation owes a great deal, was the late Jacques Fieuws, a man of many talents who had an exceptionally full and useful life. He also died of cancer on 10 November 1979 at the age of forty-eight.

The present Chairman is Mr Franz Thère. He also continues to serve as Honorary Financial Adviser and Treasurer of the Foundation's Belgian Council.

Premises for a Sue Ryder Shop at 68 Katelijnestraat, Bruges, were acquired in 1976 and was opened in April 1977. The organisers have a rota of forty volunteers and they are constantly flooded with gifts, mainly high-quality clothing (some new from clothing firms) and a small amount of bric-a-brac. Another supporter paints the Foundation's rosemary motif on small pottery stands. A second Shop is run at 179 Lange Straat, Bruges.

Fund-raising also includes galas, concerts and barbecues. Some couples about to marry ask that donations be made to the Foundation instead of sending presents and telegrams, and this also happens on the occasion of people's Silver and Golden Jubilees. During the whole year, collections of all kinds of gifts are made and taken to the warehouse by the Sue Ryder Foundation transport team. These are all for the main event of the year which is the Flea Market. Collections of an unimaginable variety of items go on throughout the preceding twelve months and for four days, the volunteers sort and price their wares in a large enclosed area called the Beaurshalle. From 7.00 p.m. on the Friday evening until 9.00–10.00 p.m. on the Sunday, simply hundreds of people stream through the Market which consists of twenty-four stalls.

There is also a stall set up by the halfway house "Rosmarijn" with handmade *haggie*. The patients themselves make candles and dried flowers, cakes, jewellery, aprons, drawings, and other handmade items to sell.

In addition a restaurant is set up, which is manned by supporters, and a flourishing trade goes on until the doors close on the Sunday evening. On average, over £16,000 is taken in two days.

Several days after the Flea Market has been held the volunteers meet for a supper. This gives them an opportunity to discuss the event in detail and suggest improvements which can be made for the next year.

*　*　*

Before establishing the Sue Ryder Home in Bruges the needs were thoroughly investigated, and it was decided that the Foundation should work with those members of society who were often misunderstood and unloved.

After the usual searches, a suitable property was found at 16 Predikherenstraat in January 1979. As with shop premises, the volunteers coped with the renovation and decoration themselves. All the furniture, curtains and linen, besides much else, were donated. The accommodation provides individual rooms for ten people, young men and women, discharged from psychiatric hospitals who are in need of a half-way house. There are also five flatlets, which provide accommodation for twenty-one people who have progressed to this type of accommodation. Four more flatlets are planned.

The essential purpose of the Home is to assist as many of the guests as possible to return to a normal life within the community. As with other Sue Ryder Homes in Belgium, the building was chosen because it is on a main street alongside the houses of the community. The principle of guests sharing responsibility for running of the Home, which includes cooking the supper, is observed here. At first it was hoped that the guests would find jobs but, as elsewhere, Belgium too has its unemployment and economic problems, so some of the guests go to workshops or to the hospital for therapy work daily, while two assist in Sue Ryder Shops. Several have moved on and have become independent, but a few ended their lives tragically elsewhere. They are free to come and go as they please.

The most competent medical advice is always available. Four consultant psychiatrists are responsible for the guests. Each guest is encouraged to remain in contact with his own psychiatrist and sees him outside the Home. The psychiatrists help check admissions and follow up what happens afterwards at the monthly meeting. The three Housemothers and two Housefathers, work on a shift basis, taking it in turns to come and work there and sleep overnight. This unusual arrangement has proved very successful in practice.

The Federal Ministry of Social Welfare in Brussels must approve the property and considers capital grants, but these take a long time to acquire, far longer than those for the running costs which are index-linked and therefore increase each year, which is a tremendous help. The gap between what the Foundation receives by way of guests' maintenance from the Ministry, and the actual cost, has to be covered by funds raised by supporters. In Belgium supplementary benefits, unemployment payments and other grants are similar to those made in Britain.

Guests are referred to the Home by hospitals, social centres and consultants. On average six to eight applications are received each month and an ever-increasing number of people with various problems is expected.

Meanwhile, in Antwerp, another group is working with people facing a crisis of one kind or another in their lives (including nervous break-downs). The intention is to try and prevent their being admitted to hospital. A house at 93/95 Kerkstraat, belonging to the parish, became a Sue Ryder Home.

The unit is a half-way house for six adults: a place where people can find a home and can make friends. To provide sheltered accommodation, there are also three houses divided into nine flats. Every Tuesday-noon they have a meal and every Tuesday evening they have a "rush-into" for the residents, old residents and friends. Together with the volunteers, they also organise walking tours and other diversions. *Duinkrantje* is the name of two-monthly periodical for the friends of the Homes. Every third Sunday of the month there is a Mass in the silent room attended by residents, friends and neighbours. No grant from the Ministry is received and the work is supported by voluntary contributions.

In Bruges, four Houses have been leased by the Sue Ryder Foundation as *Beschut Wonen* (sheltered living). These are sub-divided into seventeen flats, in which accommodation is offered to people who are discharged from the psychiatry division. Experience had taught us that most of these men and women will not adapt successfully without the kind of help we offer. Many of them, also, would be unable to afford the prohibitive cost of renting an apartment on their own. Two of these Homes are recognised by the Ministry, which allows us to recruit a full-time employee.

"Sheltered living" became an increasingly popular solution to the problem, so we rented another House. The Foundation now rents four Houses and still cannot meet the demand for this type of accommodation. There are a number of entry rules which are strictly applied:

1. applicant must have come from a psychiatry division.
2. he must have a discussion with a psychiatrist who is connected with "sheltered living". That psychiatrist decides whether the person concerned is suited to the accommodation we offer.
3. he must follow a prescribed course of therapy or he must do a job of work.

Our sheltered living scheme allows the "patient" to live alone, but with the comforting knowledge that there is always a social worker available to provide help if it is needed. Almost any problem can be solved, but there must be excellent interaction and co-operation, or the "treatment" will fail. When the individual has found a job and is mentally prepared to live on his or her own, we can say that the circle is complete and that our task has been successfully accomplished.

We also help former patients by paying their electricity bills and their rent, and helping them with their domestic accounts. We try, too, to assist them to make new friends, and we encourage them to drop in for a cup of coffee whenever they wish: from time to time we pay them a visit if we think they would be glad to see us.

In November 1991, a temporary Sue Ryder Day Centre for mentally handicapped young people was opened at Haacht, near Keerbergen, north-east of Brussels. It is hoped that it will be succeeded by a permanent Home for twenty guests. Much credit is due to many active supporters at Keerbergen. At present, ten handicapped people attend the Centre daily for occupational therapy and a meal, but they return to their homes in the evening. This gives families a much needed break.

In September 1992, in Bruges, another House with four flats was leased, and more Sue Ryder Homes and boutiques are being planned in Belgium.

The plans for a permanent Home and Day Centre involve a total cost of 45,000,000 Belgian francs (£760,000), of which eighty % will be paid by the Government. An appeal had been launched for the balance of 9,000,000 francs (£150,000).

The Foundation in Belgium also runs two Sue Ryder Shops, and there is a Sue Ryder Bookshop in Bruges.

The motto of the mediaeval Counts of Flanders was "More is in you", and we all think it can be well applied to the entire team of Foundation supporters in Bruges and beyond – which now numbers about 150 people!

I always hope to establish a Foundation in the French-speaking part of Belgium.

PART SIX

The Foundation in Britain

19

A Bag of Tools

Isn't it strange that Princes and Kings
And clowns that caper in sawdust rings
And ordinary folk like you and me
Are builders of eternity?

To each is give a bag of tools,
An hour-glass and a book of rules,
And each must build, ere his time is flown
A stumbling block or a stepping stone.

THE FOUNDATION IS A registered charity and two of the essential ingredients are voluntary contributions and personal service given by thousands of people of every age and faith. Whilst it is essential to have an underlying structure, I have always striven to keep the administration as simple as possible without impairing its effectiveness.

Ultimate authority within the Foundation lies with its Council, all of whose members are volunteers. They give generously of their time and do not draw expenses. Indeed, they incur considerable personal expense each year travelling to meetings, visiting Sue Ryder Homes and Shops and in other ways involving themselves with the activities of the Foundation.

The Council consists of men and women drawn from different walks of life, including the legal, medical, business and teaching professions, each offering his or her own individual skill and having the Foundation's aims deeply at heart. They meet every three months at Headquarters when they receive reports on all aspects of the Foundation's work – Homes, Shops, overseas work, finances and future plans. I would like to pay tribute to the late Mr H.N. Sporborg, CMG, the Council's first Chairman, to his successor, Mr John Priest, Chairman and Deputy Chairman of the Council, who, in his turn, passed on the responsibility to the present Chairman, the Reverend Robert Clifton, and also to all the Council's members, past and present, for the unfailing help and support they have offered me throughout the years. A great deal of the burden has been borne by them.

I first saw Harry Sporborg during the War when I was on a brief visit to Special Operations Executive (SOE) in Baker Street. Of course, I did not know his name at the time as everyone in the organisation was known by their initial. He was then executive to Sir Charles Hambro, Head of SOE and later he was to become Deputy to Brigadier – later Major-General – Sir Colin Gubbins, successor to Sir Charles. It was some years afterwards that, through a friend from those days, I approached him to join the Foundation and he became its Chairman.

Henry Nathan Sporborg was born of American parents, but his upbringing was thoroughly English. After Rugby Public School he read History and Law at Cambridge. It was while he was with Slaughter and May, solicitors in the City, that he was recruited into SOE and joined Sir Charles Hambro in the task of organising its Resistance movement in Scandinavia during its early and critical stages. For the purpose of cover, he was appointed Colonel in the Army and, following the end of hostilities, he was made a Commander of the Most Distinguished Order of St Michael and St George. Decorations followed from the United States, France and Norway. It was typical of Harry Sporborg in his modesty to refuse a Knighthood and another decoration offered by the British Government.

He was one of those rare people who had absolute integrity. A quiet man, he never published anything on his work with SOE because he considered that the interests of security prevented him from doing this, but he held strong views on the vital role SOE played in the War.

After the War, Harry Sporborg joined Hambros Bank and for thirty years he was one of its Directors. He held many other business appointments and was interested in more than one charity. I felt very privileged, therefore, when he told me shortly before his death that, of all his interests, St Mary's Hospital, Paddington (he was Chairman of the Board of Governors from 1964 to 1974) and the Sue Ryder Foundation were the only two charities in which he maintained an active participation.

After becoming Chairman of the Foundation, Harry witnessed its rapid growth in Britain and overseas. He was a good listener, a born leader and always a wise counsellor and true friend to me and the members of the Council. Though his health had become worse, he bravely took the Chair for the last time on 2 February 1985. On that occasion we took leave of each other.

The dreaded telex to say that he had died arrived in Delhi in March 1985 while I was working in India.

Harry received marvellous support throughout his married life from his devoted and loving wife, Mary, and they were blessed with a son and three daughters.

I was not able to return for his funeral, but attended the Service of Thanksgiving held in St Paul's Cathedral at the beginning of May 1985. During the service the choir sang Robert Louis Stevenson's words to the tune of the lovely Londonderry Air, and I thought then how they epitomised the qualities and strength of purpose that I shall always associate with Harry Sporborg.

> I would be true for there are those who trust me
> I would be pure for there are those who care
> I would be strong for there is much to suffer

> I would be brave for there is much to dare
> I would be friend for all, the foe, the friendless
> I would be giving and forget the gift
> I would be humble, for I know my weakness
> I would look up, and laugh, and love, and live.

John Priest was the natural successor to the Chair. He was a founder member and had served as Deputy Chairman during Harry Sporborg's term of office and been actively involved in the Foundation's work since 1960, as well as a close personal friend. For more than twenty years he was Chairman of the original National Appeals Committee and, every few weeks, he drove himself early on a Sunday morning from Birmingham to Headquarters to help and to attend meetings. John contributed enormously to the Foundation's appeal work and he was also, for many years, Honorary Adviser for the Sue Ryder Shops and Chairman of the Trading Team. Before his retirement he was a Director of Fyffes Group, and his business acumen and experience were especially valuable to the development of the Sue Ryder Shops. He had the happy gift of encouraging members to join in the Council's discussions and, where there were differences of opinion, of reconciling them in such a way that everyone was pleased with the outcome. Sadly, John had to retire in October 1990, but he has continued to take an active role through the examination of shop leases.

Following John's retirement, the Foundation has been fortunate to have as Chairman, the Reverend Robert Clifton, who also takes the Foundation's Retreats at Walsingham twice a year. He is a very active Chairman and takes a close interest in all aspects of the work, as well as travelling overseas when time allows, and this despite having five parishes to care for. Robert Clifton is known throughout the Foundation, having been my principal Personal Assistant for eleven years before taking holy orders.

The late Betty Clarke, the Headmistress of Benenden School, was another valued member of the Council and for many years her discerning opinions on the diverse aspects of this work were invaluable, especially when the agendas were long.

Betty was called to the Middle Temple in 1949 and would have been admirably suited to the life of a barrister, but she returned to teaching. Her concentration and, above all, her concern to get to the heart of the matter and resolve it, was recognised, and she was respected by her fellow councillors. We also greatly enjoyed her strong sense of humour and admired her faith.

Policy as determined by Council is implemented by the Finance and General Purposes Committee. Much of the detailed work relating to the Sue Ryder Homes in Britain is delegated by the Council to this Committee. Mr Bert Inman CBE and Mr Ken Baddiley OBE were Chairmen of the Homes Executive Committee. It considers all matters of policy and major problems, and tenders advice and makes recommendations to the Council when need be. It acts as a most useful link between the Council and the Homes. It was formed to exercise general oversight of all the Sue Ryder Homes in Britain. Its members have a wide range of managerial and professional experience and quickly make themselves familiar with all the established Homes. The Committee has laid down policies for the general management and development of the Homes, and has advised and assisted the House Committees in dealing with the many problems they face. At present they are deeply involved in the changing structure of the Health Service with its emphasis on care in the community and the requirement for Social Services to contract with Residential Homes for beds.

As a result, the Council and myself have been relieved of a heavy burden of work and left free to concentrate on further consolidation and extension of the Foundation's activities.

The Homes Development Executive deals with all matters concerning extensions to Sue Ryder Homes, and the repair and restoration of properties which are to become Homes in areas of Britain where the needs of the community have been established. These buildings are generally listed Grade I or Grade II and in this connection, the Foundation enjoys the co-operation of English Heritage, the Historic Buildings Council for Scotland and several conservation societies. The public are perhaps unaware that the Foundation must apply to many different authorities before any structural and conversion work can proceed. These include:

The Historic Buildings and Monuments Commission
Planning Authorities – for listed building consent and building regulations
    approval
The Fire Authority
The Health and/or Social Services – for registration

In some parts of the country, architects and quantity surveyors offer their services to the Foundation and are specifically chosen for the work, which they often undertake without charge or at reduced-scale fees. The Senior Architect, Brian Muggleton, and his quantity surveyor take responsibility for all drawings, bills of quantities and specifications, besides much work elsewhere.

Each Sue Ryder Home has a constitution drawn up for it by the Council, and is administered by a Committee whose members are responsible for the Home's day-to-day running, and who are co-opted by Headquarters. The Committee is drawn from the local community and meets regularly.

At Headquarters there is a small staff of full and part-time workers, supplemented by volunteers, whose role is to co-ordinate the work and to serve everybody in the field. It is a principle of the Foundation that administrative costs should be kept to the lowest figure compatible with efficiency, and we rely a great deal upon gifts in kind. The expansion of the Foundation's work during the past years has increased the amount of organisation and administration required.

The Foundation's shops and trading matters are controlled by a Trading Team Chaired by Mr Alan Green, a businessman who had had many years in industry. Every aspect of the shop's management is looked at on a regional basis throughout the year. Property, buying, stock control and monitoring are discussed and special attention is given to expansion both in Britain and overseas.

The purpose of the Sue Ryder Shops in any area – upmarket, middle or downmarket is:

(a) to serve and involve the community;
(b) to inform people of the work of the Foundation;
(c) to remind would-be donors about the needs in the world and, thus, to introduce them to the work;
(d) to raise urgently needed funds, and
(e) to give advice and counselling to those in need.

As the number of Sue Ryder Shops has increased over the years it has become necessary to increase the size of the organisation which supports them. In Britain we have divided the country into eight regions, in each of which a Regional Manager has been appointed. Each region is subdivided into areas and Area Managers are appointed who are responsible to the Regional Manager for the successful running of the shops on a day-to-day basis, and for ensuring that goods are properly sorted, cleaned (if necessary), ironed and coded before being put out on the rails in the Shop. The work behind the scenes in the sorting room is vital and requires skill, patience and perseverance – especially if the room is small.

The Regional Managers and the Area Managers are responsible for finding new Shops; ensuring the smooth running of the existing Shops; dealing with all matters relating to staff and volunteers; co-ordinating local appeals for donated goods; representing the Foundation with regard to specific appeals; representing the Founder by giving talks on the work of the Foundation, and visiting those who are in special need. The Area Managers are carefully chosen and receive training; many have given long and dedicated personal service. They work long hours, and I enjoy reading their reports and seeing their progress. The Foundation also benefits from the services of Regional Managers who have had long years in business and a great deal of experience in retail trading, and the public.

The number of Shops in each Area varies from four to twenty depending upon the stage of development of the Foundation in that part of the country. Each Shop is visited regularly by the Area Manager to ensure that it is being run efficiently and to give the Manageress and staff support and encouragement.

The activities of the Regional Managers are co-ordinated by the Trading Team, which meets every three months. The Team consists of all the Regional Managers, a Chartered Accountant, two or three people from the business and property world and myself. These meetings provide a most useful forum for an exchange of views and sharing of experiences, which includes the sending of reports.

After a Trading Team meeting it is usual for Regional Managers to hold a meeting of all their Area Managers back in their respective regions so that any decision made can be "passed down the line" as quickly as possible and everyone kept fully in the picture. Similar meetings are held regularly with all Shop Manageresses. This includes training sessions.

The full story of the Sue Ryder Shops is told later in this Chapter.

Sue Ryder Support Groups everywhere play a very active role in promoting the work of the Foundation and in raising funds for the Foundation's work as a whole. For more than twenty years the Friends of Sue Ryder, Cambridge and District, organised a one-day fair in the Guildhall there, with a buffet and a wide variety of stalls. Some of the Groups run Foundation shops. Each group has its Honorary Chairman, Treasurer, Secretary and Public Relations Officer.

In spite of this, money remains a perpetual problem and like everyone else, the Foundation has been severely hit by inflation. Costs of everything have soared: for instance, a folding wheelchair in 1973 cost £29 – now twenty years later, it costs a minimum of £1,000. In the same period the cost of a hoist has increased from £2,500 to £3,000.

The Foundation works in Britain and in countries overseas where the needs are known, or where it is given a property or finds a suitable one. Before a decision to open a Home is made, however, the needs must always be confirmed by the local Social Services and the Health Authorities.

In Britain the Foundation's Homes, apart from the ones for continuing care for cancer patients, are registered as Residential Care Homes or Nursing Homes, or as both under the provisions for dual registration, and certificates to that effect are issued by the registration authorities after they have satisfied themselves about staffing, fire regulations, etc.

Local authorities have a statutory responsibility for supporting people in need of care who have not the private means to pay and they have in the past sponsored many residents in the Foundation's Homes. However, the National Health Service and Community Care Act, 1990, introduced a marked charge in policy, placing much emphasis on avoiding the removal of people from their home environment. Introduced under the banner "Care in the Community", current procedures are expressed in terms of marketing a "care package", tailored to the needs of the individual client.

As was perhaps inevitable, this has spawned a whole new bureaucracy which is far removed from the expressed intentions of the Act. Now those desperate for admission find themselves beset by all kinds of delay and their relatives – or if none, their neighbours – find problems at every turn.

At the root of it all, of course, lies the demand on resources fuelled by demographic change. Add to this the growth in bureaucracy and the result, desperately sadly, is patients discharged from hospital with nowhere to go. Choice becomes a somewhat hollow term; "Care in the Community" sounds good but without enough qualified and experienced carers, and without funds, or sufficient places for those in need to choose from, the "clients" – the sick and handicapped residents or patients – find themselves needy still.

The Sue Ryder Homes for the continuing care of cancer patients, and others with a neurological conditions are registered with the Health Authorities as Nursing Homes and a certificate to that effect is also issued. In the past, an agreement was drawn up so that contractual beds were paid for by the Health Authority which covered the maintenance of the patients we were nursing. Alas, owing to the recession and cuts made by central Government to the Health Authorities, these terms have become very different indeed. Thus, responsibility for patients in need of continuing care over the past ten years has undergone a radical change. In 1992 it cost £17.5 million altogether a year to run the Sue Ryder Homes in Britain, and of this figure at least £9 million has to be found by the Foundation. Apart from this, a huge amount of fund-raising is required for essential extensions to some of the Homes, as well as necessary and expensive repairs to the properties. Each year the amount increases, but every endeavour is made to keep administration costs down. In the immediate future the Foundation will have to raise over £11 million and with the needs ever-increasing in future years it is estimated that a minimum of £16 million will be required annually. In addition, as there are the far, far more serious and desperate overseas commitments: this amount is impossible to quantify. If £16 million was available, or even an unlimited amount was available, this could be spent *very* wisely, as the needs in each country are assessed most carefully, both by the Ministers of Health and Social Welfare, who usually, unlike in Britain, are experienced and well informed people from the medical and nursing world.

Now, as at the beginning, we still do not know where or how funds will be raised. When one of the building companies with whom we were trading very kindly offered to take out life insurance on me as a means of ensuring payment of their account in the event of something happening to me, I was prompted to further deep thought about the question of fund-raising.

Despite the great difficulties and uncertainties we have encountered, I have always believed that the funds required for the Foundation's work will somehow be forthcoming; but, on the other hand, I believe equally that we must ourselves make every effort to raise these funds. Incidentally, I really dislike the word "money" and I remember, in particularly poignant surroundings, a women doctor in Poland telling me never to worry or wonder where it was coming from because it was God's money.

It is the policy of the Foundation that no Home should be parochial in outlook. Accordingly, funds are not collected for the exclusive use of a particular Home in its own area but, rather, for the work and well-being of this international Foundation as a whole. The ingenuity of supporters in thinking of new ways of raising funds for the Foundation knows no limits. Apart from raffles, fêtes, sponsored walks, concerts, auctions, and such, more unconventional methods of fund-raising have included the Leeds Court Room Swear Box Appeal, a Wellington-boot throwing competition, the Fastest Bedmaker in Town competition, the Shetland Pony Grand National, and more than sixty other similar ideas.

One year, a strenuous tour of Britain and Belgium was undertaken by the Ivo Lola Ribar Dancers from the former Yugoslavia, a group of forty-one performers, the youngest of them only eleven years old. The troupe was accompanied by eighteen heavy trunks full of regional costumes.

Walks are undertaken by an astonishing number of people, including one eighteen-year old, Barnaby Loenis, who in 1990 undertook a sponsored walk of 4,736 kilometres from the Blue Mosque in Istanbul back to London in just over five months. Barnaby raised a magnificent sum of £8,984.88. Two lads, Marek and Richard, had a wonderful experience when they walked on two pilgrimages to Poland. Richard wrote about it in an edition of the *Remembrance* magazine:

> The video ends with the Padianice pilgrimage which took place after the Wroclaw pilgrimage. Padianice is the birthplace of my mother, and so I decided to walk in that pilgrimage also in order to re-live the wonderful atmosphere of the Polish pilgrimage to Our Lady of Częstochowa, where we joined vast crowds of over 200,000 pilgrims.
>
> I think that the atmosphere of the pilgrimage comes across very well on the film of the Wrocław pilgrimage, for me it was an unbelievable experience. It was moving to witness the strength of the faith of the Polish youth: religious songs were sung non-stop during the pilgrimage, covering hundreds of miles, with nobody needing a hymm book – everyone knew the songs off by heart. I felt I was surrounded by love, everyone treated one another like sisters and brothers. It's difficult to explain to Westerners that 15,000 people could enjoy themselves during the evening get-togethers with not a single drop of alcohol between them!
>
> I will never forget the tremendous feeling of pleasure after reaching on foot from England the painting of Our Lady of Częstochowa. It's something that I would very much like to repeat this year; a friend who also walked in the pilgrimage before has said that he will go with me. It is therefore another opportunity to raise funds for the Foundation.
>
> I treated the whole walk as a personal pilgrimage to Our Lady, but realise that I should have also concentrated on the fund-raising side a bit more through our prayers.

After reading in the Press about the Foundation's work, a couple from Bradford, West Yorkshire, David and Moyra Sonley, who are very keen and experienced cyclists, have raised £560 for the Foundation, as a result of recovering money in all sorts of unlikely places. These include roadsides, in gutters, on pavements, in car parks or lay-bys, at bus stops and in bus-shelters, outside shops, supermarkets and public houses, alongside parked cars, under wayside of park seats, under beds in Youth Hostels, outside

ABOVE Patient with Sue Ryder at the Foundation's Home, Oxenhope

BELOW Volunteers who serve in the Foundation's restaurant attached to the museum, at Headquarters

ABOVE HRH The Duchess of Kent visits patients at the Sue Ryder Home, Nettlebed

BELOW HRH The Prince of Wales visiting patients with cancers at the Sue Ryder Home, Leckhampton Court

ABOVE HM The Queen speaking to volunteers from Poland and the Czech Republic during a visit to the Sue Ryder Home, Ely

BELOW Wladyslaw, the heroic R/T operator in Operation Bridge 3/Wildhorn being presented to HM Queen Elizabeth, The Queen Mother

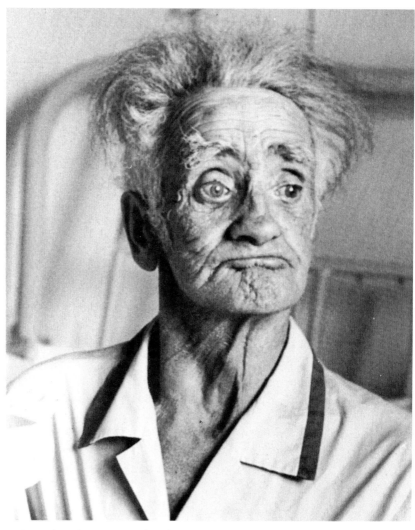

Sam, a homeless person with malignant disease at the Sue Ryder Home, Oxenhope

The Sue Ryder House in Owning, Co. Kilkenny, twenty chalets for the
elderly and those who cannot cope alone

ABOVE The Sue Ryder Home at Chantry, Ipswich, after restoration

BELOW The Sue Ryder Home at Stagenhoe Park, Whitwell, near Hitchin, Hertfordshire, where 53 long-stay patients, many of them with Huntington's Disease, live

ABOVE Marchmont House, Berwickshire, was restored and adapted to become a Sue Ryder Home for 36 patients

BELOW There are 580 Sue Ryder Shops in Britain. These shops aim to provide a service to their communities, to bring together people from all walks of life, to provide a purpose for those who are lonely or without work, to be a window to the needs of those in Britain and overseas, and to raise urgently needed funds

ABOVE The Sue Ryder Home which was the Bishop's Palace, Ely, completely restored and now housing 43 patients

BELOW The Bishop's Palace, during restoration

ABOVE Staunton Harold Hall, Leicestershire, was rescued from demolition and converted to become a Sue Ryder Home complete with a coffee shop and gift shop

BELOW Thorpe Hall, Peterborough, restored to become a Sue Ryder Home, and now housing 24 long-term and short-term patients

ABOVE Leckhampton Court before restoration work began

BELOW Leckhampton Court, Gloucestershire, after restoration, houses 30 patients

Sue Ryder with Ian Hardy, one of the Foundation's architects, in the rubble of Leckhampton Court

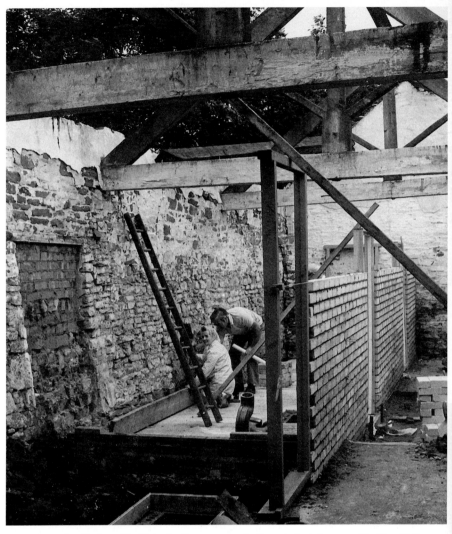

ABOVE Sue Ryder with Chris the Foreman, at the Foundation's home at Birchley Hall, Lancashire, where a cow-shed was converted to offices

ABOVE Hickleton Hall, Yorkshire, now a Sue Ryder Home
accommodating 53 patients

BELOW Cuerden Hall, Lancashire, restored to become a Sue Ryder Home for 37 patients

Lord Cheshire and Lady Ryder at Headquarters

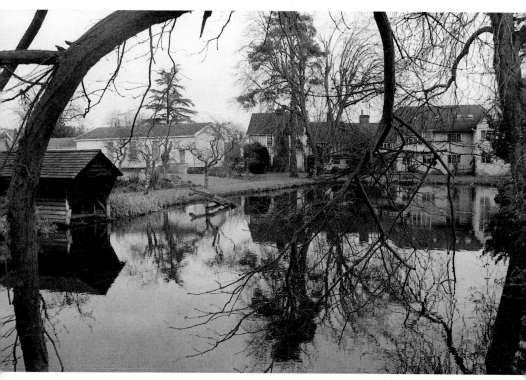

ABOVE Rear view of Cavendish, the Foundation's Headquarters

BELOW The Chapel

HH Pope John Paul II receiving Sue Ryder and her husband, Leonard Cheshire
on their Silver Wedding Day, Rome 5 April 1984

factories and work places and on country roads and lanes. In their words "one only has to look".

Mr and Mrs Soley also come as volunteers to Headquarters in August to help with the packing and dispatching of the annual *Remembrance* magazine.

I am very much aware of the deep debt of gratitude the Foundation owes to supporters who take out a Deed of Covenant or remember its work in their wills. Above all, however, we count on the individuals both here and overseas who from the start, have faithfully sent us their postal orders and cheques, usually after saving up or making some real effort. Frequently, when the Foundation has been without funds, especially at the beginning, it is these unseen people upon whom we have depended and whose letters and messages accompanying their gifts have meant so much. One letter read:

> Dear Sue Ryder
>> Have just had a lovely holiday, so here is £5 as my thanks.

Another, from a little boy read:

> Dear Sue Ryder
>> I have heard about your story and your adventure it is very exciting and I like it and I have herd about your saving peopl's live's and saving peopl in the war that get shot and badly hert and I know lot's of poor people and I hope that they are being looked after and I want a book and that is what the 5p stamp is for.
>> Love Stephen

More recently a letter from a long-standing supporter:

> Dear Lady Ryder,
>> Thank you for the 1996 issue of *Remembrance*. As usual, I have read it with interest, though with sadness because of the suffering of the people you help.
>
> There are two things I specially like about your Foundation. The first is that, at a time when many charities are run like businesses, you keep yours personal and very much encourage volunteers of various kinds. The second is that you only send out to supporters once a year and even then there is no high pressure appeal. Several charities to which I subscribe send out appeals begging for money for special purposes several times a year, saying how urgent the needs are and almost making you feel guilty if you don't respond each time. I don't like this and feel one or two appeals a year are sufficient. Apart from a few charities for which I have monthly or quarterly standing order. I do not feel I can give more than once or twice a year. No doubt your charity has pressing needs too but you show restraint in not pressurising supporters. In appreciation of this I have decided to increase my donation to £27. Will you please credit £12 of this to the Stagenhoe Park extension fund. C.A.F. voucher for £27 enclosed.
>> Yours sincerely
>> Dorothy G. Chapman (Mrs)

and a final one from a former Polish soldier:

> Dear Sue Ryder,
>
> I have just retired, at sixty five, after thirty-five years of work as a Chartered Engineer. My friends and colleagues have, without my knowledge, both made and brought presents for me which I shall treasure for as long as I shall live. There was also a collection which amounted to £120.
>
> I would be grateful if you accept this sum to help those less fortunate than myself, whose lives were shattered by the War and its aftermath, whose joys are few and whose tribulations are endless.
>
> I am a former member of the Polish Forces under British Command. Please accept my undying gratitude for the many tears you helped to dry.
>
> Yours, most sincerely,
>
> Stanislaw Rusinowski

There are other donors, too, whom I have been privileged to meet personally. I remember vividly an elderly handicapped woman sitting in her wheelchair in a small and dreary room in London. During the course of my visit she said: "There is so little I can do, but I know a bit what it is like to suffer. Please accept these crumpled notes which I have saved. I give them to you for the work with my love. I don't want thanks; it means everything for me to do this."

After a meeting in a village in Cambridgeshire, a woman in her early sixties, who looked far from well and had walked over two miles to attend, pressed 2/6d (approximately 12p) in my hand saying that she would always pray for the work and apologised for not being able to offer more.

The Foundation's *main* form of communication is through its annual magazine *Remembrance* which is sent out in August, but the contents begin to take shape in June. Every effort has to be made to collect and sift through suitable material from a mass of Press cuttings, reports, articles, correspondence and information concerning different aspects of the Foundation's work. It always seems a great effort to edit this material to give our supporters and the public generally a fair and balanced report on what has occurred during the past year. The magazine is restricted to forty-two pages because of the costs, which rise drastically every year, and we are only sorry that we cannot find more advertisers to offset these costs.

The galley proofs have to be corrected and returned by specified dates, and during the week that *Remembrance* is due to go out there is an undercurrent of excitement as the stage is set for the task of unloading copies from the printers, bagging them up and sending them out.

Before the three-ton van arrives from the printers, driven by a young girl from Bristol, the drawing room has to be emptied of furniture, except for the piano. Every available spare table and chair is brought in from different offices and rooms in the Home.

Labels are addressed from the database at Headquarters, which is meticulously kept up throughout the year. A mailsort programme is used to sort the addresses in strict postcode order so that the highest discount can be obtained from the Post Office. To this end all addresses on the database have to have the right postcode. After several different methods were tried, the manual way of looking up each address in a Post Office book proved to be the only really effective way, but it took several months of hard work before all 72,000 entries were correct.

Envelopes are filled in the drawing room. There is the characteristic smell of cardboard boxes, plastic envelopes, and rubber bands, as at least eight volunteers at a time sit side-by-side around the tables arranged down the centre of the room and put a *Remembrance* and gift catalogue into each envelope. These are then returned to their boxes and taken to another room where more volunteers are waiting to affix the labels, keeping the envelopes in strict order of postcodes. Yet more volunteers wait to "bag up", which involves putting batches of envelopes into a sack, keeping each district separate; several hundred sacks a day are filled and then stacked up ready for the postman. Having had so much practice over the years the whole operation runs like clockwork and is usually completed in the course of a week to ten days – generally with a "pat on the back" from the Post Office.

The Poles enjoy singing as they insert gift catalogues into the *Remembrance*, punctuated by such remarks as "Fernando, why are you so slow?" The atmosphere is relaxed but industrious as staff and volunteers keep up an amazing pace.

Each year different groups of helpers arrive from various countries including Poland, Czechoslovakia, Canada, Ireland, Finland, Spain, Costa Rica, Belgium, France, The Netherlands, Australia, New Zealand, Singapore, Iceland, Norway, Switzerland, Germany, from Republics of the former Yugoslavia, Mexico, Denmark, Lithuania, Russia, the Ukraine, Africa and the United States of America, and it is a delight to see how happily they work together. This intense activity, which throws us together every August, seems to crystallise our feelings for those whom we try to serve – and to redouble our determination to communicate to our supporters the news we want to spread.

One year, in the 1960s, a special effort was being made to meet the deadline for dispatch, and so the work was done in shifts without a break throughout the fifty to sixty hours it took. At about two o'clock one morning half a bottle of vermouth was produced by the shift going off duty. An eighteen-year-old volunteer from the Army happily accepted his small ration and, unknown to the rest, failed to reach his room. He decided instead to make his bed among the sacks in the long passage outside the drawing room. He fell into a deep sleep and consequently never noticed that more sacks were being dumped on top of him until he was rudely awakened by the volunteers who came to load the Post Office van in the early dawn. It was generally felt that he had been lucky to escape "posting" with the rest of the sacks!

When everything is done, a great tidying up operation takes place collecting up the rubbish, string, rubber bands, paper clips, empty boxes, torn brown wrapping paper, notes, and so on. The drawing room floor is swept whilst, outside its door, lying along the passages, are the plump stuffed Post Office sacks patiently awaiting collection – each one marked with its destination to friends of the Foundation. A pregnant silence falls upon the scene. Body and mind ache before sleep comes to soothe us all. There falls a deep and marvellous calm. While we all go and wash and gather strength, we also pray that the harvest may bear fruit for the present and coming year's work.

Shortly after the Post Office van leaves with the magazines another red post van reverses up the back drive carrying the incoming mail. The postman comes in with a sack, the huge contents of which are spilled onto the floor. The sorting can take up to an hour before the mail for the residents, staff and volunteers is distributed. Envelopes are slit and opened, while the returned *Remembrance* marked "Gone Away", "Deceased", "House demolished" are stacked ready to be entered on the computer index accordingly. It seems like a goodbye to the cheerful supporters who have died, many of whom have faithfully saved whatever they could from their small salaries or pensions over the years and written delightful letters of encouragement. Now their card is moved into the white "heavenly" drawer. Though we have never met, we seem to have known one another almost intimately through correspondence, and their notes of encouragement and support will never be forgotten. These people, from all corners of Britain and beyond, have been pillars of the Foundation.

Of the various ways in which the Foundation tries to raise funds, radio and television have proved particularly successful. Through the courtesy of the BBC I have been allowed to make two Appeals on behalf of the Foundation – one by radio, which brought a response of 14,000 letters and over £18,000 in donations, and the second by television, which raised £52,000. Writing in her diary about the first of these appeals, Mama said: "When Sue was asked what target had been in her mind before The Week's Good Cause she said, 'I don't think I've got one, but hope for a miracle', and the miracle happened."

The television Appeal proved to be exceedingly hard work; what I wanted to say had to be condensed into three minutes and thirty-six seconds and we had to cope with the technical difficulties which arose in the shooting of the film.

After the Appeal every member of staff at Headquarters, and all the residents who could help, volunteered to work in the Appeal Office, where the tables were cleared and adding and numbering machines brought in.

The first mail brought sacks of letters, but little did we know that this was to go on for seven or eight weeks non-stop; and though we had hoped and prepared for a large response, we had never expected such vast numbers of wonderful letters. As a result, we had to appeal to the Carmelite Sisters (who were responsible for our printing) and stationers in the area for further supplies.

Assembly lines were established, one being made responsible for slitting the envelopes and passing them onto the second for the opening and writing up in the card index, after which they were passed onto the then Appeals Secretary, Joy Griffith Jones, Sheila Jollands and myself for reading, marking and separating into different categories. Anthony Green, whom we called "Green's Bank", totalled the donations on a machine after each letter and card had been numbered, and these were then made up into bundles of twenty for the bank. They, in turn, had to bring in extra trestle tables and staff from other branches, who worked in the bank's cellars writing hundreds of receipts. One of the highlights of those days was when my mother came to the office window from the clothing store with a small paper parcel bearing no name or address, which was found to contain £460 in pound notes!

During the weeks following the Appeal, work went on until past ten or eleven at night, when everything would be carefully packed into boxes which were then labelled and carried upstairs to our bedroom for safety overnight. Next morning the cycle would begin again, with three-hourly announcements by "Green's Bank" giving the latest news of the grand total, which added to the excitement. The automatic typewriter FREDDIE (a gift from the Friden Typewriter Company) was in operation for more than fifteen hours a day, and added its clatter to the atmosphere.

The television broadcast was preceded by a Postal Appeal and I had signed 40,000 letters; afterwards each of the 18,000 donors had a personal letter of acknowledgement. A total of £43,000 was most gratefully received by these means.

In 1978 another National Appeal was planned, and in May of the following year, Sir Kenneth Cork, then Lord Mayor of London, kindly allowed the Foundation to launch this from the Mansion House. We will always remember his words of encouragement and support.

The very small Appeal Team consisted of five members. No professional fund-raiser was involved. Almost three years from the day of launching, the target of £500,000 was passed to reach the magic figure of £518,000.37, with expenses amounting to only £9,173. I am deeply indebted to those supporters who loaned the Foundation money on an interest-free basis and later asked for it to be treated as a gift. If this sum had not been raised the Foundation would have found itself in very serious difficulties indeed and the various objectives of the Appeal would not have been realised.

For several years I had envisaged the Foundation holding a National Appeal in November which would follow the Royal British Legion Remembrance Appeal. The whole idea of this Sue Ryder Light of Hope Appeal is to inform more people about the needs of the world – the hungry, the sick, those without medicines, medical or nursing care, the homeless and those who are unknown and unloved – and to show that we are remembering them especially during that fortnight, by showing a blue light or candle in their window, with a brief notice of explanation beside it.

We pray and hope, and indeed it is my dream, that thousands – and later millions – of blue lights will flicker throughout Britain during the Sue Ryder Light of Appeal, thus making the Foundation better known and, above all, bringing comfort and relief to those who suffer everywhere.

Scotland was the first Region to hold a Sue Ryder Light of Hope Appeal. During this week a series of fund-raising events was held throughout the country. Using publicity material such as banners, blue lamps and candles, the week was given a high profile in all the Sue Ryder Shops, so that it would bring to the attention of the public the urgent need for additional funds to consolidate and expand the work undertaken by the Foundation in this country and overseas. For this special fortnight each Sue Ryder Shop and Home was asked to hold a fund-raising event. Great imagination and a lot of hard work and planning resulted in events ranging from a skittles evening to a male cake bake. In addition to this, each Area and Region arranged activities on a larger scale, including auctions, concerts and fashion shows. Shops were asked to dress their windows in blue and white during these fund-raising weeks. In addition to this, the charter was displayed in a prominent position and a blue lamp was lit. Candles in blue cases were on sale, and members of the public were asked to light these and display them in their windows at home to publicise this special time.

During the annual fund-raising Appeal I naturally drive the length and breadth of the country attending many events, and visiting shops and Homes. I was requested to draw raffles, sign books, give short talks to schools and organisations and pose for many photographs. Local Press coverage was extremely good and some delightful pictures were used.

Church services play an extremely important role, and in each Region the Cathedral or Church is chosen which is large enough for as many of the volunteers and supporters as possible to attend, from all denominations.

Co-ordinating this week, and the events held during this short period, involved a lot of planning and organisation. It all proved to be very worthwhile and generated a great deal of enthusiasm and good will amongst all who participated.

In the 1960s we were privileged to have a well-known patron help us in our search for more suitable people to work in the field. On one occasion, the patron, accompanied by one of my Assistants, called on a firm of "headhunters" in search of such people. They had heard that the firm would give prompt and special advice and assistance without charging.

On arriving slightly ahead of the appointment, they found an ultramodern open-plan office with men and women wandering about in elegant suits with floppy silk handkerchiefs in their breast pockets calling each other "darling". One came up to them both and said, "Now, what can I do for you? Are you looking for a job?" – not recognising the famous face. They replied, "We have come for an appointment." That person floated away and another came up. On asking more or less the same question and on hearing the same reply, he said "Oh! that's our naughty Jimkins who should have returned from his lunch. Sometimes he goes out and has such a super meal that he forgets an appointment. What shall we do with him?" Then he turned to the patron and my Assistant asking for their names – which they gave him. He said, "Ah! initials won't do – I want your first names." They told him their names and he exclaimed, "Oh, mine's Andrew and you are . . . ; that's splendid; now what can I do for you – are you looking for jobs?" Each time he noted anything down, he drew out one of the many coloured felt-tip pens from a bowl on his desk and wrote on a different piece of coloured paper. After much scribbling some were screwed up and thrown – rather far – into a wastepaper basket.

As this interview was not really proceeding in the way they expected, they took leave of each other and, on going down in the lift, my Assistant said to the famous patron, "Surprising how these people exist," and he replied, "They won't for long."

Another form of fund-raising, concerts and concert tours arranged by the Foundation, have in their own way been no less successful, and took a lot of planning and organising by the late Joy Griffith Jones.

Benjamin Britten and Peter Pears gave a very fine and memorable concert in aid of the Foundation at Blickling Hall in Norfolk. Ruth, Lady Fermoy, helped to organise this particular concert. When I tried to express my thanks, I quoted from Wordsworth: "The music in my heart I bear long after it was heard no more."

In the following year a group of professional musicians from Poland offered to make a concert tour of the British Isles as their contribution to the Foundation. They performed works by Chopin, Puccini, Donizetti, Wieniawski, Verdi, and other composers. All gave their services free and gave up their annual holidays in order to make this tour.

A concert tour was a new venture for us, far more ambitious than anything hitherto attempted, which involved finding suitable concert venues up and down the country and forming a committee in each place to organise publicity, sell tickets and arrange hospitality for the artistes and those accompanying them. Most of this work fell originally upon a small team which worked tirelessly planning and making preparations for the tour.

As far as possible, the concerts were arranged geographically in order to keep mileage to a minimum, but this, of course, depended on the availability of suitable premises. Cathedrals, churches, theatres, public halls, schools and a number of private houses were chosen as locations, some of which were offered free by their owners or curators, and in every instance hospitality was provided privately or courtesy of an hotel Manager. The warmth of the welcome offered by these hosts and hostesses was to prove a source of great comfort and encouragement to the group during an extremely strenuous tour covering three to four thousand miles. Moreover, it left them with many happy memories of their first visit to Britain and gave rise to a number of friendships which have lasted ever since. Many of the artistes spoke either English or French, so language was not too much of a problem, and in fact sometimes caused a great deal of amusement!

At a few of the places, arrangements had been made for the whole party to stay in the same building, and these occasions were great opportunities for practical jokes. A tour such as this is very arduous, with its constant packing and unpacking, long drives and continually changing circumstances, and fun and laughter are essential as a means of relaxation. At one convent, for example, two of the artistes decided after the concert to change the name tags on the rooms occupied by the rest of the party. I retaliated by inventing at the last minute a new concert for the next day – which, needless to say, the artistes were willing to take in their stride. At times on the tour their tiredness was obvious but they were always concerned with rehearsing and practising.

In 1969 three more professional musicians volunteered their services, one of whom was the brilliant young violinist, Konstanty Kulka. Reviewing a performance he gave in London, the music critic of *The Daily Telegraph* wrote that the "virtuosity and brilliance of tone" displayed by this artist "were in themselves enough to make this one of the notable events here in Wigmore Hall for a long time".

The results of the original tour by the concert group were so heartening that a second tour was arranged, which took place in 1969, and a third concert group visited England in 1972, also giving performances in Bruges and Waterloo, Belgium.

The 1969 tour began at Chelmsford, going as far west as Cardiff and Cornwall and as far north as Aberdeen and Banff, so that it can almost be said to have covered the length and breadth of Britain. One of the Foundation's patrons, Sir Arthur Bliss, Master of the Queens's Musick, wrote a foreword to the programme, and Benjamin Britten, another of our patrons, sent a long greetings telegram conveying his warmest wishes. Her Royal Highness Princess Anne had graciously agreed to attend the final concert at the Queen Elizabeth Hall in London. At the last moment, she was prevented from coming by the death of her grandmother, Her Royal Highness Princess Andrew of Greece, but when she learned of the disappointment which this had caused, she gave the group the honour of receiving us in a private room at Buckingham Palace. As a schoolgirl at Benenden she had helped to carry in the luggage and sell programmes when the group performed there during the first concert tour. The artistes were given supper in the domestic science block after the concert, and it was left to the head girl of each house in the school to wait on them. Just before they sat down, the door opened and a young girl slipped in. She went up to the two artistes near her and said, "Would you mind signing my autograph book? My name is very short and easy to write: it is Anne." No one else had witnessed this and she quickly slipped out again.

For the 1972 concert tour, Benjamin Britten wrote the following Foreword to the programme:

Nearly five hundred years ago William Byrd wrote –

> Since singing is so good a thing
> I wish all men would learn to sing (or play!)

Singing or playing bring great joy to the hearts of those who sing and play, and very often (though not always!) to the ears of those who hear the singing or playing. On this occasion performers and listeners are adding an extra dimension to the music by helping unfortunate and suffering people somewhere in the world, perhaps near, perhaps far – for Sue Ryder operates wherever people need her.

As a patron of the Sue Ryder Appeal I am most grateful to all of you singers, players and listeners for your contributions to this evening.

In more ways than anyone could ever have anticipated, the tours have proved both memorable and successful. Financially, they each raised well over £15,000 for the Foundation, but, perhaps more important still, the attendant publicity in the Press and on radio and television did much to make the work of the Foundation known to those who hitherto had been unaware of its existence. A number of Sue Ryder Shops and Support Groups were established as a direct result.

One of the most pleasant memories of those long drives from concert to concert was hearing the artistes discuss classical music, operas and songs. They compared experiences and interpretations which, to my ignorant ear, were both fascinating and enlightening.

The late Sir George Clutton, who was our Road Manager, took part in the discussions and each evening, resplendent in his dinner jacket, he would sit in his chair behind the stage curtain to listen to every concert and note each artiste's performance. At one place we had a Professor from the Royal Academy of Music who took notes and later discussed them with the artistes.

Despite the weeks of detailed preparation and meetings with the groups responsible for organising the tours, there were occasions when nothing went according to plan.

During a mayoral reception I had an uneasy feeling that all was not well with the preparations for one such concert. I therefore left before lunch had ended and drove with Pat Davies, my Secretary, some sixty miles to the place where the concert was to be held. On arrival at the charming little theatre we were told that hardly any tickets had been sold and that the Manager was not due back until the late afternoon. The organisers could not be contacted, and this left us with no choice but to try and sell whatever tickets we could ourselves. While Pat stood outside the theatre approaching every pedestrian (I heard her calling, "Are you free this evening to come to a concert – a very good concert? Please take a ticket!"), I made my way to the local infirmary and asked the porter to take me to matron's office.

She was a women of singularly large build, and, while I was explaining our dilemma, she suddenly recognised me – much to my embarrassment – and rose from her desk to say how absolutely disgraceful it was that the artistes who had come so far from Poland were not receiving public support. "And you," she asked me, "now to have to go round this ancient city trying to sell the tickets at the eleventh hour?" She then rang several consultants and the nurses' home and left them all in no doubt that she expected them to attend!

From there I proceeded to the Cathedral and, during Evensong, asked the verger if he would help me by selling tickets as the congregation came out. Time was running out on me, so I then hurried to the Catholic Church and asked a rather startled priest for his full co-operation. By good fortune, rather than by good management, over 300 people eventually attended the concert. At the end of the evening we were told that the organisers had had two unexpected deaths in their groups and it was this which had reduced them to a state of disarray!

On another occasion, despite regular correspondence and at least one visit made by one of my Assistants, there had been a worrying lack of confirmation about the number of tickets sold for a concert and also the question of accommodation. This led to Sir George Clutton and ourselves deciding that it was necessary to make a telephone call two days before to find out how plans were progressing. We were shocked to hear that only £16 worth of tickets had been sold for one concert and that no firm arrangements had been made to accommodate the artistes and other members of the group. However, in the belief that we could not let down those who had bought tickets, we decided to go ourselves.

We spent our time before the concert in trying to arouse support and to get schools and other bodies involved in taking tickets. Meanwhile, a well-known local personality (wife of a retired admiral) very kindly telephoned to say that she could offer the party three beds in her large house. Fortunately, through her and other colleagues, and much to our relief, accommodation was eventually found for all the remaining artistes.

Sir George and I together took two members of the Foundation's staff to tea with our hostess. We had only twenty minutes to spare and, after being shown my room, I left the door open as Sir George and one of our colleagues were bringing our baggage upstairs. From the passage outside I heard our hostess's voice questioning Sir George as to what his helper's role was vis-à-vis myself as founder. Sir George explained politely, and I heard our hostess say "Oh, I see, he is what in the Navy we would call 'Flags'" (i.e. a Flag Lieutenant).

We returned to the hall for the rehearsal, followed by the concert, and that night I was given the opportunity by our hostess of talking about the work of the Foundation which she had followed for many years.

The next morning I drove the van to the appointed place on the sea front to load for the onward journey, but the expected volunteers did not materialise. I helped the artistes haul up their cases and instruments onto the roof rack whilst the high sea breaking against the promenade drenched us.

Our hostess called me back to her car and said, "My dear, I want to talk to you again. You must leave this sort of work to the men!" Despite my protests and my attempt to explain that I was the driver and that we had to care for the artistes' health, especially their hands and voices, she could not agree.

She then asked how long I would be away on the concert tour in other parts of the country. I said about six weeks and added that it was difficult being away from Headquarters, and that was why I had to ask two Secretaries to accompany me; also that it was difficult leaving the babies. There followed a pregnant silence, and then she put her hand on my knee and, gazing into my eyes, said, "I have always supported your Foundation and followed your work with great interest. Please do not take what I am now going to ask you too badly, but to me you are just like Sue Ryder." "Oh, yes, thank you for your continued support," I answered, wondering what was coming next. "I don't want to be inquisitive," she said, "but it has come as something of a shock to learn that you have children. I must ask you who looks after them." I then realised she thought that I was unmarried with two children! Still not realising what was in her mind I went on, "Well, my husband does try to be with them as much as possible, too," and mentioned his name which, however, meant nothing to her, and she continued, "I do hope he has a job which spares the time to help you properly." "Yes, " I murmured, "he does what he can."

On one of the first tours, the artistes were to perform in a Wren church in the City of London, with one of the artistes playing the organ. There, we were greeted by the vicar who proudly showed us round but then had to leave us to take a Communion Service in the crypt. His organist appeared briefly, but he, too, soon left us alone as he had to attend a choir practice in another church before proceeding to a luncheon in the City. Readers may imagine our dismay, as we got down onto our hands and knees in the small organ loft in a desperate attempt to find the handbook for the organ, to find that, alas, there was none! Our next task was to find a telephone directory and hunt through the pages for the firm which had built the organ. We found, to our surprise, that this firm was far away in Scotland! To add to our problems the verger appeared to be deaf. Despite the fact that we had arrived well ahead of schedule, the artistes had had no opportunity to rehearse, and the audience were by now starting to arrive. At last, and quite by chance, as we investigated the top panel of the organ above the manuals and stops, we found that one of the many switches was for the organ.

In the early '70s one energetic group of supporters organised a concert at a huge "folly" (a sham Gothic building) where the owners still made use of their own generator – which failed on this particular evening.

When I arrived it was raining. Local friends were off-loading the buffet supper from the Land and Range Rovers. In addition, there was the problem of providing enough oil lamps and candles. The gun dogs had got loose and, to the consternation of the volunteer cooks, voices could be heard calling, "Oh darling, it's too bad, the doggies have lapped up the *hors d'oeuvres*: do bring in the souffles now and find your way quickly to the different dining rooms." A Spanish couple were in service there and the butler clearly disapproved.

The large and well-known choir which had been engaged for the evening turned up nearly an hour late after getting lost in the mist. By this time some of the assembled company were beginning to show the effects of too many Pimms and an exceptionally strong cider cup.

The room where the performance took place seated only about ninety, and the unlucky ones had, therefore, to sit on the spiral staircases, which interfered with their view. Those of us sitting near the front, however, were overpowered by the strength of the youthful choir, which was accustomed to singing in cathedrals and churches. Their programme was a singularly long one, with no interval. Afterwards, the members were served a huge supper with much wine, which made them gay and boisterous and affected their otherwise good behaviour. A few conversed in Gaelic, which made it impossible for us to follow their conversation, and the evening eventually finished well past midnight. Nevertheless, the hard work and enthusiasm of the organisers succeeded in raising £400 – no mean feat and a very welcome addition to our funds.

At a well-known training station of one of the Armed Services we were greeted with cucumber sandwiches, hot scones and the order of the day. The commandant and his efficient staff were purring with happiness and satisfaction at the thought that every detail had been attended to. The artistes were eager to see the hall, try out the accoustics and then rehearse. About ten minutes after the start of the rehearsal, when I was in the midst of helping to off-load Christmas cards and other gifts for sale afterwards, Jacek Klimkiewicz, the violinist, came to me and said, "Auntie Sue, it is quite impossible for us to perform here". The piano, it appeared, was chronically out of tune (or had been misused) and, consequently, no professional artiste would feel that he could give a good performance on it.

I went immediately to the station's internal telephone and asked to speak to those concerned, who all appeared to have taken to their baths before changing into mess kit. Eventually, one officer arrived to assure me that the piano had been tuned only that morning and there was absolutely nothing he could do to improve it. I begged him to help us out of our dilemma, and finally he came up with the suggestion that we use another grand piano which was in the mess. Apparently it could be conveyed by lorry onto the stage and the cadets would give us their help in lifting it. Meanwhile, I had telephoned the closest Support Group, some of whose members were musical. They were deeply shocked but were unable to help. We managed to contact the piano tuner and, despite the distance, he came over quickly and confirmed the artistes' fears that both instruments were in an equally bad state. He told me privately that he had warned the committee that the first piano was not fit for professionals to use. For the first and, fortunately, the only time during these tours, we were forced to postpone the concert for thirty minutes whilst a discussion ensued as to which of the two pianos on the platform was the least tuneless! The programme had to be rearranged and emphasis given to the singers.

The officer commanding the station apologised to the audience for the unforeseeable delays, and his speech of welcome was excellent and very warm.

In London, one of the venues was the historic Banqueting Hall in Whitehall, which had no chairs. Jack and Mary Beevor and a group of their friends were responsible for organising this concert. Through an appeal for 900 chairs headed "Standing Room Only" in "Action Line" in the *Daily Express*, the Rank Company came to our aid. I then approached the Guards and a cheerful officer, whose name was Major R. A. G. Courage, offered free assistance to load, off-load, and move the chairs into their positions. All this received much publicity and every one of the tickets was quickly sold.

The success of the tours is, of course, due to the artistes themselves, and to the organising committees, but special mention must be made of Sir George Clutton, who was one of the Foundation's staunch supporters. Before his retirement from the diplomatic service he had been British Ambassador to the Philippines and to Poland. Sir George travelled with us as Cultural Adviser and Road Manager, sharing the difficult conditions under which the artistes lived and worked, and remaining cheerful in his manner and meticulous in his work despite all difficulties. He died in 1971 of a coronary thrombosis, and is greatly missed by the Foundation in very many ways.

Later Irena Karczewska took over as Programme Manager. Her daughter, Anna, was an exceptionally gifted concert pianist and is particularly remembered for accompanying the violin of Jacek Klimkiewicz in a beautiful rendering of Wieniawski's "Romance".

After each long day Irena found the energy to keep a meticulous diary. This was illustrated whenever possible by photographs and postcards and included a complete account of each concert, including particulars of the artistes.

There was a particularly moving concert when the group performed at Allington Castle on the evening of the Olympic tragedy at Munich in September 1972 when the Great Hall was lit by only a log fire and a menorah.

"We drove home through the snow, singing and feeling the better for having heard the artistes and bearing witness to their gaiety and courage," reads one of the many tributes received from friends and strangers after these concert tours, while another runs: "It was an occasion not to be forgotten because of their grace and dignity."

It would be very difficult to single out any individual artiste or concert for special mention; but audiences everywhere were particularly moved by Maria Bielicka's rendering of Schubert's "Ave Maria", the song she had sung to the sick and the dying in the Camps at Majdanek, Auschwitz and Ravensbrück.

Piotr Kusiewicz, who was then nineteen, was another of the many remarkable artistes who performed on behalf of the Foundation. He had studied the piano since the age of six. He completed his studies with distinction at the Musical Academy of Gdańsk. He then trained as a baritone at the Academy and joined the Gdańsk Opera Company. He has performed and won acclaim in Hungary, Britain, Switzerland and many other countries, including Czechoslovakia where he won first prize in the Karlove Vary Competition. In June 1979 Piotr took part in a performance in the Franciscan church at Kraków in the presence of Pope John Paul II. His father had performed at the Opera House in Gdańsk before him and was a survivor of Stutthoff Concentration Camp. He also performed for the Foundation both in Poland and in previous tours of Britain.

Through the late Lady Airey (an old friend of mine whose late husband, Airey Neave, served on the Council of the Foundation), Alan Kogosowski offered to give his services at a concert in London in aid of the Foundation's work in Poland. Kogosowski is a celebrated Polish/Australian pianist, born in 1952, who has made the music of Chopin his speciality.

The concert was held on the night of 17 May 1984 in Guildhall in the City of London, the last place in which Chopin himself gave a public performance (for Polish relief) before his tragically early death in 1849. Kogosowski's programme included the music that Chopin played that night.

When I arrived at the concert I was asked to say a few words at the beginning of the second half and, I tried my best to give a brief impromptu description of the contrast between our own comfort and well-being and the desperate needs among the sick, hungry, and dying in Poland.

Over 700 people attended, and they remained spellbound by the music and brilliance of the pianist. The beauty of the historic Guildhall, decorated for the occasion with huge and lovely red and white floral arrangements and red and white satin ribbons on the balconies, created a wonderful setting for the music.

The concert was filmed for television audiences in Australia, the United States and in Britain, and the audience's ecstatic applause was a just reward for Lady Airey, and all the members of her voluntary committee, who had worked so hard and joyfully for weeks beforehand. This was one of the letters we received afterwards:

> How very kind of you to give us such a wonderful evening on Thursday. To hear Chopin played so beautifully anywhere would be a delight in itself, but in that historic setting with the music flowing through one it made an altogether memorable evening which will remain with us for many years to come. I particularly liked the Fantasy in F Minor, Op. 49.

On 10 June 1984 Alan Kogosowski gave a second performance of Chopin's music at the Georgian Theatre in Richmond, Yorkshire, and a third at Marchmont House, Berwickshire.

I have many memories of these concert tours – and of the unfailing cheerfulness and comradeship displayed by the artistes on all occasions, the great friendliness with which we were received everywhere, the unforgettable music and – very especially – the lovely settings in which the concerts so often took place: the small theatres, with their fine acoustics and intimate atmosphere; the churches; and the beautiful private homes. Especially memorable was our first sight of Traquair House in Scotland, the lovely tenth-century home appearing before us suddenly as the sun broke through the mist; while at Saltram House, near Plymouth, 150 candles illuminated the room in which the artistes performed.

At the beautiful Queen Anne house of Bramham Park, near Thorner, Yorkshire, Mr and Mrs George Lane-Fox not only made all the necessary arrangements for the concert themselves, but with their committee also prepared the most delicious buffet supper which was served to performers and audience.

The concert at Bramham took place under the crystal chandeliers of the Long Gallery at the back of the house, with its mirrors reflecting the lights, and family portraits by Hoppner, Lely and Kneller looking down upon the gathering. Outside the tall windows the rose garden and the lawns stretched out, fringed with old trees and yew hedges, and the beauty of the house, the sense of continuity and tradition, and the deep feeling of peace and tranquillity provided a truly fitting setting for the music. Unhappiness and suffering seemed far away, and we who were privileged to experience that beauty and that peace could only pray that we might one day share it more fully with those who are in such need of it in the world today.

These concerts and other similar functions are now a regular feature of the Foundation's fund-raising and cultural activities, but in future we hope to save driving and fuel, and spare the artistes fatigue, by remaining in the same house for two nights at a time and radiating out from that base.

During 1970 the Royal Academy was host to an exhibition of 1,000 years of art in Poland. It attracted large crowds and it was, therefore a great privilege when the President and Council of the Academy kindly offered one evening to the Foundation in which to hold a soirée. Our guests were very moved by the many exhibits and enjoyed the evening immensely. The Foundation benefited from their presence and felt deeply indebted to the Academy and to its many friends who had organised the event so well.

* * *

For many years the Foundation held an annual Christmas Fair, which rotated among various East Anglian towns and usually ended in an auction. In the early sixties a professional auctioneer offered his services at Ipswich. He was young, very able and energetic, and proceeded to arrange everything most efficiently. Several thousand people were circulated with the news, and an advertisement was placed in *The Times* headed "Moving House". A retired Army colonel took charge of the operation as co-ordinator, and soon had been written to and rung up by countless individuals offering furniture of every style, type and size. In order to cut down the cost it was decided by the committee that we should try and persuade carriers returning empty from jobs in different parts of Britain to collect the goods – but in some cases they reached the donor's house only to find that it was impossible to get the gift out of the cellar because of its size!

Several months before the event the auctioneer stood up in the drawing room at Headquarters and announced to the Committee that he wished to have Georgian silver and good antiques on his list. Moreover, he went on to say that where we were unable to obtain such antiques ourselves, we should have no hesitation about going into the houses of friends and supporters and simply asking them outright for these items. Naturally, we were rather taken aback and hardly knew how to contain our laughter. At the same time, we did our best to explain that we were unlikely to receive the kind of antiques that he wanted!

In the last fortnight local barns were sought as storerooms and the front lawn at Headquarters was covered with every imaginable item which had been donated to us. It was suggested that one load should be sent back because the auctioneer did not think it good enough, but it was sold in the Sue Ryder Shops. Very bad weather added to our problems. Once all the assorted gifts had arrived, the auctioneer and his colleagues worked solidly from the Friday until the Tuesday making them up into lots and cataloguing them. Over 1,000 items were received.

On the morning itself the hall in which the auction was to take place had been transformed. At the beginning bidding was slow, but it went on nonstop until the evening, when my mother was handed an account for over £20 because the auctioneer had taken the disapproving shaking of her head over the initial slowness as a bid, and had knocked down to her a box containing some very rusty forks and similar useless items! But the auction was a great success and the Foundation made some £800 in all.

In October 1982 Mr John Watson and his colleague, Mr John Jenkinson, of the firm of Watson's, Auctioneers and Estate Agents of Bishop's Stortford, in Hertfordshire, kindly offered to organise a special auction in aid of the Foundation. Great efforts were needed to collect 235 lots and Mr Jenkinson personally supervised this and helped physically with the moving. The event raised £8,200. Baron Akerhielm and his wife, Lynette, were the instigators of this auction and gave a great deal of their own time to renovate some of the furniture and assisted by collecting gifts from their friends.

Auctions and fairs are, of course, part of fund-raising events. Permanent and temporary Shops, however, have, with the years, become very much part of the Foundation's way of life.

For a long time I had thought that market stalls and Shops could play a most useful role in raising funds, drawing attention to what we do and selling some of the things made especially to benefit the work of the Foundation. When the idea was first mentioned, the Committee and staff had mixed feelings as we had no professional training or experience in running a Shop; but within weeks an offer of premises on a main pedestrian thoroughfare in London came in and the rent was paid. Danuta Urbaniec, one of my Secretaries, was always willing to try her hand at anything that might be required of her and, as she had the gift of organising quickly and efficiently, she set upon what some might have considered a difficult task. The premises themselves were dilapidated and unattractive, but they were situated in a rather poor part of London where the people, both adult and children, quickly discovered that they were able to turn to the Shop and to the Foundation for assistance.

After great efforts on the part of Danuta and other members of the Foundation, the takings in a good week had, within a month or two, reached £20.

In the early days the Shop had to be stocked from our store at Headquarters, and when I went to a meeting in London I always tried to stop there on the way with a load of clothing and bric-a-brac. The butcher next door to the Shop had offered his support and said that, when necessary, the Manageress could call on him for help or use his telephone for local calls. On one occasion while we were unloading it suddenly became extremely windy and, despite the care we took, bras and other items flew out of the van and scattered themselves in the road, from where I tried desperately to retrieve them. My husband was also helping to carry cartons and bundles of clothing from the van when the butcher appeared and said to him: "The last time we met, Sir, was in 1942 when we were serving in the RAF. I was a member of the ground staff. I didn't know you were in this trade as well as Miss Ryder!"

It was not long before the Foundation's second London Shop was opened, this time in Knightsbridge opposite the Post Office, in an excellent position. The premises were scheduled for demolition, but were lent to the Foundation meanwhile for what turned out to be a period of two very profitable years. This Shop and a former wine shop adjoining it (likewise lent rent free) were also in a dilapidated condition but, although the cellar was too damp for storage, some hard work by willing local helpers and boys from St Joseph's School near Peterborough soon had the rest of the premises cleaned, renovated and ready for business. The Foundation's name was painted on the fascia by a decorator who said that two of the letters were out of line because his hand trembled every time a double-decker bus thundered past while he was working on his ladder!

Within a month or two of the Sue Ryder Shops starting in London, others – temporary or permanent – had opened up and down the country, each being set a profit-target based upon rent and other overheads.

In the late 1950s, when the Foundation became the first charity after Oxfam to open shops, countless other charities have followed the same path. As a result, the competition has grown increasingly fierce and the Sue Ryder Foundation cannot now compete with the wealthier charities in paying the very high rents charged for premises in principal shopping areas, nor do we want to upset local traders or the Chamber of Commerce.

The Foundation is always delighted to receive assistance and co-operation from commercial companies, local authorities and Government departments which offer us premises for temporary occupation while they await, for example, the grant of planning permission for their own use. These premises can be huge and the turnover very rapid.

More permanent premises for Sue Ryder Shops are also being sought, to bring them closer together and thus create "stepping stones". The Foundation would always be pleased to hear from any reader who can find suitable premises. They must be in an area where there is a steady stream of people passing by, particularly tourists and other visitors. Each Shop also needs a bank of loyal supporters, preferably volunteers, to help man the rota. Those who serve in the existing Sue Ryder Shops all seem to enjoy their hard work and the companionship they find there. Many tell me that they find the work totally absorbing and that it has become part of their life.

The majority of the Foundation's Shops are rented but we try to find as many temporary Shops as possible in prime positions in towns and cities in order to keep overheads to a minimum. Temporary Shops usually become available as a result of a change of ownership, or because they are included with other property in a scheme for renovation or for demolition prior to redevelopment. The life of such a Shop can be very brief (some times as short as a week) though it may last for as long as four years, and the Foundation must undertake to vacate the Shop at very short notice – occasionally only forty-eight hours. Nevertheless, it remains one of the most profitable ways of making money, especially if the Shop is in a particularly favourable commercial position, so the effort involved in preparing and opening the Shop is well worthwhile.

Stock for temporary Shops is supplied initially by their permanent sisters in the same or nearest area, supplemented from stores at Headquarters. Yet, one of the most heartening and amazing consequences is not only the size of these temporary Shops, but also the quality and quantity of the gifts which pour in.

The Foundation owns quite a number of freehold properties, which are bought only after very careful consideration. When a property is leased the terms of the lease are considered by a Researcher, Area Manager and Regional Manager; the draft lease is then submitted for scrutiny to two members of the Foundation's Council.

When a "possible" new Shop is found, accurate costings are carried out and, if the result is favourable, the premises are professionally valued and surveyed and the legal process is completed. As soon as possession is obtained, Area Managers move fast to carry out essential renovation work, do a complete spring clean and then move in counters, rails, a till and all the stock and other paraphernalia ready for the Shop's opening. The Shop is carpeted with material from disused lines provided by different carpet firms. Every effort is made to keep opening costs down to a minimum so that whatever is given by the public goes directly to the work of the Foundation – which is, indeed, its proper purpose.

Parallel to the preparation of the Shop for opening is the effort to find a suitable "Head girl" and volunteers to manage and run the Shop. The Shops operating in Britain are run either by the Foundation or by a Sue Ryder Support Group which gives them more independence, and the rota is organised by one or two "Head girls" or Manageresses who are appointed and paid the minimum wage in accordance with the Retail Trades (non-food) Wages Council's recommendations. They in turn are expected to encourage volunteers to help in the running of the Shop and to keep it open for as many hours as possible. In the past other helpers have been referred to the Shop from the Government Training Schemes and they have benefited from the training and experience they have received. One of them, a young man who had found himself unemployed after graduating from university, now, to his joy, has a job with the Scottish Opera Company.

Clearly, the type of Shop and clientele varies according to the area in which the Shop is situated. For instance, in a stone cottage in Shaftesbury, Dorset, which houses the Shop, the original team of helpers, several of whom had to retire due to ill health, sold textiles, small antiques and books. Shops of this type especially are patronised by people looking for wedding, birthday and other gifts.

One of the Foundation's oldest permanent Shops is at Cheadle. The staunch team there started trading in 1963 in temporary premises and, in the ensuing six years, had to move no less than seven times! The present Shop, acquired in 1969, is in an excellent position and had one of the highest turnovers recorded in a year. Originally there were forty people on the rota and although this Sue Ryder Shop still retained its rota of supporters (though some had to leave either through illness or by moving away), it is now run by Manageresses with a rota of approximately ten volunteers and they sell books and clothing (including evening dresses), bric-a-brac, paintings and household goods). The upper-floor section was similar to a boutique, while on the ground floor customers who cannot afford higher prices have a wide selection of inexpensive goods.

When it is ready to open, the existence of the Shop is advertised as widely as possible by word of mouth, local radio, posters and by any other effective means that presents itself at the time.

The Shops provide clothes, furniture and furnishings, gifts, books, toys and other goods for needy people who cannot afford to buy new goods or for anyone looking for a reasonably priced and attractive or useful gift. Valuable objects are often given and these are valued by auction houses and jewellers who give their services free. Designer clothes are especially sought after by customers. Donors and customers come from all walks of life. The presentation and window dressing are a marvel to see and many Shops win prizes, not only during the annual Sue Ryder Light of Hope Appeal, but also when they are judged by the city or town authorities.

As well as donated clothing and goods, many and varied new goods are now sold in many of the Shops, and these have played an important part in bringing in new customers to the Foundation's Shops. Attractive gift items such as tea towels, china beakers and table mats sell well, as do a fine range of birthday, anniversary and greetings cards which are obtained principally from the Medici Company who have supplied the Foundation with cards for many years. Some of the gift articles are made or designed by residents in the Foundation's Homes. Many of the most beautiful tea towels have been designed by the young women and girls who live in the Foundation's Homes at Konstancin, near Warsaw in Poland.

One of the most profitable ways of ensuring a steady income is the collection and sale of items of furniture – often acquired as a result of people asking the Foundation to come and clear a flat, cottage or house. We are always pleased to do this, making sure the premises are clean and tidy when we leave. Many of the Foundation supporters, on purchasing a new item of furniture, will offer the old unwanted item it replaces to the Foundation. Each Region has a large store in which to keep furniture whilst it is inspected for repair and restoration where necessary. Then it is priced and sent out to the larger shops that sell furniture and all manner of household goods. The Foundation also has furniture showrooms with areas arranged and furnished as bedrooms, dining rooms, sitting rooms, and so on. There is furniture of every quality and price; the cheaper items are especially useful for families or single people who have found or been given their own home after spending time in a hostel or bed and breakfast accommodation, and who are on a very restricted budget. There is a great demand for the excellent furniture in our shops, and the van, together with driver and mate, which is attached to each Region, is kept busy from dawn until dusk every day of the week.

From March 1988, second-hand upholstered furniture, and nursery goods cannot be sold unless the latest flammability requirements are met.

Second-hand furniture covers the following items: Any domestic upholstered furniture, seating, beds, sofa-beds, headboards, mattresses and children's items such as carry cots, prams and pushchairs containing upholstery. Also included are foam pillows, cushions and garden furniture containing upholstery. The Regulation does *not* apply to: sleeping bags, bedclothes, curtains and carpets. Any of the above items made before 1950 with horsehair are exempt from the new regulations, even if they have been re-upholstered since that date.

The new regulations apply to all persons who supply furniture and furnishings including those who sell second-hand furniture in the course of trading. Any trader who supplies furniture which does not meet the new flammability requirements risks prosecution, a fine of up to £5,000 and/or imprisonment of up to six months.

It has been made perfectly clear that Trading Standards would not be sympathetic when it came to charities dealing in second-hand furniture.

(Furniture not meeting the new fire regulations can be disposed of privately as this does not constitute trading.)

Supporters of the Foundation who donate furniture are very upset when we explain that we can no longer accept upholstered furniture from them.

Furniture manufactured after 1988 should bear a label stating this item meets with the regulations laid down by the EC.

Furniture sales have dropped by approximately fifty per cent since March 1990, as items such as three-piece suites and easy chairs were our biggest sellers and there was a constant demand for these. Both the Foundation and those in need are the victims. Although we feel very strongly about this legislation, it is essential, and the Foundation naturally had to agree.

I like to think that the Shops which bear my name fulfil several different purposes. The following letter, amongst many, gives me encouragement. It refers to one of the Foundation's Shops:

> I hope you will forgive my taking up your valuable time in writing to let you know how distressed I was to learn over the weekend of the imminent closure (26 May) of your local shop.
>
> The shop has made an invaluable contribution to one-parent families, pensioners, the unemployed and others on low incomes. In addition, it has become something of a social centre, where local people meet and chat. Its closure will be a real deprivation to them all.
>
> I would like to speak on behalf of all visitors to the shop and say that we will all greatly miss the two friendly and hard working ladies who over the eight years made the shop what it is – a boon to all.

I became convinced that the Foundation should also find suitable premises and run coffee shops with homemade bread, scones, cakes, and so on and thus fill a gap in towns and even some villages where few facilities exist for the visitors, tourists and local people who want to sit in pleasant surroundings and be able to enjoy meals at reasonable prices. I do so hope that more of these Sue Ryder coffee rooms may become a reality throughout the country, not only to serve the public but to make the Foundation's work better known.

The coffee room at Haworth, sadly now closed, began on a damp day one February when my colleague and I visited the Village. We spent the day combing Haworth from end to end, our hopes of finding a property there gradually decreasing as we got colder and wetter. We asked everyone – Villagers in the pub, local shopkeepers, passers-by. They all did their best to be helpful, but could tell us only what we already knew – that the price of property was exorbitant, and there were few to be found anyway. Then we remembered the sign we has seen as we entered the Village that morning: "Mr Brown – Tailor". Tired, cold and without much hope, we knocked on his door.

He seemed surprised to see us but invited us in. It was, in fact, we who were to be surprised. Mr Brown (he told us thoughtfully) was considering moving out. He had plans for a bungalow and was simply waiting for planning approval. From then on, we were able to hope that the Foundation at last could have its wished-for gift shop and coffee rooms in Haworth.

And it happened, but not without blood, sweat, tears and a great deal of hard work. The bakery downstairs had not been used for the last forty years, and the cutting rooms upstairs had to be completely renovated. The Foundation had virtually a demolition job on its hands; daunting work, but we had willing helpers from both the locality and further afield. One day, while we were fetching endless buckets of water, we heard that the front room was formerly used for funeral parties. We hoped that our own activities there would be rather less mournful and would give great pleasure and happiness to anyone who would come!

Eventually it proved possible, after considerable restoration and renovation, to convert the cottage and shop premises into what was affectionately called "Upstairs, Downstairs" – the coffee shop being upstairs and the gift shop (which is still open) below. None of this would have been possible without the staunch and devoted assistance of generous supporters led by Mr and Mrs Gordon Vestey, Miss Sheila Pawson and Mr J.F. Wood, the Honorary Treasurer. Different organisations and helpers gave service in the coffee shop. To their pride and delight, and to reward them for some of their hard work, the following appeared in Egon Ronay's *The Good Food Guide*:

> All profits made here go to the Sue Ryder Homes – so eat on! The task is not a hard one, for the Manageress is a clever cook and her eclairs, meringues and highly professional gateaux are particularly hard to resist. And, in addition to toasted snacks and sandwiches, she often turns out a daily special which could be anything from quiche and salad to apricot flan.

The Foundation's Shops and coffee rooms continue to be a meeting place for people of all ages and from all backgrounds. There is a spirit of friendliness there where everyone calling in is made welcome. They also provide a place for those who are lonely or who have problems and who want to talk to someone about them. Quite a number of people are visited in their own homes or referred to new friends.

One customer who had a drink problem came to buy clothes with the help of the volunteers and he found that they also gave him moral support.

A worried girl, who had left home because she felt unhappy and unable to cope, travelled from London and wandered into one of the Foundation's Shops in Scotland where she spent time talking to the Manageress. The girl had refused other counselling.

The Sue Ryder Shops are an example of the importance of giving personal service to others, of bringing together people of all ages and from all walks of life, and of promoting good will and strengthening the community spirit. The Foundation is most proud of this unofficial but useful form of social work carried out by the Shops, and hopes that it will be continued and extended in the future, in addition to the other, more conventional, forms of activity.

There are Sue Ryder coffee rooms at Walsingham, Cavendish, Leckhampton, Staunton Harold, Peterborough, Ely, Cuerdon, Keighley, Ipswich, and Marchmont, and we hope that in time there will be very many more, according to whatever or whatever is wanted by the community and helps the Foundation's work.

There is no doubt that these coffee shops have, in a small way, helped to spread the knowledge of the Foundation's work and it is an aspect of the total fund-raising effort which should be developed. Hopefully, both the coffee and the food served give pleasure to the public and the few moments which they spend in the coffee shop may allow them the opportunity of grasping something of the Foundation's aims and objects.

I try to visit each Area with the Foundation's local Manager every two to three years, as well as the Support Groups, and the Shops which are run independently by their local teams. If it can be arranged, a visit to a Shop will be followed by a meeting of the Support Group, to which the public are invited and during which the work of the Foundation in general and of the Shop in particular is discussed.

Each Shop has its own history, its own collection of stories, both funny and moving, and its own personalities among the customers – such as the men who come in to exchange their own worn-out shoes for a better pair without paying anything; and even, on occasion, to exchange their socks as well! There are other incidents one could mention, too, like that of the enthusiastic Manageress who disposed of her husband's best suit just back from the dry-cleaners for a few pounds. There is a system of date-coding items of clothing so that no one article remains on the rail of the Shop for more than a month. If it is then unsold it is removed to another Foundation Shop.

I do not think it would be possible to do justice in words to the amount of effort, time and devotion which has been given regularly and willingly by literally thousands of people all over the country, and which earns my deepest gratitude. Usually they come from ordinary homes: housewives – young, elderly and middle-aged – who themselves have families to care for, young people and schoolchildren. At the Shops they have scrubbed floors, cleaned, cleared, sorted, priced and served, having walked from their homes or travelled there on buses, sometimes changing several times to reach their destination, in all weathers throughout the year, year in, year out.

Where there have been husbands or other men in the background, they have normally been most willing to lend a hand. We find that men don't always enjoy serving as shop assistants, but they continue to play their vital part, and often take on the duties of Honorary Solicitor, Surveyers, Treasurer, Store Keepers or Regional Manager. Occasionally, there are surveyors who not only inspect potential new premises for the Foundation but also give up their valuable time as researchers for such premises. In several regions men work full-time to cope with repairs, renovations, maintenance and train the young unemployed too.

Since the first Sue Ryder Shop was opened in the late 1950s much has happened and changed. The Shops are now fitted out to a higher standard with better lighting and the goods are displayed professionally. There are now (in 1997) more than 570 Sue Ryder Shops in Britain. To achieve this number and geographical spread involves a lot more than perhaps even we ourselves originally envisaged. We are involved with numerous solicitors, estate agents, electricians, plumbers, handymen, and so on, many of whom generously help the Foundation by charging minimum rates for their services. To keep this number of Shops operating and successful involves other Foundation staff with legal, accounting and secretarial responsibilities, which inevitably increase.

In addition to the Shops in Britain, there are two in Belgium, one in Prague, one in Perth, Western Australia, fourteen in the Republic of Ireland, and Boutiques are opening in other countries, including Kotor and Hercog Novi in the former Yugoslavia. In Britain, during the course of the past thirty-six years, several thousand different premises have been used by the Foundation and thousands of volunteers have worked in those Shops.

I do hope that people think they are a pleasure to enter, to browse around and to buy in. The Foundation's Shops have always striven to be "upmarket" and great care is taken to ensure that in doing so our aim is to serve and to involve the community in a caring and friendly manner.

I tried to sum up our feelings about the Shops in the course of a talk I gave in 1964 in an area where the Foundation's Shop had to move to different premises no fewer than four times.

> "Being back here with you," I said, "one feels at home. We think of those who are not with us because of illness or because they have moved away from the area. In our thoughts, also, are our friends the customers, among them the old, the lonely, the sick, the young students, the pensioners, the man who uses us as his library, occasionally a young and frightened unmarried mum, or an unwanted child who looks for a toy, handmade by one of you. We think, too, of those who have worked with us but who have gone now to a brighter and happier world.
>
> "On behalf of those for whom we work – the handicapped and the sick, wherever they are, whether in this country or further afield – we would like to thank you, your husbands and friends, and many others who lift and repair and collect, and to tell you how much we depend on the service which each of you is giving and has given for many years. Although you may not meet more than a few of our patients, they know that you have them in your prayers and thoughts and in your daily actions, and I hope that God will bless each of you in your lives and in whatever you do, and that our good will will increase and bring greater service to a wider area."

20

Hickleton Hall, Yorkshire

"I Like My Choice."

FOR EIGHT YEARS THE Foundation's Home in Suffolk had cared for the handicapped, including patients from hospitals, but there were long waiting lists. Many required care, attention and affection in a Home with something close to a real family atmosphere, in addition to their need for qualified nursing staff adequately supported by other workers, including voluntary helpers. During this time the searches continued for suitable large period properties.

It was in these circumstances that in 1961 Hickleton Hall in Yorkshire was acquired.

Hickleton Hall belonged to the Woods of Hickleton and was for many years the home of the family's best-known sons, the first three Viscounts Halifax, whose motto is "I like my choice". The second Viscount (1838–1934) was for many years the foremost layman in the Anglican Church. He worked so eagerly for a close rapport with the Vatican that in many minds, friendly and hostile, Hickleton became almost synonymous with the reunion movement. It was there (as well as in the Belgian town of Malines) that senior representatives of the two Churches used to meet for discussions, sowing seeds of ecumenism which have borne fruit in our own day. Hickleton Village Church – dedicated to St Wilfrid, part Norman, part Perpendicular, and close to the Hall – was filled by the Wood family with emblems of their ecumenical interests. For years on every Thursday a candle has been lit for unity.

I first saw Hickleton Hall in November 1960 when it was threatened with demolition. It was shrouded in Yorkshire mist and half hidden by the heavy sodden branches of very beautiful trees. Accompanied by Mr D. Mutch, Lord Halifax's helpful agent, my mother and I toured the house by torchlight. We went up and down the three staircases serving the building. The very long corridor (which we nicknamed the A1) and the rusting commercial-size cooker and flagstone floor we found in the kitchen reminded me of my childhood, and the scrubbing of stone floors and cleaning of old black cast-iron ovens. Immediately I could see possibilities for the house.

The house had to be ready in six weeks to receive its first patients. I was accompanied in turn by Secretaries and Assistants from Headquarters. We lived in the two rooms in the stable block. A voluntary Secretary from

Wombwell sat at a portable typewriter sending out letters of thanks to supporters and new friends in the area. Almost every day and night messages came in, and once the telephone had been reinstalled it never ceased to ring. Volunteers had to man it and write down all messages and beg the donors to find ways of bringing their gifts there themselves.

Word went round the neighbouring villages and towns that help was needed at Hickleton Hall, and within days the rooms were filled with well over 100 people offering their services, a few of them even accompanied by their young children, who provided added distractions! The trickle became a stream and the stream became a torrent. All exterior doors wherever possible had to be locked, and a bar of wood fixed across them so that all volunteers would enter by the *main* door for registering their name and address and any trade or profession. And so they arrived, some on their own, others with friends or in a group or as representatives of organisations or schools.

We worked (as usual) from the top of the house down, and concentrated upon the repair work to window frames and the actual renovation itself. Several enthusiasts on arrival simply said "I've come to paint, luv. No, I don't need telling how to fill in and prepare – it's painting, luv, that this room needs, nowt else, to make it look right." We were taxed to the full to insist as politely and as firmly as possible that all the renovation and preparatory work must be carried out first and therefore no paint would be issued – but the strong-willed individuals and groups would then produce their own paint!

To control such large numbers was no easy task, neither was it easy to keep them from wandering about and taking over a room on the ground or other floors. The noise and excitement did not help us think clearly, but their joy and enthusiasm for saving the house and preparing the rooms for the homeless and the sick were infectious. Time went by very quickly, and within hours gifts of food started to arrive.

A good many of the volunteers stated that they could decorate, but many were inexperienced. The repair and restoration (including plastering) and decorations had to be done to a high standard and for the long term, so much tact was needed to explain to unqualified but enthusiastic helpers that the colour scheme for each room, which was typed out and pinned up to the wall (with a copy kept in the office) must be adhered to, and that paintbrushes must always be cleaned after use and then left to stand in turpentine. In many of the sixty rooms plastering and painting proceeded to the accompaniment of transistor radios blaring out at top volume. Men and women with suitable trades were allocated to form a group and take on certain rooms with a "D-Day" given for each. Hadfields, a paint firm in Surrey, supplied the paint at well below trade price, and other firms were equally generous.

There was no hot water in the Hall and the boiler was out of action – as were many of the loos. Throughout the house, water had to be heated in kettles, but in the stable block there was a small water heater, and cooking was done on a primus stove. The only furniture in the house – a table – stood in the middle of the large library, but offers of furniture came from far and wide, much of it in very good condition, and including some antiques as well as thirty harmoniums and seventy-five double beds! At no other of the Foundation's Homes has so much good furniture or so many gifts been received.

Dr Ken Jackson was the first Chairman of this Home's Committee. Both he and his wife, Joan, together with Mr Tom Siddall, the Honorary Treasurer, were to give many years of long and devoted service: they appeared unexpectedly one day in the temporary office in the stable block and offered their assistance. Dr Jackson described it as a Home which might never have started "without the unshakeable faith of those concerned". Then a local supporter came to talk to me, presenting the first donation of £5, and asked what the priorities were. When I answered "a builder", she returned within an hour with a local decorator, Pip Reast, from Doncaster, who greatly to his astonishment found himself estimating the vast quantities of paint required for the whole house. For the next six weeks he was there virtually every evening and all weekends helping to co-ordinate and supervise the large army of enthusiastic volunteers.

Just as in Poland where the rebuilding of churches and cathedrals was considered to be a priority, so here at Hickleton I felt that the chapel should be restored as soon as possible. Tom Siddall looked a little surprised when he was asked to buy on credit a deep red carpet and underfelt to cover its bare concrete floor, but he ordered it nevertheless. Two men from the Pontefract Undertakers Co-operative came forward to renovate the panelling and decorate the very high walls. The cross and candlesticks for the altar I found at a bargain price; by coincidence, they had been used in a film about a Japanese prisoner-of-war camp. Near the door of the chapel a text was discovered: "In the beginning was the Word and the Word was with God and the Word was God. All things were made by Him." The beautiful wooden carvings, which include the Crucifix hanging over the altar, a statue of Our Lady, the Sacred Heart and the Stations of the Cross, were later all carved by a resident, the late Mr Dambrowski.

The kindness and willingness of the local people were overwhelming, perhaps encouraged by the knowledge that I had been born in the county. Some offered lorries to bring the furniture to the house, while miners from Thurnscoe, Goldthorpe, and other collieries, came straight off their shifts to work at Hickleton. There was a great sense of unity and friendship, and many sang as they worked. The perpetual coal dust reminded me of my childhood in Yorkshire, and memories of Scarcroft and of other places in the West Riding came flooding back.

The drawing room and study were converted into bedrooms while the dining room was renovated and decorated by ICI and other rooms by the British Ropes Company. The lovely cornices and moulded ceilings were decorated in white and the walls were painted in Wedgwood blue. After one group had completed their renovation and decoration work, they heard that some Woods family portraits were going to be hung and they said, "Ye can't do that here now – this house is public!"

The small House Committee was originally formed to work closely with staff and volunteers: indeed, it was never necessary for the word "management" to be used, for members took part in the day-to-day running of the Home by giving service voluntarily and by sharing problems with the staff and the residents. The House Committee is responsible to the Council of the Foundation through the Homes Executive Committee.

Mrs Anna Stevens, a qualified nurse by profession and wife of a local consultant in general medicine and diseases of the chest, Dr John Stevens, MD, FRCP, had been Chairman of the House Committee since 1976, though her involvement with Hickleton began in 1962. She gave a great deal of her time to the daily running of the Home and has experienced its many joys and heartaches. Both Mrs Stevens and Mrs Ellen Bungard who succeeded her, have always appreciated the concept of the Foundation's work and seen Hickleton as part of the whole rather than as a separate entity. Ellen continues to come in every day and gives her life to the Foundation.

The Home has the largest number of residents (originally sixty-six but now registered for fifty-three), in any of the Foundation's Homes in Britain at present, and the strength of their characters has helped create the atmosphere of this Home. Many of the original residents who were admitted have died, but the humour, spiritual qualities and stubborn refusal of those living there now to accept defeat have remained.

The Foundation was also fortunate in having received the personal service of Dr John Lavric who, over twenty-three years, called each week, and sometimes more often, despite his extremely busy practice – at one time he had 3,000 patients of his own to care for. Both he and his wife and many of the original friends and helpers still give their support to both residents and fund-raising events.

Molly Trim, the Housemother, called it a community: "We set out to live a shared life," she said, "and with some it was to be a very deep sharing indeed." A New Zealander and formerly a novice in a religious order, she has served the Foundation since April 1962. Talking of the patients, she said she could never fully realise their suffering. "I aimed at giving them warmth and good food and at getting to know them. It was sometimes a humbling encounter. They always know you better than you know them, because they realise how life works. They have seen life in the raw, experienced terrible anguish. They also know what makes people react and tick."

Molly had already learned about community living from missionary work among the Maori. "They understand the individual," she says of them. "They had an outgoing joyfulness and ease. Some had time for everything. If they wanted to learn from someone, they shared his life with him, talking to him and gradually getting to know him. It was an exchange of personalities, an exchange of the essence that lies at the heart of people. The individuals here, like the Maori, couldn't be bothered with superficial relationships."

But, as with people in all situations in life, they were very different in temperament: while some showed great patience and tolerance, others were far from saintly. Some had lived close to death in hospitals, and the experience had not enriched them. Some were embittered, some distorted, some broken down. For many, independence was not a goal but a threat to be avoided at all costs. Each and every one of the individuals, the physically handicapped as well as those with psychiatric disturbances receive – at least in part – the affection and care they deserve and which we aim to give.

One resident wrote these telling words:

IF I COULD – I WOULD

If I could get up and walk away from
here – I would.

If I could bath myself, wash myself,
clean my teeth, wash my hair – I would.

If I could take myself to the toilet and sit
there in privacy – I would.

I don't like the indignity of someone having
to help me achieve such a natural function
but I can't do it alone.

If I could just reach out and get that cup
of tea and drink it myself I would – but I can't.

If I could go home and become part of my family again
and be normal, I would be happy – but I can't.

I rely on you to do all of these things for me but I
can't always stay cheerful because of this.

If I could – I would

Molly herself moved to Headquarters in December 1983 and continues to contribute to the Foundation, but in a less exacting task.

The late Sister Elizabeth Geraghty was in charge of the nursing. She had trained in Dublin and worked at Hickleton for eight years. I remember her so clearly as she sat in a chair in the office wearing an emerald green cardigan the day she came for her interview. Her energy throughout the years she worked for the Foundation, mainly for pocket money, never ceased to amaze me, and I can still see her going from room to room attending to the individual needs of the residents. Her nursing qualities and her energy will never be forgotten. One of the residents was a carrier of typhoid and Sister Elizabeth became a victim of this disease but made a slow recovery. Sadly, later, she became a victim of multiple sclerosis and was forced to retire to the country of her origin, Ireland.

Originally, a local cook, Mrs Sally Dawe, came in to prepare lunch every day. She stayed for more than eight years. Gladys, Emily and Annie worked as domestics until they too retired in their sixties. When they arrived in the morning it was customary to hear their cheerful voices asking: "Had a good night?", "What's new? Now then, tell us all about it." Elsie Wall is a member of the House Committee, and has given many years of service. Their work is complemented by volunteers from Britain and abroad, particularly during the summer holidays, who apply their youthful enthusiasm to caring for the residents with a special devotion.

The resident staff are supported by a large number of local staff who live in the neighbourhood. The unaffected cheerfulness of these helpers and volunteers and the contact they provide with the surrounding towns and villages are a vital element in making the patients feel part of the local community. At different times of the year concerts are held in this Home, as well as other events and several residents take part in making pilgrimages to Lourdes. Many of the residents here would enjoy a holiday home by the sea or sited on the edge of water, which is so therapeutic; but, alas, up to now, despite wide searches, no such property has been found. Meanwhile, a few go to holiday flats each year, but they still long for a Foundation's Holiday Home, away from their environment.

In each room I enter when I visit there is usually news. People tell me their hopes and fears; I hear about their diet, their illness, their concern at being incontinent, and memories of their homes.

Among the many patients whom I remember was Henryka who used to lie on a spinal carriage. As a child, with her family and all the inhabitants of her village, she had been arrested by the Soviets during the early hours of a day in September 1939. They were loaded onto open cattle-trucks and after many days and nights reached Siberia. Due to the unspeakable conditions in the camp, both parents died within six months of each other and Henryka's baby sister was given to a Russian family. One sister remained with Henryka, but all the other children of her family were separated and sent to Soviet orphanages.

Henryka was starving and became extremely ill. By a miracle she and her sister were found by members of General Anders's Army and survived the long journey – several thousand miles – to Persia.

She had Potts' disease (tuberculosis of the spine) and was crippled with rheumatoid arthritis, but in the privacy of her room at the Sue Ryder Home she did lovely embroidery. Henryka also made dresses and curtains for the staff, and dolls for their children. She had a very strong character and an unshakeable faith. Her humour and her interest in all whom she met will never be forgotten. Though Henryka longed for a normal life and to live independently, she came to accept, in her words, that God was asking her to offer up her suffering for the world. Cancer was diagnosed and she died bravely after visiting Lourdes in April 1983. At her Requiem Mass the priest said in his address that "we are all here because our lives have been touched by Henryka".

A local sportsman re-visiting after a long absence asked after Henryka, and now wants to do a sponsored twenty-six mile walk and name it "Henryka's Marathon".

Arthur Bennet, who was in his late fifties, was a traveller of the road. One bleak and cold day in January 1977, Robert Clifton and Molly were travelling back to Hickleton. There was snow on the ground and they noticed Arthur walking with difficulty (he disclosed later that he was suffering from a disability and sore toes and that his boots were falling apart). They asked him if he would like a lift; at first he refused, but after talking to him for some time he agreed to come with them without accepting any conditions. Naturally, being a traveller of many roads, Arthur often wanted to leave and, indeed, he would come and go as he pleased until he decided to stay permanently. After some months his sister was traced and she visited him. Arthur died at Hickleton on the 26 November 1987.

Another of the patients we have been privileged to nurse was Dr James Howat. "Dr Jim", as he was known, graduated from Cambridge University in 1952 and worked in St Mary's Hospital, Paddington, London, as a senior houseman and registrar on the medical wards. Later, he became a general practitioner in Lancashire and enjoyed his work. In 1964 he was diagnosed as having multiple sclerosis. He carried on working and looking after his patients until 1974 when he had to give it up because of increasing weakness and spasticity in his legs. His wife was able to look after him at home until 1983, when he came to live at the Sue Ryder Home, Hickleton. Dr Jim was completely dependent on the nursing staff to do everything for him, but he remained pleasant and cheerful. He had a very supportive family who visited regularly and also took him out whenever they could. His interests were very wide and included rugby, salmon fishing and classical music, and he was able to listen to his music until he died in the afternoon of 10 July 1984. His family were with him.

In 1976, after this Home had been opened for sixteen years, the opportunity arose to carry out urgently needed repairs and renovations under the supervision of the Foundation's senior Honorary Architects. A lot of the work was carried out by tradesmen under the Job Creation Programme.

I should like to take this opportunity of expressing my appreciation to the Historic Buildings Council for the grants which they have made towards completing the re-roofing of the whole of this large building and, more recently, to the essential repairs of the stonework.

At the beginning, the garden was overgrown and looked like a wilderness. The grass on the lawns was waist high. Over the years part- and full-time gardeners had tried to tackle some of its sixteen acres. In the autumn of 1982 a professional gardener, Des Wiltshire, applied to the Foundation's

Headquarters for full-time employment. He was taken on the staff at Hickleton and since then he has largely restored it into the beautiful historical Grade 2-listed garden it is today. Under his guidance and instruction boys and men doing community work through the probation service, worked in the garden. After retiring, Des was succeeded by Gordon Creaser and ably assisted by John Matthews, they all work closely with Mr J. Drake, a very experienced horticulturist. The gardens are open to the public and give joy, both to the residents and to many people from the district beyond, with its fine terraces, herbaceous borders and in the spring an abundance of particularly breathtaking snowdrops . . .

> I like to think, that, long ago,
> There fell to earth. Some flakes of snow
> Which loved this cold gray world of ours
> So much, they stayed. As snowdrop flowers.

* * *

The majority of the residents who live here are given financial aid by the local authorities, while others pay what they can afford. Nevertheless running costs and maintenance, service costs and continuous up-grading mean that fund-raising must go on *all* the time.

As is generally known, there are always great gaps in the services for the handicapped and for those who, for a variety of reasons, cannot care for themselves. Whilst "Care in the Community" has not worked as intended and frankly leaves a lot to be desired, a Domiciliary Care Unit was set up in 1995, and is led by Lynn Arrowsmith RGN, and covers the areas of Dearne and Wombwell. At present, 130 people are cared for by this team of thirty-five staff.

In addition to the nursing and the personal care given, some tasks carried out are of a more domestic nature, including shopping, firelighting and cooking meals. The carers undertake a one-day induction course, and training is now being offered in the form of NCQ Level II and the Hickleton Hall Care Service Certificate of Competence.

Very positive feedback has been received from both Goldthorpe and Wombwell Social Services stating that Hickleton Hall provides the best, most reliable quality service in the area. It has been recommended that the number of staff in the domiciliary team should be increased to provide services for people who are, at the moment, receiving care from their local Social Services. This is most encouraging news, and it is comforting to know that news of the service provided by the Sue Ryder Foundation is now spreading even further into other areas.

The Day-Care Centre has been going for a similar length of time, and attracts people from within a radius of twenty miles. The Centre is registered for ten people at any one time.

Since the beginning the Sue Ryder Home at Hickleton has sought to provide care and nursing for those who otherwise are unloved and at the edge of society. In the future we hope the day care and domiciliary service can be enlarged for the benefit of the local community. It is also hoped to provide more respite care and holiday accommodation. The aim is always to make the maximum use of the facilities we have available.

Even if the State were in a position to do much more than is the case at present, there would always be a need for voluntary initiative to complement the official services. There are, at the moment, many thousands of children and adults in Britain in need of care and, when possible, rehabilitation; and for an organisation to be effective it must establish priorities. The Foundation sees as its main task in Britain the care of the handicapped, especially patients with cancer, Motor Neurone and Huntington's Disease, and the homeless.

Grade I or Grade II properties with maximum floor areas are especially required in London, Birmingham, Manchester, and in Kent; also a holiday home/hotel by the sea or a river or perhaps in the Lake District – this remains a dream.

In any Region a Regional Appeal Team must be set up *after* the priorities are confirmed by the Social Services and Area Health Authorities. Funding from the Foundation's Headquarters is impossible, due to our great commitments elsewhere.

Birchley Hall, Lancashire

Dust as we are, the immortal spirit grows
Like harmony in music; there is a dark
Inscrutable workmanship that reconciles
Discordant elements, makes them cling together
In one society.

Wordsworth

IN LATE AUGUST 1975, a supporter and his Dutch-born wife, Mr and Mrs Woods, who lived near Wigan, awoke one morning to find *Remembrance* delivered through their letter box, and they read about developments in the North. They had been searching unsuccessfully for many years for suitable occupants to live in their house. They had a family of eight children and could not afford to keep up the place. An article in the Foundation's annual magazine made them feel that their historic house could also become a Sue Ryder Home. Their initial letter was accompanied by excellent colour photographs of the property which had all been taken on a sunny day; in the event, however, it proved to be in a poor state of repair, and except for the front garden the grounds were very overgrown. We all agreed that the house would have to be virtually rebuilt before it would be suitable for the Foundation's purposes.

Once the conveyance of the property had been completed, the Woods made arrangements to move out into their new home, which was being built beyond the boundary of the grounds. During the reconstruction of the old building they were always most hospitable and, like others in the Village, brought us over baked potatoes and warm food when this was most needed. From the moment I entered Birchley Hall, as it was known, I felt that it had great potential and that God had guided us to go there.

The fascinating history of this old house was later written up by the former owner in one of the Foundation's brochures, as follows:

> The early history of Birchley Hall is obscure, but there is documentary evidence of its existence as far back as 1202. For most of the fourteenth, fifteenth and sixteenth centuries it was in the possession of the Heton family, and some time between 1500 and 1545 one William Heton reconstructed it in the timbered style of Chester.
>
> In 1553, Birchley was sold by the Heton family to settle a debt, and the property passed to James Anderton in 1558, who rebuilt the present Hall on the site of the earlier Tudor building. The initials above the original

front door, which can be seen today with the date 1594, are those of James Anderton's brother, Thurston.

The Hall was built during a period when the Roman Catholic religion was being suppressed in England, and Catholic rites could only be practised in secret. James Anderton was himself a Catholic, and it was to serve the many Catholics in the district that he built a secret chapel at Birchley in 1618. To disguise its true purpose, the chapel was built in the form of a granary added to the original building.

This chapel still exists, and incorporates several features characteristic of the type of secret structure, including a trap door which was formerly hidden and gave access to a hiding place under the floor. (This is now bricked up.) Another hiding place within the Hall itself was discovered early in the present century, and there is a strong tradition of a secret passage leading to the nearby wood or farm buildings. Further recesses were discovered during the Hall's conversion to a Sue Ryder Home.

Because of the existence of the chapel and the presbytery in the lower part of the building, Birchley became an important mission from which Catholic priests, trained on the Continent, ministered to the local Catholics. Between 1615 and 1621, an illegal printing press was established there by Roger Anderton (a brother of James) and published some sixteen works of a religious nature. (In 1951, the then owners of Birchley Hall revived the Birchley Hall Press by publishing a number of books as a memorial to the work done in penal times.) In 1640, Birchley was sequestered for a short time because of the Royalist sympathies of the owner, James Anderton, a nephew of the first James.

As the penal laws were gradually relaxed, the chapel at Birchley was decorated, a fixed altar installed and outside steps constructed to give more convenient access. The chapel continued in use until 1928, when the Church of St Mary's, Birchley, was built and took over the function of the chapel. The Hall itself became the Dower House, and later an ordinary farmhouse. Part of it continued to provide accommodation for the local priest until the present presbytery was constructed in 1872.

During the centuries of its existence, the structure of the Hall was never altered, except for a few very minor modifications. The twentieth century saw much incidental restoration, such as the opening of windows which had been blocked, and the pointing of the exterior stonework. This work was carried out by the Middlehurst and Woods families, who owned the Hall successively. In 1968, the Woods children and students from the Upholland Seminary decorated the chapel and erected a new altar.

Arthur J. Hawkes gives the following additional information about the old house:

Birchley is reputed to be the oldest Catholic Mission in Lancashire. I have it on the authority of a local gentleman holding an official position, that about twelve years ago he accompanied an educational rambling party to Birchley, and on the floor of the present Church was a large heap of old books which, the party were informed, had a few days previously been discovered, in the course of some repairs, in the space below the old chapel floor. My informant had a clear memory, for on the top of the pile was a large and ancient edition of Ptolemy's *Geography* which he examined with great interest. What the other books were he has no recollection beyond the suggestion they were of great interest and value. Careful inquiries, however, have failed to elicit any information as to this find, though Dom F.O. Blundell, O.S.B., records that "some years ago a chalice of pewter and vestments were found in the priest's hiding place", the date of the chalice being probably early seventeenth century.

After the Foundation had acquired Birchley Hall, I received a charming letter from the former owner:

> I would like to recall that I decided to write to you after having read a copy of *Remembrance*. The list of Patrons and Trustees at the front showed me the ecumenical character of the Foundation, and perhaps most importantly, there was a description of your Mother who had recently died and who, among many great qualities, seemed to have embodied so much of the best in the Anglican tradition of Christian living.
>
> It was then that I began to hope and pray that Birchley, which had hidden and sheltered the persecuted Catholics of penal times and helped to keep alive their Faith, should now become a project and a place which, by bringing people together in caring for the suffering and those in need, would become a place of Christian reconciliation; a place wherein to "restore all things in Christ".
>
> So, God willing, the Sue Ryder Home, Birchley Hall, will give a meaning, a reason and a fulfilment to our life at Birchley.

During the first weeks before the conversion work started on the house, meetings were organised in the vicinity each evening. One meeting hall, I remember, proved hard to find despite detailed instructions, and in the pouring rain my colleagues and I, laden with cartons of Christmas cards and other gifts for sale, were inadvertently misled by passers-by who directed us up several flights of stairs to a room where judo lessons were in full swing. Those taking part in the lessons – all attired in cream judo suits – were concentrating so hard on what they were doing that we could not get a sensible answer to our question as to whether our meeting was taking place there or not. We continued our search, but soon began to feel that we should never find the right place. Eventually, however, we did so.

The hall in question had hardly changed since it was built in the late Victorian era. It had high windows, which refused to open, and retained a strong smell of many decades of children's meals. Garish colours in gloss paint were subdued in the dim light. Crude torn props and other relics of past pantomimes were evident on the platform.

A small, brave company assembled, despite the weather. When I had finished giving my talk, the Mayor (who had Chaired the meeting), gave £10 and passed the cap round. One very tall individual, with equally large shoes, solemnly announced that this town was different from others and no Foundation Shop could succeed there. "I have cleaned windows here and nobody had the right reaction," he said; but we were not put off. Later, a Foundation Shop did a brisk trade there and received excellent support. At about the same time, and from then on, a chain of Sue Ryder Shops started in the surrounding area, following the example of the one established in St Helens years before by a stalwart supporter, Mrs Heaton, and her team. They had moved fives times from cold and inconvenient premises and had not been disheartened.

At one of the public meetings to launch the Birchley Hall Appeal two men got up to speak. One said he represented my husband's Foundation and that my own Foundation was poaching in the area! I reminded him that the two Foundations should compliment each other and that I was happily married and was certainly not poaching!

The second man, a peer, said he had a "manifesto" prepared in the House of Lords which he wished to read. He walked up to the platform. Owing to his family's long association with the area it was clear that the audience expected his support, but to their astonishment he declared that no new appeal for works of charity could, or would, be acceptable in the locality. "Where are you going to get the money from?" he added. As he returned to his seat there were murmurs if indignation and a low buzz of discussion. The reaction of the audience was one of interest and incredulity. I looked at the row of people sharing the platform with me, but nobody volunteered to respond. (Later I learnt that several were in his employ and were embarrassed by his attitude.)

Trying to collect my thoughts and find the right words, I spoke about my experiences in working among the poorest of the poor and how *they* would share their last crust of bread or grain of rice, or take the shirt off their backs to help others. Moreover, the whole Foundation dedicated its work to God, and therefore endeavours of this kind were acts of faith. At this point there were cheers and a loud banging of umbrellas on the floor from Sisters representing various religious orders. The sound of this welcome support echoed about the large hall with its bad acoustics, while heavy rain beat down on the glass dome.

Instead of being able to launch an Appeal we had to be content with selling fifty-seven copies of my first autobiography *And the Morrow is Theirs*, which I autographed; but it became very clear indeed that what I had tried very humbly to say – that human beings could not be confused with money – had registered on the minds of the audience.

In St Mary's Hall in the Village of Billinge itself there followed a further public meeting, which was opened by prayers read by clergy of different denominations. Father Ashton, the Catholic priest, was Chairman.

It was at the end of this meeting, when helpers were taking up the cards and the gifts which had been laid out on tables, and humping the cartons into our vehicles, that a man wearing a red pullover and carrying a rolled umbrella approached me. He told me that the Foundation might be eligible to benefit from a Job Creation Programme (JCP) introduced that week by the Government to try to relieve the high unemployment rate. He added, however, that I would have to complete certain forms and give full details of the proposed work by the next day. All this was because the information had to be in his hands in Liverpool by Friday of the same week to go immediately before an Action Committee in London. The scheme apparently allowed organisations like ours to claim the full labour costs involved in projects such as the one we were embarked on. This conversation took place well past 11 p.m. and, although I was very tired, I remember feeling both thankful and more than a little surprised. After saying my prayers, I climbed wearily into bed to write up a list of twenty-six tradesmen and labourers who were to work in stages at this historic house.

Before we had ever heard anything about the JCP the senior Honorary Architect, Mr Stanley Bradley, on a previous visit, had stood at the top of the path and said to us, "What you really want here is £100,000," and I replied, "Well, we haven't got it, we've probably got about £5."

I woke early the next morning, and before walking over to Mass in the Village I wondered if the information about JCP scheme had been nothing but a wishful dream. But the evidence that it was true lay on the piece of paper by the bed. By 9.30 a.m. our newfound colleague, whom we nicknamed "The Umbrella Man", had kept his word and sent forms in duplicate for us to complete. Within hours of receiving these, a very nice, quiet man from Merseyside came to explain the scheme. We were told that our request meant £50,000 worth of labour, plus ten per cent of building materials, and my Assistant, Robert Clifton, and I sat down to work in an optimistic mood. We were determined to keep to the deadline given to us.

When the Honorary Architects arrived and heard that the cost of the work force might be covered by a Government grant, they exclaimed, "Is this another joke?" We assured them that it was true and of the urgency and seriousness of the situation, and they went away after a long site meeting saying that three quantity surveyors were required to check the figures. By Friday of the same week, however, the completed forms were delivered by hand, and by the following Monday the Action Committee had given their consent. It seemed like a small miracle, and all the more exciting, because it had been so unexpected. The co-operation of the planning officer, building inspector, and so on, was ensured from the start at our initial meeting in their offices, when everybody concerned came together at short notice. They shared our keenness to restore one of Lancashire's historic houses. Our thanks, too, are due to the fire officer for his help and understanding.

During the ensuing months we attended regular site meetings at the Home. I would make an early start from Headquarters to cover the 231 miles of motorway to Birchley. At lunchtime the youngest labourer would go and buy some fish and chips from the shop in the village, and we even treated ourselves to Lancashire peas.

The meetings proved as varied and lively as others elsewhere, and among those who attended them was one energetic architect, who was accompanied on occasions by his senior partner who drove miles to supervise.

Their tempers were naturally inclined to fray, and I remember one of them thumping the only table we possessed, saying, "Now, come on . . . I have told you before, if these drainage problems continue you will be for the high jump." Great efforts had been made to plan and install an inexpensive drainage scheme to replace the existing system; and at almost every site meeting we had to hammer home the fact that these plans were to be followed in the right sequence and at a predetermined speed. At the outset a bar chart was drawn up, as always, and our vigilance grew. I can remember our dismay when, on one occasion, we discovered that the new pipes were the wrong size and the new drains had been laid to fall in the wrong direction!

Our problems did not stop with drainage. The cold water supply was inadequate and the hot water system antiquated. A new main had to be laid and a new heating and hot water system installed with the usual measure of effort, frustration and pleas to cut down on time and expense.

Comments written on the walls were mostly unprintable, but the mildest of these – written when the fire alarms were being installed – read: "When the bells ring run like hell!" A further scrawl found near two dead wires read: "When feeling depressed put one in each ear and sing."

Owing to the age of the house, the walls were extremely solid and drilling proved difficult. Nevertheless, the company who installed the central heating were efficient, relatively inexpensive and very hard-working.

We divided the work force into gangs under chargehands and, despite all the problems which inevitably arose, the main house was completely restored within two years. If critics of the Job Creation Programme could see what was carried out by the unemployed tradesmen and labourers who worked so well on the project, they might change their views about the value of that maligned programme. Like all schemes, however, we had our ups and downs. The first foreman, who had all the answers and was nicknamed "the Sailor", came and went, and at one point (and not by our wishes) we were suddenly sent fifty-eight unemployed men to work on the site.

The accountant, Mr Dukes, belonged to the older generation. He had retired from his own business and was a man of unfailing courtesy and patience. Amidst all the hurly-burly and bad language he remained unruffled and generously shared his sandwiches with colleagues and visitors. Mr Dukes always wore a suit, white shirt and a tie. Everything was documented and recorded by him, and he knew exactly what was going on. He never complained about conditions, but was much concerned about the fact that I used the men's very old outside loo with no door! Almost on each visit we would be met by Mr Dukes who, after his initial friendly greetings, would say in his deep mellow voice: "I am afraid I have to tell you that there is a lack of liquidity" – in other words the dibs, or funds, had run out.

On one occasion poor Mr Dukes was tied by rope down in his chair (one of the few we had) whilst certain vandals in our employment – who had emerged from the nearby pub during the lunch break – ripped out the telephone and smashed the window. We dismissed the culprits immediately.

One morning, after I had slept a bit rough on a bedspring on the floor, Mr Dukes, who always arrived early, noticed that the window shutters of my room were still closed and became worried. He thought that I should already have been back from Mass, and I heard him solemnly announcing to my colleague (who had slept on a camp bed in the opposite room to mine), "I am very worried because Miss Ryder had a calor gas stove last night and there is no noise in the room!"

The property had now become nicknamed "The Holly Bushes" owing to the over-enthusiasm on the part of the first gardener, who pruned the lower parts of the holly bushes in the drive which screened the adjoining property – and thus destroyed the owners' privacy. Later on, the Foundation's gardener (John, from Stagenhoe) planted *Cupressus leylandii* to screen the area. These trees were the gift of a local Council's Parks and Gardens Department.

Meanwhile, Support Groups were being formed and grew in number. Parallel to these endeavours, Shop premises were found, but often only after great patience had been shown. The Foundation has always had the good fortune to count on individual supporters throughout Lancashire, and for eighteen years Mrs Eileen Wray, Chairman of the Crosby and District Support Group, and Mrs Muriel Molyneux, the Honorary Treasurer, with their colleagues, had toiled unceasingly to organise fund-raising events. They were always ready to run Shops in the deprived areas of the City of Liverpool. Constant break-ins and smashed windows did not deter them.

Within a year, through the tremendous efforts of small groups of enthusiastic supporters, Sue Ryder Shops had been established. These followed the Foundation's policy of supporting the work *as a whole*, but specific fund-raising efforts were organised by the Support Groups to keep pace with the cost of building materials for Birchley Hall over and above the ten per cent allowed for by the JCP. Companies in the area came forward, as elsewhere, and offered good terms or gifts in kind.

Hearing of the desperate shortage of funds, two anonymous donors sent £1,000 each to encourage us. Volunteers and both qualified and unqualified staff came forward and worked tirelessly. At one point I was offered on the telephone 16,000 plastic coathangers which we were expected to collect without delay. The shops had no need of any more at the time so the task of disposing of the coathangers was assigned to Nicholas, who worked on a temporary basis for the Foundation. He took on this job with great enthusiasm, but soon realised that the disposal of such a large quantity of the same rather mundane item was no easy task. Dressed in his elegant pin-striped suit (he had worked in a well-known City bank), he started at the top stores and made his way by deft persuasion through doors which would have been closed to most other people. The reaction of various managing directors, chief buyers and other executives he encountered was one of astonishment. Sadly, he was often turned away and advised to tout his wares somewhere else. During this exercise, on the brink of a hard-won sale in a man's store, the reluctant would-be buyer discovered that half of the coathangers he was about to purchase were for women's petticoats! Undaunted, Nicholas continued until the sale of all the hangers was assured, and he wrote afterwards, "Yes, my mind still boggles at the thought of all those coathangers! I shall never forget the expression on the face of the Gay Girls Warehouse Manager when I arrived with the third van load he was not expecting!"

I can vividly remember the excitement during the days which led up to the first Open Day in 1977, on a damp and dripping Sunday morning, 25 September. In no way discouraged by several days of unremitting rain, supporters of the Foundation quickly transformed the front of the Home into a world of bright stalls and bustling activity. The driveway became a second Petticoat Lane, with a long line of attractive mobile wooden stalls stretching all the way down one side.

As if to reward the optimism of those who had always been convinced that everything would eventually turn out well, the sun broke through the clouds just after midday. Then the crowds rolled in. The escorted tour round the Home soon proved so popular that long, good-humoured queues formed at the front door. Much to the amusement of all concerned, the escorted groups met and inevitably mingled with each other and became entwined on the three different floors, so that they were not easily sorted out. But no one seemed to mind! Mr Dukes gave an eloquent non-stop talk on the history of the chapel, and dozens of people crowded in to listen.

Outside, the besieged stalls did a flourishing trade in an almost unbelievable variety of goods, and only at the end of the day when the shelves were bare and the auctioneer had nothing left to sell did the large crowds from Lancashire and counties further afield finally lift their siege.

They left behind them a gallant band of weary organisers, whose infinite patience and hard work had raised more than £1,700!

There was no official opening ceremony at Birchley Hall. After the final fixes and finishes by the tradesmen, gifts of furniture, linen, blankets, etc., arrived from different parts of the country and beyond. The rooms were quickly furnished and the first residents/patients admitted. Although the rooms were not large, each resident/patient was encouraged to bring what personal possessions he or she still had left. The overall result was that they managed to create their own little homes in the rooms provided, and in doing so to express their precious, individual personalities.

The first cook, who had once run her own fish and chip shop, was a true Lancashire lass. She believed in being forthright, and on one occasion took it upon herself to telephone Headquarters to ask if the residents were to have blancmange for supper or the alternative which had been decreed by the sister-in-charge. "As cooks go she went" – but not for this reason.

The Foundation was fortunate in having Miss E. Wright, a retired health visitor, as Chairman of the Home, until 1984, and she remains a strong, knowledgeable and wise counsellor. When the Home opened, Sister Edna Curless SRN, was Matron; the present Matron is Mrs Christine Willis. Two other longstanding and active supporters of the Home were the late Dr R. Cutcliffe and the Minutes Secretary, Mrs T. Pearson.

Edward Borrows was one of the Home's first residents. He had joined his father's family business of manufacturing small industrial locomotives when he left school, but in 1910, when he was only seventeen, his father died and the business had to be sold. He then became an apprentice to the chief electrical engineer of the St Helen's Corporation. In those days apprentices received no wage but were required to pay a premium; Edward Borrows had to pay £60 a year. He never married and lived alone after his sister's death. One Christmas Day he was found in the house suffering from hypothermia and was taken to hospital. Vandals had attacked his home: they had destroyed his greenhouse, ransacked his garden and smashed many of the windows in the house and he had had wire-netting put over them. After leaving hospital, Mr Borrows came to live at the Home. He loved sketching and many of his illustrations of the novels of Dickens hung on the wall of his room – a tribute to his artistic accomplishments.

Another resident was Violetta Parsons – she was one of the most youthful ninety-year olds I have ever met. She was born at Leedstown, Cornwall, and as a young girl she became deputy organist at the Wesleyan Chapel at Camborne which had a choir of sixty; she remembered Gypsy Smith and his daughter, Zillah, preaching and singing in the Chapel.

Annie Pearson is a mild diabetic. In 1979 thrombosis set in in her left leg which had to be amputated. With others she took charge of a stall at the annual fair. She occupies a small delightful room with a french door and on arriving at the Home she was especially pleased with the mauve and blue delphinium-patterned curtains – her favourite colours. She told me her best dress was mauve. Mrs Pearson is a prominent person and very well known in the Wigan area where she was a jeweller for many years.

Dunstan Kevill suffered from very severe arthritis. He was educated at Ampleforth and joined his father's profession as a solicitor. One of his brothers is a priest in the Leeds diocese. As a young man Dunstan met a lovely girl, Bertha Middlehurst, whose family then farmed Birchley Hall. They became engaged, but at the early age of thirty-two she died and is buried in St Mary's churchyard opposite Birchley Hall. When arthritis began to take a firm hold of him – and this was obvious from his hands and wrists – he heard of the Sue Ryder Home and came to live here where once he had spent so many happy hours with Bertha. She was never forgotten and he had a photograph of her hanging in his room.

Coming from a wide variety of backgrounds, the residents naturally have equally varied interests. Mr Kevill had a deep interest in art and brought with him an oil painting, "Our Lady of the Cushion", which hangs on the wall behind the altar in the chapel. At the time of presenting his gift, Mr Kevill wrote to me:

> With regard to the picture: it was bought at the sale of contents of Scarisbrick Hall. It had been found in a ruined church in Italy by Sir Everard Scarisbrick when he was on his honeymoon some time in the last century. At first it was thought to be the work of Carlo Dolci (1616–86) but is probably by a pupil of his, or a good copy. It is very similar to a picture which was in Birchley Hall fifty years ago which included St Joseph.

It was only by a fluke that Mr Kevill obtained the picture. It appears that a representative of Sotheby's was sent up to the auction but got delayed at Crewe, so happily for the Home the picture was purchased and restored by Mr Kevill.

Several other supporters have helped with gifts for use in the chapel. A lovely brass double crucifix was given to the Home. The simple chairs were renovated and donated by the kindness of the vicar of St James's Church in Billinge, and through the kindness of another supporter four other chairs, equally suitable for the chapel, were sent to him for the Home.

The chapel is used regularly and by all denominations, both for formal services and individually by the residents and people in the Village who greatly value it. So, over the years, Mr and Mrs Woods' intentions for Birchley Hall are being fulfilled.

Plans are currently being finalised for a new two-storey extension, linked to the existing building, which will provide thirteen new single bedrooms, a new kitchen and other vitally needed facilities. At the same time improvements will be made to the existing building which, in conjunction with the new extensions, will provide increased privacy and comfort for the residents and help reduce the waiting lists. It has always been the Foundation's hope that eventually the derelict barn and other outbuildings could be converted to provide a much-needed Day-Centre, as well as a Sue Ryder Gift Shop and coffee room, which will provide facilities for residents and visitors whilst helping to raise much-needed funds; but their fulfilment will depend entirely on the generosity of supporters and members of the public.

22

Bordean House, Hampshire, and Holme Hall, East Yorkshire

Here I am.   Carrying their sheaves.

Send me to serve.

ONE MEANING OF THE word "Bordean" is Valley of the Boars, and the Valley has been inhabited from very early times. Relics of these former inhabitants and transitory visitors have confirmed their occupation of the area. A Roman camp was built on the Winchester road around AD 43, and the Jutes passed through some 400 years later when advancing on Winchester up the Meon river. These last invaders became so entrenched that the Western Saxons abandoned their efforts to dislodge them and build a boundary wall between Wessex and Sussex, parts of which still stand. It is therefore equally likely that Bordean might mean the Valley of the Boundary.

Towards the end of the seventh century, St Wilfrid, exiled Archbishop of York, landed at Selsey, having been driven from his diocese by his political enemies. It was through his efforts that the Jute-occupied area was converted to Christianity, which was many years after the surrounding predominantly Saxon communities had received the faith. The Bishop of Winchester took a personal interest in his latest acquired congregations, and Langrish and Bordean were assigned to the Church by the King of Wessex.

Bordean remained Church property until monastic lands were confiscated, when it was given to the Langrish family, Lords of the Manor of Langrish, who were dedicated royalists.

In 1947 the then owners, the Nicholsons, decided to sell the property, which was bought at that time by the Oblates of the Assumption, whose motto is "Here I am. Send me to serve." The Order ran it as a Home for elderly ladies, later renting the cellars to the Civil Defence Corps who used the very extensive basement as their Headquarters until they were dissolved in 1968.

The ghosts of Bordean are reported to be a Cavalier and a White Lady who walk the grounds from time to time, but the only recently reported occurrence was an unexplained ringing of the front door bell which was silenced, seemingly completely, by Masses being said for the souls of those who had lived in the House.

In 1974 the Sisters of the Oblates of the Assumption wrote to me asking if the Foundation could consider taking over the Home which they had created at Bordean.

French in foundation, the Oblates of the Assumption aim to be totally Catholic in outlook, in accordance with the precepts of their founder, Fr Emmanuel d'Alzon.

The purpose of the Oblates' foundation in 1865 was to assist the Fathers of the Assumption in their work for Christian unity in the Near East. Their missions in Turkey, Bulgaria, Yugoslavia, Rumania and Armenia, have been ravaged by wars several times.

The Sisters were sadly reduced in numbers and felt that as they got older they required assistance. Since opening Bordean as a Home, the Sisters had had a steady flow of twenty-four to twenty-six individuals (an exact record was never kept) staying there, who had enjoyed living with them until the end of their lives.

The House stands in a beautiful but very simple landscaped garden and is built of brick and limestone. At first sight it appears large. The rooms lie off one passage and many face south. On entering one is immediately aware of the atmosphere of peace and calm. In the small cemetery in the garden lies the grave of Father Henry Clarke, parish priest of Petersfield, an old friend who had prepared my husband for reception into the Catholic Church at Christmas 1948. Father Clarke subsequently used to stay with my mother; they had much in common and used to go the rounds of churches in East Anglia together.

Apart from the needs of those who could no longer cope on their own and remain independent, there were the needs of the Radiotherapy Centre at St Mary's Hospital, Portsmouth. Miss Irene Cade, Consultant in Radiotherapy and Oncology, wrote the following to the Foundation:

> What is the numerical need? In my own area of Portsmouth and surrounding districts in Hampshire and West Sussex, we have a population of about 600,000. In Portsmouth alone with a population of 527,000 there were 1,250 deaths from cancer in 1975, and of these were 416 under the age of sixty five, and sixty one were under the age of forty five. I stress this because there are often special problems with the younger patients. The incidence of cancer has increased over the last twenty years. In 1955 my Department saw 417 new patients, in 1974 1,150. We now do a great deal more for them – in 1955 there were 8,776 attendances for treatment, in 1975 22,491 and more patents are cured and will not reach the late stages. However, many of these will go through a difficult and frightening illness and will require convalescence for which these Sue Ryder Homes are the best place. We must not have homes exclusively for the dying. We also provide a refuge for patients who are well cared for at home but whose family temporarily require a holiday.
>
> In this way these Homes provide for a mixture of long-term fairly chronic type cancer patients, temporary short-stay patients and those in the final stages who require somewhere they can be well cared for and can die with dignity and privacy after being relieved of their pain.

Stringent fire regulations had to be complied with, which required much time, energy and fund-raising. Many local people throughout Hampshire and beyond rallied to help the cause. Amongst the parties of volunteers who helped with the decorating was a naval contingent from HMS *Mercury* whose petty officer, upon arrival at the House, commanded them not to use any "Bs" in their language while working there! Everyone felt richly rewarded when the first fête was held following the opening of the Home. The weather was perfect with blazing sunshine and the event attracted many hundreds of people.

The Foundation decided that to meet the continuing needs of the elderly and to relieve the needs which Miss Cade had identified, the Home should have ten beds for cancer patients and fourteen for the elderly and those who could not cope on their own. The mix has been successful and is appreciated by both residents and staff.

For twenty-one years Sister Hilda worked at Bordean House as Matron-in-charge of the health and nursing care of those who lived there. She retired a few years ago and still lives at the Home. Here is her inside view of it:

> In those early days, hard cash was one thing lacking. Good will, tolerance, patience and good humour were there in plenty to make up for some crea- ture comforts. With unbounded optimism we tried to augment our meagre income. Some of our early residents were not over-blessed with a bank account, and 33/- per week was accepted for full board and lodging but as surely as God helps those who help themselves (and their fellowmen) we planned to be self-supporting. The smooth green lawns of Bordean have grazed sheep for a neighbouring farmer, in return for cracked or small eggs. Unfortunately, the baa-ing of sheep and lambs was not conducive to the rest our resident family required, and that experiment ended with our contract. Then, cackling geese kept the grass down, and these were more entertaining than productive; moreover, they effectively prevented access to the pasture beyond. It needed a stout heart to intrude when Roger, the gander, patrolled the run, but they provided endless fun and entertainment for the Chaplain who was totally unafraid of Roger's sharp pecks at his old thick footgear, and also for the rest of us who watched at a respectful distance!

The ladies who were living in the House when the Foundation became responsible for it were the last of a remarkable generation. Many were Victorians or from the Edwardian era and it was a privilege to be with them and to hear of their full and varied lives. It is a source of pleasure to be able to record that they have been followed by other ladies, albeit of a later generation, to whom we are able to offer a home and who, in their turn, are able to enrich our lives from their experience.

We worked with several nuns and remember particularly the late Sister Mary.

Canon John Devine was Resident Chaplain until his death in May 1992 at the age of ninety-two years old. He is buried in the small cemetery within the grounds of Bordean House, in the company of other priests and nuns.

As in other places where the Foundation works, domiciliary visits have always been made to give support to patients and to their relatives and neighbours.

The growing number of Hospices in areas already adequately covered for the proper care of patients with cancers has had its effect on the work of the Foundation. For example when the Foundation first started at Bordean in 1976 it was the only unit of its kind in the area, and it became renowned for its high standard of medical and nursing care for many, many patients.

Alas, without proper and thorough consultation, four Hospices have since been established within a twenty-five mile radius of the Home and have thus reduced the number of patients seeking the service offered by the Foundation. As a result of this Bordean, as a Sue Ryder Home, will cease to exist. However increased domiciliary care for patients needing palliative treatment will be offered to many more people in the Portsmouth area, where a new base is to be found for the Sue Ryder nurses who co-operate and work with the district nurses.

Not every patient wants to be admitted to a Home. Many would naturally prefer to end their days in familiar surroundings, ideally with the company of their families in their own homes. For this reason, we must continue what was started at Bordean, to give increased service to the sick and dying in the community in the future.

Ever since the Foundation first took over from the Oblates of the Assumption at Bordean, hundreds of volunteers have rallied in countless ways to raise funds for the use of the Foundation at the Home.

I would like to take take this opportunity of expressing my appreciation and heartfelt gratitude to everybody who has served Bordean in such a self-less way over so many years. I hope that as many as possible will continue to do so in the future.

* * *

The Sisters of the Congregation of Oblates of the Assumption also owned another but larger property, Holme Hall, Holme-on-Spalding Moor, in East Yorkshire.

After talks with the Mother Provincial and the Treasurer of this congregation, who come over regularly from France, they agreed upon a lease between the Order and the Foundation. Their interest and offer seemed fortuitous as the Foundation had hunted and floundered in trying to find a property in this part of the country.

For just over twenty years the Sisters faithfully worked with those in their care, who were mainly people in the upper age group drawn from far and wide who could no longer cope on their own and sadly, therefore, had had to give up their independence.

When we first went to Holme Hall it was apparent that each of the residents regarded their room as their "home", which contained whatever belongings they had left in life. The individual stamp of the rooms was remarkable. Equally remarkable was the devotion of the Sisters who had dedicated their lives to God and this service.

Sister Columba (who was in charge), after taking us round this large building, repeated what the Mother Superior had said when she was first shown round in 1957: "Well, Sister, it's either an act of faith or an act of folly, and only time will tell." As at Bordean, the sisters were declining in numbers and unable to continue.

Holme Hall comprised a very large house and garden, but it was clear that its full potential had not been realised, and there was a need to encourage the link with the community made by the Sisters and so make the work which the Sisters had already done, and which the Foundation now hoped to do, better known locally.

At the time, this was a new kind of area for the Foundation to work in; it seemed very rural and unlike other parts where we had become established. Nevertheless, there was the same warmth and welcome.

Mrs Penelope Worsley came forward and, with a small band of helpers, took on responsibility for the day-to-day running of the Home. Mrs Worsley devoted many hours of each day there and it was through her great efforts that both funds and support came in. It was recognised by the Foundation from the beginning that there was a lot to do in the way of repair and renovation. Gradually, after many long meetings, the plans for the building work evolved. Meanwhile, a campaign had to be planned as to where the Foundation's support would come from. Slowly the area began to rally. The first garden fête was held in 1980, and other varied events and money-raising efforts have gradually become established and are greatly looked forward to by people in the vicinity.

The old Manor of Holme owes its name to the hill which stands behind the site of the present Hall. More than 1,000 years ago, Danish settlers in the area noticed that the hill rose out of a fen and they called it Holme, which was their word for "island". The later history of the area is notable because it was one of those widely scattered places in England where successive Lords of the Manor – at great personal risk – clandestinely kept alive the Roman Catholic religion during the most repressive years of the Reformation. As a consequence, the "old religion" never died out in Holme, although the thread of continuity at times grew desperately weak.

In 1743, besides the fourteen or fifteen Catholics who lived in the Hall, there was a local congregation of forty, all of whom, according to the custom of the time, were obliged to hear Mass in the uncomfortable chapel, not only on Sundays, but also on no less than thirty-five holy days of obligation. In the same year the Honourable Marmaduke Langdale, son of the fourth Baron, who had been given the House by his father, decided that the time had come to erect a new and more convenient chapel at Holme.

The penal laws against the Catholic religion were still on the statute books (as late as 1767 a priest was sentenced to life imprisonment at the Croydon Assizes), but the tide of religious tolerance was on its way in. The new chapel was, in fact, the first post-Reformation chapel in the East Riding of Yorkshire to be built on the ground floor expressly for Catholic worship. Previously, such chapels were constructed in upper rooms and galleries which a search party would take longer to reach, thus allowing the priest time to get into his "hole" and the rest of the people to disperse and regain their composure.

The Anglican vicar of Holme regarded the whole idea with extreme annoyance and suspicion, and it is reported that he "would frequently come and walk about near the place, saying: 'I know what they are about; but I will be up with them.'" For the vicar's benefit, "the building was ostensibly set about as an additional wing of the Hall", but everyone well knew its true purpose. However, the King himself (George III) was on the side of religious tolerance, and there was no official attempt to stop the chapel. It was duly completed and consecrated in 1766. It was a sign of the times, perhaps, that Mr Langdale employed a non-Catholic architect, Mr J. Carr, to design it.

The French Revolution, which began in 1789, had dangerous consequences for the English Catholic communities on the Continent, and over the next few years many of them returned to England as refugees. One such community was that of the English Canonesses Regular of the Holy Sepulchre, which ran a school in Liège. In the summer of 1794, they were on their way home. During their perilous journey they stopped at Rotterdam, and received there a letter from Lord Stourton – who had somehow heard about their plight – offering them Holme Hall "for an asylum" when they reached England. The offer was gratefully accepted, and the nuns soon put the House and chapel in order. The chapel itself was used alternately as a convent chapel and parish church.

One of the several owners of the Hall during the nineteenth century was Charles Langdale, who was widely regarded as the foremost English Catholic layman of his time. He was one of the first Catholics to enter Parliament after the Catholic Emancipation Act of 1829, and was responsible for founding the Holme Catholic School (which still exists).

A person whose connection with Holme Hall should never be forgotten is Gwendolen, Duchess of Norfolk, mother of the sixteenth Duke.

In 1923 the major portion of the Holme estate was sold. The Duchess, who lived at neighbouring Everingham and was a descendant through her father, Lord Herries, of the original builder of the chapel, was greatly distressed by this event; and in 1924 she purchased the Hall, chapel and presbytery and half the land. She told her aunt that she had had a vivid dream in which her father urged her to take this action. She saddled herself with a house for which she had no personal use, an "enormous barrack" of a place, damp, dilapidated, without gas or electricity, with an antiquated heating system and with rats and mice. In 1928, almost in despair at her failure to find a purchaser for Holme Hall, the Duchess made a novena to St Thèrese of Lisieux. The same year, Mother Mary Kevin of the Order of St Francis appeared on her doorstep. Mother Mary Kevin, one of the greatest figures in the missionary world in the first half of this century, was to be the outstanding personality at Holme Hall for nearly thirty years.

With the death of Mother Kevin in October 1957, Holme Hall was sold to the Oblates of the Assumption. Sister Columba, who for years was in charge at Holme Hall, wrote the following notes about those who came to live there.

Retired matrons, head teachers and even a one-time director of an art gallery could live under the same roof and share the same dining hall and sitting rooms as, say, one who had earned her living as a tightrope walker in a London circus, or another who had lived the arduous life of a fairground person for years.

Isabel was born to this life in 1886. Her birth took place in a horse-drawn caravan, and her mother did for Isabel what she had done for all her numerous children, delivered her herself. So started her life on wheels. In 1977 she applied for a place here, and it was then that we came to have a glimpse of the way of life of these sturdy people. Isabel could neither read nor write. She opted out of school when she was six. No amount of persuasion could make her join the little girls who attended the local school run by some nuns. What was her mother to do but to find her occupation at home? This meant learning the art of living as a member of the "Amusement Caterers". Eventually she became the wife of a fairground man.

"If you become a fairground man's wife," she was heard to say, "you must be prepared to do the work of a fairground man." Her descriptions of the displacements of the "convoy" each year between Easter and All Saints, from one fairground to another, would make you feel that you did not know what real work was: the heaving, the hauling, the shifting and shoving of heavy gear, the setting up or dismantling of stalls. All this while a large family was being raised. It was indeed a daunting existence. Her language was colourful and she told me how she had seen a man smoking and leaning on a tent pole on the fairground as others wanted to get the tent up. She said, "I told him if I saw him smoking again when he should be working I'd stuff the bloody cigarette right down his throat." I am sure he did not need a second warning!

This arduous way of making a living did not interfere with this brave woman's consciousness of the part God held in her life. Her night prayers, recited aloud (her hearing was failing then) revealed a person who lived habitually in the presence of God. Some two years later Isabel returned to her Maker. She particularly liked Psalm 126 and used to quote;

They go out, they go out full of tears,
carrying the seed for the sowing;

They come back, they come back
full of song, carrying their sheaves.

The Foundation is indeed privileged to carry on and, I hope, expand the work done by the Sisters for the brave people for whom Holme Hall (or HH as we affectionately know it) is now their real home.

23

Wootton House, South Yorkshire

I am! yet what I am who cares, or knows?
  My friends forsake me like a memory lost.
I am the self-consumer of my woes;
  They rise and vanish, an oblivious host,
Shadows of life, whose very soul is lost.
And yet I am – I live . . .

John Clare

FOR MANY YEARS AN elderly lady, Mrs Wootton, had written me long letters of support for this Foundation. She finally became bedridden, living alone in a Victorian house near the middle of Sheffield. When she died we found that she had left the property in her will to the Foundation.

When we first saw the building we were relieved to find the structure in good repair with the exterior recently painted. The interior had not, apparently, been touched for many years and it was covered in brown and dark green paint. Mrs Wootton had lived there up to her death in 1974, fighting hard to preserve her independence which she felt should include the right to make toast at the side of her bed. Some of the rooms in the house had been let out to students and lodgers. We later found they had made their own adaptations to the electrical wiring. The electrician was amazed that the whole house had not gone up in smoke.

As we entered the sagging back door into a room which was painted dark brown, the neglect was apparent. Many rooms were shuttered, but nevertheless I felt that the house had great potential and would make a small welcoming Home once we had removed all the belongings which had been piled up in the hall beside a huge marble statue of a lady in Classical Greek pose. The kitchen featured the original stone sink made out of one piece of local stone.

Meanwhile, the local hospital authorities were still making up their minds as to whether or not the property should be demolished to make way for a car park. Finally, we heard the good news, which left the Foundation with Wootton House and its large garden.

As always, there were no funds available to us. My colleague, Robert Clifton, slept on the floorboards before we were given beds. The whole house had to be rewired, central heating installed and stringent fire regulations complied with. The Foundation was also helped by tradesmen from the Job Creation Programme. Support came in gradually for the most pressing priorities and Joan Burton joined us as the first Housemother. Among her talents she was a professional upholsterer.

The social services encouraged the Foundation to use the building for the creation of a half-way house for men and women discharged from hospitals and hostels who were on their way back to society and who would otherwise have nowhere to go. So it has come about that the purpose of this Home is to assist such people in re-adjusting to life within the community.

In the early days the aim was for each of the residents to have a job. Often the jobs were menial and poorly paid, and one could only marvel at those who had to get up at 5 a.m. and be at work by 6 a.m. until lunch-time for a take-home wage of £23 per week. Now the position is much worse as there are virtually no jobs and most have to attend day centres instead of doing purposeful work. This can only delay their re-integration into society.

Since the Home opened, many individuals have been admitted, three of whom have married; but one of these, sadly, died later of heart failure leaving a young widow who had also lived with us. After the couple's marriage they had acquired a flat and were becoming quite independent. The others, when they come home from work, help the Housemother and warden and share as fully as possible in the running of the Home. On the whole, they are well accepted by members of the local community, some of whom visit and ask them to go out. One of the most faithful groups is still St Mark's Church nearby, but the Home also receives considerable support from numerous individuals, including professional social workers who visit in their spare time, but it must be admitted that the men and women of the Home still find satisfactory re-integration into society very difficult indeed to achieve. On the whole, these individuals, who have known acute personal deprivation, have also suffered from mental stress, and this factor, together with ignorance on the part of the public, are the main obstacles they must overcome.

Mental stress can cause extreme anguish. It is more complex than physical suffering and may be even harder to bear. Many victims of mental illness can find nobody to communicate with, and those without personal experience are very often unable to understand the agony of loneliness it can produce.

The eminent Professor of Mental Health, D. Russell Davis, describes mental illness and some of its symptoms in these words:

> The essence of mental illness may be summed up in one word: alienation. While he is ill, the patient is estranged, detached and withdrawn. He is solitary and seeks solitude. He feels that he is on his own, and that he no longer belongs to any family or any community. He is egocentric and cannot associate himself with others or espouse any cause; he does not commit himself. He breaks off transactions with others, and ceases to co-operate and to communicate. Perhaps the first sign of illness is that he

ceases to show affection and becomes indifferent or even hostile to family and friends.

He may seek reassurance from others or try to communicate his feelings, but usually fails and is often misunderstood. Indeed, he may impress those to whom he turns as unsympathetic, insensitive, and importunate, and also as dependent and passive. The feelings he displays may appear incongruous, extravagant, or false, and the ideas he expresses irrational or ridiculous. The relatives and friends from whom he has cut himself off may feel hurt or offended and condemn him. The reactions he provokes in others tend to add to his sense of apartness. When he has made a degree of recovery, he may be able to describe how well-meaning but misguided comments by others made things worse. They may have denied his illness, slighted him, shown disapproval, distaste, or repugnance, or given inappropriate advice – to pull himself together, for instance. His doctor may merely have prescribed for him without making any effort to listen or to understand him. Many patients do not seek help at all, because they know they cannot convey their feelings and do not expect to be understood or to receive help. Some are alarmed by the prospect of being questioned or of revealing themselves. Others feel that they do not deserve help. Eventually the illness may be recognised as such, often very belatedly, and the patient may then be brought to see a psychiatrist. In some cases he is not seen until after he has been admitted to hospital because he has misused drugs, perhaps in an appeal for help, but more often in an attempt to find escape or relief and bring an end to his suffering in sleep or death.

Many patients do not come to hospitals at all. Some shut themselves away in their own homes, as hermits do, and as the depressed tend to do. Some travel abroad in order to get away from family and friends. Some adopt a mode of life which keeps them out of close relationships, as vagrants do; others go to sea. Some drink on their own; others find solace in bars and clubs on the outskirts of society. Some, denied the satisfaction of human relationships, seek vicarious satisfactions in the accumulation of wealth, or in the accumulation of knowledge, or in political power – like Hitler, for instance. Others, who feel rejected by the community do not feel constrained by its laws, customs and conventions and offend against them, perhaps feeling justified in so doing because of a sense of grievance at unfair treatment. Others seek asylum in prison.

In young men and women, illness tends to arise out of crises in their relationships with parents and girl-friend or boy-friend (i.e. crises of relationship): in men and women in their thirties, illness arises out of crises in their relationships with spouses. Illness in the forties and fifties is commonly the result of a combination of stresses, due to the death of parents, the drifting apart of brothers and sisters after their parents' death, the departure of sons and daughters from home, and the consequent changes in the relationship with spouses. People in their fifties tend to become separated from their children; reunion occurs in a proportion of cases later on. In the sixties and seventies the contraction in the circle of friends and acquaintances makes a person more vulnerable when the spouse dies. Widowers are more vulnerable than widows in this as in other respects. Indeed, if anyone wants an example of society's failure to take ordinary precautions in protecting the exposed, let him consider the careless disregard of the needs of the elderly bereaved. It has been known since the end of the last century, when Durkheim pointed it out, that the suicide-rate, for instance, is very high in elderly men after bereavement, especially in those who have lost contact with their families and friends.

The Foundation is only too conscious that many more such small Homes are needed throughout the country. This particular one was the first of the Foundation's Homes in Britain to be located in a city.

24

Manorlands, West Yorkshire

The stars of the Night
I will lend thee their Light
Robert Herrick

AMONG THE MEN, WOMEN and children whom we have had the privilege of nursing in the Sue Ryder Homes in Britain, there were those who had been diagnosed as suffering from cancer. For many years it was apparent that there were many other cancer patients in equally great need, especially in areas where the Foundation had no tangible representation in the form of a Home, so supporters were always on the lookout for a suitable property situated, ideally, within ten miles of a Radiotherapy Centre.

In 1974 the Foundation was fortunate enough to acquire a family home in the Village of Oxenhope, near Keighley in Yorkshire. This pleasant Victorian House, named Manorlands, was built in 1897 by John P. Heaton, a spinner in the wool trade. One of his sons, Thomas Herbert, was killed at the Battle of the Somme in 1916, aged twenty-six. In 1911 an addition had been made to the house on the marriage of the other son, Arthur John, and later it continued to be lived in as a family home by Gordon and Monica Vestey (John Heaton's granddaughter). Mr and Mrs Vestey wanted a smaller house and so in 1974 the Foundation was able to move in.

Manorlands was opened in the same year to give continuing care to those suffering from cancer. This work is a continuation and extension of the Foundation's activities in the field of oncology which had begun overseas in 1945, especially in Poland. Since then, many thousands of child patients and adults have received treatment and had nursing care in Centres and Homes established by the Foundation.

Since its opening, this Sue Ryder Home has had the privilege of welcoming over 3,744 men and women of all ages. It contained first nine and then eleven beds, but the demand for beds was high and a purpose-built extension was added, giving twenty beds in all. In 1991 the total number of beds was reduced to eighteen to facilitate the provision of a day-care unit.

Unlike the other Homes acquired up to then, this property needed virtually no renovation, and though the extension has been added, it still retains the feeling of a family home with its sunny rooms and its windows offering superb panoramic views of the lovely gardens and the scenery of the valley, woodlands and the moors beyond. The surrounding hills are ablaze with heather in summer and, because of the altitude, the night sky at Oxenhope is especially beautiful.

Manorlands strives to give a feeling of peace and quiet, where skilled nursing is available from a caring team of trained nurses who have been specially chosen to do this work. The Home is divided into pleasantly sized rooms that offer privacy for those who want it, and companionship for those who need it. Miss Lewis was the first matron and Mrs Jill Mollitt is now in charge. There are enough staff for someone always to be available to talk, to listen, or just to sit at the bedside. Our aim is to provide a friendly and informal home, where friends and families are welcome and are encouraged to continue to help in the caring of their loved ones.

Before the Home was opened, the Foundation's familiar pattern was followed by holding preliminary meetings in Leeds and Harrogate with the health authorities, and others responsible in their respective fields, to determine the priorities. Both adults and children in hospitals and in their own homes were visited to help us assess the needs. The Marie Curie Foundation, famous for its work, had already opened its Home, Ardenlea, in Ilkley in October 1963.

In 1974 Robert Clifton and I approached Professor Charles Joslin, Professor Elect of Radiotherapy at Leeds University, who was then practising at the Cookridge Hospital. 8,000 new cases of cancer were diagnosed in a year. Later, we met representatives of the Regional Health Authority who confirmed the needs in the area, and during 1974–5, the Sue Ryder Home at Manorlands was developed. At that time Professor Joslin was also Chairman of the Advisory Committee of the Yorkshire Regional Cancer Organisation. He welcomed the Foundation to West Yorkshire and served on the House Committee at Manorlands for many years.

Up to the present time, Professor Joslin continues to act as an Honorary Medical Adviser to the Foundation and is ever ready to give us assistance and advice.

Patients were now admitted to the Home from a wide area, including Keighley, Bradford and Shipley, and occasionally from Halifax. Applications for admission may be submitted by a hospital, general practitioner or social worker. Priority for admission is always based on need, irrespective of financial status. Many patients are referred from the Radiotherapy Centre at Cookridge, Leeds, and from surrounding hospitals. In Yorkshire alone 10,000 people die of cancer each year, which means that the Home at Oxenhope can satisfy only a very small percentage of the existing needs.

I always recall and admire the courage shown by people who come to Manorlands, such as Cathie, who was in her teens and loved horses, pop music and clothes. She had had a rare type of cancer in the muscles of her neck and face since childhood and had suffered much surgery and many forms of treatment. She battled against great odds in very poor home circumstances.

Another patient I remember at the Home was "The Galloping Major" who had been a professional soldier and also had an interest in horse racing. Sadly, his marriage had foundered; then cancer of the epiglottis struck him down. Following treatment there was nowhere for him to go apart from his rather squalid lodgings, so the Foundation was glad to make a place for him. He regained his strength, had his odd bet on the horses and enjoyed the company of the local Working Men's Club. Six months later he needed terminal care. Happily, after many attempts, he and his wife were reunited. Her love for him had never died in spite of the increasing degradation the years had brought, with an inevitable loss of their friends and the need for her to find a residential job to support herself. The Major died peacefully with his wife and daughter at his bedside. Sadly, within a few months, his wife developed malignant blood cancer and died within a couple of weeks of the diagnosis being made.

The patients arrive at the Home in various states of mind, some fully alert, others under such heavy sedation that for them the drive in the ambulance is a journey into the unknown. Several come worrying about the conditions they may find here, others, again, are too ill to think or care and are beyond reasoning. All of them surely long for peace of mind, comfort and relief from pain. Little is usually said, and we can only hope that what we offer them gives assurance of a peaceful passage from this world to eternity.

Here is a short, moving piece written by a patient, for *Remembrance* 1995.

> I write today, not as an administrator or worker but as a patient of the Sue Ryder Home, Manorlands. Do you know what this means?
>
> It is not an easy thing to define. You come in helpless, hopeless and absolutely lost, not knowing what to expect or hope for – death seems an easy answer – the utter despair of life.
>
> There is much talk of what you good people may do to help, but without experiencing it yourself it is hard for you to understand just how much we need your support. Nothing seems real. Why am I here? Is there a break to be seen? Is there a future? When you are at your lowest and you have made a mess, how degrading it all feels, until one of the volunteers appears with unfailing help and tenderness. For those few moments no one is more important than you and in no time they have you back to normality.
>
> The doctors are there for you at all times to make sure you are all right, whilst getting to work on your medicine to make you feel better. The nurses and tea ladies are all there giving their support and love to everyone who needs help.
>
> I cannot speak highly enough of all these people, from the helpers to the Matron they all do wonderful work helping us all.
>
> If I ever recover, I know what I will be doing and that is helping in some small way myself. If I do not survive, I leave behind a legacy of many dedicated people who know the lowest and the highest points of life and still go on helping others.

When I was still doing relief work, one of my chief aims right from the beginning was to offer all the comfort and freedom from pain and anxiety that I could so that individuals could live as far as possible in everyday surroundings instead of in an "institutional" atmosphere. In the appalling conditions which one had to face in the immediate postWar medical teams, with little or no equipment, few medicines, dressings or bandages, I longed to be able to create "a place to live" where there would be a warm welcome and a feeling of reaching home – a condition denied to so many. I wanted to create a place which would have few rules and would not give the impression of being too clinical or too "jolly". In brief, a place where people from all walks of life could continue to be themselves and enjoy as much independence and privacy as possible.

At Manorlands there seems to be a special opportunity to try and do this, because of the scale of the House and the fortunate fact that it has retained its atmosphere of a happy family home.

The small Day Care Centre was opened in 1991, and since then over 200 patients plus in-patients have benefited. It provides occupational therapy not only for the six patients who are brought in from the community each day but also for the in-patients at Manorlands. The Centre is open five days a week and has proved to be very popular and to fill a need. The staff also provide some rehabilitation for in-patients, giving them the opportunity to prepare simple meals in readiness for their return home.

Manorlands employs two Community Liaison Sisters who undertake domiciliary visits. In 1992 they made 196 assessment visits, 767 supportive visits, from volunteer social workers and 115 bereavement visits. In co-operation with staff from Airedale Health Authority, Manorlands plans to open drop-in Centres where patients and their relatives, and the bereaved, can meet for a cup of coffee and comfort one another as well as receiving skilled counselling and help during their period of grief.

Much has been written and said about death. From sharing their last hours on earth with so many people, old and young, I feel it is such a personal and individual matter that no generalisation can ever be made about it. The conscious approach to death, both on the part of the dying and, from a different perspective, by their watching kin, affects them in so many different ways. They may be almost ascetically self-controlled, never alluding to death, resolved "not to let the side down"; or they may break down in grief or fear; or their anguish may be transparent through their silence. To all alike, we owe patience and understanding, conscious that in due course we too must follow down that self same road.

> O Lord, whose way is perfect:
> Help us, we pray thee,
> always to trust in thy goodness;
> that walking with thee and
> following thee in all simplicity,
> we may possess quiet and contented minds,
> and may cast all our care on thee,
> who carest for us.
>   Christina Rossetti

25

Nettlebed, Oxfordshire

"Let the Deed Show"
(Fleming family motto)

THE FOUNDATION DEFINES CERTAIN regions as SOS areas. Berkshire was one, where in 1978, a National Health Service working party had been discussing the necessity for a continuing care home for cancer patients for nine years.

At one of the many meetings held with the Foundation, Dr J. Bunting, the radiotherapist at the Royal Berkshire Hospital, Reading, asked how long it would take the Foundation to start a Home once a property had been found. I optimistically replied "nine months". It took the Foundation considerably longer to find the right house, but we did keep to that target once it was found. Dr Bunting subsequently confided to one of my colleagues that he never thought we could keep to the timetable once the house was acquired. He was used to the slower progress of officialdom!

From the start the need for the Home was demonstrated by the numbers applying, which illustrated why Dr Bunting was so rightly insistent upon the Foundation working in this area. Without his quiet determination and encouragement, it is hard to see how the Home would have taken root.

We visited innumerable properties, each of which was in a different state of disrepair. It was after one of many monthly meetings held in the Nurses' School of the Royal Berkshire Hospital, Reading, that we were taken to see a listed building, part of which was used as changing rooms and public loos and which we nicknamed "Stardust". Another, near Ascot, had the familiar pebble-dash exterior and institutional green and brown paint inside.

Then, at last, one of the members of the Foundation's original co-ordinating team heard about Joyce Grove, an empty Edwardian house at Nettlebed. He was taken there and left on the front steps. In his own words, "I felt like an orphan standing outside this large house wondering how on earth the Foundation could acquire it. What seemed extraordinary too was its sound structural condition after all the other properties we had visited."

He then learnt that in 1937 the property had been given by the Fleming family to St Mary's Hospital, Paddington. The Chairman of the Foundation, Mr H.N. Sporborg, was also Chairman of the Trustees of St Mary's. After talking the matter over with him, I sought the advice of the Secretary of State. The negotiations went on for several months, and when they were eventually completed the Foundation faced the task of bringing the building up to the standards required by the numerous authorities. The Foundation had to buy the House at the market price fixed by the District Valuer, despite the fact that it had originally been given to the hospital – which seemed a cruel irony. The Foundation was also asked to pay for the several tons of pre-War coal left in the cellar! We told the Area Health Authority to remove it if they wished. They left it – and we used it.

During the protracted negotiations there were many occasions when we had to work at this property, during which time it was protected by two security guards, one of whom hailed from Ireland and had a marvellous vocabulary. They treated the Foundation with great caution and visiting the House was rather like arriving at a prison. Looking back on it, their presence was a blessing in disguise during the hard winter of 1978–9.

At the initial meeting held in the Village Hall it was heartening to see the number of people who came to hear about the Foundation's work. Some had been supporters since its earliest days. Among the crowd was the Reverend Stanley Dakin who, with others, assured me of their prayers.

The Village of Nettlebed is five miles from Henley-on-Thames and nine miles from Reading. The road to the Home runs through beech woods and random clumps of trees, and rhododendrons line the drive. Until 1903 its site was occupied by a relatively modest seventeenth-century house connected, according to local legend, with Cornet Joyce, the regicide of the Civil War – a sad story. In the same year the house and the surrounding Nettlebed estate were brought by Robert Fleming, a successful merchant banker. He demolished the old house and raised the present one in its place.

The Fleming family of Nettlebed were rich, powerful and unusually distinguished. Robert's son, Valentine, and his wife, Eva, had four sons, each of whom, in his own way, achieved distinction of one kind or another.

Peter, who was eventually to inherit Nettlebed, became a celebrated author, traveller and soldier. He married the beautiful and talented actress Celia Johnson in 1935, who became a patron of the Foundation and a faithful supporter until her death in 1982.

Ian is even better known. He settled in Jamaica and there dreamed up the outrageous character of James Bond, whose lurid adventures were to make him the most celebrated secret agent ever to step out of the pages of a book.

Richard, the third son, was appointed a Director of the family firm in 1936 at the age of twenty-five. He went on, after a distinguished War service, to become a greatly respected City figure, holding a number of important Directorships.

Michael, the fourth son, was captured by the Germans while serving in France in 1940 and he later died of his wounds.

In his biography of Peter Fleming, Duff Hart-Davis described the House as "vaguely French, decidedly Gothic and totally hideous, the new Joyce Grove was a monster even when it was built. In 1913 it was struck by lightning, and after advantage had been taken of the accident to extend the house by adding a new wing, it had forty-four bedrooms besides a dozen bathrooms where, from every tap (as Peter once lugubriously remarked) there emerged a different kind of soup."

The Flemings occupied the house until the 1930s. Robert Fleming died in 1933 and his widow, Kate, lived there until her death in 1936. The house and estate then passed to Philip Fleming, who gave it to his nephew Peter. Peter decided it should be given to St Mary's, Paddington, and so it was in 1937. The house was used initially as a preliminary training school for nurses from Westminster and St Mary's Hospitals, and later for convalescent patients from St Mary's, in all for forty-one years, when it was closed because of cutbacks within the National Health Service.

This house, which had been so well maintained, bade me welcome immediately. It had large rooms with lovely moulded ceilings and cornices, mahogany panelling and doors, a wide hall and staircase, and passages through which the sun streamed. From each room the view of the gardens was beautiful. Here there was both scope and space. One could imagine the gracious living of another era, served by a large indoor and outdoor staff. Past occupiers would, I felt, be happy to know of its new purpose.

When we went round part of the stable block we found that it remained almost as it had been left, and in the room where the stable boys had slept the mattresses were still on the iron beds and the following notice in large letters reminded us of an era so close in years but really an age away: "Any man found *smoking* on these premises will be instantly dismissed. By Order of your Employer." We also found a switch in the butler's pantry which could turn off all the lights in the servants' quarters, presumably at his whim!

The lives of the young men had been cruelly shattered by the First World War and many of those employed in the house, and also in the Village, had lost their lives.

This Sue Ryder Home was eventually opened in May 1979 and, working in co-operation with the Department of Radiotherapy at the Royal Berkshire Hospital, met the urgent need in the Berkshire/South Oxfordshire/ Buckinghamshire area for facilities for the continuing care of cancer patients. Fourteen beds were put up in what had been the ballroom/drawing and billiard rooms. Part of the hall area was used as a dining room and sitting room. The library near the front door was converted into a chapel, and the dining room, renamed the Fleming Room, was let out for wedding receptions and other gatherings. Immediately opposite the front door a Sue Ryder Shop was set up and manned by volunteers.

Meanwhile, sluices, extra loos, bathrooms and wash basins were installed and all fire regulations attended to. A large shaft for a stretcher lift was prepared, and on the first floor further conversions and decoration went on before we accepted another eight patients. In early 1984, three more beds were brought into use and since then the total has increased to twenty five, up to 31 December 1992. Thus far over 4,145 patients have been nursed here, and its Domiciliary Sister makes over 300 visits to patients in their own homes each year.

The people who are admitted are those for whom there are neither suitable places in hospitals nor adequate facilities in their own homes. They may live alone and have no family or neighbours; alternatively, they may be blocking an acutely needed hospital bed. Even today there are areas in Britain, by no means excluding the Royal County of Berkshire, where there are dwellings with no hot water or indoor sanitation. In such conditions it is obviously very difficult, if not impossible, to nurse patients who are seriously ill.

Of all the Foundation's Homes, this one is the best size as it provides ample storage space and, most importantly, sufficient privacy. How tremendously the work would benefit, consolidate and grow if more such houses of this quality became available . . .

All fund-raising, both for the conversion and the running costs, was left to the Foundation. Mr G. Cashell, an eye surgeon, became the first Honorary Appeal Co-ordinator. In 1994 a minimum of £600,000 had to be raised by the Home's loyal supporters to meet the difference between the grants received from central and local funds and the running costs of the Home.

Fund-raising events previously included the Shetland Pony Grand National which was started in 1980 and proved to be the highlight of the Shetland Show and Highland Fair each year. As a result, invitations came in from many places including Olympia, Kempton Park Race Course, the Royal Highland Show and Jersey Race Course.

The "National" had a pool of twenty jockeys (boys and girls) from the age of eight who wore the silks of famous racehorse owners. A special song was composed for them to sing and this was relayed to the public before the race began.

Captain C. Middleton-Stewart and his wife, Philippa, were two stalwart supporters, and I should like to quote from a letter Philippa wrote following her husband's tragic death in 1981:

> Like so many, Colin's introduction to Sue Ryder's work came through the enthusiasm of a friend, and so it was rather to our surprise that a meeting was held in our home to try to form a Henley Support Group. The meeting was, as so often first meetings are, rather inconclusive, but very soon after that Colin became involved to the hilt in fund-raising activities. His energy was harnessed to something positive and creative; there was no time to wonder what to do with one's retirement! The telephone rang constantly, our ancient typewriter typed out, uncertainly, memos and notes; lists had to be completed, meetings to be arranged. The car was in such demand that out of consideration for my needs, Colin bought a moped on which he dashed hither and thither becoming a well known, if not slightly eccentric, figure in his white crash helmet and orange – foul weather sailing gear. Then there was the great day of the first Summer Fair; to that, as for all great occasions, Colin wore his kilt. All the hard work, all the anxieties

beforehand were forgotten. The day was an absolute success! The fair was hardly over before the next event was being planned. Colin gained much pleasure from an ever widening circle of friends, and the inspiration of people's generosity and good will.

Last Easter, he spent hours of work in the grounds preparing for the Open Day, and for the first time I felt concern that he was perhaps over-taxing himself. In June, shortly after the Open Day, he fell ill with what appeared to be bronchitis, but from then on his health steadily deteriorated. The next Summer Fair had to be planned. Colin's marvellous fund of energy was all but exhausted, and it was only sheer determination and his sense of responsibility which kept him going. By November he had to admit that he was not well enough to run the Christmas Fair, but with infinite tact the Committee eased the burden off his shoulders, and Colin was delighted that the Christmas Fair was such a success.

From November to January we lived through grey anxious days. It wasn't until after Christmas that tests for cancer were positive, and when the prime source was found Colin's condition was inoperable. Colin's courage never deserted him. At his request, I asked Matron if he might "spend a few days at the Home to stabilise his condition". How heartened I felt by her response . . . "We shall be so glad to take care of Colin." It was dusk when we drove up to the Home. As the door opened and flooded us with light, Colin was welcomed in with open arms. He must have had a sense of homecoming for though he died not long after his admission, he died so peacefully. The memory of his death will remain with me always, vivid in every detail. At a personal level the most profound experience of my life, but symbolic too of what the place means to those in need – if I may say so, a haven of understanding and love.

Like each Sue Ryder Home, Nettlebed, of necessity, runs to a routine. At 8 a.m. a report is given by the night staff to Matron or her deputy. At noon the Sisters meet to discuss drugs and the regime. At 9 p.m. the night staff receive a report from the day staff and on most Wednesdays there is a meeting of the medical and nursing staff, together with the Macmillan nurses, called "Case Conference", so that an assessment can be made of the work carried out and a check kept on the number of patients await-ing admission. Here, as elsewhere in the Foundation, the uniforms and caps worn by the nurses and others are in different colours to denote their particular job.

General practitioners, medical students and nurses, including district nurses, come to the Home for talks and instruction on pain control. Here, in this peaceful place, there is much activity. There are sixty full- and part-time staff and between thirty and forty volunteers. Their work is vital and much appreciated, as is the experienced social worker.

As in other Foundation Homes, the patients come from a variety of backgrounds, and on my visits I never cease to be amazed by what they have done in their lives. They also tell me how much more beautiful build-ings like Nettlebed are than modern ones without character or individuality. One young man, an engineer by profession, enthusiastically told me that he had listed the forty one lovely items of architectural interest which he saw about the Home.

The terrace and large lily pond delight patients who come to convalesce after surgery or radiotherapy before returning to the community; while others end their days with us peacefully and in dignity, offering their own examples of how to live courageously.

The grounds cover twenty-six acres and eight gardeners were employed there in its Fleming heyday. One of the Foundation's gardeners, who specialised in flowers, died of asthma at the age of twenty-eight, and now only one full-time gardener, a young Dutchman, with occasional help, remains.

I usually make my rounds during the evening when I often meet friends and relatives of the patients. One such friend sat by the patient's bedside right through to daybreak and staff kept her company and endeavoured to comfort her. She looked very tired and, after exchanging greetings, she went to the garden for refreshment in the early morning air.

Christine was someone else I remember. She was eighteen and came from Bishop's Stortford where she lived with her father and stepmother. She did not get on with her stepmother and was sent to boarding school in Devon. Christine felt rejected by her family and resorted to attention-seeking behaviour, including an overdose of tablets on one or two occasions. She was under the informal supervision of the Social Services Department. This young girl was courageous as far as her illness was concerned and before her operation she was cheerful, polite and smiled a lot. Post-operatively she seemed depressed.

Christine came to the Home for three weeks' post-operative convalescence and she was then going back to the hospital for a check-up prior to being discharged to a hostel for young women. However, the hostel warden had previously told her social worker that they would not be able to take her back if she was not able to work or if she needed any sort of medical supervision. Her condition improved greatly in the family atmosphere at the Home; she was obviously thriving on the love she was receiving. Her prognosis was very poor and we wanted to help her enjoy what little time she had left, so it was decided that she should not go back the hostel. At the Home, Christine had built up a very good relationship with an auxiliary (a mother of four children) who felt it would be a good idea to foster Christine for as long as she was fit enough, the Foundation's Home acting as a support. Christine had three happy weeks at her new home before her condition weakened and she came back to her other home where she was nursed among friends until she died two weeks later, peacefully and pain-free. Christine's fear was not of dying but of experiencing pain.

When I stay at the Home I like to sleep in one of the rooms in the flat kept for relatives and friends who find it necessary to stay overnight. I try to leave at 5 a.m., and the Night Sister usually accompanies me to the front door bearing news of the patients – "Nigel is a little rested now," "Tim died: we prayed together." "Give everyone my love," I reply, "I will continue to pray for them on my drives."

Once, as I drove away, dawn had broken an hour or two beforehand and shafts of sunlight glistened through the beechwoods and onto the bluebells. Further on I passed through a swirl of mist and remembered this poem:

> They that love beyond the world cannot be separated by it
> Death cannot kill what never dies.
> Nor can spirits ever be divided that love and live in the same
>   divine principal, the root and record of their friendship.
> If absence be not death, neither is theirs.
> Death is but crossing the world, as friends do the seas;
> they live in one another still.

> For they must needs be present, that love and live in that
>   which is omnipresent.
> In this Divine glass they see face to face; and their converse
>   is free as well as pure.

> This is the comfort of friends, that though they may be said
>   to die; yet their friendship and society are in the best sense
>   ever present, because immortal.

William Penn

26

St John's, Moggerhanger, Bedfordshire

> ... My marks and scars I carry with me, to be
> a witness for me, that I have fought his battles,
> who will now be my rewarder ... So he passed
> over, and the trumpets sounded for him on the
> other side.
>
> John Bunyan

THE SERIOUS NEEDS AMONGST the elderly and also the lack of facilities for cancer patients which existed in the north and south of Bedfordshire were brought to my attention by Dr T. Nicol, community physician for Bedfordshire. Dr Nicol organised and invited me to a public meeting on Monday, 1 March 1976, at Putnoe Heights Church when positive interest was shown by several members of the audience. Informal meetings had previously taken place in the north wing of the South Bedfordshire Hospital with members of the medical and nursing professions. They declared that a property must be found and converted. Tim Nicol's quiet perseverance and deep commitment to serve the community in the widest sense has had a profound effect in encouraging others to follow his example. He has been unswerving in his determination to organise support for the Foundation in Bedfordshire.

Like Cambridgeshire, Bedfordshire has no history of open villages, which consisted of owner-occupiers without allegiance to a Lord of the Manor, and as a result there is a singular lack of large properties. One house which I visited was in good condition and accessible to Bedford, but it was in the process of being sold when I went there. Several other properties about which we had been advised were either too small, too derelict, or too isolated. Inwardly I hoped that Ampthill Park House, where I had met my husband in 1955, could be acquired, but unfortunately the timing was wrong and so this beautiful place passed out of the hands of both Foundations.

Finally, someone remembered Major and Mrs Thornton at Moggerhanger. They were prepared to allow the Foundation to acquire their Victorian house, which had been built in about 1850 as a lodge, as they wished to move into a cottage adjoining the garden.

Further meetings took place, and at one held in the house of Mrs C. Robinson, a Foundation Co-ordinating Appeal Team was formed to proceed with fund-raising and to tell the public of the Foundation's intentions and the needs which existed. Support groups mushroomed throughout the country and beyond. There followed eighty-three site meetings, as the House had to be renovated and extended, and a lift and central heating installed. From small beginnings a pattern of fund-raising has emerged which could well be followed by other Appeal Teams in the future, especially where new Foundation Homes are envisaged.

The Foundation's Co-ordinating Appeal Team has to raise large and essential sums each year in addition to the grant received from the Area Health Authority and the allowances made to patients by the Department of Social Security. In 1991 the grant amounted to £121,500 and the DSS allowances came to £102,699 and these were set against the total running costs of the Home of £604,725. The shortfall of nearly £400,000 is the figure which has to be raised every year by the tremendous efforts of the Bedford Appeals Office just to break even.

Each month a diary of fund-raising events is drawn up, and in September a huge fête is organised and on one occasion the cake stall alone made £3,612! There is the sale of a Celebrity Cook Book, too, which includes favourite recipes of members of the Royal Family, showbusiness celebrities and sporting personalities.

It was Dr Nicol and his colleagues who had the original idea of organising coach parties to London and elsewhere as a fund-raising enterprise, and he passed on his role of Group Visits Organiser to a friend, retired architect, David Carter. The excursions are known as the Sue Ryder Visits and they have made a significant contribution to the costs of the Home. Around 100 trips are run each year and, in the cost of each ticket for each visit, is a donation of £2.50 to the Home. There are now around 260 people on the mailing list for the visits and they receive regular programmes of proposed trips. There is a very wide range – from factory visits, garden shows, outings to stately homes and town and country tours, to theatres, concerts, museums, art galleries and television studios. At the end of 1995, over 2,000 people made ninety visits travelling over 10,000 miles and making over £3,000 for St John's in the process. Now, David is thinking of branching out into weekend excursions and trips abroad. Members were asked recently to suggest places they would like to visit and, as a result, the group now has enough places to keep them going until the year 2000 – allowing for a few repeats!

Here is a short reflection from Ruth Dunkley, one of those many visitors:

> I first started going on the Sue Ryder visits about two years ago. On reflection I think it was probably desperation at the time as I was suffering from 'workitus' and needed some kind of release to take my mind off it at weekends. So I dutifully boarded the coach one Sunday morning and took in the delights of a morning concert at Wigmore Hall and an afternoon spent looking round an art gallery.

When I arrived home I felt rejuvenated and thoroughly relaxed. Why had the day been so rewarding? Possibly the first thing was the warm welcome I had received on the coach. Then there was the thoroughly peaceful journey on which I could read and think with no pressure around me and, as the day unfolded, I found I was surrounded by warm friendly people who were there to talk to – if I wanted.

Many outings and expeditions have followed this first one, both at weekends and in the school holidays, and what a diverse selection of culture available; plays, ballets, musicals, concerts, galleries, museums, gardens, stately homes, famous towns etc etc. I cannot pick out any particular one that I have enjoyed more than any other, but perhaps my favourite is the regular Sunday morning concert at Wigmore Hall. What more could a "workaholic" need than to sit in this beautiful building and let the mellow notes of a string quartet wash over you, followed by a glass of sherry (or two if you are with generous friends who give you their ticket!). You then drift up the road with your colleagues to enjoy an Italian pasta and a glass of wine. Maybe it is this that makes the pictures in the art gallery more remarkable, the stately home more beautiful, the gardens more striking, the artefacts in the museum more interesting. Whatever it is, the reward of the day is the peace that settles upon a befuddled brain and the thought that maybe the week to follow won't be so bad after all. I know people find the variety of outings a tonic and a joy to be part of for many different reasons. On a personal level, I have found them to be the best thing that could have happened to me. They have helped me through some difficult times both at work and at home. The diverse selection of culture has provided a true learning process, giving me a thirst for more. The convenience of travelling from door to door has been a tremendous asset. But the most important and special reason for going is the support and friendship I have received from some very special people, too. David's hard work has brought pleasure to many. With everyone's support, long may they continue.

There are regular marathons and sponsored cycle races and many schools are responsible for organising their own fund-raising projects.

Another event organised was the Motor Show. A large building was leased and dealers came to rent a space and show their cars. This has raised £5,000!

One of the highlights of 1983 was the Embroidery Exhibition staged at St Andrew's Church, Biggleswade, over the August Bank Holiday weekend. It attracted over 5,500 people, and included items on loan from the Royal Family, the Cecil family, christening robes from Hatfield House and antique and modern lace from all parts of Bedfordshire. The profits amounted to £6,150.

Not all fund-raising events are on such a large scale. We were all very touched when the following letter arrived, and deeply appreciative of the kind thought and loving effort of these children:

Dear
Lady Ryder

My Mummy is sending you a
cheque for 121 pounds, which I
collected from sponsors, when I ran
a half marathon for the Sue Ryder
Foundation— I am seven years old and
I enjoyed the run very much. I am
sending you a picture of my dad and
me wearing our medals and tee shirts.

Love from

Andrew

xox xox

John Hare, the late Bishop of Bedford, was especially concerned with the needs of people who were ill. When he died in 1976 his family wished that financial contributions given in his memory be donated to the Sue Ryder Home, St John's. His memorial appeal has since then made a very substantial contribution to the funds of the Home, and, in addition, his family gave a silver chalice and paten to the chapel.

On 27 December 1979 (the Feast of St John the Evangelist) the Chapel was dedicated by the then Bishop of St Albans, Dr Robert Runcie, and the Catholic Bishop of Northampton the Rt Rev. Charles Grant. It was one of Dr Runcie's last official appointments before he was enthroned as Archbishop of Canterbury. In his address, the Reverend Norman Hill, Vicar of Moggerhanger and Northill, said:

> How appropriate that Bishop John should be remembered here. He will be remembered in Bedford for his achievements, but here he is in a special way near work which was close to his heart, which was unfolding in his last days when he frequently with eagerness enquired after its progress.
>
> The way he pursued the vision that stirred him has so stirred others that well over £90,000 has been given in his name to this Home. Bishop John did not live to see this place become a reality, but I have no doubt that he will be helping the work of healing here with his prayers.
>
> Nothing would have been achieved, however, without the other partner in this venture, the Sue Ryder Foundation and Lady Ryder herself. She is happily present today. She would be embarrassed by any eulogies, but I have to say that we are also celebrating today yet another successful translation of the compassion which has directed the course of her life into bricks and mortar, into shelter and care for the suffering.

Naturally, every patient is different and not always easy or kind. The news concerning their symptoms or the situation in which they find themselves may, understandably, cause them to argue or express anger or resentment. Doctors, nurses, auxiliaries and volunteers bear the brunt of their feelings. Staff, too, have their problems, but these can sometimes be exchanged and discussed with patients and relatives. Thus, there is a greater feeling of togetherness. Both Dr David Marshall, past Clinical Director of the Sue Ryder Home, Oxenhope, who remains in an honorary capacity, and Father Paddy Mitchell quote the North Amerindian Sioux: "You cannot touch the wounded unless you have scarred hands." Dr Marshall goes on to say:

> Those scars may be sore and make us difficult to work with; the nurse is left after the doctor's visit – the nurse, the patient, the questions, the long nights – they have the privilege and the joy of caring but also the difficulties. And then there is the committee – do we always try and know what is needed to support staff; the irritating non-functioning of some apparatus, the way a door opens, the knowledge of a better means of doing something; the nurse doesn't always tell us or matron – but you know in families how the irritation becomes transferred and the feeling at the end of a long day "doesn't *anyone else care?*"
>
> Please remember in prayer not only our patients, but also the carers; try and understand it is hard to be a saint always, we – I – am not very good at this understanding. It needs more time, more skill, more love.

St John's Sue Ryder Home serves the area of north Bedfordshire – Huntingdon, St Neots, and surrounding areas. Occasionally, patients are taken from other areas if St John's is the most suitable Home for them. Some referrals come from the London hospitals. The first patients were admitted to the Home during the week commencing 12 May 1980; since then 2,081 patients and their families have been cared for up to the 31 December 1993. The approach to admission is as flexible as possible so that patients and their families are helped in a way that they feel is best for them. They may need assessment for pain and symptom control; a period of convalescence following treatment; respite care to give their families an opportunity for rest or a holiday; or terminal care. The initial contact is usually made on the telephone with Matron, by the nurses working with the patient's family doctor or consultant, after which a detailed medical form is completed. When the need for admission is urgent this can usually be arranged the same day. The cost of each occupied bed has now risen to £120 per day , and the total in one year is over £700,000. About fifty per cent is received from Health Authorities. This means the supporters of the Sue Ryder Home St John's have to raise over £350,000 each year, it is always hoped that patients' families and friends will contribute what they can.

One of the first patients was the Reverend Harold Phoenix who had been vicar of Moggerhanger for twenty-three years. He had been living alone and remained with the Foundation's family for a year. He always came to the meetings at the beginning and said prayers.

Mr J. was a Jewish pharmacist of forty-six who was admitted with carcinoma of the larynx with spread. He was well known in the area as a kind and caring man who took pride in providing a good service to the community where he lived and worked. His cancer was diagnosed in 1979 when he first had radiotherapy treatment. Then in 1982 he had a total laryngectomy, leaving him without a voice. He could converse using oesophageal speech and this we encouraged. He needed further radio-therapy and surgery in 1983 for spread of that carcinoma to his spine and was left with very severe, intractable pain. The management of his pain control, and its aims, was discussed with him. This he appreciated very much because of his knowledge of drugs. His pain did indeed come under control, which enabled him to enjoy listening to music again. One of our staff (a trained musician) used to listen to tapes of favourite classical pieces with him.

Mr J. died peacefully, having been with us for nearly four months, without pain and surrounded by his loving family. Two members of staff attended his funeral in the synagogue, a very moving experience indeed and a tribute to a very brave man.

I well remember Miss Beane, a former hospital matron, who, despite the severity of her illness, discussed in depth the changes she had seen throughout her career. She was critical of the changes made by the Salmon Report and was sad that some nurses no longer looked upon their work as a vocation. During one of our discussions she told me the importance of a single room to her personally, particularly in her condition, and one of her suggestions was that more paving stones instead of gravel should be put down outside to enable individuals in wheelchairs to get around more easily.

Mary was a young Irish woman diagnosed with cerebral tumour with spread. She was married and had two little children. On admission she had to be carried from the car; she couldn't stand, she was very drowsy, although her beautiful smile shone through as we introduced ourselves to her and her husband. Mary had lost all of her hair due to radiotherapy treatment and had her head covered with a pretty scarf.

During the few weeks she stayed with us she improved considerably – she walked, with two nurses at first and then on her own. Her husband was delighted and asked if it was possible for her to return home, even for a short time. We agreed to this. She remained at home, managing to cope with light housework, and being a mother to her children.

After three months at home her condition began to deteriorate and it became obvious that she needed admission for terminal care. She was re-admitted to St John's and died two weeks later, peacefully, totally trusting in God. All through her illness her strong faith had upheld her and she died still with that lovely smile, sure in the knowledge of a better life ahead, her faith literally shining out of her face.

Matron and her staff were determined from the start that the Home should be a peaceful place where all would share together the joys and sorrows of each day. The Matron now keeps alive this aim with her staff.

There are about fifty volunteers who are an essential part of the team and who come from the surrounding towns and villages. Many have worked at St John's for several years, reporting faithfully every week to do their turn on the rota. They are responsible for a variety of tasks, answering the telephone, serving the teas and coffees, arranging flowers, laying tables and preparing vegetables, as well as befriending patients and relatives.

Since the Home opened a social worker, a physiotherapist and now an aromatherapist have been added to the staff. In this way the range of support and therapy has been extended to meet the varying needs of patients. Many people are involved in the work at St John's, each having his or her own special contribution to make.

The family grows with each new patient, and their relatives and friends are encouraged to share in the care and support of their loved ones. Once pain has been controlled, anxiety relieved, and a willingness to talk realistically about the present and the future established, then each day can perhaps be accepted for whatever it will bring. From the many appreciative letters we receive from relatives I remember the following:

> I feel sure you must receive countless letters such as this. I am writing to thank you and your nurses for the care given to my aunt while she was a patient at St John's Sue Ryder Home. During my SRN training I saw many many patients in the terminal stages of carcinoma.
>
> Having spent many days at St John's I cannot tell you how happy it made us all to see Sally so settled. The first Monday I went there, someone mentioned how peaceful it was – to this she replied, "There is no peace from pain" but I feel that by the time I saw her for the last time she found peace from pain. She had nothing but praise, affection and respect for your nurses.
>
> Speaking as a relative – it was heaven to be able to sit quietly while Sally slept without someone informing you visiting time was over or to see someone else's relatives wake her up. It was lovely to talk to the Ward Sister and know she was listening and interested; not staring at the clock on the wall behind your head! To be 'phoned when things did worsen and to be told to phone at any time of the day or night if we were worried was truly appreciated. Also to be given an honest appraisal of her condition, not just told "comfortable night". I swear I'll never tell anyone that again – it means nothing when you say it and only worries the life out of you when you are told it!
>
> You really are very lucky with your staff – they'll all be remembered with great fondness by all the family. I feel I have learnt more by watching your standards of nursing care than from any intensive study block that I could have attended!

I like to feel that St John's has remained a family home and retained the informal friendly atmosphere.

27

Leckhampton Court, Gloucestershire

"I wait until my summons comes."

THREE MILES FROM CHELTENHAM and the excellent Radiotherapy
Centre there, which was provided at the general hospital by public sub-
scriptions, lies Leckhampton Court, a magnificent old building which dates
from the fourteenth century.

During previous searches in this part of Britain, I had been directed to
another beautiful Cotswold stone house ("begun about 1704") on the main
Oxford–Cheltenham road. It was in immaculate condition: the ash floorboards glistened with cleanliness, and there was a small chapel too. It was
thought to be owned by the New Zealand Bank. The last private owners
had been a couple whose only son, Lieutenant Thomas Colville, Coldstream
Guards, had been killed in the Western Desert at Longstop Hill on
Christmas Day 1942, aged twenty. His parents had put down a new floor
in the long drawing room in anticipation of giving their son a twenty-first
birthday ball.

I had been misinformed that the High Commissioner for New Zealand
knew who owned the house, and so in 1977 kindly received me in London
during a heatwave, and on hearing about this property and the land
attached expressed great interest and assured me of his good will and
support. Unhappily, the information we had received had been wrong
and the house was owned by another bank which chose to dispose of it to
a private purchaser. If only we had been able to obtain this lovely house it
would have been possible to admit patients within a short time, after
complying with fire regulations. We might thus have relieved a great deal
of human suffering in that area long, long before we were eventually able
to do so.

Several years elapsed, despite *constant* searches, before we were able
to find a suitable property in this area. On one occasion, I remember,
we went to see a depressing former workhouse with its lingering aroma of
the past.

One day we referred to the quarterly edition of the Historic Buildings List
again and decided that we should try to find a house listed called
Leckhampton Court in the Village of that name near Cheltenham. We eventually discovered the place and ventured up the drive. The grounds were so
overgrown and neglected that it took us some time to find the actual
building amongst the undergrowth – indeed we were obliged to ask

someone at the top of the drive, who was living temporarily in a caravan, if she knew where the Court was.

We made our way through the brambles and thick shrubs, past a small hen coop. As we reached an opening with a dilapidated door falling off its hinges, to our great surprise the owner appeared and when I asked if I might look around he exclaimed, "It's too late." I looked at my colleague, Robert Clifton, who murmured, "Go on, encourage him." I did so, and we were then taken on a "conducted tour" of this historic and once beautiful house. We tiptoed from one dilapidated room to the next and were left in no doubt as to the truth of the information we had been given, that the building had been virtually abandoned for ten years.

The signs of severe neglect and vandalism were shocking everywhere. Water was dripping through the shattered Cotswold slates; various fungi, including dry rot, encrusted much of the woodwork; and ferns and ivy were hanging through the ceiling. We were careful not to walk on the rotted timber floors or press against the crumbling masonry for fear of disturbing the finely balanced equilibrium which had been established between the endeavours of man and nature. The dining room was dark and shuttered, but my torchlight revealed that the panelling and floor joists had all rotted, partly because of springs of water underneath, saplings sprouted through the roof. The owner gave us a vivid description of the history of the old house and referred to one room in the south Tudor wing as King Henry's room. At one point we used a ladder to get into the remains of a room.

Leckhampton Court is one of those very old English houses which seems to have taken on a life of its own, derived from the history which it has witnessed and the events which have taken place within its walls.

The *Domesday Book* records Leckhampton as the property of a Saxon called Bitric, but William the Conqueror confiscated the estate and presented it to his wife, Matilda. Bitric was thrown into prison and so passed from the scene. Shortly afterwards Leckhampton was awarded to the powerful Norman family of Despenser.

The oldest part of the present building – the Banqueting Hall – dates from the fourteenth century. This must have belonged to the earliest recorded building on the site, which was the home of the Giffards who were Lords of the Manor of Leckhampton from 1330 to 1486. The family came from nearby Brimpsfield, and were as colourful a family as any living in that era of flamboyance and eccentricity – indeed, one John Giffard is reputed to have plundered the royal baggage on Ermine Street, an exploit for which he was hanged at Gloucester. The family was very influential locally and had links with most of the surrounding great houses. In the Leckhampton Parish Church there are effigies of the first Sir John and Lady Giffard to live at Leckhampton Court. In 1486 the Manor, together with the Court, passed to the Norwood family through the marriage of John Norwood with Eleanor, daughter of the last John Giffard, who had no sons.

The Norwoods were an old family from Kent, and most of the Court buildings which exist today were built by them. The beautiful timber-fronted wing was their creation and it was they who planned the present layout of the house on three sides of a large courtyard. Perhaps the old house breathed the Giffard spirit of adventure into the Norwoods, for they too showed much enterprise. One of their most illustrious sons was Colonel Henry Norwood, who was described in a contemporary account as "a person eminent for his loyalty in the reign of King Charles I and distinguished in the Civil Wars" – which meant in practice that there was little future for him in Cromwell's England. Leckhampton Court was, in fact, seized by the Republican forces and Henry Norwood fled to America with a party of friends. They were involved en route in an incredible series of adventures and at one time were so short of food that they decided to cast lots to determine who should be eaten. The unfortunate man who lost was, in fact, found to be dead when his companions went to claim him and, according to a reliable account, "this saved them the labour of a Butcher. They greedily fell to and notwithstanding the Accident, he proved a savoury Meal, and they buried him handsomely."

Henry Norwood then went on to establish the colony of Virginia, where the population was still fervently monarchist. After the Restoration, he returned to England, received high honours from Charles II, and was later concerned with the capture of New York from the Dutch. He then bought Leckhampton Court from his cousin and settled down in the country. He became Mayor of Gloucester and Member of Parliament for that City. He was an acquaintance of Samuel Pepys and is mentioned several times in Pepys's diary.

On the death of Henry Norwood, Leckhampton Court passed indirectly to several successive Norwoods and one of them, the Reverend Thomas, who succeeded in 1707, built the great three-storey window on the north terrace in front of the Banqueting Hall. In 1732 the central part of the north wing was destroyed by a fire, "said to have been occasioned by neglecting a chafing-dish of charcoal placed to dry a Room new-washed". Some years later the Banqueting Hall itself was completely panelled, covering the splendid decorated windows and entirely changing its character. The quotation at the head of this Chapter, "I wait until my summons comes", is taken from the tomb of William and Elizabeth Norwood.

In 1797, Charles Brandon Trye, the famous surgeon, inherited the estate when another Henry Norwood died leaving no heir; and so the third great family came into possession of Leckhampton Court. Charles Trye developed the quarries on the hill and, in order to obtain the building stone and lime, he installed the first known railway in Gloucestershire, a plateway track. Later, at his own expense, he extended his railway to the foot of the hill, to join the Leckhampton branch of Lord Sherborne's Cheltenham and Gloucester Railway. He died in 1811 after "a life exemplary of virtue and of eminent public utility".

Charles' son, Henry, who succeeded him, eventually ran heavily into debt and in 1841 was obliged to sell the estate. It realised more than £56,000 and was bought by Henry's brother, Charles, who was rector of Leckhampton. After fifty-three years, Charles demolished part of the house in front of the Banqueting Hall and moved the circular steps from the courtyard gate to the front of the entrance porch.

In 1894, the estate was split up and sold. John Hargreaves, a descendant of the great Lancashire cotton pioneer, bought the Court and the land around it and once more it became a fashionable house. Hargreaves was a close friend of the Prince of Wales (later King Edward VII) and during the Prince's affair with Lily Langtry he built the north wing in keeping with the original architectural pattern, with a special suite for the Prince and his lady above the library. The wing is still known as the King's Wing, and up to quite recently there were people at Leckhampton who could remember the Prince's carriage, with blinds discreetly drawn, making its way to and from the Court.

Through the generosity of John Hargreaves' daughter and her husband, who lived at the Court after Hargreaves' death, the house became a Voluntary Aid Detachment Hospital from 1915 to 1919. The long library in the north wing, with its fine fireplace and wood panelling, became a ward with sixteen beds. Some of the 1,700 patients treated there gave accounts of nurses dressing up as ghosts – perhaps the origin of recent unsubstantiated stories of ghosts in the Court – and recorded their appreciation of the spirit of service which existed there during the terrible years of the First World War. During the Second World War the Court was used in succession by British and American forces. In 1957 it became a preparatory school run by Dr P. Saunders.

The Foundation's involvement with Leckhampton Court was brought about by the desperate need for after-care facilities to work in conjunction with the Radiotherapy Centre at Cheltenham General Hospital where there were twenty beds for acute cases, increased to thirty beds in 1977. Originally, the Cobalt Unit Appeal raised £88,000 to build the Cancer Treatment Centre there in 1966. Later on, the Fund continued to build on its success to provide vital equipment and facilities. The National Health Service remains responsible for covering all costs of the patients and has itself provided a linear accelerator and other equipment for treatment. However, no such financial cover is given to the Sue Ryder Home when patients are transferred from the Radiotherapy Centre.

The Radiotherapy Centre at Cheltenham Hospital, which in 1993 treated over 2,000 new cases, and the Sue Ryder Home, serve a population of approximately one million. A report written in 1976 by a consultant explains why a Sue Ryder Home was felt to be necessary in the area:

> In Gloucestershire we are very fortunate that, in great measure due to the continuing generosity of the community, there are excellent treatment facilities, which are constantly being improved, and each year more patients

can be cured. The problem of continuing care however is not adequately provided for, and causes great difficulty as well as distress to many people. The figures indicate the extent of the problem. Each year over 1,500 new cancer cases occur in the county of Gloucester, and each year over 1,000 people die from this disease. In addition to this, the Area Radiotherapy and Oncology Centre, based in Cheltenham, provides a service for not only the whole of Gloucestershire, but also for Herefordshire, South Worcestershire and the adjacent areas of Gwent and Powys – a population approaching a million people. There is a desperate need for a continuing care home in this area as the nearest homes are fifty miles away and they cover large areas.

This is the sort of home which Sue Ryder envisages in Gloucestershire. We are indeed fortunate that she has selected us as one of the SOS areas. We must ensure that she is given the maximum support to enable her to turn the vision into reality.

Mrs Saunders, the former owner's American-born wife, seems to have been something of a visionary. She continued faithfully to look after the large flock of geese which, we understood, came with the building when we acquired it, in the hope that one day, in her own words "The eggs could be sold in the village and the proceeds could go towards the restoration".

During one of my many early visits, just after arriving at the Court one evening, I heard her kind voice saying: "My, you should have heard the roar at 3.25 this afternoon, when I turned to see the centre part of the building collapse! It was like a mighty ship going down!" I felt relieved about this particular collapse because that part of the building had been in a most dangerous condition. It turned out that the supporting framework to the Gothic panelling had weakened the roof structure, and consequently the walls had been pushed outward. If we had arrived at the scene some four months earlier, fully organised to carry out remedial work, I think that most of the roof structure could have been saved.

In October 1977, John Beresford, one of the Foundation's gardeners, started to cut the undergrowth and make a way through to the Court. He worked all day long and was a most conscientious man. He proceeded to clear a path which had been completely choked by brambles and all manner of undergrowth. Between October and the following March, John was joined by Mr Hughes, a retired landscape gardener in his eighties, and gradually with the aid of voluntary groups, including local schools and a work party headed by a former Mayor of Cheltenham, the wilderness was attacked. It was at this stage that the phrase "Pilgrim's Progress" came naturally to mind, and thereafter the Sue Ryder Home, Leckhampton Court, was unofficially known by that name.

A little after John began his work, a volunteer from Poland came to the Court with me and together we decided to clean out one room thoroughly – the only room "intact". We felt that the conditions surrounding us were so chaotic that it was necessary to try and bring some order and cleanliness to at least one corner. We carried buckets of cold water from near the stable block and cleared and scrubbed down the room. The work was hard but, at the end of it, it meant that at least this one room was cleaner to camp out in. There was still so much undergrowth that no problems presented themselves as regards loos!

The stone steps leading up to the door of the main entrance were extremely worn, and once the very thick undergrowth had been cut away an incongruous strip of dark red carpet was discovered on the steps.

Andrew, one of the volunteers, kept watch at night for several weeks. Large "Keep Out" notices were put up, but vandals still took an interest. Antoni from Poland, who studied at Warsaw Engineering College, and another volunteer from Spain, Adolpho, did a great deal of surveying and were an enormous help in taking dimensions of over 100 window openings in the main building; a great task, especially as they were camping out.

As the surveying work progressed and the bones of the house were uncovered, a picture of the fourteenth-century Leckhampton Court began to emerge. This is an account written by one of the Foundation's architectural staff of the impression that the newly built house might have made on a visitor:

> The first Leckhampton Court was built in about 1370. It was entered through the two-storey front porch which now stands in the centre of the Court. This entrance led straight into the Great Hall which was forty-four feet long and thirty-one feet high to the ridge. In the centre of the Hall was an open hearth which was the only source of heat in the room. The smoke encrusted and blackened the rafters and must have made the atmosphere unpleasant when the wind was in the wrong quarter.
>
> Opposite the main west door was a second entrance from the east side, and between them was the cross-passage which had doors leading off to other parts of the house.
>
> The nearest of these, right beside the front door, opened into a passage leading southwards to the kitchen. This would have been a detached building a few yards to the south of the house, to avoid the danger of fire. (In about 1500 the south wing was built, housing a new kitchen, still with an open hearth but more conveniently placed, so that hot food might still be warm when it arrived at the high table at the far end of the Hall.)
>
> The second door opened into the Butteries, where wet and dry stores were kept, and the third, at the east end of the cross-passage, led to the stairs up to the Great Chamber over the Butteries.
>
> The Great Chamber was an imposing room twenty-eight feet long. On the East wall was a stone fireplace with ornately carved head and jambs. The open roof had two arch-braced collar beam trusses, with wind-braced purlins along the roof slopes. Three windows, similar to those in the Hall, were flanked by window-seats in the deep reveals, and looked westwards across the Malvern Hills.
>
> Two doorways with arched heads led into lesser chambers at the south end. One chamber had a privy off one corner, which was later upgraded to an entrance porch from the east terrace and had a doorway inserted, with the date "1582" carved in its arched head.
>
> A little door barely two feet wide led off the Great Chamber to the room

over the porch. This room had three narrow windows and a small fireplace
and was decorated with thin red lines picking out the stonework joints on
a white background. The owner of the house would have had a small room
for personal devotions close to his own chamber and this little chamber
with its privacy and proximity would have been ideal.

The Foundation was extremely fortunate to find one dedicated and
first-class building firm, Thomas Williams (Longborough) Ltd of Moreton-
in-Marsh, who provided a wonderful team. The company's senior partner,
Cecil Williams, became a fervent supporter and has been a friend, adviser
and fund-raiser from the start. It was through his drive and enthusiasm
that the north Cotswolds were constantly raising money. His energy and
humour have never flagged. Later, in 1983, Mr Williams became Chairman
of the Foundation's Co-ordinating Team for Fund-raising for the whole
area, a member of the House Committee and in 1987 its Chairman.

Regular site meetings were held in a small hut in a clearing and later
this was erected on the forecourt. These became especially memorable
and were attended by the Senior Honorary Architect and the Foundation's
Honorary Heating Consultant, Mr A. J. Chatfield. In addition, there were
frequent visits by the Foundation's full-time architects from Headquarters,
Mr I. Hardy, and Mr P. Aitken, who worked in close collaboration with
Mr D.S. Palmer (Chief Surveyor) and Mr C. Hope (Foreman) of Messrs
Thomas Williams, and the other employees.

Considering the amount of work which had to be tackled it is not
surprising that some of our discussions became a little intense as we sat
closely together on benches round the one square table with our backs
pushed up against the wall. The enthusiastic debate, combined with the
discharge of numerous pipes, cigars and roll-ups, produced an extremely
rich atmosphere which may have caused a little displeasure to the more
reserved non-smokers but did perhaps, in some strange way, manage to
keep the ill effects of the winters at bay. Frequently the small windows in
the site hut became covered with condensation. One day we walked in and
saw the following scrawled on the wall: "Out of the gloom a voice said to
me 'Smile and be happy: things could be worse'. So I smiled and was happy,
and behold things did get worse!"

Often Mr Williams' wife, Joan, provided lunch, and in the early days
we sat on planks and the remains of a chair or sofa without springs in front
of a log fire in the Oriel Room in the Angel Wing. The stews in particular
will never be forgotten nor, for those who liked it, the ale. Ian Hardy's
enthusiasm for the building never wavered even when it meant leaving
Headquarters at 5.45 a.m. in all weathers to collect the Senior Honorary
Architect from Stamford in Lincolnshire and get to Pilgrim's by 10 a.m. for
site meetings. En route to the site we often called at the baker's as we
approached the Village to buy doughnuts to fortify us against the elements.
Ian even slept on the table in the site hut on occasions. There was an almost
Wartime atmosphere, everyone pulling together. We were all involved in

a great enterprise to save an historic house which was almost past saving and to provide a home for people who were in great need. Sleet, snow and mud during the first and second winters slowed down progress, but each of us felt the greatest happiness in seeing our goal finally realised and patients being received in the building, who clearly love and appreciate the unique atmosphere.

A decision was made at the very beginning that the ruined stable block should be converted first, and within eighteen months, Goose Bay, as we named it, was receiving its first patients. The reason why this building was called Goose Bay was that it was here that the twenty-five or thirty geese were living when the Foundation acquired the property. It took all the persuasion of the previous owner, Mrs Saunders, to carry them bodily out of their cosy home to their two new houses at the bottom of the drive (nicknamed Ryder and Cheshire Houses). Mrs Saunders told me that this had disorientated the geese and I could not help replying that I, too, was affected!

For the general public, and indeed for any visitor who comes, it must be almost impossible to appreciate what toil and effort went into converting the stables in so short a time. The result gives a feeling of intimacy and of being at home. As much as possible of the stonework and original timbers were left. The size of the rooms varies but they all give the impression of being more than bedrooms, and the largest room takes three beds. The individuals who are nursed and live there comment approvingly upon the informal atmosphere.

The local Appeal Team headed by Miss P. Challis and the late Miss P. Reddall worked unceasingly and exceeded by £17,000 the Appeal target of £150,000 set by the Foundation.

Dr David Mahy, the Consultant in Radiotherapy and Oncology at the Cheltenham General Hospital writes:

> The tremendous aesthetic appeal of the restored exterior and the comfortable interior have delighted the local citizens who knew of the magnitude of the task undertaken by the Sue Ryder Foundation. The large crowds which come to the annual Open Days in the late summer show the genuine interest of the community. The Foundation's Home is a success and the few critics of the scale of the enterprise have, when visiting the Home, changed their views and agreed that a purpose-built Home would not have been as good. Staff and patients undoubtedly appreciate the old building with its historic features – old beams, irregular corridors and odd corners as well as its modern facilities and central heating. It is always an interesting place both to work in and to visit.

The first phase of works to Pilgrim's Progress was providing thirteen beds in the Tudor Wing and was completed in 1981 and the final phase, bringing all the patients into the main building, was seventeen beds in the King's Wing in 1993, where we are now registered for thirty patients.

Goose Bay was converted into a Day Care Centre, and was opened by the Bishop of Gloucester in 1988.

The financial help which the Home received in 1992 from local health authorities, Statutory Income Support and central Government grant totalling £295,503 came to less than one-third of the running costs of the Home, which amounted to £1,011,300. The task of meeting more than two-thirds of the running costs, therefore, falls on the shoulders of the Foundation's supporters both local and national. This places a huge strain on the Foundation's resources which are needed not only for its other Homes in Britain and overseas but also to meet the desperate needs of ever-increasing numbers of sick and handicapped. Efforts are being made to extend fund-raising to cover the running costs of this Home so that it not only becomes self-supporting but also is able to contribute to the Foundation's work elsewhere – in the same way as other Homes and supporters contributed so generously to establish Leckhampton Court.

Negotiations with the Gloucestershire Health Authority in connection with contracting for the five years commencing April 1994 were indeed difficult and eventually, rather than contracting with us, the Health Authority agreed to grant aid: £310,000 p.a. up until March 1999 and a once only non-recurring grant of £500,000 payable in the first half of April 1994. The base recurring grant will be payable in April of each year. This agreement of funding will provide for nineteen patients in 1994–5 and this will reduce equally over the five-year period to provide thirteen in patients beds in 1998–9. In addition £20,000 of the recurring grant is made available to support seven-day care patients throughout the five years.

Gloucestershire Health Authority at that time were adamant in their views that patient numbers would reduce over that period of time. This has not been the case and in 1995 average number of patients proved to be twenty per day which on a 50/50 basis suggests that we are under-funded by at least £50,000; and, although we have thoroughly discussed this problem with the various Managers from Gloucestershire Health, they are not prepared to re-negotiate and say that in determining priorities they have decided not to prioritise care developments in 1996.

Cecil Williams very quickly realised the vital role of this Foundation's Home. He was in the forefront of all fund-raising and later with Mrs Gillian Rose, over twenty support groups were formed. Theirs is a never-ending task of thinking up new ways of fund-raising, ranging across the Cotswolds and indeed the majority of Gloucestershire and crossing the immediate boundaries of Hereford and Worcester.

I am always amazed by what they achieve and of the loyalty and enthusiasm which both supporters and the public show for the work year in, year out. I pray that people suffering with different conditions and those who are unloved will find the same support and assistance elsewhere.

To May 1994, 3,829 patients have been nursed in the Home. Domiciliary visits are an important element of the care provided by the Home. The Liaison Nurse has made 1,536 assessment visits and 170 bereavement visits.

Over the years the Foundation acquired its own Domiciliary Care Teams and bereavement counsellors and whenever I accompany one of them I am reminded of visits in my childhood with the district nurses, and also of countless later visits in the company of the Foundation's physicians, nurses and social workers in a variety of countries. Time and patience are essential, and so too is the gift of being a good listener. I find it is important to show that one wants to share and to be on the same wavelength.

One of the problems of a patient diagnosed with a cancer is a sense of isolation. This is clearly shown by the following extracts from a letter written by a patient from Leeds:

> I suppose one could call my problem loneliness. I do at times feel depressed, but first I had better explain. I am thirty-nine years old, was married in 1963; my husband died in 1972 leaving me with two children then aged five and seven. I remarried in 1974 and had another child in 1975. Last September I separated from my husband. So here I am now with three children aged 18,16 and 7. About two and a half years ago I was told I had cancer. The treatments and operations have failed, so you can say I am waiting to die, or for a miracle to save my life.
>
> My children know what is happening to me and it is a subject we talk about and accept. Arrangements for the children's future and funeral arrangements have all been made. The problem now is, that by accepting what is happening I suddenly find myself alone; people don't want to know, death is a taboo subject. I am a Christian and talk to the father at my local church, and while he tells me I have great courage in accepting my position it does not alleviate the problem in loneliness. My ex-husband did not want the responsibility of myself or the children. My friend of fifteen years suddenly did not want to see me anymore. My family (four brothers, four sisters, all in Liverpool) come to judge this Christian whose God is letting her die.
>
> Is there no one who understands I am still the same woman, I still want to belong to someone, be someone's friend? . . .

The work in the Foundation's Homes should complement the Domiciliary Care Teams, the importance of whose specialised knowledge in nursing and treating cancer patients cannot be over-emphasised. Whenever possible, patients naturally prefer to be nursed at home till the end of their lives. Many parents and relatives of child and adult patients often struggle under the most difficult circumstances to keep them at home, from the time of the diagnosis and through the various stages of their illness, and thus the Domiciliary Care Teams are vital. General practitioners and district nurses visit and give what time they can spare, but often many hours have to be spent by a member of the Domiciliary Care Team in listening to the doubts, questions and worries of the individual and his family.

In the case of one sixteen-year old, his parents understandably could not bring themselves to share their grief in spite of everything Matron, the nurses, clergy and others were willing to do. It would have been presumptuous for any of them to question why:

His parents could not discuss his illness with him or with anyone else. The boy was aware of his deterioration, but in their distress his parents were unable to give him much support. His father did visit him very frequently and was able to cuddle his son, often until he relaxed into sleep. The mother visited only occasionally as she felt it impossible to cope with the situation.

The illness was very sudden, unexpected and rapid, and there was no time for the parents to come to terms with it. He was thought to have injured his leg whilst playing football, but when the pain did not clear he was X-rayed and found to have a sarcoma of the right fibula. As a result of a body scan it was decided that it was safe to amputate the leg as there were no signs of any spread. However, one month later very excessive bony and chest secondaries developed and he deteriorated very rapidly and died nine days after admittance to the Home.

Often the time arrives when the individual is groping to learn about his condition. It is wrong to assume that everyone can stoically accept the truth; the right moment has to be sought to break and gently explain the bad news. Some patients have already guessed; others prefer to know all the facts and then make the necessary preparations. They may need to be assisted in doing this. Then there are those who do not want to face the truth and pretend it is just another illness; and lastly there are those who inwardly know but are not prepared to talk about it. If there is a pretence between husband and wife or next of kin a sort of game of hide and seek ensues and this brings with it great mental and physical strain. I have had the privilege of knowing many in each of these groups, but I would never presume to generalise.

While on one of my visits, I met a woman who knew that her life was coming to an end. She had worked in the mission field for many years as a physician, and we talked about prayers and poetry. Before leaving her we said the following words together which are attributed to Etienne de Grellet:

> I shall pass through this world but once
> If, therefore, there be any kindness I can show,
> or any good thing I can do, let me do it now;
> let me not defer or neglect it, for I shall not
> pass this way again.

In 1981, to the Foundation's surprise and pleasure, it was announced that the restoration work at Leckhampton Court had been awarded the first Design Award for Natural Stone, Sponsored jointly by the Stone Federation and the *Architects' Journal*. There were forty-two entries for the conservation and/or restoration category which the Foundation's Home won. Among the competing entries were Covent Garden, St Paul's Cathedral, Wells Cathedral, King's College Chapel, Sherborne Abbey and Christ Church, Oxford.

In the *Architect's Journal* of 30 September 1981 in which the announcement of the Award was made, after a brief outline of all the entries, the

following passage described why the restoration of Leckhampton Court had
been chosen:

> On visiting the site the judges quickly realised that an immense amount of
> work had been carried out with affection and care and with a great deal of
> personal involvement. The countryside around was scoured for stone and
> especially for stone roof slates, many of which were missing or smashed.
> Indeed, the roofs are a minor masterpiece with the slates graded in size
> from ridge down to eaves. Altogether a most satisfying reconstruction of a
> building which would otherwise have soon been too derelict to salvage.

In March 1982 the *Journal* featured a more detailed article and appraisal
of the restoration work and included the following account by the Senior
Honorary Architect:

> The brief for this project had two main aims: to rescue and restore a large
> country house in a very advanced stage of decay; and to produce a home
> for the continuing care of cancer patients. These aims were to be achieved
> working in association with the Historic Buildings Council and its
> Chairman, Mrs Jennifer Jenkins, and otherwise within funds subscribed by
> supporting organisations and the general public. It was intended that the
> total building cost per bed space, after deducting the HBC repair grant,
> should not exceed the cost of purpose-building on a green field site.
>
> The Sue Ryder Foundation provides a "home" for people no matter
> what their disability or state of health. The total environment of building
> character, nursing care, domestic atmosphere, comfort and facilities must
> make life as acceptable as possible to all living there. It must be each
> person's private home discreetly supported by full facilities for "heavy
> nursing". Independence, personal dignity and confidence are aided by
> facilities such as special loos, baths and ramped circulation to the lift for
> the many changes in level. Special factors arose in restoration. There were
> basic agreements with the advisers of the HBC. Namely, that the work of
> restoration must have as long a life as practicable so no risks could be taken
> with the timber, dry rot etc., and that repairs should be carried out in this
> manner and the materials of the original construction. Both these factors
> were very demanding. Every possible area of damage or defect was far
> greater than   superficial inspection would have suggested.

After the dramatic collapse of the centre section of the building which I
mentioned earlier, all that remained of the gallery was a heap of masonry.
From this heap each stone was recovered and sorted into piles according
to suitability for re-use. When the new plans were prepared this part of
the building was selected to be the chapel, and we all looked forward to the
day when it would be in use. In the months that followed it was a marvellous sight to see the masons carefully rebuilding the walls and I longed to
hear the famous hymn "He who would valiant be 'gainst all disaster . . ."
being sung there.

Finally, on 27 April 1983 the chapel was dedicated, long after several
hundred patients had been admitted to the Home. The Bishop of Gloucester,

with the Abbot of Prinknash, the Reverend C. Small (representing the Free Churches) and other clergy processed into the crowded chapel. A moving service followed. The final blessing was given by the clergy in unison:

> Go forth in peace; be of good courage;
> hold fast that which is good;
> render to no man evil for evil;
> strengthen the faint-hearted;
> support the weak;
> help the afflicted;
> honour all men;
> love and serve the Lord, rejoicing in
> the power of the Holy Spirit.
> And the blessing of God almighty,
> the Father, the Son and the Holy Spirit,
> be upon you and remain with you for ever.
> Amen

The chapel is constantly in use and early in 1986 a baby was baptised there. It was a lovely family day, but there was an underlying sadness as the baby's mother was a patient in the Home and died a few days later. She was only thirty-one years old and had another child of nineteen months. Matron was sure that the christening helped the woman's family in their grief. "They will be able to remember the joy she experienced on that day. She was surrounded by her family and friends and some of the staff. She was so cheerful and helped to make it a memorable day for us."

We are honoured to have His Royal Highness the Prince of Wales as Patron of this Sue Ryder Home and on each of his visits he has given us great encouragement and has taken a deep interest in every patient, member of staff and volunteer whom he has met. On 18 December 1992 His Royal Highness most kindly opened the Day Centre which now operates in Goose Bay. It is registered for thirty patients; since opening in 1988 up to December 1995, there have been 3,703 individual patients. The ground floor facilities include bath and shower rooms, a cubicle for hairdressing, a doctor's consulting room, and also a treatment area. There is a Sue Ryder Gift and coffee shop in the tudor wing. In-patients have been moved into the main building, which makes the running of this Home more practical and economical.

PART SEVEN

In Today Walks Tomorrow

28

Do Not Turn Away From the Handicapped And The Dying

IN 1978 AN ENVELOPE marked "No. 10 Downing Street" was among the mail placed on my desk. For some inexplicable reason I was reluctant to open the letter. To my astonishment, the letter offered me a life peerage in the Queen's Birthday Honours List. After several days of profound thought I consulted my husband and Mr Sporborg, Chairman of the Foundation. I was torn between politely declining the offer and gratefully accepting it. On the one hand, I was much averse to accepting any honour for the work I had done; on the other hand, I realised that the privilege of being able to listen and occasionally speak in the House of Lords could be used to bring the public's attention to many of the pressing needs of the people among whom I work.

After two long discussions with the Private Secretary to Mr Callaghan, the Prime Minister, I decided to accept the offer and indicated my wish to take as my title the name of the Polish capital, which has always been so close to my heart and such a part of my life. I then approached the Polish Ambassador and his wife, whom I knew very well, to seek their advice, and His Excellency exclaimed: "How excellent, you will represent Poland in the British Parliament. This will be an honour to my country and to my home city." He also telephoned Warsaw the same day to give them this news.

An exception had to be made and special permission given by Her Majesty the Queen and the Prime Minister, Mr Callaghan, for me to receive and use the title of Ryder of Warsaw, as titles with foreign names had previously been confined to Wartime leaders. Later, the following came from the Prime Minister's office:

> I thought you would like to know that our consultation with the Polish Government about your proposed title has been completed. They have expressed great satisfaction that you intend to include Warsaw in your title. I have told Garter King of Arms that this is so and he will now be able to take the necessary steps to dispose of the matter.

I thus entered into an entirely unfamiliar world. When I walk down the long corridors and sit in the Chamber I still think I shall wake up from a dream and find myself doing field work, visiting prisons and hearing the noise of endless keys clanking, or hearing the cries of those in pain, or of the sick and hungry. I was unaware of the ancient traditions and ceremonies of the House and had no inkling of the immense amount of sheer hard work that so many members undertake. It is, in fact, another job in itself and I felt embarrassed, wanting to take a full part but finding this difficult because of my commitments to the Foundation. My diaries get booked far ahead with the result that, by the time the Orders of Business are received from the House, there is often nothing one can do to change engagements already planned and accepted in order to attend the sittings.

For some, the following details of the Upper House are already well known, but, personally, I was totally unaware of what the great Royal Palace of Westminster looked like or how it functioned.

Parliament originated in the councils summoned by English kings in the eleventh, twelfth and thirteenth centuries. Assemblies of this kind, attended by varying numbers of archbishops and bishops, abbots, earls, barons, other lay magnates and royal ministers, met to give the King counsel on a wide variety of matters and to make special financial grants to him. The Parliament of Simon de Montfort in 1264 was the first to which Burghers (Citizens) of every Borough were summoned. By 1236 some of these councils were being called "parliaments". During the thirteenth century representatives of the "communities of the realm" from counties, cities and boroughs were summoned with increasing frequency to assist, their attendance in Parliament becoming unvarying after 1327. By the end of the fourteenth century they formed a separate house, the House of Commons (that is, of the local communities), with its own Speaker and Clerk.

The Lords similarly acquired identity as a separate House of Parliament and from the earliest times has been composed of lords spiritual and temporal. The lords spiritual originally consisted of the bishops and certain abbots and priors, whose membership lasted as long as they held their office. The membership of the lords temporal had become almost entirely hereditary by the fifteenth century. The lords temporal were known as "peers", indicating that amongst themselves they were equal in standing. In time, however, they became divided into five levels of rank, the most ancient being those of earl and baron, the more recent those of duke (first creation 1337), marquess (first creation 1385) and viscount (first creation 1440). In addition, from 1302 the Prince of Wales was summoned to Parliament.

In 1856 a peerage for life was conferred on Sir James Parke in order to strengthen the judicial membership of the House. In 1958 the Life Peerages Act was passed, enabling the Crown to create peerages which would expire on the death of the holder, and to confer them on women as well as men. The system of life peerages has fundamentally changed the character of the House in recent times.

When I entered the House to sit on the non-party political cross-benches, the composition of the Lords was as follows:

Women Life Peers	43
Men Life Peers	259
Women Hereditary Peers	18
Men Hereditary Peers	791
Archbishops and Bishops	26
Law Lords	18

Of these, fifty-nine were cross-benchers.

On 16 April 1996 the composition of the House is as follows:

Women Life Peers	66
Men Life Peers	314
Women Hereditary Peers	16
Men Hereditary Peers	751
Archbishops and Bishops	26
Law Lords	24

Of these, 286 are Cross-Benchers.

I was overawed by the size and architecture of the building. Sir Charles Barry, who rebuilt the Palace of Westminster after its destruction by fire in 1834, was a young and outstanding Victorian architect. His design of the building was described by Sir Hugh Casson as a "knock-out". Augustus Welby Pugin was the designer and decorator.

The royal palace covers eight acres of ground, has over 100 staircases and more than two miles of corridors. There are 2,000 members of staff, including whole teams of skilled craftsmen and tradesmen.

The Chamber of the Upper House is eighty feet long, forty-five feet wide and forty-five feet high. At its southern end, facing the Stranger's Gallery, is the Throne, designed by Pugin. The Canopy above the Throne represents the Cloth of Estate, to which lords bow on entering. When the House is sitting, the eldest sons of peers, bishops who are not members of the House, privy counsellors and certain other distinguished persons may sit on the steps of the Throne. It is only for the Opening of Parliament that peers wear their crimson and ermine robes. Then, the brass rail round the Throne is removed, and the Queen, robed and crowned, reads the Gracious Speech from the Throne while members of the House of Commons stand behind the bar of the House – a barrier which marks the boundary of the House.

In front of the Throne on ordinary sitting days is the Woolsack, so called because it was stuffed with wool from England when that was the country's main export and the source of its wealth. It now contains wool also from Wales, Scotland, Northern Ireland and the countries of the Commonwealth. The Lord Chancellor or his deputy sits on the Woolsack as Speaker of the House of Lords.

Before each day's sitting the Lord Chancellor walks in procession to the Chamber down a Division Lobby and through the Peers' Lobby with the Mace borne in front of him. Bystanders bow to the Mace, the emblem of Her Majesty's authority, as it passes. It is then placed on the Woolsack. Prayers are read by one of the bishops, and the sitting commences.

Parliamentary sessions normally begin in October or November. The House sits during about thirty-six weeks in the year. There are adjournments (normally known as "recesses") over Christmas (two–three weeks), Easter (ten days) and the Spring Bank Holiday (ten days). The Summer recess usually runs from early August to early October(twelve weeks). The House normally sits on Tuesdays, Wednesdays and Thursdays, often on Mondays, and occasionally on Fridays. Altogether there are about 140 sitting days in a year. On Mondays, Tuesdays and Wednesdays the House sits at 2.30 p.m., on Thursday at 3.00 p.m. and on Fridays at 11.00 a.m. The House sits after 10.00 p.m. on about forty days in the session.

The work of the House of Lords includes:

(i)   The Supreme Court of Appeal
(ii)   The provision of a forum for full and free debate on matters of public interest
(iii)   The revision of public bills brought from the House of Commons
(iv)   The initiation of public legislation
(v)   The consideration of delegated legislation
(vi)   The scrutiny of the activities of the executive
(vii)   The scrutiny of private legislation
(viii) The scrutiny of proposals for British and European Community legislation

Although the Lord Chancellor is Speaker of the House, he is also a member of the Government with a seat in the Cabinet, and he does not remain politically neutral as the Speaker of the House of Commons does. Nor does he have the same power as the Speaker of the House of Commons to control the proceedings of the House. In general, the House controls its own proceedings. They are regulated both by longstanding practice and by Standing Orders.

Each day's business is set out on an Order Paper. The order in which different kinds of business are taken is regulated by Standing Orders. These lay down, for example, that on all days except Wednesdays proceedings on bills come before general debates. Any lord may place business on the Order Paper and, subject to the rules concerning the order of business, items appear and are dealt with in the order in which they are "tabled" – that is, handed in to the Clerk at the Table of the House.

Each item of business is announced by the Clerk at the Table, and the member responsible then moves the motion, or asks the question, which he has tabled. He does this standing, but does not move from the place where he has been sitting. Usually he makes a speech in support of his motion or question. He may not do so, however, when asking a starred question, when he uses a standard form of words: "My Lords, I beg leave to ask the question standing in my name on the Order Paper."

After a motion has been moved, the Speaker of the House reads it out and then other lords are free to take part in the debate. If two lords rise to speak at once, and neither gives way, the House decides which it will hear first: lords indicate their preference by naming the lord they wish to hear. For the more important debates a list of speakers is prepared. This list is the responsibility of the Leader of the House and includes all those who have indicated their intention to speak. Others are not precluded from taking part, but they are expected to wait until immediately before the winding-up speeches before they speak. I found it difficult to absorb all the rules and etiquette of the House and once made the mistake of entering the Chamber during a maiden speech. Some of the most active members are the "Wheelchair Brigade" (known affectionately as the "Mobile Bench"), whose participation is so valuable. As individuals, or as a group, they are a force to be reckoned with, though diminished in numbers.

All the benches in the Chamber are equipped with small built-in loudspeakers, which are fitted in the backrests of the benches just below the ear level of the seated peers. This is a convenience which may be responsible for some of us being unjustly accused of sleeping on the red leather seats when, in fact, we are listening attentively to the debates!

One of the principles of the House is never to be rude, even to one's most determined opponents, and a written apology for transgressions is the informal rule. The courtesy and friendliness must strike every newcomer who may have thought that titles were synonymous with pomposity.

The manner in which peerages are conferred ensures a huge diversity of talent and experience, and is one of the reasons why the House of Lords is a repository of such a wide spectrum of knowledge. One of the unexpected pleasures has proved to be the informal contacts outside the Chamber. Because of the great variety of backgrounds from which members come, it is possible to learn something useful about almost any subject imaginable.

One of the nicest customs when the House is sitting late is the offer of a lift home to a member who may have no transport. My opportunity to make this offer occurred one night when I saw a member standing outside. As I drove him to his flat we talked about the events of the day. He asked if I would be attending the next day. I said, "Yes," and he thereupon encouraged me to make my maiden speech during a debate on the Health Service. This left me with very little time to prepare my text but, as it happened, (perhaps because I was closely involved with the subject of the debate), I found the occasion less awesome than taking part in the general debate later, where most speakers were experts on the subject under discussion.

Since becoming a member of the Upper House, my opinion of the value of a second chamber within the British Parliament has been immeasurably strengthened. It also seems to me that the existence of the House of Lords as a watchdog and as a brake on the activities of the House of Commons provides a very necessary safeguard. To make a proper contribution to the affairs of the House, I feel it is not only time which is needed but sound legal knowledge as well.

Copies of Hansard and other papers are sent to me daily and these should be read in order to keep abreast of the business of the House. Regrettably, only some of these can be read, for the simple reason that the Foundation's work is my life and takes up almost all of my time; but it is important to read Hansard to keep abreast of the business of the House. Ideally, I should like this to be done for me by someone who would note or summarise the questions, debates or speeches relating to issues with which I am especially concerned and who would also undertake research, and draft speeches for me. This would save me spending many precious hours reading the reports and would enable me to plan ahead and be better briefed for the sittings of the House that I want to attend. I find late-night sittings difficult to cope with, as I rise so early and my hours of sleep are already limited.

If I am in the House on a Tuesday afternoon I like to attend the House of Lords Prayer Group. This was formed in 1980 by Viscount Ingleby and Brigadier David Stileman (the Yeoman Usher) who used to meet each week for a few minutes' prayer in the Yeoman Usher's Office. Over the years, they were joined by other peers and by a few members of Parliament and by 1982, when room for the meeting became a problem, Brigadier and Mrs Stileman invited the Group to meet each Tuesday at 4.30 p.m. in their flat. This remained the meeting place until 1988 when the Stilemans retired and the meetings were transferred to the television room. Bringing us up to date, there are now three House of Lords Prayer Groups, each meeting for about an hour. One is led by Lord Ashbourne on Monday evening and another on Tuesday. Lord Elton is the co-ordinator and members take it in turns to lead the Group on Wednesday at 5 p.m. Our numbers alas are small but we remain undeterred and ever hopeful that God will hear our prayers and guide all members both in the Commons and the House of Lords to come to the right conclusions, and hear our prayers for the Queen and members and their families who are ill or in need.

Another group which I attend whenever possible is the National Prayer Breakfast. This was started by Miles and Patricia Park, following the Washington pattern. After two experimental Breakfasts the first National Prayer Breakfast sponsored by peers and Members of Parliament was held in 1985 and was attended by about 550 people. Numbers have increased steadily and around 900 people currently attend the Breakfasts which are held in the Queen Elizabeth II Conference Centre. They include overseas visitors and every Prayer Breakfast is an inspiration.

There are currently twenty-three Doorkeepers in the House, including two who look after Judicial Sittings and one who is appointed as "Red Coat". Red Coat is on duty at the peers' entrance and meets both peers and guests. Each Doorkeeper, except Red Coat, wears morning dress with a silver gilt chain round his neck. Attached to this is a gold-plated royal coat of arms and suspended below it is Black Rod's badge (Garter office badge with a rod across it). All the Doorkeepers, except the two judicial ones, have served a minimum of twenty-two years in one of the three services. Mostly, they are ex-warrant officers. The two Judicial Doorkeepers are ex-policemen with long and distinguished careers.

There are also fifteen Attendants who deliver messages and carry out numerous personal services. They dress in smart grey suits. All the staff, including the police and security staff, are unfailingly polite and courteous regardless of the extremely long hours they work. The majority of the staff know the name of each peer.

Among the many matters which claim much attention in the House, the following have *always* concerned me deeply: bad housing and the plight of those who have no homes at all; the long-term needs of the sick and disabled of all ages and their ever-increasing numbers; the unemployed; the protection of the unborn child, and the right to life of each human being; drug abuse; national defence and the nuclear deterrent (this nation spends more on tobacco and alcohol than on defence); conservation; recycling of waste; race relations; the disparity between rich and poor countries, and the importance of family life, education and discipline.

It is matters of this kind which I try – however inadequately – to bring to people's attention by speaking in the House of Lords, in the hope that my speech there may encourage a wider interest and discussion and lead eventually to practical action being taken to remove some of the burdens, or to right some of the wrongs, being borne by sections of society least able to bear them.

* * *

In 1989 the Bill for the Protection of Unborn Children was passed. I was against it as I was concerned about the experiments on human embryos. On 8 March I said:

> Let me state at the outset that I favour research which is likely to result in genuine benefit to the human race, particularly in preserving life. But in everything we do in this field we must ensure that we uphold the dignity of the human being and the sanctity of human life. I stand here in the name of internationally famous doctors, scientists and pathologists who themselves were prisoners of the Nazis.
>
> In paragraph 12.2 of the Warnock Report we are told that trans-species fertilisation between human sperm and hamster eggs is already used in the investigation of male subfertility. The report says:
>
> *Men whose sperm will fertilise a specially treated hamster egg may eventually father a child, whereas those whose sperm will not, are probably infertile.*
>
> The report goes on to tell us that although any resulting embryo does not develop beyond the two-cell stage, it is possible that other similar forms of trans-species fertilisation tests could be developed.
>
> This almost makes experiments into possibility of trans-species fertilisation sound respectable, and very plausible too. But I suggest that we

have real grounds for fears, and I am afraid also that the Voluntary Licensing Authority which was set up by the Medical Research Council gives me scant comfort.

What we assume is secure and safeguarded by legislation today or tomorrow, still gives opportunities for abuse and thus leads to further terrible acts and their similar consequences.

I would never have believed, working as I did in the ruins of Europe in 1944 to 1945, that the horrendous and horrific scenes which I witnessed among the victims of the Nazis, could possibly be the subject of debate in this House.

Following on, in December 1989 there was an Abortion Amendment to which I spoke against.

My Lords, in making my case I wish to make it clear that I fully acknowledge the sincerity of those who take a different view from mine and as a mother I understand the depths of their feelings. However, we are dealing with two separate persons, each of whom has rights, sadly rights which are in conflict with each other. On the one side we have the mother to be who has the right to live a life of her own choosing; on the other the unborn child who having been conceived by its mother and father has the right to live.

There is of course a great difference between the circumstances of these two sets of people. The mother is able to marshall her arguments force-fully and with great depth of feeling. The unborn child has no voice that we in this Chamber can hear. As yet it has no power of any kind to plead its rights, let alone defend them. Most sadly, the name of Parliament and its deliberations and decisions seems at times to replace the name of God.

With this Bill advocating abortion up to birth we are abandoning what has been the civilised standard for centuries; namely, that every human being, if he or she is to be treated by a doctor or specialist, is to be treated for his or her own particular benefit and not exploited for the perceived benefit of others.

I as a mother understand the anguish which sadly, today can rarely be relieved by the efforts of childless couples who wish to adopt. *Some adoption agencies in different parts of the country closed their lists of approved couples who were waiting to adopt because of lack of babies.*

The right revered Prelate the Bishop of Bradford said that the Churches are undecided. May I respectfully say that I believe the Catholic Church is not. I also know many other Christians and friends of the Jewish faith who share this feeling of repulsion.

This is a crossroads decision. It will determine whether our nation takes the civilised moral road or whether we compromise the principles and question the absolute sanctity of life; namely, that every stage from conception to death is to be treated with the utmost dignity and respect. I have also witnessed abortion, heard the cry of babies and seen their movements before death.

In Paul's letter to the Hebrews, it is written:

"To be alive is no man's gift, it is God's gift; and end life is no
man's right, but God's right".

We should deny this Bill a Second Reading.

Abortions are now so routine – some 170,000 a year – that consciences
have clearly been dulled as to the horror of what is being done. Not since
the Abortion Act of 1967 has there been such a pointed challenge to public
attitudes on this most deeply controversial of issues. It is no longer
possible blithely to assert that a foetus feels nothing. There is now evidence
that foetal stress-levels rise sharply if a needle is inserted merely to take
a blood sample.

For many, a woman's right to control her own reproductive system is
one of the more significant achievements of this century. Central to the
astonishing growth in abortions is the belief that a foetus has no human
characteristics and is incapable of feeling pain.

But what happens when that convenient belief is thrown into doubt? If
the scientists have got it right, the levels of pain and distress experienced
during some abortion procedures can barely be imagined.

The Catholic Church may seem a lonely and somewhat eccentric voice
on the matter of abortion but our belief is in the sacredness of life from
the moment of conception to the point of death. Christ came to give us life
in abundance, physical as well as spiritual. We must respect the greatness
of life.

Also, abortion cannot be seen in isolation. A culture that has little or no
conscience in this matter is a "culture of death" as the Pope has said on
many occasions. The consequences are an eroding of respect for life in so
many other areas too: respect for the elderly, the weak, the poor, the
marginalized.

* * *

The "Poll Tax" bill greatly concerned me because of its affect on millions
who could not afford to pay and the Sue Ryder Homes and Shops. Speaking
in June 1988 I pointed out that:

> Such proposals would cost us a staggering £500,000. This is absolutely
> dreadful, especially when we look to the Government for support and
> compassion. The Government always say that they mean to help and
> encourage charitable work. Nevertheless, it would seem that they have not
> thought sufficiently about charities when drafting the Bill. Thousands more
> bureaucrats were employed causing the country a huge amount of money.

On 4 July 1988 I spoke in a debate on Local Government Finance in favour
of an amendment which would give all registered charities 100 per cent
relief from the burden of local council rates that farms and churches had
enjoyed for decades. Had rates been levied on charity shops they would
have been a crippling burden on the Foundation which, I emphasised to the

House, exists solely for the relief of suffering. I mentioned that the Foundation cared for more than 3,000 people in Britain alone who were suffering from cancer, Huntington's Disease, Motor Neurone Disease, Parkinson's Disease, and at least seventeen other conditions or disabilities.

I continued:

We are dependent upon voluntary contributions from the public, which is aghast to think that we should be so penalised when not only do needs grow but, alas, costs increase.

I can give an illustration of one Sue Ryder Home which received £8,500 per year from two Area Health Authorities towards the £700,000 which must be raised every year to cover the full nursing and caring costs. From just 1 January to 30 June 1988 in this particular Home 109 patients attended a day care centre, staff made daily bereavement visits, 160 visits were made by a domiciliary nurse and 293 patients were cared for.

No other facilities are offered in an area with a population of over 800,000 except for ten beds in a small hospice. So pressed are the local consultants and doctors that the cobalt unit in the local hospital – again paid for by local funds – only has thirty beds . . .

. . . An absolutely crucial and important element in the fund-raising of the Foundation, and the one we rely on most throughout Britain and elsewhere, is the work carried out through our gift shops up and down the country. We already have about 350 and we hope that by 1997 or sooner we shall have raised that number to 600 or more.

The gift shops are literally the financial lifeblood of the Foundation. At the same time they use the talents of thousands of volunteers . . .

These same shops provide a service to people on low incomes. They offer a place where those people can purchase clothing, furniture, bric-a-brac or essential items at prices they can afford. The charity shops also provide a social centre for lonely people. Teenagers and children come to us for advice and help. Others who are lonely come into our shops for company. Thousands of the helpers, too, are lonely or bereaved people for whom the shops are a lifeline.

This whole work is jeopardised by the provisions in this Bill. Whatever the kind words and arguments used by the Minister and noble Lords, I can only say that if noble Lords do not amend this Bill today they will be increasing the costs of just this Foundation by a minimum of over £500,000 a year. Alas, it is no good the Government saying that discretionary relief is available. They do not have to undergo the daily hunt for premises and funds as I do. I know that in very many cases discretionary relief is not given now, and that in the future there is little hope of greater generosity on the part of hard-pressed local authorities.

In conclusion, I must say to the Government that two bad laws do not make a good one. Charitable work is trumpeted by this Government. Here is an excellent chance for them to show that they mean what they say in that regard. The removal of the rates burden will give us a greatly needed boost in a sphere of public life long held in high regard in this House. I beg to support the amendment.

In support of the amendment, Lord Wolfson said:

> ... Whatever may be the theoretical niceties, I believe that the deeply moving speech of the noble Baroness, Lady Ryder, with her immense practical experience and tireless efforts on behalf of charity, must carry great weight in every part of this House. I do not think it necessary to add to what has already been said . . . and I hope that all parts of the House will support this amendment.

At the end of the debate the House agreed to withdraw the amendment on the Government's undertaking to look again at the matter.

In a speech in the House on 14 March 1990 in the course of a debate calling attention to the gap between rich and poor in society and to the case for a social security system that meets the problems arising therefrom, I began by stressing that what was needed was the element of caring; that people should care about the welfare of each other and that Governments should care for every level of society, but especially for the poorest level.

I then spoke of my concern about the difference between public and private medicine:

> No longer can those in the public sector expect to receive the treatment they need regardless of cost. The new provision causes serious concern that a sick person who is not in the private sector will get not what he wants but what his local health authority or medical practice can afford.
>
> There are many in our society today suffering from long-term diseases and disabilities who simply cannot cope in their own homes. They need dedicated twenty-four-hour care from qualified nurses, and in an atmosphere that should be as homely and non-institutional as possible. If such people have sufficient money and can afford to pay the full cost of their care, there is a wide choice.
>
> However, if they have no money and can rely only on the DSS grant of £235, rising to only £245 in April 1990, then the choice is very limited indeed.
>
> In very many of the Sue Ryder Homes the cost per patient is over £500 per week, which has to be raised year in, year out by supporters who are becoming more and more disillusioned and bewildered by the Government's attitude. Speaking for the Foundation which bears my name, we are inundated day and night by a host of people of all ages who are literally desperate for help. I shall gladly take any noble Lord to see the dreadful conditions in which they exist.
>
> I should like noble Lords to imagine the dilemma and distress caused unnecessarily to thousands and thousands of silent sufferers. We may not think that they are vote catchers but, believe you me, the supporters who have to raise the money are. We should be ashamed that in this very materialistic society we have these shocking and deplorable gaps. Is no one in the Government going to show understanding and imagination and offer real help and not just make purring noises, referring to us as the private sector and often with remarks such as "good luck to you". This gap is not only totally wrong but shocking.

For many years, since 1948, Britain had one of the finest National Health Services, the envy of the world. Sadly, through each decade, this has been eroded. To quote the *Evening Standard* of 9 October 1996:

> London's health service is facing its worst crisis in a decade, and for the first time NHS chiefs are publicly warning it is close to breaking point.
>
> Most of the capital's health authorities are in dire financial straits, with some heading for deficits running into tens of millions. In attempts to stop the spiral of debt they are considering axing services, increasing waiting lists and closing hospitals.
>
> In the meantime, London can expect its toughest winter ever this year with over-stretched emergency departments and a shortage of beds.
>
> "Our Health authority, East London and the City, is facing a £20 million deficit, and something has got to give," says Peter Coles, chief executive of the Homerton Hospital NHS Trust, "I have never known something of this magnitude before. The authority is facing one of the worst deficits in the country. It is very serious."
>
> His view was shared by many high-ranking NHS managers contacted by the *Evening Standard*, who are risking their jobs to warn of the increasing pressures facing London's health service. Some insisted on anonymity.
>
> "The last time comparable to this was in 1987, a year of great difficulties which ended in a Government review of health services," said one health authority chief executive. "Some areas are going to have to borrow money just to get through the year. That's not crying Wolf."

Unions, pressure groups and politicians have for years been warning of the increasing strain, but this is the first time that those responsible for running the service have spoken out.

The number of accident and emergency departments in London hospitals has almost halved in six years. In 1990, the capital had sixty casualty departments, by 1994 the figure had fallen to forty eight and now it stands at thirty two.

According to Department of health statistics, London has lost an average of 2,578 beds on acute wards alone since 1990.

The number of acute hospitals which have closed between 1979 and 1995 in North and South Thames Health Authority regions stands at sixty. Hospitals which have been threatened with closure, or a diminution of services, include:

1. *Bart's*, the *London Chest Hospital* and the *Queen Elizabeth*: Scheduled to close by 2002 with services transferred.
2. *Guy's*: Will lose accident and emergency department by 1999 and most in-patient services.
3. *St Thomas'*: To become the emergency centre with most acute beds.
4. *Edgware General*: Will lose its casualty department after 1997. In-patient services will be moved to Barnet, the Royal Free and Northwick Park.
5. *Barnet General*: Will become a major general district hospital with an expanded accident and emergency department.
6. *Greenwich District Hospital*: Scheduled to close by late 1998–9. Will be replaced by the new Queen Elizabeth.

7. *Middlesex, Elizabeth Garrett Anderson and Hospital for Tropical Diseases*: Will be consolidated on the University College Hospital campus by 2002.

8. *Queen Charlotte's*: Plans approved to move Queen Charlotte's to the Hammersmith Hospital site.

9. *Oldchurch*: Set to lose its casualty department by 2000. A new accident and emergency department is to be built at Harold Wood.

I do not believe that these should be done away with, especially bearing in mind the long waiting lists and the fact that these hospitals were founded centuries ago and hundreds of people have contributed towards funding and guiding their long traditions.

Alas, the Foundation work in Britain, both to consolidate and expand, has changed beyond all recognition, and mainly due to bureaucracy and lack of funds from the Area Health Authorities and Social Services. *This fact should be publicly known and deplored.*

Another subject that is still of great concern to me is Sunday Trading. On 8 February, 1989, I said:

Why do we think about keeping Sunday holy? First, it is a day of rest, relaxation and of children being with their parents. There is the opportunity to visit friends or relatives in hospital, to walk to places of beauty and to get away from the roar of traffic and general noise created by the public. Secondly, we wake up knowing that we are not being rushed and can consider this is a calm and wholly different day. Thirdly, and most important, we remember God who declared that Sunday should be a day of worship and rest. The purpose and effect of all that is to make us better equipped for the coming week's work.

Perhaps I may remind noble Lords of this quotation from Sir Winston Churchill:

"Sunday is a Divine and priceless institution . . . the necessary pause in the national life and activity; it is the birthright of every British subject . . . and, above all, our great heritage, and one which is our responsibility, privilege and duty to hand on to posterity."

There is also the dilemma for shop assistants and even more for small retailers who are increasingly going out of business. Sunday trading will obviously accelerate this tragic trend because large stores are allowed to open for six hours on a Sunday.

It is always difficult to predict all the consequences of any piece of legislation. But the Sunday Trading Bill will accelerate the closure of thousands of small shops, putting thousands of people out of work. This will seriously affect life in rural areas, the village shop is likely to go. It will also be very difficult for the elderly and disabled and others who do not drive a car, to shop. The Bill comes at a time when there is legislation to allow shops to open twenty-four hours a day from Monday to Saturday in order to meet consumer demand. It seems all the more unnecessary for shops to open on Sundays.

* * *

A subject which has concerned me from an early age is the problem of homelessness. The following will, I hope, interest the reader.

In 1993: 70,000 Council homes were empty.
764,000 Private sector homes were empty.
17,500 Housing Association homes were empty.
48,800 Government-owned homes were empty.

900,300 empty homes.

In 1993: 5,000 Homeless were in B & B accommodation.
10,290 Homeless were in Hostels.
38,720 Homeless were in "other" accommodation.

54,010 Homeless.

In 1994 the *average* cost of remedying an "unfit" house (to make it habitable) was approximately £7,000. The total cost of remedying all "unfit" houses in the same year would have been just over one billion pounds.

In 1992–3 approximately forty-four million pounds was spent on homeless people in Bed and Breakfast accommodation.

This national disaster is above Party Politics. Building of houses has to be through Housing Associations funded through Government and this proves very restricted. Housing Associations and other organisations which specialise in this work, should be *fully* supported by central and local Government. *It* is not a political matter, indeed it is a national scandal. Personal circumstances vary widely so no generalisation can or should be made. Each individual is unique.

One local council I know of raised ten million pounds from the sale of council homes in their district. The total for Britain is estimated at five billion pounds. Each year authorities may use twenty-five per cent of receipts for repairs etc. but not for building houses, and the remaining amount from the sale has to be retained. The interest is used to cushion Council Tax or rents.

The Macmillan Government from January 1957 until October 1963, strove for, and achieved, a target of building over 300,000 council homes a year.

* * *

National Service should never have been abolished and should remain as in so many other countries for men and women after the age of eighteen; it should exist as a legal obligation for at least eighteen months to two years. If anybody objects, they must work for a community scheme. This is what we should introduce in Britain. I fully support HRH Prince Charles's idea to introduce such a scheme but alas no Government has the political will to do so. This would give discipline, respect, work, self-esteem and an opportunity for young people from all walks of life to mix with each other. It would also provide them with a skill or trade, which would be invaluable in their subsequent search for employment.

*   *   *

To ignore the appalling number of 30 million or more vehicles on the inadequate roads in Britain is sheer madness. Other countries run excellent or very good public transport at reasonable prices, and give enormous subsidies.

We are, indeed, reaping the results of the fatal Dr Beeching closures during the 1960s, of so many main and countless branch railway lines throughout Britain.

*   *   *

Within the last few years we have seen the start of the National Lottery. When legislation was brought in for a National Lottery and Scratch Cards, there were strong feelings amongst a number of peers and others to limit the amount in cash for prizes. Nobody in their right senses can truthfully say they approve of such huge individual winnings. People often spend their money on the Lottery and Scratch Cards before meeting their essential personal commitments – perhaps before remembering those in need, both in this country and overseas. Whereas extra funding had to be found, in lieu of taxes, I strongly object to the huge amounts of prize money. This could surely be shared and limited to £100–£25,000 instead of such excessive amounts. Some people think that by buying Scratch Cards and playing the Lottery they are helping this Foundation. They think, misguidedly, that a lot of their money goes to this charity. However, although an application has been made, so far we have received nothing. I feel the vast prize money is immoral and is teaching young people the wrong values and encouraging them to gamble.

*   *   *

More recently because of terrible murders, the high rise of crime and the lack of discipline and respect for authority, we as a Nation, are at last facing the necessity to take action.

In the Queen's Speech at the Opening of Parliament in October 1996, Her Majesty had this to say on the subject of the protection of the public from dangerous criminal activity:

> A Bill will be introduced to reform the sentencing and supervision of serious, dangerous and persistent offenders so as to provide greater protection for the public. Legislation will be introduced to support the fight against organised crime, including establishing a National Crime Squad. A Bill will be introduced to strengthen controls on the ownership of firearms.

The spread of violence on our streets, the shooting of the children of Dunblane, the knifing of Philip Lawrence while he tried to defend one of his pupils and the machete attack on the school-children from St Luke's has filled the nation with horror, and focused attention on the decline in our moral standards and the fragmentation of family life. Bereaved parents are calling for the banning, or at least the control, of firearms and knives.

There has been much debate on this complex and controversial issue – in both Houses of Parliament, the media and by private bodies such as the gun clubs. Lady Blatch spoke eloquently in the House of Lords on the 16 December, 1996: "As a mother who has lost a son of school age, albeit in different circumstances, I can only say that I do understand the unrelenting ache in the hearts of the families of the children." On the same day, the Earl Stafford quoted the view of a police constable of twenty-seven year's service who had said. "Banning guns will achieve very little. What we've got to do is stop the odd lunatic having them."

Who could fail to be moved by the dignity and compassion of Frances Lawrence, who wrote a manifesto after her husband's murder. First printed in *The Times*, afterwards copied widely, it is to be hoped that what she and many of us believe will help to bring about a kinder, more peaceful world. She writes:

> When a tree is cut down, it falls with a crash. As it grows, it makes no sound. The process of building is always by degrees, but destruction is sudden enough to command headlines.
>
> My hope is that out of the terrible violence that pierced the heart of my family and generated such headlines, a new ethos may be constructed in which neglected virtues are reinstated, cherished and sustained.
>
> I wish to see a nationwide movement dedicated to healing our fractured society, banishing violence, ensuring that the next generation are equipped to be good citizens and urgently debating how the moral climate can be for the better.
>
> One of the most effective crime prevention measures is, surely, action to protect and encourage family life.

* * *

During the Holy Father's visit to Britain in June 1982, he spoke at St George's Cathedral, Southwark on the subject of the anointing of the sick. I would like to quote just two paragraphs from his homily because they express exactly my own deeply held beliefs on the same matter and should have a direct bearing on the deliberations of both Houses of Parliament.

> No State has the right to contradict moral values which are rooted in the nature of man himself. These values are the precious heritage of civilisation. If society begins to deny the worth of any individual or to subordinate the human person to pragmatic or utilitarian considerations, it begins to destroy the defences that safeguard its own fundamental values.

Today I make an urgent plea to this nation. Do not neglect your sick and elderly. Do not turn away from the handicapped and the dying. Do not push them to the margins of society. For if you do, you will fail to understand that they represent an important truth. The sick, the elderly, the handicapped and the dying teach us that weakness is a creative part of human living, and that suffering can be embraced with no loss of dignity. Without the presence of these people in your midst you might be tempted to think of health, strength and power as the only important values to be pursued in life. But the wisdom of Christ and the power of Christ are to be seen in the weakness of those who share his sufferings.

29

A Time To Build

If you can keep your head when all about you
Are losing theirs and blaming it on you;
If you can trust yourself when all men doubt you,
But make allowance for their doubting too;
If you can wait and not be tired of waiting,
Or being lied about, don't deal in lies,
Or being hated don't give way to hating,
And yet don't look too good, nor talk too wise.

If you can dream – and not make dreams your master,
If you can think – and not make thoughts your aim,
If you can meet with Triumph and Disaster,
And treat those two impostors just the same;
If you can bear to hear the truth you've spoken
Twisted by knaves to make a trap for fools,
Or watch the things you gave your life to broken,
and stoop and build'em up with worn out tools.

If you can make one heap of all your winnings
And risk it on one turn of pitch and toss,
And lose, and start again at your beginnings,
And never breathe a word about your loss
If you can force your heart and nerve and sinew
To serve your turn long after they are gone,
And so hold on when there is nothing in you
Except the Will which says to them "Hold on!"

. . . If you can fill the unforgiving minute,
With sixty seconds worth of distance run,
Yours is the earth and everything that's in it . . .

                              RUDYARD KIPLING

THESE WORDS FROM KIPLING'S poem "If" remind me of Maria
Rutkowska, who taught and recited the poem secretly at night to her many
friends in the blocks in Ravensbrück, and during the endless terrible roll
calls in freezing winter or in the heat of summer. Afterwards, this same
poem was constantly repeated to me in the ruins of devastated Europe in
many poignant situations.

The poem remains firmly imprinted on my mind. It brings back to me a kaleidoscope of memories, some horrific, some full of despair, some full of hope or joyful expectation.

It has been hard to describe the events I have set down here, because it meant reliving some dreadful experiences, which include five terrible riots in Poland and the invasion of Czechoslovakia by the then Soviet Army. In writing, I have been confronted once more by the suffering and despair I have witnessed and have remembered again the faces and voices of so many people I have met, and the sea of suffering I witnessed in Ethiopia and elsewhere, where the dignity of the human spirit made me feel so humble. Children dying of disease and hunger asked in whispers how to say "Thank you" in English. I recall trying to comfort somebody and saying, "I hope the birds sang for her when her face muscles ached after weeping." I hear, too, the groans and sobs of those who had been interrogated and tortured. The sweet sickly smell of death; the black and bloated bodies of dead soldiers and civilians; the mortally wounded with missing limbs. There was a boy who asked for a taste of butter again before he died – "Oh, the cross I have borne has been so heavy"; and the woman, also dying, who asked to feel a pair of shoes – "Thank you for finding them," she said, "I hope those who walk in them will find happiness and peace." There was the child of seven in Auschwitz – "Can I taste a piece of bread before I die?"; there was an Indian with leprosy dying in the streets, homeless, amid the scurrying leaves, and Colin, a young man, lying on a London street playing "Amazing Grace" on his mouth organ.

I see before me once again crowds queuing all night and day, outside shelters or hospitals where mattresses or mats line the corridors and patients are sleeping on the floors under the beds; hospitals where the pressure is so heavy that the patients have to share the beds *if* they are to receive some care and treatment and not be turned away.

I remember patients with terminal TB meningitis, and the cry typical of that disease. I remember, too, the penetrating and overpowering smell of ulcerating cancer, and how I would pull up by the side of the road after working in both tuberculosis and cancer hospitals and get out of the van or ambulance to breathe the fresh air. There were times when there were patients with many different conditions requiring treatment, and one had to decide whose wounds to dress first, who to wash and who to give water to. We carried charcoal biscuits with us to give to patients with dysentery. One physician used these biscuits to mark the foreheads of those whom he considered should be given priority treatment, as he rated their chances higher than others.

Some of the suffering was too terrible to describe, but with it there was also courage and selflessness, hope and generosity, humour and warmth. I remember the kindness and goodness of countless people, as well as the active support which it has been my privilege to receive in all my efforts.

I remember, too, for example, the woman who walked two miles to hand me a donation of 2/6d (12.5 p); and the Borstal boys ("Borstal" named after a village in Kent where the first Institution was founded. Offenders aged fifteen to twenty-one could be detained for corrective training.) working at Hickleton who gave up their pocket money when 30/- disappeared from the collecting bowl in the front hall.

Some words come to my mind again. A patient, on the completion of a new Home, said: "I never dreamt I would have a room to myself; isn't it marvellous? Please try to thank those who have given me this privacy." Mr X – whose wife had lost her first husband, two children and her brothers during the War and was then killed herself in a road accident while visiting England under the Holiday Scheme – derived his solace from hearing and reading how happy she had been in her last few weeks. "You have made up for something of what she lost, and she lived in a fairy-land with flowers whilst with you." I am often asked how many I have worked with and for; the answer is probably about 367,500 children and adults of over fifty nationalities.

Once, a prisoner whom I was trying to help, flung at me the reproach: "I think you could have done more – that is what you are here for." I believe these words apply to my whole life and to all that I have tried to do. As I look at my life and examine my conscience, remembering my failings, I hope only that the sincerity of my endeavours will compensate, to some extent, for those failings.

There have been horrors, suffering and unhappiness, as well as frustrations and disappointments – but, in looking back on my life, I realise that the beautiful and good things have outweighed everything else, and it is of these things that I prefer to think: the smile of an Indian child as he ate his share of ice cream and sweets during a celebration; the Survivor who said that the golden dream of freedom for his country from the yoke of Nazism and Soviet tyranny had begun; the smell of incense and of hay; the sound of laughter and the sight of mellow cornfields in autumn; the beauty of mountains seen in the fading evening light or at sunrise during my long drives; returning to Britain after the War and hearing once more the pealing of church bells which I had sometimes thought I might never hear again; the sweet smell of plants and shrubs in gardens, about which, alas, I know so little; the Big Wheel of the funfair at Walton-on-the-Naze illuminated at night, during the week before the War, and the nostalgic songs we sang during the War and when we were far from home; sleeping under the stars and listening to the sounds which disturb the silence; Trunley Wood at sunrise, carpeted with anemones and cowslips; springtime in the orchard at Thurlow, the trees heavy with apple blossom; and the rooks cawing and wheeling through the air at Scarcroft.

But this is a time to look forward, a time to build, for (to quote Coleridge) "in today already walks tomorrow". In this book I have attempted to describe in an outline what the Foundation has done so far.

The past teaches us how much the future holds in promise and opportunity and how great the demands will *always* be.

If I have learned anything in a life that has seen its share of tumult, suffering and difficulties, I have learned to believe that we are made to live in harmony and that we can do so only by being compassionate and disciplined. Through compassion, the human family is bound closer together. Suffering, pain and distress, on the other hand, bring a sense of isolation and a yearning for companionship and sustained support. Compassion unites us and helps us to discover one another and ourselves. It does not cancel out suffering or evil but it offers us a way of combating it. And this way of living enriches each of us, quietly, as a gentle shower before dawn gives life to the tired soil and the thirsty bush.

Wherever we look in the world, we find human and social problems in countless forms. From time to time, a sudden disaster will call us forth from our day-to-day lives and commitments and, for a short while, will draw us together in a common desire to help. We sense the urgency of the challenge the disaster presents and we rise to the occasion.

But there is also the long term, the continuing daily need of innumerable fellow human beings – a cry that is *far* less spectacular, seemingly less urgent and, for the very reason that it is always with us, all too easily accepted as an inevitable part of life. This calls for a different kind of response, for the bit-by-bit cracking of the surface and the piece-by-piece filling of the holes – a task where there will often be no results to see and to which there will never be an end. That every human being has the right to a reasonable standard of living, to education and medical and nursing care when ill, few would deny. But the sad truth is that so many do not enjoy these rights, millions do not have food for more than the barest subsistence, nor is there any foreseeable likelihood that they will. One-third of all the people in the world go to sleep hungry at night; four out of five children on the Indian sub-continent suffer from acute malnutrition; fewer than half the babies born in Central Africa will survive their first year. When the rains are late in Ethiopia or Somalia it follows with relentless certainty that hundreds of thousands of people will be brought face to face with the horrors of starvation. In Calcutta, half a million people live in the streets, not because it is convenient, but because they have nowhere else to go. Their destitution defies description.

During one year, 12,500 million children of all nationalities die of various diseases and different causes; every day 34,300 children die; this is one child every two seconds.

All over the undeveloped world there are countless millions of children who suffer from sickness and disease and for whom even the most primitive medical care is far out of reach. Fewer than half the people of India will live to be forty.

To all these people, Britain and the other countries of Western Europe and North America represent a kind of unattainable paradise. What we take for granted – often without thought or gratitude – in terms of food, shelter and medical treatment is literally beyond the limit of their wildest fantasy. And yet we seldom share with them what we have in such relative abundance. Perhaps some of us do not know of the extent of the misery and suffering which affects such a large proportion of mankind; but most of us, if the truth be told, know but do not want to know. We subconsciously turn away from the intrusive knowledge of what goes on, for instance, in the *favelas* (shanty towns, overridden with rats) of São Paulo. The thought of it makes us uncomfortable. "What can we do about it anyhow?", we say; "and, in any event, haven't we all got enough problems of our own to worry about?"

The answer, no matter how we seek to escape it, is "No". Besides their problems, most of ours are trivial. We may worry that we cannot afford a new bicycle for Johnny for Christmas; but in Ethiopia, the parents of little Haile – who is the same age as Johnny – have problems on a different scale. They worry about whether they can keep Haile – and themselves – alive at all. Half a sack of grain until the next harvest arrives (if there is one) would be Utopia! What so many of us in the West spend each week on groceries would keep them alive for a year. As the Holy Father says, "Do not give of your abundance but of your substance".

Eventually, their problems are going to be our problems whether we like it or not. One of the most powerful lessons of history is that sooner or later people without food and shelter turn in anger on people who have both in abundance. It is the stuff of revolutions, and if they have so far been confined within national borders, this is because – in historical terms – the age of the radio and the jet aircraft arrived only yesterday. Desperate people take desperate measures; it is an inescapable fact of life.

How to attempt to close the gap and how to face up to the sacrifice which is required – so small a sacrifice by comparison with that demanded by war – still eludes the mind and the will of Governments. Yet it is people themselves who make communities and nations, and who have it within their power to create better or worse ones, even to imbue Governments with a will and a purpose that otherwise they would not have. This was illustrated by Bob Geldof's first global rock concert "Live Aid" which was held simultaneously in London and Philadelphia on 13 July 1985, and by "Sport Aid" on 25 May 1986. This proved so vividly the concern of youth and the world of entertainment. Long may others sustain their efforts and keep awake the consciences of those in different parts of the world.

I feel with Tagore that:

> I am thankful my lot lies with the humble who suffer and bear the burden
> of power, and hide their faces and stifle their sobs in the dark.

I am conscious of our own immortality, and that whatever we do, wherever it might be, does count, not only here and now but in that great future for which we have all been created. It may sometimes be that we are given that certain opportunity only once and if we fail to respond it will not be given to us again. But if we seize the opportunity, even if we should not succeed in achieving our goal, the effort involved can be offered up to God who is our Judge and who is able to turn every defeat into victory.

I have always had a deep trust in God. So many times the work has seemed impossible to cope with and decisions have proved difficult to make, but an answer has invariably been forthcoming – not necessarily the one I search for. The words written by Browning often sustain me: "Prayer is shutting out Fear with all the strength of Hope."

I find it very hard indeed to accept the growing secular emphasis in Britain, the lack of any religious instruction or reference to God at school or in life. This breeds indifference to all things spiritual and can lead to the wasteland of materialism where violence is inevitable and self-gratification the only goal.

It is sad too that the great hospitals, which certainly had a strong Christian influence, with their own chapels and prayers in the wards, are now much more entirely secular. Yet, despite all of this, one still comes across individual doctors, sisters, nurses, chaplains, teachers and a host of others whose work is clearly based upon their faith, and who bravely maintain their witness. This is really what we should all be doing. It is high time for us to declare our faith, to be more positive and definite in our lives and unashamed in our witness.

We read and witness daily in our papers, television and radio that this country can no longer be considered Christian, and that we live in a multi-racial society. True – we have people of many different religions living in Britain now, but if you look at those other religions you will find that they have a "rule of life" which they take great trouble to teach their young. It is the Christians who need to pull up their socks! In many schools there are no Christian assemblies – yet these islands have known Christianity since the early days when the Romans invaded us, and have been Christian since the time of St Ninian (c.360–c.432), St Columba (c.521–97), St Augustine (596) and St Aidan (651) and began to spread the faith.

Christianity is being eroded by people who themselves are unaware of God, by those who should be aware but fail to follow him, and there is a general drift and erosion spreading through the country where only thirty per cent of children are born to married couples.

Mercifully, many thousands pray privately and are members of prayer groups and attend church services, but they are the minority.

The heritage of Christians through the ages should be remembered, revered and followed. I remember so well prayers being said for the Royal Family as well as prayers for Russia every Sunday at the end of Mass. On certain days of the year during the War, a National Day of Prayer was held throughout the country with thousands attending to pray for our fight against the evil forces which confronted us and the fact that we were in deadly peril.

Now it is a different sort of peril – it is one of indifference, secularism and materialism. Let us pray that our leaders of all political parties and walks of life will show the nation that God and Sunday are more important that anything else.

How many children or their parents today cannot even say the Lord's Prayer? When I work in the developing countries, I am sometimes ashamed at how much spiritual teaching they give their youngsters compared with the amount given to ours, whether in their own homes or in schools. I believe it is essential that we get back to honouring God and the family way of life as He taught us in the Scriptures and through His Beloved Son.

Many, many people now are seeing the warning lights as family life breaks down. What a tremendous responsibility rests on the people who make the laws of this country and on the parents and teachers who are the guardians of family life.

The intrusion by the media is becoming worse every year. I believe that a large number of people strongly object to the power wielded by the media and their obsessive interest in stories about money, sex and people's private lives. Surely this country could follow the example of France with its Privacy Law?

Family life is the centre of any society. Our society has devalued the family and we are paying the price. Having said this, I do of course acknowledge that there are still many schools which begin their day with well prepared assemblies. These schools are a pleasure to visit and the children a joy to be with.

I am very conscious of the fact that Britain is a multi-racial country in which many faiths co-exist. I respect all genuine religions and wish to see those who hold them free to follow what they believe in. We have much to learn from many of them.

Britain, however, has been a Christian country for many centuries, and drawn moral strength from its convictions. The beauty of our literature, music and art is enriched with its traditions and if we were to lose all this, we would be indeed be the poorer, and I feel completely wrong too.

* * *

Except the Lord build the house: their
labour is but lost that build it

Except the Lord keep the city: the watchman
waketh but in vain.

It is but lost labour that ye haste to rise
up early, and so late take rest, and eat
the bread of carefulness: for so he giveth
his beloved sleep.

> Lo, children and the fruit of the womb are
> an heritage and gift that cometh of the
> Lord.
>
> Like as the arrows in the hand of the giant;
> even so are the young children.
>
> Happy is the man that hath his quiver full
> of them: they shall not be ashamed when
> they speak with their enemies in the gate.
>
> PSALM 27

The Sue Ryder Light of Hope Appeal is an annual event. The blue light has become the symbol of this appeal and it is my greatest prayer and hope that thousands of these lights will eventually flicker throughout Britain and far beyond proclaiming the summons of our charter to bring comfort and relief to those who suffer everywhere.

In many countries overseas the Foundation works in close association with religious orders. In Britain a large percentage of the Foundation's supporters, volunteers and workers are believers, and if the work is to be properly consolidated and carried forward I am convinced that the religious side of the work must be acknowledged and fitted into the structure of the Foundation which is truly ecumenical. I felt for a long time that this would mean the formation of an Association or Community which would become the core or centre of the Foundation's life. It would be the spiritual centre and power-house of prayer for the work, and some of its members would go forth into the field to sow and to reap the harvest, to serve the sick and those in need.

Since this book was first published in 1986 I have been greatly encouraged by the formation and growth of the Sue Ryder Prayer Fellowship. This group of over one hundred men and women meets twice a year at the Foundation's Retreat House in Walsingham where we are able to share our Faith and experiences, joys and sorrows and, above all, our hopes for the future. It is a fellowship of *prayer* and that must be the strength of the Foundation in the future. I always return from these gatherings greatly renewed and encouraged. The Fellowship is firmly established. In the early days it met in several different places, including St Katharine's Convent, Parmoor, which has since become a Retreat House of the Sue Ryder Foundation. The Fellowship is open to all denominations, and those who join are from all walks of life and from the different areas and countries where the Foundation works. The Fellowship also holds quiet days and retreats in the regions where all Foundation supporters, volunteers, staff and residents can meet – especially those who cannot travel to Walsingham or St Katharine's.

The immediate intention is that some of the members of the Prayer Fellowship will live as a dispersed community linked by prayer and meeting regularly to share their spiritual life and to grow together. I also hope and pray that others will join Sister Josephine, a Benedictine nun, who is living at the Foundation's Retreat House in Walsingham.

It is my prayer, and most earnest wish, that the Prayer Fellowship and the community will be at the centre of the Foundation *which is, and was, founded on faith.* The legal responsibility for the Foundation's future still rests with its Council, the majority of whose members are, as individuals, members of the Prayer Fellowship. I hope that these two bodies will grow closer and closer together and be fused in one community based on faith in God. This is how I see the work continuing in the future and after my death.

> We have to prepare for the future, and yet we do not know what it will bring.
>
> We have to find a standing ground so firm that nothing unexpected can disturb us, and so broad that it will carry any undertaking that we may have to base upon it, and so satisfying that it will take the place of all other satisfactions.
>
> There is only one thing that answers to this and that is the Will of God.
>
> Reverend Mother Stuart.

Pope John Paul II said: "We are an Easter People." This joyous attitude is the theme of this final Chapter. We must have Easter at the heart of our faith. I remember, too, Father Leo Smith writing in the Catholic Herald: "We believe in the Lord's Resurrection, in the triumph of life over death, of love over hatred, of truth over falsehood, of light over the darkness of the night."

* * *

Experience as a field worker has taught me that it is the effort made by one individual that makes all the difference to another individual's life. It has shown me that no matter who we are or what our position in life, there is always something that we can contribute if we have the desire and the will. It may be by personal service in one's spare time, by arousing the interest of other people, by organising a function, by building, by nursing, by collecting clothes or bric-a-brac for a gift shop, by going without something in order to make a small gift, or by a bequest in a will. Or, on a different level, it could be by prayer or by identifying oneself in whatever way one can with another person's predicament and need. The very fact of knowing that someone else, perhaps at the other side of the world, is interested and concerned is enough to give encouragement and new strength and to lighten the burden of the sufferer.

When compared with what needs to be achieved, all this may seem hopelessly small and inadequate, but it serves little to look at the whole sum of the problem; better that we focus our attention on what we ourselves can do or be harnessed to do.

If one has ever had the privilege of working with those who have the will and the single-mindedness to succeed, and who believe in the light at the end of the tunnel no matter how dark and how interminable the tunnel may be, one knows that almost anything can be achieved.

The War and its aftermath, followed by the struggle to maintain peace, have all been our teachers. They have taught us more clearly than ever before the oneness of the human family, the basic truth that we are all children of one Father. Surely, though we are scattered about, we are all meant to be part of a single Continent?

Yet, if we are to be whole, it will not come about easily or without sacrifice; we will have to suffer together, often be called upon to pay a heavy price. It will not be enough for the rich and the powerful to condescend to give the needy a few scaps that are left over. It is important that all of us share what we can reasonably afford and indeed more that that. Above all, we should understand the importance of personal involvement, however modest this may be.

To strive for unity in a world that remains so divided is a debt we owe to all those throughout the ages who in different ways have dedicated themselves to this cause, above all to those who have laid down their lives in its pursuit. If we are to succeed, the goal must ever be kept in mind.

What of the present and future? By disarming, we leave this country of Britain in a perilous position. Whatever the cost, we should always be up to full strength in the three Armed Services. I find to disarm is madness, especially when there are very uncertain political situations in so many parts of the world – and we must never forget that there are still huge areas of the world still gripped in the wicked system of Communism. Several countries have developed and possess nuclear weapons and we should therefore be all the more prepared to cope with fanatics. Also if the Gulf War had succeeded in ending Saddam Hussein's life then the stability of that part of the Middle East could have become more secure.

There will always be people in this country who do not want Britain involved in trying to keep the peace, but we are still a world power and must remain so and pay heed to our Chiefs-of-Staff and others. We must remain strong. Also, if we wish to live in a civilised community, we should never ignore the advice of the police and should recognise the importance of keeping the force up to strength.

We live in an age where violence of many forms abounds. There is the violence of outright war between smaller nations; the violence of internationally organised terrorism and the violence of political oppression. Our precious and hard-won liberty is being threatened, even eroded, by subversion and infiltration. We should be more aware of these underlying dangers in Britain and other countries. In the face of all this we need to renew our awareness of the all-prevailing presence of God. We need to be spiritually strong, to remain alert and watchful, praying at all times to discover the will of God. We can never afford to yield to weariness or despair. No matter what the situation in which we find ourselves, or how dark the horizon, we must not lose faith – faith in our fellow man and in ourselves as well as in the all-seeing Providence of God; faith that even though evil will always be present, within ourselves as well as in the world at large, good will finally triumph. It is through the Sue Ryder Foundation that I can express this faith as a challenge to our fellow men and women:

> Who would once more relight Creation's flame,
> Turn back to sanity a world that goes insane,
> To bridge this awful chasm of despair?
> The faint, small voice of Hope calls out,
> Do you answer? Will you dare?
>
> QEDRWL
> (L. W. Leybourne Callaghan)

CHILD OF MY LOVE

There's rosemary, that's for
remembrance; pray, love, remember . . .
HAMLET, ACT IV

As for Rosemarie, I lett it run alle
over my Garden Walls, not onlie because
my Bees love it, but also because 'tis
the Herb sacred to Remembrance, and, therefore
to Friendship.
ST THOMAS MORE

Enquiries, in writing only please, to:
   The Sue Ryder Foundation
   Cavendish
   Sudbury
   Suffolk CO10 8AY

Appendix 1

WARSAW, AUGUST/SEPTEMBER 1944

AIR SUPPLY SORTIES TO THE POLISH HOME ARMY
(by RAF from Italian airbases)

Date		Sorties	Successful	Failed to make contact	Missing/ lost
1944					
08/09	Aug	3	3	–	–
09/10	"	4	4	–	–
12/13	"	11	8	3	–
13/14	"	28	14	11	3
14/15	"	26	12	6	8
15/16	"	9	5	4	–
16/17	"	18	8	4	6
17/18	"	4	1	3	–
18/19	"	7	1	6	–
20/21	"	4	3	1	–
21/22	"	4	3	1	–
22/23	"	2	1	1	–
23/24	"	3	2	1	–
24/25	"	6	5	1	–
25/26	"	7	4	3	–
26/27	"	5	–	3	2
27/28	"	4	1	1	2
01/02	Sept	7	2	1	4
10/11	"	20	9	6	5
13/14	"	2	1	–	1
21/22	"	12	5	7	–
Totals		186	92	63	31
% age		100%	49.4%	33.8%	16.8%

Average load = 1.5 tons of supplies per aircraft

The heroic rising, in which 250,000 people were killed, was suppressed by the Nazis sixty-three days and nights later. Fifty-thousand people of all age groups were taken prisoners of war, by a quirk in the Nazi mind, marched or carried to Pruszkow and Unsus transit camp, 25 kilometers from Warsaw. Here they were segregated and transported in cattle-trucks to the concentration and death camps. It is a time which none of us who had connections with the fate of this City can bear to recount.

According to the official Report of "S" Section 1941–5, in which Professor Jan Podowski served, the following supplies were dropped to the Polish Resistance (AK: Home Army):

> 670 tons of ammunition, guns and pistols of which
> 443 tons reached the Resistance.
> 34 million dollars in notes,
> 40 thousand dollars and gold bars.

Also 19 million German marks and 50 million zlotys (Polish currency) for use only in the central and totally occupied part of Poland – called General Government. All this money, except the gold bars, was counterfeit.

Appendix 2

A list of some Death Camps where medical experiments were carried out, followed by several examples:

1. Mauthausen – Austria (near Linz)
2. Ravensbrück – Germany (North Berlin)
3. Sachsenhausen – Germany (near Berlin)
4. Auschwitz – Poland
5. Majdanek – Poland (near Lublin)
6. Neuengamme – Germany (near Hamburg)
7. Dachau – Germany (near Munich)
8. Harteim Castle (Mauthausen) – Austria
9. Buchenwald (Weimar) – Germany

In many of the concentration and death camps the SS Doctors carried out a whole range of excruciating experiments on prisoners – men, women and children – the details of these would fill a Chapter of this book. I quote from Olga Lenguel who was an inmate in Auschwitz-Birkenau:

> The German doctors had hundreds and thousands of slaves at their disposal. Since they were free to do whatever they wished, they decided to experiment with these people. It was a rich windfall which decent men and women would have scorned, but which the Nazi medical contingent gloried in.
>
> Not only did they make experiments, but they compelled many of the deportee doctors, too, to labour under the supervision of the SS physicians. Horrible as these experiments were, the men who had to conduct them might have been able to excuse themselves could they have believed that they were at least serving science, and that the sufferings of these unfortunate guinea pigs might, in the end, spare others from suffering.
>
> But there was no scientific benefit. Human beings were sacrificed by the hundreds of thousands, and that was all. So the shackled deportee doctors, almost all of whom finally ended in the crematory ovens, sabotaged the "experiments" as far as they could. Besides, such disorder and lack of method was evident in these "scientific experiments" that they were cruel games rather than serious quests for truth. Everyone has heard of heartless children who amuse themselves by tearing legs and wings off insects. Here there was one difference: the insects were human beings.
>
> One of the most common experiments, and also one of the most useless, was the inoculation of a group of inmates with a disease germ. For, in the interim, the German doctors usually lost their interest in the project. As for the guinea pigs? When they were lucky, they were sent to the hospital; when they were not, they went to the gas chamber. Only in exceptional instances were they put under observation.
>
> Often, the experiments were absolutely absurd. A German doctor conceived the idea of studying how long a human being could exist on nothing but salt water. Another submerged his human guinea pigs in ice

water and claimed he could observe the effect of the bath on internal temperatures. After undergoing such experiments, the inmates needed no hospital, but were ready for the gas chamber. One day several nurses entered the infirmary and asked, "Who cannot sleep?" About twenty inmates accepted a dose of unknown white powder, which might have had a morphine base. The next day ten were dead. The same experiments were conducted among the older women, and seventy more died the same night.

When the Germans sought new treatments for the wounds caused by American phosphorous bombs, they burned fifty Russians on the back with phosphorous. These "controls" received no medication. The men who survived were exterminated.

One of the favourite experiments was conducted on newly arrived women whose menstruation was still normal. During their periods, they were told roughly, "You will be shot in two days." The Germans wanted to know what effect such news would have on the menstrual flow. A professor of histology in Berlin even published an article in a German scientific periodical on his observation on haemorrhages provoked in women by such bad news.

Dr Mengele, the chief physician, had two favourite studies; twins and dwarfs. From the first selections, the twins of each convoy were set apart, if possible with their mothers. Then they were sent to Camp F K L. No matter what their age or sex, twins interested Mengele deeply. They were favoured and even allowed to keep their clothing and their hair. He went so far in his solicitude for twins that when they were exterminating the Czech Camp, he gave orders to spare a dozen sets of twins.

Upon arrival, twins were photographed from every possible angle. Then the experiments began, but these were disconcertingly juvenile in character. For example, one twin would be inculcated with certain chemical substances, and the doctor was to watch the reaction, if he did not happen to forget about it. But even when the doctor followed through, there was no gain for science for the simple reason that the product injected offered no particular interest. Once they used a preparation that was supposed to cause a change in the pigmentation of the hair. Many days were lost in pondering over the hair and examining it under a microscope. The result showed nothing sensational, and the experiments were allowed to lapse.

Dwarfs were Dr Mengele's greatest passion. He collected them zealously. The day he discovered a family of five dwarfs in a transport he was beside himself with joy. But his was the mania of a collector, not of a savant. His experiments and observations were carried out in an abnormal fashion. When he made transfusions, he purposely used incorrect blood types. Of course complications followed. But Mengele had no one to account to but himself. He did whatever pleased him and conducted his experiments like a mad amateur.

One experimental station which was installed some distance from the camp appeared to have a more scientific character. But only at first glance. There one could see that the "work" was only a criminal debauchery of human material and a total lack of scruples on the part of the inquirers. The experiments were theoretically intended to gather information for the

Wehrmacht. Most of the time, they consisted of tests of human endurance, resistance to cold or to heat, or to high altitudes. Hundreds of internees died in the course of these experiments in the Auschwitz station, as well as in other camps. At the price of the lives of thousands of victims, German science finally showed that a human being can subsist in ice water, at a predetermined temperature, for just so many hours. It had also been established with precision(!) how long it took for death to come after scaldings at different degrees of temperature.

I have mentioned experiments to determine the resistance of the human organism to hunger. Musulmans, especially the most emaciated specimens, were forced to drink unbelievable quantities of soup. These cramming experiments were often fatal. I heard of a few cases where the deportees, suffering horribly from hunger, volunteered for the forced feeding. The son of Prime Minister M. was so famished that he offered himself as a guinea pig for malaria experiments. The subjects of this experiment received double bread rations for a few days.

Experiments were also made in diagnostics. Interesting cases were taken from the hospital and simply killed so that they could be dissected for the purpose of an autopsy! When several cases suffered from the same ailment, they might be given treatments and, after a certain phase, be killed, so that conclusions might be drawn from the experiments. Most of the time, when a patient was killed, and no one dreamed of examining his body – there were too many dead in Auschwitz.

The German Bayer Company sent medicines in vials with no labels to indicate their contents. People suffering from tuberculosis were injected with this product. They were not sent to the gas chamber. Their overseers waited for them to die, and death came quickly. After that, parts of the lungs were taken to a laboratory chosen by Bayer.

Once the Bayer Company brought one hundred and fifty women from the Camp administration and experimented on them with unknown medicaments, perhaps for hormone tests.

The Weigel Institute of Kraków sent vaccines to the camp. These, too, had to be experimented on and "improved". The victims were chosen from French political prisoners, especially members of the French underground, whom the Germans wanted to be rid of.

About two-thousand organic preparations had to be dispatched to the University of Innsbruck. According to instructions, these preparations had to be made from absolutely healthy bodies, which had been gassed, hanged, or shot while in good health!

To enrich their racial science, the Germans regularly extracted blood. Apart from the scientific interest, the blood of the internees was used for transfusions to German wounded. 500 cc. of blood were taken from each "voluntary" donor and sent immediately to the Army. To save the lives of the Wehrmacht soldiers, the Germans forgot that Jewish blood was "of inferior quality".

I have already mentioned the "injections in the heart", as the inmates called the intracardiac injections of phenol. Sometimes, these intracardiac injections were made with benzine or petroleum. This method was used in the hospitals to kill the sick or the feeble and the "superfluous".

I spoke to a Polish doctor who was forced to give these injections to his fellow inmates for two days.

"When the SS doctor called me to the hospital," he told me, "I did not know what it was all about. He ordered me to inject the patients in the cardiac cavity. He told me that I should inject the liquid as soon as I had proof that the needle was in the cardiac cavity."

The Polish doctor followed orders, and the patients then fell dead on the floor.

In another mad experiment they laid hundreds of sick out in the blazing sun. The German wanted to know how long it would take a sick person to die under the sun without water.

Twenty miles from our Camp an experimental station which specialised in artificial insemination. To this station were sent the most endowed of the doctor inmates and the most beautiful of the women. The Germans attached great importance to these experiments. Unfortunately, I could not see the work that went on there, for this station was the most jealously guarded of all. Some data, however, I did obtain.

The Germans practiced artificial insemination on a number of women, but the investigations offered no results. I knew women who had been subjected to artificial insemination and had happened to survive, but they were ashamed to admit the experiments.

Another group was injected with the sex hormones. It had not been possible to determine the nature of the substance injected or the results the Germans obtained. After these injections, many women had abscesses which were lanced in Barrack 10.

But I am well informed on the sterilisation experiments. These took place in Auschwitz-Birkenau under the direction of a Polish doctor who was executed by the Germans a few days before the Camp was evacuated.

These experiments attempted to compare the results of the surgical methods and X-ray treatments. At the hospital, we saw numerous sick women who had come from this experimental station. They showed serious burns caused by the clumsy application of these rays. Through them and the deportee doctors we learned about the experiments. The subject was placed under X-ray radiation, which was made more and more intense. From time to time the treatment was interrupted in order to see if the subject could still copulate. All this took place under the vigilant eyes of the SS in Barrack 21. When the physician verified that the X-rays had definitely destroyed the genital faculties, this subject was dispatched to the gas chamber. Occasionally, when the irradiation took too long to produce the desired effect, the victim was castrated surgically.

In August, 1944, the Germans sterilised about one thousand boys between the ages of thirteen and sixteen. Their names and dates of sterilisation were registered. After some weeks the boys were brought to Barrack 21. In the laboratory they were questioned about the result of the first "treatment", their desires, nocturnal pollutions, loss of memory, etc.

Then the Germans forced them to masturbate. They provoked the erection by massaging the prostate glands. When this work tired the "masseur", the German "scientists" used a metal instrument, which caused the patient great pain.

The sperm was examined by a bacteriologist who determined the vitality of the spermatozoa. In 1944, the Germans sent a phosphorescent microscope to the Camp. This enabled them to see the difference between the living and the dead spermatozoa.

Sometimes the Germans made incomplete castrations: a quarter or a half of the testicle was removed. Sometimes the whole testicle was sent to Breslau in a tube sterilised with formalin (10%) for an histopathological study of the tissues. These operations were made with intrarachidian injections of novocaine. The boys were separated from the others in Barrack 21 and were closely watched. When the experiments were finished, the reward was, as usual, the gas chamber.

I remember one case of a Polish boy named Gruenwald, who was about twenty years old. Professor Klauber ordered treatment with X-rays. After two months the X-rays had not produced the desired effect. So the boy was taken to Barrack 21 for a complete castration. But the X-rays had been given in such doses that he had been seriously burned. Cancer followed and the boy suffered terribly. In January 1945, he was still alive in the hospital at Birkenau.

These methods were also applied to the women. Sometimes the Germans used short-wave rays which caused unbearable pains in the lower part of the abdomen. Then the belly of the sick women was opened to observe the lesions. The surgeons usually removed the uterus and the ovaries.

Professor Schuman and Dr Wiurd made such experiments on young girls about sixteen or seventeen years old. Of the fifty girls used for the experiment, only two survived, Bella Schimski and Dora Buyenna, both from Salonika. They told us that they had been put under short-wave rays, one plate placed on the abdomen and the other on the back. The electricity was directed towards the ovaries. The dose was so great that the subjects were gravely burned. After two months of observation, the girls had to suffer a "control" operation.

A group of young women, mostly Dutch, were subjected to a series of experiments for which only the author, Klauberg, German gynaecologist of Kattowitz, could have known the reason. With the aid of an electrical apparatus, a thick whitish liquid was infused into the genital organs of these women. It caused a terrible burning sensation. This infusion, repeated every four weeks, was each time followed by a radioscopy.

These same women were simultaneously subject to another series of experiments by an another doctor. This time it was an injection in the chest. The physician injected five cc. of a serum, whose nature I do not know, at the rate of from two to nine injections each session. The reaction came in the form of a painful swelling the size of a fist. Certain women received more than a hundred of these inoculations. Some were also injected in the gums. After a number of such experiments the women were declared useless and sent away.

Once we asked an Aryan German inmate, a former social worker, for the basic reason for the sterilisation and castration. Before his captivity he had been active in German politics and had known many eminent people. He told us that the Germans had a geopolitical reason for these experiments. If they could sterilise all non-German people still alive after their victorious war, there would be no danger of new generations of "inferior" peoples. At the same time, the living populations would be able to serve as labourers for about thirty years. After that time, the German surplus population would need all the space in these countries, and the "inferiors" would perish without descendants.

One day a large number of women, mostly Polish, were used for vivisection experiments: grafting of the bones and muscles, and various others. German surgeons arrived from Berlin to make the experiments and watch the result. The vivisections were carried out under terrible conditions. The victim was bound to the operating table in a primitive barrack, and the operation was made without aseptic care. Even after the operations, the human guinea pigs suffered terribly. They were given nothing to alleviate their sufferings.

These bone experiments were also performed at Ravensbrück, and the only ones that have full documentation that survived to this day. In the book *Beyond Human Endurance*, Ravensbrück women tell their own story. These experiments were performed on seventy-four prisoners from the Warsaw and Lublin transports, they had their operations in the period from 1 August, 1942 to 16 August, 1943. I quote from the book:

> Out of the group of seventy-four Polish women who underwent experimental operations, five died immediately after their operations: six of them were executed before their wounds had healed. The others, as inconvenient evidence of the crimes of the Nazi doctors were to be liquidated in February 1945. The assistance of everyone imprisoned in the Camp and the determination of the women who had been operated on enabled them to hide themselves among the masses of prisoners and survive their stay in the Camp despite these very difficult conditions. Out of those who were operated on, sixty-three managed to survive. Out of that number six women managed to get through to the West during evacuation and remained abroad. The rest returned to Poland. Seven of them have since died (the last on 12 January, 1969). Their death was hastened because of the operations they had in the Camp and their terrible experiences there. At present, fifty of them are living in Poland. All of them are suffering, to a greater or lesser extent, from their operations. About a quarter of their number are crippled (part of the bones and muscles having been cut away from their shins and thighs, and numerous after-effects of serious illnesses).

From *The Scourge of the Swastika* by Lord Russell:

> Between 1941 and 1942 some five hundred operations were performed on healthy persons in Dachau. The object was to instruct SS doctors and medical students. Many of the operations were of a serious nature, for example, removal of the gall bladder, and were performed by students of only two years standing. Such operations should not normally be performed except by doctors with at least four years' practice of surgery. Many of these patients either died while the operation was in progress or from post-operative complications.
>
> Malaria experiments were also carried out on some 1,200 inmates, none of whom volunteered. These experiments were carried out by a

Dr Schilling, on the personal instructions of Himmler. The victims were either bitten by mosquitoes or given injections of malaria sporozoites taken from mosquitoes. The object of the experiment was to test out certain drugs as specific for malarial fever. Thirty to forty of these "patients" died from the malaria itself and several hundreds later died from other diseases as a result of the constitution having been undermined by the disease. A number were also poisoned by overdose of neosalvarsan and pyramidon, two of the experimental drugs.

Other experiments were carried out in Dachau by Dr Sigmund Rasher, a major in the Luftwaffe. Twenty-five men were put into a specially constructed van in which air pressure could be increased or decreased. The object of the experiment was to watch the effects on the victims of high altitude or rapid descent by parachute.

Many of the inmates who were subjected to this experiment, which must have been pure torture, died from haemorrhage of lung or brain. Those who survived were coughing blood when removed from the van. The internal organs of those who had died were sent to Munich for examination; the survivors were generally put to death.

Further experiments were conducted there by a Dr Schultz and others on large numbers of Polish, Czech, and Dutch priests. A group of these were selected and given intravenous injections of pus. No after-treatment was allowed so that inflammation or general blood poisoning set in. Various drugs were then used to attempt to deal with this condition. Great pain was suffered during this experiment and most of those who did not die of septicaemia became permanent invalids.

A large number of Hungarians and gypsies were, in 1944, subjected to salt water experiments which consisted of being given nothing to eat or drink except salt water, during which time their blood, urine, and excrement were analysed.

In addition to the terrible and varied medical experiments the Nazi policy of Euthanasia was continuing.

This began with mental patients before the War, starting in six separate places and increased rapidly throughout Nazi-occupied Europe.

The killings took place by gassing patients of all age groups – unwanted Germans and then thousands of other nationalities. By 1941 the total was estimated at 70,273.

The Germans told their victims and relatives they were travelling to a Sanatorium or Nursing Home. They travelled in overcrowded cattle trucks where conditions proved appalling causing many deaths alone.

The relatives received a letter or condolence usually explaining that the patient died of influenza etc. and that on instructions from the Police, they were obliged to proceed immediately with cremation of the body. The letter always ending with "Heil Hitler."

Many reports were completed to give estimates of how much food etc. could be saved by this Euthanasia programme.

Second World War

The following are eight Concentration Camps (many auxiliary camps) from a total of over 7,000

Camp	Estimated Date	Auxiliary Camps – attached to main concentration camps	Medical Experiments –various	Number of Prisoners			Nationality	Number of SS Guards
				Held	Died	%		
Ravensbrück	November 1938	For Women – 135 For Men – 30	no exact number of victims	Women & children –132,000 Men – 20,086	Women & children –92,000 Men – 1,617	70% 8%	30	Women – 540 Men – 1000
Mauthausen +	9-08-1938	Overall 119 Camps including Gestapo establishments i.e. All Camps in Austria "under" Mauthausen		335,000 +	300,000	73%	39	80 (1940) 100+ (1944) Also HQ for Tottenkopf Death Head SS Regiment –1,250 (1940) –9,799 (1940)
Güsen I	25-05-1940			77,540				
Güsen II	09-03-1944							
Güsen III	16-12-1944							
Hartheim Castle			ditto					
Sachsenhausen	12-07-1936	120	ditto	204,537	99,775	49%	17	800+
Auschwitz Oświęcim Brzezinka	June 1940 1942	40 in Poland 4 in Czechoslovakia	ditto	5,000,000	4,000,000	80%	32	2,430 in 1944
Majdanek	1941	6	ditto	500,000	360,000	72%	51	1,228 +
Neuengamme	4-06-1940	54	ditto	106,000	55,000	52%	25+	4,500
Dachau	22-03-1933	172	ditto	25,000	148,800	59.5%	29	800+
Stutthof	August 1939 – May 1945	39	ditto	110,000	65,000	57%	25	780+

Location of camps
Mauthausen – Austria (near Linz), Ravensbrück – Germany (North Berlin), Sachsenhausen – Germany (Near Berlin), Auschwitz – Poland, Majdanek – Poland (Near Lublin), Neuengamme – Germany (Near Hamburg), Dachau – Germany (near Munich), Harteim Castle – where medical experiments were carried out.

List of Gestapo, SS and Agents
The number of Agents originally employed by the Gestapo was estimated at 32,000 but this rose in time to 54,000. These figures do not include the so-called 'stool pigeons' (voluntary or coerced), nor the quislings recruited in occupied countries. In addition the many other organisations in which the Gestapo placed its agents must be taken into account.

"SS" – The Schutz Staffel (Protection Squad)
The total establishment of the SS Einsatz Gruppen ABCD (Special Extermination Groups), which operated outside concentration and death camps, amounted to 3,000 men or more.

The Waffen "SS" raised 27 Divisions, amounting to 421,158 men.

The "SS" *Totenkopft* (Death Heath Formations) amounted to 25,000 personnel. These men and women were employed as guards throughout all concentration and death camps.

General Fighting "SS" Divisions, on all fronts, numbered 23. In 1939 there were 249,000 "SS" soldiers trained to fight without mercy and carry out horrendous atrocities on both civilians and prisoners they captured.

Appendix 3

FIRST WORLD WAR
CASUALTIES – ARMY DEAD

WESTERN FRONT – FRANCE AND BELGIUM
The number of British Army officers killed or died of wounds on the Western Front was 28,467. A further 1,682 died of sickness or accidental injuries, bringing the total to 30,149. If one adds officers from Dominion and Colonial contingents, then the total number of Army officers who died in France and Belgium was 36,722.

The number of other ranks in the British Army who were killed, or died from all causes, on the Western Front was 482,415. If one adds to these the warrant officers, non-commissioned officers (NCOs) and men from Dominion, Colonial and other contingents (such as the Royal Naval Division) then the overall figure for France and Belgium is 611,654.

GALLIPOLI – DARDANELLES CAMPAIGN
1,148 British Army and 637 Dominion and Colonial officers died from all causes in the Gallipoli campaign. Of these, 1,045 British officers and 617 others were battle casualties.

17,618 British and 14,119 Dominion and Colonial other ranks died from all causes in the Gallipoli campaign.

OTHER THEATRES OF WAR EXCLUDING THE WESTERN FRONT AND GALLIPOLI
3,506 British, Dominion and Colonial officers died from all causes in other theatres.

222,967 British, Dominion and Colonial other ranks died from all causes in other theatres.

TOTAL ARMY
908,371 British, Dominion and Colonial soldiers died on all fronts.
(Source: *Statistics of the Military Effort of the British Empire during the Great War, 1914-1920*: HMSO 1922)

ROYAL NAVY AND MERCHANT NAVY
2,342 officers and 29,866 ratings of the Royal Navy died. 14,661 merchant seamen also lost their lives.
(Source: *Statistics of the Military Effort of the British Empire during the Great War, 1914-1920*: HMSO 1922)

ROYAL FLYING CORPS, ROYAL NAVAL AIR SERVICE AND ROYAL AIR FORCE
4,579 officers and 1,587 other ranks of the British flying services lost their lives. These figures include the fatal casualties in the Royal Flying Corps and the Royal Naval Air Service. These two flying services were

amalgamated when the Royal Air Force was created as an independent service on 1 April 1918.

(Source: The British official history *The War in the Air* by Sir Walter Raleigh and H. A. Jones, Oxford University Press, 1922–1937; see Appendix XXXVI).

MISSING OR PRISONERS OF WAR

BRITISH ARMY

352,458 soldiers were listed as missing, of whom 12,238 were officers and 340,220 were other ranks. These totals include 7,348 officers and 184,054 other ranks who became prisoners of war.

ROYAL NAVY

19 officers and 60 ratings were listed as missing, 71 officers and 240 ratings were interned, and 140 officers and 642 ratings became prisoners of war.

ROYAL FLYING CORPS, ROYAL NAVAL AIR SERVICE AND ROYAL AIR FORCE

The casualty statistics for the Royal Flying Corps, the Royal Naval Air Service and the Royal Air Force give an overall figure of 3,212 airmen "missing or interned", including 2,839 officers and 373 other ranks.

(Sources: *Statistics of the Military Effort of the British Empire during the Great War, 1914–1920* and *The War in the Air*).

WOUNDED

BRITISH, DOMINION AND COLONIAL ARMIES

The total number of wounded in the British Army was 1,662,625 of whom 79,445 were officers and 1,583,180 were other ranks. With the figures added for Dominion and Colonial contingents the total was 2,090,212, including 98,025 officers and 1,992,187 other ranks.

ROYAL NAVY

The total number of wounded in the Royal Navy was 839 officers and 4,296 ratings.

ROYAL FLYING CORPS, ROYAL NAVAL AIR SERVICE AND ROYAL AIR FORCE

The total number of wounded in the flying services was 5,369 officers and 1,876 other ranks.

(Sources: *Statistics of the Military Effort of the British Empire during the Great War, 1914–1920* and *The War in the Air*).

*   *   *

SECOND WORLD WAR
(IWM Schedules as printed)
PEOPLE KILLED AND SERIOUSLY INJURED BY
VI AND V2 BOMBS

V1 (pilotless flying bombs):

Total U.K. casualties	6,184	killed
	17,981	seriously injured
	24,165	
V2 rocket:–	2,754	killed
	6,523	seriously injured
	9,277	

V1 (pilotless flying bombs):
Main offensive 12–06–44 to 5–09–44, a total of 85 days.

Actual dates when V1 launched 12–06–44 to 29–03–45 (not necessarily dropped on Britain)

V2 rocket:
As far as London is concerned from 8–9–44 to 27–3–45

Total of V1s launched: 10,492
Total of V2s launched: 1,403

Appendix 4

BATTLE OF BRITAIN

As England, despite her hopeless military situation, still shows no sign of willingness to come to terms, I have decided to prepare, and if necessary to carry out, a landing operation against her . . .

The aim of this operation is to eliminate the English motherland as a base from which war against Germany can be continued and if necessary to occupy the country completely.

Adolf Hitler, Directive No 16
16 July 1940

"The Command". RAF Fighter Command was led by its Commander-in-Chief, fifty-eight year old Air-Chief-Marshal Sir Hugh Dowding. He was a veteran of the Royal Flying Corps from 1914 and C-in-C Fighter Command from 1936.

Luftflotte 5, was based in Norway, Luftlotte 5's only significant daylight action was on 15 August 1940, and it was a dismal failure. On that day sixty-five Heinkel He111 bombers and nineteen Messerschmitt Bf110 twin-engine fighters followed by fifty Ju88 bombers endeavoured to attack Newcastle. They were repulsed with the loss of twenty-one aircraft, and did not try again in daylight. In all, on 15 August, the Luftwaffe lost aircraft and some 175 air crew; RAF fighter Command lost thirty fighters and seventeen pilots, and ten Whitleys of bomber Command were destroyed on the ground at Driffield.

The relative totals are:

	RAF aircraft	Luftwaffe aircraft
Destroyed	1,302	2,073
Damaged	845	947
	2,147	3,020

The British "heat of battle" claim 2,692 German aircraft destroyed should therefore have been 2,073 plus 947 damaged.

Twice as many of London's civil population were killed and wounded as air crews of Fighter Command lost during the whole of the Battle of Britain.

RAF Fighter Command went into the defensive battle on 1 July 1940 with 595 serviceable aircraft and four types (including 320 Hurricanes and 187 Spitfires) in fifty-four operational squadrons under four Groups with 1,054 air crew members – predominantly pilots, many of them with long service in the Royal Air Force.

The Luftwaffe opened the Battle on 1 July 1940 with 2,186 serviceable aircraft of 11 types (including 708 Bf109s, 202 Bf110s and 898 bombers) in three Luftflotten. By 31 October the number of serviceable aircraft in those three air fleets had fallen to some 1,686 (including 558 Bf109s, 157 Bf110s and 583 bombers).

In all, a total of 1,073 pilots and other aircrew members of Fighter Command were killed, missing or wounded in combat, accidents and training. Those losses amounted to more than originally entered the Battle. The losses had been replenished by an intake of 1,354 air crew members from training units, bomber and army co-operation squadrons, and hospitals whence the less seriously injured returned to flight operations.

A total of 5,811 Luftwaffe air crew were killed, missing, captured or "recovered to base" wounded in damaged aircraft. Those losses included 3,500 men killed, missing and captured in engagements with the RAF.

Of the German aircraft destroyed in combat during the Battle of Britain, approximately 860 were shot down by Hurricanes and 458 by Spitfires. This percentage ratio of 64 to 36 was also the average ratio of Hurricanes to Spitfires throughout the Battle.

In personnel, the RAF suffered one casualty for every two of its aircraft destroyed and damaged, whereas the Luftwaffe incurred nearly four times the British loss rate. This was because the RAF was fighting chiefly over home ground and because nearly half the aircraft lost by the Luftwaffe were twin-engined bombers carrying an average of four crew members.

The pilots and ground crew – "The Few". A total of 2,926 air crew took part in the Battle with Fighter command. Of these, 2,344 were British and British Commonwealth. The remaining 582 came from fourteen nations.

During the Battle, 595 RAF pilots and other crew members were killed, missing, or captured, and 478 were injured – a total of 1,072 casualities – or more than a third of the number engaged. The ground crews – men and women – kept the aircraft flying, often in the most hazardous conditions. They were also responsible for running the bital operations rooms and radar installations.

Two days later Hitler postponed the nvasion of England "indefinitely". by 1 November, Fighter Command was stronger than it had ever been, with 749 serviceable aircraft compared with 595 on 1 July 1940. The Battle of Britain had been won.

The hard-won victory of Royal Air Force Fighter Command half a century ago stands out not only as the world's first major air battle, but also for its duration and for the number of civilian casualties – some 36,000 on the British side.

Aircraft losses RAF Fighter Command and Luftwaffe

RAF Fighter Command

July	August	September	October	Totals
Total number of aircraft destroyed				
182	426	405	209	1,302

July	August	September	October	Totals
Total number of aircraft damaged				
173	222	319	131	845
Total aircraft destroyed and damaged				
355	648	724	420	2,147

Luftwaffe

Total number of aircraft destroyed				
628	742	649	414	2,073
Total number of aircraft damaged				
123	296	298	230	947
Total aircraft destroyed and damaged				
391	1,038	947	644	3,020

Appendix 5

Since 1945, when Sue Ryder's Relief work began, it is estimated that a minimum of 505,000 individuals of all ages, of over fifty nationalities, with seventeen different medical conditions have been assisted by the Sue Ryder Foundation.

In Britain alone, the numbers of people helped since the Sue Ryder Homes opened, until June 1997 were:

In-patients	33,272
Patients in Day Centres	30,672
Visits by Domiciliary Care Teams	36,084
Visits by Bereavement Counsellors	9,634

Acknowledgements

Many people have given me the most invaluable assistance in research and in checking historical details. I thank all of them, and I should in particular like to express my appreciation to the following for permissions to use copyright material:

Baring, Maurice, *The Collected Poems of Maurice Baring* (New York: AMS Press).

Brittain, Vera, *Testament of Youth* (London: Victor Gollancz), and with the permission of the Literary Executors for the Vera Brittain Estate.

The late Lord Cheshire of Woodall, the citation for his Victoria Cross is reproduced by kind permission of Her Majesty's Stationery Office.

Churchill, Sarah, *A Thread in the Tapestry* (London: Andre Deutsch).

Dragic, Dr Djordje, *Partisan Hospitals in Yugoslavia* (Zarod: Vojnoizdaracki).

Gilbert, Martin, *Auschwitz and the Allies* (London: Michael Joseph).

Hart-Davis, Duff, *Peter Fleming* (London: Jonathan Cape).

Hillary, Richard, *The Last Enemy* (London: Macmillan).

Iranek-Osmecki, Kazimierz, *He Who Saves One Life* (New York: Crown Publishers).

Lileyko, Jerzy, *A Companion Guide to the Royal Castle in Warsaw* (Warsaw: Interpress).

Majdalany, Fred, *Cassino – Portrait of a Battle* (London: Longman).

Mayne, Richard, *– Prague's Cruel Spring* (London: Encounter).

Moravec, Frantisek, *Master of Spies* (London: The Bodley Head).

Schlabrendorff, Fabian von, *The Secret War Against Hitler* (Belmont: David S. Lake Publishers).

Wavell, Field Marshal Lord, *Other Men's Flowers* (London: Jonathan Cape), and with the permission of his Executors.

I also extend my thanks to the following:

Aerospace magazine
The late Rt Revd Agnellus Andrew, OFM, Bishop of Numana
The Auschwitz Museum
Battle of Britain by Francis K. Mason
Mr Terry Blatch
Lord Bullock
Bundesarchiv
The late Lady Hermione Cobbold
The Commonwealth War Graves Commission
Gervase Cowell, Chairman of the Historical Committee, Special Forces Club

The Daily Telegraph
Mr Richard Dunning
Five Chimneys by Olga Lengyel published in 1947
Mrs Nina K. Freebody
Miss B. Gazdzik
The late Herbert Goodacre
Mr J.J. Harding HB(A), from the Army Historical Branch at the
    Ministry of Defence
The late Dr Michael Hargrave
House of Lords Library
The Imperial War Museum
The late Wanda Kiedrzynsta
Hannes Kramer
Mr L.W. Leybourne Callaghan
The London Transport Museum
Mahn und Gedenkstatte Ravensbrück in Germany –
    Monika Herzog
Professor C.D. Marsden
Viscount Mersey
Norges Hjemmefront Museum, Oslo (Norwegian Resistance
    Museum)
Mr P. O'Connor
The Polish Underground Movement (1939–1945) Study Trust
Mrs Pam Richards
Professor D. Russell Davis, MA, MD, Cantab., FRCP, DPM
Mr Geoffrey Sparrow
Duncan Stuart CMG, SOE Advisor to the Foreign &
    Commonwealth Office
The Times newspaper
The Wiener Library
Mr Simon Wiesenthal at the Documentation Centre, Vienna
WTS/FANY
Yad Vashem, The Holocaust Martyrs' & Heroes' Remembrance
    Authority in Jerusalem
Zycie Warszawy (Warsaw Life)

INDEX

"SR" indicates Lady Ryder of Warsaw.
Individual Homes are indexed under "Sue Ryder Homes".